Encyclopaedia of the Musical Film

Encyclopaedia
of the Musical Film

STANLEY GREEN

OXFORD UNIVERSITY PRESS
New York   Oxford

Oxford University Press

Oxford   New York   Toronto
Delhi   Bombay   Calcutta   Madras   Karachi
Petaling Jaya   Singapore   Hong Kong   Tokyo
Nairobi   Dar es Salaam   Cape Town
Melbourne   Auckland

and associated companies in
Beirut   Berlin   Ibadan   Nicosia

First published in 1981 by Oxford University Press, Inc.,
200 Madison Avenue, New York, New York 10016

First issued as an Oxford University Press paperback, 1988

Oxford is a registered trademark of Oxford University Press

Library of Congress Cataloging in Publication Data
Green, Stanley.
Encyclopaedia of the musical film.
1. Moving-pictures, Musical—Dictionaries. I. Title.
PN1995.M86G7   791.43'75'03   81-735
ISBN 0-19-502958-5   AACR2
ISBN 0-19-505421-0 (pbk.)

2 4 6 8 10 9 7 5 3

Printed in the United States of America
on acid free paper

PREFACE

Following the basic format of my previous *Encyclopaedia of the Musical Theatre,* and something of a companion volume to it, this ready-reference encyclopaedia contains succinct information regarding the musical screen's most prominent individuals, productions, and songs. Though emphasis is on the Hollywood output (including feature-length cartoons), British musical films and selected original television musicals are also covered.

It is not always easy to determine what is and what is not a musical film, so there seems little point in trying to establish strict eligibility criteria. My standards of determination, admittedly loose, are based on a combination of factors: the number of songs or musical selections, the manner and length of their presentation, the musical contributions of leading members of the cast, and the subject matter of the film. There are of course exceptions. Those motion pictures considered beyond the scope of this survey are Western musicals (the Gene Autry and Roy Rogers kind), short subjects, documentary musicals, foreign-language musicals, and silent films with accompanying scores. All dates of productions are according to the years listed in *Film Daily Year Book*.

The individuals receiving entries in the book have been chosen from among actors, actresses, on-camera musicians, composers, lyricists, directors, choreographers, and producers. All such entries contain year-by-year listings of every musical production with which they were associated. A name in parentheses preceded by ''né'' or ''née'' is name at birth; other names in parentheses—first, middle, or nick—are those that are not used professionally.

Under entries for actors and actresses, the roles that were played appear in italics in parentheses following the film titles.

Under entries for composers and lyricists, the names of the collaborators—except if otherwise indicated—appear in parentheses following the film titles.

Production entries include major performers and their roles, as well as all the songs performed on the screen and by whom. Also titles of songs that were intended to be in the films but were discarded or cut out before their release.

Song entries include those primarily written for or first introduced in films. They also include a small number that may have been introduced on Broadway or elsewhere but which subsequently became even more closely identified with screen performances. This also allows for "theme" songs sung over credits, or elsewhere on the soundtrack, of nonmusicals. Disallowed are songs "inspired" by films without being an actual part of them, even though their music may have been part of the background scores. (No, Dorothy Lamour didn't sing "The Moon of Manakoora" in *The Hurricane,* so don't try to find it here.)

Books dealing with specific individuals or screen productions are mentioned at the end of such entries; others dealing with various aspects of the subject may be found in the General Bibliography. Soundtrack and other original-cast recordings (excluding unauthorized releases) are also in the back of the book.

I have sought and received information from a number of people, primarily Don Koll and Dan Langan. I thank them all, including Louis Botto, John Cocchi, Ray Evans, Ted Fetter, Hugh Fordin, Arthur Hove, Ed Jablonski, Ephraim Katz, Michael Kerker, Leonard Maltin, Larry Moore, Alfred Simon, and two close relatives, Susan Green and Rudy David Green. Miles Kreuger, who read the galleys, was most generous with valued comments and recommendations. The staff of the Billy Rose Theatre Collection of the New York Public Library has, as usual, been most helpful. And Elliott Serkin's interest and encouragement will always be appreciated.

But no one deserves more gratitude than my wife, Kay, who put in the long hours advising, checking, reading, and rereading. She shares credit for the book's virtues and is blameless for its faults.

May 1981   S.G.

The *Encyclopaedia of the Musical Film* has been updated for this edition to include such pertinent information as necrology, additional films under existing entries, and additional Oscar winners. Factual errors, misspellings, and typos have also been corrected.

August 1987   S.G.

CONTENTS

Encyclopaedia of the Musical Film

A

"**Aba Daba Honeymoon, The**" Music by Walter Donovan; lyric by Arthur Fields. A Congo romance between a monkey and a chimpanzee results in a June wedding presided over by a baboon, and followed by their honeymoon. Debbie Reynolds and Carleton Carpenter became permanently identified with this snappy 1914 vaudeville number when they revived it as a song-and-dance routine in *Two Weeks with Love* (MGM 1950). The song had been previously performed on screen by Paul Whiteman's orchestra in *King of Jazz* (Univ. 1930).

Abbott, George (Francis), director, producer, screenwriter; b. Forestville, NY, June 25, 1887. One of the musical stage's most prolific and influential directors, Abbott was in charge of 32 Broadway shows, thirteen of which were brought to the screen and three of which he directed and produced himself. Bib: *Mister Abbott* by Abbott (1963).

Asterisk indicates Mr. Abbott was also co-producer and screenwriter of the following:
1929 Why Bring That Up?
1940 Too Many Girls (also prod.)
1957 The Pajama Game *
1958 Damn Yankees *

Abbott and Costello, actors. (William Alexander) Bud Abbott, b. Asbury Park, NJ, Oct. 2, 1895; d. Woodland Hills, Cal., April 24, 1974. Lou Costello (né Louis Francis Cristillo), b. Paterson, NJ, March 6, 1906; d. Beverly Hills, March 3, 1959. Durable roughhouse comedy team, with Abbott the sharp-featured operator forever taking advantage of his childlike roly-poly partner. The duo performed their classic "Who's on First?" routine in two films, *One Night in the Tropics* and *The Naughty Nineties*. Costello was also famous for his catch-phrase, "I'm a ba-a-ad boy," which he'd bleat whenever apprehended for a misdeed. After headlining in burlesque and vaudeville, the team won a Universal contract following appearances in a Broadway revue and on radio. In all, they acted in 36 feature films. Bib: *Who's on First?* ed. Richard Anobile (1972); *Bud and Lou* by Bob Thomas (1977).

1940 One Night in the Tropics (*Abbott; Costello*)
1941 Buck Privates (*Slicker Smith; Herbie Brown*)
In the Navy (*Smokey Adams; Pomeroy Watson*)
Hold That Ghost (*Chuck Murray; Ferdinand Jones*)
Keep 'Em Flying (*Blackie Benson; Heathcliffe*)
1942 Ride 'Em Cowboy (*Duke; Willoughby*)
Rio Rita (*Doc; Wishy*)
Pardon My Sarong (*Algy Shaw; Wellington Pflug*)
1943 It Ain't Hay (*Grover Mockridge; Wilbur Hoolihan*)
Hit the Ice (*Flash Fulton; Tubby McCoy*)
1944 In Society (*Eddie; Albert*)
Lost in a Harem (*Pete Johnson; Harvey Garvey*)
1945 The Naughty Nineties (*Dexter Broadhurst; Sebastian Dinwiddie*)
Abbott and Costello in Hollywood (*Buzz Kurtis; Abercrombie*)
Here Come the Coeds (*Slats McCarthy; Oliver Quackenbush*)
1951 Comin' Round the Mountain (*Al Stewart; Wilbert Smith*)
1952 Lost in Alaska (*Tom Watson; George Bell*)
1956 Dance with Me, Henry (*Uncle Bud; Pops Henry*)

"**About a Quarter to Nine**" Music by Harry Warren; lyric by Al Dubin. Leading a top-hatted male chorus in a nightclub floor show in *Go Into Your Dance* (Warner 1935), Al Jolson looks forward to his date with Ruby Keeler. Song also sung by Jolson (voice dubbed for Larry Parks) in *The Jolson Story* (Col. 1946).

"**Abraham**" Music & lyric by Irving Berlin. Rhythmic celebration of Abraham Lincoln's birthday in *Holiday*

Inn (Par. 1942) by Bing Crosby and Marjorie Reynolds (with Martha Mears' voice), both in blackface, plus Louise Beavers. Music also used for tap dance by Vera-Ellen and George Chakiris (then known as George Kerris) in *White Christmas* (Par. 1954).

"Ac-Cent-Tchu-Ate the Positive" Music by Harold Arlen; lyric by Johnny Mercer. Revivalistic exhortation—with appropriate lessons from Noah and Jonah and warning "Don't mess with Mr. In-Between"—propounded by Bing Crosby and Sonny Tufts in *Here Come the Waves* (Par. 1944). In the film, the number was performed in a Navy show, with Crosby and Tufts both in blackface.

"Accidents Will Happen" Music by James Van Heusen; lyric by Johnny Burke. A romantically tenacious castaway hopes for a change of heart. Introduced in *Mr. Music* (Par. 1950) by Bing Crosby and Dorothy Kirsten.

Adams, Lee. *See* **Strouse and Adams.**

Adamson, Harold, lyricist; b. Greenville, NJ, Dec. 10, 1906; d. Beverly Hills, Aug. 17, 1980. Though he contributed songs to Broadway revues and musicals, Adamson is chiefly known for his work on such films as *The Great Ziegfeld* ("You"), *You're a Sweetheart* (title song), and *Higher and Higher* ("I Couldn't Sleep a Wink Last Night," "A Lovely Way To Spend an Evening," "The Music Stopped"). Other movie songs: "Did I Remember?," "It's a Most Unusual Day," "My Resistance Is Low," "When Love Goes Wrong" (in *Gentlemen Prefer Blondes*), and "An Affair To Remember." Adamson's major collaborators were composers Burton Lane, Herbert Stothart, Jack King, Walter Donaldson, Jimmy McHugh (with whom he worked on 19 movies), Jule Styne, Johnny Green, Hoagy Carmichael, Harry Warren, and co-lyricist Leo McCarey. Those who introduced Adamson's songs include Lily Pons, Alice Faye, Deanna Durbin, Frank Sinatra, Jane Powell, Marilyn Monroe, Jane Russell, and Perry Como.

1933	Dancing Lady (Lane)
1934	Bottoms Up (Lane)
1935	Reckless (Lane; King)
	Here Comes the Band (Lane; Donaldson)
1936	The Great Ziegfeld (Donaldson)
	Banjo on My Knee (McHugh)
1937	Merry-Go-Round of 1938 (McHugh)
	Hitting a New High (McHugh)

	You're a Sweetheart (McHugh)
	Top of the Town (McHugh)
1938	Mad About Music (McHugh)
	Road to Reno (McHugh)
	That Certain Age (McHugh)
1943	Hit Parade of 1943 (Styne)
	Around the World (McHugh)
	Higher and Higher (McHugh)
1944	Four Jills in a Jeep (McHugh)
	Bathing Beauty (Green)
	Something for the Boys (McHugh)
1945	Bring on the Girls (McHugh)
	Nob Hill (McHugh)
	Doll Face (McHugh)
1947	Calendar Girl (McHugh)
	Hit Parade of 1947 (McHugh)
	Smash Up (McHugh)
1948	If You Knew Susie (McHugh)
1953	Gentlemen Prefer Blondes (Carmichael)
1955	Jupiter's Darling (Lane)
1957	An Affair To Remember (Warren-McCarey)

Adler, (Lawrence) Larry, harmonica player; b. Baltimore, Feb. 10, 1914. Nightclub and concert virtuoso who performed specialty in films, most memorably playing "Night Over Shanghai" in *The Singing Marine*.

1934	Many Happy Returns
	Operator 13
1936	Big Broadcast of 1937
1937	The Singing Marine
1944	Music for Millions
1948	Three Daring Daughters

Adler, Richard, composer, lyricist; b. New York, Aug. 3, 1921. With co-composer-lyricist Jerry Ross, Adler wrote the scores for two Broadway musicals, *The Pajama Game* and *Damn Yankees,* that were transferred to the screen. Alone he has written stage and television musicals, ballets, and concert pieces. Adler was once married to actress Sally Ann Howes.

1957	The Pajama Game (Ross)
	Little Women (tv)
1958	Damn Yankees (Ross)
	The Gift of the Magi (tv)
1966	Olympus 7-0000 (tv) (also prod.)

"Affair To Remember, An" Music by Harry Warren; lyric by Harold Adamson & Leo McCarey; French lyric by Tanis Chandler. Title song—and romantic theme melody—of 1957 Fox film, first sung by Vic Damone over credits. During story, it was performed in scene at Villefranche, in which Cary Grant's aunt, Cathleen Nesbitt, a former concert pianist, plays the music for Grant and Deborah Kerr. Miss Kerr, with Marni Nixon's dubbed voice, then sings it in French. Also sung by Kerr-Nixon as sign-off piece in a Boston nightclub. Composer Warren once revealed that he tried twenty-five different melodies before getting the one that he felt had the proper "classical" sound. The film for which the song was written was a remake of *Love Affair* (1939), and originally the song was given that title. When it was found that RKO had sold Fox the rights to everything *but* the title, it had to be changed and the lyrics adjusted accordingly. But the new title was still not contained in the lyric; the closest it came was in the final four bars: "a love affair to remember."

"Afraid To Dream" Music by Harry Revel; lyric by Mack Gordon. Don Ameche confessed his romantic insecurity in *You Can't Have Everything* (Fox 1937). Song also sung in film by Tony Martin and Alice Faye.

"After Sundown" Music by Nacio Herb Brown; lyric by Arthur Freed. Soulful Latin-flavored ballad sung by Bing Crosby off camera during a montage of romantic scenes involving Bing and Marion Davies in *Going Hollywood* (MGM 1933).

"Again" Music by Lionel Newman; lyric by Dorcas Cochran. Though not written specifically for a film, the song was identified with Ida Lupino, who talk-sang it as a road-house entertainer in *Road House* (Fox 1948).

Ager, Milton, composer; b. Chicago, Oct. 6, 1893; d. Los Angeles, April 6, 1979. Former vaudeville pianist who became publisher and wrote songs for stage and early talkies. Best-remembered film song was "Happy Days Are Here Again," with Jack Yellen.

1929 Honky Tonk (Yellen)
1930 Chasing Rainbows (Yellen)
 King of Jazz (Yellen)
 They Learned About Women (Yellen)

"Ah Still Suits Me" Music by Jerome Kern; lyric by Oscar Hammerstein II. Kern and Hammerstein added this song of shiftless contentment to Universal's 1936 film version of *Show Boat*. Paul Robeson sang it while shelling peas in the kitchen of the showboat, and Hattie McDaniel, as his wife, supplied verbal counterpoint as she berated him for his laziness. (In the scene a box of Aunt Jemima Pancake Mix was prominently displayed on the table. Coincidentally, Tess Gardella, known as Aunt Jemima, had played Miss McDaniel's role in the original stage production of *Show Boat*.) Title of song is now customarily written "I Still Suits Me."

"Ain't It a Shame About Mame?" Music by James V. Monaco; lyric by Johnny Burke. Jaunty tale of the misfortunes that befall a regular gal when she ups and marries Sir Reginald What's-His-Name. Introduced in *Rhythm on the River* (Par. 1940) by Mary Martin at an audition of songs she's written with Bing Crosby.

Akst, Harry, composer; b. New York, Aug. 15, 1894; d. Hollywood, March 31, 1963. Vaudeville pianist, band leader, then Hollywood composer, primarily for Warner and Fox. With lyricist Grant Clarke, he wrote "Am I Blue?," which Ethel Waters sang in *On with the Show*. Others who sang Akst songs in films: Ted Lewis, Jane Withers, Harry Richman, Tony Martin. Others with whom he wrote: Benny Davis, Lew Brown, Sidney Clare.

1929 On with the Show (Clarke)
 Is Everybody Happy? (Clarke)
 The Show of Shows (pianist only)
1930 So Long, Letty (Clarke)
 Song of the Flame (Clarke)
 Leathernecking (Davis)
1931 June Moon (pianist only)
1933 42nd Street (pianist only)
1934 Stand Up and Cheer (Brown)
1935 Paddy O'Day (Clare)
1936 Can This Be Dixie? (Clare)
 The Music Goes Round (Brown)
 Star for a Night (Clare)
1937 The Holy Terror (Clare)
 Sing and Be Happy (Clare)
1938 Rascals (Clare)
1943 Harvest Melody (Davis)

Alberghetti, Anna Maria, actress, singer; b. Pesaro, Italy, May 15, 1936. Dark-haired, wide-eyed actress with classically trained voice who made her concert debut at Carnegie Hall in 1949. In addition to films she has also appeared on Broadway in *Carnival*, in nightclubs, and on television.

1951 The Medium (Italy) (*Monica*)
 Here Comes the Groom (*Theresa*)
1953 The Stars Are Singing (*Katri Wallenska*)
1957 10,000 Bedrooms (*Nina Martelli*)
1958 Aladdin (tv) (*Princess*)

1959 A Bell for Adano (tv) (*Tina*)
1960 Cinderfella (*Princess Charmaine*)

Alda, Robert (né Alphonso Roberto D'Abruzzo), actor, singer; b. New York, Feb. 26, 1914. Film debut as George Gershwin in Warner's *Rhapsody in Blue;* later usually played heavies. The father of Alan Alda, he also acted on Broadway in *Guys and Dolls*. (Died 1986.)

1945 Rhapsody in Blue (*George Gershwin*)
1946 Cinderella Jones (*Tommy Coles*)
1947 The Man I Love (*Mickey Toresca*)
1948 April Showers (*Billy Shay*)

Alexander's Ragtime Band (1938). Music & lyrics by Irving Berlin; screenplay by Kathryn Scola, Lamar Trotti, Richard Sherman.

A 20th Century-Fox film produced by Darryl F. Zanuck; associate producer, Harry Joe Brown; directed by Henry King; choreography, Seymour Felix; art directors, Bernard Herzbrun, Boris Leven; costumes, Gwen Wakeling; music director, Alfred Newman; cameraman, J. Peverell Marley; editor, Barbara McLean.

Cast: Tyrone Power (*Alexander, né Roger Grant*); Alice Faye (*Stella Kirby*); Don Ameche (*Charlie Dwyer*); Ethel Merman (*Jerry Allen*); Jack Haley (*Davey Lane*); Helen Westley (*Aunt Sophie*); Jean Hersholt (*Prof. Heinrich*); John Carradine (*taxi driver*); Paul Hurst (*Bill Mulligan*); Wally Vernon (*Wally*); Ruth Terry (*Ruby Lane*); Douglas Fowley (*Snapper*); Eddie Collins (*Cpl. Collins*); Chick Chandler (*Louie*); Dixie Dunbar (*dancer*); Robert Gleckler (*Dirty Eddie*); Joe King (*Charles Dillingham*); Charles Coleman (*waiter*); The King's Men (*army quartet*); Cully Richards (*musician*); Jane Jones, Mel Kalish, Otto Fries (*singing trio*); Jack Pennick (*sergeant*); Charles Tannen (*secretary*); Lon Chaney Jr. (*photographer*); Grady Sutton (*Babe*).

Songs: "Alexander's Ragtime Band" - Faye, with Power, Ameche, Haley, Richards/ "Ragtime Violin" - Jones, Kalish, Fries/ "That International Rag" - Faye, with Haley, Chandler/ "Everybody's Doin' It" - Faye, chorus; dance by Vernon, Dunbar/ "Now It Can Be Told" - Ameche; Faye/ "This Is the Life" - Vernon/ "When the Midnight Choo-Choo Leaves for Alabam' " - Faye/ "For Your Country and My Country" -Douglas/ "I Can Always Find a Little Sunshine at the YMCA" - King's Men/ "Oh, How I Hate To Get Up in the Morning" - Haley, soldiers/ "We're on Our Way to France" - soldiers/ "Say It with Music" - Merman/ "A Pretty Girl Is Like a Melody" - Merman/ "Blue Skies" - Merman, Faye/ "Pack Up Your Sins

and Go to the Devil" - Merman/ "What'll I Do?" - chorus/ "My Walking Stick" - Merman/ "Remember" - Faye/ "Everybody Step" - Merman/ "All Alone" - Faye/ "Marie" - chorus/ "Easter Parade" - Ameche/ "Heat Wave" - Merman, chorus. Unused: "Marching Along with Time."

Alexander's Ragtime Band was the first in a series of big-budget musicals that used period locales and glossed-over history as backdrop for a procession of familiar melodies. In this case, it was the output of Irving Berlin through which the film covered the story of the ups, downs, and ups of a classically trained bandleader (Tyrone Power), his composer-pianist friend (Don Ameche), and the singer they both love (Alice Faye). Though their saga covers the period 1911 to 1937, none of the principals ages a day as they progress from humble beginnings in San Francisco, through World War I, international acclaim, and on up to a sellout concert at Carnegie Hall. Primarily because Alexander, like Berlin, put on a wartime soldier show, many mistakenly have believed the movie to be based on the composer's life—though the Carnegie Hall ending could just as easily have indicated Benny Goodman's. The film, which was in production for over a year and utilized 85 sets, was something of a nostalgic follow-up to *In Old Chicago*, also starring Power, Ameche, and Faye, though that film had used songs far more sparingly. After *Alexander's* success, Fox followed it with other period musicals: *Rose of Washington Square* (Faye, Power); *Lillian Russell* (Faye, Ameche); *Tin Pan Alley* (Faye, Grable, Payne); *Hello, Frisco, Hello* (Faye, Payne); *The Dolly Sisters* (Grable, Payne, Haver), etc.

"Alfie" Music by Burt Bacharach; lyric by Hal David. Theme song of nonmusical film *Alfie* (Par. 1966), which sums up hedonism of leading character, played by Michael Caine, through series of questions ("What's it all about, Alfie?"). Lyricist David once admitted that he was reluctant to take on assignment because a song about a man with so uninteresting a name as Alfie did not excite him. Number was sung on soundtrack by Cher.

"All God's Chillun Got Rhythm" Music by Bronislaw Kaper & Walter Jurmann; lyric by Gus Kahn. Revivalistic number introduced by Ivie Anderson and Crinoline Choir in *A Day at the Races* (MGM 1937). The scene begins with Harpo Marx as a flute-playing Pied Piper attracting a horde of shanty-town Negroes who think he's Gabriel. They then dance through the town proclaiming the happiness derived from the one thing that all God's chillun got.

"All I Do Is Dream of You" Music by Nacio Herb Brown; lyric by Arthur Freed. Confession of a romantic idler, introduced by Gene Raymond in *Sadie McKee* (MGM 1934). Also sung by uncredited French singer in *Broadway Melody of 1936* (MGM 1935); Debbie Reynolds in *Singin' in the Rain* (MGM 1952); Miss Reynolds and Bobby Van in *The Affairs of Dobie Gillis* (MGM 1953); Twiggy in *The Boy Friend* (MGM 1971).

"All I Want Is Just One Girl" Music by Richard A. Whiting; lyric by Leo Robin. In the revue *Paramount on Parade* (Par. 1930) a scene called "A Park in Paris" offered Maurice Chevalier, as a gendarme, observing the numerous park-bench lovers and singing of his desire to find the one girl for him. Song reprised in film by Mitzi Green imitating Charlie Mack (of Moran & Mack) and Chevalier.

All That Jazz (1979). Screenplay by Robert Alan Aurthur & Bob Fosse.

A 20th Century-Fox and Columbia film produced by Daniel Melnick and Robert Alan Aurthur; directed by Bob Fosse; choreography, Fosse; production design, Philip Rosenberg; fantasy design, Tony Walton; costumes, Albert Wolsky; music director, Ralph Burns; orchestrations, Burns; cameraman, Giuseppe Rotunno; editor, Alan Heim; Technicolor.

Cast: Roy Scheider (*Joe Gideon*); Jessica Lange (*Angelique*); Ann Reinking (*Kate Jagger*); Leland Palmer (*Audrey Paris*); Cliff Gorman (*David Newman*); Ben Vereen (*O'Connor Flood*); Erzsebet Foldi (*Michelle*); William LeMassena (*Jonesy Hecht*); Deborah Geffner (*Victoria*); Sandahl Bergman (*featured dancer*); Keith Gordon (*Young Joe*).

Songs: "On Broadway" (Barry Mann-Cynthia Weil-Jerry Leiber-Mike Stoller) - George Benson (soundtrack)/ "Take Off with Us" (Stan Lebowsky-Fred Tobias) - Bergman, chorus/ "Everything Old Is New Again" (Peter Allen-Carole Sager) - Peter Allen (soundtrack); dance by Reinking, Foldi/ "After You've Gone" (Henry Creamer-Turner Layton) - Palmer/ "There'll Be Some Changes Made" (W. B. Overstreet-Billy Higgins) - Reinking/ "Some of These Days" (Shelton Brooks) - Foldi/ "Bye Bye Love" - (B. & F. Bryant) - Vereen, Scheider.

Like Bob Fosse, the film's director and co-author, the leading character, Joe Gideon, is a hard-driving, self-absorbed, death-obsessed, chain-smoking Broadway director-choreographer, with an understanding ex-wife (Leland Palmer suggesting Gwen Verdon), a patient mistress (Ann Reinking suggesting Ann Reinking), and an adoring daughter (Erzsabet Foldi suggesting Nicole Fosse). Also like Fosse, Gideon suffers from a heart attack which—unlike Fosse's—proves fatal. Beginning with a crackling chorus-line audition, *All That Jazz* offers authentic glimpses of the creation and creators of a musical show until the last half hour when the emphasis shifts to Gideon's coronary. After Gideon literally bares his heart to the audience during open-heart surgery, a razzle-dazzle song-and-dance fantasy brings his life and the film to an end.

The unusual joint sponsorship of *All That Jazz* by two rival film companies came about when Fox invested in it after Columbia had threatened to halt production because of soaring costs.

"All the Way" Music by James Van Heusen; lyric by Sammy Cahn. Song pledging total devotion sung by Frank Sinatra (as Joe E. Lewis) in *The Joker Is Wild* (Par. 1957). Scene was the opening night at a swank Chicago nightclub; song later reprised by voice of Sinatra on record. Because of the ballad's popularity, the film itself later became known as *All the Way*—though the lyric revealed a far stronger romantic commitment than the character in the story actually possessed.

"All Through the Day" Music by Jerome Kern; lyric by Oscar Hammerstein II. Sung by Larry Stevens in *Centennial Summer* (Fox 1946) during a demonstration of magic lantern slides at the Philadelphia Centennial Exposition in 1876. In the ballad, the singer reveals that he spends his days dreaming about the night ("Down falls the sun . . . Down smiles the moon"), when he can be alone with his beloved.

"All You Want To Do Is Dance" Music by Arthur Johnston; lyric by Johnny Burke. Amorous frustration felt by one whose ballroom partner is more interested in dancing than in romancing. Sung by Bing Crosby in *Double or Nothing* (Par. 1937).

Allen, Fred, (né John Florence Sullivan), actor; b. Cambridge, Mass., May 31, 1894; d. New York, March 17, 1956. Allen was a deadpan comic distinguished by heavily pouched eyes and a flat nasal twang. After beginning in vaudeville, where he specialized in topical humor, he appeared in five Broadway musicals but reached his greatest fame on radio in the 30s and 40s. His wife, Portland Hoffa, was a member of his comedy troupe. Bib: *Much Ado About Me* by Allen (1956).

1935 Thanks a Million (*Ned Lyman*)
1938 Sally, Irene and Mary (*Gabriel Green*)
1940 Buck Benny Rides Again (voice only)
     Love Thy Neighbor (*Fred Allen*)

Allen, Gracie. *See* **Burns and Allen.**

"All's Fair in Love and War" Music by Harry Warren; lyric by Al Dubin. This lighthearted battle-of-the-sexes song was written to accommodate a Busby Berkeley military spectacle in *Gold Diggers of 1937* (Warner 1936). It was sung by Dick Powell to Joan Blondell, who then led a company of 70 white-helmeted girls carrying flags and drums through all sorts of marching drills. Because of budget restrictions, Berkeley staged the number without sets—only a sound stage covered with shiny black surfacing.

Allyson, June (née Ella Geisman), actress, singer; b. The Bronx, NY, Oct. 7, 1923(?). Husky-voiced, diminutive, blonde June Allyson was the spunky, lip-quivering heroine of a series of youthful MGM musicals, including *Two Sisters from Boston* and *Good News*, both opposite Peter Lawford. She's also remembered for her Universal loanout as James Stewart's wife in *The Glenn Miller Story*. Miss Allyson's early appearances were in the chorus and in featured roles of Broadway musicals, most notably *Best Foot Forward*, which won her a Hollywood contract. Her first husband was Dick Powell.

1943 Best Foot Forward (*Minerva*)
     Girl Crazy (specialty)
     Thousands Cheer (specialty)
1944 Meet the People (*Annie*)
     Two Girls and a Sailor (*Patsy Deyo*)
1945 Music for Millions (*Barbara Ainsworth*)
1946 Two Sisters from Boston (*Martha Canford Chandler*)
     Till the Clouds Roll By (specialty)
1947 Good News (*Connie Lane*)
1948 Words and Music (specialty)
1954 The Glenn Miller Story (*Helen Miller*)
1956 The Opposite Sex (*Kay*)
     You Can't Run Away from It (*Ellie Andrews*)

"Alone" Music by Nacio Herb Brown; lyric by Arthur Freed. Romantic mating call from one lonely heart to

another. First sung on board an ocean liner in *A Night at the Opera* (MGM 1935) by Kitty Carlisle and Allan Jones; reprised by Harpo Marx as harp solo. Also sung by Judy Garland in *Andy Hardy Meets Debutante* (MGM 1940).

Alter, Louis, composer; b. Haverhill, Mass., June 18, 1902; d. New York, Nov. 3, 1980. Began career as vaudeville pianist, then wrote songs for Broadway musicals. Best-known film contributions: "You Turned the Tables on Me," "Twilight on the Trail," and "A Melody from the Sky" (all with lyricist Sidney Mitchell); "Rainbow on the River" (Paul Francis Webster); "Dolores" (Frank Loesser); "Do You Know What It Means To Miss New Orleans" (Eddie DeLange). Also wrote with Jack Scholl.

1935 Going Highbrow (Scholl)
1936 Trail of the Lonesome Pine (Mitchell)
     Rainbow on the River (Webster)
1937 Make a Wish (Webster)
1947 New Orleans (DeLange)

Altman, Robert, director; b. Kansas City, Mo., Feb. 20, 1922. Prolific, imaginative director who scored first hit with *M*A*S*H*, then made major contribution with musical *Nashville*. Bib: *Robert Altman* by Judith Kass (1978).

1975 Nashville (also prod.)
1979 A Perfect Couple (also script, prod.)
1980 Popeye

Alton, Robert (né Robert Alton Hart), choreographer; b. Bennington, Vt., Jan. 28, 1897; d. Hollywood, June 12, 1957. Broadway choreographer of 30s and early 40s (*Anything Goes, Pal Joey*) who was associated with MGM musicals between 1944 and 1953.

1936 Strike Me Pink
1941 You'll Never Get Rich
1944 Broadway Rhythm
     Bathing Beauty
1946 The Harvey Girls
     Ziegfeld Follies
     Till the Clouds Roll By
1947 Good News
1948 The Pirate
     Easter Parade
     The Kissing Bandit
     Words and Music
1949 The Barkleys of Broadway
     In the Good Old Summertime
1950 Annie Get Your Gun
     Pagan Love Song (also dir.)

1951 Show Boat
1952 The Belle of New York
1953 I Love Melvin
     Call Me Madam
1954 White Christmas
     The Country Girl
     There's No Business Like Show Business
1955 The Girl Rush (also co-prod.)

"Always and Always" Music by Edward Ward; lyric by Bob Wright & George Forrest. Pledge of eternal devotion sung by Joan Crawford to Alan Curtis in *Mannequin* (MGM 1937).

"Am I Blue?" Music by Harry Akst; lyric by Grant Clarke. Torchy lament of a woman whose man has gone, leaving her "the sad and lonely one." Introduced by Ethel Waters wearing a bandanna and carrying a basket of cotton in a plantation scene of a Broadway-bound musical in *On with the Show* (Warner 1929). Also sung by Charlotte Greenwood in *So Long, Letty* (Warner 1930); Joan Leslie in *The Hard Way* (Warner 1942); Nan Wynn in *Is Everybody Happy?* (Col. 1943); Barbra Streisand in *Funny Lady* (Col. 1975). In her autobiography, *His Eye Is on the Sparrow*, Miss Waters revealed that Harry Akst, who had written "Dinah," had come to her dressing room while she was singing in Los Angeles and offered her the new song. When she sang it for Darryl Zanuck he signed her for two weeks' work in *On with the Show*. In another Akst-Clarke song, "Birmingham Bertha," also sung by Miss Waters in the film, she related the further tale of the woman who goes to Chicago to get even with the man who done her wrong.

"Am I in Love?" Music by Harry Warren; lyric by Al Dubin. He's got all the symptoms so it must be the real thing. Crooned by Kenny Baker in *Mr. Dodd Takes the Air* (Warner 1937); also by Gene Nelson in *She's Working Her Way Through College* (Warner 1952).

"Amado Mio" Music & lyric by Doris Fisher & Allan Roberts. Sultry ballad sung in a Rio de Janeiro nightclub in *Gilda* (Col. 1944) by Rita Hayworth (with Anita Ellis' voice).

Ameche, Don (né Dominic Felix Amici), actor, singer; b. Kenosha, Wis., May 31, 1908. Ameche was the toothy, mustached, leading man of Fox musicals, appearing with Alice Faye (five times), and Sonja Henie and Betty Grable (twice each). Among songs he intro-

duced: "Afraid To Dream," "Now It Can Be Told" (in *Alexander's Ragtime Band*), "Down Argentina Way," "You'd Be So Nice To Come Home To." He also appeared in many nonmusicals (including *Alexander Graham Bell*) and Broadway musicals (*Silk Stockings*). Since Ameche's last film appearance in 1966, he has devoted himself primarily to the stage.

1936 Ramona (*Alessandro*)
     One in a Million (*Bob Harris*)
1937 You Can't Have Everything (*George McRea*)
1938 In Old Chicago (*Jack O'Leary*)
     Happy Landing (*Jimmy Hall*)
     Alexander's Ragtime Band (*Charlie Dwyer*)
     Josette (*David Brossard*)
1939 The Three Musketeers (*D'Artagnan*)
     Swanee River (*Stephen Foster*)
1940 Lillian Russell (*Edward Solomon*)
     Down Argentine Way (*Ricardo Quintero*)
1941 That Night in Rio (*Larry Martin/ Baron Manuel Duarte*)
     Moon Over Miami (*Phil O'Neil*)
     Kiss the Boys Goodbye (*Lloyd Lloyd*)
1943 Something To Shout About (*Ken Douglas*)
1944 Greenwich Village (*Kenneth Harvey*)
1949 Slightly French (*John Gayle*)
1957 Junior Miss (tv) (*Harry Graves*)

American in Paris, An (1951). Music by George Gershwin; lyrics by Ira Gershwin; screenplay by Alan Jay Lerner.

An MGM film produced by Arthur Freed; directed by Vincente Minnelli; choreography, Gene Kelly; art directors, Cedric Gibbons, Preston Ames; costumes, Irene Sharaff, Orry-Kelly, Walter Plunkett; music director, Johnny Green; orchestrations, Green, Saul Chaplin; cameramen, Alfred Gilks, John Alton; editor, Adrienne Fazan; Technicolor.

Cast: Gene Kelly (*Jerry Mulligan*); Leslie Caron (*Lise Bourvier*); Oscar Levant (*Adam Cook*); Georges Guetary (*Henri Baurel*); Nina Foch (*Milo Roberts*); Eugene Borden (*Georges Mattieu*); Martha Bammatre (*Mathilde Mattieu*); Anna Q. Nilsson (*Kay Jensen*); Paul Maxey (*John McDowd*); Mary Young (*flower seller*); Lucien Planzoles, Christian Pasques, Anthony Mazola (*boys in street*); George Davis (*François*), Dudley Field Malone (*Winston Churchill*).

Songs: "Nice Work If You Can Get It" - Guetary/ "Embraceable You" - dance by Caron/ "Fascinating Rhythm" - Levant, piano/ "By Strauss" - Guetary, Kelly, Levant; dance by Kelly, Guetary, Young, Borden, Bammatre/ "I Got Rhythm" - Kelly, with Planzoles, Pasques, Mazola, others/ "Tra-La-La" - Kelly, Levant; dance by Kelly with Levant, piano/ "Love Is Here To Stay" - Kelly; dance by Kelly & Caron/ "I'll Build a Stairway to Paradise" (lyric with B. G. De-Sylva) - Guetary, with showgirls/ "I Don't Think I'll Fall in Love Today" - Levant, piano/ "Concerto in F 3rd Movement" - Levant, piano/ " 'S Wonderful" - Guetary, Kelly; dance by Kelly/ "Liza" - Levant, piano/ "An American in Paris" (ballet) - Kelly, Caron, dancers. Unused: "My Cousin in Milwaukee," "A Foggy Day," "The Half of It Dearie, Blues," "But Not for Me," "Love Walked In," "I've Got a Crush on You."

The film's genesis was a vague notion producer Freed had about doing a musical about an American—prefer-ably a dancer—in Paris. Ira Gershwin agreed to sell him the title but only on condition that no songs other than those by the Gershwin brothers would be used. It was further decided to incorporate the Gershwin sym-phonic suite at the end of the film, though no one knew just how. The idea for the story evolved from an article in *Life* magazine about American artists studying in Paris under the GI Bill of Rights. Screenwriter Alan Jay Lerner focused his tale on expatriate painter Gene Kelly who needs only one look at Leslie Caron to fall in love with her. Complications arise, however, because she is betrothed to an older man, a music-hall entertainer (Georges Guetary), who had saved her life during the Resistance. The artist, too, has a would-be protector of sorts, a rich American woman, played by Nina Foch, which put Kelly in something of a chaste variation on the situation he had encountered in his first hit, the Broadway musical *Pal Joey*. To keep the plot going, Kelly and Guetary become friends through mutual con-fidant Oscar Levant without being aware that each loves the same girl. Eventually, of course, Guetary makes the noble sacrifice to true love.

Original plans called for about half the movie to be filmed in Paris, but financial considerations dictated that the entire film be shot in Culver City. Among those ini-tially considered for Kelly's dancing and romantic part-ner were Cyd Charisse and Vera-Ellen; Kelly, however, held out for Miss Caron, an authentic Parisienne whom he had seen in a ballet in Paris two years before. Guetary won the role of the French singer over Carl Brisson and Maurice Chevalier.

The "American in Paris" ballet was tied rather loosely into the story as the means through which Kelly, brooding over his lost love, thinks about Paris and what the city has meant to him. Since he played the role of an artist, all locales in the 17-minute work were depicted in the styles of such painters as Dufy (Place de la Con-corde), Renoir (Pont Neuf), Utrillo (Montmartre), Rousseau (the zoo), Van Gogh (Place de l'Opéra), and Toulouse-Lautrec (Moulin Rouge). The ballet took six weeks to rehearse and one month to shoot. Bib: *The Magic Factory* by Donald Knox (1973).

Anchors Aweigh (1945). Music mostly by Jule Styne; lyrics mostly by Sammy Cahn; screenplay by Isobel Lennart from short story "You Can't Fool a Marine" by Natalie Marcin.

An MGM film produced by Joe Pasternak; directed by George Sidney; choreography, Gene Kelly, Stanley Do-nen; cartoon sequence directed by Fred Quimby; art di-rectors, Cedric Gibbons, Randall Duell; costumes, Irene, Kay Dean; music director, George Stoll; camera-men, Robert Planck, Charles Boyle; editor, Adrienne Fazan; Technicolor.

Cast: Frank Sinatra (*Clarence Doolittle*); Kathryn Grayson (*Susan Abbott*); Gene Kelly (*Joe Brady*); José Iturbi (*José Iturbi*); Dean Stockwell (*Donald Martin*); Carlos Ramirez (*Carlos*); Henry O'Neill (*Admiral Ham-mond*); Leon Ames (*Commander*); Rags Ragland (*police sergeant*); Edgar Kennedy (*police captain*); Pamela Britton (*Brooklyn girl*); Henry Armetta (*hamburger man*); Billy Gilbert (*café manager*); Sharon McManus (*Mexican girl*); James Burke (*studio cop*); Grady Sutton (*Bertram Kramer*); Charles Coleman (*butler*); Harry Barris (*sailor*).

Songs: "We Hate To Leave" - Sinatra, Kelly, chorus/ "Lullaby" (Brahms) - Sinatra/ "I Begged Her" - Sin-atra, Kelly/ "If You Knew Susie" (Joseph Meyer-B. G. DeSylva) - Sinatra, Kelly/ "Jealousy" (Jacob Gade-Vera Bloom) - Grayson/ "What Makes the Sunset?" - Sinatra/ "All of a Sudden My Heart Sings" (Herpin-Harold Rome) - Grayson/ "Donkey Serenade" (Rudolf Friml) - Iturbi, piano/ "The King Who Couldn't Dance" incl. "The Worry Song" (Sammy Fain-Ralph Freed) - Kelly: dance by Kelly, Jerry the Mouse/ The Charm of You" - Sinatra/ "Mexican Hat Dance" (F. A. Partichela) - Kelly, McManus/ "Hungarian Rhap-sody No. 2" (Liszt) - Iturbi, piano, with piano students/ "I Fall in Love Too Easily" - Sinatra/ "La Cumpar-sita" (Matos Rodriguez) - dance by Kelly/ "Waltz Ser-enade" (Tchaikovsky-Earl Brent) - Grayson, with Iturbi, studio orch./ "Anchors Aweigh" (Alfred Miles - Charles Zimmerman) - chorus, with Iturbi, Navy band.

The theme of sailors on leave in a big city, which had already been the concern of *Follow the Fleet,* was the basic idea of Frank Sinatra's first starring film at MGM. With Gene Kelly as the brash sailor, and Sinatra as the shy one, the movie put them ashore in Hollywood, where they become involved in furthering Kathryn Grayson's singing career and take every chance they get to sing and dance. Kelly's major dancing stints were in a "Mexican Hat Dance" routine with Sharon McManus, and in the highly imaginative "King Who Couldn't Dance" number, the first time the screen was able to combine live-action dance routines with animated cartoon characters (in this case Jerry the Mouse, co-star of the *Tom and Jerry* series of shorts). In all, Sinatra and Kelly made three films together. The third, *On the Town,* again found them as sailors on shore leave, this time in New York.

"And You'll Be Home" Music by James Van Heusen; lyric by Johnny Burke. Ariose advice to find happiness by following one's dreams and one's heart, sung by Bing Crosby in *Mr. Music* (Par. 1950).

Anderson, (Edward) Eddie "Rochester", actor, singer; b. Oakland, Cal., Sept. 18, 1905; d. Los Angeles, Feb. 28, 1977. A short, gravel-voiced black comic, Anderson won lasting fame as Jack Benny's radio and television valet Rochester, who always had an impertinent quip to cut his penny-pinching master down to size. He was associated with Benny from 1937 to 1964, during which time they also appeared together in three films. Anderson's most important screen role was in *Cabin in the Sky.*

1936	Show Boat (*young Negro*)
	The Music Goes Round (bit)
1937	Melody for Two (*Exodus Johnson*)
1938	Gold Diggers in Paris (*doorman*)
	Going Places (*groom*)
1939	Man About Town (*Rochester*)
	Honolulu (*Washington*)
1940	Buck Benny Rides Again (*Rochester*)
	Love Thy Neighbor (*Rochester*)
1941	Birth of the Blues (*Louie*)
	Kiss the Boys Goodbye (*George*)
1943	Star Spangled Rhythm (specialty)
	Cabin in the Sky (*Little Joe Jackson*)
	What's Buzzin' Cousin? (*Rochester*)
	Broadway Rhythm (*Eddie*)
1945	I Love a Bandleader (*Newton H. Newton*)

Anderson, Maxwell, lyricist; b. Atlantic, Pa., Dec. 15, 1888; d. Stamford, Conn., Feb. 28, 1959. Poetic playwright (*Mary of Scotland, Winterset*) whose two Broadway musicals with composer Kurt Weill were transferred to the screen. Also adapted his own play *High Tor* as a television musical with composer Arthur Schwartz, and wrote songs for one Hollywood film with Allie Wrubel.

1944	Knickerbocker Holiday (Weill)
1956	High Tor (tv) Schwartz) (also script)
1959	Never Steal Anything Small (Wrubel)
1974	Lost in the Stars (Weill)

Andrews, Julie (née Julia Elizabeth Wells), actress, singer; b. Walton-on-Thames, Eng., Oct. 1, 1935. Following her Broadway successes in *The Boy Friend, My Fair Lady,* and *Camelot,* Miss Andrews brought her spring-clear voice and spoonful-of-sugar charm to such major family-entertainment musical films as *Mary Poppins, The Sound of Music,* and *Thoroughly Modern Millie.* She also appeared in the first television version of *Cinderella* (introducing "In My Own Little Corner"). Later, Miss Andrews turned to more sophisticated film fare, both with songs (*Darling Lili,* in which she sang "Whistling Away the Dark") and without. First married to designer Tony Walton, she is the wife of producer Blake Edwards. Bib: *Julie Andrews* by John Cottrell (1968); *Julie Andrews* by Robert Windeler (1970).

1956	High Tor (tv) (*Lise*)
1957	Cinderella (tv) (*Cinderella*)
1964	Mary Poppins (*Mary Poppins*)
1965	The Sound of Music (*Maria Rainer von Trapp*)
1967	Thoroughly Modern Millie (*Millie*)
1968	Star! (*Gertrude Lawrence*)
1969	Darling Lili (*Lili Smith*)
1982	Victor/Victoria (*Victoria Grant*)

Andrews Sisters, singers, actresses. (Patricia) Patti, b. Minneapolis, Feb. 16, 1920; Maxine, b. Minneapolis, Jan. 3, 1918; LaVerne, b. Minneapolis, July 6, 1915; d. May 8, 1967. Rhythmic vocal trio whose distinctive harmonizing first won notice with "Bei Mir Bist du Schon." Made many records and appeared in modest-budget musicals at Universal (1940–44), including three with Abbott and Costello. Among film songs they introduced: "You're a Lucky Fellow Mr. Smith," "Boogie Woogie Bugle Boy," "Pennsylvania Polka." Patti and Maxine also starred on Broadway in *Over Here,* and Maxine (aka Maxene) later had a solo singing act.

The Andrews Sisters always kept their real names for their film roles:

1940 Argentine Nights
1941 Buck Privates
     In the Navy
     Hold That Ghost
1942 What's Cookin'?
     Private Buckaroo
     Give Out, Sisters
1943 How's About It?
     Always a Bridesmaid
1944 Follow the Boys
     Moonlight and Cactus
     Swingtime Johnny
     Hollywood Canteen
1946 Make Mine Music (soundtrack only)
1947 Road to Rio
1948 Melody Time (soundtrack only)

"Angel Eyes" Music by Matt Dennis; lyric by Earl Brent. Boozy lament ("Drink up, all you people") of a torch-carrying nightclub entertainer, introduced by composer Dennis in *Jennifer* (AA 1953).

"Animal Crackers in My Soup" Music by Ray Henderson; lyric by Ted Koehler & Irving Caesar. Sung in *Curly Top* (Fox 1935) by Shirley Temple at the Lakeside Orphanage to entertain the other children during lunch. After singing, Miss Temple skips up and down between the rows of tables as the kids beat time with their silverware.

Ann-Margret (née Ann-Margaret Olsson), actress, singer, dancer; b. Valsobyn, Sweden, April 28, 1941. Leggy personification of outdoorsy sensuality who has been a headliner in nightclubs as well as a film star; has also appeared in many nonmusicals.

1962 State Fair (*Emily*)
1963 Bye Bye Birdie (*Kim McAfee*)
1964 The Pleasure Seekers (*Fran Hobson*)
     Viva Las Vegas (*Rusty Martin*)
1966 The Swinger (*Kelly Olsson*)
1975 Tommy (*Norma Walker*)

Annie Get Your Gun (1950). Music & lyrics by Irving Berlin; screenplay by Sidney Sheldon from Broadway musical by Dorothy & Herbert Fields and Berlin.

An MGM film produced by Arthur Freed; associate producer, Roger Edens; directed by George Sidney; choreography, Robert Alton; art directors, Cedric Gibbons, Paul Groesse; costumes, Helen Rose, Walter Plunkett; music director, Adolph Deutsch; cameraman, Charles Rosher; editor, James Newcom; Technicolor.

Cast: Betty Hutton (*Annie Oakley*); Howard Keel (*Frank Butler*); Louis Calhern (*Buffalo Bill Cody*); J. Carrol Naish (*Chief Sitting Bull*); Edward Arnold (*Pawnee Bill*); Keenan Wynn (*Charlie Davenport*); Benay Venuta (*Dolly Tate*); Clinton Sundberg (*Foster Wilson*); James H. Harrison (*Mac*); Bradley Mora (*Little Jake*); Diana Dick (*Nellie*); Susan Odin (*Jessie*); Eleanor Brown (*Minnie*).

Songs: "Colonel Buffalo Bill" - Wynn, Venuta, Keel/ "Doin' What Comes Natur'lly" - Hutton/ "The Girl That I Marry" - Keel/ "You Can't Get a Man with a Gun" - Hutton/ "There's No Business Like Show Business" - Wynn, Calhern, Keel, Hutton/ "They Say It's Wonderful" - Hutton, Keel/ "My Defenses Are Down" - Keel/ "I'm an Indian, Too" - Hutton/ "I Got the Sun in the Morning" - Hutton/ "Anything You Can Do" - Hutton, Keel. Unused: "Let's Go West Again," "Moonshine Lullaby."

One of Broadway's classic musical comedies came about simply because co-librettist Dorothy Fields wanted to write a show with Ethel Merman as Annie Oakley. The composer was to have been Jerome Kern, but his death just before production started brought producers Rodgers and Hammerstein to Irving Berlin. MGM bought the screen rights for Judy Garland to play the sharp-shooting, tomboyish hillbilly who joins Buffalo Bill's Wild West Show and promptly falls in love with star attraction Frank Butler. Love turns into bickering rivalry, however, which is only resolved when—despite the contentious duet, "Anything You Can Do"—Annie lets Frank best her in a shooting contest. When illness forced the studio to remove Miss Garland from the project, Betty Hutton, in her only assignment away from Paramount, was given the choicest role of her screen career. The five-month shooting delay also resulted in Louis Calhern being cast as Buffalo Bill after the death of Frank Morgan. Howard Keel, in his first movie, won the part of Frank Butler over John Raitt. As a film, *Annie Get Your Gun* remained close to its source though it was able to take advantage of the camera for outdoor sequences, particularly the spectacular "There's No Business Like Show Business" finale. The movie was the biggest musical hit of 1950.

The success of *Annie Get Your Gun* was apparently the chief inspiration for Warner's *Calamity Jane* (1953), in which buckskin-wearing, trigger-happy "Calám"

(Doris Day) had a feuding romance with mild Bill Hickock (also played by Howard Keel).

"Anniversary Song" Music by Ion Ivanovici, adapted by Saul Chaplin; lyric by Chaplin & Al Jolson. Originally a Rumanian waltz known as "Valurile Dunarii"—and in translations, "Donauwellen" and "Danube Waves"—the sentimental piece was the only "new" song in *The Jolson Story* (Col. 1946). It was sung by Larry Parks (with Al Jolson's voice) while sitting on the veranda of his California house at a small dinner party honoring his parents' 50th wedding anniversary. Jolson sang it again for Parks in *Jolson Sings Again* (Col. 1949). The Ivanovici music had first been heard in the movies as a piano piece supposedly played by Gustav von Seyffertitz and Marlene Dietrich in *Dishonored* (Par. 1931).

"Any Moment Now" Music by Jerome Kern; lyric by E. Y. Harburg. In which a brief meeting stirs anticipation of a lasting love. First sung by Deanna Durbin in *Can't Help Singing* (Univ. 1944).

Anything Goes (1936). Music by Cole Porter, Frederick Hollander, Richard A. Whiting, Hoagy Carmichael; lyrics by Porter, Leo Robin, Edward Heyman; screenplay by Howard Lindsay, Russel Crouse, and Guy Bolton from Broadway musical by Lindsay, Crouse, Bolton, P. G. Wodehouse, and Porter.

A Paramount film produced by Benjamin Glazer; directed by Lewis Milestone; art directors, Hans Dreier, Ernst Fegte; music director, Victor Young; cameraman, Karl Struss; editor, Eda Warren.

Cast: Bing Crosby (*Billy Crocker*); Ethel Merman (*Reno Sweeney*); Charlie Ruggles (*Rev. Dr. Moon*); Ida Lupino (*Hope Harcourt*); Grace Bradley (*Bonnie LeTour*); Arthur Treacher (*Sir Evelyn Oakleigh*); Richard Carle (*Bishop Dobson*); Margaret Dumont (*Mrs. Wentworth*); Robert McWade (*Elisha J. Whitney*); Avalon Boys Quartet.

Songs: "Anything Goes" (Porter) - Merman/ "I Get a Kick Out of You" (Porter) - Merman/ "There'll Always Be a Lady Fair" (Porter) - Avalon Boys/ "Sailor Beware" (Whiting-Robin) - Crosby/ "Moonburn" (Carmichael-Heyman) - Crosby/ "My Heart and I" (Hollander-Robin) - Crosby/ "You're the Top" (Porter) - Merman, Crosby/ "Shanghai-Di-Ho" (Hollander-Robin) - Merman, Crosby.

Anything Goes, the quintessential Broadway musical comedy of the mid-30s, was transferred to the screen with basically the same story, four of the original Cole Porter songs, and Ethel Merman repeating her stage role. Otherwise, there were four new songs, and William Gaxton was replaced by Bing Crosby, Victor Moore by Charlie Ruggles (though W. C. Fields had been slated for the role), and Bettina Hall by Ida Lupino. The principal locale was a transatlantic liner going from New York to Southampton, and the main characters were Reno Sweeney, a former evangelist turned nightclub singer; her friend Billy Crocker; Public Enemy No. 13 masquerading as the Rev. Dr. Moon; and Hope Harcourt, a society belle so beloved by Billy that he stows away just to be near her. The denouement is achieved when Reno snags the titled Englishman to whom Hope is affianced, Billy gets Hope, and Moon is officially declared harmless. There was general disappointment that the film had retained so little of the Porter score (with "You're the Top" undergoing a complete revision in the lyric) and that Victor Moore did not repeat the role with which he was so closely identified.

Twenty years later, another Paramount film called *Anything Goes* again starred Bing Crosby (along with Jeanmaire, Mitzi Gaynor, Donald O'Connor, and Phil Harris) and kept five of the original Cole Porter songs (though lyricist Ted Fetter was called in to make uncredited alterations to "You're the Top" and "Anything Goes"). The movie also added "It's De-Lovely" from another Porter show and assigned James Van Heusen and Sammy Cahn to come up with three new numbers. But apart from an ocean voyage (from Le Havre to New York), this release bore scant resemblance to any *Anything Goes* that had gone before.

"Anywhere I Wander" Music & lyric by Frank Loesser. A wanderer's loneliness expressed by Danny Kaye as *Hans Christian Andersen* (Goldwyn 1952). Note that the song has an unusually short refrain of 12 bars.

"Applause, Applause" Music by Burton Lane; lyric by Ira Gershwin. To bell ringers, singers, monologists, ventriloquists, animal trainers, magicians, musical-saw musicians, actors, pianists—in short, anyone on a stage—there is no sound that's greater than. Introduced in *Give a Girl a Break* (MGM 1953) by Gower Champion and Debbie Reynolds in finale of a Broadway revue.

"Apple for the Teacher, An" Music by James V. Monaco; lyric by Johnny Burke. In which a student expresses his desire to be kept after school to learn romance from the teacher. Sung by Linda Ware in *The Star Maker* (Par. 1939); also by Gene Autry in *The Last Roundup* (Col. 1947).

"April Love" Music by Sammy Fain; lyric by Paul Francis Webster. Ballad of young love sung by Pat Boone entertaining fellow guests at a dance in film of same name (Fox 1957). Song later reprised by Boone and Shirley Jones.

"April Played the Fiddle" Music by James V. Monaco; lyric by Johnny Burke. Springtime stirrings of romance revealed by Bing Crosby in *If I Had My Way* (Univ. 1940).

Arden, Eve (née Eunice Quedens), actress; b. Mill Valley, Cal., April 30, 1912. Tall, wide-eyed unflappable mistress of the one-line, off-the-shoulder putdown. Miss Arden, who did not assume her professional name until she appeared on Broadway in *Ziegfeld Follies of 1934*, has acted in some 60 films, many nonmusical, and has had her own television series, *Our Miss Brooks*. She repeated her stage role in the film version of *Let's Face It*, and scored particular success in *Cover Girl*.

1929	Song of Love (*Mazie*)
1933	Dancing Lady (*southern actress*)
1938	Cocoanut Grove (*Sophie de Lemma*)
	Having Wonderful Time (*Henrietta*)
1939	At the Circus (*Peerless Pauline*)
1940	No, No, Nanette (*Winnie*)
1941	Ziegfeld Girl (*Patsy Dixon*)
	San Antonio Rose (*Gabby Trent*)
	Sing for Your Supper (*Barbara Stevens*)
1943	Hit Parade of 1943 (*Belinda Wright*)
	Let's Face It (*Maggie Watson*)
1944	Cover Girl (*Stonewall Jackson*)
1945	Pan-Americana (*Hoppy*)
	Earl Carroll Vanities (*Tex Donnolly*)
	Patrick the Great (*Jean Matthews*)
1946	The Kid from Brooklyn (*Ann Westley*)
1947	Song of Scheherazade (*Mme. de Talavera*)
1948	One Touch of Venus (*Molly Grant*)
1949	My Dream Is Yours (*Vivian Martin*)
1950	Tea for Two (*Pauline Hastings*)
1978	Grease (*Principal McGee*)
1982	Grease II (*Principal McGee*)

"Aren't You Glad You're You?" Music by James Van Heusen; lyric by Johnny Burke. Song of self-appreciation sung by Bing Crosby in *The Bells of St. Mary's* (RKO 1945) to buck up the spirits of an unhappy young girl (Joan Carroll).

"Aren't You Kind of Glad We Did?" Music by George Gershwin; lyric by Ira Gershwin. Double-entendre conversational duet sung by Betty Grable and Dick Haymes in *The Shocking Miss Pilgrim* (Fox 1947). After having spent the day together and gone to a restaurant for dinner, the unrepentant dyad express mock concern that fellow Bostonians in 1874 will find their behavior scandalous because they'd been unchaperoned. Originally written (but unused) in the early 1930s, the song first dealt with a romantic if impecunious couple expressing satisfaction at being married. For the film, as Ira Gershwin put it in his book *Lyrics on Several Occasions,* he changed the number "from an Epithalamium of the Depression to a mid-Victorian Colloquy."

Arlen, Harold (né Hyman Arluck), composer; b. Buffalo, Feb. 15, 1905. Distinctive composer of richly melodic, penetrating ballads and bright rhythm numbers whose work has been greatly influenced by blues and jazz. Arlen's most celebrated film score was for *The Wizard of Oz* with lyricist E. Y. Harburg ("Over the Rainbow," "We're Off To See the Wizard"); other major screen assignments were *Blues in the Night* with Johnny Mercer ("Blues in the Night," "This Time the Dream's on Me") and *A Star Is Born* with Ira Gershwin ("The Man That Got Away," "It's a New World"). Other Hollywood songs: "Let's Fall in Love," "Lydia, the Tattoed Lady," "That Old Black Magic," "Hit the Road to Dreamland," "Happiness Is a Thing Called Joe," "My Shining Hour," "One for My Baby," "Let's Take the Long Way Home," "Ac-Cen-Tchu-Ate the Positive," "Now I Know," "Hooray for Love," "For Every Man There's a Woman." Lyricists with whom Arlen worked include Ted Koehler, Lew Brown, Leo Robin, Ralph Blane, Dorothy Fields, and himself. Judy Garland, Groucho Marx, Bing Crosby, Ethel Waters, Fred Astaire, Dinah Shore, Betty Grable, Ezio Pinza, and Tony Martin were all identified with the composer's Hollywood output.

Arlen began his career as a singer with dance bands, then indited songs for nightclub revues (*Cotton Club Parade*), and graduated to Broadway musicals (*Bloomer Girl, House of Flowers,* etc.). Bib: *Harold Arlen: Happy with the Blues* by Edward Jablonski (1961). (Died New York, April 23, 1986.)

1934 Let's Fall in Love (Koehler)
1936 Strike Me Pink (Brown)
     The Singing Kid (Harburg)
     Stage Struck (Harburg)
     Gold Diggers of 1937 (Harburg)
1939 The Wizard of Oz (Harburg)
     At the Circus (Harburg)
1941 Blues in the Night (Mercer)
1942 Star Spangled Rhythm (Mercer)
1943 Cabin in the Sky (Harburg)
     The Sky's the Limit (Mercer)
1944 Up in Arms (Koehler)
     Here Come the Waves (Mercer)
1948 Casbah (Robin)
1950 My Blue Heaven (Blane, Arlen)
     The Petty Girl (Mercer)
1951 Mr. Imperium (Fields)
1953 Down Among the Sheltering Palms (Blane)
     The Farmer Takes a Wife (Fields)
1954 A Star Is Born (Gershwin)
     The Country Girl (Gershwin)
1962 Gay Purr-ee (Harburg)

Armstrong, (Daniel) Louis ("Satchmo"), trumpeter, singer, actor; b. New Orleans, July 4, 1900; d. New York, July 6, 1971. Jazz's most esteemed trumpeter appeared in more films (both with and without his orchestra) than any other jazzman. Among songs he introduced were "Jeepers Creepers," "Do You Know What It Means To Miss New Orleans?," and "A Kiss To Build a Dream On." Armstrong started his career as cornetist with bands led by Kid Ory, Joe "King" Oliver, and Fletcher Henderson. He began his durable recording career under his own name in 1925, formed his band in 1930, and performed almost to the end.

1936 Pennies from Heaven (Henry)
1937 Artists and Models (specialty)
     Every Day's a Holiday (band leader)
1938 Doctor Rhythm (specialty)
1939 Going Places (Gabe)
1943 Cabin in the Sky (Devil's Trumpeter)
1944 Jam Session (specialty)
     Atlantic City (specialty)
     Hollywood Canteen (specialty)
1947 New Orleans (Louis Armstrong)
     Carnegie Hall (specialty)
1948 A Song Is Born (specialty)
1951 Here Comes the Groom (specialty)
     The Strip (specialty)
1952 Glory Alley (Shadow Johnson)
1954 The Glenn Miller Story (Louis Armstrong)
1956 High Society (Louis Armstrong)
1959 The Five Pennies (Louis Armstrong)

1961 Paris Blues (Wild Man Moore)
1965 When the Boys Meet the Girls (specialty)
1966 A Man Called Adam (Willie Ferguson)
1969 Hello, Dolly! (specialty)

Arnaz, Desi (né Desiderio Alberto Arnaz y de Acha III), actor, singer, bandleader; b. Santiago, Cuba, March 2, 1917. Energetic interpreter of Latin-American numbers, who won greatest fame as the exasperated husband in the television series *I Love Lucy,* co-starring and co-produced with his then wife Lucille Ball. Arnaz's first Hollywood role was re-creating his Broadway part in *Too Many Girls.* His and Miss Ball's children are Lucie Arnaz and Desi Arnaz, Jr., both actors. Bib: *A Book* by Arnaz (1976). (Died Dec. 2, 1986.)

1940 Too Many Girls (Manuelito Lynch)
1941 Four Jacks and a Jill
1946 Cuban Pete (Desi Arnaz)
1949 Holiday in Havana (Carlos Estrada)

"Arthur Murray Taught Me Dancing in a Hurry" Music by Victor Schertzinger; lyric by Johnny Mercer. This explosive account of a crash course in ballroom dancing was Betty Hutton's first hit and set the style for the kind of propulsive number with which she was most closely identified. Miss Hutton introduced it singing with Jimmy Dorsey's orchestra at the Swingland Dance Hall, San Francisco, in *The Fleet's In* (Par. 1942). It is said that Arthur Murray at first objected to the song on the grounds that it belittled his teaching methods, but he soon came to appreciate its publicity value.

"As Time Goes By" Music & lyric by Herman Hupfeld. First sung by Frances Williams in the 1931 Broadway musical *Everybody's Welcome,* this tribute to the durability of fundamental romantic things has become far more closely associated with Dooley Wilson's tear-stained rendition in the nonmusical film *Casablanca* (Warner 1942). As Ingrid Bergman and Humphrey Bogart's love theme, it served to bring back memories of blissful days in Paris after the estranged pair, seeing each other again in Rick's Place, ask Wilson to play it. But neither one said, "Play it again, Sam."

Astaire, Fred (né Frederick Austerlitz), actor, dancer, singer, choreographer; b. Omaha, Neb., May 10, 1899. Combining the unsurpassed grace and inventiveness of his dancing, a light but expressive singing voice, and an engaging, boyish personality, Fred Astaire was the screen's foremost song-and-dance man. Though he later turned to nondancing roles, his elegantly unalterable image was established in the series of musicals he made first at RKO with Ginger Rogers (*The Gay Divorcee, Roberta, Top Hat, Follow the Fleet, Swing Time, Shall We Dance*), and later, primarily at MGM, with a succession of leading ladies, including Eleanor Powell (*Broadway Melody of 1940*), Rita Hayworth (*You'll Never Get Rich, You Were Never Lovelier*), Lucille Bremer (*Ziegfeld Follies*), Judy Garland and Ann Miller (*Easter Parade*), Miss Rogers again (*The Barkleys of Broadway*), Vera-Ellen (*Three Little Words*), Jane Powell (*Royal Wedding*), Cyd Charisse (*The Band Wagon, Silk Stockings*), Leslie Caron (*Daddy Long Legs*), and Audrey Hepburn (*Funny Face*). Astaire also co-starred with Bing Crosby in *Holiday Inn* and *Blue Skies,* and danced with Gene Kelly in *Ziegfeld Follies* and *That's Entertainment Part 2*. The dancer's most frequent choreographic assistant was Hermes Pan.

Astaire introduced—either singing or dancing—songs by some of our most eminent songwriters: Vincent Youmans, Gus Kahn, and Edward Eliscu ("The Carioca," "Orchids in the Moonlight," "Flying Down to Rio"); Con Conrad and Herb Magidson ("The Continental"); Jerome Kern and Dorothy Fields ("I Won't Dance," "The Way You Look Tonight," "A Fine Romance," "Never Gonna Dance"); Irving Berlin ("Top Hat, White Tie and Tails," "Isn't This a Lovely Day?," "The Piccolino," "Cheek to Cheek," "Let Yourself Go," "Let's Face the Music and Dance," "I'm Putting All My Eggs in One Basket," "Change Partners," "I Used To Be Color Blind," "You're Easy To Dance With," "A Couple of Swells," "It Only Happens When I Dance with You"); George and Ira Gershwin ("Beginner's Luck," "Let's Call the Whole Thing Off," "Shall We Dance?," "They All Laughed," "They Can't Take That Away from Me," "A Foggy Day," "Nice Work If You Can Get It"); Cole Porter ("I've Got My Eyes on You," "I Concentrate on You"); Kern and Johnny Mercer ("You Were Never Lovelier," "Dearly Beloved," "I'm Old-Fashioned"); Harold Arlen and Mercer ("My Shining Hour," "One for My Baby"); Burton Lane and Alan Jay Lerner ("You're All the World to Me"); Harry Warren and Arthur Freed ("This Heart of Mine"); Arthur Schwartz and Howard Dietz ("That's Entertainment"); Mercer alone ("Something's Gotta Give").

Astaire began his career at the age of seven in a vaudeville act with his sister Adele. Together, they became Broadway's top dancing team, appearing in ten musicals (including *Lady, Be Good!, Funny Face,* and *The Band Wagon*), three of which they successfully took to London. After Adele's retirement, Fred teamed with Claire Luce in *Gay Divorce* (the only stage role he repeated in films). He also made many records, and appeared in musical and dramatic television programs. Bib: *Steps in Time* by Astaire (1959); *The Fred Astaire & Ginger Rogers Book* by Arlene Croce (1972); *Starring Fred Astaire* by Stanley Green (1973); *Fred Astaire* by Michael Freedland (1976). (Died Los Angeles, June 22, 1987.)

Asterisk indicates appearance with Miss Rogers:

1933	Dancing Lady (*Fred Astaire*)
	Flying Down to Rio* (*Fred Ayres*)
1934	The Gay Divorcee* (*Guy Holden*)
1935	Roberta* (*Huck Haines*)
	Top Hat* (*Jerry Travers*)
1936	Follow the Fleet* (*Bake Baker*)
	Swing Time* (*John "Lucky" Garnett*)
1937	Shall We Dance* (*Pete Peters*)
	A Damsel in Distress (*Jerry Halliday*)
1938	Carefree* (*Tony Flagg*)
1939	The Story of Vernon and Irene Castle* (*Vernon Castle*)
1940	Broadway Melody of 1940 (*Johnny Brett*)
	Second Chorus (*Danny O'Neill*)
1941	You'll Never Get Rich (*Robert Curtis*)
1942	Holiday Inn (*Ted Hanover*)
	You Were Never Lovelier (*Robert Davis*)
1943	The Sky's the Limit (*Fred Atwell*)
1945	Yolanda and the Thief (*Johnny Riggs*)
1946	Ziegfeld Follies (specialties)
	Blue Skies (*Jed Potter*)
1948	Easter Parade (*Don Hewes*)
1949	The Barkleys of Broadway * (*Josh Barkley*)
1950	Three Little Words (*Bert Kalmar*)
	Let's Dance (*Don Elwood*)
1951	Royal Wedding (*Tom Bowen*)
1952	The Belle of New York (*Charles Hall*)
1953	The Band Wagon (*Tony Hunter*)
1955	Daddy Long Legs (*Jervis Pendleton*)
1957	Funny Face (*Dick Avery*)
	Silk Stockings (*Steve Canfield*)
1968	Finian's Rainbow (*Finian McLonergan*)
1974	That's Entertainment (narrator)
1976	That's Entertainment Part 2 (narrator)

"At Last" Music by Harry Warren; lyric by Mack Gordon. Ballad proclaiming a long-awaited romance, first played by Glenn Miller's orchestra as an instrumental in a New York nightclub in *Sun Valley Serenade* (Fox 1941). Again performed by the Miller orchestra in *Or-*

chestra Wives (Fox 1942), this time with vocals by Ray Eberle and Lynn Bari (dubbed by Pat Friday).

"At the Balalaika" Music by George Posford, adapted by Herbert Stothart; lyric by Robert Wright & George Forrest. With different words (by Eric Maschwitz), the languid tango was first sung in a London musical, *Balalaika* (1936). It is best known in its revised version in the 1939 MGM film also called *Balalaika,* in which it was initially presented by Ilona Massey and the Russian Art Choir at the Café Balalaika. Later it was reprised by Walter Woolf King (in the trenches) and by Nelson Eddy (back at the café).

"At the Codfish Ball" Music by Lew Pollack; lyric by Sidney Mitchell. In *Captain January* (Fox 1936), Shirley Temple—later joined by Buddy Ebsen—entertains the citizens of a small fishing town by singing and dancing in the street. The perky number was something of a piscine successor to Miss Temple's "Animal Crackers in My Soup."

"Aurora" Music by Roberto Roberti; lyric by Harold Adamson. Rhythmic paean to a Brazilian beauty, the number was sung by the Andrews Sisters, backed by Ted Lewis' orchestra, in an outdoor nightclub in *Hold That Ghost* (Univ. 1941).

Avalon, Frankie (né Francis Thomas Avallone), singer, actor; b. Philadelphia, Sept. 18, 1940. Teenage singing idol who made series of sabulous musicals with Annette Funicello. Did take-off on himself in *Grease.*

1957	Jamboree (specialty)
1963	Beach Party (*Frankie*)
1964	Muscle Beach Party (*Frankie*)
	Bikini Beach (*Frankie*)
1965	Ski Party (*Todd Armstrong*)
	Beach Blanket Bingo (*Frankie*)
	Jet Set
	I'll Take Sweden (*Kenny Klinger*)
1966	Fireball 500 (*Dave*)
1967	How To Stuff a Wild Bikini (*Frankie*)
1978	Grease (*Teenage Idol*)
1987	Back to the Beach (*Frankie*)

B

"Babbitt and the Bromide, The" Music by George Gershwin; lyric by Ira Gershwin. Though introduced by Fred Astaire and his sister Adele in the 1927 Broadway musical *Funny Face,* this comic song-and-dance number became even more closely identified with Fred Astaire and Gene Kelly, who performed it in *Ziegfeld Follies* (MGM 1946). The piece concerns two "sub-sti-an-tial" solid citizens who meet on the avenue one day, meet again ten years later, and meet for the third time in Heaven. At each encounter, they are unable to express themselves in any way other than such examples of bromidic babbittry as "Hello! Howa you? Howza folks? What's new?" Fred and Gene's only other dance routine together was in *That's Entertainment Part 2* (MGM 1976).

Babes in Arms (1939). Screenplay by Jack McGowan & Kay Van Riper from Broadway musical by Richard Rodgers & Lorenz Hart.

An MGM film produced by Arthur Freed; directed by Busby Berkeley; art director, Merrill Pye; costumes, Dolly Tree; music director, George Stoll; music adapted by Roger Edens; orchestrations, Leo Arnaud, George Bassman; cameraman, Ray June; editor, Frank Sullivan.

Cast: Mickey Rooney (*Mickey Moran*); Judy Garland (*Patsy Barton*); Charles Winninger (*Joe Moran*); Guy Kibbee (*Judge Black*); June Preisser (*Rosalie Essex*); Grace Hayes (*Florrie Moran*); Betty Jaynes (*Molly Moran*); Douglas McPhail (*Don Brice*); Rand Brooks (*Jeff Steele*); Leni Lynn (*Dody Martini*); John Sheffield (*Bobs*); Henry Hull (*Madox*); Barnett Parker (*William*); Ann Shoemaker (*Mrs. Barton*); Margaret Hamilton (*Martha Steele*).

Songs: "Good Morning" (Nacio Herb Brown-Arthur Freed) - Garland, Rooney/ "You Are My Lucky Star" (Brown-Freed) - Jaynes/ "Broadway Rhythm" (Brown-Freed) - Garland/ "Babes in Arms" (Rodgers-Hart) - McPhail, Garland, Rooney, babes/ "Where or When" (Rodgers-Hart) - McPhail, Jaynes, Garland/ "I Cried for You" (Gus Arnheim, Abe Lyman-Freed) - Garland/ "Daddy Was a Minstrel Man" (Roger Edens) - Garland/ "Oh, Susannah" (Stephen Foster) - Garland, Rooney/ "Ida, Sweet as Apple Cider" (Eddie Leonard) - Rooney/ "Moonlight Bay" (Percy Wenrich-Edward Madden) - chorus/ "I'm Just Wild About Harry" (Eubie Blake-Noble Sissle) - Garland/ "God's Country" (Harold Arlen-E. Y. Harburg) - Rooney, McPhail, Garland, Jaynes. Unused: "Let's Take a Walk Around the Block" (Arlen-Harburg), "I Wish I Were in Love Again" (Rodgers-Hart).

Richard Rodgers always considered *Babes in Arms* the best of all the film versions of the Rodgers and Hart stage musicals—despite the fact that only two of his original songs were sung on the screen. Although other numbers were added and the names of the characters were changed, the movie retained the basic outline of the Broadway libretto: children of old-time vaudevillians avoid being sent to a work farm by staging their own show. The film, however, added a romantic and a professional complication for Judy Garland in the person of a former Shirley Temple-type movie star (June Preisser), and Mickey Rooney's part, that of the brash young man who puts the show together, was made predominant. *Babes in Arms* had three important firsts: the first movie to co-star Rooney and Garland (she had just finished *The Wizard of Oz*); the first to be produced by Arthur Freed, thus inaugurating what was to be the Freed Unit; the first MGM picture to be directed and choreographed by Busby Berkeley. The film's success sparked three other Rooney-Garland-Freed-Berkeley

"Why-don't-us-kids-put-on-our-own-show" musicals—*Strike Up the Band, Babes on Broadway,* and *Girl Crazy.*

"Baby Doll" Music by Harry Warren; lyric by Johnny Mercer. In *The Belle of New York* (MGM 1952) wealthy playboy Fred Astaire woos Salvation Army lass Vera-Ellen by singing this light, airy song of affection. Naturally, he breaks down her resistance and they dance all around the mission. The song had originally been intended for Gene Kelly to sing in *Take Me Out to the Ball Game* (MGM 1949), but it was cut before the film's release.

"Baby, It's Cold Outside" Music & lyric by Frank Loesser. Though Loesser wrote it as a piece he and his wife could perform at parties, this comic conversational duet—between a wolfish swain and his nervous date—was sung in *Neptune's Daughter* (MGM 1949) by Ricardo Montalban and Esther Williams, then by Red Skelton and Betty Garrett.

"Baby, Take a Bow" Music by Jay Gorney & Lew Brown; lyric by Brown. Shirley Temple's bow as Fox's premiere attraction was made with the help of this musical sendoff in *Stand Up and Cheer* (1934), in which it was sung as part of a production number with top-hatted James Dunn. To show Miss Temple as a child vaudeville performer in Fox's *Young People,* made six years later, part of this footage was spliced into a version of the song featuring Jack Oakie and Charlotte Greenwood (dressed as a baby).

Bacharach, Burt, composer; b. Kansas City, Mo., May 12, 1928. Also active as pianist and conductor, Bacharach has composed scores for nonmusical films, including *Alfie* (which contained the title song) and *Butch Cassidy and the Sundance Kid* ("Raindrops Keep Fallin' on My Head"). On these and many other songs his collaborator was lyricist Hal David. Also wrote with Paul Anka.

1972   Lost Horizon (David)
1980   Together? (Anka)

"Back Bay Polka" Music by George Gershwin; lyric by Ira Gershwin. Sung by four improper Bostonians—poet Allyn Joslyn, composer Charles Kemper, lexicographer Lillian Bronson, and painter Arthur Shields, who are joined by Elizabeth Patterson and Betty Grable—in

The Shocking Miss Pilgrim (Fox 1947). In the film, which takes place in 1874, the singers poke fun at the city's then prevalent stern moral code aimed at people found embracing, showing individuality, drinking anything stronger than lemonade, reading unapproved books, or whose family tree doesn't date from the Pilgrims.

Bacon, Lloyd, director; b. San Jose, Cal., Jan. 16, 1890; d. Burbank, Nov. 15, 1955. Remembered for his quick-paced, atmospheric Warner Bros. showbiz musicals between 1928 and 1936 (e.g., *42nd Street, Footlight Parade*), with six choreographed by Busby Berkeley and six with songs by Harry Warren and Al Dubin. Dick Powell was in six films directed by Bacon; Al Jolson, Joan Blondell and Dan Dailey were in three each. The son of actor Frank Bacon, the director began his Hollywood career in 1921; after leaving Warner in 1943, he was with Fox for ten years.

1928   The Singing Fool
1929   Honky Tonk
        Say It with Songs
1930   So Long, Letty
        She Couldn't Say No
1932   The Crooner
1933   42nd Street
        Footlight Parade
1934   Wonder Bar
1935   In Caliente
        Broadway Gondolier
1936   Cain and Mabel
        Gold Diggers of 1937
1938   Cowboy from Brooklyn
1941   Navy Blues
1946   Wake Up and Dream
1947   I Wonder Who's Kissing Her Now
1948   You Were Meant for Me
        Give My Regards to Broadway
1951   Call Me Mister
        Golden Girl
1953   The "I Don't Care" Girl
        Walking My Baby Back Home
1954   The French Line

"Bad in Every Man, The" Music by Richard Rodgers; lyric by Lorenz Hart. Torchy lament sung in a Harlem nightclub by tan-faced Shirley Ross in *Manhattan Melodrama* (MGM 1934). This version of the song had the third of four sets of lyrics written for the same melody. The first was called "Prayer" and intended for Jean Harlow to sing (or mouth) in *Hollywood Party* (MGM

1934), but the scene was cut. The second lyric turned it into the title song for *Manhattan Melodrama* (also called "It's Just That Kind of a Play"); after that lyric was rejected it became "The Bad in Every Man." The fourth version—as "Blue Moon"—became the only hit Rodgers and Hart ever wrote that was not originally introduced in a stage or screen musical. "Blue Moon" was also sung by Mel Tormé in *Words and Music* (MGM 1948); Valentina Cortesa in *Malaya* (MGM 1949); Jane Froman (for Susan Hayward) in *With a Song in My Heart* (Fox 1952); Robert DeNiro and Mary Kay Place in *New York, New York* (UA 1977); and Sha Na Na in *Grease* (Par. 1978).

Bailey, Pearl (Mae), singer, actress; b. Newport News, Va., March 29, 1918. Miss Bailey's slurred, casual singing style and her comic delivery have made her a top attraction on records, in nightclubs, and in Broadway musicals (most notably, *Hello, Dolly!*). Bib: *The Raw Pearl* by Miss Bailey (1968).

1947 Variety Girl (specialty)
1948 Isn't It Romantic? (*Addie*)
1954 Carmen Jones (*Frankie*)
1956 That Certain Feeling (*Gussie*)
1958 St. Louis Blues (*Aunt Hagar*)
1959 Porgy and Bess (*Maria*)

Baker, (Kenneth Lawrence) Kenny, actor, singer; b. Monrovia, Cal., Sept. 30, 1912. Baker's high tenor voice and air of boyish innocence made him something of a successor to Dick Powell. He first attracted notice on the Jack Benny radio shows of the mid-30s, and introduced such songs as "Am I in Love?," "Remember Me," "Love Is Here To Stay," "Love Walked In," and "Spring Again." (Died Cal., Aug. 10, 1985.)

1935 King of Burlesque (*Arthur*)
      Big Broadcast of 1936 (vocals for Henry Wadsworth)
1937 The King and the Chorus Girl (*singer*)
      Turn Off the Moon (*Kenny Baker*)
      Mr. Dodd Takes the Air (*Claude Dodd*)
      52nd Street (*Benny*)
1938 The Goldwyn Follies (*Danny Beecher*)
      Radio City Revels (*Kenny*)
1939 At the Circus (*Jeff Wilson*)
      The Mikado (*Nanki Poo*)
1940 The Hit Parade of 1941 (*David Farraday*)
1943 Silver Skates (*Danny*)
      Stage Door Canteen (specialty)

1944 Doughboys in Ireland (*Danny O'Keefe*)
1945 The Harvey Girls (*Terry O'Halloran*)
1947 Calendar Girl (*Byron Jones*)

Ball, Lucille (Desiree), actress; b. Jamestown, NY, Aug. 6, 1910. Miss Ball won her greatest fame as the wide-eyed blonde comic heroine of the television series, *I Love Lucy,* produced with and co-starring her first husband, Desi Arnaz. In Hollywood films, the actress began as a Goldwyn Girl, then wise-cracked her way up to stardom. Her children are Desi Jr. and Lucie Arnaz.

1933 Broadway Through a Keyhole (*girl at beach*)
      Roman Scandals (*slave girl*)
1934 Moulin Rouge (chorus)
      Murder at the Vanities (chorus)
      Bottoms Up (girl)
      Kid Millions (show girl)
1935 Roberta (*mannequin*)
      Old Man Rhythm (*coed*)
      Top Hat (*flower shop girl*)
      I Dream Too Much (*Gwendolyn Dilley*)
1936 Follow the Fleet (*Kitty Collins*)
      That Girl from Paris (*Claire Williams*)
1938 Joy of Living (*Salina*)
      Go Chase Yourself (*Carol Meely*)
      Having Wonderful Time (*Miriam*)
1939 That's Right, You're Wrong (*Sandra Sand*)
1940 Dance, Girl, Dance (*Bubbles*)
      Too Many Girls (*Consuelo Casey*)
1942 Seven Days' Leave (*Jerry*)
1943 DuBarry Was a Lady (*May Daly*)
      Best Foot Forward (*Lucille Ball*)
      Thousands Cheer (specialty)
1944 Meet the People (*Julie Hampton*)
1945 Abbott and Costello in Hollywood (guest bit)
1946 Ziegfeld Follies (specialty)
      Easy To Wed (*Gladys Benton*)
1950 Fancy Pants (*Agatha Floud*)
1974 Mame (*Mame Dennis Burnside*)

Band Wagon, The (1953). Music by Arthur Schwartz; lyrics by Howard Dietz; screenplay by Betty Comden & Adolph Green.

An MGM film produced by Arthur Freed; directed by Vincente Minnelli; associate producer, Roger Edens; choreography, Fred Astaire, Michael Kidd; art directors, Cedric Gibbons, Preston Ames, Oliver Smith; costumes, Mary Ann Nyberg; music director, Adolph Deutsch; orchestrations, Conrad Salinger, Skip Martin, Alexander Courage; cameraman, Harry Jackson; editor, Albert Akst; Technicolor.

Cast: Fred Astaire (*Tony Hunter*); Cyd Charisse (vocals by India Adams) (*Gabrielle Gerard*); Oscar Levant (*Lester Marton*); Nanette Fabray (*Lily Marton*); Jack Buchanan (*Jeffrey Cordova*); James Mitchell (*Paul Byrd*); Robert Gist (*Hal Benton*); Thurston Hall (*Col. Tide*); Ava Gardner (guest bit); LeRoy Daniels (*boot-black*).

Songs: "By Myself" - Astaire/ "A Shine on Your Shoes" - Astaire; dance by Astaire, Daniels/ "That's Entertainment" - Buchanan, Fabray, Levant, Astaire; reprised with Charisse (Adams) added/ "The Beggar Waltz" - dance by Charisse, Mitchell, ballet corps/ "Dancing in the Dark" - dance by Astaire, Charisse/ "You and the Night and the Music" - chorus, dance by Astaire, Charisse/ "Something To Remember You By" - girls, boys/ "High and Low" - girls, boys/ "I Love Louisa" - Astaire, with Levant, Fabray, girls, boys/ "New Sun in the Sky" - Charisse (Adams)/ "I Guess I'll Have To Change My Plan" - Astaire, Buchanan/ "Louisiana Hayride" - Fabray, chorus/ "Triplets" - Astaire, Fabray, Buchanan/ "The Girl Hunt" ballet (narration by Alan Jay Lerner) - Astaire; dance by Astaire, Charisse, dancers. Unused: "Got a Bran' New Suit," "Sweet Music," "Two-Faced Woman, "You Have Everything," "Alone Together," "Never Marry a Dancer," "The Private Eye."

On the Broadway stage, *The Band Wagon* was a revue with disconnected songs, dances, and sketches. Opening in 1931, it starred Fred and Adele Astaire, Frank Morgan, and Helen Broderick and featured over a dozen songs by Arthur Schwartz and Howard Dietz. On the screen *The Band Wagon* retained the services of Fred Astaire, kept five of the songs, added seven from other Schwartz-Dietz shows plus "That's Entertainment" and "The Girl Hunt" ballet (both written for the film), and had an original story that superficially recalled Astaire's own career. Like Astaire, the hero is an aging, legendary Hollywood song-and-dance man who had once starred on Broadway at the New Amsterdam Theatre (in *The Band Wagon*). Unlike Astaire, however, he is washed up in Hollywood and must make a comeback in a Broadway musical. Also involved are a beautiful ballerina (Cyd Charisse), a married writing team (Nanette Fabray and Oscar Levant, suggesting Betty Comden and Adolph Green, the unmarried writing team of the script), and a temperamental director (originally intended for Clifton Webb, Jack Buchanan's role was a cross between Orson Welles and José Ferrer).

Though the mood was generally satirical, the story of *The Band Wagon* was essentially the ancient backstage tale of the Broadway-bound show saved from disaster by last-minute personnel changes. But here, instead of a youngster taking over from an old-timer, it's the old-timer who takes over from a pretentious director (with Levant delivering the Mickey Rooney line, "Gosh, with all this raw talent around, why can't us kids get together and put on ourselves a show!"). The film was not the first to use *The Band Wagon*'s stage songs. In 1949, Fox bought the rights to the show and put three of its numbers in *Dancing in the Dark* (about a washed-up actor, William Powell, who discovers a young actress to star in the show's screen version). Since Fox also owned the show's title, MGM producer Arthur Freed had to buy it from the rival studio to replace the working title of *I Love Louisa*.

The fourth Freed-produced musical to be fashioned around the catalogue of a major songwriter or team, *The Band Wagon* followed *Easter Parade* (Irving Berlin), *An American in Paris* (George and Ira Gershwin), and *Singin' in the Rain* (Nacio Herb Brown and Freed himself). It was also Astaire's last film under his MGM contract, though he did return to the studio four years later in *Silk Stockings*, when his co-star was again Cyd Charisse.

Bari, Lynn (née Marjorie Schuyler Fisher), actress; b. Roanoke, Va., Dec. 18, 1915. After five years of chorus work and bits, dark-haired, apple-cheeked Lynn Bari graduated to playing "other-woman" roles in Fox musicals.

1933   Dancing Lady (*chorus*)
1934   Stand Up and Cheer (*chorus*)
1935   George White's Scandals (*chorus*)
       Music Is Magic (*cashier*)
       Thanks a Million (*telephone operator*)
1936   Sing, Baby, Sing (*telephone operator*)
       Pigskin Parade (*coed*)
1937   On the Avenue (*chorus*)
       Sing and Be Happy (*chorus*)
       You Can't Have Everything (*bit*)
1938   Rebecca of Sunnybrook Farm (*bit*)
       Walking Down Broadway (*Sandra DeVoe*)
       Battle of Broadway (*Marjorie Clark*)
       Josette (*Mrs. Dupree*)
1940   Lillian Russell (*Edna McCauley*)
1941   Sun Valley Serenade (*Vivian Dawn*)
       Moon Over Her Shoulder (*Susan Rossiter*)
1942   Orchestra Wives (*Janie*)

1943 Hello, Frisco, Hello (*Bernice Croft*)
1944 Sweet and Low Down (*Pat Sterling*)
1946 Margie (*Isabel Palmer*)
1951 On the Sunny Side of the Street
1952 Has Anybody Seen My Gal? (*Harriet Blaisdell*)
      I Dream of Jeanie (*Mrs. McDowell*)

Barkleys of Broadway, The (1949). Music by Harry Warren; lyrics by Ira Gershwin; screenplay by Betty Comden & Adolph Green.

An MGM film produced by Arthur Freed; directed by Charles Walters; associate producer, Roger Edens; choreography, Fred Astaire, Robert Alton, Hermes Pan; art directors, Cedric Gibbons, Edward Carfagno; costumes, Irene, Valles; music director, Lennie Hayton; orchestrations, Hayton, Conrad Salinger; vocal arrangements, Robert Tucker; cameraman, Harry Stradling; editor, Albert Akst; Technicolor.

Cast: Fred Astaire (*Josh Barkley*); Ginger Rogers (*Dinah Barkley*); Oscar Levant (*Ezra Miller*); Billie Burke (*Millie Belney*); Jacques François (*Jacques Pierre Barredout*); Gale Robbins (*Shirlene May*); George Zucco (*judge in play*); Hans Conried (*Ladislaus Ladi*); Inez Cooper (*Pamela Driscoll*); Joyce Matthews (*Genevieve*).

Songs: "Swing Trot" - dance by Astaire, Rogers/ "Sabre Dance" (Khatchaturian) - Levant, piano/ "You'd Be Hard To Replace" - Astaire/ "Bouncin' the Blues" - dance by Astaire, Rogers/ "My One and Only Highland Fling" - Astaire, Rogers/ "A Weekend in the Country" - Astaire, Rogers, Levant/ "Shoes with Wings On" - Astaire/ "Concerto in B-flat Minor" (Tchaikovsky) - Levant, piano/ "They Can't Take That Away from Me" (music, George Gershwin) - Astaire; dance by Astaire, Rogers/ "Manhattan Downbeat" - Astaire, chorus; dance by Astaire, Rogers, chorus. Unused: "The Courtship of Elmer and Ella," "Natchez on the Mississip'," "These Days," "There Is No Music," "The Poetry of Motion," "Call On Us Again," "Taking No Chances with You," "Second Fiddle to a Harp," "Minstrels on Parade."

After the success of *Easter Parade,* producer Arthur Freed was quick to follow it with another musical co-starring Fred Astaire and Judy Garland. Tentatively titled *You Made Me Love You,* it found most of the production crew of the previous movie again on hand: director Walters, associate producer Edens, choreographer Alton, art director Gibbons, music arranger Salinger, vocal arranger Tucker, cameraman Stradling, and editor Akst. And though the screenplay was an original by

Comden and Green and new songs were written by Harry Warren and Ira Gershwin (their only screen association), the story borrowed from the other film by showing what might have happened if a song-and-dance team similar to the bickering pair in *Easter Parade* had become the Lunt and Fontanne of the musical stage. Though enjoying apparently unbroken success, the female half, urged by an egotistical playwright, seeks fulfillment in meaningful drama—only, of course, to discover that she's happier in musical comedy.

During the film's preparation, Miss Garland's illness made it impossible for her to continue and she was replaced by Ginger Rogers, thus reuniting Astaire and Rogers after nine years for their tenth screen appearance together. Because of the cast change, some of the songs had to be discarded and there was one addition: "They Can't Take That Away from Me," which George and Ira Gershwin had written for Fred and Ginger's *Shall We Dance.* Another reminder of the team's past glory was the joyful, seemingly spontaneous "Bouncin' the Blues" dance routine performed as part of a rehearsal.

Barrymore, John (né John Sidney Blythe), actor; b. Philadelphia Feb. 15, 1882; d. Hollywood, June 29, 1942. Member of celebrated theatrical family whose best-remembered role in a musical was in *Maytime*. Bib: *Goodnight, Sweet Prince* by Gene Fowler (1944); *The Barrymores* by Hollis Alpert (1964).

1929 The Show of Shows (specialty)
1937 Maytime (*Nicolai Nazaroff*)
1938 Romance in the Dark (*Zoltan Jason*)
      Hold That Coed (*Gov. Harrigan*)
1941 Playmates (*John Barrymore*)

Bart, Lionel (né Lionel Begleiter), composer, lyricist; b. London, Aug. 1, 1930. Of Bart's six London stage musicals, *Lock Up Your Daughters* (music by Laurie Johnson) and *Oliver!,* his biggest hit, were transferred to the screen.

1968 Oliver! (alone)
1969 Lock Up Your Daughters (Johnson)

Barton, James, actor, singer; b. Gloucester, NJ, Nov. 1, 1890; d. Mineola, NY, Feb. 19, 1962. Grizzled song-and-dance man, famed for his realistic drunk routine, who appeared in vaudeville and Broadway musicals (*Paint Your Wagon*).

1950 The Daughter of Rosie O'Grady (*Dennis O'Grady*)
      Wabash Avenue (*Harrigan*)

1951   Here Comes the Groom (*Pa Jones*)
        Golden Girl (*Crabtree*)

Basie, (William) Count, pianist, bandleader; b. Red Bank, NJ, Aug. 21, 1904. Basie organized his first jazz band in 1936 and continued as leader for over 45 years. His film appearances were only with his orchestra. (Died Hollywood, Fla., April 26, 1984.)

1943   Hit Parade of 1943
        Top Man
        Crazy House
        Reveille with Beverly
        Stage Door Canteen
1957   Jamboree
1960   Cinderfella
1974   Blazing Saddles

Baxter, Warner, actor; b. Columbus, Ohio, March 29, 1889; d. Beverly Hills, May 7, 1951. Dapper, man-of-authority type with pencil-thin mustache, Baxter began his film career in 1923. He appeared in over sixty sound films, with *42nd Street* his best-remembered musical.

1930   Happy Days (minstrel specialty)
1933   42nd Street (*Julian Marsh*)
        I Loved You Wednesday (*Philip Fletcher*)
1934   Stand Up and Cheer (*Lawrence Cromwell*)
1935   Under the Pampas Moon (*Cesar Campo*)
        King of Burlesque (*Kerry Bolton*)
1937   Vogues of 1938 (*George Curson*)
1944   Lady in the Dark (*Kendall Nesbitt*)

"Be a Clown" Music & lyric by Cole Porter. In *The Pirate* (MGM 1948) Gene Kelly, about to be hanged as a pirate, is granted a last-minute request to perform. With the dancing Nicholas Brothers included in the act, the tumbling, prancing, cavorting trio clown their way through this dithyrambic celebration of the joys that come only to those who play the fool. After winning his freedom, Kelly reprises the number at the end of the film with Judy Garland, with both sporting putty noses and wearing baggy costumes. Kelly was directly responsible for Cole Porter writing "Be a Clown." Feeling that the movie needed a knockout comic number, he persuaded the composer to add it to the score after the other songs had been completed. Four years later, it was the inspiration—if that's the right word—for "Make 'Em Laugh," which Nacio Herb Brown and Arthur Freed wrote for Donald O'Connor in *Singin' in the Rain*.

"Be Careful It's My Heart" Music & lyric by Irving Berlin. Plea for cardiac consideration ("It's not my

watch you're holding, it's my heart") introduced by Bing Crosby in *Holiday Inn* (Par. 1942). In the scene, Crosby is rehearsing with Marjorie Reynolds for a nightclub show planned for Valentine's Day. Behind Crosby's back, Fred Astaire enters the room and, properly smitten with Miss Reynolds, wafts her across the floor.

"Be My Love" Music by Nicholas Brodszky; lyric by Sammy Cahn. Booming ballad ("There'll be no one but you for me ETERNALLY . . .") for Mario Lanza and Kathryn Grayson in *The Toast of New Orleans* (MGM 1950). Also sung by Connie Francis in *Looking for Love* (MGM 1964).

Beatles, The, singers, actors, musicians, composers, lyricists. George Harrison, b. Liverpool, Eng., Feb. 25, 1943. John (Winston) Lennon, b. Liverpool, Oct. 9, 1940; d. New York, Dec. 8, 1980 (murdered). (James) Paul McCartney, b. Liverpool, June 18, 1942. Ringo Starr (né Richard Starkey), b. Liverpool, July 7, 1940. Influential singing group who, beginning in 1964, spearheaded the international rock and roll craze. In contrast to their frequently frenetic songs and interpretations, the Beatles as an acting quartet were low-key performers, with each one only a slight variation of the others. Their first two films—*A Hard Day's Night* is considered a classic—were directed by Richard Lester; their third was a surrealistic cartoon; their fourth used their songs but did not use them. Lennon and McCartney were responsible for their best-known screen songs: "A Hard Day's Night," "And I Loved Her," "Help!" Bib: *The Beatles* by Hunter Davies (1968); *The Beatles* by Julius Fast (1968).

1964   A Hard Day's Night
1965   Help!
1968   Yellow Submarine (voices only)
1978   Sgt. Pepper's Lonely Hearts Club Band (comp., lyr. only)

Beaumont, Harry, director; b. Abilene, Kansas, Feb. 10, 1888; d. Santa Monica, Dec. 22, 1966. Ex-vaudevillian who became an early contract director at MGM and who was responsible for its first major film musical, *The Broadway Melody*.

1929   The Broadway Melody
1930   Lord Byron of Broadway
        Children of Pleasure

"Beautiful Girl" Music by Nacio Herb Brown; lyric by Arthur Freed. Marriage proposal to a gorgeous creature (in which "picture" rhymes with "mixture"), sung by Bing Crosby as he casually cuts a record in *Going Hollywood* (MGM 1933). Also sung in *Stage Mother* (MGM 1933) and by Jimmie Thompson in *Singin' in the Rain* (MGM 1952).

"Because You're Mine" Music by Nicholas Brodszky; lyric by Sammy Cahn. Mario Lanza's follow-up to "Be My Love," supplied by the same writers, was heard in *Because You're Mine* (MGM 1952).

Bedknobs and Broomsticks. See Mary Poppins.

Beggar's Opera, The (1952). Music by Sir Arthur Bliss; lyrics by John Gay, Christopher Fry; screenplay by Denis Cannan and Fry from London musical by Gay.

A British Lion film produced by Laurence Olivier and Herbert Wilcox; directed by Peter Brook; art director, William C. Andrews; costumes, George Wakhevitch; music director, Muir Mathieson; arrangements, Sir Arthur Bliss; cameraman, Guy Green; editor, Reginald Beck; Technicolor.

Cast: Laurence Olivier (*Capt. Macheath*); Stanley Holloway (*Lockit*); Dorothy Tutin (vocals by Adele Leigh) (*Polly Peachum*); George Devine (vocals by John Cameron) (*Peachum*); Mary Clare (vocals by Edith Coates) (*Mrs. Peachum*); Hugh Griffith (*beggar*); Daphne Anderson (vocals by Jennifer Vyvyan) (*Lucy Lockit*); Athene Seyler (vocals by Edith Coates) (*Mrs. Trapes*); Yvonne Furneux (*Jenny Diver*); Margot Grahame (vocal by Joan Cross) (*actress*); Kenneth Williams (*Jack*); Denis Cannan (*footman*); Edith Coates (*Mrs. Coaxer*); George Rose (*turnkey*); Eric Pohlmann (*innkeeper*); Laurence Naismith (*Matt of the Mint*).

Songs: "My Heart Was So Free" - Olivier/ "How Shall I Change a Dull Day?" - Tutin (Leigh)/ "Can Love Be Controlled by Advice?" - Tutin (Leigh)/ "In the Days of My Youth" - Seyler (Coates), Holloway, Anderson (Vyvyan)/ "O Lucy, What Made You Sink So Low?" - Holloway, Seyler (Coates), Devine (Cameron), Clare (Coates)/ "O Ponder Well" - Tutin (Leigh)/ "And We Shall See Spinning Together" - Olivier/ "Pretty Polly Say" - Olivier/ "Were I Laid on When I Was Down Greenland Coast" - Tutin (Leigh), Olivier/ "O What Pain It Is To Part" - Olivier, Tutin (Leigh)/ "Fill Every Glass" - tavern singers/ "To Arms" - tavern singers/ "If the Heart of a Man" - Oli-vier/ "Youth's the Season Made for Joy" - Olivier/ "At the Gallows I'll Serve Her with Pleasure" - Olivier/ "Paddington Green" - Holloway/ "And the Beef We Have Roasted and Ate" - Devine (Cameron), Holloway/ "Man May Escape from Rope and Gun" - Olivier/ "How Happy Would I Be with Either" - Olivier/ "What Now, Madam Flirt?" - Anderson (Vyvyan), Tutin (Leigh)/ "No Power on Earth" - Tutin (Leigh)/ "Rest You, Sleep You" - Tutin (Leigh)/ "I'm Like a Skiff on the Ocean Toss'd" - Anderson (Vyvyan)/ "Come, Sweet Lass" - Olivier, Anderson (Vyvyan)/ "Feed the Dear Heart" - Tutin (Leigh), Anderson (Vyvyan)/ "O Cruel Cruel Cruel Case" - Olivier/ "Since Laws Were Made for Ev'ry Degree" - Olivier/ "Would I Might Be Hang'd" - Anderson (Vyvyan), Tutin (Leigh)/ "Reprieve!" - cast.

As the first musical starring Laurence Olivier and the first movie directed by Peter Brook, *The Beggar's Opera* was intended to be nothing less than the outstanding British musical film of all time. The production, however, was beset by friction—Olivier and Brook were frequently at odds—and the finished product, while praised by many, was a boxoffice disaster. The story was based on the first British ballad opera—or musical comedy—which was written by John Gay in 1728 as a satire on both corrupt politicians and florid Italianate opera. The film opens in Newgate Prison where Captain Macheath, a highwayman, meets a beggar who has written an opera that makes Macheath a far more dashing figure than he actually is. In a device similar to one later used in *Man of La Mancha,* the opera then takes over: redcoated Macheath, betrayed by his wife Polly's parents, is taken to Newgate where he escapes with the aid of Lucy Lockit, the jailer's daughter. Recaptured in a gambling house, he is sentenced to be hanged at dawn, but the beggar gets the idea of having Macheath reprieved at the last minute to the general rejoicing of the London multitude. Of the leading actors in the cast, only Olivier and Holloway did their own singing; Olivier also did his own riding and dueling.

Gay's story also furnished Kurt Weill and Bertolt Brecht with the idea for their *Die Dreigroschenoper* (*The Threepenny Opera*), presented in Berlin on the 200th anniversary of the original production. Set in London during the reign of Queen Victoria, its sardonic view of society and jangly beer-hall tunes soon won it a large following. In the original cast was Lotte Lenya (Kurt Weill's wife) who repeated her role of Jenny in the 1930 film version and also in Marc Blitzstein's record-breaking off-Broadway production in the 50s. In 1965, a second film version, in both German and English, had a cast headed by Curt Jurgens (Macheath), Hildegard Knef (Jenny), and Sammy Davis, Jr. (Street Singer).

"(I've Got) Beginner's Luck" Music by George Gershwin; lyric by Ira Gershwin. After tailing the unresponsive Ginger Rogers early in *Shall We Dance* (RKO 1937), Fred Astaire finally gets a chance to talk to her on the deck of an ocean liner. Following an awkward attempt at conversation, he breaks into song to express the exhilaration he feels at discovering "The first time that I'm in love I'm in love with you." Ira Gershwin later used the "beginner-becoming-a-winner" idea in "Sure Thing" (music by Jerome Kern) in *Cover Girl* (Col. 1944).

Bells of St. Mary's, The. *See Going My Way.*

Benchley, Robert (Charles), actor; b. Worcester, Mass., Sept. 15, 1889; d. New York, Nov. 21, 1945. Ambling, amiable performer who turned to acting after establishing himself as a humorist and theatre critic. Benchley, who also made a number of short subjects, played leading comic roles in two Fred Astaire films, *You'll Never Get Rich* and *The Sky's the Limit* (in which he delivered a version of his famed "Treasurer's Report" monologue). Bib: *Robert Benchley* by Nathaniel Benchley (his son) (1955).

1933	Dancing Lady (*Ward King*)	
1937	Broadway Melody of 1938 (*Duffy*)	
1941	Nice Girl? (*Oliver Dana*)	
	The Reluctant Dragon (*Robert Benchley*)	
	You'll Never Get Rich (*Martin Cortland*)	
1943	The Sky's the Limit (*Phil Harriman*)	
1944	The National Barn Dance (*Mitchum*)	
1945	Pan-Americana (*Charlie*)	
	Duffy's Tavern (specialty)	
	The Stork Club (*Tom Curtis*)	
	Road to Utopia (narrator)	

Bennett, Joan, actress; b. Palisades, NJ, Feb. 27, 1910. Cool, fragile-looking nonsinging leading lady, who appeared opposite Bing Crosby in two films. Miss Bennett, the daughter of actor Richard Bennett and the sister of actress Constance Bennett, was married to writer Gene Markey and producer Walter Wanger.

1930	Puttin' on the Ritz (*Dolores Fenton*)
	Maybe It's Love (*Nan Sheffield*)

1932	Careless Lady (*Sally Brown*)
1935	Mississippi (*Lucy Rumford*)
	Two for Tonight (*Bobbie Lockwood*)
1937	Vogues of 1938 (*Wendy Van Klettering*)
1938	Artists and Models Abroad (*Patricia Harper*)
1945	Nob Hill (*Harriet Carruthers*)
1957	Junior Miss (tv) (*Grace Graves*)

Benny, Jack (né Benjamin Kubelsky), actor; b. Chicago, Feb. 14, 1894; d. Beverly Hills, Dec. 26, 1974. Casual, subtle comedian whose well-timed responses and air of injured innocence helped make him a durable favorite in radio and television. In general, the parsimonious, vain character depicted on the air was usually transferred to Benny's movie roles, most of them seen in Paramount films. The comedian was married to Mary Livingstone (née Sadie Marks), who appeared with him on radio; others in his troupe, some of whom also acted in his movies, were Eddie Anderson (as his valet, Rochester), Kenny Baker (followed by Dennis Day); and Phil Harris. Bib: *Jack Benny* by Irving Fein (1976); *The Jack Benny Show* by Milt Josefsberg (1977); *Jack Benny* by Mary Benny (1978).

1929	Hollywood Revue of 1929 (*Jack Benny*)	
1930	Chasing Rainbows (*Eddie*)	
	Lord Byron of Broadway (radio announcer)	
1934	Transatlantic Merry-Go-Round (*Chad Denby*)	
1935	Broadway Melody of 1936 (*Bert Keeler*)	
1936	The Big Broadcast of 1937 (*Jack Carson*)	
	College Holiday (*J. Davis Bowster*)	
1937	Artists and Models (*Mac Brewster*)	
1938	Artists and Models Abroad (*Buck Boswell*)	
1939	Man About Town (*Bob Temple*)	
1940	Buck Benny Rides Again (*Jack Benny*)	
	Love Thy Neighbor (*Jack Benny*)	
1944	Hollywood Canteen (specialty)	
1952	Somebody Loves Me (guest bit)	
1957	Beau James (guest bit)	
1962	Gypsy (guest bit)	

Bergen, Edgar (né Edgar John Bergren), actor; b. Chicago, Feb. 16, 1903; d. Las Vegas, Sept. 30, 1978. Ventriloquist whose school-marmish personality contrasted so well with that of his brash, wisecracking dummy, Charlie McCarthy, that he was a radio favorite for over 30 years. The father of actress Candice Bergen, he occasionally appeared without his dummy in dramatic roles.

The ventriloquist and his dummy were known as Edgar Bergen and Charlie McCarthy in all the following films:
1938   The Goldwyn Follies

1939 Charlie McCarthy, Detective
1942 Here We Go Again
1943 Around the World
     Stage Door Canteen
1944 Song of the Open Road
1946 Fun and Fancy Free
1979 The Muppet Movie

Bergman, Alan, and Marilyn (Keith), lyricists. Alan, b. Brooklyn, Sept. 11, 1925. Marilyn, b. Brooklyn, Nov. 10, 1929. Husband-wife lyric-writing team who have written such movie songs as "The Windmills of Your Mind" (with Michel Legrand), "The Way We Were" (Marvin Hamlisch), and "What Are You Doing the Rest of Your Life?" (Legrand).

1983 Yentl (Legrand)

Berkeley, Busby (né Busby Berkeley William Enos), choreographer, director; b. Los Angeles, Nov. 29, 1895; d. Palm Springs, March 14, 1976. Broadway dance director who achieved legendary fame by creating flamboyant movie routines—kaleidoscopic patterns shot from above were a trademark—demonstrating that choreography could be achieved with a camera as well as with feet. Berkeley was responsible for staging production numbers in a variety of locales and with a variety of themes. He put dancers on a honeymooners' train (*42nd Street*) and in a Honeymoon Hotel (*Footlight Parade*). He made endless numbers of girls cavort in Central Park (*Gold Diggers of 1933*), frolic by a waterfall (*Footlight Parade*), dress like Ruby Keeler (*Dames*), and go through close-order military drills (*Gold Diggers of 1937*). And he had girls swirling about playing violins (*Gold Diggers of 1933*), harps (*Fashions of 1934*), and pianos (*Gold Diggers of 1935*). More dramatic themes were New York's bustling, menacing Times Square ("Forty Second Street"), the Depression's indifference to war heroes ("Remember My Forgotten Man"), and the tragic consequences of a pleasure-mad society ("Lullaby of Broadway"). Later, the choreographer made striking use of color, especially in *The Gang's All Here*.

Berkeley worked on eleven films with Dick Powell (four of them with Ruby Keeler), six with Judy Garland (four of them with Mickey Rooney), and four with Eddie Cantor. He was with Warner from 1933 to 1938, and with MGM from 1939 to 1954, serving as director as well as dance director on a dozen musicals. Bib: *The Busby Berkeley Book* by Tony Thomas & Jim Terry (1973).

Asterisk indicates Mr. Berkeley was also director:
1930 Whoopee
1931 Palmy Days
     Flying High
1932 The Kid from Spain
1933 42nd Street
     Gold Diggers of 1933 (also *call boy*)
     Footlight Parade
     Roman Scandals
1934 Wonder Bar
     Fashions of 1934
     Twenty Million Sweethearts
     Dames
1935 Gold Diggers of 1935*
     Go Into Your Dance
     In Caliente
     Bright Lights*
     I Live for Love*
     Stars Over Broadway
1936 Stage Struck*
     Gold Diggers of 1937
1937 The Singing Marine
     Varsity Show
     Hollywood Hotel*
1938 Gold Diggers in Paris
     Garden of the Moon*
1939 Broadway Serenade
     Babes in Arms*
1940 Strike Up the Band*
1941 Ziegfeld Girl
     Lady, Be Good
     Babes on Broadway*
1942 Born To Sing
     For Me and My Gal (dir. only)
1943 Cabin in the Sky
     Girl Crazy
     The Gang's All Here*
1946 Cinderella Jones*
1948 Romance on the High Seas
1949 Take Me Out to the Ball Game (dir. only)
1950 Two Weeks with Love
1951 Call Me Mister
     Two Tickets to Broadway
1952 Million Dollar Mermaid
1953 Small Town Girl
     Easy To Love
1954 Rose Marie
1962 Jumbo

Berle, Milton (né Milton Berlinger), actor; b. New York, July 12, 1908. A toothy, wisecracking, anything-for-a-laugh comedian, Berle began career in vaudeville, became headliner in nightclubs, and also appeared on

Broadway. His greatest fame was as host of television variety series (1948–55). Bib: *Milton Berle: An Autobiography* with Haskel Frankel (1974).

1937   Radio City Revels (*Teddy*)
       New Faces of 1937 (*Wellington Wedge*)
1941   Sun Valley Serenade (*Nifty Allen*)
       Tall, Dark and Handsome (*Frosty*)
       Rise and Shine (*Seabiscuit*)
1949   Always Leave Them Laughing (*Kip Cooper*)
1960   Let's Make Love (*Milton Berle*)
1972   Journey Back to Oz (voice of *Cowardly Lion*)
1979   The Muppet Movie (guest bit)

Berlin, Irving (né Israel Baline), composer, lyricist; b. Temun, Russia, May 11, 1888. Pre-eminent, self-taught songwriter whose works had a special knack of expressing the emotions of the average American. A master at composing honest, direct melodies combined with simple but artfully constructed lyrics, Berlin was successful in all three major areas of popular music—Tin Pan Alley, Broadway, and Hollywood.

On screen the Berlin musicals were frequently a combination of the new and the old. Those major films with all or mostly all new songs were *Top Hat* ("Isn't This a Lovely Day?," "Top Hat, White Tie and Tails," "Cheek to Cheek," "No Strings," "The Piccolino"); *Follow the Fleet* ("Let Yourself Go," "I'm Putting All My Eggs in One Basket," "Let's Face the Music and Dance"); *On the Avenue* ("I've Got My Love to Keep Me Warm," "This Year's Kisses," "You're Laughing at Me"); *Carefree* ("I Used To Be Color Blind," "Change Partners"); *Holiday Inn* ("White Christmas," "Be Careful It's My Heart," "You're Easy to Dance With"); *White Christmas* ("Count Your Blessings Instead of Sheep"). The movie with about half new songs and half old was *Easter Parade* ("Better Luck Next Time," "A Couple of Swells"). Those films with predominantly old songs were *Alexander's Ragtime Band* ("Now It Can Be Told"); *Blue Skies* ("You Keep Coming Back Like a Song"); *There's No Business Like Show Business* ("A Man Chases a Girl"). Those adapted from Broadway musicals were *Louisiana Purchase; This Is the Army; Annie Get Your Gun; Call Me Madam*. Other film songs include "Marie," "Puttin' on the Ritz," "With You," "Let Me Sing and I'm Happy," and "I Poured My Heart into a Song."

Berlin ballads were sung in six musicals starring Fred Astaire, three of them with Ginger Rogers, two with Bing Crosby. Others identified with his songs: Harry Richman, Al Jolson, Dick Powell, Alice Faye, Ethel Merman, Howard Keel, Betty Hutton, Donald O'Connor, Danny Kaye, and Judy Garland. Bib: *Irving Berlin* by Michael Freedland (1974).

1929   Hallelujah
1930   Puttin' on the Ritz
       Mammy
1935   Top Hat
1936   Follow the Fleet
1937   On the Avenue
1938   Alexander's Ragtime Band
       Carefree
1939   Second Fiddle
1941   Louisiana Purchase
1942   Holiday Inn
1943   This Is the Army (also specialty)
1946   Blue Skies
1948   Easter Parade
1950   Annie Get Your Gun
1953   Call Me Madam
1954   White Christmas
       There's No Business Like Show Business

Berman, Pandro S., producer; b. Pittsburgh, March 28, 1905. Berman produced seven of the ten musicals co-starring Fred Astaire and Ginger Rogers, one with Astaire alone and two with Miss Rogers alone. The producer was with RKO from 1931 to 1939, with MGM from 1940 to 1965; among his nonmusicals were *Stage Door, Gunga Din,* and *Father of the Bride*.

Asterisk indicates Astaire-Rogers film:
1933   Melody Cruise
1934   Hips Hips Hooray
       The Gay Divorcee*
1935   Roberta*
       Top Hat*
       In Person
       I Dream Too Much
1936   Follow the Fleet*
       Swing Time*
       That Girl from Paris
1937   Shall We Dance*
       A Damsel in Distress
1938   Having Wonderful Time
       Carefree*
1941   Ziegfeld Girl
1942   Rio Rita
1947   Living in a Big Way
1952   Lovely To Look At
1957   Jailhouse Rock

Bernie, Ben (né Benjamin Anzelovitz), bandleader, actor; b. New York, May 30, 1891; d. Beverly Hills, Oct. 20, 1943. Popular orchestra conductor who appeared in nightclubs and on radio, and who capitalized on avuncular personality and nasal comic patter. His "feud" with columnist Walter Winchell prompted the "old maestro's" last two films.

1934 Shoot the Works (*Joe Davis*)
1935 Stolen Harmony (*Jack Conrad*)
1937 Wake Up and Live (*Ben Bernie*)
Love and Hisses (*Ben Bernie*)

Bernstein, Leonard, composer; b. Lawrence, Mass., Aug. 25, 1918. Music director of the NY Philharmonic (1956–69) and composer of symphonic, choral, and Broadway scores. The two transferred to the screen were in collaboration with lyricists Betty Comden and Adolph Green, and Stephen Sondheim. Bernstein's one background film score was for *On the Waterfront*. Bib: *Leonard Bernstein* by John Briggs (1961).

1949 On the Town (Comden, Green)
1961 West Side Story (Sondheim)

Best Foot Forward (1943). Music & lyrics by Hugh Martin & Ralph Blane; screenplay by Irving Brecher & Fred Finklehoffe from Broadway musical by Martin, Blane, and John Cecil Holm.

An MGM film produced by Arthur Freed; directed by Edward Buzzell; choreography, Charles Walters; art directors, Cedric Gibbons, Edward Carfagno; costumes, Irene; music director, Lennie Hayton; orchestrations, Conrad Salinger, Jack Matthias, LeRoy Holmes, George Bassman, Leo Arnaud; cameraman, Leonard Smith; editor, Blanche Sewell.

Cast: Lucille Ball (vocal by Gloria Grafton) (*Lucille Ball*); William Gaxton (*Jack O'Riley*); Virginia Weidler (*Helen Schlessinger*); Tommy Dix (*Bud Hooper*); Nancy Walker (*Blind Date*); June Allyson (*Minerva Pierce*); Kenny Bowers (*Dutch Miller*); Gloria DeHaven (*Ethel*); Jack Jordan (*Hunk Hoyt*); Beverly Tyler (*girl at prom*); Chill Wills (*Chester Short*); Henry O'Neill (*Major Reeber*); Donald MacBride (*Capt. Bradd*); Sara Haden (*Miss Talbott*); Harry James and His Orchestra.

Songs: "Wish I May, Wish I Might" - Allyson, Bowers, DeHaven, Jordan, Haden, MacBride, cadets, girls/ "Three Men on a Date" - Dix, Bowers, Jordan/ "Two O'Clock Jump" (Harry James, Count Basie, Benny Goodman) - James orch./ "Ev'ry Time" - Weidler/ "Flight of the Bumble Bee" (Rimsky-Korsakov) - James orch./ "The Three B's" - Allyson, Walker, DeHaven, James orch./ "I Know You by Heart" - James orch./ "Shady Lady Bird" - James orch./ "My First Promise" - Tyler/ "Alive and Kicking" - Walker, James orch./ "You're Lucky" - Ball (Grafton)/ "Buckle Down, Winsocki" - Dix, cadets, girls. Unused: "That's How I Love the Blues," "What Do You Think I Am?"

On Broadway the 1941 musical *Best Foot Forward* was a breezy, youthful show about the complications that arise when, as a publicity stunt, movie star Gale Joy (played by Rosemary Lane) accepts an invitation to a prom at Winsocki Prep. In MGM's screen version the basic plot and teenage high spirits were retained, though the prep school was turned into a military academy (the US was then at war) and the movie star became Lucille Ball (played by Lucille Ball). The film kept seven of the 14 original Martin and Blane songs (surprisingly "Just a Little Joint with a Jukebox" was discarded) and added three new numbers by the team (including the rousing "Wish I May, Wish I Might") plus two Harry James specialties. June Allyson and Nancy Walker made their Hollywood debuts in roles they had originated in the Broadway *Best Foot Forward* (their "Three B's" routine with Gloria DeHaven was one of the film's standouts), but other actors from the show were signed for different parts from the ones they had played. Tommy Dix, who had introduced "Buckle Down, Winsocki" in a minor role, sang the number on screen in the leading role of the cadet whose invitation to Lucille Ball gets him into trouble with girlfriend Virginia Weidler. Kenny Bowers and Jack Jordan, also in the Broadway show, reversed their almost indistinguishable parts for the film.

Soon after *Best Foot Forward* had opened on Broadway, Columbia's Harry Cohn offered to buy the movie rights for a project involving Rita Hayworth (as the movie star), Shirley Temple (as the jilted prom date), and Glenn Miller's orchestra. MGM's Arthur Freed (who first wanted Lana Turner for *his* movie star) secured the rights by putting up more money and also, as part of the agreement, lending Gene Kelly to Columbia for *Cover Girl*.

"Best Things Happen When You're Dancing, The" Music & lyric by Irving Berlin. In *White Christmas* (Par. 1954) Danny Kaye expressed the sentiment to Vera Ellen while dancing in a Miami nightclub, after which the couple continued their dance on a deserted veranda. Both the song's meaning and the way the number was staged, so reminiscent of the "Cheek to Cheek" routine in *Top Hat,* indicate that the piece had been written for Fred Astaire, the film's intended co-star who had to bow out because of illness.

"Better Luck Next Time" Music & lyric by Irving Berlin. Introduced by Judy Garland in *Easter Parade* (MGM 1948). Convinced that her dancing partner, Don Hewes (Fred Astaire), still loves his former partner, unhappy Hannah Brown (Miss Garland) sits dejectedly at a bar and pours her heart out "because there ain't gonna be no next time for me."

"Between You and Me" Music & lyric by Cole Porter. Song of total adoration, used in *Broadway Melody of 1940* (MGM 1940) for George Murphy's audition as Eleanor Powell's leading man.

"Beyond the Blue Horizon" Music by Richard A. Whiting & W. Franke Harling; lyric by Leo Robin. Introduced by Jeanette MacDonald in *Monte Carlo* (Par. 1930). In the film's "Blue Express Scene" the music is coordinated with the accelerated sound of locomotive wheels as the train picks up momentum on its way to Monte Carlo. While expressing the hope that the engine will speed her to a bright tomorrow, Miss MacDonald leans out of her compartment window to acknowledge the waving and singing of the peasants in the fields. The actress also sang the piece in the wartime musical *Follow the Boys* (Univ. 1944), in which the original lyric's "rising sun" was changed to "shining sun" to avoid any possible Japanese association.

"Bibbidi-Bobbidi-Boo" Music by Al Hoffman & Jerry Livingston; lyric by Mack David. Sung by the Fairy Godmother (voice of Verna Felton) to cheer up Cinderella as she prepares her for the royal ball. From Walt Disney's animated version of *Cinderella* (RKO 1949).

Big Broadcast of 1938 (1938). Music by Ralph Rainger; lyrics by Leo Robin; screenplay by Walter DeLeon, Francis Martin, and Ken Englund from story by Frederick Hazlitt Brennan.

A Paramount film produced by Harlan Thompson; directed by Mitchell Leisen; choreography, LeRoy Prinz; art director, Hans Dreier, Ernst Fegte; costumes, Edith Head; cartoon sequence, Leon Schlesinger; music director, Boris Morros; cameramen, Harry Fishbeck, Gordon Jennings; editors, Eda Warren, Chandler House.

Cast: W. C. Fields (*T. Frothingwell Bellows/ S. B. Bellows*); Bob Hope (*Buzz Fielding*); Dorothy Lamour (*Dorothy Windham*); Shirley Ross (*Cleo Fielding*); Martha Raye (*Martha Bellows*); Lynne Overman (*Scoop McPhail*); Leif Erickson (*Robert Hayes*); Ben Blue (*Mike*); Grace Bradley (*Grace Fielding*); Rufe Davis (*Turnkey*); Patricia Wilder (*Honey Chile*); Lionel Pape (*Lord Droopy*); Dorothy Howe (*Joan Fielding*); Russell Hicks (*Capt. Stafford*); Shep Fields Orchestra (specialty); Tito Guizar (specialty); Kirsten Flagstad (specialty).

Songs: "This Little Ripple Had Rhythm" - Fields orch./ "Don't Tell a Secret to a Rose" - Guizar/ "Zuni Zuni" (Guizar) - Guizar/ "You Took the Words Right Out of My Heart" - Lamour, Erickson/ "Brunnhilde's Battle Cry" (Wagner, *Die Walkure*) - Flagstad/ "Thanks for the Memory" - Hope, Ross/ "Mama, That Moon Is Here Again" - Raye/ "The Waltz Lives On" - Ross, chorus/ "Truckin'" (Rube Bloom-Ted Koehler) - Raye. Unused: "Sawing a Woman in Half" (Jack Rock)

Since Warner's series of *Gold Diggers* films and MGM's series of *Broadway Melodys* were concerned with stage entertainments, Paramount varied the backstage format by offering a series of musicals dealing with broadcasting. With less elaborately mounted production numbers than the other two studios', the four *Big Broadcast* movies (and the similarly structured *International House*) had slim plots and relied heavily on specialty numbers and sketches. The first one, released in 1932, was primarily a showcase for Bing Crosby, making his acting debut in a feature-length film. He sang two early hits, "Please" and "Here Lies Love," both written by Ralph Rainger and Leo Robin, who would be associated with all subsequent movies in the series. On hand for routines and specialty appearances were Burns and Allen, the Boswell Sisters, Cab Calloway, Kate Smith, Arthur Tracy, and Vincent Lopez and his orchestra. Stuart Erwin played the harried radio-station owner; Frank Tuttle directed.

Though avoiding the *Big Broadcast* appellation, Paramount's *International House* in 1933 was very much part of the series since it featured specialty acts (including Rudy Vallee, Cab Calloway, Stoopnagle and Budd, and Baby Rose Marie) seen on an experimental television apparatus emanating from China. Under Edward Sutherland's direction, leading roles were played by

W. C. Fields, Stuart Erwin, Peggy Hopkins Joyce, and Burns and Allen.

Two years later, *Big Broadcast of 1936* revived the radio rubric and optimistically added the following year. This one, directed by Norman Taurog, found harried station owner Jack Oakie involved with a pioneering television invention called "radio eye," which allowed for appearances by Bing Crosby (singing "I Wished on the Moon," with a Dorothy Parker lyric), Burns and Allen, Amos 'n' Andy, Ethel Merman (doing Gordon and Revel's "It's the Animal in Me," in a scene that had been cut from *We're Not Dressing*), the Vienna Boys Choir, Bill Robinson, Mary Boland and Charlie Ruggles, and Ray Noble and his orchestra.

Jack Benny joined *Big Broadcast of 1937,* which also involved Ray Milland, Shirley Ross, Martha Raye, Burns and Allen, and vignette musical appearances by Benny Goodman and his orchestra, Leopold Stokowski and a symphony orchestra, and harmonica-player Larry Adler. It was directed by Mitchell Leisen.

Big Broadcast of 1938 was the most notable in the series chiefly because of W. C. Fields' antics on the golf course and at the billiard table, and Bob Hope's screen debut in which he sang "Thanks for the Memory" with Shirley Ross. This year's plot concerned a transatlantic race between two mammoth ocean liners, the *Gigantic* and the *Colossal*. The *Gigantic* wins because of an invention that picks up electronic impulses from the radio station on shore which then furnishes power to two huge propellers. The ship also provides daily broadcasts featuring such oddly assorted attractions as Shep Fields' orchestra, Tito Guizar, and Kirsten Flagstad, and ending with the uncharacterstically elaborate production, "The Waltz Lives On."

Birth of the Blues (1941). Screenplay by Harry Tugend & Walter DeLeon from story by Tugend.

A Paramount film produced by B. G. DeSylva, Monta Bell; directed by Victor Schertzinger; art directors, Hans Dreier, Ernst Fegté; costumes, Edith Head; music director, Robert Emmett Dolan; orchestrations, Dolan; cameraman, William Mellor; editor, Paul Weatherwax.

Cast: Bing Crosby (clarinet by Danny Polo) (*Jeff Lambert*); Mary Martin (*Betty Lou Cobb*); Brian Donlevy (cornet by Poky Carriere) (*Memphis*); Eddie "Rochester" Anderson (*Louie*); Jack Teagarden (*Pepper*); J. Carrol Naish (*Blackie*); Carolyn Lee (*Aunt Phoebe Cobb*); Ruby Elzy (*Ruby*); Harry Barris (*Suds*);

Harry Rosenthal (*pianist*); Perry Botkin (*Leo*); Ronnie Cosbey (*Jeff as a boy*).

Songs: "The Birth of the Blues" (Ray Henderson - B. G. DeSylva, Lew Brown) - Crosby/ "Memphis Blues" (Handy) - Crosby with band/ "By the Light of the Silvery Moon" (Gus Edwards - Edward Madden) - Crosby/ "Tiger Rag" (Original Dixieland Jazz Band) - Crosby (Polo) and band/ "Waiting at the Church" (Fred Leigh-Henry Pether) - Martin/ "Cuddle Up a Little Closer" (Karl Hoschna-Otto Harbach) - Martin/ "Wait 'til the Sun Shines, Nellie" (Harry Von Tilzer-Andrew Sterling) - Crosby, Martin with band/ "My Melancholy Baby" (Ernie Burnett) - Crosby/ "The Waiter, and the Porter and the Upstairs Maid" (Johnny Mercer) - Crosby, Martin, Teagarden with band/ "St. Louis Blues" (Handy) - Elzy.

In the early 1940s Hollywood discovered the world of jazz music and jazz musicians. The first major-studio effort, Paramount's *Birth of the Blues,* was primarily an easy-going Bing Crosby vehicle roughly based on the formation of Nick LaRocca's Original Dixieland Jazz Band, supposedly the first white group to play black music. With band vocalist Mary Martin (it was her best movie role), dubbed cornetist Brian Donlevy, and authentic jazz trombonist Jack Teagarden in tow, Crosby leads his Basin Street Hot-Shots as they struggle to be heard in New Orleans. Eventually they win favor in local night spots and, when last seen, are heading up the river to Chicago. The songs were mostly traditional jazz numbers and sentimental ballads, vocally highlighted by the Crosby-Martin duet, "Wait Till the Sun Shines, Nellie." B. G. DeSylva, the film's producer, was co-lyricist of the title song.

Coincidentally, two other movies about jazz musicians arrived soon after *Birth of the Blues.* Warner's *Blues in the Night,* with songs by Harold Arlen and Johnny Mercer, had a cast led by Priscilla Lane, Richard Whorf, and Jack Carson. Anatole Litvak directed. Then came RKO's *Syncopation,* the second to deal with the early years of jazz. Adolphe Menjou, Jackie Cooper, and Bonita Granville were the chief players, and William Dieterle was director.

"Black Market" Music & lyric by Frederick Hollander. Cynical, war-weary offer of goods to be traded—principally passion for rations—made by Marlene Dietrich in Berlin cabaret scene in *A Foreign Affair* (Par. 1948).

"Black Moonlight" Music by Arthur Johnston; lyric by Sam Coslow. Dolorous dirge of suicidally inclined Harlem resident (''What am I doing up here in a daze/ As I gaze on the cold river bay?''), introduced by Kitty Kelly in *Too Much Harmony* (Par. 1933).

"Blah Blah Blah" Music by George Gershwin; lyric by Ira Gershwin. Satire on movie-type vacuous love songs, with romantic clichés separated by trios of ''blahs.'' Performed in *Delicious* (Fox 1931) by El Brendel, Manya Roberti, and chorus to show a group of Russian immigrants how easy it is to write songs. Melody was originally called ''I Just Looked at You'' (lyric by Ira Gershwin and Gus Kahn) intended for but unused in Broadway musical *Show Girl* (1929); then called ''Lady of the Moon'' (lyric by Ira alone) intended for *Ming Toy* (1929) but musical was never produced.

Blaine, Vivian (née Vivian Stapleton), actress, singer; b. Newark, NJ, Nov. 21, 1921. Though Miss Blaine's fame rests primarily on her nose-clogged Miss Adelaide in *Guys and Dolls* (both stage and screen), she had been previously starred in a series of Fox musicals in the mid-40s (including *State Fair,* in which she sang ''That's for Me'' and ''It's a Grand Night for Singing''). She also introduced ''On the Boardwalk at Atlantic City'' in *Three Little Girls in Blue.* Don Ameche, Perry Como, Dick Haymes, and Frank Sinatra were among her leading men.

1943	Jitterbugs (*Susan Cowan*)
1944	Greenwich Village (*Bonnie*)
	Something for the Boys (*Blossom Hart*)
1945	State Fair (*Emily Edwards*)
	Nob Hill (*Sally Templeton*)
	Doll Face (*Doll Face*)
1946	If I'm Lucky (*Linda*)
	Three Little Girls in Blue (*Liz*)
1952	Skirts Ahoy (*Una Yancy*)
1955	Guys and Dolls (*Miss Adelaide*)

Blair, Janet (née Martha Janet Lafferty), actress, singer; b. Altoona, Pa., April 23, 1921. Former singer with Hal Kemp's band who usually played pert, well-scrubbed, girl-next-door types, both in musicals and nonmusicals. Introduced ''You'd Be So Nice To Come Home To'' in *Something To Shout About.*

1942	Broadway (*Billie Moore*)
1943	Something To Shout About (*Jean Maxwell*)
1945	Tonight and Every Night (*Judy Kane*)
1946	Tars and Spars (*Christine Bradley*)

1947	The Fabulous Dorseys (*Jane Howard*)
1968	The One and Only Genuine Original Family Band (*Mama Bower*)

Blane, Ralph (né Ralph Uriah Hunsecker), composer, lyricist; b. Broken Arrow, Okla., July 26, 1914. Began career as singer with Hugh Martin in vocal quartet in Broadway musicals. Blane and Martin each wrote half the score of *Best Foot Forward,* later filmed. In Hollywood, the team's most notable achievement was *Meet Me in St. Louis,* whence came ''The Boy Next Door,'' ''The Trolley Song,'' and ''Have Yourself a Merry Little Christmas.'' Other Blane-Martin songs include ''Love'' (*Ziegfeld Follies*) and ''Pass That Peace Pipe,'' with Roger Edens (*Good News*). Though he wrote both words and music for ''Girls Were Made To Take Care of Boys,'' Blane often worked as lyricist only, collaborating with such composers as Harry Warren (''The Stanley Steamer''), Harold Arlen, and Josef Myrow, and with co-lyricist Robert Wells. June Allyson, Judy Garland, Mickey Rooney, Lena Horne, Dennis Morgan, Betty Grable, Dan Dailey, Mitzi Gaynor, Doris Day, Jane Powell, and Vic Damone sang film songs by Ralph Blane.

1943	Best Foot Forward (*Martin*)
1944	Meet Me in St. Louis (*Martin*)
1945	Abbott and Costello in Hollywood (*Martin*)
1948	Summer Holiday (*Warren*)
	One Sunday Afternoon (*alone*)
1949	My Dream Is Yours (*Warren*)
1950	My Blue Heaven (*Arlen*)
1952	Skirts Ahoy (*Warren*)
1953	Down Among the Sheltering Palms (*Arlen*)
1954	The French Line (*Myrow-Wells*)
	Athena (*Martin*)
1955	The Girl Rush (*Martin*)
1957	The Girl Most Likely (*Martin*)

Blondell, (Rose) Joan, actress; b. New York, Aug. 30, 1909; d. Santa Monica, Dec. 25, 1979. Blonde, round-faced, saucer-eyed comedienne who usually played the wisecracking but vulnerable chorus girl in Warner backstage musicals between 1933 and 1937. She appeared opposite James Cagney, Dick Powell, and Bing Crosby, and introduced ''Remember My Forgotten Man'' in *Gold Diggers of 1933.* Second and third of her three husbands were Powell and producer Michael Todd. Bib: *Center Door Fancy* by Miss Blondell (1972).

1933	Gold Diggers of 1933 (*Carol King*)
	Footlight Parade (*Nan Prescott*)

1934 Dames (*Mabel Anderson*)
1935 Broadway Gondolier (*Alice Hughes*)
1936 Colleen (*Minnie Hawkins*)
       Stage Struck (*Peggy Revere*)
       Gold Diggers of 1937 (*Norma Perry*)
1937 The King and the Chorus Girl (*Dorothy*)
1939 East Side of Heaven (*Mary Wilson*)
1940 Two Girls on Broadway (*Molly Mahoney*)
1956 The Opposite Sex (*Edith*)
1957 This Could Be the Night (*Crystal*)
1978 Grease (*Vi*)

Blore, Eric, actor; b. London, Dec. 23, 1887; d. Los Angeles, March 1, 1959. Blore was a fussy, bumptious comic with an expressive round face whose specialty was playing Wodehousean butlers, waiters, valets, and hotel managers. Prior to his years in Hollywood—where he is best remembered for his five appearances in support of Fred Astaire and Ginger Rogers—he had acted in and written for the London and New York theatre.

1933 Flying Down to Rio (*Butterbass*)
1934 The Gay Divorcee (*waiter*)
1935 Folies Bergère (*François*)
       Old Man Rhythm (*Phillips*)
       Top Hat (*Bates*)
       I Dream Too Much (*Roger*)
       To Beat the Band (*Hawkins*)
1936 Swing Time (*Gordon*)
1937 Shall We Dance (*Cecil Flintridge*)
       Hitting a New High (*Cosmo*)
1938 Joy of Living (*Potter*)
       Swiss Miss (*Edward*)
1940 Music in My Heart (*Griggs*)
       The Boys from Syracuse (*Pinch*)
1941 Road to Zanzibar (*Charles Kimble*)
       Redhead (*Digby*)
1943 The Sky's the Limit (*Jackson*)
       Happy Go Lucky (*Vespers*)
1945 Penthouse Rhythm (*Ferdy Pelham*)
       Easy To Look At (*Billings*)
1948 Romance on the High Seas (*ship doctor*)
1949 Ichabod and Mr. Toad (voice of *Mr. Toad*)
       Love Happy (*Mackinaw*)
1950 Fancy Pants (''*Sir Wimbley*'')

"Blossoms on Broadway" Music by Ralph Rainger; lyric by Leo Robin. Romance turns the bustling thoroughfare into a romantic country lane. Introduced by Shirley Ross in film of same name (Par. 1937).

Blue, Ben (né Benjamin Bernstein), actor; b. Montreal, Sept. 12, 1901; d. Los Angeles, March 7, 1975. Wispy comedian and pantomimist with breathless delivery who appeared mostly in Paramount and MGM musicals; later primarily in nightclubs.

1934 College Rhythm (bit)
1936 Follow Your Heart (*Ben Blue*)
       College Holiday (*stagehand*)
1937 Turn Off the Moon (*Luke*)
       High, Wide and Handsome (*Samuel*)
       Artists and Models (*Jupiter Pluvius*)
       Thrill of a Lifetime (*Skipper*)
1938 Big Broadcast of 1938 (*Mike*)
       College Swing (*Ben Volt*)
       Cocoanut Grove (*Joe Delemma*)
1939 Paris Honeymoon (*Sitska*)
1942 For Me and My Gal (*Sid Simms*)
       Panama Hattie (*Rowdy*)
1943 Thousands Cheer (*Chuck*)
       Broadway Rhythm (*Felix Gross*)
1944 Two Girls and a Sailor (*Ben*)
1946 Two Sisters from Boston (*Wrigley*)
       Easy To Wed (*Spike Dolan*)
1947 My Wild Irish Rose (*Hopper*)
1948 One Sunday Afternoon (*Nick*)

"Blue Gardenia" Music by Lester Lee; lyric by Bob Russell. Sung by Nat King Cole in Hawaiian restaurant scene in nonmusical film of same name (Warner 1953).

"Blue Hawaii" Music by Ralph Rainger; lyric by Leo Robin. Nocturnal invitation to romance on a balmy tropical island, sung by Bing Crosby in *Waikiki Wedding* (Par. 1937). Though the film already had Harry Owen's "Sweet Leilani," Robin persuaded Rainger to write the music to this song. It became a hit despite Rainger's feeling that his music was inferior and at first protested its publication. The song was also sung by Elvis Presley (over credits) in *Blue Hawaii* (Par. 1961).

"Blue Moon." *See* **"Bad in Every Man, The"**

Blue Skies (1946). Music & lyrics by Irving Berlin; screenplay by Arthur Sheekman, adapted by Allan Scott from idea by Berlin.

A Paramount film produced by Sol C. Siegel; directed by Stuart Heisler; choreography, Hermes Pan; art directors, Hans Dreier, Hal Pereira; costumes, Edith Head, Waldo Angelo; music director, Robert Emmett Dolan; vocal arrangements, Joseph J. Lilley; cameramen, Charles Lang, Jr., William Snyder; editor, LeRoy Stone; Technicolor.

Cast: Bing Crosby (*Johnny Adams*); Fred Astaire (*Jed Potter*); Joan Caulfield (*Mary O'Dare Adams*); Billy DeWolfe (*Tony*); Olga San Juan (*Nita Nova*); Jimmy Conlin (*Jeffrey*); Cliff Nazarro (*Cliff*); Roy Gordon (*Charles Dillingham*); Jack Norton (*drunk*); Frank Faylen (*Mack*).

Songs: ''A Pretty Girl Is Like Melody'' - chorus; dance by Astaire/ ''I've Got My Captain Working For Me Now'' - Crosby, DeWolfe/ ''You'd Be Surprised'' - San Juan/ ''All by Myself'' - Crosby/ ''Serenade to an Old Fashioned Girl'' - Caulfield, chorus/ ''Puttin' on the Ritz'' - Astaire/ ''(I'll See You in) C-U-B-A'' - Crosby, San Juan/ ''A Couple of Song and Dance Men'' - Crosby, Astaire/ ''You Keep Coming Back Like a Song'' - Crosby/ ''Always'' - chorus/ ''Blue Skies'' - Crosby/ ''The Little Things in Life'' - Crosby/ ''Not for All the Rice in China'' - Crosby/ ''Russian Lullaby'' - Crosby/ ''Everybody Step'' - Crosby/ ''How Deep Is the Ocean?'' - chorus, Crosby/ ''(Running Around in Circles) Getting Nowhere'' - Crosby/ ''Heat Wave'' - San Juan, chorus; dance by Astaire/ ''Any Bonds Today?'' - Crosby/ ''This Is the Army, Mr. Jones'' - Crosby/ ''White Christmas'' - Crosby.

The success of *Holiday Inn* made it seem inevitable that Bing Crosby would be again teamed with Fred Astaire. Yet the second pairing was due almost exclusively to misfortune. Producer-director Mark Sandrich originally signed the classically trained hoofer Paul Draper to appear with Crosby in *Blue Skies,* but Sandrich died soon after shooting had begun. His replacements, producer Siegel and director Heisler, then brought in Fred Astaire to succeed Draper. *Blue Skies,* like its predecessor, was a movie with a plot manufactured to accommodate a hefty catalogue of Irving Berlin songs, with the emphasis more on the old (17) than the new (4). Again Crosby and Astaire played former song-and-dance partners who vie for the affection of one girl (here Joan Caulfield) and again her preference is Crosby (she even gets to marry him twice). In the previous film, the plot gimmick had been to use appropriate songs in a nightclub open only on holidays; in the new film, whose time span was 1919 to 1946, it was to use appropriate songs in a variety of ''theme'' nightclubs. Among the standout numbers was the Astaire dance—accompanied by a row of mini-size Astaires—to ''Puttin' on the Ritz.'' This was the final scene filmed and was intended as Astaire's farewell to dancing (he did retire but then returned to the screen two years later in *Easter Parade*). In 1954 Astaire was again signed to co-star with

Crosby—in *White Christmas*—a variation on *Holiday Inn* again featuring a profusion of Berlin songs. But illness forced his replacement first by Donald O'Connor, then, when O'Connor took sick, by Danny Kaye.

''Bluebirds in the Moonlight'' Music by Ralph Rainger; lyric by Leo Robin. At a dinner honoring Gulliver in Max Fleischer's feature-length cartoon, *Gulliver's Travels* (Par. 1939), the Lilliputians entertain by singing this bouncy number of appreciation. King Little, in fact, is so delighted that he dances on the table with Gulliver's fingers.

Blues in the Night. See Birth of the Blues.

''Blues in the Night'' Music by Harold Arlen; lyric by Johnny Mercer. Lament about a two-timing woman sung by William Gillespie in a jail cell in *Blues in the Night* (Warner 1941). Because Arlen wanted the song to have the impact of authentic folk blues, he used the traditional three-stanza, twelve-bar pattern of the musical form. After Mercer had set words to the melody, the composer offered only one suggestion: take lines appearing on the fourth page of the typed lyric—beginning ''My mamma done tol' me when I was in knee pants''—and move them to the opening of the song. The number impressed everyone so highly that the film, originally titled *Hot Nocturne,* became known as *Blues in the Night.* Song also sung by John Garfield (comic gangster version) in *Thank Your Lucky Stars* (Warner 1943).

Blyth, Ann (Marie), actress, singer; b. Mount Kisco, NY, Aug. 16, 1928. Dark-haired, square-jawed leading lady with well-trained voice who began at Universal, then became an alternative to Kathryn Grayson in MGM musicals of the early 50s. Miss Blyth appeared in films with Donald O'Connor, Bing Crosby, Mario Lanza (introducing ''The Loveliest Night of the Year'' in *The Great Caruso*), and Howard Keel.

1944	Chip off the Old Block (*Glory Marlowe III*)	
	The Merry Monahans (*Sheila DeRoyce*)	
	Babes on Swing Street (*Carol Curtis*)	
	Bowery to Broadway (*Bessie Jo Kirby*)	
1948	Top o' the Mornin' (*Conn McNaughton*)	
1951	The Great Caruso (*Dorothy Benjamin Caruso*)	
1954	The Student Prince (*Kathie Ruder*)	
	Rose Marie (*Rose Marie LeMaitre*)	
1955	Kismet (*Marsinah*)	
1957	The Helen Morgan Story (*Helen Morgan*)	

"Boa Noite" Music by Harry Warren; lyric by Mack Gordon. Romantic goodnight sung by Don Ameche in Rio de Janeiro night club in *That Night in Rio* (Fox 1941); reprised by Alice Faye (in her bedroom) singing to Ameche (in his bedroom).

Bock and Harnick. (Jerrold Lewis) Jerry Bock, composer; b. New Haven, Conn., Nov. 23, 1928. Sheldon Harnick, lyricist; b. Chicago, Apr. 30, 1924. Major Broadway team (*Fiorello!*, *She Loves Me*, *Fiddler on the Roof*) who wrote seven scores together, with only *Fiddler* making it to the screen.

    1966   The Canterville Ghost (tv)
    1971   Fiddler on the Roof

"Bojangles of Harlem" Music by Jerome Kern; lyric by Dorothy Fields. Rhythmic tribute to dancing star Bill Robinson introduced in *Swing Time* (RKO 1936). Presented as the floorshow at the Silver Sandal, a plush New York nightclub, the number is sung by the tan-faced chorus girls to Fred Astaire as the beloved Bojangles (his only appearance in blackface) who is emulated by both tough guys in Harlem poolrooms and kids coming out of schoolrooms. Fred joins the dancing girls, then follows with a solo featuring three huge shadows projected on the wall behind him. Lyricist Dorothy Fields once revealed that the composer, who was more comfortable creating flowing, longline melodies, was able to get into the spirit of the number only after Astaire had spent an afternoon tapping all around Kern's hotel suite.

Boland, Mary, actress; b. Philadelphia, Jan. 28, 1880; d. New York, June 23, 1965. Fluttery, social-climbing type who appeared in many Paramount comedies with Charlie Ruggles as her long-suffering spouse. Made Broadway debut in 1905 and starred in two stage musicals.

    1934   Melody in Spring (*Mary Blodgett*)
              Down to Their Last Yacht (*Queen of Molakamokalu*)
    1935   Two for Tonight (*Mrs. J. S. K. Smythe*)
              Big Broadcast of 1936 (specialty)
    1936   College Holiday (*Carola Gaye*)
    1938   Artists and Models Abroad (*Isabel Channing*)
    1940   New Moon (*Valerie de Rossac*)
              Hit Parade of 1941 (*Emily Potter*)
              One Night in the Tropics (*Kitty Marblehead*)

Boles, John, actor, singer; b. Greenville, Texas, Oct. 28, 1895; d. San Angelo, Texas, Feb. 27, 1969. Strong-jawed, wooden, mustached Broadway operetta baritone who appeared in film musicals with Bebe Daniels, Evelyn Laye, Gloria Swanson, Gladys Swarthout (twice), and Shirley Temple (twice). Boles, who acted mostly in Fox musicals, introduced "It Happened in Monterey" in *King of Jazz*.

    1929   The Desert Song (*Pierre Birabeau*)
              Rio Rita (*Capt. James Stewart*)
    1930   Song of the West (*Harry Stanton*)
              King of Jazz (specialty)
              Captain of the Guard (*Rouget de l'Isle*)
              One Heavenly Night (*Mirko*)
    1932   Careless Lady (*Stephen Illington*)
    1933   My Lips Betray (*King Rupert*)
    1934   Stand Up and Cheer (specialty)
              Wild Gold (*Steve Miller*)
              Bottoms Up (*Hal Reade*)
              Music in the Air (*Bruno Mahler*)
    1935   Redheads on Parade (*John Bruce*)
              Curly Top (*Edward Morgan*)
              The Littlest Rebel (*Capt. Herbert Cary*)
    1936   Rose of the Rancho (*Jim Kearney*)
    1938   Romance in the Dark (*Antal Kovach*)
    1943   Thousands Cheer (*Col. Jones*)

Bolger, (Raymond Wallace) Ray, actor, dancer, singer; b. Dorchester, Mass., Jan. 10, 1904. Bolger's agile, spidery dancing and unassuming comic personality were seen at their best in such films as *The Wizard of Oz* (singing "If I Only Had a Brain"), *The Harvey Girls* (dancing "On the Atchison, Topeka and Santa Fe"), and *Where's Charley?* (repeating his stage role). The actor began his Broadway career in 1926, won stardom with *On Your Toes* and *By Jupiter*, and apppeared in nightclubs, television, and concerts. (Died Jan. 15, 1987.)

    1936   The Great Ziegfeld (*Ray Bolger*)
    1937   Rosalie (*Bill Delroy*)
    1938   Sweethearts (*Fred*)
    1939   The Wizard of Oz (*Hunk/Scarecrow*)
    1940   Sunny (*Bunny Billings*)
    1941   Four Jacks and a Jill
    1943   Stage Door Canteen (specialty)
    1945   The Harvey Girls (*Chris Maule*)
    1949   Look for the Silver Lining (*Jack Donahue*)
    1952   April in Paris (*S. Winthrop Putnam*)
              Where's Charley? (*Charley Wykeham*)
    1961   Babes in Toyland (*Barnaby*)
    1976   The Entertainer (tv) (*Billy Rice*)
    1985   That's Dancing! (narrator)

"Bonjour, Paris!" Music by Roger Edens; lyric by Leonard Gershe. Exuberant greeting in *Funny Face* (Par. 1957) from Fred Astaire, Kay Thompson, and Audrey Hepburn as they enjoy separate, split-screen tours of the city, and end up giggling together on the Eiffel Tower.

"Boogie Woogie Bugle Boy" Music by Hughie Prince; lyric by Don Raye. The Andrews Sisters trumpeted this salute to Company B's notably rhythmic bugler in *Buck Privates* (Univ. 1941).

Boone, (Charles Eugene) Pat, actor, singer; b. Jacksonville, Fla., June 1, 1934. Bland, clean-cut singing idol of the 50s whose trademark was white buckskin shoes. His successful recording career led him to Hollywood, where he was identified with such pieces as "Friendly Persuasion" (on film soundtrack) and "April Love." He is the father of singer Debbie Boone.

1957 Bernardine (*Beau Wilson*)
       April Love (*Nick Conover*)
1958 Mardi Gras (*Paul Newell*)
1959 Journey to the Center of the Earth (*Alec McEwen*)
1961 All Hands on Deck (*Lt. Donald*)
1962 State Fair (*Wayne Frake*)
1963 The Main Attraction (*Eddie*)

"Born Free" Music by John Barry; lyric by Don Black. Stirring theme of film of same name (Col. 1966), sung on soundtrack by Matt Monro.

"Born in a Trunk" Music by Roger Edens (uncredited); lyric by Leonard Gershe. Elaborate show-business saga of the rise of an ambitious singer (Judy Garland), performed as part of a movie being shown in *A Star Is Born* (Warner 1954). During the number, Miss Garland sang all or part of the following songs: "Swanee," "I'll Get By," "You Took Advantage of Me," "Black Bottom," "Peanut Vendor," "Melancholy Baby." This segment, added after director George Cukor had finished his work, was directed by Richard Barstow assisted by Roger Edens.

Born To Dance (1936). Music & lyrics by Cole Porter; screenplay by Jack McGowan & Sid Silvers from story by McGowan, Silvers, B. G. DeSylva.

An MGM film produced by Jack Cummings; directed by Roy Del Ruth; choreography, Dave Gould; art director, Cedric Gibbons; costumes, Adrian; music director, Alfred Newman; orchestrations, Roger Edens; editor, Blanche Sewell; cameraman, Ray June.

Cast: Eleanor Powell (*Nora Paige*); James Stewart (*Ted Barker*); Virginia Bruce (*Lucy James*); Una Merkel (*Jenny Saks*); Sid Silvers (*Gunny Saks*); Frances Langford (*Peggy Turner*); Raymond Walburn (*Capt. Percival Digby*); Alan Dinehart (*McKay*); Buddy Ebsen (*Mush Tracy*); Juanita Quigley (*Sally Saks*); Georges and Jalna (*dancers*); Reginald Gardiner (*policeman*); Barnett Parker (*floorwalker*); The Foursome (*singers*); Helen Troy (*telephone operator*).

Songs: "Rolling Home" - Foursome, Silvers, Ebsen, Stewart, sailors/ "Rap Tap on Wood" - Powell, Foursome/ "Hey, Babe, Hey" - Stewart, Silvers, Ebsen, Langford; dance by Powell, Stewart, Merkel, Silvers, Langford, Ebsen/ "Entrance of Lucy James" - sailors/ "Love Me, Love My Pekinese" - Bruce/ "Easy To Love" - Stewart; dance by Powell/ "I've Got You Under My Skin" - dance by Georges & Jalna; sung by Bruce/ "Swingin' the Jinx Away" - Langford, Ebsen, Foursome, chorus; dance by Ebsen, Powell. Unused: "Goodbye, Little Dream, Goodbye," "It's De-Lovely," "Who but You."

Released the year between *Broadway Melody of 1936* and *Broadway Melody of 1938*, MGM's *Born to Dance* could easily have qualified as *Broadway Melody of 1937*. All three films had the same tapping star (Eleanor Powell), tapping comic (Buddy Ebsen), director (Roy Del Ruth), writers (Jack McGowan and Sid Silvers), and choreographer (Dave Gould), and all were concerned with how Eleanor gets her big break on Broadway. Composer-lyricist Cole Porter was signed to write the score for *Born To Dance* even before the story had been written. At first there were plans to do a revue based on the Broadway show *As Thousands Cheer,* but the studio eventually settled on an unproduced musical-comedy libretto about two sailors and the hostess of a Lonely Hearts Club in New York. As work progressed the number of sailors was increased to three (Allan Jones, Buddy Ebsen, and Sid Silvers) who would be romantically paired with three girls at the club (Eleanor Powell, Judy Garland, and Una Merkel). A fourth girl, a bored socialite (Frances Langford), was added to threaten the Powell-Jones combination. Along the way Jones was replaced by James Stewart, and Miss Garland by Miss Langford, whose original role was then taken by Virginia Bruce, with the part changed to that of a bitchy musical-comedy star. In the time-honored tradition of backstage musicals, neophyte Powell gets to replace Miss Bruce in the show *Great Guns!* before opening night—with nary a soul concerned that one is a dancer and the other a singer. *Born To Dance* almost marked the screen debut of Sonja Henie, who was to have appeared in a brief ice-skating sequence, but she wanted too much money; so instead of Jimmy taking Eleanor to a skating rink, they go off to a fancy nightclub to see ballroom dancers Georges and Jalna.

Borzage, Frank, director; b. Salt Lake City, April 23, 1893; d. Hollywood, June 19, 1962. Primarily a director of sentimental "women's" pictures, Borzage began his career acting in and directing silent films. His most memorable: *Seventh Heaven, A Farewell to Arms*.

1930	Song o' My Heart
1934	Flirtation Walk
1935	Shipmates Forever
1936	Hearts Divided
1941	Smilin' Through
1942	Seven Sweethearts
1943	Stage Door Canteen
	His Butler's Sister

Boswell, (Constance) Connie, singer; b. New Orleans, Dec. 3, 1907; d. New York, Oct. 10, 1976. She began as member of close-harmony trio with sisters, Martha and Vet, in the 20s; as the Boswell Sisters the team won fame on radio and records, then broke up in 1935 with Connie continuing as a solo act. In films she introduced "Whispers in the Dark" and "Sand in My Shoes." Miss Boswell, who changed the spelling of her first name to Connee in the early 40s, was a victim of polio and always sang from a wheelchair.

Miss Boswell sang with sisters in first three films:
1932	The Big Broadcast
1934	Moulin Rouge
	Transatlantic Merry-Go-Round
1937	Artists and Models
1941	Kiss the Boys Goodbye
1942	Syncopation
1946	Swing Parade of 1946
1959	Senior Prom

"Boulevard of Broken Dreams, The" Music by Harry Warren; lyric by Al Dubin. Minor-key, pseudo-French lament about the street of sorrows where gigolo meets gigolette and dreams are broken and forgotten. Introduced by Constance Bennett (sporting French accent) in production number in a Broadway theatre in *Moulin Rouge* (UA 1934).

"Boy Next Door, The" Music & lyric by Hugh Martin & Ralph Blane. In *Meet Me in St. Louis* (MGM 1944), Judy Garland, who lives at 5135 Kensington Avenue,

expresses her longing for the handsome new neighbor, Tom Drake, who has moved into 5133. Though the girl pines, "The boy next door affection for me won't display," it's odd that she could have expected any sign of affection since, earlier in the song, she had revealed that they have never even met. In 1954, Vic Damone sang the ballad as "The Girl Next Door" in *Athena* (MGM).

"Boys in the Back Room, The" Music by Frederick Hollander; lyric by Frank Loesser. In a flashy cowgirl outfit, Marlene Dietrich introduced the rousing drinking song as a frontier saloon entertainer in *Destry Rides Again* (Univ. 1939).

Bracken, (Edward Vincent) Eddie, actor; b. Astoria, NY, Feb. 7, 1920. Fast-moving, always-in-a-jam Joecollege type who went to Hollywood to repeat his role in *Too Many Girls,* then appeared mostly in Paramount films (including nonmusical *Hail the Conquering Hero*).

1940	Too Many Girls (*JoJo Jordan*)
1942	The Fleet's In (*Barney Waters*)
	Sweater Girl (*Jack Mitchell*)
	Star Spangled Rhythm (*Jimmy Webster*)
1943	Happy Go Lucky (*Wally Case*)
1944	Rainbow Island (*Toby Smith*)
1945	Bring On the Girls (*J. Newport Bates*)
	Out of This World (*Herbie Fenton*)
	Duffy's Tavern (specialty)
1947	Ladies' Man (*Henry Haskell*)
1950	Summer Stock (*Orville Wingate*)
1951	Two Tickets to Broadway (*Lew Conway*)
1952	About Face (*Boff Roberts*)

Bradley, Grace, actress, singer, dancer; b. Brooklyn, Sept. 21, 1913. Roundfaced, well-proportioned redhead who played second leads in Paramount musicals. Married actor William Boyd.

1933	The Way to Love (*sunburned lady*)
	Too Much Harmony (*Verne LaMonte*)
	Girl Without a Room (*Nada*)
1935	Stolen Harmony (*Jean Loring*)
	Old Man Rhythm (*Marian Beecher*)
1936	Rose of the Rancho (*Flossie*)
	Anything Goes (*Bonnie LeTour*)
	Three Cheers for Love (*Eve Bronson*)
	Sitting on the Moon (*Polly Blair*)
1937	Wake Up and Live (*Jean Roberts*)
1938	Big Broadcast of 1938 (*Grace Fielding*)
1941	There's Magic in Music (*Maidie Duvalle*)

Breaux, Marc, and Deedee Wood, choreographers. Marc (Charles) Breaux, b. Carenco, La., Nov. 3. (Audrey Donella) Deedee Wood, b. Boston, June 7, 1927. Husband-wife team who began on Broadway as chorus dancers, then assisted choreographer Michael Kidd on *Li'l Abner* and became choreographers of *Do Re Mi*. In Hollywood, their best-known work was for *Mary Poppins*.

1959   Li'l Abner (Wood only)
1964   Mary Poppins
1965   The Sound of Music
1967   The Happiest Millionaire
1968   Chitty Chitty Bang Bang
1974   Huckleberry Finn
1976   The Slipper and the Rose (Breaux only)

Breen, Bobby, actor, singer; b. Toronto, Nov. 4, 1927. Boy soprano noted for his birdlike trilling who was RKO's answer to Fox's Shirley Temple. Introduced "Rainbow on the River"; later became a nightclub singer.

1936   Let's Sing Again (*Billy Gordon*)
       Rainbow on the River (*Philip*)
1937   Make a Wish (*Chip*)
1938   Hawaii Calls (*Billy Couter*)
       Breaking the Ice (*Tommy Martin*)
1939   Fisherman's Wharf (*Tony*)
       Way Down South (*Tim*)
1942   Johnny Doughboy (specialty)

Bremer, Lucille, actress, dancer; b. Amsterdam, NY, Feb. 21, 1923. Expressionless beauty who appeared in Arthur Freed musicals and managed to dance with Fred Astaire in two of them.

1944   Meet Me in St. Louis (*Rose Smith*)
1945   Yolanda and the Thief (*Yolanda Acquaviva*)
1946   Ziegfeld Follies (specialty)
       Till the Clouds Roll By (*Sally*)

Brendel, (Elmer G.) El, actor; b. Philadelphia, March 25, 1890; d. Hollywood, April 9, 1964. Brendel was an eternally grinning rube comic with a "yumpin'-yim-miny" accent who provided innocent humor mostly in Fox musicals.

1929   The Cock-Eyed World (*Olson*)
       Sunny Side Up (*Eric Swenson*)
       Hot for Paris (*Axel Olson*)
1930   Happy Days (minstrel specialty)
       Movietone Follies of 1930 (*Axel Swenson*)
       Just Imagine (*Single O*)
       The Golden Calf (*Knute Olson*)
1931   Delicious (*Jansen*)
1933   My Lips Betray (*Stigmat*)

1937   The Holy Terror (*Axel Swenson*)
       Blonde Trouble (*window washer*)
1938   Happy Landing (*bandmaster*)
1938   Little Miss Broadway (*Ole*)
1940   If I Had My Way (*Axel Swenson*)
1949   The Beautiful Blonde from Bashful Bend (*Jorgensen*)

Brice, Fanny (née Fanny Borach), actress, singer; b. New York, Oct. 29, 1891; d. Hollywood, May 29, 1951. Miss Brice, one of the great clowns of the Broadway musical stage, made her NY debut in 1910. Her basic Yiddish-accented character, with her mischievous eyes and half-moon smile, was best seen on the screen in *The Great Ziegfeld*. She was married to and divorced from producer Billy Rose; the most popular song she introduced in films was "I'd Rather Be Blue." Film bios: *Funny Girl* and *Funny Lady,* both with Barbra Streisand as Miss Brice. Bib: *The Fabulous Fanny* by Norman Katkov (1953).

1928   Night Club (specialty)
       My Man (*Fanny Brand*)
1930   Be Yourself (*Fanny Field*)
1936   The Great Ziegfeld (*Fanny Brice*)
1938   Everybody Sing (*Olga Chekaloff*)
1946   Ziegfeld Follies (specialty)

Bricusse, Leslie, composer, lyricist, screen writer; b. London, Jan. 29, 1931. Bricusse first won notice with his London and New York stage hit, *Stop the World—I Want to Get Off,* written with Anthony Newley, which was filmed in 1966 and in 1978. Among his movie songs are "Talk to the Animals," "Thank You Very Much," and "Candy Man."

Asterisk indicates Mr. Bricusse also wrote script:
1966   Stop the World—I Want To Get Off* (Newley)
1967   Doctor Dolittle*
1969   Goodbye, Mr. Chips
1970   Scrooge* (also prod.)
1971   Willy Wonka and the Chocolate Factory (Newley)
1976   Peter Pan (tv)* (Newley)
1978   Sammy Stops the World* (Newley)
1982   Victor/Victoria (Mancini)

Brisson, Carl (né Carl Brisson Pederson), actor, singer, dancer; b. Copenhagen, Dec. 24, 1895; d. Copenhagen, Sept. 26, 1958. A teeth-flashing, dimpled, top-hatted personification of Continental charm, Brisson won success on the London stage in the 1920s and acted in British screen musicals before his brief career in Hollywood. His best-known film song was "Cocktails for Two" in

Murder at the Vanities. Brisson was the father of stage producer Frederick Brisson and father-in-law of Rosalind Russell.

1930 Song of Soho (Eng.) (*Carl*)
1933 Prince of Arcadia (Eng.) (*Prince Peter*)
1934 Two Hearts in Waltz Time (Eng.) (*Carl Hoffman*)
Murder at the Vanities (*Eric Lander*)
1935 All the King's Horses (*King Rudolph/ Carlo Rocco*)
Ship Café (*Chris Anderson*)

"Broadway Melody" Music by Nacio Herb Brown; lyric by Arthur Freed. This rousing anthem to the thoroughfare that "always wears a smile" was sung by Charles King on three occasions in *The Broadway Melody* (MGM 1929): 1) auditioning it for music publisher James Gleason as a song he's just written for the latest Francis Zanfield (*sic*) revue; 2) teaching it to Bessie Love and Anita Page in their hotel room while Miss Love accompanies him on the ukulele; 3) belting it during a rehearsal of the Zanfield show. In the last, clad in top hat, white tie and tails, he struts across the stage with a chorus line behind him and a painted skyline backdrop bearing the words "MELODY" on one side and "BROADWAY" on the other. (This last scene was included in the 1944 Two Cities film, *This Happy Breed*, in a sequence showing the London presentation of *The Broadway Melody*.) Song was later sung by Harry Stockwell in *Broadway Melody of 1936* (MGM) and Gene Kelly in *Singin' in the Rain* (MGM 1952).

All three of MGM's subsequent *Broadway Melody* films also featured "Broadway" songs: "Broadway Rhythm" (1936) and "Your Broadway and My Broadway" (1938) were again by Brown and Freed; "Don't Monkey with Old Broadway" (1940) was by Cole Porter.

Broadway Melody, The (1929). Music by Nacio Herb Brown; lyrics by Arthur Freed: screenplay by Edmund Goulding, Norman Houston, James Gleason.

An MGM film produced by Irving Thalberg; directed by Harry Beaumont; art director, Cedric Gibbons; costumes, David Cox; cameraman, John Arnold; editors, Sam S. Zimbalist (sound), William Levenway (silent).

Cast: Charles King (*Eddie Kerns*); Anita Page (*Queenie Mahoney*); Bessie Love (*Harriet "Hank" Mahoney*); Jed Prouty (*Uncle Jed*); Kenneth Thomson (*Jock Warriner*); Mary Doran (*Flo*); Eddie Kane (*Francis Zanfield*); Edward Dillon (*Dillon*); James Gleason (*James Gleason*); Nacio Herb Brown (*pianist*); James Burrows (*singer*); Biltmore Trio (*singers*).

Songs: "Broadway Melody" - King, with Brown, piano; reprised by King with Page, Love/ "Harmony Babies" - Love, Page/ "Love Boat" - Burrows/ "You Were Meant for Me" - King/ "Truthful Parson Brown" (Willard Robison) - Biltmore Trio/ "Wedding of the Painted Doll" - Burrows; dance by chorus/ "The Boy Friend" - Love, Page. Unused: "Lovely Lady."

Though *The Broadway Melody* was initially planned as a part-talkie, producer Irving Thalberg, after seeing the early sound rushes, decided to film it as MGM's first 100% all-talking motion picture, or—as its ads proclaimed—"ALL TALKING! ALL SINGING! ALL DANCING!" It was also the first movie to use songs both within a story and as part of a Broadway show being performed, and it was the first to have an original score created specifically for its use. (Brown and Freed won the assignment after competing with Fred Fisher and Billy Rose.) Greeted as a cinema milestone by press and public, the film became the first talkie seen by most of the United States, since it was chosen by a majority of exhibitors as their premier sound attraction (though as a precaution, MGM also released a silent version for the still unconverted).

In plot and setting *The Broadway Melody* may have had a number of stage antecedents, but it succeeded in setting the pattern for decades of show business stories. Its tale was concerned with song-and-dance-and-songwriting man, Eddie Kerns (Charles King), who is engaged to marry vaudevillian "Hank" Mahoney (Bessie Love) but falls in love with—and eventually marries—her kid sister Queenie (Anita Page). But what mattered most to audiences were the seemingly authentic backstage ambiance (auditions, wisecracking chorus girls, etc.) and spectacular onstage production numbers (one in color) of the latest Francis Zanfield (*sic*) extravaganza, *The Broadway Melody*.

Originally, the title of the film was to have been *Whoopee*, but, when Eddie Cantor opened in a Broadway show with that name, *The Broadway Melody* was substituted. Before Misses Love and Page were signed, Vivian and Rosetta Duncan, a vaudeville and musical-comedy team, whose career supposedly furnished the basic idea for the story, were considered to have the inside track. As something of a consolation, the Duncans then went into a similar backstage yarn, *It's a Great Life*. Charles King and Bessie Love tried with little success to score another hit together in *Chasing Rainbows*, also with a similar format. The title *Broadway Melody*—with appropriate years affixed—was later used in 1936,

1938, and 1940 for a series of show business musicals all featuring the tapping of Eleanor Powell. The basic plot of the 1929 movie was reused in 1940 in the MGM film *Two Girls on Broadway,* directed by S. Sylvan Simon. But here, the Mahoney sisters (Joan Blondell and Lana Turner) and Eddie Kerns (George Murphy) aspired to fame not in the theatre but in nightclubs.

Broadway Melody of 1936 (1935). Music by Nacio Herb Brown; lyrics by Arthur Freed; screenplay by Jack McGowan, Sid Silvers, and Harry Conn from story by Moss Hart.

An MGM film produced by John Considine, Jr.; directed by Roy Del Ruth; choreography, Dave Gould, Albertina Rasch; art director, Cedric Gibbons; costumes, Adrian; music director, Alfred Newman; orchestrations, Roger Edens; cameraman, Charles Rosher; editor, Blanche Sewell.

Cast: Jack Benny (*Bert Keeler*); Eleanor Powell (*Irene Foster*); Robert Taylor (*Bob Gordon*); Una Merkel (*Kitty Corbett*); Frances Langford (*singer*); Sid Silvers (*Snoop Blue*); Buddy Ebsen (*Buddy Burke*); June Knight (*Lillian*); Vilma Ebsen (*Sally*); Harry Stockwell (*singer*); Nick Long, Jr. (*Basil Newcombe*); Paul Harvey (*editor*); Robert Wildhack (*Hornblow*); Don Wilson (*radio announcer*).

Songs: "Broadway Melody" - Stockwell/ "You Are My Lucky Star" - Langford; reprised by Eleanor Powell/ "I've Got a Feelin' You're Foolin' " - Knight, Taylor; dance by Knight, Long/ "Sing Before Breakfast" - Ebsens, Powell/ "All I Do Is Dream of You" - unidentified French singer/ "On a Sunday Afternoon" - Ebsens, chorus/ "Broadway Rhythm" - Langford; dance by Ebsens, Knight, Long, Powell, chorus.

Broadway Melody of 1938 (1937). Music by Nacio Herb Brown; lyrics by Arthur Freed; screenplay by Jack McGowan & Sid Silvers.

An MGM film produced by Jack Cummings; directed by Roy Del Ruth; choreography, Dave Gould; art director, Cedric Gibbons; costumes, Adrian; music director, George Stoll; orchestrations, Roger Edens, Leo Arnaud, Murray Mutter; cameraman, William Daniels; editor, Blanche Sewell.

Cast: Robert Taylor (*Steve Raleigh*); Eleanor Powell (*Sally Lee*); George Murphy (*Sonny Ledford*); Buddy Ebsen (*Peter Trot*); Sophie Tucker (*Alice Clayton*); Judy Garland (*Betty Clayton*); Binnie Barnes (*Caroline Whip-*

ple); Charles Igor Gorin (*Nicki Papaloopas*); Billy Gilbert (*George Papaloopas*); Willie Howard (*waiter*); Raymond Walburn (*Herman Whipple*); Charley Grapewin (*James Blakeley*); Barnett Parker (*Jerry Jason*); Helen Troy (*Emma Snipe*); Robert Wildhack (*sneezer*); Carole Landis (bit).

Songs: "Toreador Song" (Bizet, *Carmen*) - Gorin/ "Follow in My Footsteps" - Murphy, Ebsen, Powell/ "Yours and Mine" - Powell/ "Everybody Sing" - Garland, with Tucker, Parker, actors/ "Some of These Days" (Shelton Brooks) - Tucker/ "I'm Feelin' Like a Million" - Murphy, Powell/ "Largo al Factotum" (Rossini, *The Barber of Seville*) - Gorin/ "Dear Mr. Gable" ("You Made Me Love You") (James Monaco-Joseph McCarthy; Roger Edens) - Garland/ "Your Broadway and My Broadway" - Tucker, Gorin; dance by Murphy, Powell, Ebsen, Garland, chorus.

If Warner could have its *Gold Diggers* series, MGM could have its *Broadway Melodys*. The title of the 1929 movie was dusted off in the mid-30s with the year 1936 appended, and it also served for backstage musicals in 1938 and 1940. (Also very much part of the series was *Born to Dance,* which could just as easily have been called *Broadway Melody of 1937.*) In both 1936 and 1938 editions, Robert Taylor appeared as the producer-songwriter of a new musical show (titled *Broadway Rhythm* in the former and *Broadway Melody* in the latter), with Eleanor Powell as the newcomer who, after the prerequisite vicissitudes, wins both Taylor and stardom. Both films were concerned with the problems of raising money, and each used a gimmick to ensure the production's success: the 1936 entry had Miss Powell pass herself off as a celebrated French actress; the 1938 entry had Miss Powell come up with the needed capital when her opera-loving horse wins a race after hearing the strains of "Largo al Factotum." (A similar situation had occurred in *A Day at the Races* and would later pop up again in *Going Places.*) Both these editions ended with glittering singing and tapping tributes to the thoroughfare known as Broadway. As for production staffs, they both shared the same composer, lyricist, screenwriters, director, choreographer, art director, costume designer, orchestrator, and editor.

But there were distinctive elements. The 1936 movie had a generally stronger original score and the comic presence of Jack Benny; the 1938 movie gave us such memorable moments as Sophie Tucker belting "Some of These Days" and Judy Garland singing her heart out to "Dear Mr. Gable."

Broadway Melody of 1940 (1940). Music & lyrics by Cole Porter; screenplay by Leon Gordon & George Oppenheimer from story by Jack McGowan & Dore Schary.

An MGM film produced by Jack Cummings; directed by Norman Taurog; choreography, Fred Astaire, Bobby Connolly; art director, Cedric Gibbons; costumes, Adrian, Valles; music director, Alfred Newman; orchestrations, Edward Powell, Leo Arnaud, Charles Henderson; music supervisor, Roger Edens; cameramen, Oliver T. Marsh, Joseph Ruttenberg; editor, Blanche Sewell.

Cast: Fred Astaire (*Johnny Brett*); Eleanor Powell (*Clare Bennett* née *Brigit Callahan*); George Murphy (*King Shaw*); Frank Morgan (*Bob Casey*); Ian Hunter (*Bert Matthews*); Florence Rice (*Amy Blake*); Lynne Carver (*Emmy Lou Lee*); Douglas McPhail (*masked singer*); Trixie Frischke (*juggler*); Herman Bing (*artist*); Jack Mulhall (*George*); Barbara Jo Allen (Vera Vague) (*receptionist*); Joe Yule (*Dan*); The Music Maids (*quartet*).

Songs: "Please Don't Monkey with Broadway" - Astaire, Murphy/ "All Ashore" (Roger Edens) - Powell, sailors/ "Between You and Me" - Murphy; dance by Powell, Murphy/ "I've Got My Eyes on You" - Astaire/ "Jukebox Dance" - Astaire, Powell/ "I Concentrate on You" - McPhail; dance by Astaire, Powell/ "Begin the Beguine" - Carmen D'Antonio (vocal by Lois Hodnett), Music Maids; dance by Astaire, Powell. Unused: "I Happen To Be in Love" "I'm So in Love with You."

In her two previous *Broadway Melody* films as well as in *Born To Dance*, Eleanor Powell was a struggling young dancer trying for her first break in the theatre. In *Broadway Melody of 1940*, as a daring departure, she was an established Broadway star who helps Fred Astaire get *his* big chance. The film, though, was less concerned with the creation of a show than with the problems arising when the wrong man, George Murphy (playing Astaire's dancing partner), was selected as Eleanor's co-star instead of Fred. The picture, Astaire's first away from RKO, where he had been since 1934, was memorable for uniting the screen's two leading dancers and it provided ample opportunity for both, particularly in the lengthy "Begin the Beguine" finale.

Broadway Melody of 1940 was the fourth and last of MGM's *Broadway Melody* series. A fifth, *Broadway Melody of 1943*, scheduled for Miss Powell and Gene Kelly, was cancelled.

"Broadway Rhythm" Music by Nacio Herb Brown; lyric by Arthur Freed. Heralded by its musical exclamation ("Gotta dance! Gotta dance!"), this pulsating tribute to the Great White Way was introduced in *Broadway Melody of 1936* (MGM 1935) by Frances Langford in flashy tuxedo as part of a nightclub floorshow. Number then danced by Vilma and Buddy Ebsen, June Knight and Nick Long, Jr., climaxed by Eleanor Powell tapping away in top hat and spangly tails backed by formally attired chorus boys. Song also sung by Judy Garland in *Babes in Arms* (MGM 1939), and by Gene Kelly in *Singin' in the Rain* (MGM 1952). Each of MGM's other three *Broadway Melody* films also had its own "Broadway" song: "Broadway Melody" in *The Broadway Melody* (1929); "Your Broadway and My Broadway" in *Broadway Melody of 1938;* and "Don't Monkey with Old Broadway" in *Broadway Melody of 1940*. Except for the last, which was by Cole Porter, the others were by Brown and Freed.

Broderick, Helen, actress; b. Philadelphia, 1891; d. Beverly Hills, Sept. 25, 1959. Miss Broderick's deadpan, sharp-tongued delivery provided a witty, worldly touch to such Hollywood musicals as the Astaire-Rogers *Top Hat* and *Swing Time*. A headliner in vaudeville and a Broadway star (until 1933), she was the mother of actor Broderick Crawford.

1935	Top Hat (*Madge Hardwicke*)
	To Beat the Band (*Frieda MacCreery*)
1936	Swing Time (*Mabel Anderson*)
1937	Life of the Party (*Pauline*)
1938	Radio City Revels (*Gertie*)
	Road to Reno (*Aunt Minerva*)
1939	Naughty but Nice (*Aunt Martha*)
	Honeymoon in Bali (*Lorna Smith*)
1940	No, No, Nanette (*Mrs. Smith*)
1941	Nice Girl? (*Cora Foster*)
1943	Stage Door Canteen (guest bit)
1944	Chip off the Old Block (*Glory Marlowe Sr.*)
1946	Because of Him (*Nora*)

Brodszky, Nicholas, composer; b. Russia, 1905; d. Hollywood, Dec. 24, 1958. Operetta composer who worked in Hungary before writing for films in England and US. Brodszky's Hollywood output, while at MGM, included "Be My Love," "Because You're Mine," "I'll Never Stop Loving You." Mario Lanza, Jane Powell, Kathryn Grayson, Dean Martin, Ann Blyth, and

June Allyson introduced his songs. Among his collaborators were lyricists Sammy Cahn, Leo Robin, and Paul Francis Webster.

1950 The Toast of New Orleans (Cahn)
1951 Rich, Young and Pretty (Cahn)
1953 Small Town Girl (Robin)
     Latin Lovers (Robin)
1954 The Student Prince (Webster)
1956 Meet Me in Las Vegas (Cahn)
     The Opposite Sex (Cahn)
1957 Ten Thousand Bedrooms (Cahn)
     Let's Be Happy (Eng.) (Webster)

Brooks, Jack, lyricist; b. Liverpool, Eng., Feb. 14, 1912; d. Hollywood, Nov. 8, 1971. With Universal 1941–49, then MGM, Paramount. Brooks worked chiefly with composers Norman Berens, Edgar Fairchild, Hoagy Carmichael ("Ole Buttermilk Sky"), Saul Chaplin, Walter Scharf, Jack Hope and Lyle Moraine, and Harry Warren ("That's Amore").

1941 Melody Lane (Berens)
1942 Don't Get Personal (Berens)
1945 Here Come the Co-eds (Fairchild)
     Penthouse Rhythm (Berens)
     That Night with You (misc.)
1947 Song of Scheherezade (Rimsky-Korsakoff)
1948 The Countess of Monte Cristo (Chaplin)
1949 Yes, Sir, That's My Baby (Scharf)
1952 Son of Paleface (Hope, Moraine)
1953 The Caddy (Warren)
1955 Artists and Models (Warren)
1960 Cinderfella (Warren)

Brown, (Joseph Evans) Joe E., actor; b. Holgate, Ohio, July 28, 1892; d. Hollywood, July 6, 1973. Wide-mouthed, quizzical-looking, acrobatic comedian who made his Broadway bow in 1919. Brown acted in over forty-five Hollywood films, mostly comedies without music, until 1963. Bib: *Laughter Is a Wonderful Thing* by Brown (1956).

1929 On with the Show (*Ike*)
     Sally (*Grand Duke Constantine*)
1930 Song of the West (*Hasty Howell*)
     Hold Everything (*Gink Schiner*)
     Top Speed (*Elmer Peters*)
     The Lottery Bride (*Hoke Curtis*)
     Maybe It's Love (*Speed Hansen*)
1935 Bright Lights (*Joe Wilson*)
1936 Sons o' Guns (*Jimmy Canfield*)
1942 Joan of Ozark (*Cliff Little*)
1943 Chatterbox (*Rex Vane*)

1944 Casanova in Burlesque (*Joe Kelly Jr.*)
     Pin-Up Girl (*Eddie*)
     Hollywood Canteen (guest bit)
1951 Show Boat (*Cap'n Andy Hawks*)
1959 Some Like It Hot (*Osgood Fielding III*)

Brown, Lew (né Louis Brownstein), lyricist, screenwriter; b. Odessa, Russia, Dec. 10, 1893; d. New York, Feb. 5, 1958. With partners, co-lyricist B. G. DeSylva and composer Ray Henderson, Brown created a series of youthful, fast-stepping Broadway musicals between 1925 and 1930; of these *Good News* (filmed twice) and *Follow Thru* were brought to the screen with at least some of the original songs. In Hollywood the trio collaborated on songs for Al Jolson ("Sonny Boy"), Janet Gaynor ("Sunny Side Up," "I'm a Dreamer, Aren't We All?," "If I Had a Talking Picture of You"), and Gloria Swanson. On Broadway, Brown also wrote *Yokel Boy,*—later filmed—with Sam Stept and Charles Tobias. Other movie collaborators with whom Brown worked were composers Harry Akst, Jay Gorney ("Baby, Take a Bow"), Harold Arlen, Sammy Fain ("That Old Feeling"), and Nacio Herb Brown. Among other singers who introduced his songs were Shirley Temple, Harry Richman, Eddie Cantor, and Harriet Hilliard. Film bio: *The Best Things in Life Are Free,* with Ernest Borgnine as Brown.

Unless otherwise noted, the following had songs written with Messrs. DeSylva and Henderson; asterisk indicates Mr. Brown also wrote script:

1928 The Singing Fool
1929 Say It with Songs
     Sunny Side Up*
1930 Good News
     Follow Thru
     Just Imagine*
1931 Indiscreet*
1934 Stand Up and Cheer (Akst)*
1936 The Music Goes Round (Akst)
     Strike Me Pink (Arlen)
1937 New Faces of 1937 (Fain)
1942 Yokel Boy (Stept-Tobias)
1943 Swing Fever (Fain, NH Brown)
1947 Good News
1956 The Best Things in Life Are Free

Brown, Nacio Herb, composer; b. Deming, New Mexico, Feb. 22, 1896; d. San Francisco, Sept. 28, 1964. Brown and lyricist Arthur Freed were the major songwriters of MGM musicals—and nonmusicals—between

1929 and 1937. They created such pieces as "Wedding of the Painted Doll," "Broadway Melody," and "You Were Meant for Me" (from *The Broadway Melody*); "Singin' in the Rain"; "Pagan Love Song"; "Should I?"; "Temptation"; "All I Do Is Dream of You"; "Alone" (*A Night at the Opera*); "I've Got a Feelin' You're Foolin'," "Broadway Rhythm," and "You Are My Lucky Star" (*Broadway Melody of 1936*); "Would You?" (*San Francisco*). Most of these were used as the basis of the score of *Singin' in the Rain*. Other songs: "Paradise" (with Gordon Clifford) and "You Stepped Out of a Dream" (Gus Kahn). Other Hollywood collaborators: Leo Robin, Edward Heyman, Earl Brent. Charles King, Bing Crosby, Allan Jones, Kitty Carlisle, Frances Langford, Eleanor Powell, Tony Martin, and Jeanette MacDonald were among those most closely associated with Brown's songs. The composer also collaborated with Richard A. Whiting and B. G. DeSylva on the Broadway musical, *Take a Chance*, which was filmed. Brown was once married to actress Anita Page.

1929   The Broadway Melody (Freed) (also *pianist*)
        Hollywood Revue of 1929 (Freed)
1930   Lord Byron of Broadway (Freed)
        Good News (Freed)
1933   Going Hollywood (Freed)
        Take a Chance (Whiting-DeSylva)
1934   Sadie McKee (Freed)
        Student Tour (Freed)
1935   Broadway Melody of 1936 (Freed)
1937   Broadway Melody of 1938 (Freed)
1943   Wintertime (Robin)
1944   Greenwich Village (Robin)
1948   On an Island with You (Heyman)
        The Kissing Bandit (Heyman, Brent)
1952   Singin' in the Rain (Freed)

Bruce, Virginia (née Helen Virginia Briggs), actress, singer; b. Minneapolis, Sept. 29, 1910. Cool, delicate-featured blonde adept at other-woman roles who appeared in films between 1929 and 1960. Introduced "I've Got You Under My Skin" in *Born To Dance*. (Died Hollywood, Feb. 24, 1982.)

1929   Why Bring That Up? (bit)
        The Love Parade (*Lady in Waiting*)
1930   Lilies of the Field (*Pearl*)
        Paramount on Parade (specialty)
        Safety in Numbers (*Alma McGregor*)
        Let's Go Native (*secretary*)
        Whoopee (show girl)
1935   Here Comes the Band
        Metropolitan (*Anne Merrill*)

1936   The Great Ziegfeld (*Audrey Lane*)
        Born To Dance (*Lucy James*)
1937   When Love Is Young (*Wanda Werner*)
1939   Let Freedom Ring (*Maggie Adams*)
1942   Pardon My Sarong (*Joan Marshall*)
1944   Brazil (*Nicky Henderson*)

Brynner, Yul (né Youl Bryner), actor; b. Sakhalin, Russia, July 11, 1915. Glabrous, exotic romantic lead in some 30 films whose Broadway success in *The King and I* resulted in his most closely identified role and his only screen musical. (Died New York, Oct. 10, 1985.)

1956   The King and I (*King*)

Buchanan, (Walter John) Jack, actor, singer, dancer, director, producer; b. Helensburgh, Scotland, April 2, 1890; d. London, Oct. 21, 1957. Buchanan was a dapper, reedy-voiced song-and-dance man whose career was primarily devoted to the London stage (where he made his debut in 1912). He starred in British film musicals between 1932 and 1938 (repeating stage roles in both *That's a Good Girl* and *This'll Make You Whistle*), and scored a late hit in the US film, *The Band Wagon* (introducing "That's Entertainment"). His leading ladies included Jeanette MacDonald (*Monte Carlo*), Gertrude Lawrence, Anna Neagle, and Elsie Randolph (three films). Bib: *Top Hat & Tails* by Michael Marshall (1978).

1929   Paris (US) (*Guy Pennell*)
1930   Monte Carlo (US) (*Count Rudolph Falliere*)
1932   Goodnight, Vienna (*Capt. Max Schlettoff*)
1933   Yes, Mr. Brown (*Nicholas Baumann*) (also co-dir.)
        That's a Good Girl (*Jack Barrow*) (also dir.)
1935   Brewster's Millions (*Jack Brewster*)
        Come Out of the Pantry (*Lord Robert Brent*)
1936   Lime Light (guest bit)
        When Knights Were Bold (*Sir Guy Devere*)
        This'll Make You Whistle (*Bill Hopping*)
1937   The Sky's the Limit (*Dave Harber*) (also prod.)
1938   Sweet Devil (prod. only)
        Break the News (*Teddy Enton*) (also prod.)
1953   The Band Wagon (US) (*Jeffrey Cordova*)

"Buds Won't Bud" Music by Harold Arlen; lyric by E. Y. Harburg. Nothing goes right "when the love you love won't love you." After being dropped from the score of the 1937 Broadway musical, *Hooray for What!*, the number was sung by Judy Garland in *Andy Hardy Meets Debutante* (MGM 1940) but cut from film. First sung on screen by Ethel Waters in *Cairo* (MGM 1942).

Bullock, Walter, lyricist; b. Shelburn, Ind., May 6, 1907; d. Los Angeles, Aug. 19, 1953. Bullock wrote songs for three Shirley Temple films and collaborated with composers Lew Pollack, Victor Schertzinger, Marvin Hatley, Harold Spina, Sam Pokrass, Alfred Newman, and Jule Styne. His best-known piece was "When Did You Leave Heaven?" (with Richard A. Whiting), sung by Tony Martin in *Sing, Baby, Sing.*

1936	Follow Your Heart (Schertzinger)
1937	Nobody's Baby (Hatley)
	52nd Street (Spina)
1938	Sally, Irene and Mary (Spina)
	Little Miss Broadway (Spina)
	Just Around the Corner (Spina)
1939	The Three Musketeers (Pokrass)
1940	The Blue Bird (Newman)
	Hit Parade of 1941 (Styne)

Burke, Billie (née Mary William Ethelbert Burke), actress; b. Washington, DC, Aug. 7, 1885; d. Beverly Hills, May 14, 1970. Patrician, fluttery, redheaded Billie Burke was a stellar attraction of the London and NY theatres before making her film debut in 1915. Her best-remembered role in a musical was as the Good Witch in *The Wizard of Oz.* The wife of stage producer Florenz Ziegfeld, she was played in *The Great Ziegfeld* by Myrna Loy. Bib: *With a Feather on My Nose* (1949) and *With Powder on My Nose* (1959), both by Miss Burke.

1929	Glorifying the American Girl (guest bit)
1938	Everybody Sing (*Diana Bellaire*)
1939	The Wizard of Oz (*Glinda*)
1940	Irene (*Mrs. Vincent*)
	Hullabaloo (*Penny Merryweather*)
1942	What's Cookin'? (*Angela Courtney*)
1943	You're a Lucky Fellow, Mr. Smith (*Aunt Harriet*)
1945	Swing Out, Sister (*Jessica*)
1946	Breakfast in Hollywood (*Mrs. Cartwright*)
	The Bachelor's Daughters (*Molly*)
1950	The Barkleys of Broadway (*Millie Belney*)
1953	Small Town Girl (*Mrs. Livingston*)
1960	Pepe (guest bit)

Burke, (Joseph A.) Joe, composer; b. Philadelphia, March 18, 1884; d. Upper Darby, Pa., June 9, 1950. Before being succeeded by composer Harry Warren, Burke was lyricist Al Dubin's partner in writing songs for early Warner musicals. The team's "Painting the Clouds with Sunshine" and "Tiptoe Through the Tulips" were heard in *Gold Diggers of Broadway.*

1929	Gold Diggers of Broadway
	Sally

1930	She Couldn't Say No
	Hold Everything
	Top Speed
	Life of the Party
	Oh, Sailor Behave!

Burke, Johnny, lyricist; b. Antioch, Cal., Oct. 3, 1908; d. New York, Feb. 25, 1964. Former dance-band pianist who wrote lyrics for 23 Bing Crosby movies at Paramount with the following composers: Arthur Johnston ("Pennies from Heaven," "One, Two, Button Your Shoe," "All You Want To Do Is Dance," "The Moon Got in My Eyes"); James V. Monaco ("I've Got a Pocketful of Dreams," "On the Sentimental Side," "East Side of Heaven," "An Apple for the Teacher," "April Played the Fiddle," "Only Forever," "Too Romantic"); and James Van Heusen ("Moonlight Becomes You," "Road to Morocco," "Sunday, Monday or Always," "Swingin' on a Star," "Aren't You Glad You're You?," "But Beautiful"). Others who introduced songs with Burke lyrics were Dorothy Lamour ("It Could Happen to You," "Personality"), Mary Martin ("Ain't It a Shame About Mame?"), Bob Hope, Betty Hutton, Dinah Shore ("Like Someone in Love"), Ginger Rogers (who danced to "Suddenly It's Spring"), and Ann Blyth. Burke's words were also mated to melodies by Victor Schertzinger, Johann Strauss, Richard Heuberger, and Rudolf Friml.

1936	Go West, Young Man (Johnston)
	Pennies from Heaven (Johnston)
1937	Double or Nothing (Johnston)
1938	Doctor Rhythm (Monaco)
	Sing You Sinners (Monaco)
1939	East Side of Heaven (Monaco)
	The Star Maker (Monaco)
1940	Road to Singapore (Monaco; Schertzinger)
	If I Had My Way (Monaco)
	Rhythm on the River (Monaco)
	Love Thy Neighbor (Van Heusen)
1941	Road to Zanzibar (Van Heusen)
	Playmates (Van Heusen)
1942	Road to Morocco (Van Heusen)
1943	Dixie (Van Heusen)
1944	Going My Way (Van Heusen)
	And the Angels Sing (Van Heusen)
	Belle of the Yukon (Van Heusen)
1945	Road to Utopia (Van Heusen)
1946	Cross My Heart (Van Heusen)
	London Town (Eng.) (Van Heusen)
1947	Welcome Stranger (Van Heusen)
	Road to Rio (Van Heusen)

1948 The Emperor Waltz (Van Heusen; Strauss; Heuberger)
Mystery in Mexico (Van Heusen)
1949 A Connecticut Yankee in King Arthur's Court (Van Heusen)
Top o' the Morning (Van Heusen)
1950 Riding High (Van Heusen)
Mister Music (Van Heusen)
1952 Road to Bali (Van Heusen)
1953 Little Boy Lost (Van Heusen)
1956 The Vagabond King (Friml)

Burns, Bob, actor; b. Van Buren, Ark., Aug. 2, 1896; d. San Fernando Valley, Cal., Feb. 2, 1956. Rube comic, inventor of a valve-instrument called a bazooka, and Martha Raye's foil in five Paramount musicals.

1935 The Singing Vagabond
1936 Rhythm on the Range (*Buck*)
Big Broadcast of 1937 (*Bob Black*)
1937 Waikiki Wedding (*Shad Buggle*)
Mountain Music (*Bob Burnside*)
1938 Radio City Revels (*Lester*)
Tropic Holiday (*Breck Jones*)
1944 Belle of the Yukon (*Sam Slade*)

Burns and Allen, actors. George Burns (né Nathan Birnbaum), b. New York, Jan. 20, 1896. (Grace Ethel Cecile Rosalie) Gracie Allen, b. San Francisco, July 26, 1902; d. Hollywood, Aug. 28, 1964. Burns would puff on his cigar, ask about his wife's brother, and express nearly exhausted patience as Gracie would chirp her way through a series of birdbrain nonsequiturs. The basic routine established the pair as vaudeville headliners and took them to radio, films (mostly for Paramount), and television. After Miss Allen retired in 1958, Burns continued as solo comic and film actor (*The Sunshine Boys*). Bib: *I Love Her, That's Why* (1955), *Living It Up* (1976), *The Third Time Around* (1979) all by Burns.

Unless otherwise noted, the team was known as George Burns and Gracie Allen in the following:
1932 The Big Broadcast
1933 International House
College Humor
1934 We're Not Dressing
Many Happy Returns
1935 Love in Bloom
Here Comes Cookie
Big Broadcast of 1936
1936 Big Broadcast of 1937 (*Mr. & Mrs. Platt*)
College Holiday (*George Hyman; Calliope Dove*)
1937 A Damsel in Distress

1938 College Swing (*George Jonas; Gracie Alden*)
1939 Honolulu (*Joe Duffy; Millie DeGrasse*)
1944 Two Girls and a Sailor (Gracie only specialty)
1978 Sgt. Pepper's Lonely Hearts Club Band (George only as *Mayor Kite*)
Movie Movie (George only as narrator)

"But Beautiful" Music by James Van Heusen; lyric by Johnny Burke. Philosophical view of love as both funny and sad, quiet and mad, etc., sung by Bing Crosby in *Road to Rio* (Par. 1947).

Butler, David, director; b. San Francisco, 1895; d. Arcadia, Cal., June 14, 1979. Silent screen actor who directed films chiefly at Fox (1927–37) and Warner (1943–54), and whose most memorable song-and-dance movies were *Sunny Side Up, Road to Morocco, Where's Charley?,* and *Calamity Jane.* Among actors who were in Butler-directed musicals: Doris Day and Dennis Morgan (six each); Jack Carson (four); Shirley Temple, Janet Gaynor and Charles Farrell, Bing Crosby, Gordon MacRae, Ray Bolger, Kay Kyser (three each).

1929 Fox Movietone Follies
Sunny Side Up (also script)
1930 High Society Blues
Just Imagine
1931 Delicious
1933 My Weakness
1934 Bottoms Up
1935 The Littlest Rebel
1936 Captain January
Pigskin Parade
1937 Ali Baba Goes to Town
You're a Sweetheart
1938 Kentucky Moonshine
Straight, Place and Show
1939 East Side of Heaven
That's Right, You're Wrong (also prod.)
1940 If I Had My Way (also prod.)
You'll Find Out (also prod.)
1941 Playmates (also prod.)
1942 Road to Morocco
1943 Thank Your Lucky Stars (also guest bit)
1944 Shine on Harvest Moon
1946 The Time, the Place and the Girl
1947 My Wild Irish Rose
1948 Two Guys from Texas
1949 Look for the Silver Lining
It's a Great Feeling (also guest bit)
1950 The Daughter of Rosie O'Grady
Tea for Two

1951 Lullaby of Broadway
Painting the Clouds with Sunshine
1952 Where's Charley? (Eng.)
April in Paris
By the Light of the Silvery Moon
1953 Calamity Jane
1961 The Right Approach

Butterworth, Charles (Edward), actor; b. South Bend, Ind., July 26, 1896; d. Los Angeles, June 14, 1946. Befuddled comedian of slight build with distinctive nasal voice who always appeared to be sniffing something. Butterworth went to Hollywood after a Broadway career that had begun in 1926; on screen he usually played naïve millionaires, professors, or noblemen.

1930 Life of the Party (*Col. Joy*)
1932 Love Me Tonight (*Count de Savignac*)
1933 My Weakness (*Gerald Gregory*)
1934 The Cat and the Fiddle (*Charles*)
Hollywood Party (*Harvey Klemp*)
Student Tour (*Prof. Lippincott*)
1935 The Night Is Young (*Willy*)
1936 Rainbow on the River (*Barrett*)
1937 Swing High, Swing Low (*Harry Raskin*)
Every Day's a Holiday (*Larmuadou Graves*)
1938 Thanks for the Memory (*Biney*)
1939 Let Freedom Ring (*The Mackeral*)
1940 The Boys from Syracuse (*Duke of Ephesus*)
Second Chorus (*J. Lester Chisholm*)
1941 Road Show (*Harry Whitman*)
Sis Hopkins (*Horace Hopkins*)
1942 Give Out Sisters (*Prof. Woof*)
What's Cooking? (*J. P. Courtney*)
1943 This Is the Army (*Eddie Dibble*)
Always a Bridesmaid (*Col. Winchester*)
The Sultan's Daughter (*Sultan*)
1944 Follow the Boys (*Louie Fairweather*)
Dixie Jamboree (*Professor*)

"Buttons and Bows" Music & lyric by Jay Livingston & Ray Evans. Bouncy lament for the comforts back home in the East, sung by Bob Hope in a covered wagon in *The Paleface* (Par. 1948). Also sung (with new lyric) by Roy Rogers, Jane Russell, and Hope in *Son of Paleface* (Par. 1952).

Buzzell, Edward ("Eddie"), director, actor; b. Brooklyn, Nov. 13, 1896. Former Broadway comic actor who appeared in early talkies, primarily shorts, then became director. At MGM worked with Eleanor Powell, Red Skelton, the Marx Brothers, and Esther Williams in two musicals each. (Died Los Angeles, Jan. 11, 1985.)

Unless otherwise noted, Mr. Buzzell was director of the following:
1929 Little Johnny Jones (*Johnny Jones* only)
1935 The Girl Friend
1939 Honolulu
At the Circus
1940 Go West
1942 Ship Ahoy
1943 Best Foot Forward
1946 Easy To Wed
1949 Neptune's Daughter
1955 Ain't Misbehavin'

"By a Waterfall" Music by Sammy Fain; lyric by Irving Kahal. Dick Powell sang the profluent love song to Ruby Keeler in a woodland setting as part of a movie theatre stage revue in *Footlight Parade* (Warner 1933). After he falls asleep, Dick's dream becomes a Busby Berkeley spectacle in which Ruby doffs her clothes and joins a bevy of nymphs sliding and diving into the water. Somehow this turns into a huge pool, where the girls continue to cavort and where, seen from overhead, they form all kinds of prismatic patterns. Back in the opening scene, a fully clothed Ruby splashes water on Dick's shoes, which awakens him in time to finish the song.

C

"**Ça, C'est L'Amour**" Music & lyric by Cole Porter. Macaronic ballad sung by Taina Elg to Gene Kelly in *Les Girls* (MGM 1957) as they glide in a rowboat on a French lake. Melodically the song is reminiscent of Porter's "C'est Magnifique" from the Broadway musical *Can-Can*.

Cabaret (1972). Music by John Kander; lyrics by Fred Ebb; screenplay by Jay Allen & Hugh Wheeler from Broadway play *I Am a Camera* by John Van Druten and musical by Joe Masteroff, Kander, & Ebb, both of which were based on *Berlin Stories* by Christopher Isherwood.

An Allied Artists-ABC film produced by Cy Feuer; directed by Bob Fosse; choreography, Fosse; art directors, Rolf Zehetbauer, Jurgen Kierbach; costumes, Charlotte Flemming; music director, Ralph Burns; orchestrations, Burns; cameraman, Geoffrey Unsworth; editor, David Bretherton; Technicolor.

Cast: Liza Minnelli (*Sally Bowles*); Michael York (*Brian Roberts*); Helmut Griem (*Maximilian Von Heune*); Joel Grey (*Master of Ceremonies*); Marisa Berenson (*Natalia Landauer*); Fritz Wepper (*Fritz Wendel*); Elizabeth Neumann-Viertel (*Fraulein Schneider*); Greta Keller (*voice on phonograph*); Oliver Collignon (vocal by Mark Lambert) (*Young Nazi*); Angelika Koch, Louise Quick (chorus girls).

Songs: "Willkommen" - Grey, chorus/ "Mein Herr" - Minnelli/ "Maybe This Time" - Minnelli/ "Money, Money" - Grey & Minnelli/ "Two Ladies" - Grey, Koch, Quick/ "Tomorrow Belongs to Me" - Collignon (Lambert)/ "Heiraten" - Keller/ "If You Could See Her" - Grey/ "Cabaret" - Minnelli.

Like the 1966 Broadway musical from which it was adapted, *Cabaret* took a sophisticated, candid look at German decadence in the last years of the Weimar Republic, using the metaphor of a sleazy cabaret, the Kit Kat Club, presided over by an epicene master of ceremonies. To an even greater extent, however, it confined its musical selections to the nightclub's garish floorshow, the only exceptions being "Heiraten" and "Tomorrow Belongs to Me." The film differed from the stage *Cabaret* by eliminating the character of the Jewish fruit dealer, lessening the importance of the landlady, and adding two characters—a wealthy Jewish girl and her penniless suitor—who had been in both the Isherwood book and Van Druten's nonmusical Broadway version, *I Am a Camera*. On stage, *Cabaret*'s hedonistic yet vulnerable Sally Bowles (played by Jill Haworth) had been English and her lover, Clifford Bradshaw (Bert Convy), had been American. In the film version, possibly because the character was played by Liza Minnelli, Sally was American and her lover, Brian Roberts, was English. Joel Grey, as the Master of Ceremonies, a part conceived for the stage *Cabaret,* was the only member of that cast to repeat his role in the movie. One screen character who had been in neither the stage play nor the stage musical was an oily bisexual aristocrat who has liaisons with both Sally and Brian. For the film, which was shot in Germany, director Fosse used a boldly cinematic approach, with much use of cross-cutting, that gave it the look of a work created expressly for the screen.

Cabin in the Sky (1943). Music by Vernon Duke, Harold Arlen; lyrics by John Latouche, E. Y. Harburg; screenplay by Joseph Schrank from Broadway musical by Lynn Root, Duke, Latouche.

An MGM film produced by Arthur Freed; associate producers, Albert Lewis, Roger Edens (uncredited); directed by Vincente Minnelli; choreography, Busby Berkeley (uncredited); art directors, Cedric Gibbons,

Leonid Vasian; costumes, Irene, Gile Steele; music director, George Stoll; music adaptation, Edens; orchestrations, George Bassman, Conrad Salinger; choral arrangements, Hall Johnson; cameraman, Sidney Wagner; editor, Harold Kress.

Cast: Ethel Waters (*Petunia Jackson*); Eddie "Rochester" Anderson (*Little Joe Jackson*); Lena Horne (*Georgia Brown*); Louis Armstrong (*Devil's Trumpeter*); Duke Ellington Orchestra; Rex Ingram (*Lucius Berry/ Lucifer Jr.*); Kenneth Spencer (*Rev. Green/ Lord's General*); John W. Sublett aka Bubbles (*Domino Johnson*); Oscar Polk (*Deacon/ Fleetfoot*); Mantan Moreland, Willie Best, Fletcher Rivers aka Moke, Leon James aka Poke (*Idea Men*); Ford L. Washington aka Buck (*Messenger Boy/ Paradise pianist*); Butterfly McQueen (*Lily*); Ernest Whitman (*Jim Henry*); Hall Johnson Choir.

Songs: "Li'l Black Sheep" (Arlen-Harburg) - choir, Waters/ "Old Ship of Zion" (trad.) - choir/ "Happiness Is a Thing Called Joe" (Arlen-Harburg) - Waters/ "Cabin in the Sky" (Duke-Latouche) - Waters, Anderson/ "Taking a Chance on Love" (Duke-Latouche, Ted Fetter) - Waters, with Anderson, guitar/ "Life's Full of Consequence" (Arlen-Harburg) - Anderson, Horne/ "Going Up" (Duke Ellington) - Ellington orch., dancers/ "Shine" (Ford Dabney-Cecil Mack) Bubbles/ "Honey in the Honeycomb" (Duke-Latouche) - Horne, reprised by Waters. Unused: "Ain't It the Truth," "I Got a Song" (both by Arlen-Harburg).

A critically well-received but financially unsuccessful Broadway musical of 1940, *Cabin in the Sky* was a parable of Southern Negro life. Little Joe, a shiftless gambler is—apparently—fatally shot in a crap game, but his good wife, Petunia, prays so hard that the Lord grants him six months to redeem himself. The Lord's General and Lucifer Jr. do battle for Joe's soul, which the latter, aided by temptress Georgia Brown, seems to have little difficulty winning. But when Petunia is shot in a dancehall the Lord again shows mercy and lets her squeeze her errant mate through the Pearly Gates. (Note elements here of such other musicals as *The Green Pastures, Carousel,* and *Damn Yankees.*)

In the film version, the first movie to be directed entirely by Vincente Minnelli, the original plot outline was faithfully followed, except that it all turns out to be a dream. Ethel Waters, as Petunia, repeated her stage role (it was her only starring part in a screen musical), as did Rex Ingram as Lucifer Jr. Eddie "Rochester" Anderson won the part of Little Joe over Dooley Wilson, who had

originated it, because he was then better known, and Lena Horne was given her first acting opportunity as Georgia (thus turning a predominantly dancing role, played on stage by Katherine Dunham, to a predominantly singing one). Three songs were retained from the Broadway score by Vernon Duke and John Latouche, with three new pieces contributed by Harold Arlen and E. Y. Harburg. Keen eyes will also recognize stock footage of the cyclone in *The Wizard of Oz* being used for the windstorm that destroys the dancehall.

Caesar, (Isidore) Irving, lyricist; b. New York, July 4, 1895. Primarily a Broadway lyricist whose musical, *No, No, Nanette,* written with composer Vincent Youmans, was filmed three times (the last time as *Tea for Two*), and who, with Ray Henderson and Ted Koehler, gave Shirley Temple "Animal Crackers in My Soup."

1930	No, No, Nanette (Youmans)
1934	George White's Scandals (Henderson)
1935	Curly Top (Henderson, Koehler)
1940	No, No, Nanette (Youmans)
1950	Tea for Two (Youmans)

Cagney, James (Francis), actor, dancer, singer; b. New York, July 17, 1899. Fast-moving, fast-talking, pugnacious actor, formerly of the Broadway stage, identified with both gangster melodramas (*The Public Enemy, Angels with Dirty Faces*) and musicals (*Footlight Parade, Yankee Doodle Dandy, Love Me or Leave Me*). From 1930 to 1953 Cagney was with Warner, under whose aegis he gave his memorable song-and-dance performance as George M. Cohan. Actresses who have played opposite him in musicals include Joan Blondell, Joan Leslie, Virginia Mayo, and Doris Day. Bib: *Films of James Cagney* by Homer Dickens (1972); *Cagney by Cagney* (1976): *Cagney: The Actor as Auteur* by Patrick McGilligan (1980). (Died March 30, 1986.)

1933	Footlight Parade (*Chester Kent*)
1937	Something To Sing About (*Terry Rooney*)
1942	Yankee Doodle Dandy (*George M. Cohan*)
1950	West Point Story (*Elwin Bixby*)
1951	Starlift (guest bit)
1955	Love Me or Leave Me (*Marty "Gimp" Snyder*)
	The Seven Little Foys (*George M. Cohan*)
1959	Never Steal Anything Small (*Jake MacIllaney*)

Cahn, Sammy (né Samuel Cohen), lyricist; b. New York, June 18, 1913. A prolific, adaptable writer, Cahn worked steadily in Hollywood during the 40s and 50s contributing songs to nonmusicals as well as musicals.

Among the composers with whom he has been paired: Jule Styne ("I've Heard That Song Before," "I'll Walk Alone," "There Goes That Song Again," "The Charm of You," "I Fall in Love Too Easily," "Time After Time," "It's Magic," "Three Coins in the Fountain"); Nicholas Brodszky ("Be My Love," "Because You're Mine," "I'll Never Stop Loving You"); and James Van Heusen ("Love and Marriage," "The Tender Trap," "All the Way," "High Hopes," "The Second Time Around," "Pocketful of Miracles," "Call Me Irresponsible," "My Kind of Town"). Others with whom Cahn has written include Saul Chaplin, Axel Stordahl, and Paul Weston ("I Should Care"), Ray Heindorf, Vernon Duke, Sammy Fain, Arthur Schwartz, Sylvia Fine, and Harry Warren. Frank Sinatra has introduced the most Cahn hits on the screen; other singers associated with his songs are Doris Day, Bing Crosby, Mario Lanza, Jackie Gleason, Kathryn Grayson, Gene Kelly, Dean Martin, Danny Kaye, Marilyn Monroe, and Ann-Margret. Cahn also wrote lyrics for stage musicals, including *High Button Shoes,* and has appeared in nightclubs and on Broadway in a program of his own songs. Bib: *I Should Care* by Cahn (1974).

1941 Rookies on Parade (Chaplin)
     Time Out for Rhythm (Chaplin)
     Go West Young Lady (Chaplin)
1942 Youth on Parade (Styne)
     Johnny Doughboy (Styne)
1943 Thumbs Up (Styne)
1944 Knickerbocker Holiday (Styne)
     Step Lively (Styne)
     Carolina Blues (Styne)
1945 Tonight and Every Night (Styne)
     Anchors Aweigh (Styne)
1946 Tars and Spars (Styne)
     Cinderella Jones (Styne)
     The Kid from Brooklyn (Styne)
     Earl Carroll Sketch Book (Styne)
1947 Ladies' Man (Styne)
     It Happened in Brooklyn (Styne)
1948 Romance on the High Seas (Styne)
     Two Guys from Texas (Styne)
1949 It's a Great Feeling (Styne)
     Always Leave Them Laughing (Heindorf)
1950 The Toast of New Orleans (Brodszky)
     The West Point Story (Styne)
1951 Rich, Young and Pretty (Brodszky)
     Two Tickets to Broadway (script only)
     Double Dynamite (Styne)
1952 She's Working Her Way Through College (Duke)
     April in Paris (Duke)

1953 Peter Pan (Fain)
     Three Sailors and a Girl (Fain) (also prod.)
1955 You're Never Too Young (Schwartz)
     Our Town (tv) (Van Heusen)
1956 Anything Goes (Van Heusen)
     The Court Jester (Fine)
     Meet Me in Las Vegas (Brodszky)
     Pardners (Van Heusen)
     The Opposite Sex (Brodszky)
1957 Ten Thousand Bedrooms (Brodszky)
     Beau James (*auditioning songwriter* only)
1958 Rock-a-Bye Baby (Warren)
1959 Say One for Me (Van Heusen)
1960 Let's Make Love (Van Heusen)
     High Time (Van Heusen)
1962 Road to Hong Kong (Van Heusen)
1964 Robin and the Seven Hoods (Van Heusen)
     The Pleasure Seekers (Van Heusen)
1967 Jack and the Beanstalk (tv) (Van Heusen)
1972 Journey Back to Oz (Van Heusen)
1974 That's Entertainment Part 2 (narrator only)
1982 Heidi's Song (Lane)

Calamity Jane. *See **Annie Get Your Gun**.*

"Californ-i-ay" Music by Jerome Kern; lyric by E. Y. Harburg. Rollicking tribute—sung by Deanna Durbin and Robert Paige in *Can't Help Singing* (Univ. 1944)—to the state where "The hills have more splendor, The girls have more gender."

"Call Me Irresponsible" Music by James Van Heusen; lyric by Sammy Cahn. Confession of an irresponsible, unreliable, undependable, unpredictable, impractical dreamer. In *Papa's Delicate Condition* (Par. 1963), pajama-clad Jackie Gleason, having gone on a drinking spree because his wife has left him, sings it in his bedroom after awakening with a hangover. Van Heusen and Cahn had written the song in 1956 as one of five numbers intended for a musical version of the same story to star Fred Astaire. The movie was never made, but seven years later, when Paramount decided to film it with Gleason, "Call Me Irresponsible" was the only song to be retained.

Call Me Madam (1953). Music & lyrics by Irving Berlin; screenplay by Arthur Sheekman from Broadway musical by Howard Lindsay, Russel Crouse, and Berlin.

A 20th Century-Fox film produced by Sol C. Siegel; directed by Walter Lang; choreography, Robert Alton; art directors, Lyle Wheeler, John DeCuir; costumes, Irene Sharaff; music director, Alfred Newman; associate music director, Ken Darby; cameraman, Leon Shamroy; editor, Robert Simpson; Technicolor.

Cast: Ethel Merman (*Sally Adams*); George Sanders (*Cosmo Constantine*); Donald O'Connor (*Kenneth Gibson*); Vera-Ellen (vocals by Carole Richards) (*Princess Maria*); Billy DeWolfe (*Pemberton Maxwell*); Helmut Dantine (*Prince Hugo*); Walter Slezak (*Tantinnin*); Steven Geray (*Sebastian*); Ludwig Stossel (*Grand Duke*); Lilia Skala (*Grand Duchess*); Charles Dingle (*Sen. Brockway*); Emory Parnell (*Sen. Parnell*); Leon Belasco (*leader*); Walter Woolf King (*Secretary of State*); Fritz Feld (*hat clerk*); Johnny Downs (*cameraman*).

Songs: "The Hostess with the Mostes' " - Merman/ "Can You Use Any Money Today?" - Merman/ "Marrying for Love" - Sanders/ "It's a Lovely Day Today" - O'Connor, Vera-Ellen (Richards)/ "That International Rag" - Merman/ "The Ocarina" - Vera-Ellen (Richards)/ "What Chance Have I?" - O'Connor/ "The Best Thing for You" - Merman, Sanders/ "Something To Dance About" - O'Connor, Vera-Ellen (Richards)/ "You're Just in Love" - Merman, O'Connor.

Apart from *Anything Goes, Call Me Madam* was the only Broadway musical in which Ethel Merman repeated her original role on the screen. The role, which was written for her, was that of a Washington hostess (based on Perle Mesta) who becomes Ambassador to Lichtenburg, a mythical European kingdom, and the humor was derived from contrasting Ethel's earthiness with State Department protocol and Old World customs. On the screen, basically a photographed play, eight of the original 13 Irving Berlin songs were retained, plus two of his from other sources. Merman was given her best opportunity in films, and she was aided by the casting of two dancers, Donald O'Connor and Vera-Ellen, as young lovers. In a romantic role opposite the star, George Sanders had his only chance to sing in the movies.

Calloway, (Cabell) Cab, singer, actor, bandleader; b. Rochester, NY, Dec. 24, 1907. Exuberant bandleader-singer whose hi-de-ho scat singing made him a popular entertainer in nightclubs (especially the Cotton Club in NY), in theatres, and on records. Acted on Broadway in *Hello, Dolly!* (1967). Bib: *Of Minnie the Moocher and Me* by Calloway (1976).

Except for the last two films, Mr. Calloway performed with his band in the following:

1932	The Big Broadcast
1933	International House
1936	The Singing Kid
1937	Manhattan Merry-Go-Round
1943	Stormy Weather
1944	Sensations of 1945
1958	St. Louis Blues (*Blade*)
1980	The Blues Brothers (*Curtis*)

"Can I Forget You?" Music by Jerome Kern; lyric by Oscar Hammerstein II. Saddened at the thought of leaving, Irene Dunne sang this canorous farewell to Randolph Scott in *High, Wide and Handsome* (Par. 1937).

"Candy Man, The" Music & lyric by Anthony Newley & Leslie Bricusse. Sung by candy-store owner Aubrey Wood dispensing chocolate bars to children in *Willy Wonka and the Chocolate Factory* (Par. 1971).

Canova (Juliet) Judy, actress, singer; b. Jacksonville, Fla., Nov. 20, 1916. Hillbilly entertainer who yodeled and clowned her way mostly through low-budget Republic musicals, usually with members of her family. (Died Hollywood, Aug. 5, 1983.)

1935	Going Highbrow (*Annie*)
	In Caliente (*singer*)
1937	Thrill of a Lifetime (*Judy*)
	Artists and Models (*Toots*)
1941	Sis Hopkins (*Sis Hopkins*)
	Puddinhead (*Judy Goober*)
1942	Sleepytime Gal (*Bessie Cobb*)
	True to the Army (*Daisy Hawkins*)
	Joan of Ozark (*Judy Hull*)
1943	Chatterbox (*Judy Boggs*)
	Sleepy Lagoon (*Judy Joyner*)
1944	Louisiana Hayride (*Judy Crocker*)
1945	Hit the Hay (*Judy Stevens*)
1946	Singin' in the Corn (*Judy McCoy*)
1951	Honeychile (*Judy*)
1952	Oklahoma Annie (*Judy*)
	The WAC from Walla Walla (*Judy*)
1954	Untamed Heiress (*Judy*)
1955	Carolina Cannonball (*Judy*)
	Lay That Rifle Down (*Judy*)

"Can't Buy Me Love" Music & lyric by John Lennon & Paul McCartney. Sung on soundtrack of *A Hard Day's Night* (UA 1964) by the Beatles as the quartet (John Lennon, Paul McCartney, George Harrison, Ringo Starr) enjoy an imaginary game of soccer in an open field.

"Can't Get Out of This Mood" Music by Jimmy McHugh; lyric by Frank Loesser. Torchy lament ("Heartbreak, here I come") sung by Ginny Simms in *Seven Days' Leave* (RKO 1942).

"Can't Help Falling in Love" Music & lyric by George Weiss, Hugo Peretti, Luigi Creatore. As a birthday present to an old lady in *Blue Hawaii* (Par. 1961), Elvis Presley offers an Austrian musicbox and sings the sentimental waltz it supposedly contains.

"Can't Help Singing" Music by Jerome Kern; lyric by E. Y. Harburg. In the film of the same name (Univ. 1944), Deanna Durbin and Robert Paige joined voices in this lilting confession of the happiness they feel with the coming of spring.

Cantor, Eddie (né Isidore Itzkowitz), actor, singer; b. New York, Jan. 31, 1892; d. Hollywood, Oct. 10, 1964. Slight, wiry, eye-popping comedian-singer, usually cast as a mousy innocent who eventually turns heroic and foils the machinations of schemers and tough guys. A major Broadway star (*Ziegfeld Follies, Kid Boots, Whoopee*) before making a series of six films for Samuel Goldwyn. Among songs he introduced on the screen were "My Baby Just Cares for Me" (*Whoopee*) and "Keep Young and Beautiful" (*Roman Scandals*). Also had successful radio career and made many records. Film bio: *The Eddie Cantor Story,* with Keefe Brasselle as Cantor (who dubbed the singing). Bib: *Take My Life* by Cantor (1957).

1929 Glorifying the American Girl (specialty)
1930 Whoopee (*Henry Williams*)
1931 Palmy Days (*Eddie Simpson*)
1932 The Kid from Spain (*Eddie Williams*)
1933 Roman Scandals (*Eddie*)
1934 Kid Millions (*Eddie Wilson*)
1936 Strike Me Pink (*Eddie Pink*)
1937 Ali Baba Goes to Town (*Aloysius Babson*)
1940 Forty Little Mothers (*Gilbert Thompson*)
1943 Thank Your Lucky Stars (*Eddie Cantor/Joe Simpson*)
1944 Hollywood Canteen (guest bit)
     Show Business (*Eddie Martin*)
1948 If You Knew Susie (*Sam Parker*)
1952 The Story of Will Rogers (*Eddie Cantor*)
1953 The Eddie Cantor Story (vocals for Keefe Brasselle)

Capra, Frank, director, producer; b. Bisaquino, Sicily, May 18, 1897. Famed for his sentimental, socially slanted comedies (including those anent Messrs. Deeds, Smith, and Doe), Capra also directed two musicals with Bing Crosby. Bib: *The Name Above the Title* by Capra (1971).

1950 Riding High
1951 Here Comes the Groom

"Carioca, The" Music by Vincent Youmans; lyric by Edward Eliscu & Gus Kahn. The nickname given to a native of Rio de Janeiro was made the title of a new Brazilian dance—actually a modified samba—that was introduced in *Flying Down to Rio* (RKO 1933). At an outdoor Rio nightspot, the Carioca Casino, the number is first performed by the Brazilian Turunas and demonstrated by the dancing guests. Intrigued by the music and the steps that require partners to press their foreheads together, Fred Astaire and Ginger Rogers join the dancers who, admiringly, soon give the team the floor to themselves. They are followed by 25 couples as, one after another, three vocalists—including Etta Moten—sing the words. After 16 North Brazilians perform a more animated version, they are replaced by Fred and Ginger dancing atop seven white grand pianos forming a circular dancefloor. Two subsequent Astaire-Rogers films ended with the couple supposedly introducing new dance or music sensations: "The Continental" in *The Gay Divorcee* and "The Piccolino" in *Top Hat*.

Carlisle, Kitty (née Catherine Holtzman), actress, singer; b. New Orleans, Sept. 3, 1914. Dark-haired actress-singer with operatic training who won starring roles on Broadway after debut in *Champagne, Sec* (1933). In films twice appeared opposite both Bing Crosby and Allan Jones, and introduced "Love in Bloom," and "Alone." She was married to playwright and occasional screenwriter Moss Hart. In 1976 Miss Carlisle became chairman of the NY State Council on the Arts.

1934 Murder at the Vanities (*Ann Ware*)
     She Loves Me Not (*Midge Mercer*)
     Here Is My Heart (*Princess Alexandra*)
1935 A Night at the Opera (*Rosa Castaldi*)
1943 Larceny with Music (*Pamela Mason*)
1945 Hollywood Canteen (guest bit)

Carlisle, Mary, actress; b. Boston, Feb. 3, 1912. Roundfaced, coed-type blonde who was Bing Crosby's leading lady in three films. Retired from screen in 1942.

1933 College Humor (*Barbara Shirrel*)
     Sweetheart of Sigma Chi (*Vivian*)

1934 Palooka (*Ann*)
      Million Dollar Ransom (*Francesca*)
1935 The Old Homestead (*Nancy*)
1937 Double or Nothing (*Vicki Clark*)
1938 Doctor Rhythm (*Judy Marlowe*)
1939 Hawaiian Nights (*Millie*)
      Rovin' Tumbleweed (*Mary*)

Carmichael, (Hoagland Howard) Hoagy, composer, lyricist, actor, singer, pianist; b. Bloomington, Ind., Nov. 22, 1899. Began as singer-pianist on records and with Jean Goldkette's orchestra; had first success as composer with "Star Dust." Wrote film songs mostly for Paramount and was usually seen on screen as the dour, hollow-cheeked pianist hunched over the keyboard. Among Carmichael's best-know Hollywood songs: "Small Fry," Two Sleepy People," "Heart and Soul" (in film short), "How Little We Know," "Ole Buttermilk Sky," "In the Cool Cool Cool of the Evening," "My Resistance Is Low." In addition to writing his own lyrics, he worked with Frank Loesser, Johnny Mercer, Edward Heyman, Harold Adamson, Stanley Adams, Paul Francis Webster, Janice Torre and Fred Spielman, and Jack Brooks. The composer's songs have been sung in movies by Carmichael himself (in a twangy, nasal voice), Bing Crosby, Donald O'Connor, Bob Hope, Shirley Ross, Dick Powell, Jane Russell, and Marilyn Monroe. Bib: *The Stardust Road* (1946) and *Sometimes I Wonder* (1965), both by Carmichael. (Died Rancho Mirage, Cal. Dec. 27, 1981.)

1941 Road Show (alone)
      Mr. Bug Goes to Town (Loesser)
1943 True to Life (Mercer)
1944 To Have and Have Not (Mercer; Webster) (also
      Cricket)
1946 Canyon Passage (Brooks; alone) (also *Hi Linnet*)
1947 Night Song (Spielman, Torre) (also *Chick Morgan*)
1950 Young Man with a Horn (*Smoke Willoughby* only)
1952 The Las Vegas Story (Adamson; alone) (also *Happy*)
1953 Gentlemen Prefer Blondes (Adamson)
1955 Timberjack (Mercer; Webster) (also *Jingles*)

Carminati, Tullio (né Count Tullio Carminati de Brambilla), actor, singer; b. Zara, Dalmatia, Italy, Sept. 21, 1894; d. Rome, Feb. 26, 1971. Suave continental actor who made stage debut in Rome (1913), appeared on Broadway in *Music in the Air* (1932), and is best remembered as Grace Moore's leading man in film, *One Night of Love*. Introduced song "Paris in the Spring."

1934 Moulin Rouge (*Victor LeMaire*)
      One Night of Love (*Monteverdi*)

1935 Let's Live Tonight (*Nick Kerry*)
      Paris in Spring (*Paul DeLille*)
1937 London Melody (Eng.) (*Marius Andreani*)
      Sunset in Vienna (Eng.) (*Toni*)

Caron, Leslie (Claire Margaret), actress, dancer; b. Paris, July 1, 1931. Miss Caron was a ballet dancer in Paris when Gene Kelly recommended her as his dancing lead in *An American in Paris*. Her spunky gamine quality—always sure to make men feel that she needed protection—was also appreciated in other musicals, *Daddy Long Legs* (opposite Fred Astaire) and *Gigi,* as well as in such efforts as *Lili* and *The Glass Slipper*, which qualify as musicals only because of their extended dance sequences. "Hi-Lili, Hi-Lo" and "The Night They Invented Champagne" were introduced by Miss Caron and her voice dubber Betty Wand. The actress later turned to dramatic roles.

1951 An American in Paris (*Lise Bourvier*)
1952 Glory Alley (*Angela*)
1953 Lili (*Lili*)
1955 The Glass Slipper (*Ella*)
      Daddy Long Legs (*Julie André*)
1958 Gigi (*Gigi*)

Carousel (1956). Music by Richard Rodgers; lyrics by Oscar Hammerstein II; screenplay by Henry & Phoebe Ephron from Broadway musical by Rodgers & Hammerstein based on Benjamin F. Glazer's version of Ferenc Molnar's play *Liliom*.

A 20th Century-Fox film produced by Henry Ephron; directed by Henry King; choreography, Rod Alexander, Agnes deMille; art directors, Lyle Wheeler, Jack Martin Smith; costumes by Mary Wills; music director, Alfred Newman; associate, Ken Darby; cameraman, Charles G. Clarke; editor, William Reynolds; DeLuxe color; CinemaScope.

Cast: Gordon MacRae (*Billy Bigelow*); Shirley Jones (*Julie Jordan Bigelow*); Cameron Mitchell (*Jigger Craigin*); Barbara Ruick (*Carrie Pipperidge*); Claramae Turner (*Nettie Fowler*); Robert Rounseville (*Enoch Snow*); Gene Lockhart (*Starkeeper*); Audrey Christie (*Mrs. Mullin*); Susan Luckey (*Louise*); William LeMassena (*Heavenly Friend*); John Dehner (*David Bascombe*); Jacques d'Amboise (*dancer*).

Songs: "Carousel Waltz" - Orchestra/ "You're a Queer One, Julie Jordan" - Ruick, Jones/ "Mister Snow" - Ruick/ "If I Loved You" - Jones, MacRae/ "When the Children Are Asleep" - Rounseville, Ruick/ "June Is Bustin' Out All Over" - Turner, Ruick, chorus/ "Soliloquy" - MacRae/ "Blow High, Blow Low" - Mitchell, chorus/ "A Real Nice Clambake" - Ruick, Turner, Rounseville, Mitchell, chorus/ "There's Nothin' So Bad for a Woman" - Mitchell/ "What's the Use of Wond'rin'?" - Jones/ "You'll Never Walk Alone" - Turner. Unused: "Geraniums in the Winder," "The Highest Judge of All."

Faithfully adapted from the 1945 Rodgers and Hammerstein Broadway musical, featuring John Raitt and Jan Clayton, *Carousel* told the story of a swaggering, ne'er-do-well carnival barker who marries the simple factory girl Julie, kills himself in an attempted robbery, and returns to earth to instill a measure of confidence in his timid, unhappy daughter. Originally, Frank Sinatra had been signed for the role of Billy, but he walked off the set during early days of filming because of his objection to the movie being shot in both 35 mm Cinema-Scope and 55 mm CinemaScope (though it was released only in 35). Gene Kelly might have taken over the part, but he refused to have his voice dubbed, and so *Carousel* followed *Oklahoma!* with Gordon MacRae playing opposite Shirley Jones. The film was shot on location at Boothbay Harbor, Maine, and Zoma Beach, California.

Carpenter, Carleton, actor, singer; b. Bennington, Vt., July 10, 1926. Slim, gawky MGM juvenile who sang "Aba Daba Honeymoon" with Debbie Reynolds in *Two Weeks with Love*. Also has acted in nonmusicals and on Broadway.

1950   Three Little Words (*Dan Healy*)
        Summer Stock (*Artie*)
        Two Weeks with Love (*Billy Finlayson*)

Carr, Allan (né Allan Solomon), producer, screenwriter; b. Chicago, May 27, 1941. Artists' manager who became associated with producer Robert Stigwood (1975–78) before going into independent production.

1977   Saturday Night Fever
1978   Grease (also co-script)
1980   Can't Stop the Music (also co-script)
1982   Grease II

Carroll, John (né Julian LaFaye), actor, singer; b. Mandeville, La., 1907; d. Hollywood Hills, April 24, 1979. Dark-haired, mustached second lead in major films and first lead in minors who often played Latin types. Made many nonmusicals.

1930   Monte Carlo (officer at wedding)
1936   Hi, Gaucho (*Lucio*)
1938   Rose of the Rio Grande (*El Gato*)

1940   Go West (*Terry Turner*)
1941   Sunny (*Larry Warren*)
        Lady, Be Good (*Buddy Crawford*)
1942   Rio Rita (*Ricardo Montera*)
1943   Hit Parade of 1943 (*Rick Farrell*)
1947   Fiesta (*Jose Ortega*)
1950   Hit Parade of 1951 (*Eddie Paul*)
1953   The Farmer Takes a Wife (*Jotham Klore*)

Carroll, Nancy (née Ann Veronica LaHiff), actress, singer; b. New York Nov. 19, 1905; d. New York, Aug. 6, 1965. Red-haired, round-faced, wide-eyed Nancy Carroll was often teamed with Charles "Buddy" Rogers in early Paramount talkies. Later returned to the theatre, where she had begun her career. Bib: *Films of Nancy Carroll* by Paul Nemcik (1969).

1929   The Shopworn Angel (*Daisy Heath*)
        Close Harmony (*Marjorie Merwin*)
        Dance of Life (*Bonnie*)
        Sweetie (*Barbara Pell*)
1930   Honey (*Olivia Dangerfield*)
        Paramount on Parade (specialty)
        Follow Thru (*Lora Moore*)
1934   Transatlantic Merry-Go-Round (*Sally Marsh*)
1935   After the Dance (*Ann Taylor*)
1938   That Certain Age (*Grace Bristow*)

Carson, (John Elmer) Jack, actor, singer; b. Carmen, Manitoba, Canada, Oct. 27, 1910; d. Encino, Cal., Jan. 2, 1963. Beefy, swaggering first or second lead in Warner musicals (1941–49), usually with Dennis Morgan and/or Doris Day. Carson, who introduced "A Gal in Calico," was active in films to 1961.

1938   Having Wonderful Time (*Emil Beatty*)
        Carefree (*Connors*)
1939   Destry Rides Again (*Jack Tyndall*)
1940   Love Thy Neighbor (*Policeman*)
1941   Navy Blues (*Buttons Johnson*)
        Blues in the Night (*Leo Powell*)
1942   The Hard Way (*Albert Runkel*)
1944   Shine on Harvest Moon (*The Great Georgetti*)
        Hollywood Canteen (guest bit)
1946   Two Guys from Milwaukee (*Buzz Williams*)
        The Time, the Place and the Girl (*Jeff Howard*)
1947   Love and Learn (*Jingles*)
1948   April Showers (*Joe Tyme*)
        Romance on the High Seas (*Peter Virgil*)
        Two Guys from Texas (*Danny Foster*)
1949   It's a Great Feeling (*Jack Carson*)
        My Dream Is Yours (*Doug Blake*)

1953 Dangerous When Wet (*Windy Webb*)
1954 Red Garters (*Jason Carberry*)
     A Star Is Born (*Matt Libby*)
1955 Ain't Misbehavin' (*Hal North*)

Castle, (Nicholas) Nick, choreographer; b. Brooklyn, March, 21, 1910; d. Los Angeles, Aug. 28, 1968. Durable dance director with vaudeville experience, Castle worked mostly at Fox, MGM, and Paramount with such performers as George Murphy, Shirley Temple (four films), Betty Grable (*Down Argentine Way*), Vivian Blaine, Ann Miller, Dan Dailey, Judy Garland and Gene Kelly (*Summer Stock*), Fred Astaire, and Mitzi Gaynor.

1937 Love and Hisses
1938 Rebecca of Sunnybrook Farm
     Rascals
     Little Miss Broadway
     Hold That Coed
     Straight, Place and Show
1939 The Little Princess
     Swanee River
1940 Young People
     Down Argentine Way
1941 Buck Privates
     Hold That Ghost
     Hellzapoppin
1942 Ride 'Em Cowboy
     Moonlight Masquerade
     Joan of Ozark
     Orchestra Wives
     Johnny Doughboy
1943 Mayor of 44th Street
     Stormy Weather
     This Is the Army
     What's Buzzin' Cousin?
1944 Show Business
     Something for the Boys
1945 Nob Hill
     Mexicana
1946 Earl Carroll Sketchbook
     Thrill of Brazil
1948 Lulu Belle
1949 You're My Everything
1950 Nancy Goes to Rio
     Summer Stock
1951 Royal Wedding
     Rich, Young and Pretty
     The Strip
1952 Skirts Ahoy
     Everything I Have Is Yours
     Stars and Stripes Forever
1953 Here Come the Girls

1954 Red Garters
1955 Seven Little Foys
     You're Never Too Young
1956 Anything Goes
     Bundle of Joy
1958 Sing, Boy, Sing
     Rock-a-Bye Baby
1962 State Fair

" 'Cause My Baby Says It's So" Music by Harry Warren; lyric by Al Dubin. In *The Singing Marine* (Warner 1937), Marine Dick Powell, after entering a radio amateur talent contest, scored a hit with this breezy song of naïve trustfulness.

Centennial Summer. See Meet Me in St. Louis.

"Certain Smile, A" Music by Sammy Fain; lyric by Paul Francis Webster. Whispery ballad introduced by Johnny Mathis on soundtrack of nonmusical film of the same name (Fox 1958).

Chakiris George, actor, singer, dancer; b. Norwood, Ohio, Sept. 16, 1933. Dark, intense actor, something of a forerunner of John Travolta. Known as George Kerris 1947–56; scored biggest success in *West Side Story*.

1947 Song of Love (member St. Luke Choristers)
1953 Gentlemen Prefer Blondes (dancer)
1954 Brigadoon (dancer)
     White Christmas (dancer)
1955 The Girl Rush (dancer)
1956 Meet Me in Las Vegas (dancer)
1961 West Side Story (*Bernardo*)
1967 The Young Girls of Rochefort (*Etienne*)

Champion, Marge and Gower, dancers, actors, choreographers. Marge (née Marjorie Celeste Belcher), b. Los Angeles, Sept. 2, 1921. Gower, b. Geneva, Ill., June 22, 1920, d. New York, Aug. 25, 1980. Youthful-looking, married (but later divorced) dance team whose beaming smiles and flashing legs enlivened MGM musicals. Marge was also model for Disney cartoon characters Snow White in *Snow White and the Seven Dwarfs* and Blue Fairy in *Pinocchio*. Gower became top Broadway director-choreographer (*Bye Bye Birdie, Hello, Dolly!, 42nd Street*).

One asterisk indicates Marge without Gower; two indicate Gower without Marge:
1939 The Story of Vernon and Irene Castle* (*Irene's friend*)
1946 Till the Clouds Roll By** (specialty)
1950 Mr. Music (specialty)

1951 Show Boat (*Ellie May & Frank Schultz*)
1952 Everything I Have Is Yours (*Pamela & Chuck Hubbard*)
Lovely to Look At (*Clarisse & Jerry Ralby*)
1953 Give a Girl a Break (*Madelyn Corlane; Ted Sturges*) (Gower also chor.)
1955 Jupiter's Darling (*Meta; Varius*)
Three for the Show (*Gwen Howard; Vernon Lownes*)
1957 The Girl Most Likely** (chor. only)

"Change Partners" Music & lyric by Irving Berlin. In *Carefree* (RKO 1938), while gliding around a country-club dancefloor with another partner, Fred Astaire implored Ginger Rogers to get rid of hers and dance with him.

"Changing My Tune" Music by George Gershwin; lyric by Ira Gershwin. A sudden change in fortune, and one who had "wanted a permit to make me a hermit," now sees only a bright future. Introduced by Betty Grable in *The Shocking Miss Pilgrim* (Fox 1947), whose score was assembled from manuscripts discovered after George Gershwin's death.

Chaplin, Saul, (né Saul Kaplan), composer, conductor, arranger, producer; b. Brooklyn, Feb. 19, 1912. Arranger turned composer (combining both skills for "Anniversary Song") who became film producer in 1957. Among his lyric-writing partners: Sammy Cahn, Walter Samuels, Eddie DeLange, Jack Brooks, Johnny Mercer, Al Jolson.

1941 Go West, Young Lady (Cahn)
Rookies on Parade (Cahn)
Time Out for Rhythm (Cahn)
1943 Redhead from Manhattan (Samuels)
1944 Cowboy Canteen (Samuels)
1946 Meet Me on Broadway (DeLange)
1948 Countess of Monte Cristo (Brooks)
1957 Les Girls (co-prod. only)
1958 Merry Andrew (Mercer) (also co-prod.)
1960 Can-Can (co-prod. only)
1965 The Sound of Music (co-prod. only)
1968 Star! (prod. only)
1976 That's Entertainment Part 2 (co-prod. only)

"Charade" Music by Henry Mancini; lyric by Johnny Mercer. The game of love recalled in this "sad little serenade" by a vocal group on soundtrack of the non-musical film starring Cary Grant and Audrey Hepburn (Univ. 1963).

Charisse, Cyd (née Tula Ellice Finklea), actress, dancer; b. Amarillo, Texas, March 8, 1921. Long-limbed beauty who began career as dancer with Ballet Russe; won screen fame with Fred Astaire in *The Band Wagon* and *Silk Stockings,* and with Gene Kelly in *Singin' in the Rain* and *Brigadoon.* Singing principally dubbed by Marion Doenges, Eileen Wilson, India Adams, Carol Richards. Between 1943 and 1944 Miss Charisse was known as Lily Norwood. Bib: *The Two of Us* by Miss Charisse & Tony Martin (her husband) (1976).

1944 Something to Shout About (*Lily*)
1946 The Harvey Girls (*Deborah Andrews*)
Ziegfeld Follies (specialty)
Till the Clouds Roll By (specialty)
1947 Fiesta (*Conchita*)
The Unfinished Dance (*Ariane Bouchet*)
1948 On an Island with You (*Yvonne Torro*)
The Kissing Bandit (specialty)
Words and Music (specialty)
1952 Singin' in the Rain (specialty)
Sombrero (*Lola de Torrano*)
1953 The Band Wagon (*Gabrielle Gerard*)
Easy To Love (guest bit)
1954 Deep in My Heart (specialty)
1955 Brigadoon (*Fiona Campbell*)
It's Always Fair Weather (*Jackie Leighton*)
1956 Meet Me in Las Vegas (*Maria Corvier*)
1957 Silk Stockings (*Nina "Ninotchka" Yoshenko*)
1962 Black Tights (*Widow*)

"Charm of You, The" Music by Jule Styne; lyric by Sammy Cahn. Willowy ballad in which the charm of one's beloved is compared to an oddly convoluted and surprisingly limited number of pleasures. Soulfully introduced by Frank Sinatra in *Anchors Aweigh* (MGM 1945).

"Chattanooga Choo-Choo" Music by Harry Warren; lyric by Mack Gordon. Chugging narrative of a train passenger who anticipates departing at approximately 3:45 from Track 24, Pennsylvania Station, New York, reading a magazine, traveling through Baltimore, dining in the diner, feasting on ham and eggs in North Carolina, and being welcomed by a certain party upon his arrival in the Tennessee city. Performed in *Sun Valley Serenade* (Fox 1941) at an informal rehearsal by Glenn Miller's orchestra, with vocals by Tex Beneke and Paula Kelly and the Modernaires. The scene is immediately followed by a song-and-dance version featuring Dorothy Dandridge and the Nicholas Brothers in costume and on a stage with a painted backdrop of the choo-choo itself. Song was also sung by Dan Dailey in *You're My Everything* (Fox 1949) and by Frances Langford and The Modernaires, backed by James Stewart leading the Miller band, in *The Glenn Miller Story* (Univ. 1954). Composer Warren also wrote two other locomotive numbers: "Shuffle Off to Buffalo" (with Al Dubin) in *42nd Street* (Warner 1933) and "On the Atchison, Topeka and the Santa Fe" (with Johnny Mercer) in *The Harvey Girls* (MGM 1946).

"Cheek to Cheek" Music & lyric by Irving Berlin. At a fashionable Lido resort in *Top Hat* (RKO 1935), Fred Astaire woos Ginger Rogers on the dancefloor by revealing the unrivalled bliss he finds while dancing with her cheek on his. The song is unusual in that it has two releases, or middle sections, the first beginning "Oh, I'd love to climb a mountain," the second "Dance with me I want my arms about you." Berlin based the chief melody of the song on his verse to the 1917 "Smile and Show Your Dimple" (whose refrain provided the model for another famous tune, "Easter Parade"). "Cheek to Cheek," with a different lyric, was also sung by the Ritz Brothers in *On the Avenue* (Fox 1937).

Chevalier, Maurice (Auguste), actor, singer; b. Paris, Sept. 12, 1888; d. Paris, Jan. 1, 1972. With his straw hat rakishly tilted, his lower lip roguishly jutted, and his strutting air of *joi de vivre,* Chevalier epitomized the carefree, amorous Parisian boulevardier. Originally, a headliner in French music halls, cabarets, and revues (frequently with singer Mistinguett), he was over forty when he became one of Paramount's most popular stars. He was teamed with Jeanette MacDonald in four films (*The Love Parade, One Hour with You, Love Me Tonight, The Merry Widow*), and with Claudette Colbert in two (*The Big Pond, The Smiling Lieutenant*). Four were directed by Ernst Lubitsch. Among songs Chevalier introduced were "Louise," "My Love Parade," "My Ideal," "You Brought a New Kind of Love to Me," "One Hour with You," "Isn't It Romantic?," and "Mimi." "I Remember It Well," "Thank Heaven for Little Girls," and "I'm Glad I'm Not Young Anymore" were all sung in *Gigi*. The singer appeared frequently on television and made many records. Bib: *The Man in the Straw Hat* (1949), *With Love* (1960), and *I Remember It Well* (1970) all by Chevalier; *Chevalier* by Gene Ringgold & DeWitt Bodeen (1973).

1929	Innocents of Paris (*Maurice Marny*)
	The Love Parade (*Count Alfred Renard*)
1930	Paramount on Parade (specialty)
	The Big Pond (*Pierre Mirande*)
	Playboy of Paris (*Albert*)
1931	The Smiling Lieutenant (*Lt. Niki*)
1932	One Hour with You (*Dr. André Bertier*)
	Love Me Tonight (*Maurice Courtelin*)
1933	A Bedtime Story (*René, Vicomte de St. Denis*)
	The Way to Love (*François*)
1934	The Merry Widow (*Danilo*)
1935	Folies Bergère (*Eugene Charlier/Fernand, Baron Cassini*)
1936	The Beloved Vagabond (Eng.) (*André Paragot*)
1938	Break the News (Eng.) (*François Verrier*)
1958	Gigi (*Honoré Lachaille*)
1960	Can-Can (*Pierre Barrière*)
	Pepe (specialty)
1962	Jessica (*Father Antonio*)
	In Search of the Castaways (*Prof. Paganel*)
1964	I'd Rather Be Rich (*Philip Dulaine*)

"Chica Chica Boom Chic" Music by Harry Warren; lyric by Mack Gordon. Samba introduced in *That Night in Rio* (Fox 1941) by Carmen Miranda in production number at mammoth Rio de Janeiro nightclub; joined by Don Ameche, costumed as US naval officer, and dancing chorus.

"Chim Chim Cheree" Music & lyric by Richard M. Sherman & Robert B. Sherman. Rollicking number sung by happy chimneysweep Dick Van Dyke in *Mary Poppins* (Disney 1964) to buck up spirits of unhappy children Karen Dotrice and Matthew Garber; later Julie Andrews joined in. Earlier in the film, Van Dyke sang different words to the same melody as a one-man band street entertainer and also as a sidewalk chalk artist.

"Chitty Chitty Bang Bang" Music & lyric by Richard M. Sherman & Robert B. Sherman. Caractacus Potts (Dick Van Dyke) and his two children (Heather Ripley and Adrian Hill) sang this staccato love song to their "fine four-fendered friend" in the film of the same name (UA 1968).

Chocolate Soldier, The. See My Fair Lady.

Churchill, Frank E., composer; b. Rumford, Me., Oct. 20, 1901; d. Castaic, Cal., May 14, 1942. Composer of songs primarily for Walt Disney cartoons, Churchill wrote such pieces as "Who's Afraid of the

Big Bad Wolf?'' (for short *The Three Little Pigs*) and ''Whistle While You Work,'' ''Some Day My Prince Will Come,'' and ''Heigh Ho'' (for *Snow White and the Seven Dwarfs*). Larry Morey, Ann Ronell, Paul Francis Webster, Ned Washington, and Edward Plumb were lyricists with whom Churchill worked.

1937	Snow White and the Seven Dwarfs (Morey)
1938	Breaking the Ice (Webster)
1941	Dumbo (Washington)
	The Reluctant Dragon (also lyr.)
1942	Bambi (Plumb)

Claire, Bernice (née Bernice Claire Jahnigan), actress, singer; b. Oakland, Cal. Blonde leading lady of early talkie musicals, co-starred in first three with Alexander Gray. Also appeared with Gray in vaudeville.

1930	No, No, Nanette (*Nanette*)
	Song of the Flame (*Aniuta*)
	Spring Is Here (*Betty Bradley*)
	Top Speed (*Virginia Rollins*)
1931	Kiss Me Again (*Fifi*)
1933	Moonlight and Pretzels

Clare, Sidney, lyricist; b. New York, Aug. 15, 1892; d. Los Angeles Aug. 29, 1972. Vaudeville dancer-comedian who became Hollywood lyricist. ''Keeping Myself for You,'' with Vincent Youmans, was added to *Hit the Deck* (1930); ''On the Good Ship Lollipop,'' with Richard A. Whiting for *Bright Eyes* (1934), became Shirley Temple's most closely associated song. Other composer collaborators: Oscar Levant, Jay Gorney, Sam Stept, Harry Akst, Lew Pollack.

1929	Street Girl (Levant)
	Tanned Legs (Levant)
1930	Love Comes Along (Levant)
1933	Jimmy and Sally (Gorney)
1934	Wild Gold (Gorney)
	Transatlantic Merry-Go-Round (Whiting)
1935	This Is the Life (Stept)
	Music Is Magic (Levant)
	Paddy O'Day (Akst)
1936	Song and Dance Man (Pollack)
	Can This Be Dixie? (Akst)
	Star for a Night (Akst)
1937	The Holy Terror (Akst)
	Sing and Be Happy (Akst)
1938	Rascals (Akst)

Clark, Petula (Sally Owen), actress, singer; b. West Ewell, Surrey, Eng., Nov. 15, 1932. Child actress in films, then pop singing star whose career hit peak in mid-60s.

1946	London Town (Eng.) (*Peggy Sanford*)
1968	Finian's Rainbow (*Sharon McLonergan*)
1969	Goodbye Mr. Chips (*Katherine Chipping*)

Clarke, Grant, lyricist; b. Akron, Ohio, May 14, 1891; d. Los Angeles, May 16, 1931. Clarke's most famous film song was ''Am I Blue?,'' written with his most frequent collaborator, Harry Akst.

1929	On with the Show (Akst)
	Is Everybody Happy? (Akst)
1930	So Long, Letty (Akst)
	Song of the Flame (Akst)

Clooney, Rosemary, actress, singer; b. Maysville, Ky., May 23, 1928. Blonde, mellow-voiced ballad singer, best known for successful recording career. Most popular movie was *White Christmas*, in which she sang ''Count Your Blessings.'' Miss Clooney was once married to actor-director José Ferrer. Bib: *This for Remembrance* by Miss Clooney (1977).

1953	The Stars Are Singing (*Terry Brennan*)
	Here Come the Girls (*Daisy Crockett*)
1954	Red Garters (*Calaveras Kate*)
	White Christmas (*Betty Haynes*)
	Deep in My Heart (specialty)

''Closer You Are, The'' Music by Jule Styne; lyric by Leo Robin. Seated at a piano in an open-air restaurant in New York, songwriter Tony Martin sang his latest balladic effort to Janet Leigh in *Two Tickets to Broadway* (RKO 1951).

''Cocktails for Two'' Music by Arthur Johnston; lyric by Sam Coslow. At five o'clock in a secluded rendezvous that overlooks the avenue, a hand-holding couple enjoy each other's company while sipping cocktails. Presented on screen as a production number in *Murder at the Vanities* (Par. 1934), in which it was sung by Carl Brisson. According to lyricist Coslow, the song was written because the repeal of Prohibition sparked the idea for a romantic piece about an imbibing twosome. Danced by Miriam Hopkins in *She Loves Me Not* (Par. 1934); parodied by Spike Jones and His City Slickers in *Ladies Man* (Par. 1947); and groaned à la Dietrich by Danny Kaye in *On the Double* (Par. 1961).

''Coffee in the Morning (and Kisses in the Night)'' Music by Harry Warren; lyric by Al Dubin. Sung in

Moulin Rouge (UA 1934) first by Constance Bennett in rehearsal, then as part of production number (with Miss Bennett in black wig and sporting French accent), accompanied by Russ Columbo, the Boswell Sisters, and a dancing chorus. Lest the Hays Office think that the song advocated an immoral dalliance, the lyric revealed it was actually a wedding proposal: "It isn't formal, but with a wedding ring it's natural and normal . . ."

Cohan, George M(ichael), actor, singer, dancer, composer, lyricist; b. Providence, RI, July 4, 1878; d. New York, Oct. 5, 1942. Broadway's multi-talented song-and-dance man (he was also librettist, playwright, director, and producer) appeared in only one movie musical—and that one had songs by Rodgers and Hart. Two of Cohan's stage musicals, *Little Johnny Jones* and *Little Nellie Kelly,* however, were adapted to the screen, and his songs were heard in his film bio, *Yankee Doodle Dandy* (in which James Cagney played his part). Bib: *George M. Cohan* by Ward Morehouse (1943); *George M. Cohan* by John McCabe (1973)

Unless otherwise noted, Mr. Cohan was composer lyricist of the following:
1930 Little Johnny Jones
1932 The Phantom President (*Theodore Blair/Doc Varney* only)
1940 Little Nellie Kelly
1942 Yankee Doodle Dandy

Cole, Jack, choreographer, dancer; b. New Brunswick, NJ, April 27, 1914; d. Los Angeles, Feb. 16, 1974. Jazz-influenced dance director, who also specialized in dances of the Orient. Cole choreographed 12 Broadway musicals, including *Kismet* and *Man of La Mancha;* in Hollywood, he worked primarily with Rita Hayworth, Gene Kelly, Danny Kaye, Betty Grable, Mitzi Gaynor, Marilyn Monroe, and Jane Russell.

1941 Moon Over Miami (also dancer)
1944 Cover Girl
1945 Eadie Was a Lady
Tonight and Every Night (also dancer)
1946 Tars and Spars
The Jolson Story
The Thrill of Brazil
1947 Down to Earth
1951 On the Riviera
Meet Me After the Show
1952 The Merry Widow

1953 The I Don't Care Girl
The Farmer Takes a Wife
Gentlemen Prefer Blondes
1954 There's No Business Like Show Business
1955 Three for the Show
Gentlemen Marry Brunettes
Kismet (also dancer)
1957 Designing Woman (also dancer)
Les Girls
1959 Some Like It Hot
1960 Let's Make Love

Cole, (Nathaniel Adams) Nat "King," singer, pianist, actor; b. Montgomery, Ala., March 17, 1919; d. Santa Monica, Feb. 15, 1965. Syrupy-voiced singer and tinkly pianist who made records, appeared in nightclubs and on television, and who sang a song or two in musical and nonmusical films. His only acting role was in *St. Louis Blues.* Bib: *Nat "King" Cole* by Maria Cole (his wife) (1971).

1943 Here Comes Elmer
Pistol Packin' Mamma
1944 Pin-Up Girl
Stars on Parade
Swing in the Saddle
1945 See My Lawyer
1946 Breakfast in Hollywood
1949 Make Believe Ballroom
1953 Small Town Girl
1958 St. Louis Blues (*W. C. Handy*)
1965 Cat Ballou

Coleman, Cy (né Seymour Kaufman), composer; b. New York, June 14, 1929. Broadway composer whose only work transferred to the screen so far has been *Sweet Charity* (lyrics by Dorothy Fields). He also wrote background score for *Father Goose,* whence came "Pass Me By" (lyric by Carolyn Leigh).

1969 Sweet Charity (Fields)

Colonna, (Gerard) Jerry, actor, singer; b. Boston, Sept. 17, 1904. Colonna's teeth-clenched manner of speaking, piercing long-held notes, bulging eyes, and handlebar mustache made him a frequently imitated comic. He was Bob Hope's radio sidekick and appeared with Hope in four screen musicals. (Died Nov. 21, 1986.)

1937 Rosalie (*Joseph*)
1938 Little Miss Broadway (musician)
Garden of the Moon (band singer)
College Swing (*Prof. Yasha Koloski*)
1939 Naughty but Nice (*Allie Grey*)

1940 Melody and Moonlight (*Abner Kellogg*)
      Road to Singapore (*Achilles Bombanassa*)
1941 Ice Capades (*Jerry Colonna*)
      Sis Hopkins (*Professor*)
      You're the One (*Dr. Colonna*)
1942 True to the Army (*Pvt. J. Wethersby Bates*)
      Ice Capades
      Priorities on Parade (*Jeep Jackson*)
      Star-Spangled Rhythm (specialty)
1944 Atlantic City (*Professor*)
1946 Make Mine Music (voice only)
1947 Road to Rio (*Cavalry Captain*)
1951 Alice in Wonderland (voice of *March Hare*)
1956 Meet Me in Las Vegas (specialty)
1957 Pinocchio (tv) (*Ringmaster*)
1962 Road to Hong Kong (guest bit)

Columbo, (Ruggerio Eugenio de Rudolpho) Russ, singer, actor, composer; b. Philadelphia, Jan. 14, 1908; d. Hollywood, Sept. 2, 1934 (shotgun accident). Early singing idol of radio whose crooning, caressing style was similar to Bing Crosby's. Began as band singer with Gus Arnheim orchestra in 1929, then fronted own band and made records. Wrote songs with Grace Hamilton and Jack Stern.

1929 Street Girl (*band singer*)
      Dynamite
1933 Broadway Through a Keyhole (*Clark Brian*)
1934 Moulin Rouge (*Russ Columbo*)
      Wake Up and Dream (*Paul Scotti*) (also songs w. Hamilton, Stern)

Comden and Green, lyricists, screenwriters. Betty Comden, b. Brooklyn, May 3, 1917. Adolph Green, b. The Bronx, Dec. 2, 1915. Inseparable writing team chiefly associated with Broadway musicals, who collaborated with composers Leonard Bernstein on *On the Town* and Jule Styne on *Bells Are Ringing* (both filmed). In Hollywood, they turned out scripts for Arthur Freed musicals at MGM, including three with show-business themes (*The Barkleys of Broadway, Singin' in the Rain, The Band Wagon*), and they wrote songs with Roger Edens, André Previn, and Styne. Comden and Green's songs were sung on the screen by Gene Kelly, Frank Sinatra, Ann Miller, Dolores Gray, Judy Holliday (with whom the writers had begun their career performing in a nightclub act), and Shirley MacLaine.

Unless otherwise noted, Comden and Green wrote scripts for the following; films for which they also wrote lyrics indicated by names of composers in parentheses:
1944 Greenwich Village (bit parts only)

1947 Good News
1949 Take Me Out to the Ball Game (lyr. only) (Edens)
      The Barkleys of Broadway
      On the Town (Bernstein; Edens)
1952 Singin' in the Rain
1953 The Band Wagon
1955 It's Always Fair Weather (Previn)
1960 Bells Are Ringing (Styne)
1964 What a Way To Go (Styne)
1967 I'm Getting Married (tv) (Styne)

"Come Blow Your Horn" Music by James Van Heusen; lyric by Sammy Cahn. Swinging exhortation to put up a bold front ("Make like a little lamb and wham you're shorn"), offered by Frank Sinatra on soundtrack of his nonmusical film of same name (Par. 1963).

"Come Saturday Morning" Music by Fred Karlin; lyric by Dory Previn. Singing over the credits of *The Sterile Cuckoo* (Par. 1969), The Sandpipers liltingly look forward to being with their friend.

Como, (Pietro Ronald) Perry, singer, actor; b. Cannonsburg, Pa., May 18, 1912. Casual, durable crooner with slightly nasal voice and cardigan-sweater cosiness who enjoyed large following on radio, television, and records. Began career as band vocalist with Ted Weems orchestra in 1936, then became single. Acted opposite Vivian Blaine in first three films.

1944 Something for the Boys (*Sgt. Laddie Green*)
1945 Doll Face (*Nicky Ricci*)
1946 If I'm Lucky (*Allen Clark*)
1948 Words and Music (*Eddie Anders*)

Connolly, (Robert) Bobby, choreographer; b. 1890; d. Encino, Cal., Feb. 29, 1944. Broadway dance director (1926–34) who shared the choreographic load with Busby Berkeley at Warner during the 30s. At MGM (1939–43) Connolly's major films were *The Wizard of Oz, Broadway Melody of 1940,* and *For Me and My Gal.*

1933 Moonlight and Pretzels
      Take a Chance
1934 Flirtation Walk
1935 Sweet Adeline
      Sweet Music
      Go Into Your Dance
      Stars Over Broadway
      Broadway Hostess
1936 Colleen
      The Singing Kid
      Sons o' Guns

1937 The King and the Chorus Girl
Ready, Willing and Able
1938 Swing Your Lady
Fools for Scandal
1939 Honolulu
The Wizard of Oz
At the Circus
1940 Broadway Melody of 1940
Two Girls on Broadway
1942 Ship Ahoy
For Me and My Gal
1943 I Dood It

Conrad, Con (né Conrad K. Dober), composer; b. New York, June 18, 1891; d. Van Nuys, Cal., Sept. 28, 1938. Best remembered in Hollywood for "The Continental" in *The Gay Divorcee*, and "Midnight in Paris" (both lyrics by Herb Magidson) in *Here's to Romance*. Other collaborators: Sidney Mitchell, Archie Gottler, Jack Meskill.

1929 Fox Movietone Follies (Mitchell-Gottler)
Broadway (Mitchell-Gottler)
The Cockeyed World (Mitchell-Gottler)
1930 Let's Go Places (Mitchell-Gottler)
Movietone Follies of 1930 (Meskill)
1934 The Gift of Gab (Magidson)
The Gay Divorcee (Magidson)

"Constantly" Music by James Van Heusen; lyric by Johnny Burke. Romantic pledge made by Dorothy Lamour and overheard by Bing Crosby in *Road to Morocco* (Par. 1942).

"Continental, The" Music by Con Conrad; lyric by Herb Magidson. Lengthy—72-bar—song about the introduction of a daring new dance sensation that includes both kissing and singing. In *The Gay Divorcee* (RKO 1934), Fred Astaire, kept prisoner by Erik Rhodes in a hotel room with Ginger Rogers, hears the melody played by the orchestra at an outdoor dancefloor below. Ginger explains that "It's the newest thing over here" and sings the inviting words, which makes them both determined to partake in the revels. Deceiving their dim-witted captor, they slip out of the room and bound onto the dancefloor. As the other dancers deferentially back off to give them room, Astaire and Rogers perform the intricate steps and are soon joined by a dancing chorus. The words are reprised by Rhodes and new ones are sung by Lillian Miles itemizing all the places in Europe where the dance has become the rage. As a finale Fred and Ginger lead the dancers through a tango and a series of Russian dance variations. The entire musical presentation took 17 minutes. The following year, introducing "I Won't Dance" in *Roberta,* Miss Rogers sang the lines, "When you dance you're charming and you're gentle/ Specially when you do 'The Continental.' "

"Cooking Breakfast for the One I Love" Music by Henry Tobias; lyric by Billy Rose. "My baby likes bacon and that's what I'm makin'," sang Fanny Brice in *Be Yourself* (UA 1930), as she happily prepared the meal for sleeping Robert Armstrong.

"Cosi-Cosa" Music by Bronislaw Kaper & Walter Jurmann; lyric by Ned Washington. Merry-making number—apparently inspired by "Funiculi–Funcula"—sung by Allan Jones entertaining a shipload of immigrants in *A Night at the Opera* (MGM 1935). Song was also sung by Jones in *Everybody Sing* (MGM 1938).

Coslow, (Samson) Sam, lyricist, composer; b. New York, Dec. 27, 1902. As lyricist, Coslow wrote some of his most durable songs—"Moon Song," "The Day You Came Along," "Down the Old Ox Road," "Learn To Croon," "Thanks," "Cocktails for Two," "My Old Flame"—with composer Arthur Johnston for Paramount films starring Kate Smith, Bing Crosby, Carl Brisson, and Mae West. He also wrote lyrics for "Sing You Sinners," with music by W. Franke Harling. As composer as well as lyricist, Coslow was responsible for "You'll Have To Swing It" and "It's Love Again." Among his other composer collaborators were Richard A. Whiting, Newell Chase, Ralph Rainger, Sammy Fain, Barry Trivers, Al Siegel, Frederick Hollander, Kurt Weill, and Burton Lane; he also worked with lyricist Leo Robin. Nancy Carroll, Lillian Roth, Marlene Dietrich, Dennis King, Martha Raye, Jessie Matthews, and Dorothy Lamour all introduced Coslow songs. Bib: *Cocktails for Two* by Coslow (1977). (Died April 2, 1982.)

1929 Dance of Life (Whiting-Robin)
1930 The Vagabond King (Chase-Robin)
Honey (Harling)
1932 This Is the Night (Rainger)
Blonde Venus (Rainger)
1933 Hello, Everybody (Johnston)
College Humor (Johnston)
Too Much Harmony (Johnston)
1934 Murder at the Vanities (Johnston)
Many Happy Returns (Johnston)
Belle of the Nineties (Johnston)

1935 All the King's Horses (alone)
     Coronado (Whiting)
     Goin' to Town (Fain)
1936 It's Love Again (Eng.) (alone)
1937 Turn Off the Moon (alone)
     Mountain Music (alone)
     Thrill of a Lifetime (Hollander)
     This Way Please (Siegel)
     Every Day's a Holiday (Trivers)
1938 Love on Toast (Lane)
     You and Me (Weill)
1945 Out of This World (alone)
1947 Copacabana (alone)

Costello, Lou. *See* **Abbott and Costello.**

"Count Your Blessings Instead of Sheep" Music & lyric by Irving Berlin. Inspirational prescription for insomniacs, sung by Bing Crosby and Rosemary Clooney in a Vermont lodge in *White Christmas* (Par. 1954).

"Couple of Song and Dance Men, A" Music & lyric by Irving Berlin. Hokey vaudeville-type number for Bing Crosby and Fred Astaire in *Blue Skies* (Par. 1946). Cliff Nazarro was the pianist. Similar routine was performed by Crosby and Donald O'Connor singing "Ya Gotta Give the People Hoke" in *Anything Goes* (Par. 1956).

"Couple of Swells, A" Music & lyric by Irving Berlin. Appearing as hoboes in a Broadway revue in *Easter Parade* (MGM 1948), Judy Garland and Fred Astaire, sporting battered top hats and missing front teeth, delight in mocking the social pretensions they see all about them as they walk up a fashionable avenue. The song was written after producer Arthur Freed had asked Berlin to write a "fun number" for Judy and Gene Kelly (the originally intended co-star); when "Let's Take an Old-Fashioned Walk" was rejected (it would later reappear in the Broadway musical, *Miss Liberty*), the songwriter came up with "A Couple of Swells." In setting and content the number is close to Noël Coward's "Men About Town," which Coward and Gertrude Lawrence sang in the one-act musical *Red Peppers* (1936), and Berlin's own "Slumming on Park Avenue," sung by Alice Faye in *On the Avenue* (Fox 1937). Other clownish duets in Arthur Freed musicals around that time were the Garland-Kelly "Be a Clown" in *The Pirate* (MGM 1948) and the Jane Powell-Fred Astaire "Liar Song" in *Royal Wedding* (MGM 1951).

Courtneidge, (Esmerelda) Cicely, actress, singer; b. Sydney, Australia, April 1, 1893; d. London, April 26, 1980. Dame of the British Empire 1972. Cicely Courtneidge was an elegant, knockabout comedienne who wore funny hats and acted with her husband, Jack Hulbert, in both London stage musicals and British films. Introduced "There's Something About a Soldier" in *Soldiers of the King*. Bib: *Cicely* by Miss Courtneidge (1953); *The Little Woman's Always Right* by Hulbert (1975).

Asterisk indicates appearance with Mr. Hulbert:
1930 Elstree Calling* (specialty)
1932 Happily Ever After* (*Illustrated Ida*)
1933 Soldiers of the King (*Maisie Marvello*)
     Aunt Sally (*Sally Bird*)
1935 A Perfect Gentleman (US) (*April*)
1936 Everybody Dance (*Lady Kate*)
1937 Take My Tip* (*Lady Hattie Pilkington*)
1940 Under Your Hat* (*Kay Millett*)

Cover Girl (1944). Music by Jerome Kern; lyrics by Ira Gershwin; screenplay by Virginia Van Upp, adapted by Marion Marsonnet & Paul Gangelin from story by Erwin Gelsey.

A Columbia film produced by Arthur Schwartz; directed by Charles Vidor; choreography, Gene Kelly, Stanley Donen, Seymour Felix, Jack Cole; art directors, Lionel Banks, Cary Ordell; costumes, Travis Banton, Gwen Wakeling, Muriel King; music director, Morris Stoloff; orchestrations, Carmen Dragon, Saul Chaplin; cameramen, Rudolph Maté, Allen Davey; editor, Viola Lawrence; Technicolor.

Cast: Rita Hayworth (vocals by Martha Mears) (*Rusty Parker/ Maribelle Hicks*); Gene Kelly (*Danny McGuire*); Lee Bowman (*Noel Wheaton*); Phil Silvers (*Genius*); Jinx Falkenburg (*Jinx*); Leslie Brooks (*Maurine Martin*); Eve Arden (*Cornelia "Stonewall" Jackson*); Otto Kruger (*John Coudair*); Jess Barker (*Young John Coudair*); Anita Colby (*Anita Colby*); Ed Brophy (*Bartender*); Thurston Hall (*Tony Pastor*); Curt Bois (*chef*); Jack Norton (*drunk*); Robert Homans (*Pop*); Stanley Clements (*elevator boy*); Shelley Winters (*girl*).

Songs: "The Show Must Go On" - Hayworth, Brooks, girls/ "Who's Complaining?" - Silvers, with Hayworth, Brooks, girls/ "Sure Thing" - Hayworth (Mears), boys/ "Make Way for Tomorrow" (lyric with E. Y. Harburg) - Hayworth (Mears), Kelly, Silvers/ "Put Me to the Test" - Kelly; dance by Kelly, Hayworth/ "Long Ago and Far Away" - Hayworth

(Mears), Kelly/ "Poor John" (Fred Leigh-Henry Pether) - Hayworth (Mears), buskers/ "Alter-Ego Dance" - Kelly/ "Cover Girl" - chorus; dance by Hayworth, boys. Unused: "Time: The Present," "What I Love To Hear," "That's the Best of All," "Tropical Night."

Cover Girl was the third major musical Rita Hayworth made at Columbia (the other two: *You'll Never Get Rich, You Were Never Lovelier*). This time she was partnered by Gene Kelly (borrowed from MGM), who established himself in it as a major dancer, choreographer, and actor. The story concerns Rusty Parker, a dancer at Danny McGuire's Brooklyn night spot, who gets a chance to be a Broadway star after winning a magazine cover-girl contest. Eventually she returns to Danny. There is also a flashback (recalling *Evergreen*) that relates the story of the publisher's infatuation with Rusty's grandmother, a turn-of-the-century singer at Tony Pastor's Music Hall, who also gives up wealth and position to marry the man she loves. Produced by Arthur Schwartz, himself primarily a composer, *Cover Girl* had songs by Jerome Kern (he'd already written the music for Miss Hayworth's *You Were Never Lovelier*) who joined with lyricist Ira Gershwin for their only collaboration. Though no actor at Columbia was deemed suitable for the male lead, the film was put into production even before Kelly was signed. The dancer-choreographer's most memorable creations were "Make Way for Tomorrow," exuberantly performed with Miss Hayworth and Phil Silvers, and the dramatic "Alter-Ego" number in which he was made to appear as if he were dancing with himself on a deserted street. Thirty-six years later Kelly played another character named Danny McGuire in the film *Xanadu*.

Prompted by the success of *Cover Girl*, Columbia boss Harry Cohn bought the screen rights to Rodgers and Hart's *Pal Joey* for Kelly (he had been Joey on Broadway) and Hayworth (as the naïve young girl), plus Vivienne Segal (repeating her stage role as the worldly older woman). But MGM refused to release Kelly, and Cohn had to wait 13 years before filming the property with Rita Hayworth (now cast as the worldly older woman), Frank Sinatra, and Kim Novak.

Coward, Noël (Peirce), composer lyricist, actor, screen writer; b. Teddington, Eng., Dec. 16, 1899; d. Jamaica, WI, March 26, 1973. Knighted 1970. Prolific writer associated with the London stage, who specialized in smart, satirical plays and revues and sentimental operettas. One of the operettas, *Bitter Sweet*, was filmed twice, and three one-act plays from his collection *Tonight at 8:30*, including the musical *Red Peppers*, were filmed under the title, *Meet Me Tonight*. Coward's major screen achievement was the wartime saga *In Which We Serve*. Bib: *Present Indicative* (1937) and *Future Indefinite* (1954) both by Coward; *Noël Coward Song Book* (1953); *Theatrical Companion to Noël Coward* by Joe Mander & Raymond Mitchenson (1957); *Lyrics of Noël Coward* 1965); *A Talent To Amuse* by Sheridan Morley (1969); *The Life of Noël Coward* by Cole Lesley (1976).

1933   Bitter Sweet (Eng.)
1941   Bitter Sweet (US)
1952   Meet Me Tonight (Eng.) (also script)
1967   Androcles and the Lion (US tv) (*Julius Caesar* only)

Crain, Jeanne, actress; b. Barstow, Cal., May 25, 1925. Originally kid-sister type who appeared primarily in nonmusicals. At Fox between 1943 and 1950 her best-remembered musical role was in *State Fair*, in which she introduced "It Might as Well Be Spring" (with Louanne Hogan's voice).

1943   The Gang's All Here (girl at party)
1945   State Fair (*Margy Frake*)
1946   Centennial Summer (*Julia Rogers*)
          Margie (*Margie McDuff*)
1948   You Were Meant for Me (*Peggy Arnold*)
1950   I'll Get By (guest bit)
1955   Gentlemen Marry Brunettes (*Connie Jones*)
          The Second Greatest Sex (*Liza McClure*)
1957   The Joker Is Wild (*Lettie Page*)

Crawford, Joan (née Lucille LeSueur), actress; b. San Antonio, Texas, March 23, 1904; d. New York, 10, 1977. More than any other actress Joan Crawford epitomized the glamorous, homegrown Hollywood star. Customarily cast as an ambitious working girl who rises to the top and wins her man, she was a wide-eyed, full-lipped, square-shouldered mainstay of MGM movies from the late 20s through 1943. Though not primarily identified with musicals, Miss Crawford began her career as a Charleston dancer and was Fred Astaire's first dancing partner in films (*Dancing Lady*). She also introduced the song "Always and Always." The actress's first two (of four) husbands were Douglas Fairbanks, Jr., and Franchot Tone. Bib: *A Portrait of Joan* by Miss Crawford (1962); *Films of Joan Crawford* by Lawrence Quirk (1968); *Joan Crawford* by Bob Thomas (1978).

1929   Hollywood Revue of 1929 (specialty)
1933   Dancing Lady (*Janie Barlow*)

1934 Sadie McKee (*Sadie McKee*)
1939 Ice Follies of 1939 (*Mary McKay*)
1944 Hollywood Canteen (guest bit)
1946 Humoresque (*Helen Wright*)
1949 It's a Great Feeling (guest bit)
1953 Torch Song (*Jenny Stewart*)

Crosby, (Harry Lillis) Bing, actor, singer; b. Tacoma, Wash., May 2, 1903; d. Madrid, Oct. 14, 1977. The most popular and durable singing actor of the American musical screen was usually cast as an amiable nonconformist whose easygoing personality was projected through a series of tailor-made roles. Crosby's resonant, intimate crooning style was first heard in vaudeville, then as a member of a singing trio, the Rhythm Boys, with Paul Whiteman's Orchestra. After making his screen debut with the orchestra, he appeared on his own radio program in the early 1930s which won him a wide following. Crosby soon became the major star attraction at Paramount, where he remained under contract for 24 years. He acted in seven "Road" pictures with Bob Hope, in all but one with Dorothy Lamour as the romantic lead. Other notable film roles were in *Anything Goes* (two versions), *Pennies from Heaven, Sing You Sinners, Holiday Inn, Going My Way, Blue Skies, White Christmas, The Country Girl* (his major dramatic effort), and *High Society.* He appeared opposite Mary Carlisle in three films, and in two each with Kitty Carlisle, Joan Bennett, Shirley Ross, Mary Martin, Ethel Merman, Fred Astaire, Jane Wyman, Grace Kelly.

Among songs Crosby introduced were "Three Little Words," "Please," "The Day You Came Along," "Learn To Croon," "Temptation," "Thanks," "June in January," "Love in Bloom," "Love Is Just Around the Corner," "Love Thy Neighbor," "May I?," "Down by the River," "I Wished on the Moon," "It's Easy To Remember," "Soon," "I'm an Old Cowhand," "Empty Saddles," "Pennies from Heaven," "Blue Hawaii," "Sweet Leilani," "I've Got a Pocketful of Dreams," "Small Fry," "The Funny Old Hills," "East Side of Heaven," "Only Forever," "Too Romantic," "Be Careful It's My Heart," "White Christmas," "Constantly," "Moonlight Becomes You," "Road to Morocco," "Ac-Cent-Tchu-Ate the Positive," "Swinging on a Star," "But Beautiful," "Sunday, Monday or Always," "In the Cool Cool Cool of the Evening," "Zing a Little Zong," "Count Your Blessings," "True Love," "The Second Time Around." Most of Crosby's songs were written by composer James Van Heusen and lyricist Johnny Burke; others who

wrote for him were Arthur Johnston, Sam Coslow, Ralph Rainger, Leo Robin, Johnny Mercer, James V. Monaco, Harold Arlen, Harry Warren, and Irving Berlin. Crosby, who also appeared on a weekly radio program for decades, recorded more songs than any other singer in history. After the death of his first wife, actress Dixie Lee, the singer married actress Kathryn Grant. Both his brother, Bob Crosby, and his son, Gary Crosby, had screen careers.

Bib: *The Story of Bing Crosby* by Ted Crosby (his brother) (1946); *The Incredible Crosby* by Barry Ulanov (1948); *Call Me Lucky* by Bing Crosby (1953); *Films of Bing Crosby* by Robert Bookbinder (1977); *Bing* by Charles Thompson (1975); *The One and Only Bing* by Bob Thomas (1977).

1930 King of Jazz (band singer)
     Check and Double Check (voice only)
1931 Reaching for the Moon (singer)
     Confessions of a Co-Ed (singer)
1932 The Big Broadcast (*Bing Crosby*)
1933 College Humor (*Fred Danvers*)
     Too Much Harmony (*Eddie Bronson*)
     Going Hollywood (*Bill Williams*)
1934 We're Not Dressing (*Steve Jones*)
     She Loves Me Not (*Paul Lanton*)
     Here Is My Heart (*J. Paul Jones*)
1935 Mississippi (*Tom Grason*)
     Two for Tonight (*Gilbert Gordon*)
     Big Broadcast of 1936 (specialty)
1936 Anything Goes (*Billy Crocker*)
     Rhythm on the Range (*Jeff Larrabee*)
     Pennies from Heaven (*Larry*)
1937 Waikiki Wedding (*Tony Marvin*)
     Double or Nothing (*Lefty Boylan*)
1938 Doctor Rhythm (*Dr. Bill Remsen*)
     Sing You Sinners (*Joe Beebe*)
1939 Paris Honeymoon (*Lucky Lawton*)
     East Side of Heaven (*Danny Martin*)
     The Star Maker (*Larry Earl*)
1940 Road to Singapore (*Josh Mallon*)
     If I Had My Way (*Buzz Blackwell*)
     Rhythm on the River (*Bob Summers*)
1941 Road to Zanzibar (*Chuck Reardon*)
     Birth of the Blues (*Jeff Lambert*)
1942 Holiday Inn (*Jim Hardy*)
     Road to Morocco (*Jeff Peters*)
     Star Spangled Rhythm (specialty)
1943 Dixie (*Dan Emmett*)
1944 Going My Way (*Father Chuck O'Malley*)
     Here Come the Waves (*Johnny Cabot*)
1945 Out of This World (vocals for Eddie Bracken)
     Duffy's Tavern (specialty)
     The Bells of St. Mary's (*Father Chuck O'Malley*)

1946 Road to Utopia (*Duke Johnson/ Junior Hooten*)
1946 Blue Skies (*Johnny Adams*)
1947 Welcome Stranger (*Dr. Jim Pearson*)
Variety Girl (specialty)
Road to Rio (*Scat Sweeney*)
1948 The Emperor Waltz (*Virgil Smith*)
1949 A Connecticut Yankee in King Arthur's Court (*Hank Martin*)
Top o' the Mornin' (*Joe Mulqueen*)
Ichabod and Mr. Toad ("Ichabod" narrator)
1950 Riding High (*Dan Brooks*)
Mr. Music (*Paul Merrick*)
1951 Here Comes the Groom (*Pete Garvey*)
1952 Just for You (*Jordan Blake*)
Road to Bali (*George Cochran*)
1953 Scared Stiff (guest bit)
Little Boy Lost (*Bill Wainwright*)
1954 White Christmas (*Bob Wallace*)
The Country Girl (*Frank Elgin*)
1956 Anything Goes (*Bill Benson*)
High Tor (tv) (*Van Van Dorn*)
High Society (*C. K. Dexter Haven*)
1959 Say One for Me (*Father John Conroy*)
1960 Let's Make Love (*Bing Crosby*)
High Time (*Harvey Howard*)
Pepe (*Bing Crosby*)
1962 Road to Hong Kong (*Harry Turner*)
1964 Robin and the Seven Hoods (*Alan A. Dale*)

Crosby, (George Robert) Bob, actor, singer, bandleader; b. Spokane, Wash., Aug. 23, 1913. Bing's boyish-looking younger brother appeared in films both with and without his orchestra. He began his career as a singer with the Dorsey Brothers Orchestra in 1935, then fronted own band specializing in Dixieland. After the band broke up, he became a radio and television personality, primarily during the 50s.

1940 Let's Make Music (*Bob Crosby*)
1941 Rookies on Parade (*Duke Wilson*)
Sis Hopkins (*Jeff Farnsworth*)
1943 Presenting Lily Mars (specialty)
Reveille with Beverly (specialty)
Thousands Cheer (specialty)
1944 Kansas City Kitty (*Jimmy*)
Meet Miss Bobby Sox (*Bob Crosby*)
My Gal Loves Music (*Mel Murry*)
Pardon My Rhythm (specialty)
The Singing Sheriff (*Bob Richards*)
1951 Two Tickets to Broadway (*Bob Crosby*)
1952 Road to Bali (guest bit)
1953 When You're Smiling (specialty)
1959 The Five Pennies (*Will Paradise*)
Senior Prom (specialty)

Crosland, Alan, director; b. New York, Aug. 10, 1894; d. Beverly Hills, July 16, 1936. Historically important as the director of the first film with synchronized music (*Don Juan,* 1926) and first part-talkie (*The Jazz Singer,* 1927). At Warner through 1931.

1927 The Jazz Singer
1929 On with the Show
1930 Song of the Flame
Big Boy
Viennese Nights
1931 Children of Dreams
1935 King Solomon of Broadway

"Cryin' for the Carolines" Music by Harry Warren; lyric by Sam Lewis & Joe Young. Homesick lament ("Anyone can see what's troublin' me") expressed by the Brox Sisters in *Spring Is Here* (Warner 1930).

"Cuban Love Song" Music by Jimmy McHugh; lyric by Dorothy Fields. Ardent pledge of devotion offered by Lawrence Tibbett in *Cuban Love Song* (MGM 1931).

Cugat, Xavier (né Francisco de Asis Javier Cugat Mingall de Bru y Deulofeo), bandleader, actor; b. Gerona, Spain, Jan. 1, 1900. Beginning as a danceband violinist, Cugat fronted the most celebrated Latin-American dance orchestra in US nightclubs, films, and on records. In Hollywood, he usually played himself—or a variation thereof—and both he and his band were spotlighted in MGM musicals between 1944 and 1949. His third and fourth wives were singers Abbe Lane and Charo. Bib: *Rumba Is My Life* by Cugat (1949).

1936 Go West, Young Man
1942 You Were Never Lovelier
1943 The Heat's On
Stage Door Canteen
1944 Bathing Beauty
Two Girls and a Sailor
1945 Weekend at the Waldorf
1946 Holiday in Mexico
No Leave, No Love
1947 This Time for Keeps
1948 On an Island with You
A Date with Judy
Luxury Liner
1949 Neptune's Daughter
1955 Chicago Syndicate

Cukor, George, director; b. New York, July 7, 1899. Major director of large-scale dramas, comedies, and costume epics (*Dinner at Eight, David Copperfield,*

Camille, The Philadelphia Story) whose chief musicals were *A Star Is Born* and *My Fair Lady*. Began career as stage director-actor-producer; entered films in 1929 as dialogue director of *All Quiet on the Western Front*. Bib: *Cukor & Co.* by Gary Carey (1971); *On Cukor* by Gavin Lambert (1972). (Died, Los Angeles, Jan. 24, 1983.)

1932	One Hour with You (part)
1954	A Star Is Born
1957	Les Girls
1960	Let's Make Love
	Song Without End (part)
1964	My Fair Lady
1976	The Blue Bird

Cummings, Irving, director; b. New York, Oct. 9, 1888; d. Hollywood, April 18, 1959. Cummings became a director, mostly at Fox, after having been an actor in silent films. He worked on four musicals each with Shirley Temple and Betty Grable (including *Down Argentine Way*), three each with Carmen Miranda and Don Ameche. His son, Irving Cummings, Jr., produced *Double Dynamite*.

1930	Cameo Kirby
1935	Curly Top
1936	Poor Little Rich Girl
1937	Vogues of 1938
	Merry-Go-Round of 1938
1938	Little Miss Broadway
	Just Around the Corner
1940	Lillian Russell
	Down Argentine Way
1941	That Night in Rio
	Louisiana Purchase
1942	My Gal Sal
	Springtime in the Rockies
1943	Sweet Rosie O'Grady
1945	The Dolly Sisters
1951	Double Dynamite

Cummings, Jack (né Jacob Kominsky), producer; b. New Brunswick, Can., 1900. Between 1936 and 1955, Cummings produced musicals exclusively for MGM (where uncle Louis B. Mayer was studio boss). Among his credits: *Born To Dance, Broadway Melody* (1938 and 1940 versions), *Kiss Me, Kate,* and *Seven Brides for Seven Brothers.* Red Skelton acted in eight of his films, Eleanor Powell in five, Howard Keel in four.

1936	Born To Dance
1937	Broadway Melody of 1938
1938	Listen, Darling
1939	Honolulu
1940	Broadway Melody of 1940
	Two Girls on Broadway
	Go West
1942	Ship Ahoy
1943	I Dood It
1944	Broadway Rhythm
	Bathing Beauty
1946	Easy To Wed
1947	It Happened in Brooklyn
	Fiesta
1949	Neptune's Daughter
1950	Three Little Words
	Two Weeks with Love
1951	Excuse My Dust
	Texas Carnival
1952	Lovely To Look At
1953	Sombrero
	Kiss Me, Kate
	Give a Girl a Break
1954	Seven Brides for Seven Brothers
1955	Interrupted Melody
1959	The Blue Angel
1960	The Second Time Around
1964	Viva Las Vegas

Cummings, (Clarence) Robert (Orville), actor, singer; b. Joplin, Mo., June 9, 1910. Youthful-looking, dark-haired actor usually cast as Ivy League playboy in musicals. Appearing in over 60 films through 1966; also had his own television series.

1935	Millions in the Air (*Jimmy*)
1936	Three Cheers for Love (*Jimmy Tuttle*)
1937	Hideaway Girl (*Michael Winslow*)
1938	College Swing (*radio announcer*)
	You and Me (*Jim*)
1939	Three Smart Girls Grow Up (*Harry Loren*)
	The Under Pup (*Dennis King*)
	Charlie McCarthy, Detective (*Scotty Hamilton*)
1940	Spring Parade (*Harry Marten*)
	One Night in the Tropics (*Steve Harper*)
1941	Moon Over Miami (*Jeff Bolton*)
	It Started with Eve (*Jonathan Reynolds*)
1950	The Petty Girl (*George Petty*)
1954	Lucky Me (*Dick Carson*)
1963	Beach Party (*Prof. Sutwell*)

Curtiz, Michael (né Mikhaly Kertesz), director; b. Budapest, Dec. 24, 1888; d. Hollywood, April 11, 1962. Prolific, protean director whose output of over 100 films stretched from 1926 through 1962. At Warner until 1953, his most celebrated musical was *Yankee Doodle Dandy* (nonmusicals included *Captain Blood, The Adventures of Robin Hood,* and *Casablanca*). Doris Day sang in four of his films; others with whom he worked were Al Jolson, James Cagney, Bing Crosby, Danny Kaye, and Elvis Presley.

1930 Mammy
     Bright Lights
1935 Bright Lights (prod. only)
1942 Yankee Doodle Dandy
1943 This Is the Army
1946 Night and Day
1948 Romance on the High Seas

1949 My Dream Is Yours (also prod.)
     It's a Great Feeling (guest bit only)
1950 Young Man with a Horn
1951 I'll See You in My Dreams
1953 The Jazz Singer
1954 White Christmas
1956 The Vagabond King
     The Best Things in Life Are Free
1957 The Helen Morgan Story
1958 King Creole

D

Dailey, (Daniel James) Dan (Jr.), actor, singer, dancer; b. New York, Dec. 14, 1914; d. Los Angeles, Oct. 16, 1978. Rangy, sandy-haired, self-confident song-and-dance man primarily identified with Fox musicals (1947–54), who appeared opposite Betty Grable in four backstage sagas (including *Mother Wore Tights* in which he introduced "You Do"). Also acted in many nonmusicals; returned to stage in 1962.

1940	Hullabaloo (*Bob Strong*)
1941	Ziegfeld Girl (*Jimmy Walters*)
	Lady, Be Good (*Bill Pattison*)
1942	Panama Hattie (*Dick Bullitt*)
	Give Out Sisters (*Bob Edwards*)
1947	Mother Wore Tights (*Frank Burt*)
1948	You Were Meant for Me (*Chuck Arnold*)
	Give My Regards to Broadway (*Bert Norwick*)
	When My Baby Smiles at Me (*Skid Johnson*)
1949	You're My Everything (*Tim O'Connor*)
1950	My Blue Heaven (*Jack Moran*)
	I'll Get By (guest bit)
1951	Call Me Mister (*Shep Dooley*)
1952	Meet Me at the Fair (*Doc Tilbee*)
1953	The Girl Next Door (*Bill Carter*)
1954	There's No Business Like Show Business (*Terry Donahue*)
1955	It's Always Fair Weather (*Doug Hallerton*)
1956	Meet Me in Las Vegas (*Chuck Rodwell*)
	The Best Things in Life Are Free (*Ray Henderson*)
1960	Pepe (*Ted Holt*)

Dale, Virginia, actress, dancer, singer; b. 1918. Roundfaced, honey blonde who appeared mostly in Paramount musicals; best remembered as Fred Astaire's dancing partner in *Holiday Inn*.

1938	Start Cheering (*Mabel*)
1940	Buck Benny Rides Again (*Virginia Dale*)
	Love Thy Neighbor (*Virginia Astor*)
1941	Dancing on a Dime (*Dolly Stewart*)
	Las Vegas Nights (*Patsy Lynch*)
	The Singing Hill
	Kiss the Boys Goodbye (*Gwen Abbott*)
1942	Holiday Inn (*Lila Dixon*)

Daley, Cass (née Catherine Dailey), actress, singer; b. Philadelphia, July 17, 1915; d. Hollywood, March 22, 1975. Bony, buck-toothed comedienne whose grotesque antics enlivened a decade of Paramount musicals.

1942	The Fleet's In (*Cissie*)
	Star Spangled Rhythm (*Mimi*)
1943	Crazy House (*Sadie Silverfish*)
	Riding High (*Tess Connors*)
1945	Out of This World (*Fanny*)
	Duffy's Tavern (specialty)
1947	Ladies Man (*Geraldine Ryan*)
	Variety Girl (specialty)
1952	Here Comes the Groom (specialty)
1954	Red Garters (*Minnie Redwing*)

Dames. See Gold Diggers of 1933.

"Dames" Music by Harry Warren; lyric by Al Dubin. In a scene from a Broadway revue in *Dames* (Warner 1934), Dick Powell, playing a producer, tells potential backers that dames are the most important ingredient in any show. A covey of lovelies is introduced (including "Miss Warren" and "Miss Dubin"), and the scene dissolves into a Busby Berkeley celebration of the allure of chorus girls. They are seen waking, bathing, dressing, and rushing to the theatre where they delight in forming a variety of geometric patterns.

Damn Yankees. See Pajama Game, The.

Damone, Vic (né Vito Rocco Farinola), actor, singer; b. Brooklyn, June 12, 1928. Dark-haired, resonant-voiced singer of slight build, who has made records and appeared in nightclubs.

1951 Rich, Young and Pretty (*André Milan*)
      The Strip (*Vic Damone*)
1954 Athena (*Johnny Nyle*)
      Deep in My Heart (specialty)
1955 Hit the Deck (*Rico Ferrari*)
      Kismet (*Caliph*)
1956 Meet Me in Las Vegas (guest bit)
1957 An Affair To Remember (voice only)
1965 Dangerous Christmas of Red Riding Hood (tv)
      (*Woodsman*)

Damsel in Distress, A (1937). Music by George Gershwin; lyrics by Ira Gershwin; screenplay by P. G. Wodehouse, Ernest Pagano, S. K. Lauren from novel by P. G. Wodehouse and play by Wodehouse & Ian Hay.

An RKO-Radio film produced by Pandro S. Berman; directed by George Stevens; choreography, Fred Astaire, Hermes Pan; art director, Van Nest Polglase; music director, Victor Baravalle; orchestrations, Robert Russell Bennett, Ray Noble, George Bassman; cameraman, Joseph August; editor, Henry Berman.

Cast: Fred Astaire (*Jerry Halliday*); George Burns (*George Burns*); Gracie Allen (*Gracie Allen*); Joan Fontaine (*Lady Alyce Marshmorton*); Reginald Gardiner (vocal by Mario Berini) (*Keggs*); Ray Noble (*Reggie*); Constance Collier (*Lady Caroline Marshmorton*); Montagu Love (*Lord John Marshmorton*); Harry Watson (*Albert*); Jan Duggan, Mary Dean, Pearl Amatore, Betty Rome (*madrigal singers*).

Songs: "I Can't Be Bothered Now" - Astaire/ "The Jolly Tar and the Milkmaid" - Astaire, Duggan, Dean, Amatore, Rome, singers/ "Put Me to the Test" - dance by Astaire, Burns, Allen/ "Stiff Upper Lip" - Allen; dance by Astaire, Burns, Allen, fairgoers/ "Sing of Spring" - singers/ "Things Are Looking Up" - Astaire; stroll by Astaire, Fontaine/ "A Foggy Day" - Astaire/ "Nice Work If You Can Get It" - Duggan, Dean, Amatore, Astaire; reprised as drum solo & dance by Astaire/ "Ah, che a voi perdoni Iddio" (Flotow, *Marta*) - Gardiner (Berini). Unused: "Pay Some Attention to Me."

Because Ginger Rogers was anxious to get out from under Fred Astaire's shadow and into the limelight as a dramatic actress, the RKO sachems agreed that, after seven pictures together, Fred and Ginger would temporarily go their own ways. For Fred's leading lady in *A Damsel in Distress*, the studio tried but failed to get Ruby Keeler (a questionable choice) and Jessie Matthews (unquestionably an ideal choice), then settled on nondancing Joan Fontaine under the naïve notion that this would avoid comparisons with Ginger. It was also decided that the featured comedians in the cast would also be unassociated with previous Astaire movies—Burns and Allen, Reginald Gardiner (as an Eric Blore butler), and Ray Noble. Behind the scenes, however, was the accustomed producer, Pandro Berman, plus George Stevens as director (he had been responsible for *Swing Time*), and George and Ira Gershwin for the sparkling score (they had done *Shall We Dance*).

And the story certainly contained reminders of past Astaire-Rogers vehicles, primarily *Top Hat*. Again Fred played a popular American dancer named Jerry who, while appearing in London, falls in love at first sight and leaves the city to woo his beloved. After the inevitable misunderstandings—accompanied by much singing and dancing—he wins the lady and ends up skipping off to be married. (There were also reminiscent elements of the Chevalier-MacDonald charmer *Love Me Tonight* in the tale of a commoner who rescues a lovelorn aristocrat in a castle.) But *A Damsel in Distress* did have its own memorable moments, particularly Astaire's drum solo and dance to "Nice Work If You Can Get It," the Burns and Allen nonsequitur humor, and the trio's wacky dance—to "Stiff Upper Lip"—in the fun house at a nearby fair.

Dancing Lady. *See **42nd Street**.*

"Dancing on a Dime" Music by Burton Lane; lyric by Frank Loesser. Lilting piece advocating a crowded dancefloor as perfect for a romantic time. Sung by Grace McDonald and Robert Paige in Paramount film of the same name (1941).

Dandridge, Dorothy, actress, singer; b. Cleveland, Nov. 9, 1923; d. W. Hollywood, Sept. 8, 1965. Though she introduced the lively "Chattanooga Choo-Choo" in *Sun Valley Serenade*, Miss Dandridge is best remembered in Hollywood as the doomed heroine of *Carmen Jones* and of *Porgy and Bess*. Bib: *Everything and Nothing* by Miss Dandridge (1970).

1937 A Day at the Races (child singer)
1941 Sun Valley Serenade (singer)
1943 Hit Parade of 1943 (specialty)
1944 Atlantic City (specialty)
1954 Carmen Jones (*Carmen Jones*)
1959 Porgy and Bess (*Bess*)

Daniels, (Virginia) Bebe, actress, singer; b. Dallas, Jan. 14, 1901; d. London, March 16, 1971. Dark-haired actress who appeared in early Hollywood musicals including *Rio Rita* and *42nd Street* (introducing "You're Getting To Be a Habit with Me"). Moved to England with husband Ben Lyon, where they became a popular radio team. Bib: *Life with the Lyons* by Miss Daniels & Lyon (1953); *Bebe and Ben* by Jill Allgood (1975).

1929	Rio Rita (*Rita Ferguson*)
1930	Love Comes Along (*Peggy*)
	Dixiana (*Dixiana*)
1933	42nd Street (*Dorothy Brock*)
	The Song You Gave Me (Eng.) (*Mitzi Hensen*)
	A Southern Maid (Eng.) (*Dolores/Juanita*)
1935	Music Is Magic (*Diane DeValle*)
1941	Hi, Gang! (Eng.) (*Victory Girl*)

Dare, (Daniel) Danny, choreographer, producer; b. 1905. Dare's major work as dance director was for *Holiday Inn;* later—as Daniel Dare—he became a producer at Paramount.

1936	Three Cheers for Love
1937	52nd Street
1938	Start Cheering
1942	Holiday Inn
	Star Spangled Rhythm
1944	Here Come the Waves
1945	Bring on the Girls
	Incendiary Blonde
	Duffy's Tavern (also asst. prod.)
	Road to Utopia
1947	Variety Girl (also prod.)
	Road to Rio (prod. only)
1948	Isn't It Romantic? (also prod.)

Darin, Bobby (né Robert Walden Cassotto), actor, singer, composer, lyricist; b. The Bronx, NY, May 14, 1936; d. Hollywood, Dec. 20, 1973. Pop record star with flip, neo-Sinatra image; also songwriter.

1960	Pepe (specialty)
1962	Too Late Blues (*Ghost Wakefield*)
	State Fair (*Jerry Dundee*)
1964	The Lively Set (comp., lyr. only)

"Dark Is the Night" Music by Nicholas Brodszky; lyric by Sammy Cahn. The end of a romance sorrowfully expressed by Jane Powell in *Rich, Young and Pretty* (MGM 1951).

David, Hal, lyricist; b. New York, May 25, 1921. Collaborator of composer Burt Bacharach, with whom he wrote such film hits as "Alfie" and "Raindrops Keep Fallin' on My Head." David, who also worked with Marty Nevins, was president of ASCAP 1980–1986. He is the brother of lyricist Mack David. Bib: *What the World Needs Now* by David (1968).

1951	Two Gals and a Guy (Nevins)
1972	Lost Horizon (Bacharach)

David, Mack, lyricist; b. New York, July 5, 1912. Lyricist of many theme songs for films and television. Best-known movie song: "Bibbidi Bobbidi Boo" from *Cinderella,* with Al Hoffman and Jerry Livingston. With Livingston, he also wrote songs for four Jerry Lewis-Dean Martin comedies. He is the brother of lyricist Hal David.

1949	Cinderella (Livingston, Hoffman)
1950	At War with the Army (Livingston)
1951	Sailor Beware (Livingston)
1952	Jumping Jacks (Livingston)
1953	Scared Stiff (Livingston)

Davies, Marion (née Marion Cecilia Douras), actress, singer; b. New York, Jan. 3, 1897; d. Los Angeles, Sept. 22, 1961. Blonde, wide-eyed, round-faced actress, who began career as show girl in New York. Entered silent films in 1917 when patron William Randolph Hearst set up Cosmopolitan Productions as a showcase for her talents. In musicals, she was co-starred opposite such players as Bing Crosby, Dick Powell, and Clark Gable. Bib: *Marion Davies* by Fred Lawrence Guiles (1972).

1929	Hollywood Revue of 1929 (specialty)
	Marianne (*Marianne*)
1930	The Florodora Girl (*Daisy*)
1932	Blondie of the Follies (*Blondie McClune*)
1933	Going Hollywood (*Sylvia Bruce*)
1934	Operator Thirteen (*Gail Loveless*)
1936	Hearts Divided (*Betsy Patterson*)
	Cain and Mabel (*Mabel O'Dare*)
1937	Ever Since Eve (*Marge Winton*)

Davis, (Madonna Josephine) Joan, actress; b. St. Paul, June 29, 1907; d. Palm Springs, May 23, 1961. Gawky comedienne with almost perpetual expression of total hopelessness, who appeared in Fox musicals between 1937 and 1941. Acted opposite Bert Lahr in three films, Eddie Cantor in two. Later had own television series, *I Married Joan.*

1935	Millions in the Air (singer)
1937	The Holy Terror (*Lil*)
	On the Avenue (*Miss Katz*)
	Wake Up and Live (*Spanish dancer*)
	Sing and Be Happy (*Myrtle*)
	Thin Ice (*bandleader*)
	Life Begins in College (*Inez*)

Love and Hisses (*Joan*)
1938   Sally, Irene and Mary (*Irene Keene*)
Josette (*Mary Morris*)
My Lucky Star (*Mary Boop*)
Hold That Coed (*Lizzie Olsen*)
Just Around the Corner (*Kitty*)
1941   Sun Valley Serenade (*Miss Carstairs*)
Hold That Ghost (*Camille Brewster*)
Two Latins from Manhattan (*Joan Daley*)
1942   Yokel Boy (*Molly Malone*)
1943   Around the World (*Joan*)
1944   Show Busines (*Joan Mason*)
Beautiful but Broke (*Dottie*)
Kansas City Kitty (*Polly Jasper*)
1945   George White's Scandals of 1945 (*Joan Mason*)
1948   If You Knew Susie (*Susie Parker*)

Davis, Johnny "Scat," actor, singer, trumpeter. Roundfaced trumpeter-vocalist who got his start with Fred Waring's orchestra and burst on the screen as an excessively ebullient scat singer and actor. Introduced "Hooray for Hollywood" in *Hollywood Hotel*.

1937   Varsity Show (*Buzz Bolton*)
Hollywood Hotel (*Georgia*)
1938   Cowboy from Brooklyn (*Jeff Hardy*)
Garden of the Moon (*Slappy Harris*)
1944   You Can't Ration Love (*Kewpie*)
Knickerbocker Holiday (*Tenpin*)

Davis, Sammy, Jr., actor, singer, dancer, musician; b. New York, Dec. 8, 1925. Multi-talented entertainer who began with his father and uncle in vaudeville (the Will Mastin Trio), then became nightclub and television headliner. A flamboyant performer, Davis' film work was especially notable in *Porgy and Bess*. Bib: *Yes I Can* by Davis, Jane & Burt Boyar (1965), *Hollywood in a Suitcase* by Davis (1980).

1956   Meet Me in Las Vegas (voice only)
1959   Porgy and Bess (*Sportin' Life*)
1960   Pepe (specialty)
1964   Robin and the Seven Hoods (*Will*)
Three Penny Opera (*Street Singer*)
1966   A Man Called Adam (*Adam Johnson*)
1968   Sweet Charity (*Big Daddy*)
1978   Sammy Stops the World (*Littlechap*)
1982   Heidi's Song (voice of *Head Ratte*)
1985   That's Dancing! (narrator)

Day, Dennis (né Eugene Dennis McNulty), actor, singer; b. New York, May 21, 1917. Noted for his high tenor voice and his air of trusting innocence, Day achieved fame primarily as a regular on Jack Benny's radio and television programs.

1940   Buck Benny Rides Again (*Dennis Day*)
1942   The Powers Girl (*Dennis Day*)
1943   Sleepy Lagoon (*Lancelot Hillie*)
1944   Music in Manhattan (*Stanley*)
1948   Melody Time (voice only)
1950   I'll Get By (*Freddy Lee*)
1951   The Golden Girl (*Mart Taylor*)
1953   The Girl Next Door (*Reed Appleton*)

Day, Doris (née Doris Mary Anne von Kappelhoff), actress, singer; b. Cincinnati, April 3, 1924. Former band singer with Les Brown's orchestra who won Hollywood fame for honeyed voice, sunny smile, short blonde hair, and freckles. After a number of Warner musicals (1948–54), mostly with Gordon MacRae, Gene Nelson, and Jack Carson, Miss Day won greatest recognition in MGM's *Love Me or Leave Me*. Among songs she introduced: "It's Magic," "Secret Love," "Que Sera Sera," and "I'll Never Stop Loving You." During 60s, she was identified with series of naïve sex comedies. Bib: *Doris Day: Her Own Story* by A. E. Hotchner (1975); *Films of Doris Day* by Christopher Young (1977).

1948   Romance on the High Seas (*Georgia Garrett*)
1949   It's a Great Feeling (*Judy Adams*)
My Dream Is Yours (*Martha Gibson*)
1950   Young Man with a Horn (*Jo Jordan*)
Tea for Two (*Nanette Carter*)
West Point Story (*Jan Wilson*)
1951   Lullaby of Broadway (*Melinda Howard*)
On Moonlight Bay (*Marjorie Winfield*)
Starlift (*Doris Day*)
I'll See You in My Dreams (*Grace LeBoy Kahn*)
1952   April in Paris (*Ethel "Dynamite" Jackson*)
1953   By the Light of the Silvery Moon (*Marjorie Winfield*)
Calamity Jane (*Jane*)
1954   Lucky Me (*Candy Williams*)
Young at Heart (*Laurie Tuttle Sloane*)
1955   Love Me or Leave Me (*Ruth Etting*)
1957   The Pajama Game (*Babe Williams*)
1962   Jumbo (*Kitty Wonder*)

"Day Dreaming" Music by Harry Warren; lyric by Johnny Mercer. In *Gold Diggers in Paris* (Warner 1938) Rudy Vallee and Rosemary Lane sang of an imaginary romance they hoped would come true.

"Day You Came Along, The" Music by Arthur Johnston; lyric by Sam Coslow. Hyperbolically romantic view of the memorable occasion ("the most eventful day in history") expressed by Judith Allen in a vaudeville scene and reprised by Bing Crosby in *Too Much Har-*

mony (Par. 1933). Note that the song's title—or a variation thereof—occurs nine times in the lyric.

"Days of Wine and Roses" Music by Henry Mancini; lyric by Johnny Mercer. Lament for lost youth, sung by vocal group on soundtrack of Jack Lemmon-Lee Remick nonmusical film of same name (Warner 1962). Note that composer Mancini created his complete melody from just two nearly identical 16-bar sections, and that lyricist Mercer matched his efforts with a poignant lyric that said what was needed in exactly two sentences.

"Dear Heart" Music by Henry Mancini; lyric by Jay Livingston & Ray Evans. Waltzing theme of nonmusical *Dear Heart* (Warner 1965), expressing longing for reunion, sung by chorus on soundtrack during credits. Though the film, which starred Glenn Ford and Geraldine Page, was originally to have been called *The Out of Towners,* the title was changed to take advantage of the song's potential success.

"Dear Mister Gable" (**"You Made Me Love You"**) Music by James V. Monaco; lyric by Joseph McCarthy; revised by Roger Edens. The popular standard, "You Made Me Love You," which dates from 1913, was outfitted by Roger Edens with a new 12-bar verse and spoken patter for Judy Garland to reintroduce at a birthday party for Clark Gable. It caused such a sensation that a spot was found in *Broadway Melody of 1938* (MGM 1937) for Judy to sing it to Gable's photograph as she writes him a letter in her room.

"Dearly Beloved" Music by Jerome Kern; lyric by Johnny Mercer. Romantic entreaty introduced by Fred Astaire, backed by Xavier Cugat's orchestra, at a wedding reception in *You Were Never Lovelier* (Col. 1942). Note the striking similarity between this melody and a section of the Love Duet from Puccini's *Madama Butterfly* (first heard in the violin solo following Cio-Cio San's line, "Or son contenta").

De Haven, Gloria (Mildred), actress, singer; b. Los Angeles, July 23, 1925. Band singer (Bob Crosby, Jan Savitt) who appeared in Hollywood musicals, mostly at MGM, and introduced "The Stanley Steamer" in *Summer Holiday.* The daughter of actor Carter DeHaven, she played her own mother in *Three Little Words.* John Payne was the first of her four husbands.

1943	Best Foot Forward (*Ethel*)
	Thousands Cheer (specialty)
1944	Broadway Rhythm (*Patsy Demming*)
	Two Girls and a Sailor (*Jean Deyo*)
	Step Lively (*Christine Marlowe*)
1946	Summer Holiday (*Muriel McComber*)
1949	Yes, Sir, That's My Baby (*Sara Jane Winfield*)
1950	Three Little Words (*Mrs. Carter DeHaven*)
	Summer Stock (*Abigail Falbury*)
	I'll Get By (*Terry Martin*)
1951	Two Tickets to Broadway (*Hannah Mowbray*)
1952	Down Among the Sheltering Palms (*Angela Toland*)
1954	So This Is Paris (*Janie Mitchell*)
1955	The Girl Rush (*Taffy Tremaine*)

DeLange, (Edgar) Eddie, lyricist; b. Long Island City, NY, Jan. 12, 1904; d. Los Angeles, July 13, 1949. Became Hollywood lyricist after career as mid-30s bandleader in partnership with Will Hudson (with whom he wrote "Moonglow"). His composer collaborators included Josef Myrow, Saul Chaplin, and Louis Alter ("Do You Know What It Means To Miss New Orleans?").

1946	If I'm Lucky (Myrow)
	Meet Me on Broadway (Chaplin)
1947	New Orleans (Alter)

"Delishious" Music by George Gershwin; lyric by Ira Gershwin. Charmed by the way Scottish immigrant Janet Gaynor pronounces the song's title, writer Raul Roulien—in *Delicious* (Fox 1931)—penned a number based on the rhyming of "delishee-us," "caprishee-us," "ambishee-us," and "repetishee-us"—as well as "selecshee-on," "affecshee-on," and "connecshee-on." Also sung by Joan Leslie (with Sally Sweetland's voice) in *Rhapsody in Blue* (Warner 1945).

Del Rio, Dolores (née Lolita Dolores Asunsolo de Martinez), actress; b. Durango, Mexico, Aug. 3, 1905. Dark-eyed exotic beauty who made 25 Hollywood films between 1925 and 1967, mostly dramas. Musical highlight: dancing to "Orchids in the Moonlight" with Fred Astaire in *Flying Down to Rio.* (Died April 11, 1983.)

1933	Flying Down to Rio (*Belinha de Rezende*)
1934	Wonder Bar (*Ynez*)
1935	I Live for Love (*Donna Alvarez*)
	In Caliente (*Rita Gomez*)

Del Ruth, Roy, director; b. Philadelphia, Oct. 18, 1895; d. Sherman Oaks, Cal., April 27, 1961. After directing silent films, Del Ruth worked at Warner, UA

(*Kid Millions*), MGM (two *Broadway Melodys, Born to Dance*), and Fox (*On the Avenue*). He directed Gordon MacRae in five musicals, Doris Day and Eleanor Powell in three each; also Eddie Cantor, Maurice Chevalier, Dick Powell, Alice Faye, Sonja Henie, Bing Crosby, Nelson Eddy, and James Cagney. Del Ruth was married to actress Winnie Lightner.

1929	The Desert Song
	Gold Diggers of Broadway
1930	Hold Everything
	Life of the Party
1934	Kid Millions
1935	Folies Bergère
	Broadway Melody of 1936
	Thanks a Million
1936	Born To Dance
1937	On the Avenue
	Broadway Melody of 1938
1938	Happy Landing
	My Lucky Star
1939	The Star Maker
1941	The Chocolate Soldier
1943	DuBarry Was a Lady
1944	Broadway Rhythm
1949	Always Leave Them Laughing
1950	The West Point Story
1951	On Moonlight Bay
	Starlift
1952	About Face
1953	Three Sailors and a Girl

de Paul, Gene, composer; b. New York, June 17, 1919. Former danceband pianist whose Hollywood output was written with lyricists Don Raye ("Mister Five by Five," "I'll Remember April," and "Milkman, Keep Those Bottles Quiet") and Johnny Mercer ("When You're in Love" from de Paul's most highly regarded score, *Seven Brides for Seven Brothers*). On Broadway, dePaul and Mercer wrote the score for *Li'l Abner,* which was later filmed. Grace McDonald, Dick Foran, Nancy Walker, Jane Powell, Howard Keel, June Allyson, and Jack Lemmon were among those who introduced dePaul songs.

1941	In the Navy (Raye)
	Moonlight in Hawaii (Raye)
	Keep 'Em Flying (Raye)
	Behind the Eight Ball (Raye)
	Hellzapoppin (Raye)
1942	Ride 'Em Cowboy (Raye)
	Pardon My Sarong (Raye)

1943	Hi' Ya Chum (Raye)
	Larceny with Music (Raye)
1944	Broadway Rhythm (Raye)
1948	A Song Is Born (Raye)
1949	Ichabod and Mr. Toad (Raye)
1954	Seven Brides for Seven Brothers (Mercer)
1956	You Can't Run Away from It (Mercer)
1959	Li'l Abner (Mercer)

De Sylva, (George Gard) B. G. ("Buddy"), lyricist, producer, screenwriter; b. New York, Jan. 27, 1895; d. Los Angeles, July 11, 1950. With partners, co-lyricist Lew Brown and composer Ray Henderson, DeSylva created a series of eight youthful, fast-moving Broadway musicals between 1925 and 1930, of which *Good News* (filmed twice) and *Follow Thru* were brought to the screen with at least partially original scores. Another Broadway musical, *Take a Chance,* written with Richard A. Whiting, Nacio Herb Brown, and Vincent Youmans, was also filmed. In Hollywood, DeSylva, Brown, and Henderson collaborated on songs for Al Jolson ("Sonny Boy"), Janet Gaynor ("Sunny Side Up," "I'm a Dreamer, Aren't We All?," "If I Had a Talking Picture of You"), and Gloria Swanson. DeSylva also wrote "Wishing" for Irene Dunne in *Love Affair.* In addition to being both a lyricist and screen writer, he was also a producer, first at Fox (four musicals with Shirley Temple), then at Paramount, where he was executive producer 1939–44. In 1942 DeSylva was a co-founder of Capitol Records. Film bio: *The Best Things in Life Are Free,* with Gordon MacRae as DeSylva.

Unless otherwise noted, the following had songs written with Messrs. Brown & Henderson; one asterisk indicates he was also screenwriter & producer; two asterisks indicate he was producer only:

1928	The Singing Fool
1929	Say It with Songs
	Sunny Side Up (also script)
1930	Good News
	Follow Thru
	Just Imagine*
1931	Indiscreet*
1933	My Weakness (Whiting)*
	Take a Chance (Whiting, N. Brown; Youmans)*
1935	Under the Pampas Moon**
	The Littlest Rebel**
	Captain January**
1936	Sing, Baby, Sing**
	Poor Little Rich Girl**
1937	Merry-Go-Round of 1938**
	You're a Sweetheart**

1941 Birth of the Blues **
1943 Lady in the Dark **
1946 The Stork Club **
1947 Good News
1956 The Best Things in Life Are Free

DeWolfe, Billy (né William Andrew Jones), actor; b. Wollaston, Mass., Feb. 18, 1907; d. Los Angeles, March 5, 1974. DeWolfe was an androgynous floor-walker-type comic actor who appeared in Paramount films between 1943 and 1949. Though sporting a hairline mustache, the actor made a specialty of impersonating a soused matron, an act he also performed on stage and in nightclubs.

1943 Dixie (*Mr. Bones*)
1945 Duffy's Tavern (*Doctor*)
1946 Blue Skies (*Tony*)
1947 The Perils of Pauline (*Timmy*)
     Variety Girl (specialty)
1948 Isn't It Romantic? (*Horace Frazier*)
1950 Tea for Two (*Larry Blair*)
1951 Lullaby of Broadway (*Lefty Mack*)
1953 Call Me Madam (*Pemberton Maxwell*)

"Diamonds Are Forever" Music by John Barry; lyric by Don Black. The reasons why they'll always be a girl's best friend, caressingly revealed by Shirley Bassey on the soundtrack of James Bond film of the same name (UA 1971).

"Dickey-Bird Song, The" Music by Sammy Fain; lyric by Howard Dietz. Avian announcement of the arrival of spring, chirped by mother Jeanette MacDonald and daughters Jane Powell, Mary Eleanor Donahue (dubbed by Beverly Jean Garbo), and Ann E. Todd (Pat Hyatt) in *Three Daring Daughters* (MGM 1948).

"Did I Remember?" Music by Walter Donaldson; lyric by Harold Adamson. Sung by Jean Harlow (Virginia Verrill's voice) in cabaret scene in *Suzy* (MGM 1936), then reprised by Cary Grant—with improvised lyric—to show that he'd been listening to every word she sang. Melodically, the ballad is similar to "Fancy Our Meeting" (by Joe Meyer, Phil Charig, Ira Gershwin) introduced in London stage musical, *That's a Good Girl* (1928).

"Did You Ever See a Dream Walking?" Music by Harry Revel; lyric by Mack Gordon. Art Jarrett and Ginger Rogers sang of a romantic vision that obligingly came to life in *Sitting Pretty* (Par. 1933).

Dieterle, (Wilhelm) William, director; b. Rheinpfalz, Germany, July 15, 1893; d. Ottobrunn, W. Germany, Dec. 9, 1972. Became Hollywood director in 1926, later specialized in costume dramas including lives of Pasteur, Zola, Juarez, Ehrlich, and Reuter.

1931 Her Majesty Love
1933 Adorable
1934 Fashions of 1934
1942 Syncopation
1956 Magic Fire (Eng.)

Dietrich, (Maria Magdalene) Marlene, actress, singer; b. Berlin, Dec. 27, 1901. Along with Greta Garbo, Miss Dietrich—at least to US audiences—epitomized the exotic foreign movie star. Though this Lorelei figure, celebrated for her world-weary air, her shapely legs, and her sensuous, husky voice, never appeared in a film musical per se, a number of her movies cast her as an entertainer in locales ranging from a German beer hall (*The Blue Angel*, filmed in Berlin in both German and English), to a North African cabaret (*Morocco*), to New York and Paris nightclubs (*Blonde Venus*), to a Western saloon (*Destry Rides Again*), to a South Seas honkytonk (*Seven Sinners*). Except for *Song of Songs,* all of Miss Dietrich's films through 1935 were directed by her mentor, Josef von Sternberg. "Falling in Love Again" was the song most closely identified with her, though she also had success with "The Boys in the Backroom," "I've Been in Love Before," and "Golden Earrings." Bib: *Dietrich* by Leslie Frewin (1967); *Films of Marlene Dietrich* by Homer Dickens (1968); *Marlene Dietrich* by Sheridan Morley (1977); *Marlene* by Charles Higham (1977).

1930 The Blue Angel (*Lola-Lola Frohlich*)
     Morocco (*Amy Jolly*)
1932 Blonde Venus (*Helen Faraday*)
1933 Song of Songs (*Lily Czepanek*)
1939 Destry Rides Again (*Frenchy*)
1940 Seven Sinners (*Bijou*)
1944 Follow the Boys (specialty)
1948 A Foreign Affair (*Erika von Schlütow*)

Dietz, Howard, lyricist; b. New York, Sept. 8, 1896. For over 30 years Dietz was MGM's chief of advertising and publicity while at the same time—mostly in collaboration with composer Arthur Schwartz—pursuing a career as Broadway lyricist. The team's songs for the 1931 revue *The Band Wagon* provided the basis for the scores for two films, *Dancing in the Dark* and *The Band Wagon* (which also contained "That's Entertainment"). Bib:

Dancing in the Dark by Dietz (1974). (Died New York, July 30, 1983.)

1934	Hollywood Party (prod., script)
1936	Under Your Spell (Schwartz)
1949	Dancing in the Dark (Schwartz)
1953	The Band Wagon (Schwartz)

"Ding-Dong! The Witch Is Dead" Music by Harold Arlen; lyric by E. Y. Harburg. Joyously sung by the Munchkins in *The Wizard of Oz* (MGM 1939) upon the accidental death of the Wicked Witch of the North.

Disney, (Walter Elias) Walt, producer; b. Chicago, Dec. 5, 1901; d. Burbank, Dec. 15, 1966. Pioneering legendary leader in the field of film animation who began his Mickey Mouse cartoon shorts in 1928. Nine years later, he created the first full-length cartoon, *Snow White and the Seven Dwarfs,* and through subsequent animated and live-action features continued to offer a world of imagination and adventure that always had a special appeal to the young. Bib: *The Disney Story* by Diane Disney Miller (his daughter) (1957); *The Disney Version* by Richard Schickel (1968); *The Art of Walt Disney* by Christopher Finch (1973); *Walt Disney: An American Original* by Bob Thomas (1976); *The Disney Films* by Leonard Malten (1978).

1934	Hollywood Party (cartoon sequence, voice of *Mickey Mouse* only)
1937	Snow White and the Seven Dwarfs
1940	Pinocchio
	Fantasia
1941	The Reluctant Dragon (also in film)
	Dumbo
1942	Bambi
1943	Saludos Amigos
1945	The Three Caballeros
1946	Make Mine Music
	Song of the South
1947	Fun and Fancy Free
1948	Melody Time
	So Dear to My Heart
1949	Ichabod and Mr. Toad
1950	Cinderella
1951	Alice in Wonderland
1953	Peter Pan
1955	The Lady and the Tramp
1956	Davy Crockett and the River Pirates
	Westward Ho the Wagons
1957	Perri
1959	Sleeping Beauty
1961	One Hundred and One Dalmatians
	The Parent Trap

	Babes in Toyland
1962	In Search of the Castaways
1963	Summer Magic
	The Sword in the Stone
1964	Mary Poppins
1967	The Jungle Book
	The Happiest Millionaire

"Dissertation on the State of Bliss" (**"Love and Learn Blues"**). Music by Harold Arlen; lyric by Ira Gershwin. Philosophical view of the ambivalence of love, sung at a bar by Jacqueline Fontaine in *The Country Girl* (Par. 1954), joined in by a tipsy Bing Crosby. Though the title of the song does not appear in the lyric, it was used because three previous songs had been called "Love and Learn."

Dixon, Lee, actor, dancer; b. Brooklyn, Jan. 22, 1914; d. New York, Jan. 8, 1953. Gangly, curly-haired dancing actor who appeared in Warner musicals; later created role of Will Parker in Broadway musical *Oklahoma!*.

1936	Gold Diggers of 1937 (*Boop Oglethorpe*)
1937	Ready, Willing and Able (*Pinky Blair*)
	The Singing Marine (*Slim Baxter*)
	Varsity Show (*Johnny "Rubberlegs" Stevens*)

Dixon, Mort, lyricist; b. New York, March 20, 1892; d. Bronxville, March 23, 1956. Warner contractee who collaborated with composer Allie Wrubel and is best remembered for "Flirtation Walk" and "The Lady in Red." His songs were introduced by Dick Powell, Wini Shaw, Everett Marshall, Dolores Del Rio.

1934	Flirtation Walk
	Happiness Ahead
1935	Broadway Hostess
	I Live for Love
	In Caliente

"Do I Love You Because You're Beautiful?" Music by Richard Rodgers; lyric by Oscar Hammerstein II. Or are you beautiful because I love you? Philosophical query posed by Prince Charming Jon Cypher and Julie Andrews in television production, *Cinderella* (CBS 1957). Also sung by Stuart Damon in remake (1965). In his book, *Musical Stages,* Rodgers wrote that the line, "Am I making believe I see in you?," bothered Hammerstein because he had once written a song called "Make Believe" and also because he wanted a stronger expression. But since the composer remained unconvinced that substituting "telling my heart" for "making believe" would make any appreciable difference, the phrase remained as originally written.

"Do You Know What It Means To Miss New Orleans?" Music by Louis Alter; lyric by Eddie De-Lange. Warmly insinuating tribute, introduced by Billie Holiday and Louis Armstrong in *New Orleans* (UA 1947).

"Doin' the Uptown Lowdown" Music by Harry Revel; lyric by Mack Gordon. Sung by Frances Williams in nightclub sequence in *Broadway Thru a Keyhole* (UA 1933). The song, which was somewhat in the style of Irving Berlin's "Puttin' on the Ritz," was concerned with a new dance craze that was making Harlem a popular tourist attraction ("Bankers with their Cinderelatives/ Listening to those hot high yallertives").

"Dolores" Music by Louis Alter; lyric by Frank Loesser. "Not Marie or Emily or Doris," sang Bert Wheeler in *Las Vegas Nights* (Par. 1941), only his Dolores was the girl for him. Tommy Dorsey's orchestra provided the accompaniment.

Donaldson, Walter, composer; b. Brooklyn, Feb. 15, 1893; d. Santa Monica, July 15, 1947. Prolific pop composer whose Broadway musical *Whoopee* was transferred to the screen, and whose Hollywood output included such songs as "My Baby Just Cares for Me," "You," "You Never Looked So Beautiful Before," and "Did I Remember?" Gus Kahn and Harold Adamson were his lyric-writing partners.

1930   Whoopee (Kahn)
1934   Kid Millions (Kahn)
        Operator 13 (Kahn)
1936   The Great Ziegfeld (Adamson)

Donen, Stanley, director, choreographer, producer; b. Columbia, SC April 13, 1924. Broadway dancer who went to Hollywood as protégé of Gene Kelly, whom he assisted as choreographer in Columbia's *Cover Girl,* and with whom he was associated at MGM on *Anchors Aweigh, Take Me Out to the Ball Game, On the Town, Singin' in the Rain, It's Always Fair Weather.* On his own as director, Donen won recognition for *Royal Wedding, Seven Brides for Seven Brothers,* and *Funny Face.* Donen has also worked with Frank Sinatra, Esther Williams, Fred Astaire, Jane Powell, Donald O'Connor, Debbie Reynolds, Howard Keel, Dan Dailey, Cyd Charisse, Audrey Hepburn, and Doris Day. Also directed nonmusicals, including *Charade.*

Unless otherwise noted, Mr. Donen was choreographer or co-choreographer of the following; asterisk indicates he was director but not choreographer:

1943   Best Foot Forward (dancer) (asst. chor.)
1944   Cover Girl (asst. chor.)
        Jam Session
        Kansas City Kitty
        Hey, Rookie
1945   Anchors Aweigh
1946   Holiday in Mexico
        No Leave, No Love
1947   Living in a Big Way
        This Time for Keeps
1948   Big City
        A Date with Judy
        The Kissing Bandit
1949   Take Me Out to the Ball Game (also script)
        On the Town (also co-dir.)
1951   Royal Wedding*
1952   Singin' in the Rain (also co-dir.)
1953   Give a Girl a Break (also dir.)
1954   Seven Brides for Seven Brothers*
        Deep in My Heart*
1955   It's Always Fair Weather (also co-dir.)
1957   Funny Face*
        The Pajama Game* (also co-prod.)
1958   Damn Yankees* (also co-prod.)
1973   The Little Prince* (also prod.)
1978   Movie Movie* (also prod.)

"Donkey Serenade, The" Music by Rudolf Friml & Herbert Stothart; lyric by Robert Wright & George Forrest. Timing the music to the hoofbeats of a team of donkeys in *The Firefly* (MGM 1937), Allan Jones, Robert Spindola, and guitarist Manuel Alvarez Maciste serenaded Jeanette MacDonald as she rode in a coach over the Spanish mountains. The song is actually two musical pieces put together. The main flowing theme had been written by Friml in 1920 as a piano-teaching piece called "Chanson"; later, with a lyric by Sigmund Spaeth, Dailey Paskman, and Irving Caesar, it became known as "Chansonette." The second theme, the one with the clip-clop rhythm, was composed by Stothart specifically for the film. The music was also played by pianist José Iturbi in *Anchors Aweigh* (MGM 1945), and sung by Dean Martin and Jerry Lewis in *My Friend Irma* (Par. 1949).

Donohue, (John Francis) Jack, choreographer, director; b. New York, Nov. 3, 1908. Staged dances at Fox (four films with Shirley Temple), Paramount, MGM (five with Esther Williams), and Warner. Began directing nonmusicals in 1950. (Died Cal., March 27, 1984.)

1934	George White's Scandals
	Music in the Air
1935	Under Pressure
	Lottery Lover
	The Little Colonel
	Curly Top
	Under the Pampas Moon
	Music Is Magic
	Thanks a Million
	The Littlest Rebel
1936	Captain January
1937	You're in the Army Now (Eng.)
1941	Louisiana Purchase
1942	The Fleet's In
	The Powers Girl
1943	Best Foot Forward
	Girl Crazy
1944	Broadway Rhythm
	Bathing Beauty
	Lost in a Harem
1946	Two Sisters from Boston
	Easy To Wed
1947	It Happened in Brooklyn
	On an Island with You
1949	Neptune's Daughter
1950	The Duchess of Idaho
1953	Calamity Jane
1954	Top Banana
	Lucky Me (also dir.)
1961	Babes in Toyland (also dir.)

"Don't Fence Me In" Music by Cole Porter; lyric by Porter & Robert Fletcher (uncredited). The original version of this loping tribute to the unfettered life was a poem written by a Montana miner, engineer, and historian named Robert Fletcher. After purchasing the rights to it for $150 in the mid-30s, Porter used only the title and a couple of phrases in creating the song, originally intended for a Fox film, *Adios Argentina,* which was never made. Somehow the song found its way to Warner, where it was first intended as a theme for the screen bio of Will Rogers but it wasn't used. Eventually, Roy Rogers and the Sons of the Pioneers introduced it in Warner's *Hollywood Canteen* (1944), in which it was reprised by the Andrews Sisters. Rogers also sang it in *Don't Fence Me In* (Republic 1945).

"Don't Give Up the Ship" Music by Harry Warren; lyric by Al Dubin. Stirring tribute to the US Navy sung by Dick Powell and cadets in *Shipmates Forever* (War-

ner 1935). The song, now an official anthem of the US Naval Academy, was the precursor of the Warren-Dubin "Song of the Marines," sung by Powell in *The Singing Marine* (Warner 1937).

"Don't Let the Moon Get Away" Music by James V. Monaco; lyric by Johnny Burke. Called on to entertain at a roadside nightclub in *Sing You Sinners* (Par. 1938), Bing Crosby obliged with this jaunty appeal for instant romantic gratification.

"Don't Say Goodnight" Music by Harry Warren; lyric by Al Dubin. A waltzing successor to the same writers' "Shadow Waltz" (in Warner's *Gold Diggers of 1933*), the song was introduced by Dick Powell in *Wonder Bar* (Warner 1934). In this one, Busby Berkeley had the swirling girls reflected in huge mirrors.

Dorsey, (James) Jimmy, bandleader, saxophonist, actor; b. Shenandoah, Pa., Feb. 29, 1904; d. New York, June 12, 1957. A leading figure of the swing band era, Dorsey began career fronting an orchestra with his brother, Tommy. Won success on his own after forming own band; made many recordings. Introduced "I Remember You" and "Tangerine" in *The Fleet's In.* Film bio: *The Fabulous Dorseys,* with Dorsey as himself. Bib: *The Dorsey Years* by Herb Sanford (1980).

1941	Lady, Be Good
1942	The Fleet's In
1943	I Dood It
1944	Four Jills in a Jeep
	Lost in a Harem
	Hollywood Canteen
1947	The Fabulous Dorseys (*Jimmy Dorsey*)
1948	Music Man (*Jimmy Dorsey*)
1949	Make Believe Ballroom

Dorsey, (Thomas) Tommy, bandleader, trombonist, actor; b. Shenandoah, Pa., Nov. 19, 1905; d. Greenwich, Conn., Nov. 26, 1956. A leading figure of the swing band era, Dorsey began career fronting an orchestra with his brother, Jimmy. Won success on his own after forming own band; made many recordings. Introduced "Dolores" in *Las Vegas Nights.* Film bio: *The Fabulous Dorseys,* with Dorsey as himself. Bib: *The Dorsey Years* by Herb Sanford (1980).

1941	Las Vegas Nights
1942	Ships Ahoy
1943	Presenting Lily Mars
	DuBarry Was a Lady

Girl Crazy
Swing Fever
1944 Broadway Rhythm
1945 The Thrill of a Romance
1947 The Fabulous Dorseys (*Tommy Dorsey*)
1948 A Song Is Born
1951 Disc Jockey

"Double Trouble" Music by Ralph Rainger & Richard A. Whiting; lyric by Leo Robin. Romantic dilemma of "trying to be true to two," confessed by Lyda Roberti, Jack Oakie, Henry Wadsworth, and chorus in *Big Broadcast of 1936* (Par. 1935).

"Down Argentina Way" Music by Harry Warren; lyric by Mack Gordon. Panegyric to the South American country ("I'll bet an old castanet/ That you can never forget Argentina") introduced in a New York nightclub in *Down Argentine Way* (Fox 1940). In the scene, Don Ameche soulfully sings it in Spanish to Betty Grable who then reprises it as a hip-swiveling song-and-dance number. Note that the name of the country is a noun in the song title and an adjective in the film title.

"Down by the River" Music by Richard Rodgers; lyric by Lorenz Hart. Bing Crosby sang this littoral love song in *Mississippi* (Par. 1935) as he pledged a love as deep and as lasting as the river.

"Down the Old Ox Road" Music by Arthur Johnston; lyric by Sam Coslow. Despite its seeming innocence, the lyric reveals that taking a girl down the Old Ox Road means more than a stroll ("This old tradition's not a place but just a proposition"). Introduced by Professor Bing Crosby and smooching collegians, including Jack Oakie and Mary Kornman, in *College Humor* (Par. 1933).

Downs, Johnny, actor, dancer; b. Brooklyn, Oct. 10, 1913. Joe College-type who breezed and tapped his way through low-budget musicals, mostly at Republic and Universal. Acted opposite Eleanore Whitney in four pictures, Jane Frazee in three.

1934 Babes in Toyland (bit)
1935 Coronado (*Johnny Marvin*)
1936 The First Baby (*Johnny Ellis*)
     Pigskin Parade (*Chip Carson*)
     College Holiday (*Johnny Jones*)
1937 Turn Off the Moon (*Terry Keith*)

Thrill of a Lifetime (*Stanley*)
Blonde Trouble (*Fred Stevens*)
1938 Hold That Coed (*Dink*)
     Swing, Sister, Swing (*Johnny Bennett*)
1939 Hawaiian Nights (*Ted Hartley*)
     Laugh It Off (*Steve Hannis*)
1940 I Can't Give You Anything but Love (*Bob Gunther*)
     Sing, Dance, Plenty Hot (*Johnny*)
     Slightly Tempted (*Jimmy Duncan*)
     Melody and Moonlight (*Danny O'Brien*)
1941 Redhead (*Ted Brown*)
     Moonlight in Hawaii (*Pete*)
     Sing Another Chorus (*Andy Peyton*)
     All American Coed (*Bob Sheppard*)
     Behind the Eight Ball (*Danny*)
1943 Harvest Melody (*Tommy*)
     Campus Rhythm (*Scoop*)
1944 Trocadero (*Johnny*)
     Twilight on the Prairie
1945 Rhapsody in Blue (*dancer*)
1946 The Kid from Brooklyn (*M. C.*)
1953 Call Me Madam (*cameraman*)
     Cruisin' Down the River (*Thad Jackson*)
     Here Come the Girls (*Bob*)

Drake, Dona (née Rita Novello), actress, singer, dancer; b. Mexico City, 1920. Bouncy, button-cute second lead of wartime Paramount musicals, known as Rita Rio in 1930s.

1936 Strike Me Pink (*dancer*)
1941 Louisiana Purchase (*Beatrice*)
1942 Road to Morocco (*Mihirmah*)
     Star-Spangled Rhythm (*specialty*)
1943 Let's Face It (*Muriel*)
     Salute for Three (*Dona*)
1944 Hot Rhythm (*Mary*)

"Dream Lover" Music by Victor Schertzinger; lyric by Clifford Grey. In her royal bedchamber in *The Love Parade* (Par. 1929), Queen Louise (Jeanette MacDonald) awakens and sings of the imaginary sweetheart she's just dreamed about. Virginia Bruce was among her ladies in waiting.

"Dreamer, The" Music by Arthur Schwartz; lyric by Frank Loesser. In *Thank Your Lucky Stars* (Warner 1943) lethargic farmgirl Dinah Shore (in a charity revue) yearns for her lover who has gone away to serve and pledges that she will "stay a dreamer till he's home once more." Number later reprised in show as a scat-sung version by jitterbugging Olivia DeHavilland, George Tobias, and Ida Lupino.

"Dreaming Out Loud" Music & lyric by Sam Coslow. Frances Langford with matrimony on her mind in *Dreaming Out Loud* (RKO 1940).

Dubin, Al, lyricist; b. Zurich, June 10, 1891; d. New York, Feb. 11, 1945. In partnership with composer Harry Warren, Dubin supplied songs for the bulk of Warner musicals during the 1930s, including *42nd Street, Footlight Parade,* and four *Gold Diggers* movies. Among their songs: "Forty-Second Street," "Shuffle Off to Buffalo," "You're Getting To Be a Habit with Me," "Young and Healthy," "Shadow Waltz," "We're in the Money," "Honeymoon Hotel," "Keep Young and Beautiful," "The Boulevard of Broken Dreams," "I Only Have Eyes for You," "Fair and Warmer," "About a Quarter to Nine," "She's a Latin from Manhattan," "Don't Give Up the Ship," "Lullaby of Broadway," "September in the Rain," "The Words Are in My Heart," "All's Fair in Love and War," "With Plenty of Money and You," "Am I in Love?," " 'Cause My Baby Says It's So," "Remember Me," "Song of the Marines." Prior to working with Warren, Dubin collaborated with composer Joe Burke ("Painting the Clouds with Sunshine" and "Tip Toe Through the Tulips," both from *Gold Diggers of Broadway*); other partners were Walter Jurmann and James V. Monaco. Dubin's songs were introduced by such singers as Dick Powell, Eddie Cantor, Al Jolson, Wini Shaw, James Melton, Kenny Baker, Rudy Vallee, and John Payne.

1929 Gold Diggers of Broadway (Burke)
      Sally (Burke)
1930 She Couldn't Say No (Burke)
      Hold Everything (Burke)
      Top Speed (Burke)
      Life of the Party (Burke)
      Oh, Sailor Behave (Burke)
1931 Her Majesty Love (Jurmann)
1933 42nd Street (Warren) (also *songwriter*)
      Gold Diggers of 1933 (Warren)
      Footlight Parade (Warren)
      Roman Scandals (Warren)
1934 Moulin Rouge (Warren)
      Wonder Bar (Warren)
      Twenty Million Sweethearts (Warren)
      Dames (Warren)
1935 Gold Diggers of 1935 (Warren)
      Go Into Your Dance (Warren)
      Broadway Gondolier (Warren)
      Shipmates Forever (Warren)
      Stars Over Broadway (Warren)

1936 Colleen (Warren)
      Hearts Divided (Warren)
      Cain and Mabel (Warren)
      Gold Diggers of 1937 (Warren)
      Sing Me a Love Song (Warren)
1937 Melody for Two (Warren)
      Mr. Dodd Takes the Air (Warren)
      The Singing Marine (Warren)
1938 Gold Diggers in Paris (Warren)
      Garden of the Moon (Warren)
1943 Stage Door Canteen (Monaco)

Duchin, (Edwin Frank) Eddy, bandleader, pianist; b. Boston, April 1, 1909; d. New York, Feb. 9, 1951. Slim, dapper society bandleader-pianist who appeared with his orchestra in two films, and was the subject of film bio, *The Eddy Duchin Story* (Col. 1956), with Tyrone Power as Duchin and Carmen Cavallero dubbing his piano.

1935 Coronado
1937 Hit Parade of 1937

Duke, Vernon (né Vladimir Dukelsky), composer; b. Parafianovo, Russia, Oct. 10, 1903; d. Santa Monica, Jan. 16, 1969. Broadway composer with classical background who completed George Gershwin's score for *The Goldwyn Follies*. His only stage musical transferred to the screen was *Cabin in the Sky,* written with John Latouche; in Hollywood he collaborated with lyricists Ira Gershwin and Sammy Cahn. Kenny Baker, Ethel Waters, Lena Horne, Gene Nelson, Doris Day, and Ray Bolger sang Duke's songs on the screen. Bib: *Passport to Paris* by Duke (1955).

1938 The Goldwyn Follies (Gershwin)
1943 Cabin in the Sky (Latouche)
1952 She's Working Her Way Through College (Cahn)
      April in Paris (Cahn)

Duna, Steffi (née Stephanie Berindey), actress, dancer; b. Budapest, 1913. Ballet dancer with the Budapest Opera who became identified as a Hollywood Latin. Danced in first three-color Technicolor film, *La Cucaracha* (short); also played dramatic roles.

1936 Hi, Gaucho (*Inez de Alvarez*)
      Dancing Pirate (*Serafina*)
1938 Rascals (*Stella*)
1939 Way Down South (*Pauline*)
1940 The Girl from Havana (*Chita*)

Dunbar, (Christina Elizabeth) Dixie, actress, dancer; b. Montgomery, Ala., Jan. 19, 1919. Pert, peppy, tappy performer with Broadway and nightclub experience who appeared in Fox musicals. Retired at 19.

1934 George White's Scandals (*Patsy Day*)
1935 King of Burlesque (*Marie*)
1936 The First Baby (*Maude Holbrook*)
     Sing, Baby, Sing (*telephone operator*)
     Pigskin Parade (*Ginger Jones*)
     One in a Million (*Goldie*)
1937 Sing and Be Happy (*Della Dunn*)
     Life Begins in College (*Polly*)
1938 Rebecca of Sunnybrook Farm (*receptionist*)
     Alexander's Ragtime Band (specialty)
     Walking Down Broadway (*Tiny Bronson*)
     The Freshman Year (*Dotty*)

Dunn, James (Howard), actor; b. New York, Nov. 2, 1905; d. Santa Monica, Sept. 3, 1967. Affable, round-faced actor who appeared with Sally Eilers, Shirley Temple, and Claire Trevor in Fox nonmusicals as well as musicals. Remembered for dramatic role in *A Tree Grows in Brooklyn*.

1932 Dance Team (*Jimmy Mulligan*)
1933 Jimmy and Sally (*Jimmy O'Connor*)
     Take a Chance (*Duke Stanley*)
1934 Stand Up and Cheer (*Jimmy Dugan*)
     Baby, Take a Bow (*Eddie Ellison*)
     365 Nights in Hollywood (*Jimmy Dale*)
     Bright Eyes (*Loop*)
1935 George White's Scandals (*Eddie Taylor*)

Dunne, Irene (Marie), actress, singer; b. Louisville, Dec. 20, 1901. Patrician star of musicals (*Roberta, Show Boat, High, Wide and Handsome*), dramas (*Back Street, Love Affair*), and comedies (*The Awful Truth*) who appeared in 40 films before her retirement in 1952. Introduced "Lovely To Look At," "The Folks Who Live on the Hill," "Can I Forget You?," and "Wishing." Miss Dunne began her career on the Broadway musical stage; her appearance in the touring *Show Boat* won her a Hollywood contract.

1930 Leathernecking (*Daphne Witherspoon*)
1935 Sweet Adeline (*Addie Schmidt*)
     Roberta (*Princess Stephanie*)
1936 Show Boat (*Magnolia Hawks Ravenal*)
1937 High, Wide and Handsome (*Sally Watterson Cortlandt*)
1938 Joy of Living (*Maggie Garret*)
1939 Love Affair (*Terry McKay*)
1950 Never a Dull Moment (*Kay Kingsley*)

Durante, (James Francis) Jimmy, actor; b. New York, Feb. 10, 1893; d. Santa Monica, Jan. 29, 1980.

Endearingly raucous clown whose "schnozzola," gravel voice, and stiff-kneed strut made him one of the screen's most engaging personalities. Originally in vaudeville, then Broadway musicals (including *Jumbo, Red, Hot and Blue!*), Durante proved particularly durable in films, with some of his best work in MGM musicals between 1944 and 1948. Also appeared in successful television series and in nightclubs. Bib: *Schnozzola* by Gene Fowler (1951).

1930 Roadhouse Nights (*Daffy*)
1931 The Cuban Love Song (*O. O. Jones*)
1932 Blondie of the Follies (*Jimmy*)
     The Phantom President (*Curly Cooney*)
1933 Broadway to Hollywood (*Hollywood Character*)
1934 Palooka (*Knobby Walsh*)
     George White's Scandals (*Happy Donnelly*)
     Hollywood Party (*Jimmy*)
     Strictly Dynamite (*Moxie Slaight*)
     Student Tour (*Hank*)
1936 Land Without Music (Eng.) (*Jonah J. Whistler*)
1938 Start Cheering (*Willie Gumbatz*)
     Sally, Irene and Mary (*Jefferson Twitchell*)
     Little Miss Broadway (*Jimmy Clayton*)
1940 Melody Ranch (*Cornelius J. Courtney*)
1944 Two Girls and a Sailor (*Billy Kipp*)
     Music for Millions (*Andrews*)
1945 Two Sisters from Boston (*Spike*)
1947 It Happened in Brooklyn (*Nick Lombardi*)
     This Time for Keeps (*Ferdi Farro*)
1948 On an Island with You (*Buckley*)
1950 The Great Rupert (*Amendola*)
     The Milkman (*Breezy Albright*)
1957 Beau James (*Jimmy Durante*)
1960 Pepe (guest bit)
1962 Jumbo (*Pop Wonder*)
1966 Alice Through the Looking Glass (tv) (*Humpty Dumpty*)

Durbin, (Edna Mae) Deanna, actress, singer; b. Winnipeg, Canada, Dec. 4, 1921. Discovered by Universal producer Joe Pasternak (who was in charge of nine of her films), Miss Durbin sang with a classically trained voice and projected an effusive personality through a series of Singing-Miss-Fixit roles. Winning stardom after her first movie, she was heard in such pieces as "Someone To Care for Me," "Can't Help Singing," "More and More," and "Spring Will Be a Little Late This Year" (in her major dramatic film, *Christmas Holiday*), as well as operatic and concert arias. Miss Durbin retired in 1948.

1936 Three Smart Girls (*Penny Craig*)
1937 One Hundred Men and a Girl (*Patricia Cardwell*)

1938 Mad About Music (*Gloria Harkinson*)
That Certain Age (*Alice Fullerton*)
1939 Three Smart Girls Grow Up (*Penny Craig*)
First Love (*Connie Harding*)
1940 It's a Date (*Pamela Drake*)
Spring Parade (*Ilonka Tolnay*)
1941 Nice Girl? (*Jane Dana*)
It Started with Eve (*Anne Terry*)
1943 The Amazing Mrs. Holliday (*Ruth Holliday*)
Hers to Hold (*Penny Craig*)
His Butler's Sister (*Ann Carter*)
1944 Can't Help Singing (*Caroline Frost*)
1945 Lady on a Train (*Nicki*)
1946 Because of Him (*Kim Walker*)
1947 I'll Be Yours (*Louise Ginglebusher*)
Something in the Wind (*Mary Collins*)
1948 Up in Central Park (*Rosie Moore*)
For the Love of Mary (*Mary Peppertree*)

Dvorak, Ann (née Ann McKim), actress, dancer; b. New York, Aug. 2, 1911; d. Honolulu, Dec. 10, 1979. Dark-haired, wide-eyed, intense actress who often played hard-luck dames (*Scarface, Three on a Match*) in over 60 films between 1929 and 1951. In musicals, she appeared opposite Dick Powell, Maurice Chevalier, Rudy Vallee, and Phil Regan.

1929 Hollywood Revue of 1929 (chorus)
1930 Lord Byron of Broadway (chorus)
1932 The Crooner (*Judy*)
1933 College Coach (*Claire Gore*)
The Way to Love (*Madeleine*)
1935 Sweet Music (*Bonnie Haydon*)

Bright Lights (*Fay Wilson*)
Thanks a Million (*Sally Mason*)
1937 Manhattan Merry-Go-Round (*Ann Rogers*)
1945 Flame of the Barbary Coast (*Flaxen Tarry*)
Masquerade in Mexico (*Helen Grant*)
1946 Abilene Town ((*Rita*)
The Bachelor's Daughters (*Terry*)

Dwan, (Joseph Aloysius) Allan, director, producer; b. Toronto, April 3, 1885. Versatile director who began his career in 1911 and ended it 47 years later. Most of his films through 1941 were made at Fox; among musical stars he directed were Gloria Swanson, Jimmy Durante, Shirley Temple, Don Ameche, the Ritz Brothers, Jack Oakie, Kay Kyser, and Nelson Eddy. Bib: *Allan Dwan* by Peter Bogdanovich (1971). (Died Woodland Hills, Cal., Dec. 21, 1981.)

Asterisk indicates Mr. Dwan was also producer or associate producer:
1930 What a Widow! *
1934 Hollywood Party (uncredited)
1936 Song and Dance Man
1938 Rebecca of Sunnybrook Farm
Josette
1939 The Three Musketeers
1940 Young People
1941 Rise and Shine
1942 Here We Go Again *
1943 Around the World *
1947 Calendar Girl *
Northwest Outpost *
1952 I Dream of Jeanie
1953 Sweethearts on Parade *

E

"Earful of Music, An" Music by Walter Donaldson; lyric by Gus Kahn. Listening to music plus dancing with one's beloved equal total bliss. Number introduced by Ethel Merman as a saleswoman in a music store at the beginning of *Kid Millions* (Goldwyn 1934).

"East Side of Heaven" Music by James V. Monaco; lyric by Johnny Burke. Ballad in anticipation of a nocturnal rooftop rendezvous with a poor but devoted angel who lives in a New York tenement. Introduced by Bing Crosby in film of same name (Univ. 1939).

Easter Parade (1948). Music & lyrics by Irving Berlin; screenplay by Sidney Sheldon, Frances Goodrich, and Albert Hackett from story by Goodrich & Hackett.

An MGM film produced by Arthur Freed; directed by Charles Walters; associate producer, Roger Edens; choreography, Fred Astaire, Robert Alton, Walters; art directors, Cedric Gibbons, Jack Martin Smith; costumes, Irene, Valles; music director, Johnny Green; orchestrations, Conrad Salinger, Mason Van Cleave, Leo Arnaud; vocal arrangements, Robert Tucker; music supervisor, Edens; cameraman, Harry Stradling; editor, Albert Akst; Technicolor.

Cast: Judy Garland (*Hannah Brown*); Fred Astaire (*Don Hewes*); Peter Lawford (*Johnny Harrow*); Ann Miller (*Nadine Hale*): Jules Munshin (*François*); Clinton Sundberg (*Mike*); Richard Beavers (*singer*); Benay Venuta (*bar patron*).

Songs: "Happy Easter" - Astaire/ "Drum Crazy" - Astaire/ "It Only Happens When I Dance with You" - Astaire; dance by Astaire, Miller; reprised by Garland/ "Everybody's Doin' It" - chorus/ "I Want To Go Back to Michigan" - Garland/ "Beautiful Faces Need Beautiful Clothes" - dance by Astaire, Garland/ "A Fella with an Umbrella" - Lawford, Garland/ "I Love a Piano" - Garland; dance by Astaire, Garland/ "Snooky Ookums" - Astaire, Garland/ "Ragtime Violin" - Astaire; dance by Astaire, Garland/ "When the Midnight Choo-Choo Leaves for Alabam' " - Astaire, Garland/ "Shaking the Blues Away" - Miller/ "Steppin' Out with My Baby" -Astaire, chorus/ "A Couple of Swells" - Astaire, Garland/ "The Girl on the Magazine Cover" - Beavers/ "Better Luck Next Time" - Garland/ "Easter Parade" - Garland, Astaire. Unused: "I Love You—You Love Him," "Mr. Monotony," "Let's Take an Old-Fashioned Walk," "A Pretty Girl Is Like a Melody."

With a generous array of Irving Berlin songs (10 old, 7 new), *Easter Parade* was originally planned to capitalize on the successful teaming of Gene Kelly with Judy Garland in *The Pirate*. Kelly, however, broke his ankle soon after rehearsals began, and Fred Astaire, who had been in semi-retirement since *Blue Skies,* was glad to take over the assignment. Another accident, Cyd Charisse's, was responsible for Ann Miller getting the second female lead in the picture. The story, something of a variation on the Kelly-Garland *For Me and My Gal,* was concerned with what happens when dancing star Astaire teams with unknown Garland after regular partner Miller has left him to star in the *Ziegfeld Follies* (actually no performer was ever "starred" in a *Follies*). The new team has professional problems when Fred tries to turn Judy into a replica of Ann and personal problems when Judy suspects Fred of still being in love with her. The plot, of course, served mainly to accommodate the bountiful songs and dances, including such memorable moments as the ragtime numbers performed by Astaire and Garland, Astaire's slow-motion dance to "Steppin' Out with My Baby," the team's mischievous "Couple of Swells" routine, and Garland's torchy "Better Luck Next Time." The film covered the period from the day before Easter Sunday 1912 to Easter Sunday 1913, when Fred and Judy, arm in arm, take the traditional stroll down New York's Fifth Avenue.

"Easy To Love" Music & lyric by Cole Porter. During a nocturnal stroll in New York's Central Park, James Stewart—in *Born To Dance* (MGM 1936)—breaks into song to reveal to Eleanor Powell exactly how he feels about her. After Eleanor reveals how she feels about Jimmy, she performs a billowy, high-kicking dance all around a statue as her beau conducts an imaginary orchestra with a stick. A passing policeman (Reginald Gardiner), unimpressed with Stewart's musical ability, takes another stick and gives a vivid demonstration of how a real maestro whips his musicians into a symphonic frenzy. Later, during a rehearsal of a Broadway-bound revue, the song is reprised by Frances Langford and danced to by Buddy Ebsen. The composer originally wrote the song for William Gaxton to sing in the Broadway musical *Anything Goes* (1934), but it was dropped in favor of "All Through the Night." "Easy To Love" was also sung in *Night and Day* (Warner 1946) and by Tony Martin in *Easy To Love* (MGM 1953).

Ebb, Fred. *See* **Kander and Ebb.**

"Ebony Rhapsody" Music by Arthur Johnston; lyric by Sam Coslow. A production number in *Murder at the Vanities* (Par. 1934) opened with an old-fashioned prelude sung by Carl Brisson and Kitty Carlisle, then changed pace with an updated, syncopated variation on Liszt's Second Hungarian Rhapsody featuring Gertrude Michael and Duke Ellington's orchestra.

Ebsen, (Christian Rudolf) Buddy, actor, dancer; b. Belleville, Ill., April 2, 1908. Gangly, contortionistic dancer with aw-shucks personality who was spotlighted in two *Broadway Melody* movies (the first with his sister Vilma) and *Born To Dance*. Later won acclaim in nonmusical *Breakfast at Tiffany's* and fame in two television series, *Beverly Hillbillies* and *Barnaby Jones*. Ebsen also danced in Broadway revues and musical comedies.

1935	Broadway Melody of 1936 (*Ted Burke*)
1936	Captain January (*Paul Roberts*)
	Born To Dance (*Mush Tracy*)
	Banjo on My Knee (*Buddy*)
1937	Broadway Melody of 1938 (*Peter Trot*)
1938	Girl of the Golden West (*Alabama*)
	My Lucky Star (*Buddy*)
1941	They Met in Argentina (*Duke*)

1942	Sing Your Worries Away (*Tommy Jones*)
1954	Red Garters (*Ginger Pete*)
1968	The One and Only Genuine Original Family Band (*Papa Bowers*)

Eddy, Nelson, actor, singer; b. Providence, RI, June 29, 1901; d. Miami Beach, March 6, 1967. With his wavy blond hair, slightly flabby face, and assorted uniforms, baritone Nelson Eddy was the Hollywood image of the operetta hero during the 1930s. The eight MGM musicals he starred in with Jeanette MacDonald were primarily films that re-created the lush world of Victor Herbert (*Naughty Marietta, Sweethearts*), Rudolf Friml (*Rose Marie*), Sigmund Romberg (*Maytime, New Moon*), and Noël Coward (*Bitter Sweet*). Eddy made many records and sang in concerts and nightclubs. Among songs he introduced were "In the Still of the Night," "Rosalie," and "At the Balalaika." Other leading ladies included Eleanor Powell, Ilona Massey, Risë Stevens, and Susanna Foster. Bib: *Films of Jeanette MacDonald and Nelson Eddy* by Eleanor Knowles (1975).

Asterisk indicates appearance with Miss MacDonald:

1933	Broadway to Hollywood (*John Sylvester*)
	Dancing Lady (singer)
1934	Student Tour (singer)
1935	Naughty Marietta* (*Capt. Jim Warrington*)
1936	Rose Marie* (*Sgt. Bruce*)
1937	Maytime* (*Paul Allison*)
	Rosalie (*Dick Thorpe*)
1938	The Girl of the Golden West* (*Ramerez*)
	Sweethearts* (*Ernest Lane*)
1939	Let Freedom Ring (*Steve Logan*)
	Balalaika (*Prince Peter Karagin*)
1940	New Moon* (*Charles Henri, duc de Villiers*)
	Bitter Sweet* (*Carl Linden*)
1941	The Chocolate Soldier (*Karl Lang*)
1942	I Married an Angel* (*Willi Palaffi*)
1943	Phantom of the Opera (*Anatole Carron*)
1944	Knickerbocker Holiday (*Brom Broeck*)
1946	Make Mine Music (voice only)
1947	Northwest Outpost (*Capt. Jim Laurence*)

Edens, Roger, composer, lyricist, producer; b. Hillsboro, Texas, Nov. 9, 1905; d. Hollywood, July 13, 1970. Multifaceted musical talent who went to Hollywood in 1934 as arranger for Ethel Merman. Soon joined MGM in that capacity, also as adapter, supervisor, composer, and lyricist. From 1945 to 1954 he was associate producer to Arthur Freed; on his own he produced *Deep in My Heart* and *Funny Face*. As composer he also worked with lyricists Arthur Freed, Ralph Freed,

Earl Brent, Betty Comden and Adolph Green, Kay Thompson, Hugh Martin and Ralph Blane, and Leonard Gershe. Among his songs: "Our Love Affair," "It's a Great Day for the Irish," "Pass That Peace Pipe," "The French Lesson."

Unless otherwise noted, beginning in 1945 Mr. Edens was associate producer; films for which he composed songs indicated by names of lyricists in parentheses:

1939 Babes in Arms (alone)
1940 Strike Up the Band (A. Freed)
     Little Nellie Kelly (alone)
1941 Ziegfeld Girl (R. Freed; also alone)
     Lady, Be Good (alone)
     Babes on Broadway (alone)
1945 Yolanda and the Thief
1946 The Harvey Girls
     Ziegfeld Follies (R. Freed; Brent; Thompson)
1947 Good News (Comden-Green; Martin-Blane)
1948 The Pirate
     Easter Parade
     Words and Music
1949 Take Me Out to the Ball Game (Comden-Green)
     The Barkleys of Broadway
     On the Town (Comden-Green)
1950 Annie Get Your Gun
     Pagan Love Song
1951 Royal Wedding
     Show Boat
     An American in Paris
1952 The Belle of New York
     Singin' in the Rain (Comden-Green)
1953 The Band Wagon
1954 Brigadoon
     Deep in My Heart (prod.)
1957 Funny Face (prod.) (Gershe)
1962 Jumbo (alone)
1964 The Unsinkable Molly Brown
1969 Hello, Dolly!

Edwards, Blake (né William Blake McEdwards), director, producer, screenwriter; b. Tulsa, July 26, 1922. Began as writer, then became director and producer with such nonmusical hits as *Breakfast at Tiffany's, Days of Wine and Roses,* the *Pink Panther* series, and *10.* Married to Julie Andrews, whom he directed in *Darling Lili.*

Unless otherwise noted, Mr. Edwards was director-screenwriter of the following:

1953 All Ashore (script only)
1955 Bring Your Smile Along
1956 He Laughed Last
1960 High Time (dir. only)
1969 Darling Lili (also prod.)
1982 Victor/Victoria (also co-prod.)

Edwards, (Clifton A.) Cliff ("Ukulele Ike"), actor, singer; b. Hannibal, Mo., June 14, 1895; d. Hollywood, July 17, 1971. Edwards' high-pitched voice introduced "Singin' in the Rain" in *Hollywood Revue of 1929* and "When You Wish Upon a Star" in *Pinocchio.* A vaudeville headliner who also appeared in Broadway musicals, he acted in over 100 films.

1929 Hollywood Revue of 1929 (specialty)
     Marianne (*Soapy*)
     So This Is College (*Windy*)
1930 Lord Byron of Broadway (*Joe*)
     Montana Moon (*Froggy*)
     Good News (*Kearney*)
     Those Three French Girls (*Owly*)
1931 The Prodigal (*Snipe*)
1933 Take a Chance (*Louie Webb*)
1934 George White's Scandals (*Stew Hart*)
1935 George White's Scandals (*Dude Holloway*)
1938 The Girl of the Golden West (*Minstrel Joe*)
1940 Pinocchio (voice of *Jiminy Cricket*)
1941 Dumbo (voice of *Jim Crow*)
     Prairie Stranger
1943 Salute for Three (*Foggy*)
1946 Fun and Fancy Free (voice of *Jiminy Cricket*)

"Eeny Meeny Meiny Mo" Music by Matty Malneck; lyric by Johnny Mercer. Rhythmic number based on variation on nursery rhyme ("Even Mr. Crosby bings it") introduced by lyricist Johnny Mercer in *To Beat the Band* (RKO 1935).

Eliscu, Edward, lyricist; b. New York, April 2, 1902. Broadway lyricist whose major Hollywood songs were for *Flying Down to Rio*—"The Carioca," "Orchids in the Moonlight," and the title number, all written with Vincent Youmans and Gus Kahn. Other collaborators: Henry Myers and Jay Gorney.

1933 Flying Down to Rio (Kahn-Youmans)
1943 The Heat's On (Myers, Gorney)
1944 Hey, Rookie (Myers, Gorney)

Ellington, (Edward Kennedy) Duke, composer, pianist, bandleader; b. Washington, DC, April 29, 1899; d. New York, May 24, 1974. Eximious jazz composer-arranger who formed his first band in 1918 and continued conducting until the last year of his life. On screen he made only specialty appearances with his orchestra (introducing "Three Little Words" and "My Old Flame"), but he did write scores for films, including *Anatomy of a Murder.* Bib: *Music Is My Mistress* by Ellington (1975).

1930 Check and Double Check
1934 Murder at the Vanities
       Belle of the Nineties
1937 Hit Parade of 1937
1942 Cabin in the Sky
1943 Reveille with Beverly
1961 Paris Blues (comp. only)

Enright, (Raymond E.) Ray, director; b. Anderson, Ind., March 25, 1896; d. Hollywood, April 3, 1965. Warner director who worked with Dick Powell on six musicals, including *Twenty Million Sweethearts* with Ginger Rogers and *Dames* with Ruby Keeler.

1930 Song of the West
       Golden Dawn
       Dancing Sweeties
1934 Twenty Million Sweethearts
       Dames
1936 Sing Me a Love Song
1937 Ready, Willing and Able
       The Singing Marine
1938 Swing Your Lady
       Gold Diggers in Paris
       Hard To Get
       Going Places
1939 Naughty but Nice

Errol, Leon, actor; b. Sydney, Australia, July 3, 1881; d. Hollywood, Oct. 12, 1951. Bandy-legged, sour-faced, bald comic actor who appeared in Broadway musicals from 1910 to 1929 before beginning screen career. Teamed with Lupe Velez in late 30s for series of mostly nonmusical films.

1930 Paramount on Parade (specialty)
       One Heavenly Night (*Otto*)
1931 Her Majesty Love (*Baron Von Schwarzdorf*)
1934 We're Not Dressing (*Hubert*)
1935 Coronado (*Otto Wray*)
1937 Make a Wish (*Brennan*)
1939 Dancing Coed (*Pops Marlow*)
       The Girl from Mexico (*Uncle Matt*)
1941 Six Lessons from Madam LaZonga (*Alvarez*)
       Moonlight in Hawaii (*Spencer*)
       Melody Lane (*McKenzie*)
1943 Strictly in the Groove (*Durham*)
       Follow the Band (*Mike O'Brien*)
       Cowboy in Manhattan (*Hank*)
       Gals, Inc. (*Cornelius V. Rensington III*)
       Higher and Higher (*Drake*)
1944 Hat Check Honey (*Dan Briggs*)
       Slightly Terrific (*Tuttle*)
       Twilight on the Prairie
       Babes on Swing Street (*Malcolm Curtis*)

1945 Under Western Skies (*Willie*)
1946 Riverboat Rhythm (*Matt Lindsay*)
1949 Variety Time
1951 Footlight Varieties

Etting, Ruth, singer; b. David City, Neb., Nov. 23, 1896; d. Colorado Springs, Sept. 24, 1978. Blonde torch singer, primarily a nightclub and recording artist. Film bio: *Love Me or Leave Me,* with Doris Day as Miss Etting.

1933 Roman Scandals (*Olga*)
1934 Hips Hips Horray (*Ruth Etting*)
       Gift of Gab (*Ruth*)

Evans, Ray. *See* **Livingston and Evans.**

Evergreen (1934). Music by Richard Rodgers, Harry M. Woods; lyrics by Lorenz Hart, Harry M. Woods; screenplay by Marjorie Gaffney & Emlyn Williams from London musical by Benn W. Levy and Rodgers & Hart.

A Gaumont-British film produced by Michael Balcon; directed by Victor Saville; choreography, Buddy Bradley; art director, Alfred Junge; music director, Louis Levy; cameraman, Glen MacWilliams; editor, Ian Dalrymple.

Cast: Jessie Matthews (*Harriet Green/ Harriet Green Jr.*); Sonnie Hale (*Leslie Benn*); Betty Balfour (*Maudie, Lady Shropshire*); Barry Mackay (*Tommy Thompson*); Ivor MacLaren (*Marquis of Staines*); Hartley Power (*George Treadwell*).

Songs: "Daddy Wouldn't Buy Me a Bow-Wow" (Joseph Tabrar) - Matthews/ "I Wouldn't Leave My Wooden Hut for You" - Matthews, Balfour/ "When You've Got a Little Springtime in Your Heart" (Woods) - Matthews/ "If I Give In to You" (Rodgers-Hart) - Matthews/ "Tinkle Tinkle Tinkle" (Woods) - Hale/ "Little Brown Jug" (Joseph Winner) - dance/ "Dear Dear" (Rodgers-Hart) - Matthews, Mackay/ "Dancing on the Ceiling" (Rodgers-Hart) - Matthews/ "Just by Your Example" (Woods) - dance by Matthews/ "Over My Shoulder" (Woods) - Matthews.

Of her nine films as reigning star of British musicals in the 1930s, Jessie Matthews enjoyed her greatest international success in *Evergreen*. Adapted from the 1930 London stage musical (whose title was written *Ever Green*), the movie told how Harriet Green, the daughter of an Edwardian stage star who had disappeared, becomes a sensation in London by posing as her own mother at the age of 60 (though 40 would have been more logical). She is aided in the deception by her boy-friend-press agent, Tommy Thompson (Barry Mackay), and a temperamental director, Leslie Benn (Sonnie Hale, Miss Matthews' husband at the time). Eventually, she confesses all and wins the sympathy of the public. The main point of difference with the stage musical is that in the earlier version she impersonated her own grandmother to become a success in Paris, and admitted the ruse because she had fallen in love with her unsuspecting leading man, Tommy Thompson (then played by Mr. Hale). Though Rodgers and Hart had written the score for *Ever Green,* they were unavailable to write additional numbers for *Evergreen* and so Harry Woods, another American songwriter, was called in.

Fred Astaire, appearing on the London stage in 1934 in *Gay Divorce,* was initially sought to play the role of Tommy in the film, but RKO would not release him.

"Evergreen" Music by Barbra Streisand; lyric by Paul Williams. Emotional declaration of undying love introduced by Barbra Streisand in *A Star Is Born* (Warner 1976). The first presentation is at a recording session with Miss Streisand singing it to—and at times with—Kris Kristofferson; the second is by Miss Streisand heard over the final credits.

"Every Day" Music by Sammy Fain; lyric by Irving Kahal. Daily amatory rededication pledged by Rudy Vallee in *Sweet Music* (Warner 1935).

"Everybody Sing" Music by Nacio Herb Brown; lyric by Arthur Freed. Buoyant exhortation introduced by Judy Garland in *Broadway Melody of 1938* (MGM 1937), accompanied by a group including Sophie Tucker and Barnett Parker. Scene took place in reception room of Broadway producer Robert Taylor.

"Ev'ryone Says 'I Love You' " Music by Harry Ruby; lyric by Bert Kalmar. Recurrent theme in *Horsefeathers* (Par. 1932) used to serenade Thelma Todd by 1) Zeppo Marx, as she has breakfast in bed; 2) Chico Marx on the piano; 3) Harpo Marx on the harp) 4) Groucho Marx, accompanying himself on the guitar as the lady paddles a canoe on a lake. Both vocal versions have different lyrics.

"Everything I Have Is Yours" Music by Burton Lane; lyric by Harold Adamson. Art Jarrett as a band singer introduced the ballad during a formal party in *Dancing Lady* (MGM 1933), with Joan Crawford supplying the "la-da-da's" while dancing in the arms of Franchot Tone. Also sung by Ezio Pinza in *Strictly Dishonorable* (MGM 1951) and Monica Lewis in *Everything I Have Is Yours* (MGM 1952).

"Everything Stops for Tea" Music by Al Hoffman & Al Goodhart; lyric by Maurice Sigler. Perky explanation of the British custom, sung by Jack Buchanan in *Come Out of the Pantry* (UA 1935).

"Everything's Been Done Before" Music by Jack King & Edwin H. Knopf; lyric by Harold Adamson. Since all the pleasures associated with falling in love have been around for a long time, why not do what's been done before? Allan Jones introduced the tripping ballad as part of a theatrical production in *Reckless* (MGM 1935).

"Everything's in Rhythm with My Heart" Music by Al Hoffman & Al Goodhart; lyric by Maurice Sigler. Buoyant expression of someone rhythmically in tune with the whole world ("The flowers that grow and the breezes that blow seem to go with the flow of my song"), sung by Jessie Matthews in *First a Girl* (Gaumont-Brit. 1935).

F

"Face to Face" Music by Sammy Fain; lyric by Sammy Cahn. Girl is with boy and the most unbelievable things seem to be happening. Jane Powell auditioned the ballad in *Three Sailors and a Girl* (Warner 1953) while riding in a taxi.

Fain, Sammy (né Samuel Feinberg), composer; b. New York, June 17, 1902. Former vaudeville and radio singer whose Hollywood songs were written with lyricists Irving Kahal ("You Brought a New Kind of Love to Me," "By a Waterfall"), Sam Coslow, Lew Brown ("That Old Feeling"), E. Y. Harburg, Jack Yellen, Ralph Freed, Mack Gordon, Bob Hilliard, Jerry Seelen, Sammy Cahn, Paul Francis Webster ("Secret Love," "Love Is a Many-Splendored Thing," "April Love," "A Certain Smile"), and co-composer Pierre Norman. Fain's screen songs were identified with Maurice Chevalier, Dick Powell, Rudy Vallee, Mae West, Harriet Hilliard, Kathryn Grayson, Betty Grable, Jane Powell, Doris Day, Howard Keel, Dean Martin, and Pat Boone.

1930	Young Man of Manhattan (Norman-Kahal)
1933	Footlight Parade (Kahal)
	College Coach (Kahal)
1934	Harold Teen (Kahal)
	Dames (Kahal) (also *Buttercup Baumer*)
1935	Sweet Music (Kahal)
	Goin' to Town (Coslow)
1937	New Faces of 1937 (Brown)
1944	Meet the People (Harburg)
1945	George White's Scandals of 1945 (Yellen)
1946	Two Sisters from Boston (Freed)
	No Leave, No Love (Freed)
1951	Call Me Mister (Gordon)
	Alice in Wonderland (Hilliard)
1953	The Jazz Singer (Seelen)
	Peter Pan (Cahn)
	Three Sailors and a Girl (Cahn)
	Calamity Jane (Webster)
1954	Lucky Me (Webster)
1956	Hollywood or Bust (Webster)
1957	April Love (Webster)
1958	Mardi Gras (Webster)
1959	A Diamond for Carla (tv) (Webster)
	The Big Circus (Webster)

"Fair and Warmer" Music by Harry Warren; lyric by Al Dubin. Love is all that's needed to turn cloudy skies to clear. Spiritedly sung by Dick Powell in *Twenty Million Sweethearts* (Warner 1934).

"Faithful Forever" Music by Ralph Rainger; lyric by Leo Robin. In the Max Fleischer cartoon *Gulliver's Travels* (Par. 1939), Jonathan Swift may be surprised to know, "Faithful" is the official song of the Kingdom of Lilliput and "Forever" the official song of the neighboring Kingdom of Lupescu. When war breaks out over which song will be played at the wedding of Lilliputian Princess Glory and Lupescuan Prince David, Gulliver comes up with the solution: "Sing 'Faithful' and 'Forever' together as one song." Which Glory (with Jessica Dragonette's voice) and David (with Lanny Ross') are only too happy to do.

"Falling in Love Again" Music by Frederick Hollander; lyric by Sammy Lerner from German by Robert Liebmann. The moodily enticing piece will forever be associated with the sight of Marlene Dietrich, wearing silver top hat and thigh-high stockings, as she appeared on stage in *The Blue Angel* (Par. 1930) and crooned her siren song to Emil Jannings. Filmed in Berlin, the English-language movie was simultaneously made in German (as *Der blaue Engel*), in which the song was offered as *"Ich bin von Kopf bis Fuss auf Liebe eingestellt."*

"Fancy Free" Music by Harold Arlen; lyric by Johnny Mercer. "Spring is here but it can't catch me," sang the romantically unattached Joan Caulfield in this lilting waltz in *The Petty Girl* (Col. 1950).

"Fancy Meeting You" Music by Harold Arlen; lyric by E. Y. Harburg. Song of romantic reincarnation ("Forever since the world began/ I was your prehistoric man") sung by Dick Powell to Jeanne Madden in a museum in *Stage Struck* (Warner 1936).

Fantasia (1940). A Walt Disney film released by RKO-Radio; production supervisor, Ben Sharpsteen; story directors, Joe Grant, Dick Huemer; sequences directed by Samuel Armstrong, James Algar, Bill Roberts, Paul Satterfield, Hamilton Luske, Jim Handley, Ford Beebe, T. Hee, Norman Ferguson, Wilfred Jackson; supervising animators, Fred Moore, Vladimir Tytla, Wolfgang Reitherman, Joshua Meador, Ward Kimball, Eric Larson, Arthur Babbitt, Oliver Johnston, Don Towsley; art directors, Robert Cormack, Al Zinnen, Curtiss Perkins, Arthur Byram, Bruce Bushman, McLaren Stewart, Dick Kelsey, John Hubley, Hugh Hennesey, Kenneth Anderson, J. Gordon Legg, Herbert Ryman, Yale Gracey, Lance Nolley, Kendall O'Connor, Harold Doughty, Ernest Nordli, Kay Nielsen, Terrell Stapp, Charles Payzant, Thor Putnam; music director, Edward H. Plumb; editor, Stephen Csillag; Technicolor; Fantasound.

Cast: Leopold Stokowski and the Philadelphia Orchestra; Deems Taylor (narrator); Mickey Mouse (*Sorcerer's Apprentice*).

Selections: "Toccata and Fugue in D Minor" (Bach)/ "The Nutcracker Suite" (Tchaikovsky)/ "The Sorcerer's Apprentice" (Dukas) - Mickey Mouse/ "The Rite of Spring" (Stravinsky)/ "Pastoral Symphony" (Beethoven)/ "Dance of the Hours" (Ponchielli)/ "Night on Bald Mountain" (Mussorgsky)/ "Ave Maria" (Schubert-Rachel Field) - chorus dir. by Charles Henderson, Julietta Novis, soloist. Unused: "Clair de Lune" (Debussy).

The first—and so far only—attempt to combine visual images with concert music, *Fantasia* evolved from a cartoon short based on Paul Dukas' "L'Apprenti Sorcier" with Mickey Mouse as the Apprentice and Leopold Stokowski conducting a local symphony orchestra. At Stokowski's urging, Disney expanded the short into a feature-length cartoon by adding seven other classical works, with the maestro directing his own Philadelphia Orchestra, and with radio commentator Deems Taylor to introduce the selections. Though criticized by purists for tampering with the scores and for using visual means to interpret a nonvisual art form, Disney and his staff of over 1000 succeeded in creating an imaginative, purely cinematic work which, since the 70s, has become something of a cult film with pot-puffing young America. The interpretive approaches included abstract (Bach's "Toccata and Fugue"), narrative ("The Sorcerer's Apprentice," which was followed by Mickey Mouse and Leopold Stokowski, both in silhouette, shaking hands), balletic ("The Nutcracker Suite" and "Dance of the Hours"), primeval ("The Rite of Spring"), comically mythological ("Pastoral Symphony"), wildly ritualistic ("Night on Bald Mountain"), and serenely spiritual ("Ave Maria").

Disney initially planned to vary the order of selections and even replace certain works with other classical pieces. He also intended to show *Fantasia* at a limited number of theatres with special Fantasound—or stereo—equipment. After the film's first showing, however, wartime restrictions forced Disney to put *Fantasia* into general release with standard sound.

Two other episodic musical films were created by the Disney studio, though these used popular numbers sung and performed on the soundtrack by popular performers: *Make Mine Music* (1946) featured Nelson Eddy, Dinah Shore, Benny Goodman's orchestra, the Andrews Sisters, Andy Russell, and The Pied Pipers; *Melody Time* (1948) featured Roy Rogers, Ethel Smith, Buddy Clark, The Andrews Sisters again, Fred Waring's orchestra, Frances Langford, and Dennis Day.

"Faraway Part of Town, The" Music by André Previn; lyric by Dory Langdon. Introduced in *Pepe* (Col. 1960) by the voice of Judy Garland heard on a record. Number then used for dance by Shirley Jones and Dan Dailey around the garden of a Hollywood mansion.

"Farewell, Amanda" Music & lyric by Cole Porter. Breezy end-of-the-affair number performed in *Adam's Rib* (MGM 1949) by David Wayne as a song he's just written in honor of the character played by Katharine Hepburn.

Farrell, Charles, actor; b. Onset Bay, Mass., Aug. 9, 1901. Arrow-collar, arrow-straight leading man who appeared in 12 movies with Janet Gaynor (four of them musical). Sang "If I Had a Talking Picture of You" in

Sunny Side Up. Most closely associated role was in silent film *Seventh Heaven.*

1929	Sunny Side Up (*Jack Cromwell*)
1930	Happy Days (guest bit)
	High Society Blues (*Eddie Granger*)
1931	Delicious (*Larry Beaumont*)
1933	Girl Without a Room (*Tom Duncan*)
1937	Moonlight Sonata (Eng.) (*Eric Molnar*)
1938	Just Around the Corner (*Jeff Hale*)

Faye, Alice (née Alice Jeane Leppert), actress, singer; b. New York, May 5, 1915. Between 1938 and 1943, the blonde, throaty-voiced singing actress with the snub nose, pouting lips, and hourglass figure was Fox's reigning singing star, appearing in such lavish period productions as *In Old Chicago, Alexander's Ragtime Band* (singing "Now It Can Be Told"), *Rose of Washington Square, Lillian Russell, Tin Pan Alley* ("You Say the Sweetest Things, Baby"), and *Hello, Frisco, Hello* ("You'll Never Know"). In more up-to-date entertainments Miss Faye was also on hand to introduce such pieces as "I'm Shooting High," "Sing, Baby, Sing," "Goodnight, My Love," "Never in a Million Years," "There's a Lull in My Life," "This Year's Kisses" (in *On the Avenue*), "You Can't Have Everything," "You're a Sweetheart," "A Journey to a Star," and "No Love, No Nothin'" (last two in *The Gang's All Here*). The actress was co-starred with Don Ameche in five musicals, John Payne in four, and Tyrone Power in three. Once married to Tony Martin, she is the wife of Phil Harris. Bib: *Films of Alice Faye* by W. Franklyn Moshier (1974).

1934	George White's Scandals (*Mona Vale*)
	She Learned About Sailors (*Jean Legoi*)
	365 Nights in Hollywood (*Alice Perkins*)
1935	George White's Scandals (*Honey Walters*)
	Every Night at Eight (*Dixie Dean*)
	Music Is Magic (*Peggy Harper*)
1936	King of Burlesque (*Pat Doran*)
	Poor Little Rich Girl (*Jerry Dolan*)
	Sing, Baby, Sing (*Jean Warren*)
	Stowaway (*Susan Parker*)
1937	On the Avenue (*Mona Merrick*)
	Wake Up and Live (*Alice Huntley*)
	You Can't Have Everything (*Judith Wells*)
	You're a Sweetheart (*Betty Bradley*)
1938	Sally, Irene and Mary (*Sally Day*)
	In Old Chicago (*Belle Fawcett*)
	Alexander's Ragtime Band (*Stella Kirby*)
1939	Rose of Washington Square (*Rose Sargent*)
1940	Lillian Russell (*Lillian Russell*)

	Tin Pan Alley (*Katie Blane*)
1941	That Night in Rio (*Baroness Cecilia Duarte*)
	The Great American Broadcast (*Vicki Adams*)
	Weekend in Havana (*Nan Spencer*)
1943	Hello, Frisco, Hello (*Trudy Evans*)
	The Gang's All Here (*Eadie Allen*)
1944	Four Jills in a Jeep (speciality)
1962	State Fair (*Melissa Frake*)
1978	The Magic of Lassie (*waitress*)

Felix, Seymour, choreographer; b. New York, Oct. 23, 1892; d. 1961. Prolific dance director with Broadway and nightclub background who staged the "Pretty Girl Is Like a Melody" sequence in *The Great Ziegfeld.* Other major films: *Sunny Side Up, On the Avenue, Alexander's Ragtime Band, Yankee Doodle Dandy, Cover Girl, Mother Wore Tights.*

1929	Sunny Side Up
1930	Just Imagine
1932	Stepping Sisters (also dir.)
1934	The Cat and the Fiddle
	Hollywood Party
	Kid Millions
1935	The Girl Friend
1936	The Great Ziegfeld
1937	On the Avenue
	Vogues of 1938
1938	Alexander's Ragtime Band
1939	Broadway Serenade
	Rose of Washington Square
1940	Lillian Russell
	Tin Pan Alley
1941	Navy Blues
1942	Yankee Doodle Dandy
1943	Let's Face It
1944	Cover Girl
	Atlantic City
	Greenwich Village
1945	The Dolly Sisters
1946	Do You Love Me?
	Three Little Girls in Blue
1947	Mother Wore Tights
1948	Give My Regards to Broadway
	When My Baby Smiles at Me
1949	Oh, You Beautiful Doll
1951	Golden Girl
1952	Down Among the Sheltering Palms
1953	The "I Don't Care" Girl

"Fella with an Umbrella, A" Music & lyric by Irving Berlin. During a sudden downpour in New York, Peter Lawford—in *Easter Parade* (MGM 1948)—introduces himself to Judy Garland and snatches a street vendor's huge umbrella to protect her. Because of his disarming, if brash, manner, Judy finds herself revealing all kinds of personal information. As for himself, Peter confesses, "I'm just a fella, a fella with an umbrella . . . ."

Fiddler on the Roof (1971). Music by Jerry Bock; lyrics by Sheldon Harnick; screenplay by Joseph Stein from Broadway musical by Stein, Bock, and Harnick based on stories by Sholom Aleichem including "Tevye's Daughters."

A United Artists film produced by the Mirisch Production Co. & Norman Jewison; directed by Jewison; choreography, Tom Abbott, based on original by Jerome Robbins; art directors, Robert Boyle, Michael Stringer; costumes, Elizabeth Haffenden, Joan Bridge; music director, John Williams; orchestrations, Williams; violin soloist, Isaac Stern; cameraman, Oswald Morris; editors, Anthony Gibbs, Robert Lawrence; DeLuxe color; PanaVision.

Cast: Topol (*Tevye*); Norma Crane (*Golde*); Leonard Frey (*Motel*); Molly Picon (*Yente*); Paul Mann (*Lazar Wolf*); Rosalind Harris (*Tzeitel*); Michele Marsh (*Hodel*); Neva Small (*Chava*); Michael Glaser (*Perchik*); Patience Collier (*Grandma Tzeitel*); Ruth Madoc (*Fruma Sarah*); Shimen Ruskin (*Mordcha*); Tutte Lemkow (*Fiddler*).

Songs: Tradition" - Topol, villagers, Stern/ "Matchmaker, Matchmaker" - Harris, Marsh, Small/ "If I Were a Rich Man" - Topol/ "Sabbath Prayer" - Topol, Crane, villagers, Stern/ "To Life" - Topol, Mann, villagers, Russians/ "Miracle of Miracles" - Frey/ "Tevye's Dream" - Topol, Crane, Collier, Madoc, villagers/ "Sunrise, Sunset" - Topol, Crane, Glaser, Marsh, villagers, Stern/ "Wedding Celebration" - villagers, dance by men/ "Do You Love Me?" - Topol, Crane/ "Far from the Home I Love" - Marsh/ "Chavaleh" - Topol/ "Chava ballet" - dance by Small, Harris, Marsh/ "Anatevka" - Topol, Crane, Mann, Picon, Ruskin, villagers, Stern. Unused: "Now I Have Everything," "I Just Heard."

The long-running Broadway and international stage success was transformed to the screen by its original librettist, and its choreography was based on Jerome Robbins' original dances. The faithfulness to source was evident throughout the film version, which starred Topol (he was the London Tevye) in the part originated by the older, less virile and more comedic Zero Mostel. The film expanded the original concept of the stage work chiefly by showing the houses and animals of a real Rus-

sian village in 1905 (actually photographed near Zagreb, Yugoslavia), while retaining the fantasy quality by using colors associated with Marc Chagall. The focus of the story was the efforts of Tevye, a dairyman, to retain tradition in the face of change, particularly as revealed through his relationships with his three oldest daughters and the men they marry.

In 1979 *Fiddler on the Roof* was re-released in Dolby Stereo with its running time shortened by 38 minutes.

Fields, Dorothy, lyricist; b. Allenhurst, NJ, July 15, 1904; d. New York, March 28, 1974. Also distinguished as a Broadway lyricist-librettist, Miss Fields first won recognition in Hollywood for her songs with composer Jerome Kern for two Fred Astaire-Ginger Rogers films: *Roberta* ("I Won't Dance" and "Lovely To Look At," both also in the movie's remake, *Lovely To Look At*) and *Swing Time* ("A Fine Romance," "The Way You Look Tonight"). Her lyrics were also combined with the music of Jimmy McHugh ("Cuban Love Song," "I Feel a Song Comin' On," "I'm in the Mood for Love"), Fritz Kreisler ("Stars in My Eyes"), Oscar Levant, Harold Arlen, Arthur Schwartz, Harry Warren, and, for television, Burton Lane. Of the eleven stage musicals for which Miss Fields wrote lyrics, the two that were filmed were *Up in Central Park* (with Sigmund Romberg) and *Sweet Charity* (Cy Coleman). Lawrence Tibbett, Lily Pons, Irene Dunne, Grace Moore, Allan Jones, Deanna Durbin, Ezio Pinza, Betty Grable, and Shirley MacLaine were among those who sang her songs in movies. Miss Fields was the daughter of comedian-producer Lew Fields and sister of stage and screenwriters Joseph Fields and Herbert Fields.

1930	Love in the Rough (McHugh)
1931	Cuban Love Song (McHugh)
1935	Roberta (Kern)
	Hooray for Love (McHugh)
	Every Night at Eight (McHugh)
	In Person (Levant)
	I Dream Too Much (Kern)
1936	The King Steps Out (Kreisler)
	Swing Time (Kern)
1938	Joy of Living (Kern) (also script)
1940	One Night in the Tropics (Kern)
1943	Stage Door Canteen (guest bit only)
1948	Up in Central Park (Romberg)
1951	Mr. Imperium (Arlen)
	Excuse My Dust (Schwartz)
	Texas Carnival (Warren)
1952	Lovely To Look At (Kern)

1953   The Farmer Takes a Wife (Arlen)
          Junior Miss (tv) (Lane)
1968   Sweet Charity (Coleman)

Fields, Gracie (née Grace Stansfield), actress, singer; b. Rochdale, Eng., Jan. 9, 1898; d. Capri, Italy, Sept. 27, 1979. Dame of the British Empire 1979. Good-humored, everybody's-pal-type singing actress with flair for comic dialect numbers and swooping long-line ariosos. The epitome of the hard-working Englishwoman, ''Our Gracie'' became the highest paid actress in the world, though her musical films—all made in Britain except the last—were successes only in her own country. Miss Fields introduced ''Sally'' in her first film, sang ''The Biggest Aspidistra in the World'' in *Keep Smiling,* made many records, appeared on the variety stage and in nightclubs, had her own radio programs both in England and the US, and was a great favorite with the troops during World War II. The second of her three husbands was film director Monty Banks. Bib: *Sing as We Go* by Miss Fields (1961).

1931   Sally in Our Alley (*Sally Winch*)
1932   Looking on the Bright Side (*Gracie*)
1933   This Week of Grace (*Gracie Milroy*)
          Love, Life and Laughter (*Nellie Gwyn*)
1934   Sing as We Go (*Gracie Platt*)
1935   Look Up and Laugh (*Gracie Pearson*)
1936   Queen of Hearts (*Gracie Perkins*)
1937   The Show Goes On (*Sally Scowcroft*)
1938   We're Going To Be Rich (*Kit Dobson*)
          Keep Smiling (*Gracie Gray*)
1939   Shipyard Sally (*Sally Fitzgerald*)
1943   Stage Door Canteen (US) (specialty)

Fields, W. C. (né William Claude Dukenfield), actor; b. Philadelphia, Apr. 9, 1879; d. Pasadena, Dec. 25, 1946. Bulbous-nosed comedian who established the character of the cynical con man, mumbling and drawling his disdain for children, pets, and the eternal inconveniences of everyday life. Also appeared in silent films and nonmusicals (*David Copperfield, The Bank Dick*). Fields began his career in vaudeville in 1897, appeared in seven editions of the *Ziegfeld Follies* on Broadway, and had his greatest stage success in *Poppy,* in which he also appeared on the screen. Bib: *W. C. Fields: His Follies and Fortunes* by Robert Lewis Taylor (1949); *W. C. Fields by Himself,* ed. Ronald Fields (grandson) (1972).

1931   Her Majesty Love (*Torrek*)
1933   International House (*Prof. Quail*)

1935   Mississippi (*Comm. Jackson*)
1938   Big Broadcast of 1938 (*T. Frothingwell Bellows/ S. B. Bellows*)
1944   Follow the Boys (specialty)
          Song of the Open Road (specialty)
          Sensations of 1945 (specialty)

"Fill the World with Love" Music & lyric by Leslie Bricusse. Anthem-like chorale sung by schoolboys in *Goodbye Mr. Chips* (MGM 1969).

"Fine Romance, A" Music by Jerome Kern; lyric by Dorothy Fields. Self-described ''Sarcastic Love Song'' introduced by Ginger Rogers and Fred Astaire in *Swing Time* (RKO 1936). In a snow-filled rustic retreat a sudden chill develops between the young lovers, who take turns describing the other as being cold as yesterday's mashed potatoes, calmer than the seals in the Arctic, and as hard to land as the *Ile de France.* Song also sung by Virginia O'Brien in *Till the Clouds Roll By* (MGM 1946).

Fisher, Doris, composer, lyricist; b. New York, May 2, 1915. Miss Fisher and her composer-lyricist partner, Allan Roberts, contributed songs to about a dozen Columbia films. Their best known was ''Put the Blame on Mame'' in *Gilda,* one of their two films starring Rita Hayworth.

1946   Gilda
          The Thrill of Brazil
          Singin' in the Corn
          Talk About a Lady
1947   Cigarette Girl
          Down to Earth

Fitzgerald, Ella, singer, actress; b. Newport News, Va., April 25, 1918. Pre-eminent, jazz-influenced singer who has won renown primarily for concerts and recordings.

1942   Ride 'Em Cowboy (*Ruby*)
1955   Pete Kelly's Blues (*Maggie Jackson*)
1958   St. Louis Blues (specialty)

"Flirtation Walk" Music by Allie Wrubel; lyric by Mort Dixon. ''Because with you there's nothing that won't come true,'' sang West Pointer Dick Powell to Ruby Keeler as they strolled through the Military Academy's famed landmark in *Flirtation Walk* (Warner (1934).

Flying Down to Rio (1933). Music by Vincent Youmans; lyrics by Edward Eliscu & Gus Kahn; screenplay by Cyril Hume, H. W. Hanemann, and Erwin Gelsey from play by Anne Caldwell and story by Louis Brock.

An RKO-Radio film produced by Louis Brock; directed by Thornton Freeland; choreography, Fred Astaire, Dave Gould; assistant choreographer, Hermes Pan; art directors, Van Nest Polglase, Carroll Clark; costumes, Walter Plunkett; music director, Max Steiner; cameraman, J. Roy Hunt; editor, Jack Kitchin.

Cast: Dolores Del Rio (*Belinha de Rezende*); Gene Raymond (*Roger Bond*); Raul Roulien (*Julio Rubeiro*); Ginger Rogers (*Honey Hale*); Fred Astaire (*Fred Ayres*); Blanche Friderici (*Dona Elena*); Franklin Pangborn (*Hammerstein*); Eric Blore (*Butterbass*); Walter Walker (*de Rezende*); Etta Moten (*singer*); Paul Porcasi (*Mayor*); Luis Alberni (*casino manager*); Clarence Muse (*caddy*); Betty Furness, Movita Casteneda (*hotel guests*); Mary Kornman (*Belinha's friend*).

Songs: "Music Makes Me" - Rogers/ "The Carioca" - Moten, two uncredited singers; dance by Astaire, Rogers, Brazilians/ "Orchids in the Moonlight" - Roulien; dance by Astaire, Del Rio/ "Flying Down to Rio" - Astaire; dance by aerial chorus.

Flying Down to Rio was created with the idea of combining songs, dances, and aviation with a South American background. Apart from its spectacular finale, in which girls danced on the wings of airplanes apparently in flight, the movie is best remembered for the "Carioca" number, which put Fred Astaire and Ginger Rogers on the dance floor together for the first time. The team did not have the leading roles; these went to Dolores Del Rio, as a wealthy Brazilian, and Gene Raymond (in a part originally intended for Joel McCrea), as a bandleader-songwriter-aviator who wins Dolores from her countryman Raul Roulien. The film's score was the last written by composer Vincent Youmans.

"Flying Down to Rio" Music by Vincent Youmans; lyric by Edward Eliscu & Gus Kahn. Buoyant title song of the 1933 RKO film used for spectacular aerial "floorshow" that provided the movie's finale. Because a new hotel in Rio de Janeiro has been denied an entertainment permit for its opening day, bandleader Gene Raymond gets the idea of putting on the show *above* the hotel. Thus, as Fred Astaire sings the number, a fleet of airplanes appears with chorus girls strapped to the wings. Wearing surprisingly revealing costumes, the girls perform a series of leggy if constricted dance routines, with

featured performances by trapeze artists and apache dancers. Choreographer Dave Gould even included a moment of terror as one girl falls off her plane but is miraculously caught on the wings of another one that swoops right under it.

"Foggy Day (in London Town), A" Music by George Gershwin; lyric by Ira Gershwin. Atmospheric ballad describing a lonely, brumous day that suddenly burst into sunlight when the right person appeared. Despite the locale specified in the lyric, the song was performed in *A Damsel in Distress* (RKO 1937) by a formally clad Fred Astaire while strolling over the fog-covered grounds of an English country castle.

"Folks Who Live on the Hill, The" Music by Jerome Kern; lyric by Oscar Hammerstein II. Sitting on a hilltop in *High, Wide and Handsome* (Par. 1937), Irene Dunne and Randolph Scott discuss the home they will build there someday. Then, with Scott's head in her lap, Miss Dunne expresses in song the happiness it will bring them not only when they are young but even when—as "Darby and Joan who used to be Jack and Jill"—their children are grown up and gone.

Follow the Fleet (1936). Music & lyrics by Irving Berlin; screenplay by Dwight Taylor & Allan Scott from Broadway play *Shore Leave* by Hubert Osborne.

An RKO-Radio film produced by Pandro S. Berman; directed by Mark Sandrich; choreography, Fred Astaire, Hermes Pan; art director, Van Nest Polglase; costumes, Bernard Newman; music director, Max Steiner; cameraman, David Abel; editor, Henry Berman.

Cast: Fred Astaire (*Bake Baker*); Ginger Rogers (*Sherry Martin*); Randolph Scott (*Bilge Smith*); Harriet Hilliard (*Connie Martin*); Astrid Allwyn (*Iris Manning*); Ray Mayer (*Dopey Williams*); Russell Hicks (*Jim Nolan*); Lucille Ball (*Kitty Collins*); Betty Grable, Joy Hodges, Jennie Gray (*singing trio*); Tony Martin, Frank Jenks (*sailors*); Dorothy Fleisman, Bob Cromer (*contest dancers*).

Songs: "We Saw the Sea" - Astaire, sailors/ "Let Yourself Go" - Rogers, with Grable, Hodges, Gray; dance by Astaire, Rogers, Fleisman, Cromer, others; reprised as dance by Rogers/ "Get Thee Behind Me, Satan" - Hilliard/ "I'd Rather Lead a Band" - Astaire; dance by Astaire, sailors/ "But Where Are You?" - Hilliard/ "I'm Putting All My Eggs in One Basket" - Astaire, Rogers; "Let's Face the Music and Dance" - Astaire; dance by Astaire, Rogers. Unused: ''Moonlight Maneuvers,'' ''With a Smile on My Face.''

The 1922 Broadway play *Shore Leave* had the distinction of serving as the basis for both the successful stage musical *Hit the Deck* (whose Vincent Youmans score included ''Hallelujah'' and ''Sometimes I'm Happy'') and the successful screen musical *Follow the Fleet.* For the latter, Irving Berlin wrote his second score for Fred Astaire and Ginger Rogers, who were co-starring in their fourth film. (Berlin almost didn't get the assignment. Though his songs for the team's *Top Hat* had been a major factor in its popularity, some of the RKO brass felt that the new movie should have songs by Harry Warren and Al Dubin, then much in demand after winning an Academy Award for ''Lullaby of Broadway.'' But producer Pandro Berman insisted on Berlin.)

In both *Shore Leave* and *Hit the Deck* the plot concerned a New England girl (named Connie Martin in the former and Loulou Martin in the latter) and her infatuation with a marriage-shy sailor (named Bilge Smith in both). In *Follow the Fleet,* with Harriet Hilliard as Connie and Randolph Scott as Bilge, their story became secondary to one involving two newly created characters: sailor Bake Baker, Bilge's buddy, and dancehall singer Sherry Martin, Connie's sister, a former vaudeville team who meet again at the Paradise Ballroom in San Francisco. As Bake and Sherry, Fred and Ginger provided a contrasting comic romance as they had previously done in *Roberta* (in which Scott also played Astaire's pal), thus eliminating the customary character comedians that populated most of the team's movies. Except for a divorcée's palatial estate, the film's chief locales—a battleship, a dancehall, and a steam schooner—made it the least opulent of any that starred Astaire and Rogers—even though the ship's deck accommodated an entire complement of tapping sailors, the dancehall was surrounded by a luxurious garden, and the schooner easily had enough room for an elaborate musical show. But the image-change was most noticeable in the casting of Astaire as a gum-chewing gob, which not only lowered his social standing but severely limited his wardrobe. Still, the musical show on the schooner was reason enough for him to don white tie and tails for his—and Miss Rogers'—stunning dance to ''Let's Face the Music and Dance.''

Footlight Parade (1933). Music by Harry Warren, Sammy Fain; lyrics by Al Dubin, Irving Kahal; screenplay by Manuel Seff & James Seymour.

A Warner Bros. film produced by Hal B. Wallis; directed by Lloyd Bacon; choreography, Busby Berkeley; art director, Anton Grot; costumes, Orry-Kelly; music director, Leo F. Forbstein; cameraman, George Barnes; editor, George Amy.

Cast: James Cagney (*Chester Kent*); Joan Blondell (*Nan Prescott*); Ruby Keeler (*Bea Thorn*); Dick Powell (*Scotty Blair*); Guy Kibbee (*Silas Gould*); Frank McHugh (*Francis*); Ruth Donnelly (*Harriet Gould*); Claire Dodd (*Vivian Rich*); Hugh Herbert (*Charlie Bowers*); Herman Bing (*Fralick*); Billy Barty (*little boy*); Dave O'Brien (chorus); Hobart Cavanaugh (*idea man*); Jimmy Conlin (*uncle*); Billy Taft (*singer*).

Songs: ''Ah, the Moon Is Here'' (Fain-Kahal) - Powell, McHugh/ ''Sittin' on a Backyard Fence'' (Fain-Kahal) - Keeler, Taft/ ''Honeymoon Hotel'' (Warren-Dubin) -Powell, Keeler, others/ ''By a Waterfall'' (Fain-Kahal) - Powell, with Keeler, chorus/ ''Shanghai Lil'' (Warren-Dubin) - Cagney, Keeler, chorus.

The last of Warner's three legendary backstage musicals released in 1933, *Footlight Parade* differed from its predecessors, *42nd Street* and *Gold Diggers of 1933,* in that it had an original story dealing not with the creation of a Broadway musical but with the creation of a series of mini-musicals, known as 'prologues,'' which were offered in major movie houses during the early years of sound films. More than the other two, it focused its attention on one person, the kinetic, imaginative director, played by James Cagney, forever beset by personal and professional problems. (Though possibly based on choreographer Busby Berkeley, the character has its latter-day counterpart in Joe Gideon in *All That Jazz*.) The film also was oddly structured in that all three of its spectacular prologues—''Honeymoon Hotel,'' ''By a Waterfall,'' and ''Shanghai Lil''—were offered one after the other during the last half-hour of the picture.

But there were inescapable links with both other 1933 musicals. Again the cast included callow youths Dick Powell and Ruby Keeler and pompous character actor Guy Kibbee. And again the credits included the same choreographer, co-scriptwriter (James Seymour), songwriters (though here Warren and Dubin shared the load with Fain and Kahal), music director, and costume designer. And as Keeler had done in *42nd Street* and Powell in *Gold Diggers,* Cagney here takes over the leading role (in ''Shanghai Lil'') when the regular actor is unable to go on, thus marking his first major appearance as a hoofer on the screen.

"For Every Man There's a Woman" Music by Harold Arlen; lyric by Leo Robin. Philosophical view of the inevitability of love which was offered in *Casbah* (Univ. 1948) in three different settings: 1) by Tony Martin on a balcony overlooking the Casbah in Algiers; 2) by Martin to Marta Toren while dancing in a Casbah nightclub; 3) by Yvonne DeCarlo to Martin in her tobacco shop as she mocks his love for Miss Toren.

"For Me and My Gal" Music by George W. Meyer; lyric by Edgar Leslie & E. Ray Goetz. High-spirited song-and-dance number performed by vaudevillians Judy Garland and Gene Kelly in film of the same name (MGM) 1942. The scene was a small restaurant in Clifton Junction, Ohio, in 1916—the year before the song was actually written.

"For You" Music by Werner Heymann; lyric by Ted Koehler. Total devotion emotionally pledged by Kenny Baker in production number in *The King and the Chorus Girl* (Warner 1937).

"For You, For Me, For Evermore" Music by George Gershwin; lyric by Ira Gershwin. Dick Haymes and Betty Grable discover each other in *The Shocking Miss Pilgrim* (Fox 1947) and look forward to unending happiness. The ballad's music, discovered after George Gershwin's death, was written in Hollywood in 1936.

Foran, (John Nicholas) Dick, actor, singer; b. Flemington, NJ, June 18, 1910; d. Panorama City, Cal., Aug. 10, 1979. Rugged, red-haired lead and second lead who appeared in some 200 features—mostly Westerns—during a 44-year career. Introduced "I'll Remember April."

1934	Stand Up and Cheer (specialty)
1935	Lottery Lover
	Shipmates Forever (*Gifford*)
	Song of the Saddle (*Frank Wilson*)
1938	Cowboy from Brooklyn (*Sam Thorne*)
1941	In the Navy (*Dynamite Dugan*)
	Keep 'Em Flying (*Jimmy Roberts*)
	Behind the Eight Ball (*Bill Edwards*)
1942	Ride 'Em Cowboy (*Broncho Bob Mitchell*)
	Private Buckaroo (*Lou Prentice*)
1943	Hi, Buddy (*Dave O'Connor*)

Forrest, George. *See* **Wright and Forrest.**

Forrest, Sally (née Katherine Scully Feeney), actress, dancer; b. San Diego, May 28, 1928. Slim, blonde dancer who rose from MGM chorus to featured leads; later appeared in dramatic roles.

1946	Till the Clouds Roll By (dancer)
1948	Are You With It? (dancer)
	The Pirate (dancer)
1949	Take Me Out to the Ball Game (dancer)
1951	Excuse My Dust (*Liz Bullitt*)
	The Strip (*Jane Tafford*)

42nd Street (1933). Music by Harry Warren; lyrics by Al Dubin; screenplay by James Seymour & Rian James from novel by Bradford Ropes.

A Warner Bros. film produced by Darryl F. Zanuck; directed by Lloyd Bacon; choreography, Busby Berkeley; art director, Jack Okey; costumes, Orry-Kelly; music director, Leo F. Forbstein; cameraman, Sol Polito; editor, Thomas Pratt.

Cast: Warner Baxter (*Julian Marsh*); Bebe Daniels (*Dorothy Brock*); George Brent (*Pat Denning*); Ruby Keeler (*Peggy Sawyer*); Dick Powell (*Billy Lawler*); Ginger Rogers (*"Anytime Annie" Lowell*); Una Merkel (*Lollie Fleming*); Guy Kibbee (*Abner Dillon*); Ned Sparks (*Thomas Barry*); George E. Stone (*Andy Lee*); Allen Jenkins (*Mac MacElroy*); Eddie Nugent (*Terry Neil*); Henry B. Walthall (*old actor*); Clarence Nordstrom (*juvenile lead*); Harry Warren, Al Dubin (*songwriters*); Harry Akst (*pianist*); Jack LaRue (*tough guy*); Louise Beavers (*Pansy*); Toby Wing (*"Young and Healthy" girl*); Tom Kennedy (*Slim Murphy*); Charles Lane (*librettist*).

Songs: "It Must Be June" - chorus; reprised by Daniels, Powell/ "You're Getting To Be a Habit with Me" - Daniels/ "Shuffle Off to Buffalo" - Keeler, Nordstrom, with Merkel, Rogers, chorus/ "Young and Healthy" - Powell, with Wing, chorus/ "Forty-Second Street" - Keeler, Powell; dance by Keeler, chorus.

Once the sound revolution saturated the screen with musicals, the public soon tired of song-and-dance spectacles, and their numbers dwindled to a handful in 1931 and 1932. *42nd Street* brought them back. No matter that its backstage tale of heartbreak and success contained ingredients that had been part of such pioneering efforts as *The Broadway Melody* and Warner's own *On with the Show* and *The Gold Diggers of Broadway*. What gave *42nd Street* its seminal importance were the large-scale routines by choreographer Busby Berkeley—"Young and Healthy," "Shuffle Off to Buffalo,"

"Forty-Second Street"—that, more than in any previous film, took full advantage of the mobility of the camera and the opportunities for imaginative film editing. By not confining his production numbers to the limitations of a real stage, Berkeley put movie audiences into a fantasy world impossible to achieve in any other entertainment media.

42nd Street came about because Darryl Zanuck, then production head at Warner, simply felt that the time was right to bring back musicals. Jack Warner opposed the idea, but Zanuck went ahead anyway, with the film's musical sequences shot at night so that the studio boss would be unaware of what was going on. Allegedly it was only when he saw the first screening of the completed movie that Warner was aware that the picture was a musical.

The picture traces the creation of *Pretty Lady,* a Broadway-bound musical comedy (though its sequences seem totally disconnected), from the first rehearsals to the out-of-town opening in Philadelphia (why the opening shown on screen was not in a 42nd Street theatre remains a mystery). Along the way the story introduces various characters concerned with the production: the ruthless ailing director, Warner Baxter (whose screen name, Julian Marsh, suggests the prolific Broadway director Julian Mitchell); juvenile leads Ruby Keeler (in her movie debut) and Dick Powell; aging star Bebe Daniels (in a role originally intended for Kay Francis) and her ne'er-do-well lover George Brent; wise-cracking chorus girls Ginger Rogers and Una Merkel; plus assorted producers, writers (Warren and Dubin in bit parts), staff members, and backers. *42nd Street* also used a Cinderella plot device—borrowed from *On with the Show* and found with variations in many subsequent musicals—in which the unknown performer takes over from the show's lead. The situation gave Baxter the immortal line that ended his pep talk to replacement Ruby Keeler: "Sawyer, you're going out a youngster, but you've got to come back a star."

After the huge success of *42nd Street,* the formula was quickly applied again to *Gold Diggers of 1933* and *Footlight Parade.* All three had choreography by Berkeley, songs by Warren and Dubin, and Dick Powell singing to Ruby Keeler. And MGM's *Dancing Lady,* late in 1933, also gave us a story of a Broadway-bound musical (called *Dancing Lady*) in which a tough director (Clark Gable) replaces his star with a chorus girl (Joan Crawford) and uses a finale ("That's the Rythm of the Day") to show the frantic pace of modern living.

In 1980 an elaborate Broadway musical version of *42nd Street* starred Jerry Orbach (Julian) and Tammy Grimes (Dorothy), with the original Warren-Dubin numbers augmented by their songs from other films. The show was directed and choreographed by Gower Champion, who died the day the musical opened.

"Forty-Second Street" Music by Harry Warren; lyric by Al Dubin. Spirited invitation to that "naughty, bawdy, gaudy, sporty" thoroughfare introduced in a Busby Berkeley production number in a Broadway-bound musical in *42nd Street* (Warner 1933). First sung and tapped by Ruby Keeler as, literally, a taxi dancer performing on the roof of a Checker Cab, then developed into a panorama of the area as various types, including dancing girls, illustrate the frantic nature of the locale. In a hotel room viewed from outside, we see two lovers fighting so furiously that the girl jumps out of the window into the waiting arms of a boy below. Their dance is terminated when the jealous hotel-room lover stabs the girl. Viewing the melodramatic scene from a bar, Dick Powell sings part of the lyric, and the number ends with chorus girls mounting stairs and holding up huge cards of cutout buildings forming the Manhattan skyline. For some reason, Ruby and Dick get the final closeup.

Fosse, (Robert Louis) Bob, director, choreographer, actor, dancer; b. Chicago, June 23, 1927. Fosse made his name on Broadway with his jazzy, jagged dance routines for *The Pajama Game* and *Damn Yankees,* both of whose screen versions he also choreographed. He then became a pre-eminent director-choreographer of a series of dazzlingly stylized concept musicals, beginning with *Sweet Charity* (also filmed) and including *Pippin* and *Chicago.* His movie career began at MGM, where he acted and danced in three films (including *Kiss Me, Kate,* which also marked his first choreographic effort), later he returned to direct such screen successes as *Cabaret* and the autobiographical *All That Jazz.* Fosse was married to dancers Mary Ann Niles, Joan McCracken, and Gwen Verdon (all divorced). (Died Washington, DC, Sept. 23, 1987.)

Unless otherwise noted, Mr. Fosse was choreographer of the following (asterisk indicates he was also director):

1953 The Affairs of Dobie Gillis (*Charlie Trask* only)
      Kiss Me, Kate ("*Hortensio*") (also part-chor.)
      Give a Girl a Break (*Bob Dowdy* only)
1955 My Sister Eileen (also *Frank Lippincott*)
1957 The Pajama Game

1958 Damn Yankees (also dancer)
1968 Sweet Charity *
1972 Cabaret *
1975 The Little Prince (*Snake* only)
1979 All That Jazz * (also script)

Foster, Susanna (née Suzanne DeLee Flanders Larson), actress, singer; b. Chicago, Dec. 6, 1924. Miss Foster began her screen career as Paramount's teenage singing rival to Universal's Deanna Durbin; by 1943 she had become Universal's singing replacement for Miss Durbin. One of her distinctions was her ability to sing F above high C.

1939 The Great Victor Herbert (*Peggy*)
1941 There's Magic in Music (*Toodles LaVerne*)
     Glamour Boy (*Joan Winslow*)
1943 Phantom of the Opera (*Christine DuBois*)
     Top Man (*Connie Allen*)
1944 Follow the Boys (specialty)
     This Is the Life (*Angela*)
     Bowery to Broadway (*Peggy Fleming*)
     The Climax (*Angela*)
1945 Frisco Sal (*Sally*)
     That Night with You (*Penny*)

Foy, Eddie, Jr. (né Edwin Fitzgerald, Jr.), actor, singer, dancer; b. New Rochelle, NY, Feb. 4, 1905. Spry, slight, sharp-featured song-and-dance entertainer who repeated his Broadway stage role in *The Pajama Game* in the screen version. The son of comedian Eddie Foy, he began his career in his father's family vaudeville act; on screen he played Foy Senior in both musical and nonmusical films and narrated his father's film bio, *The Seven Little Foys,* starring Bob Hope. He was the brother of director-producer Bryan Foy. (Died July 15, 1983.)

1929 Queen of the Night Clubs (*Eddie Parr*)
1930 Leathernecking (*Chick Evans*)
1933 Broadway Thru a Keyhole (*Eddie Foy, Jr.*)
1937 Turn Off the Moon
1940 Lillian Russell (*Eddie Foy, Sr.*)
1941 Rookies on Parade (*Cliff Dugan*)
     Puddin' Head (*Harold Montgomery*)
     Four Jacks and a Jill
1942 Yokel Boy (*Joe Ruddy*)
     Yankee Doodle Dandy (*Eddie Foy, Sr.*)
     Moonlight Masquerade (*Lord Percy Ticklederry*)
     Joan of Ozark (*Eddie McCable*)
1943 Dixie (*Pelham*)
1944 And the Angels Sing (*Fuzzy Johnson*)
1951 Honey Chile (*Eddie Price*)
1953 The Farmer Takes a Wife (*Fortune Friendly*)
1954 Lucky Me (*Duke*)

1955 The Seven Little Foys (narrator)
1957 The Pajama Game (*Hinesy*)
1960 Bells Are Ringing (*J. Otto Pranz*)
1966 Olympus 7-0000 (tv) (*Casey*)

Francis, Connie (née Concetta Franconero), singer, actress; b. Newark, NJ, Dec. 12, 1938. Short, dark-haired singer, best known for many hit records and theatre and nightclub appearances.

1956 Rock Rock Rock (vocals for Tuesday Weld)
1957 Jamboree (specialty)
1960 Where the Boys Are (*Angie*)
1963 Follow the Boys (*Bonnie Pulaski*)
1964 Looking for Love (*Libby Caruso*)
1965 When the Boys Meet the Girls (*Ginger Gray*)

Frazee, Jane (née Mary Jane Frahse), actress, singer; b. Duluth, Minn., July 18, 1918. Nightclub and radio singer who became leading lady in low-budget Universal, Republic, and Columbia musicals. Appeared opposite Robert Paige seven times, Roy Rogers four, and Johnny Downs and Allan Jones three each. (Died 1985.)

1940 Melody and Moonlight (*Kay Barnett*)
1941 Buck Privates (*Judy Gray*)
     Angels with Broken Wings (*Jane Lord*)
     San Antonio Rose (*Hope Holloway*)
     Moonlight in Hawaii (*Toby*)
     Sing Another Chorus (*Edna*)
     Hellzapoppin (*Kitty*)
1942 What's Cookin'? (*Anne Payne*)
     Almost Married (*Gloria Dobson*)
     Moonlight Masquerade (*Vikki Forrester*)
     Get Hep to Love (*Ann Winters*)
     Moonlight in Havana (*Gloria Jackson*)
     Don't Get Personal (*Mary Reynolds*)
     When Johnny Comes Marching Home (*Joyce*)
1943 Hi' Ya Chum (*Sunny*)
     Rhythm of the Islands (*Joan Holton*)
1944 Rosie the Riveter (*Rosie Warren*)
     Kansas City Kitty (*Eileen Hasbrook*)
     She's a Sweetheart (*Maxine Lecour*)
     Beautiful but Broke (*Sally Richards*)
     Swing in the Saddle
     Cowboy Canteen
1947 Calendar Girl (*Patricia O'Neil*)
     Springtime in the Sierras (*Taffy Baker*)
1948 The Gay Ranchero (*Betty Richards*)
     Under California Stars
     Grand Canyon Trail (*Carol Martin*)

Freed, Arthur, producer, lyricist; b. Charleston, SC, Sept. 9, 1894; d. Hollywood, April 12, 1973. Hollywood's highly esteemed prolific producer of musical films, Freed began his career as an MGM executive with *The Wizard of Oz,* on which he was assistant producer. With the creation of his own Freed Unit at the studio, he put together a series of major, frequently innovative works led by *Babes in Arms, Cabin in the Sky, Girl Crazy, Meet Me in St. Louis, The Harvey Girls, Ziegfeld Follies, The Pirate, Easter Parade, On the Town, Annie Get Your Gun, Show Boat, An American in Paris, Singin' in the Rain, The Band Wagon,* and *Gigi.* Among directors and choreographers who worked on his films were Vincente Minnelli (11 musicals), Robert Alton (11), Gene Kelly (8), Busby Berkeley (8), Charles Walters (8), Stanley Donen (4). Actors who made multiple appearances in Freed's musical productions include Judy Garland (14), Gene Kelly (12), Cyd Charisse (9), Fred Astaire (8), Mickey Rooney (6), Red Skelton (4), June Allyson (4), and Howard Keel (4). Among song and script writers associated with his films were Betty Comden and Adolph Green (8), Harry Warren (6), Alan Jay Lerner (4), plus Cole Porter, Ira Gershwin, Irving Berlin, Johnny Mercer, Harold Arlen, E. Y. Harburg, Frederick Loewe, Burton Lane, and Ralph Freed (his brother). Roger Edens began working with Freed as composer, lyricist, and adapter in 1939; later he was his associate producer on 19 musicals.

Before his career as producer, Freed was an MGM lyricist whose partnership with composer Nacio Herb Brown resulted in the scores for such films as *The Broadway Melody* ("Broadway Melody," "You Were Meant for Me," "The Wedding of the Painted Doll") and *Broadway Melody of 1936* ("You Are My Lucky Star," "I've Got a Feelin' You're Foolin'," "Broadway Rhythm"). Other songs by the team were "Singin' in the Rain," "Pagan Love Song," "Should I?," "Temptation," "All I Do Is Dream of You," "Alone," and "Would You?" (Most of these were in *Singin' in the Rain.*) Freed also wrote with composers Al Hoffman and Al Goodhart ("Fit as a Fiddle"), Roger Edens ("Our Love Affair"), and Harry Warren ("This Heart of Mine"). Charles King, Cliff Edwards, Bing Crosby, Allan Jones, Kitty Carlisle, Jeanette MacDonald, Robert Taylor, Frances Langford, Judy Garland, Mickey Rooney, and Fred Astaire were among those who introduced Arthur Freed songs. Bib: *The MGM Years* by Lawrence Thomas (1972); *The World of Entertainment* by Hugh Fordin (1975).

Beginning in 1939 Mr. Freed was a producer; films for which he wrote lyrics are indicated by composers' names in parentheses:

1929	The Broadway Melody (Brown)
	Hollywood Revue of 1929 (Brown)
1930	Lord Byron of Broadway (Brown)
	Good News (Brown)
1933	Going Hollywood (Brown)
1934	Sadie McKee (Brown)
	Student Tour (Brown)
1935	Broadway Melody of 1936 (Brown)
1937	Broadway Melody of 1938 (Brown)
1939	The Wizard of Oz (asst. prod. only)
	Babes in Arms (Brown)
1940	Strike Up the Band (Edens)
	Little Nellie Kelly
1941	Lady, Be Good
	Babes on Broadway
1942	Panama Hattie
	For Me and My Gal
1943	Cabin in the Sky
	DuBarry Was a Lady
	Best Foot Forward
	Girl Crazy
1944	Meet Me in St. Louis (also vocal for Leon Ames)
1945	Yolanda and the Thief (Warren)
1946	The Harvey Girls
	Ziegfeld Follies
1947	Till the Clouds Roll By
	Good News
1948	Summer Holiday
	The Pirate
	Easter Parade
	Words and Music
1949	Take Me Out to the Ball Game
	The Barkleys of Broadway
	On the Town
1950	Annie Get Your Gun
	Pagan Love Song (Warren)
1951	Royal Wedding
	Show Boat
	An American in Paris
1952	The Belle of New York
	Singin' in the Rain (Brown)
1953	The Band Wagon
1954	Brigadoon
1955	It's Always Fair Weather
	Kismet
1956	Invitation to the Dance
1957	Silk Stockings
1958	Gigi
1960	Bells Are Ringing

Freed, Ralph, lyricist; b. Vancouver, BC, Canada, May 1, 1907; d. Los Angeles, Feb. 13, 1973. Brother of lyricist-producer Arthur Freed, his best-known song was "How About You?," music by Burton Lane, in *Babes on Broadway*. Other collaborators: Frank Skinner, Sammy Fain, Jimmy McHugh.

1939   She Married a Cop (Lane)
1941   Babes on Broadway (Lane)
1944   Two Girls and a Sailor (McHugh, etc.)
1945   No Leave, No Love (Fain)
1946   Holiday in Mexico (Fain, etc.)
        Two Sisters from Boston (Fain)
1947   This Time for Keeps (Fain; Lane)

Freeland, Thornton, director; b. Hope, ND, Feb. 10, 1898. Freeland's major musicals were *Whoopee* (first Eddie Cantor hit) and *Flying Down to Rio* (first Astaire-Rogers film).

1930   Be Yourself
        Whoopee
1933   Flying Down to Rio
1934   George White's Scandals
1935   Brewster's Millions (Eng.)
1937   Paradise for Two (Eng.)
1938   Hold My Hand (Eng.)
        Gaiety Girls (Eng.)
1941   Too Many Blondes

"French Lesson, The" Music by Roger Edens; lyric by Betty Comden & Adolph Green. Rudimentary language exercise (to a melody reminiscent of Rodgers and Hart's "How To Win Friends and Influence People") performed by librarian June Allyson to help football player Peter Lawford pass an important test in *Good News* (MGM 1947). Rumor has it that Lawford, who is actually proficient in French, had to coach Miss Allyson in the pronunciations.

"Friend of Yours, A" Music by James Van Heusen; lyric by Johnny Burke. In *The Great John L.* (UA 1945), Lee Sullivan gave musical advice to keep the others from guessing how serious things really were.

"Friendly Persuasion" (**"Thee I Love"**) Music by Dimitri Tiomkin; lyric by Paul Francis Webster. Gently bucolic piece sung on soundtrack of nonmusical film of the same name (AA 1956) by Pat Boone. The movie, which was about Quaker farmers, was originally to have been called *Thee I Love,* with the lyric to the title song written accordingly. When the name was changed, lyricist Webster justified the song's new title by substituting the line, "Lips have I to kiss thee too in friendly persuasion."

Friml, Rudolf, composer; b. Prague, Dec. 1, 1879; d. Hollywood, Nov. 12, 1972. Between 1912 and 1934, Friml created a series of rich, robust Broadway operettas, three of which received the Hollywood treatment: *The Firefly,* with lyricist Otto Harbach (new story); *Rose-Marie,* with Harbach, Oscar Hammerstein II, and Herbert Stothart (three versions, the first silent, the second with altered story, the third with added Friml songs); and *The Vagabond King,* with Brian Hooker (filmed twice, the second time with added Friml songs). "The Donkey Serenade," with co-composer Stothart and lyric by Robert Wright and George Forrest, is Friml's best-remembered movie song. Other screen collaborators: J. Keirn Brennan, Gus Kahn, Edward Heyman, Paul Francis Webster, Johnny Burke. In films Friml's songs were sung by Jeanette MacDonald (four movies), Nelson Eddy, Allan Jones, Nino Martini, Ann Blyth, Howard Keel, and Kathryn Grayson.

1930   The Vagabond King (Hooker)
        The Lottery Bride (Brennan)
1936   Rose Marie (Stothart-Harbach, Hammerstein)
1937   The Firefly (Harbach; Stothart-Wright, Forrest)
        Music for Madame (Kahn)
1947   Northwest Outpost (Heyman)
1954   Rose Marie (Stothart-Harbach, Hammerstein; Webster)
1956   The Vagabond King (Hooker; Burke)

"From Russia with Love" Music & lyric by Lionel Bart. Matt Monro introduced this moodily romantic piece on the soundtrack of the James Bond film of the same name (UA 1964).

"From the Top of Your Head (to the Tip of Your Toes)" Music by Harry Revel; lyric by Mack Gordon. "You have so many thrillables, I'm all out of syllables," sang a buoyant Bing Crosby in *Two for Tonight* (Par. 1935), to extol the charms of Joan Bennett.

"From This Moment On" Music & lyric by Cole Porter. Exuberant ballad heralding the beginning of a carefree romantic life ("No more blue songs/ Only whoop-de-doo songs"), which Cole Porter had written for the 1950 Broadway musical *Out of This World,* but which, inexplicably, was dropped. It was, however, added to the film version of *Kiss Me, Kate* (MGM 1953) and was sung and danced by Tommy Rall (he did most of the singing), Ann Miller, Bobby Van, and Bob Fosse in a scene from a musical-stage version of Shakespeare's *The Taming of the Shrew.* Though the number was otherwise directed by Hermes Pan, a 45-second dance performed by Fosse and Carol Haney marks Fosse's debut as a choreographer.

"Fuddy Duddy Watchmaker, The" Music by Jimmy McHugh; lyric by Frank Loesser. Bouncy number of an ancient watchmaker's skill at making a watch tick with a beautiful beat ("I dunno how he does it but he does it"). Betty Hutton expressed proper awe in *Happy Go Lucky* (Par. 1943).

Funicello, Annette, actress, singer; b. Utica, NY, Oct. 22, 1942. Former Walt Disney juvenile lead (then known as "Annette"), who teamed in 1963 for some gritty musical escapades with Frankie Avalon.

1961	Babes in Toyland (*Mary Contrary*)	
1963	Beach Party (*Dolores*)	
1964	Muscle Beach Party (*Deedee*)	
	Bikini Beach (*Deedee*)	
1965	Beach Blanket Bingo (*Deedee*)	
1966	Fireball 500 (*Jane*)	
1967	How To Stuff a Wild Bikini (*Deedee*)	
	Pajama Party (*Connie*)	
1987	Back to the Beach (*Deedee*)	

Funny Face (1957). Music mostly by George Gershwin; lyrics mostly by Ira Gershwin; screenplay by Leonard Gershe from his unproduced musical *Wedding Day*.

A Paramount film produced by Roger Edens; directed by Stanley Donen; choreography, Fred Astaire, Eugene Loring; art directors, Hal Pereira, George W. Davis; costumes, Edith Head; music director, Adolph Deutsch; orchestrations, Conrad Salinger, Mason Van Cleave, Alexander Courage, Skip Martin; cameraman, Ray June; editor, Frank Bracht; Technicolor; VistaVision.

Cast: Fred Astaire (*Dick Avery*); Audrey Hepburn (*Jo Stockton*); Kay Thompson (*Maggie Prescott*); Michel Auclair (*Emil Flostre*); Robert Flemyng (*Paul Duval*); Virginia Gibson (*Babs*); Dovima (*Marion*).

Songs: "Think Pink!" (Roger Edens-Leonard Gershe) - Thompson/ "How Long Has This Been Going On?" - Hepburn/ "Funny Face" - Astaire; dance by Astaire, Hepburn/ "Bonjours, Paris!" (Edens-Gershe) - Astaire, Thompson, Hepburn/ "Let's Kiss and Make Up" - Astaire/ "He Loves and She Loves" - Astaire; dance by Astaire, Hepburn/ "On How To Be Lovely" (Edens-Gershe) - Thompson, Hepburn/ "Marche Funèbre" (Edens) - uncredited French singer/ "Clap Yo' Hands" - Astaire, Thompson/ " 'S Wonderful" -Astaire, Hepburn.

Except for the title, the presence of Fred Astaire, and the retention of four Gershwin songs, the movie *Funny Face* bore no resemblance to the 1927 Broadway musical, in which Astaire had co-starred with his sister Adele. (The screen version of *that* production, called *She Knew What She Wanted*, had been made in England in 1936.) Hollywood's *Funny Face* came about only after a series of complicated negotiations involving MGM (which had writer Gershe, producer Edens, and director Donen under contract), Warner Bros. (which owned the rights to the Gershwin songs Edens wanted to use), and Paramount (which had contracts with Audrey Hepburn and Fred Astaire). Eventually, Warner sold the rights to MGM, and MGM lent Gershe, Edens, and Donen to Paramount. The story, based on a libretto Gershe had written for an unproduced stage musical, dealt with a fashion photographer (Astaire) and a Greenwich Village intellectual (Hepburn) whose heart melts under the romantic influence of Paris, where she has gone as a model. (Astaire's next film, *Silk Stockings,* also used Paris in a similar manner, though this time the city helps break down the resistance of a doctrinaire Communist agent.)

In the stunningly photographed *Funny Face,* Astaire's character (Dick Avery), was based on photographer Richard Avedon (the movie's visual consultant), Kay Thompson's magazine editor was modeled on Carmel Snow of *Harper's Bazaar,* and Michel Auclair's Professor Flostre, the founder of Empathicalism, was a fairly heavy-handed putdown of Jean-Paul Sartre, the founder of Existentialism. Though the weather was often uncooperative, most of the film's exterior shooting was done on location in Paris. Choreographically, the film was most distinguished by Astaire's courtyard solo to "Let's Kiss and Make Up" and the Astaire-Hepburn misty morning dance to "He Loves and She Loves." *Funny Face* also marked the first—of two—musicals Miss Hepburn has made to date, and the one in which she did her own singing.

Funny Girl (1968). Music by Jule Styne; lyrics by Bob Merrill; screenplay by Isobel Lennart from Broadway musical by Lennart, Styne, and Merrill based on the life of Fanny Brice.

A Columbia film produced by Ray Stark and William Wyler; directed by Wyler, Herbert Ross (uncredited); choreography, Ross; production designed by Gene Callahan; art director, Robert Luthardt; costumes, Irene Sharaff; music director, Walter Scharf; cameraman,

Harry Stradling; editors, Maury Winetrode, William Sands; Technicolor; PanaVision.

Cast: Barbra Streisand (*Fanny Brice*); Omar Sharif (*Nick Arnstein*); Kay Medford (*Rose Brice*); Anne Francis (*Georgia James*); Walter Pidgeon (*Florenz Ziegfeld*); Lee Allen (*Eddie Ryan*); Mae Questel (*Mrs. Strakosh*); Tommy Rall (*dancer*).

Songs: "I'm the Greatest Star" - Streisand/ "If a Girl Isn't Pretty" - Medford, Questel/ "Roller Skate Rag" - chorus; dance by Streisand/ "I'd Rather Be Blue Over You" (Fred Fisher-Billy Rose) - Streisand/ "Second Hand Rose" (James Hanley-Grant Clarke) - Streisand/ "His Love Makes Me Beautiful" - chorus, Streisand/ "People" - Streisand/ "You Are Woman, I Am Man" - Sharif, Streisand/ "Don't Rain on My Parade" - Streisand/ "Sadie, Sadie" - Streisand/ "The Swan" - Streisand; dance by Streisand, Rall/ "Funny Girl" - Streisand/ "My Man" (Maurice Yvain-Channing Pollock) - Streisand.

After appearing as Fanny Brice in her first starring role on the stage and the screen, Barbra Streisand emerged as a greater attraction than the woman she portrayed. The 1964 Broadway musical, in which Miss Streisand played opposite Sydney Chaplin, was the fulfillment of a dream long held by producer Ray Stark, who was also Miss Brice's son-in-law. Originally conceived as a screen musical, it seemed more appropriate, at least initially, for the stage. The show weathered many problems, including changes of director and postponements of the opening, but went on to achieve a run of over three years.

The movie version, also produced by Stark, was written by the original librettist (who was primarily a screenwriter anyway). It also retained seven of the Styne-Merrill songs, and added three new pieces by the team and three period numbers identified with Miss Brice ("My

Man," her trademark song, provided the finale). Kay Medford of the Broadway company and Lee Allen of the London company were also in the film. Though the story—about Fanny's stormy romance with her husband Nick Arnstein, and the problems caused by his shady financial dealings—remained basically the same, the screen version took full advantage of the medium for musical and dramatic effectiveness. "Don't Rain on My Parade" was now sung by Miss Streisand as she rushes through a railway station, rides on a train, drives a car, and stands on the bridge of a tugboat sailing past the Statue of Liberty.

One controversy developed over directing credit. Though he actually directed over half the film, Herbert Ross, who was also the choreographer, had to be content with the billing "Musical Numbers Directed by . . ." Ross, however, did get to direct and choreograph *Funny Lady,* the sequel to *Funny Girl,* again starring Miss Streisand. Released in 1975, it took up the story of Fanny's unhappy second marriage to songwriter-producer Billy Rose (played by James Caan). The film had six new songs by John Kander and Fred Ebb, plus nine old ones by assorted writers, including Rose.

A previous film musical based on the Fanny Brice-Nick Arnstein romance was released by Fox in 1939. Though claiming to be "entirely fictional," *Rose of Washington Square* starred Alice Faye and Tyrone Power in a saga so close to reality (Alice even sang "My Man") that Miss Brice sued the studio. The case was settled out of court.

"Funny Old Hills, The" Music by Ralph Rainger; lyric by Leo Robin. Bing Crosby sang this echolalic, rhythmic number in *Paris Honeymoon* (Par. 1939).

G

Gable, (William) Clark, actor; b. Cadiz, Ohio, Feb. 1, 1901; d. Los Angeles, Nov. 16, 1960. Gable was Hollywood's pre-eminent man's-man movie star. Though he appeared in three musicals, the only solo he sang on the screen was "Puttin' on the Ritz" in the nonmusical *Idiot's Delight*. In a career that covered 67 film appearances, his major roles were in *It Happened One Night, Mutiny on the Bounty,* and *Gone with the Wind*. Carole Lombard was the third of his five wives. Bib: *The King* by Charles Samuels (1963); *Films of Clark Gable* by Gabe Essoe (1970); *Long Live the King* by Lyn Tornabene (1977).

1933	Dancing Lady (*Patch Gallagher*)
1936	San Francisco (*Blackie Norton*)
	Cain and Mabel (*Larry Cain*)

"Gal in Calico, A" Music by Arthur Schwartz; lyric by Leo Robin. The loping tale of a rodeo cowboy who hopes to marry a calico-clad gal and settle down in Santa Fe. Sung in *The Time, the Place and the Girl* (Warner 1946) by Dennis Morgan and Jack Carson in a Broadway-bound revue. In the scene, Morgan and Carson, as cowboys, serenade Martha Vickers as she is donning a dress of the prescribed fabric, and the number ends with chorus girls rope-twirling in a corral. The melody of the song had been written in 1934 with a different lyric (by Howard Dietz) for a radio series, *The Gibson Family*.

Gallagher, Richard "Skeets," actor; b. Terre Haute, Ind., July 28, 1891; d. Santa Monica, May 22, 1955. Blond, breezy former vaudevillian and Broadway actor who appeared in early Paramount musicals.

1929	Close Harmony (*Johnny Bay*)
	Pointed Heels (*Donald Ogden*)
1930	Honey (*Charles Dangerfield*)
	Paramount on Parade (m.c.)

	Let's Go Native (*Jerry*)
	Love Among the Millionaires (*Roots*)
1933	Too Much Harmony (*Johnny Dixon*)
1936	Hats Off (*Buzz Morton*)
1941	Zis Boom Bah

Gardiner, (William) Reginald, actor; b. Wimbledon, Eng., Feb. 27, 1903, d. Westwood, Cal., July 8, 1980. Though usually cast as an uppity butler or nobleman, Gardiner made his US screen debut in *Born To Dance* as a nonspeaking NY policeman with an urge to conduct a symphony orchestra. Actor, who first appeared on London stage, won fame for impersonations of trains and wallpaper.

1934	How's Chances? (Eng.) (*Dersingham*)
1936	Born To Dance (*policeman*)
1937	A Damsel in Distress (*Keggs*)
1938	Everybody Sing (*Jerrold Hope*)
	Sweethearts (*Norman Trumpett*)
1943	Sweet Rosie O'Grady (*Duke Charles*)
1945	The Dolly Sisters (*Duke*)
1946	Do You Love Me? (*Herbert Benham*)
1947	I Wonder Who's Kissing Her Now (*Will Hough*)
1948	That Lady in Ermine (*Alberto*)
1950	Wabash Avenue (*English Eddie*)
	I'll Get By (guest bit)
1955	Ain't Misbehavin' (*Piermont Rogers*)
1958	Rock-a-Bye Baby (*Henry Herman*)

Gardner, Ava (Lavinia), actress; b. Grabtown, NC, Dec. 24, 1922. Dark-haired sultry beauty, mostly in dramas, whose major musical role was in *Show Boat*. She was married to and divorced from Mickey Rooney, Artie Shaw, and Frank Sinatra. Bib: *Ava* by David Hanna (1974); *Ava Gardner* by Judith Kass (1977).

1941	Babes on Broadway (bit)
1943	DuBarry Was a Lady (bit)
	Swing Fever (bit)

1944   Two Girls and a Sailor (bit)
        Music for Millions (bit)
1948   One Touch of Venus (*Venus/Venus Jones*)
1951   Show Boat (*Julie LaVerne*)
1953   The Band Wagon (guest bit)
1976   The Blue Bird (*Luxury*)

Garland, Judy (née Frances Ethel Gumm), actress, singer; b. Grand Rapids, Minn., June 10, 1922; d. London, June 22, 1969. The poignant, smiling-through-tears waif who could overcome all obstacles—at least on the screen—Judy Garland was MGM's major female musical attraction of the 1940s. The catch in the throat, the tremolo in the voice, the clutch of the hand all helped her performances convey such personal intensity that she forged a far stronger emotional bond with her audience than any other performer on the screen. Among the highlights of her movie career—her "Dear Mr. Gable" confession in *Broadway Melody of 1938* . . . the enduring children's fantasy, *The Wizard of Oz* (singing "Over the Rainbow") . . . the "backyard musicals" with Mickey Rooney, such as *Babes in Arms* ("Good Morning"), *Strike Up the Band* ("Our Love Affair"), and *Babes on Broadway* ("How About You?") . . . the three appearances with Gene Kelly, *For Me and My Gal, The Pirate* ("Be a Clown"), and *Summer Stock* ("Get Happy") . . . those sentimental journeys into America's past, *Meet Me in St. Louis* ("The Boy Next Door," "Have Yourself a Merry Little Christmas," "The Trolley Song"), *The Harvey Girls* ("On the Atchison, Topeka and the Santa Fe"), and *In the Good Old Summertime* ("I Don't Care") . . . singing and dancing with Fred Astaire in *Easter Parade* ("A Couple of Swells") . . . and her dramatic comeback in *A Star Is Born* ("The Man That Got Away").

Miss Garland, whose emotional problems were responsible for the termination of her MGM contract in 1950, also made many records, gave sellout concerts, had her own television series, and worked on five films after *A Star Is Born*. The first three of her five husbands were composer David Rose, director Vincente Minnelli, and producer Sid Luft. She is also the mother of Liza Minnelli and Lorna Luft. Bib: *Judy* by Joe Morella & Edward Epstein (1970); *Judy* by Gerold Frank (1975); *Judy Garland* by Anne Edwards (1975); *Rainbow* by Christopher Finch (1975).

1936   Pigskin Parade (*Sairy Dodd*)
1937   Broadway Melody of 1938 (*Betty Clayton*)
1938   Everybody Sing (*Judy Bellaire*)
        Listen, Darling (*Pinkie Wingate*)
        Love Finds Andy Hardy (*Betsy Booth*)
1939   The Wizard of Oz (*Dorothy Gale*)
        Babes in Arms (*Patsy Barton*)
1940   Andy Hardy Meets Debutante (*Betsy Booth*)
        Strike Up the Band (*Mary Holden*)
        Little Nellie Kelly (*Nellie Kelly*)
1941   Ziegfeld Girl (*Susan Gallagher*)
        Babes on Broadway (*Penny Morris*)
1942   For Me and My Gal (*Jo Hayden*)
1943   Presenting Lily Mars (*Lily Mars*)
        Girl Crazy (*Ginger Gray*)
        Thousands Cheer (specialty)
1944   Meet Me in St. Louis (*Esther Smith*)
1946   The Harvey Girls (*Susan Bradley*)
        Ziegfeld Follies (specialty)
        Till the Clouds Roll By (*Marilyn Miller*)
1948   The Pirate (*Manuela*)
        Easter Parade (*Hannah Brown*)
        Words and Music (specialty)
1949   In the Good Old Summertime (*Veronica Fisher*)
1950   Summer Stock (*Jane Falbury*)
1954   A Star Is Born (*Esther Blodgett Maine*)
1960   Pepe (voice only)
1962   Gay Purr-ee (voice of *Mewsette*)
        I Could Go on Singing (*Jenny Bowman*)

Garrett, Betty, actress, singer; b. St. Joseph, Mo., May 23, 1919. Squeaky-voiced, round-eyed comic actress who appeared in Broadway revue, *Call Me Mister,* before making Hollywood debut. She played opposite Frank Sinatra in *Take Me Out to the Ball Game* and *On the Town* and sang "Baby, It's Cold Outside" in *Neptune's Daughter.* Miss Garrett, who has also acted in dramatic roles, was married to the late Larry Parks.

1948   Big City (*Shoo-Shoo Grady*)
        Words and Music (*Peggy McNeil*)
1949   Take Me Out to the Ball Game (*Shirley Delwyn*)
        Neptune's Daughter (*Betty Barrett*)
        On the Town (*Hildy*)
1955   My Sister Eileen (*Ruth Sherwood*)

Gaxton, William (né Arturo Antonio Gaxiola), actor, singer; b. San Francisco, Dec. 2, 1893; d. New York, Feb. 2, 1963. Gaxton was a slick-haired, chunky, nervously energetic Broadway musical-comedy lead (*A Connecticut Yankee, Of Thee I Sing*), who duplicated a stage role only in the screen version of *Fifty Million Frenchmen* (but the songs were cut). Otherwise, he was Hollywood's idea of what a press agent looked and talked like.

1943   Stage Door Canteen (guest bit)
       Best Foot Forward (*Jack O'Riley*)
       Something To Shout About (*Willard Samson*)
       The Heat's On (*Tony Ferris*)
1945   Diamond Horseshoe (*Joe Davis, Sr.*)

Gay Divorcee, The (1934). Music by Cole Porter, Harry Revel, Con Conrad; lyrics by Porter, Mack Gordon, Herb Magidson; screenplay by George Marion Jr., Dorothy Yost, Edward Kaufman from Broadway musical *Gay Divorce* by Samuel Hoffenstein, Kenneth Webb, and Porter based on play by Dwight Taylor taken from unproduced play, *An Adorable Adventure,* by J. Hartley Manners.

An RKO-Radio film produced by Pandro S. Berman; directed by Mark Sandrich; choreography, Fred Astaire, Dave Gould, Hermes Pan; art directors, Van Nest Polglase, Carroll Clark; costumes, Walter Plunkett; music director, Max Steiner; cameraman, David Abel; editor, William Hamilton.

Cast: Fred Astaire (*Guy Holden*); Ginger Rogers (*Mimi Glossop*); Alice Brady (*Hortense Ditherwell*); Edward Everett Horton (*Egbert Fitzgerald*); Erik Rhodes (*Rodolfo Tonetti*); Eric Blore (*waiter*); Betty Grable (*hotel guest*); Lillian Miles (*singer*); E. E. Clive (*customs inspector*).

Songs: "Don't Let It Bother You" (Revel-Gordon) - chorus; dance by Astaire/ "A Needle in a Haystack" (Conrad-Magidson) - Astaire/ "Let's K-nock K-nees" (Revel-Gordon) - Grable, Horton/ "Night and Day" (Porter) - Astaire; dance by Astaire, Rogers/ "The Continental" (Conrad-Magidson) - Rogers, Rhodes, Miles; dance by Astaire, Rogers, chorus.

To take advantage of the success Astaire and Rogers had achieved in *Flying Down to Rio,* RKO decided to build an entire movie around their talents. The vehicle chosen was based on *Gay Divorce,* a 1932 Broadway musical which had marked Astaire's final appearance in New York (and his only one without sister Adele). The first problem for the screen version was the title, since a divorce, according to the Hays office, could never be gay. They did, however, permit the adjective to apply to a divorcee. The film also brought Astaire and Rogers together with producer Pandro S. Berman (he was in charge of seven of their movies) and director Mark Sandrich (he did five).

Though some changes beside the title were made when the musical went before the camera, the basic story was retained. Fred, now cast as a dancer rather than a writer, is mistakenly thought by Ginger to be a professional corespondent with whom she must spend the night at an English resort to win a divorce. Complications arise when the real corespondent, a dandified Italian shows up at the hotel, but all is straightened out by next morning's breakfast. Of Cole Porter's original Broadway score of 10 songs, only "Night and Day" (one of Astaire and Rogers' most magical routines) was used in the film; otherwise, four new numbers—including "The Continental"—were supplied by two Hollywood teams. In addition to Astaire, two actors repeated their stage roles in the movie: Erik Rhodes as the corespondent and Eric Blore as a fussy waiter. (*The Gay Divorcee* and *Top Hat,* the third Astaire-Rogers vehicle, are compared under the latter title.)

Gaynor, Janet (née Laura Gainor), actress; b. Philadelphia, Oct. 6, 1906. Diminutive, spunky heroine—something of a transitional figure between Mary Pickford and Shirley Temple—who appeared in Fox musicals and nonmusicals. Her most memorable musical was *Sunny Side Up,* appearing opposite her frequent co-star Charles Farrell, in which she sang "I'm a Dreamer, Aren't We All?," "Sunny Side Up," and "If I Had a Talking Picture of You." (Died Sept. 14, 1984.)

1929   Sunny Side Up (*Molly Carr*)
1930   Happy Days (guest bit)
       High Society Blues (*Eleanor Divine*)
1931   Delicious (*Heather Gordon*)
1933   Adorable (*Princess Marie Christine*)
1957   Bernardine (*Mrs. Wilson*)

Gaynor, Mitzi (née Francesca Mitzi de Czanyi von Gerber), actress, singer, dancer; b. Chicago, Sept. 4, 1930. A leggy, lively, round-faced performer, Miss Gaynor appeared mostly in Fox musicals and enjoyed her biggest success in *South Pacific.* She retired from films in 1963 and has since appeared in nightclubs and on television.

1950   My Blue Heaven (*Gloria Adams*)
1951   Golden Girl (*Lotta Crabtree*)
1952   Bloodhounds of Broadway (*Emily Ann Stackerlee*)
1953   The "I Don't Care" Girl (*Eva Tanguay*)
       Down Among the Sheltering Palms (*Rozouila*)
1954   There's No Business Like Show Business (*Katy Donahue*)
1956   Anything Goes (*Patsy Blair*)
1957   The Joker Is Wild (*Martha Stewart*)
       Les Girls (*Joy Henderson*)
1958   South Pacific (*Nellie Forbush*)

"Georgy Girl" Music by Tom Springfield; lyric by Jim Dale. Jaunty advice to a seemingly carefree but actually lonely girl to "shed those dowdy feathers and fly." Sung by The Seekers on soundtrack of nonmusical film, *Georgy Girl* (Col. 1966), in which the title role was played by Lynn Redgrave.

Gershwin, George (né Jacob Gershvin), composer; b. Brooklyn, Sept. 26, 1898; d. Beverly Hills, July 11, 1937. The dominant Broadway composer to emerge during the 1920s, Gershwin created a ceaseless flow of brisk, infectious rhythms and affectingly poignant ballads that were sung in 23 musicals in New York and two in London. With the exception of *Song of the Flame,* written with Otto Harbach and Oscar Hammerstein II, all of his Broadway musicals adapted for the screen were written with his brother, lyricist Ira Gershwin: *Tip-Toes* (silent); *Oh, Kay!* (silent); *Funny Face* (made in England as *She Knew What She Wanted*); *Rosalie* (no Gershwin songs); *Girl Crazy* (filmed three times, the last retitled *When the Boys Meet the Girls*); and *Porgy and Bess* (with co-lyricist DuBose Heyward). Original movie musicals with songs from Gershwin's stage scores were *Lady, Be Good, An American in Paris, Rhapsody in Blue* (the composer's film bio, with Robert Alda as Gershwin), and *Funny Face.* Original Gershwin music was heard in such Hollywood attractions as *Shall We Dance* ("Shall We Dance?," "They All Laughed," "Beginner's Luck," "They Can't Take That Away from Me," "Let's Call the Whole Thing Off "); *A Damsel in Distress* ("Nice Work If You Can Get It," "A Foggy Day"); *The Goldwyn Follies* ("Love Is Here To Stay," "Love Walked In"); *The Shocking Miss Pilgrim* ("Changing My Tune," "For You, For Me, For Evermore").

Among those who sang Gershwin songs on the screen were Janet Gaynor, Fred Astaire, Ginger Rogers, Kenny Baker, Ann Sothern, Judy Garland, Mickey Rooney, Betty Grable, Dick Haymes, Gene Kelly, Audrey Hepburn, and Sammy Davis, Jr. Bib: *George Gershwin,* ed. by Merle Armitage (1938); *George Gershwin: A Study in American Music* by Isaac Goldberg & Edith Garson (1958); *George and Ira Gershwin Song Book* (1960); *The Gershwin Years* by Edward Jablonski & Lawrence Stewart (1973); *The Gershwins* by Robert Kimball & Alfred Simon (1973).

Unless otherwise noted, the following had songs written with Ira Gershwin:

1930 Song of the Flame (Harbach, Hammerstein)

1931 Delicious
1932 Girl Crazy
1936 She Knew What She Wanted (Eng.)
1937 Shall We Dance
      A Damsel in Distress
1938 The Goldwyn Follies
1941 Lady, Be Good
1943 Girl Crazy
1945 Rhapsody in Blue
1947 The Shocking Miss Pilgrim
1951 An American in Paris
1957 Funny Face
1959 Porgy and Bess (also Heyward)
1964 Kiss Me, Stupid
1965 When the Boys Meet the Girls

Gershwin, Ira (né Israel Gershvin), lyricist; b. New York, Dec. 6, 1896. Composer George Gershwin and lyricist Ira Gershwin formed the most successful sibling songwriting team ever to work in the Broadway musical theatre. Of the 14 shows they wrote together, those adapted for the screen were *Tip-Toes* (silent); *Oh, Kay!* (silent); *Funny Face* (made in England as *She Knew What She Wanted*); *Rosalie* (no Gershwin songs); *Girl Crazy* (filmed three times, the last retitled *When the Boys Meet the Girls*); and *Porgy and Bess* (with co-lyricist DuBose Heyward). Songs from the brothers' stage musicals were also sung in the following original movie musicals: *Lady, Be Good, An American in Paris, Rhapsody in Blue* (the composer's bio), and *Funny Face.* Songs they wrote for the screen were introduced in such Hollywood fare as *Shall We Dance* ("Shall We Dance?," "They All Laughed," "Beginner's Luck," "They Can't Take That Away from Me," "Let's Call the Whole Thing Off "); *A Damsel in Distress* ("Nice Work If You Can Get It," "A Foggy Day"); *The Goldwyn Follies* ("Love Is Here To Stay," "Love Walked In"); *The Shocking Miss Pilgrim* ("Changing My Tune," "For You, For Me, For Evermore"). After George's death in 1937, Ira collaborated with composers Vernon Duke, Aaron Copland, Jerome Kern (*Cover Girl,* including "Long Ago and Far Away"), Kurt Weill (their stage musical, *Lady in the Dark,* was filmed), Harry Warren (*The Barkleys of Broadway*), Burton Lane, and Harold Arlen (*A Star Is Born,* including "The Man That Got Away").

Among those who sang Gershwin lyrics in movies were Janet Gaynor, Fred Astaire, Ginger Rogers, Kenny Baker, Ann Sothern, Judy Garland, Mickey Rooney, Gene Kelly, Betty Grable, Dick Haymes, Bing Crosby, Audrey Hepburn, and Sammy Davis, Jr. Bib: *Lyrics on*

Several Occasions by Gershwin (1959); *George and Ira Gershwin Song Book* (1960); *The Gershwin Years* by Edward Jablonski & Lawrence Stewart (1973); *The Gershwins* by Robert Kimball & Alfred Simon (1973). (Died Beverly Hills, Aug. 17, 1983.)

Unless otherwise noted, the following had songs written with George Gershwin:

1931	Delicious
1932	Girl Crazy
1936	She Knew What She Wanted (Eng.)
1937	Shall We Dance
	A Damsel in Distress
1938	The Goldwyn Follies (also Duke)
1941	Lady, Be Good
1943	Girl Crazy
	The North Star (Copland)
1944	Lady in the Dark (Weill)
	Cover Girl (Kern)
1945	Where Do We Go from Here? (Weill)
	Rhapsody in Blue
1947	The Shocking Miss Pilgrim
1949	The Barkleys of Broadway (Warren)
1951	An American in Paris
1953	Give a Girl a Break (Lane)
1954	A Star Is Born (Arlen)
	The Country Girl (Arlen)
1957	Funny Face
1959	Porgy and Bess (also Heyward)
1964	Kiss Me, Stupid
1965	When the Boys Meet the Girls

"Get Happy" Music by Harold Arlen; lyric by Ted Koehler. In 1930 Ruth Etting had scored a hit with this song in Ruth Selwyn's *9:15 Revue* on Broadway, but it remained for Judy Garland to turn it into a classic in *Summer Stock* (MGM 1950). Wearing a floppy black hat, abbreviated black costume, and black tights and accompanied by a rhythmic male chorus, she charged through the revivalistic number with such nerve-tingling drive that it became one of the highlights of her career. Actually, the scene was inserted in the movie about two months after regular shooting had stopped because director Charles Walters felt that a rousing song-and-dance routine was needed for the finale. In ill health at the time, Miss Garland weighed about twenty pounds less than she had during the previously filmed sequences.

"Get Thee Behind Me, Satan" Music & lyric by Irving Berlin. A girl's fear of falling in love was expressed by Harriet Hilliard—after meeting Randolph Scott—in *Follow the Fleet* (RKO 1936). Berlin originally wrote the ballad to be sung by Ginger Rogers in the previous years's *Top Hat,* but it was deleted. The lyric's biblical reference to temptation may be found in both Matthew XVI, verse 23 and Luke IV, verse 8.

"(Running Around in Circles) Getting Nowhere" Music & lyric by Irving Berlin. Philosophical lullaby about meaningless activity (a greyhound chasing its tail, a squirrel on a treadmill, a rider on a carousel) sung by Bing Crosby to daughter Karolyn Grimes in *Blue Skies* (Par. 1946).

Gibson, Virginia (née Virginia Gorski), actress, dancer, singer; b. St. Louis, April 9, 1926. Broadway ingenue who appeared in Warner and MGM musicals (most notable: *Seven Brides for Seven Brothers*).

1950	Tea for Two (*Mabel*)
1951	Painting the Clouds with Sunshine (*June*)
	Starlift (guest bit)
1952	About Face (*Betty Long*)
1953	She's Back on Broadway (*Angela Korinna*)
1954	Seven Brides for Seven Brothers (*Liza Pontipee*)
	Athena (*Niobe Mulvain*)
1957	Funny Face (*Babs*)

Gigi (1958). Music by Frederick Loewe; lyrics by Alan Jay Lerner; screenplay by Lerner from novel by Colette.

An MGM film produced by Arthur Freed; directed by Vincente Minnelli; production design, Cecil Beaton; art directors, William Horning, Preston Ames; costumes, Beaton; music director, André Previn; orchestrations, Conrad Salinger; cameramen, Joseph Ruttenberg, Georges Barsky; editor, Adrienne Fazan; MetroColor; CinemaScope.

Cast: Leslie Caron (vocals by Betty Wand) (*Gigi*); Maurice Chevalier (*Honoré Lachailles*); Louis Jourdan (*Gaston Lachailles*); Hermione Gingold (*Madame Alvarez*); Eva Gabor (*Liane d'Exelmans*); Jacques Bergerac (*Sandomir*); Isabel Jeans (*Aunt Alicia*); John Abbott (*Manuel*); Monique Van Vooren (*showgirl*); Edwin Jerome (*Charles*).

Songs: "Thank Heaven for Little Girls" - Chevalier/ "It's a Bore" - Chevalier, Jourdan/ "The Parisians" - Caron (Wand)/ "Gossip" - Parisians/ "She Is Not Thinking of Me" - Jourdan/ "The Night They Invented Champagne" - Caron (Wand), Jourdan, Gingold/ "I Remember It Well" - Chevalier, Gingold/ "Gigi" - Jourdan/ "I'm Glad I'm Not Young Anymore" -Chevalier/ "Say a Prayer for Me Tonight" - Caron (Wand). Background: "A Toujours."

Arthur Freed's penultimate musical production was a frothy tale set in turn-of-the-century Paris that reunited the producer with three key people with whom he had worked on *An American in Paris:* Alan Jay Lerner, Vincente Minnelli, and Leslie Caron. *Gigi* was unique in a number of respects. Its score was the first written for the screen by the Broadway team of Lerner and Loewe (their only other would be *The Little Prince*). Its story, based on a 60-page novel by Colette about a girl raised by a family of elegant cocottes who gets a worldly man-about-town to propose marriage, was considerably more sophisticated than that of most screen musicals. And it was the first American musical film to be shot almost entirely in Paris, not only at such distinctive locales as Maxim's, the Bois de Boulogne, the Palais de Glace, and the Tuileries, but also in interiors that ordinarily might have been filmed in Hollywood. (Two numbers *were* filmed in Hollywood, but that was because the shooting had run overtime. They were "I Remember It Well" and "The Night They Invented Champagne," the latter directed by Charles Walters.)

Colette's novella had previously been turned into a French movie sans music in 1950 (starring Danielle Delorme) and into a Broadway play by Anita Loos in 1954 (starring Audrey Hepburn). Two years later, the London company was headed by Leslie Caron, who had, as early as 1951, been mentioned for the role of Gigi in a possible adaptation as a screen musical. Gaston, the wealthy bored Parisian who suddenly realizes that little Gigi has grown up before his very eyes, was a part originally intended for Dirk Bogarde; when he proved unavailable, it went to Louis Jourdan. Gaston's gadabout Uncle Honoré, a minor character in Colette's book, was expanded to fit the personality of the epitomical boulevardier, Maurice Chevalier. Three celebrated actresses—Gladys Cooper, Ina Claire, and Yvonne Printemps—all turned down the role of Gigi's elegant Aunt Alicia before it was awarded to Isabel Jeans.

Because it contained musical echoes of Lerner and Loewe's own *My Fair Lady* and because it also dealt with a tomboyish young girl who is transformed into a stylish young lady who wins the heart of a confirmed bachelor, *Gigi* was regarded as something of a Gallic variation on the previous musical. Fifteen years later Lerner adapted *Gigi* as a stage musical; its production, with Alfred Drake (Honoré), Daniel Massey (Gaston), Maria Karnilova (Mme. Alvarez), Agnes Moorehead (Alicia), and Karin Wolfe (Gigi), became the first Broadway version of a movie musical to retain virtually the complete score.

"Gigi" Music by Frederick Loewe; lyric by Alan Jay Lerner. Ruminant song of discovery, as Gaston (Louis Jourdan), in *Gigi* (MGM 1958), becomes aware that he has fallen in love with a girl (Leslie Caron) he has always treated as a child. The song is similar in style and purpose to "I've Grown Accustomed to Her Face," which Lerner and Loewe had previously written for Henry Higgins in the Broadway musical *My Fair Lady* (1956).

Gingold, Hermione (Ferdinanda), actress, singer; b. London, Dec. 9, 1897. A raffish yet regal comedienne with a buzz-saw voice, Miss Gingold scored her first success in London revues. She sang "I Remember It Well" with Maurice Chevalier in *Gigi,* and repeated her stage role in the film version of *A Little Night Music.* (Died New York, May 24, 1987.)

 1958 Gigi (*Mme. Alvarez*)
 1962 Gay Purr-ee (voice of *Mme. Rubens-Chatte*)
    The Music Man (*Eulalie Shinn*)
 1964 I'd Rather Be Rich (*Miss Grimshaw*)
 1978 A Little Night Music (*Mme. Armfeldt*)

"Girl Friend of the Whirling Dervish, The" Music by Harry Warren; lyric by Al Dubin & Johnny Mercer. Novelty item of the sad experience of the Hindu holy man who gets involved with a two-timer who gives him the runaround. Sung by nightclub bandleader John Payne, with Johnny "Scat" Davis, Jerry Colonna (as the girl friend), Ray Mayer, and Joe Venuti in *Garden of the Moon* (Warner 1938).

"Girl on the Police Gazette, The" Music & lyric by Irving Berlin. Song of romantic attachment to tights-clad cover girl of the once racy tabloid. Presented in *On the Avenue* (Fox 1937) as part of a Broadway revue in which it is sung by Dick Powell, in derby and with mustache, as he contemplates the picture of cover girl Alice Faye. Scene then reveals typical gay-Nineties sights—barber shop (complete with quartet), horsedrawn trolley, amusement park, outdoor beer garden, the exterior of the Gaiety Theatre and its stage door. When Miss Faye comes out of the door Powell presents her with a bouquet and requests a picture—but she's insulted when he asks for one in tights. In 1915 Berlin had written a song of similar intent, "The Girl on the Magazine Cover," which was later sung in *Easter Parade* (MGM 1948).

"Girls Were Made To Take Care of Boys" Music & lyric by Ralph Blane. They do it by sharing sorrows and joys, offering help and guidance, and showing affection and understanding. Boys, on the other hand, take care of girls by providing material pleasures and comforts. A pre-women's lib sentiment introduced by Dorothy Malone in *One Sunday Afternoon* (Warner 1948).

"Give a Little Whistle" Music by Leigh Harline; lyric by Ned Washington. Warning signal (''And always let your conscience be your guide'') proposed by Jiminy Cricket (voice of Cliff Edwards) to Pinocchio (Dickie Jones) in the Disney cartoon feature, *Pinocchio* (1940).

"Give Her a Kiss" Music by Richard Rodgers; lyric by Lorenz Hart. In *The Phantom President* (Par. 1932), George M. Cohan and Claudette Colbert drive to a country lane. There they park and listen to the assorted birds and frogs urging the timid suitor to take advantage of the romantic situation.

"Give Me the Simple Life" Music by Rube Bloom; lyric by Harry Ruby. Jaunty philosophical ballad advocating a life without ''worrying, hustling or hurrying,'' sung by John Payne and June Haver in *Wake Up and Dream* (Fox 1946).

Gleason, (Herbert John) Jackie, actor; b. Brooklyn, Feb. 26, 1916. Rotund comic who perfected the character of the outwardly aggressive but inwardly insecure bungler on his television series. Gleason introduced ''Call Me Irresponsible'' in nonmusical film, *Papa's Delicate Condition.* (Died Ft. Lauderdale, June 24, 1987.)

1941　Navy Blues (*Tubby*)
1942　Orchestra Wives (*Beck*)
　　　Springtime in the Rockies (*Commissioner*)

Glenn Miller Story, The (1954). Screenplay by Valentine Davies & Oscar Brodney based on the life of Glenn Miller.

A Universal film produced by Aaron Rosenberg; directed by Anthony Mann; choreography, Kenny Williams; art directors, Bernard Herzbrun, Alexander Golitzen; music director, Joseph Gershenson; music associate, Henry Mancini; cameraman, William Daniels; editor, Russell Schoengarth.

Cast: James Stewart (trombone dubbed by Joe Yukl) (*Glenn Miller*); June Allyson (*Helen Burger Miller*); Henry Morgan (piano dubbed by Lyman Gandee) (*Chummy MacGregor*); Charles Drake (*Don Haynes*); George Tobias (*Si Schribman*); Frances Langford (*Frances Langford*); Louis Armstrong (*Louis Armstrong*); Gene Krupa (*Gene Krupa*); Ben Pollack (*Ben Pollack*); Barton MacLane (*Gen. Hap Arnold*); Sig Rumann (*Kranz*); Irving Bacon (*Miller*); Kathleen Lockhart (*Mrs. Miller*); The Modernaires; Ruth Hampton (*singer*).

Songs: ''Basin Street Blues'' (Williams) - Armstrong, Krupa, jazzmen/ ''Over the Rainbow'' (Arlen-Harburg) - orchestra/ ''I Know Why'' (Warren-Gordon) - orchestra/ ''String of Pearls'' (Gray-DeLange) - orchestra/ ''Pennsylvania 6-5000'' (Gray-Sigman) -orchestra/ ''Tuxedo Junction'' (Hawkins-Johnson-Dash) - orchestra/ ''St. Louis Blues'' (Handy) - band/ ''In the Mood'' (Garland-Razaf) - band/ ''Chattanooga Choo-Choo'' (Warren-Gordon) - Langford, Modernaires, band/ ''We Must Be Vigilant'' (Meacham-Leslie) - band/ ''Little Brown Jug'' (Winner) - band.

A legendary figure of the big-band era (he died in an airplane crash over the English Channel during World War II), Glenn Miller was the subject of the screen's most popular treatment of the life of a bandleader. A highly sentimentalized tale, it was notable for James Stewart's winning portrayal of Miller, and for the faithful duplication of the distinctive Glenn Miller sound (Joe Yukl, who played the trombone for Stewart, had once replaced Miller in the Dorsey Brothers Orchestra). Other bandleader bios: *The Fabulous Dorseys* (Tommy and Jimmy as themselves), *The Benny Goodman Story* (Steve Allen), *The Eddy Duchin Story* (Tyrone Power), *The Gene Krupa Story* (Sal Mineo), *The Five Pennies* (Danny Kaye as Red Nichols).

"Go Into Your Dance" Music by Harry Warren; lyric by Al Dubin. Dancing as an antidote to the blues prescribed by Al Jolson in a nightclub production in the film of the same name (Warner 1935).

Goddard, Paulette (née Pauline Marion Levy), actress; b. Great Neck, NY, June 3, 1911. Nonsinging, dark-haired leading lady who usually appeared in light comedy roles. Second, third and fourth of her husbands were Charles Chaplin, Burgess Meredith, and Erich Maria Remarque.

1932　The Kid from Spain (chorus)
1934　Kid Millions (chorus)
1936　The Bohemian Girl (*gypsy*)
1940　Second Chorus (*Ellen Miller*)
1941　Pot o' Gold (*Molly*)
1942　Star-Spangled Rhythm (specialty)
1945　Duffy's Tavern (specialty)
1947　Variety Girl (guest bit)

Going My Way (1944). Music mostly by James Van Heusen; lyrics mostly by Johnny Burke; screenplay by Frank Butler & Frank Cavett from story by Leo McCarey.

A Paramount film produced and directed by Leo McCarey; art directors, Hans Dreier, William Flannery; costumes, Edith Head; music director, Robert Emmett Dolan; cameraman, Lionel Linden; editor, LeRoy Stone.

Cast: Bing Crosby (*Father Chuck O'Malley*); Risë Stevens (*Genevieve Linden*); Barry Fitzgerald (*Father Fitzgibbon*); Frank McHugh (*Father Timothy O'Dowd*); Jean Heather (*Carol James*); Gene Lockhart (*Haines Sr.*); James Brown (*Haines Jr.*); Porter Hall (*Belknap*); Fortunio Bonanova (*Tomaso Bozanni*); Stanley Clements (*Tony Scaponi*); Carl "Alfalfa" Switzer (*Herman Langerhank*); William Frawley (*Max Dolan*); Adeline DeWalt Reynolds (*Molly Fitzgibbon*); Robert Mitchell Boychoir.

Songs: "The Day After Forever" - Heather, Crosby/ "Silent Night" (Franz Gruber-anon.) - Crosby, Boychoir/ "Too-ra-loo-ra-loo-ral" (J. R. Shannon) - Crosby/ "Habanera" (Bizet-Meilhac, Halévy, *Carmen*) Stevens, chorus/ "Going My Way" - Crosby, Boychoir/ "Ave Maria" (Schubert-Scott) - Crosby, Stevens, Boychoir/ "Swinging on a Star" - Crosby, Boychoir.

Though initially concerned about being believable as a priest, Bing Crosby agreed to star in *Going My Way* primarily because of his admiration for writer-director Leo McCarey. McCarey, whose original title for the movie was *The Padre*, began filming only a rough outline, which resulted in many improvised scenes and a shooting schedule that stretched to six months. In the movie Crosby played a regular-guy priest at odds with crotchety Father Barry Fitzgerald, whom he has been sent to supervise (though without Fitzerald's knowledge) at St. Dominick's Church. One of Crosby's tasks is to settle a real-estate debt, which he does by selling his song, "Swinging on a Star," to a music publisher. The film ends on Christmas Eve when—as arranged by Crosby and his friend opera star Risë Stevens—Fitzerald's 90-year-old Irish mother (played by 82-year-old Adeline DeWalt Reynolds) has a reunion with the son she hasn't seen in 45 years.

Crosby and McCarey were involved in a similar tale the following year called *The Bells of St. Mary's* (but at RKO not Paramount), with Ingrid Bergman the counterpart of Barry Fitzgerald. Crosby and Fitzgerald teamed again in *Welcome Strangers* (Par. 1947), only this time they were bickering doctors. The third and last time Crosby played a priest was in *Say One for Me* (Fox 1957).

Gold Diggers of 1933 (1933). Music by Harry Warren; lyrics by Al Dubin; screenplay by Erwin Gelsey & James Seymour; dialogue by David Boehm & Ben Markson from Broadway play *The Gold Diggers* by Avery Hopwood.

A Warner Bros. film produced by Hal B. Wallis; directed by Mervyn LeRoy; choreography, Busby Berkeley; art director, Anton Grot; costumes, Orry-Kelly; music director, Leo F. Forbstein; cameraman, Sol Polito; editor, George Amy.

Cast: Warren William (*J. Lawrence Bradford*); Joan Blondell (*Carol King*); Aline MacMahon (*Trixie Lorraine*); Ruby Keeler (*Polly Parker*); Dick Powell (*Brad Roberts* né *Robert Treat Bradford*); Ginger Rogers (*Fay Fortune*); Ned Sparks (*Barney Hopkins*); Guy Kibbee (*Faneuil Peabody*); Clarence Nordstrom (*Don Gordon*); Sterling Holloway (*delivery boy*); Ferdinand Gottschalk (*club member*); Hobart Cavanaugh (*dog salesman*); Etta Moten (*singer*); Billy Barty (*baby in park*); Tammany Young (*Gigolo Eddie*); Busby Berkeley (*call boy*).

Songs: "We're in the Money" ("The Gold Digger's Song") - Rogers, chorus/ "Shadow Waltz" - Powell; reprised by Powell, Keeler, chorus/ "I've Got To Sing a Torch Song" - Powell/ "Pettin' in the Park" - Powell, Keeler with MacMahon, Barty, chorus/ "Remember My Forgotten Man" - Blondell, Moten, chorus.

A stuffy Bostonian, concerned that a relative has taken up with a chorus girl, hastens to New York to buy off the alleged gold digger. To make him look foolish, another chorus girl passes herself off as the relative's girl, and in the course of a night on the town gets the gentleman drunk. Apparently chastened by the experience, the Bostonian somehow comes to realize that all girls in the theatre are not bad and the two end up as man and wife. This bare outline was enough to provide the general plot of a 1919 play, *The Gold Diggers* (with Ina Claire and Bruce McRae), and its silent film treatment; a 1929 screen musical, *Gold Diggers of Broadway* (Nancy Welford and Conway Tearle); a 1933 screen musical, *Gold Diggers of 1933* (Joan Blondell and Warren William); and a 1951 screen musical, *Painting the Clouds with Sunshine* (Virginia Mayo and Tom Conway).

The 1933 movie version, easily the most memorable,

was the second of three major backstage musicals—the others were *42nd Street* and *Footlight Parade*—that Warner offered during the same year. Put into production even before *42nd Street* was released, the film, originally called *High Life,* was first conceived without any lavish musical routines. After the tremendous success of *42nd Street,* however, Busby Berkeley was called in and allowed to let his kaleidoscopic imagination run wild. Also on hand from the previous picture: songwriters Warren and Dubin, music director Forbstein, cameraman Polito, and actors Dick Powell (as the stuffy Bostonian's brother, an aspiring songwriter), Ruby Keeler (the one he sings his songs to), Ginger Rogers, Ned Sparks, Clarence Nordstrom, and Guy Kibbee.

Of the three 1933 Warner musicals, *Gold Diggers of 1933* was the one to deal most directly with the Depression. Not only did it cover the difficulties of finding backers to invest in elaborate Broadway shows, it also depicted the cramped tenement quarters and day-to-day financial worries of actresses Ruby Keeler, Joan Blondell, Aline MacMahon, and Ginger Rogers. Even the two musical numbers that opened and closed the movie took varying views of the country's shattered economy: the prematurely optimistic "We're in the Money," with Miss Rogers leading the coin-clad chorus girls, and the stirring "Remember My Forgotten Man"—also serving as the finale of the show, *Forgotten Melody*—with its appeal in behalf of war veterans. One device that linked the film to both *42nd Street* and *Footlight Parade*—and to numerous other backstage musicals—was having a leading performer in the show replaced by another. Here juvenile lead Nordstrom, suffering from lumbago, is reluctantly succeeded by publicity-shy Powell.

Gold Diggers of 1933 was released only four years after its Technicolor model, *Gold Diggers of Broadway.* The earlier musical version, directed by Roy Del Ruth, is best remembered for Nick Lucas warbling "Tip Toe Through the Tulips" and "Painting the Clouds with Sunshine," both by lyricist Dubin and his then partner, composer Joe Burke. Among the cast's acquisitive ladies were Winnie Lightner, Ann Pennington, and Lilyan Tashman.

Warner produced three more films with *Gold Diggers* in their titles. *Gold Diggers of 1935* abandoned the Broadway milieu in favor of The Wentworth Plaza, a New Hampshire summer resort where a charity show is to be presented. This time, poor medical student Dick Powell, working as a desk clerk, sings to wealthy Gloria Stuart. More obvious gold-digging was done by temper-

amental Russian director Adolphe Menjou fleecing socialite Alice Brady, and secretary Glenda Farrell blackmailing snuff expert Hugh Herbert. The songs were again by Warren and Dubin and the choreography was again by Busby Berkeley (who also directed the film). Berkeley's standout creations: the white piano number, "The Words Are in My Heart," and the moralistic urban commentary, "Lullaby of Broadway," sung by Wini Shaw.

Dick Powell again had the lead in *Gold Diggers of 1937,* with Joan Blondell a more animated romantic vis-à-vis than his previous ladies. Here Powell is an insurance salesman tricked into selling a million-dollar policy to ailing theatre producer Victor Moore. Aided by Miss Blondell and Glenda Farrell (gold-digging again), Powell keeps the producer well and happy enough to let the insurance man take over Moore's Broadway show and put Blondell in the lead. Though four of the songs were by Harold Arlen and E. Y. Harburg, the two interpolations by Warren and Dubin became the most popular. "With Plenty of Money and You" was a pecuniary variation on "We're in the Money," and "All's Fair in Love and War" was a decidedly more lighthearted military spectacle by Busby Berkeley than "Remember My Forgotten Man." Lloyd Bacon directed.

The last in the series, *Gold Diggers in Paris,* released in 1938, offered a new locale and—except for Hugh Herbert—a new set of leading players. With Rudy Vallee (in a role refused by Dick Powell) and Rosemary Lane, the movie had to do with misunderstandings caused when Vallee's nightclub troupe is invited to appear at the Paris Exposition under the mistaken impression that it's a ballet company. Ray Enright directed the film whose Busby Berkeley routines were appreciably less elaborate than in the past. The best-known number in the score was Warren and Dubin's "The Latin Quarter."

There were variations on the *Gold Diggers* series in other Warner musicals of the 30s, though *Dames* followed the format so closely that it could easily have been called *Gold Diggers of 1934.* Dick Powell played a songwriter-singer trying to raise money for a new show, Ruby Keeler was the aspiring actress he loved, and Joan Blondell was the wisecracking, gold-digging trouper. Also on hand were the dependably gullible Guy Kibbee and Hugh Herbert. The movie even had the last-minute substitution in the Broadway production, though here the real switch was that Miss Blondell went on for Ruby Keeler (but it was only in the first scene). Directed by Ray Enright, *Dames* was distinguished by its Ruby Keeler tribute, "I Only Have Eyes for You," a Busby Berkeley creation based on the song by Warren and Dubin.

The *Gold Diggers* appellation was never affixed to a movie title after the Paris excursion in 1938, but in 1951 Warner resurrected the original *Gold Diggers* plot and used it as the basis for *Painting the Clouds with Sunshine*. This version, directed by David Butler, offered stuffy Bostonian Tom Conway trying to curb dancing brother Gene Nelson's infatuation for Lucille Norman, a member of a Las Vegas sister act with Virginia Mayo and Virginia Gibson. No problem, really, since Lucille preferred Dennis Morgan. Apart from the title song and "Tip-Toe Through the Tulips," which had been first sung in *Gold Diggers of Broadway*, the songs in *Painting the Clouds with Sunshine* were standards unassociated with previous *Gold Diggers* movies.

Bib: *Gold Diggers of 1933* ed. by Arthur Hove (1980).

"Golden Earrings" Music by Victor Young; lyric by Jay Livingston & Ray Evans. According to the lyric, an old gypsy story holds that love will come to one who wears the prescribed aureate adornment. Murvyn Vye sang the minor-key melody in the film of the same name (Par. 1947) in a scene with Marlene Dietrich.

"Goldfinger" Music by John Barry; lyric by Leslie Bricusse & Anthony Newley. "The man with the Midas touch" was described by Shirley Bassey on the soundtrack of the James Bond film (UA 1964). Gert Frobe played Goldfinger.

Goldwyn, Samuel (né Samuel Goldfisch), producer; b. Warsaw, Aug. 27, 1881; d. Los Angeles, Jan. 31, 1974. Colorful Hollywood pioneer who co-produced early feature *The Squaw Man* (1914) and became the industry's leading independent producer. Noted for the quality of his films (*Dodsworth, Dead End, The Little Foxes, The Best Years of Our Lives*), Goldwyn produced 62 features between 1929 and 1959. Eddie Cantor and Danny Kaye starred in six Goldwyn musicals each; other major musicals were *Guys and Dolls* (Frank Sinatra, Marlon Brando) and *Porgy and Bess* (Sidney Poitier, Dorothy Dandridge). Bib: *The Great Goldwyn* by Alva Johnston (1937); *Goldwyn* by Arthur Marx (1976), *Samuel Goldwyn Presents* by Alvin Marill (1976).

1930	Whoopee
	One Heavenly Night
1931	Palmy Days
1932	The Kid from Spain
1933	Roman Scandals
1934	Kid Millions
1936	Strike Me Pink
1938	The Goldwyn Follies
1939	They Shall Have Music
1944	Up in Arms
1945	Wonder Man
1946	The Kid from Brooklyn
1947	The Secret Life of Walter Mitty
1948	A Song Is Born
1952	Hans Christian Andersen
1955	Guys and Dolls
1959	Porgy and Bess

"Good Morning" Music by Nacio Herb Brown; lyric by Arthur Freed. Cheery greeting first sung by Judy Garland and Mickey Rooney in a publisher's office in *Babes in Arms* (MGM 1939). Also sung and danced by Gene Kelly, Debbie Reynolds, and Donald O'Connor in *Singin' in the Rain* (MGM 1952).

Good News (1947). Music mostly by Ray Henderson; lyrics mostly by B. G. DeSylva & Lew Brown; screenplay by Betty Comden & Adolph Green from Broadway musical by DeSylva, Laurence Schwab, Brown, Henderson.

An MGM film produced by Arthur Freed; directed by Charles Walters; associate producer, Roger Edens; choreography, Robert Alton, Walters; art directors, Cedric Gibbons, Edward Carfagno; costumes, Helen Rose, Valles; music director, Lennie Hayton; vocal arrangements, Kay Thompson; cameraman, Charles Schoenbaum; editor, Albert Akst; Technicolor.

Cast: June Allyson (*Connie Lane*); Peter Lawford (*Tommy Marlowe*); Patricia Marshall (*Pat McClellan*); Joan McCracken (*Babe Doolittle*); Mel Tormé (*Danny*); Robert Strickland (*Peter Van Dyne III*); Ray McDonald (*Bobby Turner*); Donald MacBride (*Coach Johnson*); Clinton Sundberg (*Prof. Burton Kenyon*); Tom Dugan (*Pooch*); Lon Tindall (*Beef*).

Songs: "Good News" incl. "Tait Song" (lyric, Roger Edens, Kay Thompson) - McCracken, students/ "Be a Ladies' Man"(added lyric, Edens, Thompson) - Lawford, McDonald, Dugan, Tindall, Tormé/ "Lucky in Love" - Marshall, McCracken, Tormé, Allyson, Lawford/ "The French Lesson" (Roger Edens-Comden,

Green) - Allyson, Lawford/ "The Best Things in Life Are Free" - Allyson; reprised by Tormé/ "Pass That Peace Pipe" (Edens-Hugh Martin, Ralph Blane) - McCracken, McDonald, students/ "Just Imagine" - Allyson/ "Varsity Drag" - Allyson with Lawford, students. Unused: "An Easier Way" (Edens-Comden, Green).

Broadway's quintessential collegiate musical of the 20s—with its flat-chested flappers and slick-haired sheiks—was filmed by MGM in 1930 and in 1947. The second version marked the first film directed by choreographer Charles Walters and the first with a screenplay by Comden and Green. With six of the 12 stage songs (plus two new numbers), the film stuck closely to the original 1927 libretto as it told of the romance between poor but bright Connie (June Allyson) and conceited football hero Tom (Peter Lawford). Tom is almost prevented from playing in Tait's big game because he's failed French (on stage he failed astronomy). Van Johnson and Mickey Rooney had been sought for the male lead before it went to London-born Lawford.

In the 1930 movie *Good News,* Connie was played by Mary Lawlor (from the 1927 Broadway cast), Tom by Stanley Smith, Pat by Lola Lane, Babe by Bessie Love, Bobby by Gus Shy (also on Broadway), Flo by Penny Singleton (then known as Dorothy McNulty), and Pooch by Cliff Edwards, with Abe Lyman's orchestra providing the music. Six of the original Broadway numbers were retained, four new ones were added.

Goodman, (Benjamin David) Benny, bandleader, clarinetist; b. Chicago, May 30, 1909. The "King of Swing" began his career as clarinetist with Ben Pollack's orchestra, then organized his own band in 1934. His personal appearances, broadcasts, and records helped launch the swing era, and his dominance of the field lasted from 1936 through 1944. Most film appearances were with his orchestra. Film bio: *The Benny Goodman Story,* with Steve Allen as Goodman (and Goodman playing clarinet). Bib: *Benny: King of Swing* by Stanley Baron (1979). (Died June 13, 1986.)

1936 The Big Broadcast of 1937
1937 Hollywood Hotel
1942 The Powers Girl
      Syncopation
1943 The Gang's All Here
      Stage Door Canteen
1944 Sweet and Lowdown

1946 Make Mine Music (clarinet only)
1948 A Song Is Born (*Prof. Magenbruch*)
1955 The Benny Goodman Story (clarinet for Steve Allen)

"Goodnight, Lovely Little Lady" Music by Harry Revel; lyric by Mack Gordon. Bing Crosby, as a sailor aboard a yacht, sang this lullaby to quiet a pet bear in *We're Not Dressing* (Par. 1934).

"Goodnight, My Love" Music by Harry Revel; lyric by Mack Gordon. Tender nighty-night as Shirley Temple tries putting herself to sleep in *Stowaway* (Fox 1936); later reprised by Alice Faye dancing with Robert Young on the moonlit deck of a ship.

"Goodnight, Vienna" Music by George Posford; lyric by Eric Maschwitz. Jack Buchanan, in *Goodnight, Vienna* (UA 1932), bids a dreamy, evocative farewell to the "enchanted city of Columbine and Pierrot."

Gordon, Mack (né Morris Gittler), lyricist; b. Warsaw, June 21, 1904; d. New York, March 1, 1959. Gordon was under contract to Paramount (1933–36) and Fox (1936–50), working primarily with composers Harry Revel and Harry Warren. With Revel, he wrote "Did You Ever See a Dream Walking?," "Love Thy Neighbor," "Once in a Blue Moon," "Stay as Sweet as You Are," "May I?," "With My Eyes Wide Open I'm Dreaming," "Take a Number from One to Ten," "Without a Word of Warning," "Paris in the Spring," "Goodnight, My Love," "I Feel Like a Feather in the Breeze," "May I Have the Next Romance with You?," "You Hit the Spot," "Afraid To Dream," "Never in a Million Years," "There's a Lull in My Life," "You Can't Have Everything," and "You Say the Sweetest Things, Baby." With Warren: "Down Argentina Way," "Chattanooga Choo-Choo," "I Know Why," "I Yi Yi Yi Yi," "At Last," "I Had the Craziest Dream," "I've Got a Gal in Kalamazoo," "Serenade in Blue," "You'll Never Know," "My Heart Tells Me," "The More I See You." Gordon also occasionally wrote his own music ("Here Comes Cookie") and he collaborated with such other composers as Max Rich, Abner Silver, Ted Snyder, Harry Owen, James V. Monaco ("I Can't Begin To Tell You"), Charles Henderson, Josef Myrow ("On the Boardwalk at Atlantic City," "You Make Me Feel So Young," "You Do," "It Happens Every Spring"), and Sammy Fain. His songs were introduced by, among others, Bing Crosby, Jack Haley,

Lanny Ross, Jack Oakie, Lyda Roberti, Gracie Allen, Shirley Temple, Alice Faye, Jessie Matthews, Don Ameche, Carmen Miranda, Betty Grable, Dick Haymes, Judy Garland, and the orchestras of Glenn Miller and Harry James.

1929	Song of Love (Rich)
	Pointed Heels (Rich)
1930	Swing High (Silver, Snyder)
1933	Broadway Thru a Keyhole (Revel)
	Sitting Pretty (Revel) (also *publisher*)
1934	We're Not Dressing (Revel)
	Shoot the Works (Revel)
	She Loves Me Not (Revel)
	College Rhythm (Revel)
1935	Love in Bloom (Revel)
	Stolen Harmony (Revel)
	Paris in Spring (Revel)
	Two for Tonight (Revel)
	Collegiate (Revel) (also *song coach*)
1936	Poor Little Rich Girl (Revel)
	Stowaway (Revel)
1937	Head Over Heels (Eng.) (Revel)
	Everybody Dance (Eng.) (Revel)
	Wake Up and Live (Revel)
	This Is My Affair (Revel)
	You Can't Have Everything (Revel)
	Ali Baba Goes to Town (Revel)
	Love and Hisses (Revel)
1938	Josette (Revel)
	Love Finds Andy Hardy (Revel)
	My Lucky Star (Revel)
	Thanks for Everything (Revel)
1940	Star Dust (alone)
	Young People (Warren)
	Down Argentine Way (Warren)
1941	That Night in Rio (Warren)
	The Great American Broadcast (Warren)
	Sun Valley Serenade (Warren)
	Weekend in Havana (Warren)
1942	Song of the Islands (Owen)
	Orchestra Wives (Warren)
	Iceland (Warren)
	Springtime in the Rockies (Warren)
1943	Sweet Rosie O'Grady (Warren)
1944	Pin-Up Girl (Monaco)
	Sweet and Low Down (Monaco)
	Irish Eyes Are Smiling (Monaco)
1945	Diamond Horseshoe (Warren)
	The Dolly Sisters (Monaco; Henderson; Revel)
1946	Three Little Girls in Blue (Myrow) (also prod.)
1947	Mother Wore Tights (Myrow)
1950	Wabash Avenue (Myrow)
	Summer Stock (Warren)

1951	Call Me Mister (Fain)
1953	I Love Melvin (Myrow)
	The Girl Next Door (Myrow)
1956	Bundle of Joy (Myrow)

Gorney, Jay, composer; b. Bialystok, Dec. 12, 1896. Originally a composer for the Broadway stage, Gorney went to Hollywood in 1933, first at Fox later at Columbia. Shirley Temple and James Dunn introduced his "Baby, Take a Bow" (lyric by Lew Brown) in *Stand Up and Cheer*. Other collaborators: Sidney Clare, E. Y. Harburg, Don Hartman, Edward Eliscu, Henry Myers.

1933	Jimmy and Sally (Clare)
	Moonlight and Pretzels (Harburg)
1934	Wild Gold (Clare)
1935	Lottery Lover (Hartman)
	Redheads on Parade (Hartman)
1943	The Heat's On (Eliscu, Myers)
1944	Hey, Rookie (Eliscu, Myers)

"Gotta Have Me Go with You" Music by Harold Arlen; lyric by Ira Gershwin. Judy Garland, Jack Harmon, and Don McCabe sang the spirited formula for unadulterated bliss as part of a Hollywood benefit show in *A Star Is Born* (Warner 1954). During the performance James Mason, as an inebriated actor, attempted to join in the trio's dance routine.

Gould, Dave, choreographer; b. Budapest, 1905; d. June 3, 1969. Responsible for spectacular finales of *Flying Down to Rio* (airplanes) and *Born To Dance* (battleship). Other major films: *The Gay Divorcee, Folies Bergère,* two *Broadway Melodys*.

1933	Melody Cruise
	Flying Down to Rio
1934	Hips Hips Hooray
	Hollywood Party
	The Gay Divorcee
1935	Folies Bergère
	Broadway Melody of 1936
1936	Born To Dance
1937	A Day at the Races
	Broadway Melody of 1938
1938	Breaking the Ice
1939	Everything's on Ice
1940	The Boys from Syracuse
1942	Rhythm Parade (also co-dir.)
1944	Lady, Let's Dance
	Casanova in Burlesque
	My Best Gal
	Rosie the Riveter

Gould, Morton, composer; b. Richmond Hill, NY, Dec. 10, 1913. Concert composer, conductor, and pianist who wrote music for two Broadway shows, plus film and television background scores. Lyricist collaborator: Edward Heyman.

1945   Delightfully Dangerous (Heyman) (also in film)

Grable, (Ruth Elizabeth) Betty, actress, singer, dancer; b. S. St. Louis, Dec. 18, 1916; d. Santa Monica, July 3, 1973. Something of a successor to Alice Faye at Fox—though their careers overlapped for a time—this blonde dancing actress with the admired legs and buoyant personality was a musical star for over ten years. Miss Grable, who won notice in the Broadway musical, *DuBarry Was a Lady,* appeared in such colorful films as *Down Argentine Way* (singing "Down Argentina Way"), *Tin Pan Alley, Sweet Rosie O'Grady* ("My Heart Tells Me"), *The Dolly Sisters* ("I Can't Begin To Tell You"), *The Shocking Miss Pilgrim* ("Changing My Tune," "For You, For Me, For Evermore"), and her biggest hit, *Mother Wore Tights* ("You Do"). She starred opposite Dan Dailey in four films, John Payne in three, and Don Ameche, Victor Mature, and Dick Haymes in two each. Her husbands were actor Jackie Coogan and bandleader Harry James (both divorced).

1930   Let's Go Places (chorus)
       Movietone Follies of 1930 (chorus)
       Whoopee (chorus)
1931   Palmy Days (chorus)
1932   The Kid from Spain (chorus)
1933   Sweetheart of Sigma Chi (*band singer*)
       Melody Cruise (*stewardess*)
1934   Student Tour (*Cayenne*)
       The Gay Divorcee (*hotel guest*)
1935   Nitwits (*Mary*)
       Old Man Rhythm (*Sylvia*)
1936   Collegiate (*Dorothy*)
       Follow the Fleet (*singer*)
       Pigskin Parade (*Laura Watson*)
1937   This Way Please (*Jane Morrow*)
       Thrill of a Lifetime (*Gwen*)
1938   College Swing (*Betty*)
       Give Me a Sailor (*Nancy Larkin*)
1939   Man About Town (*Susan*)
1940   Down Argentine Way (*Glenda Crawford*)
       Tin Pan Alley (*Lily Blane*)
1941   Moon Over Miami (*Kay Latimer*)
1942   Footlight Serenade (*Pat Lambert*)
       Song of the Islands (*Eileen O'Brien*)
       Springtime in the Rockies (*Vicky*)

1943   Coney Island (*Kate Farley*)
       Sweet Rosie O'Grady (*Madeleine Marlowe*)
1944   Four Jills in a Jeep (specialty)
       Pin-Up Girl (*Lorry Jones*)
1945   Diamond Horseshoe (*Bonnie Collins*)
       The Dolly Sisters (*Jenny Dolly*)
1946   Do You Love Me? (guest bit)
1947   The Shocking Miss Pilgrim (*Cynthia Pilgrim*)
       Mother Wore Tights (*Myrtle Burt*)
1948   That Lady in Ermine (*Francesca/Angelina*)
       When My Baby Smiles at Me (*Bonnie Kane*)
1949   The Beautiful Blonde from Bashful Bend (*Freddie Jones*)
1950   Wabash Avenue (*Ruby Summers*)
       My Blue Heaven (*Molly Moran*)
1951   Call Me Mister (*Kay Hudson*)
       Meet Me After the Show (*Delilah*)
1953   The Farmer Takes a Wife (*Molly Larkin*)
1955   Three for the Show (*Julie Lowndes*)

Grant, Cary (né Alexander Archibald Leach), actor; b. Bristol, Eng., Jan. 18, 1904. Stylish, durable lead in light comedies and dramas who appeared in musicals opposite Marlene Dietrich, Mae West (twice), and Grace Moore, and played Cole Porter in film bio *Night and Day*. Also sang—after a fashion—"Did I Remember?" in *Suzy* (1936). Bib: *Films of Cary Grant* by Donald Deschner (1971). (Died Davenport, Iowa, Nov. 29, 1986.)

1932   This Is the Night (*Stepan*)
       Blonde Venus (*Nick Townsend*)
1933   She Done Him Wrong (*Capt. Cummings*)
       I'm No Angel (*Jack Clayton*)
1934   Kiss and Make-Up (*Dr. Maurice Lamar*)
1937   When You're in Love (*Jimmy Hudson*)
1946   Night and Day (*Cole Porter*)
1957   An Affair To Remember (*Nickie Ferrante*)

Gravet, Fernand (né Fernand Martens), actor; b. Brussels, Dec. 25, 1904; d. Paris, Nov. 2, 1970. Continental charmer—known as Fernand Gravey in Europe and Fernand Graavey in England—who acted mostly in French plays and films. Appeared opposite Anna Neagle in two British screen musicals; played Johann Strauss, Jr., in Hollywood's first biography of a composer.

1933   Bitter Sweet (Eng.) (*Carl Linden*)
       Early to Bed (Eng.) (*Carl*)
1934   The Queen's Affair (Eng.) (*Carl*)
1937   The King and the Chorus Girl (*Alfred*)
1938   Fools for Scandal (*René*)
       The Great Waltz (*Johann Strauss, Jr.*)

Gray, Alexander, actor, singer; b. Wrightsville, Pa. Jan. 8, 1902; d. Oct. 4, 1975. Singing lead of early talkies who co-starred with Bernice Claire in three films, also appeared with her in vaudeville.

1929 The Show of Shows (specialty)
   Sally (*Blair Farrell*)
1930 No, No, Nanette (*Tom Trainor*)
   Song of the Flame (*Prince Volodya*)
   Spring Is Here (*Terry Clayton*)
   Viennese Nights (*Otto*)
1933 Moonlight and Pretzels

Gray, Dolores, actress, singer; b. Chicago, June 7, 1924. Amply proportioned blonde song belter with Broadway and London stage experience; also night-clubs, television.

1955 It's Always Fair Weather (*Madeline Bradbille*)
   Kismet (*Lalume*)
1956 The Opposite Sex (*Sylvia*)

Gray, Lawrence, actor, singer; b. San Francisco, July 28, 1898; d. Mexico City, Feb. 2, 1970. Early talkies leading man who acted in two films with Marion Davies, one with Marilyn Miller. Became film executive in mid-30's.

1929 Marianne (*Stagg*)
   It's a Great Life (*Jimmy Dean*)
1930 Florodora Girl (*Jack*)
   Spring Is Here (*Steve Alden*)
   Children of Pleasure (*Danny Regan*)
   Sunny (*Tom Warren*)
1935 The Old Homestead (*Bob*)
1936 Dizzy Dames (*Terry*)

Grayson, Kathryn (née Zelma Kathryn Elizabeth Hedrick), actress, singer; b. Winston-Salem, NC, Feb. 9, 1922. MGM's successor to Jeanette MacDonald was the coolly proper, amply bosomed diva of such offerings as *Anchors Aweigh, That Midnight Kiss, Show Boat,* and *Kiss Me, Kate.* Howard Keel was her romantic interest in three films; Mario Lanza (with whom she sang "Be My Love"), Frank Sinatra and Gene Kelly in two each. Miss Grayson was once married to singer-actor Johnny Johnston.

1942 Rio Rita (*Rita Winslow*)
   Seven Sweethearts (*Billie VanMaaster*)
1943 Thousands Cheer (*Kathryn Jones*)
1945 Anchors Aweigh (*Susan Abbott*)
1946 Ziegfeld Follies (specialty)
   Two Sisters from Boston (*Abigail Chandler*)
   Till the Clouds Roll By (specialty)

1947 It Happened in Brooklyn (*Ann Fielding*)
1948 The Kissing Bandit (*Teresa*)
1949 That Midnight Kiss (*Prudence Budell*)
1950 The Toast of New Orleans (*Suzette Micheline*)
   Grounds for Marriage (*Ina Massine*)
1951 Show Boat (*Magnolia Hawks Ravenal*)
1952 Lovely To Look At (*Stephanie*)
1953 The Desert Song (*Margot*)
   So This Is Love (*Grace Moore*)
   Kiss Me, Kate (*Lilli Vanessi*)
1956 The Vagabond King (*Catherine de Vaucelles*)

Grease (1978). Music & lyrics mostly by Jim Jacobs & Warren Casey; screenplay by Bronte Woodard, adapted by Allan Carr from Broadway musical by Jacobs & Casey.

A Paramount film produced by Robert Stigwood and Allan Carr; directed by Randal Kleiser; choreography, Patricia Birch; art director, Philip Jefferies; music director, Louis St. Louis; music supervisor, Bill Oakes; guitar soloist, Peter Frampton; cameraman, Bill Butler; editor, John F. Burnett; PanaVision.

Cast: John Travolta (*Danny Zuko*); Olivia Newton-John (*Sandy Alston*); Stockard Channing (*Betty Rizzo*); Jeff Conaway (*Kenickie*); Didi Conn (*Frenchie*); Eve Arden (*Principal McGee*); Frankie Avalon (*Teen Angel*); Joan Blondell (*Vi*); Edd Byrnes (*Vince Fontaine*); Sid Caesar (*Coach Calhoun*); Alice Ghostley (*Mrs. Murdock*); Dody Goodman (*Blanche*); Sha-Na-Na (*Johnny Casino & the Gamblers*); Barry Pearl (*Doody*); Dinah Manoff (*Marty Marishino*); Fannie Flagg (*Nurse Wilkins*); Frankie Valli (singer over credits).

Songs: "Grease" (Barry Gibb) - Valli, with Frampton, guitar/ "Summer Nights" - Travolta, Newton-John/ "Look at Me, I'm Sandra Dee" - Channing/ "Hopelessly Devoted to You" (John Farrar) - Newton-John/ "Greased Lightnin'" - Travolta/ "Beauty School Dropout" - Avalon/ "Rock 'n Roll Is Here To Stay" (D. White) - Sha-Na-Na/ "Those Magic Changes" -Sha-Na-Na/ "Hound Dog" (Jerry Leiber-Mike Stoller) - Sha-Na-Na/ "Born To Hand Jive" - Sha-Na-Na/ "Blue Moon" (Richard Rodgers-Lorenz Hart) -Sha-Na-Na/ "Sandy" (Louis St. Louis-Scott Simon) -Travolta/ "There Are Worse Things I Could Do" -Channing/ "You're the One That I Want" (Farrar) - Travolta, Newton-John/ "We Go Together" - Travolta, Newton-John, cast. Unused: "It's Raining on Prom Night," "Tears on My Pillow," "Mooning," "Freddy, My Love," "Rock 'n Roll Party Queen."

Grease opened in New York in 1972, won a cult following attracted to its satirical view of high school greasers of the 50s, and had a record-breaking run of seven and a half years. Even while the show was still running on Broadway, the movie version was released and achieved the All-Time Boxoffice record for a musical. The dances were staged by the original choreographer, Patricia Birch, and the two leading male roles were both played by actors who had appeared in different parts on the stage: John Travolta had toured as Doody and played it briefly on Broadway; Jeff Conaway had been Danny for a year and a half in the Broadway company. Five songs were dropped from the original Jacobs-Casey score and five new numbers were added, plus two oldies. Though it changed the locale of Rydell High School from an ethnic urban center to Southern California, the movie scrupulously maintained the show's basic attitude of mocking individuality and advocating conformity at its most tasteless and promiscuous.

"Grease" Music & lyric by Barry Gibb. Rhythmic assertion ("Grease is the word./ It's got a groove./ It's got a meaning") sung by Frankie Valli, accompanied by Peter Frampton's guitar, over cartoon credits of film (Par. 1978).

Great Caruso, The (1951). Screenplay by Sonia Levien & William Ludwig from Dorothy Caruso's biography of her husband, Enrico Caruso.

An MGM film produced by Joe Pasternak; directed by Richard Thorpe; opera sequences staged by Peter Herman Adler; art directors, Cedric Gibbons, Gabriel Scognamillo; music director, Adler; supervisor, Johnny Green; music adaptation, Irving Aaronson; cameraman, Joseph Ruttenberg; editor, Gene Ruggiero; Technicolor.

Cast: Mario Lanza (*Enrico Caruso*); Ann Blyth (*Dorothy Benjamin Caruso*); Dorothy Kirsten (*Louise Heggar*); Jarmila Novotna (*Maria Selka*); Richard Hageman (*Carlo Santi*); Carl Benton Reid (*Park Benjamin*); Eduard Franz (*Giulio Gatti-Casazza*); Ludwig Donath (*Alfredo Brazzi*); Alan Napier (*Jean de Reszke*); Peter Edward Price (*Caruso as a boy*).

Songs & Arias: "Mattinata" (Leoncavallo - Lanza/ "Mama Mia" (trad.) - Lanza/ "La donna mobile" (Verdi-Piave, *Rigoletto*) - Lanza/ "Numi, Pieta" (Verdi-Ghislanzoni, *Aida*) - Kirsten/ "Celeste Aida" (*Aida*) - Lanza/ "Torna a Surriento" (DeCurtis) - Lanza/ "O Paradiso" (*Aida*) - Lanza, Kirsten/ "Che gelida manina" (Puccini-Giacosa, Illica, *La Bohème*) - Lanza/ "Sweethearts" (Victor Herbert-Robert B.

Smith) - Kirsten/ "Vesti la Giubba" (Leoncavallo, *Pagliacci*) - Lanza/ "Ave Maria" (Bach, Gounod) - Lanza, choir/ "The Loveliest Night of the Year" (Juventino Rosas-Irving Aaronson-Paul Francis Webster) - Blyth/ "Sextet" (Donizetti-Cammarano, *Lucia di Lammermoor*) - Lanza, Kirsten, mezzo, tenor, baritone, bass/ "Because" (D'Hardelot-Teschemacher) - Lanza/ "M'Appari" (Flotow-Riese, *Martha*) - Lanza/ " 'Tis the Last Rose of Summer" (Thomas Moore, *Martha*) - Kirsten, Lanza.

The screen's most popular attraction dealing with the world of opera skimmed the life of the Metropolitan's legendary tenor so that it became a succession of triumphs with only a few glossed-over conflicts or setbacks. As Caruso, Mario Lanza won the greatest acclaim of his career as the movie took the story from Caruso's humble beginnings in Naples, through his idyllic marriage (unmentioned was the fact of the singer's former wife and family), to his death of pleurisy at the age of 48 (Lanza died at 38). The movie, however, was occupied mostly with showing scenes from six of the tenor's most celebrated operas. Three other biographies of opera stars were produced in the wake of the film's success: *So This Is Love* (1953), with Kathryn Grayson as Grace Moore (Miss Moore had played Jenny Lind in *A Lady's Morals* in 1930); *Melba* (1953), with Patrice Munsel as Nellie Melba; and *Interrupted Melody* (1955), with Eleanor Parker (dubbed by Eileen Farrell) as Marjorie Lawrence.

Great Ziegfeld, The (1936). Music mostly by Walter Donaldson; lyrics mostly by Harold Adamson; screenplay by William Anthony McGuire based on life of Florenz Ziegfeld.

An MGM film produced by Hunt Stromberg; directed by Robert Z. Leonard; choreography, Seymour Felix; art director, Cedric Gibbons; costumes, Adrian; music director, Arthur Lange; orchestrations, Frank Skinner; cameraman, Oliver T. Marsh; editor, William S. Gray.

Cast: William Powell (*Florenz Ziegfeld Jr.*); Myrna Loy (*Billie Burke*); Luise Rainer (*Anna Held*); Virginia Bruce (*Audrey Lane*); Frank Morgan (*Jack Billings*); Fanny Brice (*Fanny Brice*); Ray Bolger (*Ray Bolger*); Nat Pendleton (*Sandow*); Harriet Hoctor (specialty); Reginald Owen (*Sam Sampson*); Jean Chatburn (*Mary Lou*); Ernest Cossart (*Sidney*); Joseph Cawthorn (*Dr. Florenz Ziegfeld Sr.*); A. A. Trimble (*Will Rogers*); Buddy Doyle (*Eddie Cantor*); Herman Bing (*Schultz*); William Demarest (*Gene Buck*); Raymond Walburn

(*Sage*); Charles Judels (*Pierre*); Jean Holland (*Patricia Ziegfeld*); Paul Irving (*Abe Erlanger*); Stanley Morner (Dennis Morgan) (voice of Allan Jones) (*singer*); Marcelle Corday (*Marie*); Esther Muir (*"Sarah Bernhardt"*); Robert Greig (*Joseph Urban*); Charles Trowbridge (*Julian Mitchell*); Edwin Maxwell (*Diamond Jim Brady*); Ruth Gillette (*Lillian Russell*); Virginia Grey (chorus).

Songs: "Won't You Come and Play with Me?" (Anna Held) - Rainer/ "It's Delightful To Be Married" (Vincent Scott-Held) - Rainer/ "If You Knew Susie" (Joseph Meyer-B. G. DeSylva) - Doyle/ "Shine on Harvest Moon" (Nora Bayes-Jack Norworth) - chorus/ "A Pretty Girl Is Like a Melody" (Irving Berlin) - Morner (Jones), chorus/ "You Gotta Pull Strings" - chorus/ "She's a Follies Girl" - Bolger, girls/ "You" - chorus/ "You Never Looked So Beautiful Before" - boys/ "Yiddle on Your Fiddle" (Berlin) - Brice/ "Queen of the Jungle" - Brice, chorus/ "My Man (Maurice Yvain-Channing Pollock) - Brice/ "A Circus Must Be Different in a Ziegfeld Show" (Con Conrad-Herb Magidson) chorus; dance by Hoctor. Unused: "It's Been So Long."

The Great Ziegfeld was the first of the show-business biographical epics in which a highly romanticized account of the life of a showman (or actor or composer) is the peg on which to hang a number of familiar songs and spectacularly staged routines, and to introduce a variety of colorful characters, both real and fictitious. Originally, Universal was to have made the Ziegfeld biography, but after the producer's former associate William Anthony McGuire had worked on the screenplay for about a year, the studio abandoned the project as too expensive and sold the rights to MGM. Other former Ziegfeld associates were initially to have been in the film, but Marilyn Miller withdrew after she was offered only a secondary role, and appearances by Ann Pennington, Gilda Gray, and Leon Errol ended up on the cutting room floor. Fanny Brice, Ray Bolger, and Harriet Hoctor did appear in specialty numbers, though Bolger had never been in a Ziegfeld show. While most of the real people portrayed in the movie were identified by name, "Audrey Lane" was supposedly Lillian Lorraine, one of Ziegfeld's most celebrated loves, and "Jack Billings" was rival producer Charles Dillingham.

With airy, urbane William Powell playing the craggy, dour impresario, the lengthy motion picture traced his flamboyant career from the days he managed strongman Sandow at the Chicago World's Fair in 1893 through his volatile relationship with first wife Anna Held (Luise Rainer) and his more compatible relationship with second wife Billie Burke (Myrna Loy). It showed Ziegfeld launching his annual *Follies* in 1907 and his *Midnight Frolic* in 1915, included his setbacks and recoveries, and ended with his death at 65 still dreaming of past and future glories. Miss Rainer's memorable laughing-and-crying telephone scene (recalling Bessie Love's similar scene in *The Broadway Melody*) was put in the film over the objection of studio boss Louis B. Mayer, who did not want Anna Held brought back in the story after the couple's divorce.

The mammoth "Pretty Girl Is Like a Melody" scene, which ended the first half of the movie, cost a record $220,000. Added after the regular shooting had been finished, and staged by Seymour Felix, the number featured a 32-foot-high volute consisting of 175 steps and weighing 100 tons. As it revolved in an ascending manner, formally clad Dennis Morgan (then known as Stanley Morner) sang the *Follies* theme song (with Allan Jones' voice!), and 182 singers, dancers, and musicians performed interpolated musical snippets ranging from *Pagliacci* to *Rhapsody in Blue*. As the Spirit of the *Follies*, Virginia Bruce, ended the scene perched atop the huge structure as waves of satin curtains descended in folds all around it.

There were two additional "Ziegfeld" movies from MGM: the 1941 *Ziegfeld Girl* (in which the producer was never shown but which did feature Judy Garland, Lana Turner, Hedy Lamarr, James Stewart, Tony Martin, and Jackie Cooper) and the 1946 all-star revue, *Ziegfeld Follies* (with Powell again as Ziegfeld). In 1929, Ziegfeld himself supervised *Glorifying the American Girl* (the slogan used for the *Follies*) which was about a girl (Mary Eaton) who becomes the leading lady of a *Follies*-type revue. *Rose of Washington Square* (Fox 1939), *Blue Skies* (Par. 1946), *Easter Parade* (MGM 1948), *Love Me or Leave Me* (MGM 1955), and *Funny Girl* (Col. 1968) all contained scenes supposedly taking place during *Ziegfeld Follies* productions. Ziegfeld was also portrayed in films by Paul Henreid in *Deep in My Heart* (MGM 1954) and Walter Pidgeon in *Funny Girl*.

Green, Adolph. *See* **Comden and Green.**

Green, Alfred E., director; b. Perris, Cal., 1889; d. Hollywood, Sept. 4, 1960. Green, who began in movies during the early silent days, achieved his biggest success with *The Jolson Story*.

1930 Sweet Kitty Bellairs
1935 Sweet Music
     Here's to Romance
1936 Colleen
1937 Mr. Dodd Takes the Air
1940 Shooting High
1943 The Mayor of 44th Street
1946 Tars and Spars
     The Jolson Story
1947 The Fabulous Dorseys
     Copacabana
1951 Two Gals and a Guy
1953 The Eddie Cantor Story
1954 Top Banana

Green, John ("Johnny"), composer; b. New York, Oct. 10, 1908. An arranger-conductor with Paramount in the early 30s, Green was general music director at MGM between 1949 and 1958. His best-known film song was "I Cover the Waterfront" (lyric by Edward Heyman) written to promote the 1933 talkie, and his best-known background score was for *Raintree County*. During the 30s he was featured pianist with his own dance band, making records (most notably with Fred Astaire) and appearing on radio. Among his lyric-writing collaborators: E. Y. Harburg, Ted Koehler, Harold Adamson, Robert Franklin, Ted Duncan, Ralph Blane, Leo Robin.

1930 The Sap from Syracuse (Harburg)
1938 Start Cheering (Koehler) (also specialty)
1944 Bathing Beauty (Adamson)
1946 Easy To Wed (Franklin; Duncan; Blane)
1947 Something in the Wind (Robin)

Green, Mitzi (née Elizabeth Keno), actress, singer; b. New York, Oct. 22, 1920; d. Huntington Harbour, Cal., May 24, 1969. Precocious child actress in early talkies and *Our Gang* shorts, who wore her hair in bangs, had a talent for mimicry, and introduced "Sing You Sinners." Also appeared on Broadway in *Babes in Arms*.

1930 Honey (*Doris*)
     Paramount on Parade (specialty)
     Love Among the Millionaires (*Penelope*)
1932 Girl Crazy (*Tessie Deegan*)
1934 Transatlantic Merry-Go-Round (*Mitzi*)
1952 Lost in Alaska (*Rosette*)
     Bloodhounds of Broadway (*Tessie Sammis*)

Greenwood, (Frances) Charlotte, actress, singer, dancer; b. Philadelphia, June 25, 1890; d. Beverly Hills, Jan. 18, 1978. Gangly blonde comedienne with exuber-

ant personality whose specialty was flat-footed high kicks. Began in vaudeville, then achieved Broadway success in *So Long, Letty* (1916), and repeated the part on the screen. Prominent in Fox musicals of the 40s in which she usually played mothers and aunts; remembered for her role in *Oklahoma!* Bib: *Never Too Tall* by Miss Greenwood (1947).

1930 So Long, Letty (*Letty Robbins*)
1931 Palmy Days (*Miss Martin*)
     Flying High (*Pansy*)
1940 Star Dust (*Lola Langdon*)
     Young People (*Kitty Ballentine*)
     Down Argentine Way (*Binnie Crawford*)
1941 Moon Over Miami (*Aunt Susie*)
     Tall, Dark and Handsome (*Winnie*)
1942 Springtime in the Rockies (*Phoebe Grey*)
1943 The Gang's All Here (*Mrs. Peyton Potter*)
1946 Wake Up and Dream (*Sara March*)
1949 Oh, You Beautiful Doll (*Anna Breitenbach*)
1953 Dangerous When Wet (*Ma Higgins*)
1955 Oklahoma! (*Eller Murphy*)
1956 The Opposite Sex (*Lucy*)

Grey, Clifford, lyricist; b. Birmingham, Eng., Jan. 5, 1887; d. Ipswich, Eng., Sept. 25, 1941. Prolific London and New York lyricist-librettist with two stage works—*Sally*, with Jerome Kern, and *Hit the Deck*, with Leo Robin and Vincent Youmans—transferred to the screen. Maurice Chevalier introduced his songs in *The Love Parade* ("My Love Parade"), music by Victor Schertzinger, and *The Smiling Lieutenant*, music by Oscar Straus. Grey also wrote film scores with Herbert Stothart and Franz Lehar.

1929 The Love Parade (Schertzinger)
     Devil May Care (Stothart)
     Sally (Kern)
1930 Hit the Deck (Robin-Youmans)
     The Rogue Song (Stothart, Lehar)
1931 The Smiling Lieutenant (Straus)
1955 Hit the Deck (Robin-Youmans)

Guizar, Tito, actor, singer; b. Mexico, 1909. Guitar-strumming, delicate-featured troubadour who appeared in films in both Mexico and Hollywood. Also sang in nightclubs.

1935 Under the Pampas Moon (café singer)
1938 Big Broadcast of 1938 (specialty)
     Tropic Holiday (*Ramon*)
1939 St. Louis Blues (*Rafael San Ramos*)
1941 Blondie Goes Latin (*Don Rodriguez*)
1944 Brazil (*Miguel Soaves*)

1946   The Thrill of Brazil (*Tito Guizar*)
1948   The Gay Ranchero (*Nicki Lopez*)

Guys and Dolls (1955). Music & lyrics by Frank Loesser; screenplay by Joseph L. Mankiewicz from Broadway musical by Abe Burrows & Loesser based on short story "The Idyll of Miss Sarah Brown" by Damon Runyon.

A Samuel Goldwyn film released by MGM; directed by Joseph L. Mankiewicz; choreography, Michael Kidd; production design, Oliver Smith; art director, Joseph Wright; costumes, Irene Sharaff; music director, Jay S. Blackton; orchestrations, Skip Martin, Nelson Riddle, Alexander Courage, Al Sendrey; cameraman, Harry Stradling; editor, Daniel Mandell; Eastman Color; CinemaScope.

Cast: Marlon Brando (*Sky Masterson*); Jean Simmons (*Sarah Brown*); Frank Sinatra (*Nathan Detroit*); Vivian Blaine (*Miss Adelaide*); Robert Keith (*Lt. Brannigan*); Stubby Kaye (*Nicely-Nicely Johnson*); B. S. Pully (*Big Jule*); Johnny Silver (*Benny Southstreet*); Sheldon Leonard (*Harry the Horse*); Danny Dayton (*Rusty Charlie*); George E. Stone (*Society Max*); Regis Toomey (*Arvid Abernathy*); Kathryn Givney (*Gen. Cartwright*); Veda Ann Borg (*Laverne*): Renée Renor (*Cuban singer*).

Songs: "Fugue for Tinhorns" - Kaye, Silver, Dayton/ "Follow the Fold" - Simmons, Toomey, Salvation Army workers/ "The Oldest Established" - Sinatra, Brando, Kaye, Silver, Stone, Leonard, gamblers/ "I'll Know" - Brando, Simmons/ "Pet Me, Papa" - Blaine, chorus/ "Adelaide's Lament" - Blaine/ "Guys and Dolls" - Sinatra, Kaye, Silver/ "Adelaide" - Sinatra/ "A Woman in Love" - uncredited singer, Renor; reprised by Simmons, Brando/ "If I Were a Bell" - Simmons/ "My Time of Day" - orchestra only/ "Take Back Your Mink" - Blaine, chorus/ "Luck Be a Lady" - dance by gamblers, sung by Brando/ "Sue Me" - Blaine, Sinatra / "Sit Down, You're Rockin' the Boat" - Kaye. Unused: "A Bushel and a Peck," "More I Cannot Wish You," "I've Never Been in Love Before."

The classic 1950 Broadway musical was brought to the screen with a deliberate attempt to create a fantasy world that would circumvent the realism usually imposed by the camera. This was done by taking the opposite approach from the one first used in *On the Town:* instead of showing actual New York City locales, *Guys and Dolls* offered a stylized, two-dimensional city, similar to a stage production, that was felt would provide a more congenial setting for the Damon Runyon characters. Unfortunately, the attempt at less realism only made the people and situations less believable. The plot, remaining faithful to its source, focused on Nathan Detroit, the harried proprietor of "the oldest established permanent floating crap game in New York"; Miss Adelaide, Nathan's allergy-afflicted fiancée of 14 years; Sky Masterson, the self-assured highroller; and Miss Sarah Brown, of the Save-a-Soul Mission, who is the means of Sky's reformation.

Producer Samuel Goldwyn cast his leading roles somewhat against type with Frank Sinatra (who had wanted to play Sky) as Nathan, Marlon Brando (whose singing was his own) as Sky, and Jean Simmons (in her only movie musical) as Miss Sarah. They replaced the more authentic originals, Sam Levene, Robert Alda, and Isabel Bigley, though others in the film—Vivian Blaine, Stubby Kaye, Johnny Silver, and B. S. Pully, as well as choreographer Michael Kidd—were recruited from the Broadway company. For the movie, the songwriter substituted "Pet Me, Papa" for "A Bushel and a Peck," and "A Woman in Love" for "I've Never Been in Love Before."

H

Hale, Sonnie (né John Robert Hale-Monro), actor, singer, director; b. London, May 1, 1902; d. London, June 9, 1959. Hale was married to Jessie Matthews during her reign as queen of British film musicals, appearing with her in three movies (including *Evergreen*) and directing her in three. Active in the London musical theatre from 1921 to 1948, he was the son of actor Robert Hale, brother of Binnie Hale, and, before marrying Miss Matthews, husband of Evelyn Laye.

1932	Happy Ever After (*Willie*)
	Tell Me Tonight (*Alexander Koretsky*)
1933	Early to Bed (*Helmut*)
1934	Evergreen (*Leslie Benn*)
	My Song for You (*Charlie*)
	My Heart Is Calling (*Alphonse Rosée*)
1935	First a Girl (*Victor*)
1936	It's Love Again (*Freddie Rathbone*)
1937	Head Over Heels (dir. only)
	Gangway (dir. only)
1938	Sailing Along (dir. only)
1946	London Town (*Charlie*)

Haley, (John Joseph) Jack, actor, singer; b. Boston, Aug. 10, 1899; d. Los Angeles, June 6, 1979. An eye-rolling comic actor usually playing a naïve, easily duped character, Haley is best remembered on screen for his performance as the Tin Woodman in *The Wizard of Oz* (singing "If I Only Had a Heart"). During the 1930s he acted mostly in Fox films, introducing such songs as "Wake Up and Live" and "Never in a Million Years" (dubbed by Buddy Clark). Haley was also featured in Broadway musicals, including *Follow Thru* and *Higher and Higher,* both of which were subsequently filmed. Producer Jack Haley, Jr., is his son.

1930	Follow Thru (*Jack Martin*)
1933	Sitting Pretty (*Pete Pendleton*)
1935	The Girl Friend (*Henry*)

	Redheads on Parade (*Peter Mathews*)
	Coronado (*Chuck Hornbostel*)
1936	Pigskin Parade (*Slug Winters*)
	Poor Little Rich Girl (*Jimmy Dolan*)
1937	Wake Up and Live (*Eddie Kane*)
1938	Rebecca of Sunnybrook Farm (*Orville Smithers*)
	Alexander's Ragtime Band (*Davey Lane*)
	Hold That Coed (*Wilbur*)
	Thanks for Everything (*Henry Smith*)
1939	The Wizard of Oz (*Hickory/Tin Woodman*)
1941	Navy Blues (*Powerhouse Bolton*)
	Moon Over Miami (*Jack*)
1942	Beyond the Blue Horizon (*Squidge*)
1943	Higher and Higher (*Mike O'Brien*)
1944	Take It Big (*Jack North*)
1945	George White's Scandals (*Jack Williams*)
	Sing Your Way Home (*Steve*)
1946	People Are Funny (*Pinky Wilson*)

Hall, Alexander, director; b. Boston, 1894; d. San Francisco, July 30, 1968. Hall entered films in 1932 and directed such musical stars as Shirley Temple, Mae West, Gladys Swarthout, Rita Hayworth, and Mario Lanza. He was once married to actress Lola Lane.

1933	Torch Singer
1934	Little Miss Marker
1935	Goin' to Town
1936	Give Us This Night
1947	Down to Earth
1952	Because You're Mine
1953	Let's Do It Again

Hallelujah, I'm a Bum (1933). Music by Richard Rodgers; lyrics & rhythmic dialogue by Lorenz Hart; screenplay by S. N. Behrman from story by Ben Hecht.

A United Artists film produced by Joseph M. Schenck; directed by Lewis Milestone; art director, Richard Day; music director, Alfred Newman; cameraman, Lucien Andriot; editor, W. Duncan Mansfield.

Cast: Al Jolson (*Bumper*); Madge Evans (*June Marcher*); Frank Morgan (*Mayor John Hastings*); Harry Langdon (*Egghead*); Chester Conklin (*Sunday*); Edgar Connor (*Acorn*); Tammany Young (*Orlando*); Tyler Brooke (*mayor's secretary*); Bert Roach (*John*); Louise Carver (*Ma Sunday*); Richard Rodgers (*photographer's assistant*); Lorenz Hart (*bank teller*),

Songs: "I Gotta Get Back to New York" - Jolson/ "My Pal Bumper" - Connor, Jolson, Langdon, bums/ "Hallelujah, I'm a Bum" - Jolson/ "Laying the Cornerstone" - Morgan, officials, children/ "Dear June" - Jolson/ "Bumper Found a Grand" - Connor, Langdon, Jolson, bums/ "What Do You Want with Money?" - Jolson/ "Hallelujah, I'm a Bum" (different song) -Jolson/ "Kangaroo Court" - Jolson, Langdon, Connor, bums/ "I'd Do It Again" - Jolson/ "You Are Too Beautiful" - Jolson. Unused: "Sleeping Beauty."

Following their successful expansion of the use of film music in *Love Me Tonight*, Rodgers and Hart tried rhythmic and rhymed conversation in *Hallelujah, I'm a Bum*, through which they attempted to affect a smoother transition from dialogue to song. The film, the only musical to deal directly with homeless people during the Depression, focused on squatters who must live in New York's Central Park. The basic plot concerns their leader (Al Jolson), who unknowingly falls in love with the fiancée of his friend the Mayor (Frank Morgan, who succeeded Roland Young after the latter took ill).

Hallelujah, I'm a Bum offered Lewis Milestone his first chance to direct a musical when the original director, Harry D'Abbabie D'Arrast, walked out over a disagreement with Jolson. The movie was one of the few at the time to have musical sequences shot on exterior locations. All the scenes in Central Park were filmed at the Riviera Country Club in Pacific Palisades, which necessitated the studio orchestra being at the club to accompany the action. Both Rodgers and Hart appeared briefly in the picture: Rodgers is seen as a grinning photographer's assistant as the Mayor poses with a large Italian family; Hart gets a closeup and some brief dialogue as a teller in a bank where Jolson has gotten a job to impress Madge Evans. Another curiosity: two different songs are named "Hallelujah, I'm a Bum."

"Hallowe'en" Music by Harold Arlen; lyric by Ralph Blane & Arlen. Though Irving Berlin had already written anthems celebrating most of the American holidays, the one he missed—as the verse to the song points out— was Hallowe'en, and the refrain proceeds to make amends for the omission. The lighthearted paean was presented in *My Blue Heaven* (Fox 1950) as an impromptu entertainment by Jane Wyatt, Betty Grable, Dan Dailey, and David Wayne.

Hamlisch, Marvin, composer; b. New York, June 2, 1944. Hamlisch scored his first film, *The Swimmer*, in 1968. Since then he has supplied scores and theme songs for other nonmusicals (including the title song from *The Way We Were*, written with Marilyn and Alan Bergman) and one semi-musical, *Starting Over* (with lyricist Carole Bayer Sager). He also composed the score for Broadway musicals *A Chorus Line* and *They're Playing Our Song*, and television musical *The Entertainer* (with lyricists Robert Joseph and Tim Rice).

Hammerstein, Oscar (Greeley Clendenning) II, lyricist, screenwriter; b. New York, July 12, 1895; d. Doylestown, Pa., Aug. 23, 1960. A major contributor to the development of the American musical theatre, Hammerstein worked primarily in the areas of operetta (with co-librettist-lyricist Otto Harbach and composers Rudolf Friml, Herbert Stothart, Sigmund Romberg, George Gershwin, and Emmerich Kalman) and musical play (music by Jerome Kern, Vincent Youmans, and Georges Bizet), and he is particularly celebrated for his 18-year partnership with Richard Rodgers. As lyricist, Hammerstein was adept at creating idiomatic, poetic expressions, often dealing with the interrelationships of such themes as nature, music, home, and love. He wrote 35 musicals in New York and two in London, of which there were a record number of 26 less or more faithful screen adaptations: *Rose-Marie* (three times, the first silent); *Sunny* (twice); *Song of the Flame; Show Boat* (three times, the first part-talkie); *The Desert Song* (three times); *Golden Dawn; The New Moon* (twice, the first with new story); *Rainbow* (retitled *Song of the West*); *Sweet Adeline; Music in the Air; Very Warm for May* (retitled *Broadway Rhythm*, with one Hammerstein song); *Oklahoma!; Carmen Jones; Carousel; South Pacific; The King and I; Flower Drum Song; The Sound of Music.*

In Hollywood, Hammerstein wrote lyrics to the music of Romberg, Kern, Erich Wolfgang Korngold, Johann Strauss, Jr., Ben Oakland, and Rodgers. His chief original screen musicals were *High, Wide and Handsome* ("The Folks Who Live on the Hill," "Can I Forget You?"), and *State Fair* ("It's a Grand Night for Singing," "It Might as Well Be Spring"). For television he wrote *Cinderella* ("In My Own Little Corner," "Do I Love You Because You're Beautiful?"). Other film songs: "You Will Remember Vienna," "When I Grow Too Old To Dream," "I'll Take Romance," "All Through the Day" (for *Centennial Summer*), and "A Kiss To Build a Dream On" (with Bert Kalmar and Harry Ruby). Among those who sang Hammerstein lyrics on the screen were John Boles, Grace Moore, Lawrence Tibbett, Gloria Swanson, Irene Dunne, Evelyn Laye, Jeanette MacDonald, Nelson Eddy, Gladys Swarthout, Allan Jones, Paul Robeson, Helen Morgan, Miliza Korjus, Lanny Ross, Anna Neagle, Dennis Morgan, Gordon MacRae, Ann Blyth, Shirley Jones, Julie Andrews, Mitzi Gaynor, Pat Boone, Bobby Darin, and Ann-Margret. Bib: *Lyrics* by Hammerstein (1949); *Some Enchanted Evenings* by Deems Taylor (1952); *Rodgers and Hammerstein Song Book* (1958); *Getting To Know Him* by Hugh Fordin (1977); *The Sound of Their Music* by Frederick Nolan (1978); *Rodgers & Hammerstein Fact Book* ed. Stanley Green (1980); *The Rodgers & Hammerstein Story* by Green (1980).

Asterisk indicates Mr. Hammerstein also wrote script:
1929 Show Boat (Kern)
       The Desert Song (Harbach-Romberg)
1930 Song of the West (Youmans)
       Song of the Flame (Harbach-Gershwin, Stothart)
       Golden Dawn (Harbach-Kalman, Stothart)
       Viennese Nights (Romberg)*
       New Moon (Romberg)
       Sunny (Harbach-Kern)
1931 Children of Dreams (Romberg)*
1934 Music in the Air (Kern)
1935 Sweet Adeline (Kern)
       The Night Is Young (Romberg)
1936 Rose Marie (Harbach-Friml, Stothart)
       Give Us This Night (Korngold)
       Show Boat (Kern)*
1937 Swing High, Swing Low (script only)
       High, Wide and Handsome (Kern)*
1938 The Great Waltz (Strauss)
       The Lady Objects (Oakland)
1939 The Story of Vernon and Irene Castle (script only)
1940 New Moon (Romberg)
1941 Sunny (Harbach-Kern)
1943 The Desert Song (Harbach-Romberg)
1945 State Fair (Rodgers)*
1951 Show Boat (Kern)
1953 The Desert Song (Harbach-Romberg)
1954 Rose Marie (Harbach-Friml, Stothart)
       Carmen Jones (Bizet)
1955 Oklahoma! (Rodgers)

1956 Carousel (Rodgers)
       The King and I (Rodgers)
1957 Cinderella (tv) (Rodgers)*
1958 South Pacific (Rodgers)
1961 Flower Drum Song (Rodgers)
1962 State Fair (remake) (Rodgers)
1965 The Sound of Music (Rodgers)
       Cinderella (tv remake) (Rodgers)

"Hang Your Heart on a Hickory Limb" Music by James V. Monaco; lyric by Johnny Burke. Bouncy warning that, since love brings pain, the safest course is to avoid it. Then, on the other hand, it can also be argued that "love is worth the trouble it can be." Bing Crosby first sang the number in *East Side of Heaven* (Univ. 1939). The idea for the lyric came from an old rhyme in which a daughter's request for permission to go swimming is granted by her mother but only with the stipulation, "Hang your clothes on a hickory limb/ And don't go near the water." Coincidentally, the same rhyme also prompted another song of the same year, "Yes, My Darling Daughter" by Jack Lawrence.

Hans Christian Andersen (1952). Music & lyrics by Frank Loesser; screenplay by Moss Hart from story by Myles Connolly.

A Samuel Goldwyn film released by RKO-Radio; directed by Charles Vidor; choreography, Roland Petit; art directors, Richard Day, Antoni Clavé; costumes, Clavé, Mary Wills; music director, Walter Scharf; orchestrations, Jerome Moross; cameraman, Harry Stradling; editor, Danel Mandell; Technicolor.

Cast: Danny Kaye (*Hans Christian Andersen*); Farley Granger (*Niels*); Jeanmaire (*Doro*); Joey Walsh (*Peter*); Erik Bruhn ("*Hussar*"); Roland Petit ("*Prince*"); Philip Tonge (*Otto*); John Qualen (*Burgomaster*); Peter Votrian (*Lars*).

Songs: "The King's New Clothes" - Kaye/ "I'm Hans Christian Andersen" - Kaye/ "Wonderful Copenhagen" - uncredited singer, Kaye, Walsh/ "Thumbelina" - Kaye/ "Ice Skating Ballet" - Jeanmaire, Bruhn, dancers/ "Ugly Duckling" - Kaye/ "Dream Fantasy" - dance by Kaye, Jeanmaire, Granger/ "Anywhere I Wander" - Kaye/ "Inchworm" - Kaye/ "No Two People" - Kaye, Jeanmaire, dancers/ "The Little Mermaid" (music, Franz Liszt) - dance by Jeanmaire, Petit, dancers.

Created as "a fairy tale about a great spinner of fairy tales," the movie told how Andersen, a cobbler in Odense in 1830, so bewitched the local school children with his stories that town officials were only too happy when he took off for Copenhagen. There he made a pair of slippers for a ballerina, fell unrequitedly in love with her, and wrote the story of "The Little Mermaid" which the ballerina's husband turned into a 17-minute ballet. After returning to Odense, the heartsick storyteller now found his talents appreciated by everyone. Since this was a total distortion of Andersen's life, even prompting Danish opposition to the film before it was completed, producer Goldwyn made sure that the movie was preceeded by a printed denial of any biographical intent.

It had taken Goldwyn five years to find the kind of story he wanted (he'd already rejected 21 completed manuscripts), though the elaborate, colorful film was best appreciated for the ballets (four in all, comprising some 25 percent of the footage), the generous Frank Loesser score (including four songs based on Andersen's tales), and the restrained performance of Danny Kaye. In 1974 Beverley Cross made a stage adaptation of the movie, which was presented in London under the shortened title, *Hans Andersen*. Tommy Steele played Hans. The story stuck a little closer to facts by having him fall in love with Jenny Lind rather than a ballet dancer. One Andersen fairy tale that was not included in the movie had provided the basis for the ballet in the 1948 Michael Powell-Emeric Pressburger film, *The Red Shoes*, starring Moira Shearer. In 1962, two other creators of fairy tales were depicted by Laurence Harvey and Karl Bohm in *The Wonderful World of the Brothers Grimm*. An MGM-Cinerama release, it was directed by George Pal and Henry Levin and had songs by Bob Merrill.

"Happiness Is a Thing Called Joe" Music by Harold Arlen; lyric by E. Y. Harburg. Song of romantic contentment sung in *Cabin in the Sky* (MGM 1943) by Petunia Jackson (Ethel Waters) about her newly reformed gambling husband, Li'l Joe (Eddie "Rochester" Anderson). Also sung by Susan Hayward in *I'll Cry Tomorrow* (MGM 1955).

"Happy Days Are Here Again" Music by Milton Ager; lyric by Jack Yellen. Sung by Charles King in *Chasing Rainbows* (MGM 1930) in a scene in which a group of World War I soldiers get word of the Armistice. Because the studio permitted the song's music publisher to release the optimistic number prior to the film's opening, George Olsen's orchestra played it at the Hotel Pennsylvania in New York soon after the Wall Street crash. Later, when Olsen featured it to great suc-

cess during a Hollywood engagement, MGM production chief Irving Thalberg wanted to know why it wasn't being used in an MGM picture. When told that it was, though the movie was still unreleased, the studio executive ordered the entire scene reshot so that the number might be given a more elaborate presentation. The song was later sung in *Beau James* (Par. 1957), in *This Earth Is Mine* (Univ. 1959), and by a busload of tourists in *The Night of the Iguana* (MGM 1964). It was also closely associated with Franklin D. Roosevelt's presidential campaign of 1932.

Harburg, E. Y. ("Yip") (né Isidore Hochberg), lyricist; b. New York, April 8, 1896. Harburg's puckish, adroitly rhymed, frequently socially conscious lyrics were primarily associated with Broadway musicals, including such major works as *Bloomer Girl* and *Finian's Rainbow* (filmed in 1968). His most memorable screen assignment was *The Wizard of Oz* ("We're Off To See the Wizard," "Over the Rainbow"), written with composer Harold Arlen for Judy Garland. With Arlen he also wrote "Lydia the Tattooed Lady" for Groucho Marx in *At the Circus* and "Happiness Is a Thing Called Joe" for Ethel Waters in *Cabin in the Sky*. Other collaborators were Johnny Green, Jay Gorney, Arthur Schwartz, Burton Lane, Jerome Kern ("Can't Help Singing," "More and More"), Sammy Fain, and Earl Robinson. Among screen performers who sang Harburg lyrics were Al Jolson, Dick Powell, Kenny Baker, Jeanette MacDonald, Lena Horne, Deanna Durbin, Fred Astaire, and Petula Clark. (Died Los Angeles, March 5, 1981.)

1930	The Sap from Syracuse (Green)	
1933	Moonlight and Pretzels (Gorney)	
1936	The Singing Kid (Arlen)	
	Stage Struck (Arlen)	
	Gold Diggers of 1937 (Arlen)	
1939	The Wizard of Oz (Arlen)	
	At the Circus (Arlen)	
1942	Ship Ahoy (Lane)	
	Cairo (Schwartz)	
1943	Cabin in the Sky (Arlen)	
1944	Meet the People (Fain, Arlen, Lane) (also prod.)	
	Can't Help Singing (Kern)	
1946	California (Robinson)	
1962	Gay Purr-ee (Arlen)	
1968	Finian's Rainbow (Lane)	

Hard Day's Night, A (1964). Music & lyrics by John Lennon & Paul McCartney; screenplay by Alun Owen.

A United Artists film produced by Walter Shenson; directed by Richard Lester; art director, Ray Simm; costumes, Julie Harris; music director, George Martin; cameraman, M. Silverlock; editor, John Jympson.

Cast: John Lennon (*John*); Paul McCartney (*Paul*); George Harrison (*George*); Ringo Starr (*Ringo*); Wilfred Brambell (*Grandfather*); Norman Rossington (*Norm*); Victor Spinetti (*Director*); John Junkin (*Shake*); Anna Quayle (*Millie*); Kenneth Haigh (*Simon*).

Songs: "A Hard Day's Night"/ "I Should Have Known Better"/ "I Want To Be Your Man"/ "Don't Bother Me" (George Harrison)/ "All My Loving"/ "If I Fell"/ "Can't Buy Me Love"/ "And I Love Her"/ "I'm Happy Just To Dance with You"/ "Tell Me Why"/ "She Loves You." All sung by The Beatles.

The quartet's casual charm, the pulsating musical score, Richard Lester's frenetic and inventive film cutting, and Alun Owen's cheeky script all contributed to the only rock-and-roll movie accepted as a classic. When United Artists first decided to make the low-budget film, it was simply to capitalize on the near-hysterical adulation of the Beatles so that its record company would be able to cut the soundtrack album. To this end a story was devised as a fictionalized documentary revolving around a day in the lives of the celebrated group. As shooting neared completion, however, the picture was still without a name, a problem remedied by Ringo Starr's chance reference to an all-night recording session as "a hard day's night."

As a unit, the Beatles made one other movie, *Help!* (UA 1965), also directed by Lester, which involved them in James Bond intrigue. The British movie, *Catch Us If You Can* (1965), with the Dave Clark Five, was something of a Beatles movie spinoff. Bib: *The Beatles in "A Hard Day's Night"* (1978).

"Hard Day's Night, A" Music & lyric by John Lennon & Paul McCartney. Title song of film (UA 1964) introduced on soundtrack by The Beatles (John Lennon, Paul McCartney, George Harrison, Ringo Starr) during opening scenes showing the group being pursued by pubescent fans. The song, which was added to the film after the other numbers had been recorded, was inspired by Ringo Starr's characterization of an all-night recording session.

Hardy, Oliver. *See* **Laurel and Hardy.**

Harline, Leigh, composer; b. Salt Lake City, Utah, March 26, 1907; d. Los Angeles, Dec. 10, 1969. Member Walt Disney music department, 1932–41; then free-

lance conductor, arranger, composer, scoring many nonmusical films. Best-known song was "When You Wish Upon a Star," lyric by Ned Washington, from *Pinocchio.* Also collaborated with Mort Greene.

1940 Pinocchio (Washington)
1947 Beat the Band (Greene)

Harling, W. Franke, composer; b. London, Jan. 18, 1887; d. Sierra Madre, Cal., Nov. 22, 1958. Composed film background scores, operas, tone poems, and music for "Sing You Sinners" (lyric by Sam Coslow) and "Beyond the Blue Horizon" (with Richard A. Whiting and Leo Robin).

1930 Honey (Coslow)
     Monte Carlo (Whiting-Robin)

Harnick, Sheldon. *See* **Bock and Harnick.**

Harris, Phil, actor, singer, bandleader; b. Linton, Ind., June 24, 1906. Usually appearing as the self-confident if bumbling ladies' man, curly-haired Harris was also prominent as music director for Jack Benny's radio series. He made many records and is married to Alice Faye.

1933 Melody Cruise (*Alan Chandler*)
1937 Turn Off the Moon (*Phil Harris*)
1939 Man About Town (*Ted Nash*)
1940 Dreaming Out Loud (*Peter Atkinson*)
     Buck Benny Rides Again (*Phil Harris*)
1946 I Love a Bandleader (*Phil Burton*)
1950 Wabash Avenue (*Uncle Mike*)
1951 Starlift (guest bit)
     Here Comes the Groom (specialty)
1956 Anything Goes (*Steve Blair*)
1967 The Jungle Book (voice of *Baloo the Bear*)
1970 The Aristocats (voice of *J. Thomas O'Malley*)
1973 Robin Hood (voice of *Little John*)

Harrison, George. *See* **Beatles, The.**

Harrison, (Reginald Carey) Rex, actor; b. Huyton, Eng., March 5, 1908. Urbane, versatile stage and screen actor whose Professor Higgins taught phonetics to Liza Doolittle and whose Dr. Dolittle learned to talk to the animals. Among his six wives were Lilli Palmer (divorced), Kay Kendall (died), and Rachel Roberts (divorced). Bib: *Rex* by Harrison (1974).

1964 My Fair Lady (*Prof. Henry Higgins*)
1967 Doctor Dolittle (*Dr. John Dolittle*)

Hart, Lorenz (Milton), lyricist; b. New York, May 2, 1895; d. New York, Nov. 22, 1943. Hart was noted for his worldly, at times cynical outlook, the peppery playfulness of his lyrics, and his ability at polysyllabic rhyming. Except for his words to Franz Lehar's music in the 1934 film version of *The Merry Widow*, he worked exclusively with composer Richard Rodgers; together they wrote the scores for 26 musicals in New York and three in London. Of these, 12 were transferred to the screen with varying degrees of faithfulness and success: *Present Arms* (retitled *Leathernecking*); *Spring Is Here*; *Heads Up!*; *Ever Green*; *Jumbo*; *On Your Toes* (though two ballets were retained, music was used only in background); *Babes in Arms*; *I Married an Angel*; *The Boys from Syracuse*; *Too Many Girls* ("You're Nearer" added); *Higher and Higher* (Rodgers and Hart songs replaced); *Pal Joey*. Stage songs also in film bio, *Words and Music*, with Mickey Rooney as Hart.

For the screen, Rodgers and Hart made major contributions to three innovative musicals: *Love Me Tonight* ("Lover," "Isn't It Romantic?," "Mimi"); *The Phantom President* ("Give Her a Kiss"); and *Hallelujah, I'm a Bum* ("You Are Too Beautiful"). They also wrote "Soon," "It's Easy To Remember" and "Down by the River" for Bing Crosby's *Mississippi*. Among others who sang Hart's lyrics in movies were Maurice Chevalier, Jeanette MacDonald, George M. Cohan, Al Jolson, Jessie Matthews, Judy Garland, Allan Jones, Martha Raye, Perry Como, Ann Sothern, Lena Horne, Frank Sinatra, and Jimmy Durante. Bib: *Rodgers & Hart Song Book* (1951); *Musical Stages* by Rodgers (1975); *Rodgers and Hart* by Samuel Marx & Jan Clayton (1976); *Thou Swell, Thou Witty* by Dorothy Hart (his sister-in-law) (1976); *Rodgers and Hammerstein Fact Book* ed. Stanley Green (1980).

Unless otherwise noted, following had songs written with Mr. Rodgers:

1930	Spring Is Here
	Leathernecking
	Heads Up
1931	The Hot Heiress
1932	Love Me Tonight
	The Phantom President
1933	Hallelujah, I'm a Bum (also *bank teller*)
1934	Hollywood Party
	Evergreen (Eng.)
	The Merry Widow (Lehar)
1935	Mississippi
1936	Dancing Pirate
1938	Fools for Scandal
1939	Babes in Arms
1940	The Boys from Syracuse
	Too Many Girls
1941	They Met in Argentina
1942	I Married an Angel
1948	Words and Music
1957	Pal Joey
1962	Jumbo

Harvey, Lilian (née Helene Lilian Muriel Pape), actress, singer, dancer; b. Horsey, Eng., Jan 19, 1906; d. Antibes, France, July 27, 1968. Petite blonde international film star celebrated for her series of German musical films with Willy Fritsch (e.g., *Der Kongress Tanzt/ Congress Dances*), some released in English. In addition, she made films in Hollywood, Britain, and France.

1932	Congress Dances (Ger.) (*Chrystal Weinzinger*)
	Happy Ever After (Ger.) (*Jou-Jou*)
1933	Heart Song (Ger.) (*Juliette*)
	My Weakness (US) (*Looloo Blake*)
	My Lips Betray (US) (*Lili Wieler*)
1934	I Am Suzanne (US) (*Suzanne*)
1935	Let's Live Tonight (US) (*Kay Routledge*)
	Invitation to the Waltz (Eng.) (*Jenny Peachey*)

Harvey Girls, The (1946). Music by Harry Warren; lyrics by Johnny Mercer; screenplay by Edmund Beloin, Nathaniel Curtis, Harry Crane, James O'Hanlon, and Samson Raphaelson from book by Samuel Hopkins Adams and story by Eleanore Griffin & William Rankin.

An MGM film produced by Arthur Freed; directed by George Sidney; associate producer, Roger Edens; choreography, Robert Alton; art directors, Cedric Gibbons, William Ferrari; costumes, Helen Rose, Valles; music director, Lennie Hayton; orchestrations, Conrad Salinger; cameraman, George Folsey; editor, Albert Akst; Technicolor.

Cast: Judy Garland (*Susan Bradley*); John Hodiak (*Ned Trent*); Ray Bolger (*Chris Maule*); Angela Lansbury (*Em*); Preston Foster (*Judge Sam Purvis*); Virginia O'Brien (*Alma*); Kenny Baker (*Terry O'Halloran*); Cyd Charisse (vocals by Marion Doenges) (*Deborah Andrews*); Marjorie Main (*Sonora Cassidy*); Chill Wills (*H. H. Hartsey*); Selena Royle (*Miss Bliss*); Jack Lambert (*Marty Peters*); Ben Carter (*John Henry*); Horace (Stephen) McNally ("*Gold Dust*" *McLean*).

Songs: "In the Valley Where the Evening Sun Goes Down" - Garland/ "Wait and See" - Lansbury; reprised by Baker/ "On the Atchison, Topeka and the Santa Fe" - Carter, Main, Bolger, O'Brien, Garland, Harvey girls, cowboys; reprised as dance by Bolger/

"The Train Must Be Fed" (Roger Edens) - Royle, Main, Harvey girls/ "Oh, You Kid" - Lansbury, girls/ "It's a Great Big World" - Garland, O'Brien, Charisse (Doenges)/ "The Wild Wild West" - O'Brien/ "Swing Your Partner Round and Round" - Harvey girls; dance by Bolger, Garland, Main, Charisse, Harvey girls. Unused: "March of the Doagies," "Hayride," "My Intuition."

Spurred by the rip-roaring reception afforded the Broadway musical, *Oklahoma!*, producer Arthur Freed felt that the screen, so appropriate for westerns, would prove equally suitable for western musicals. Because MGM already owned the rights to *The Harvey Girls*, which had been originally scheduled as a nonmusical for Lana Turner, Freed was able to secure it as a musical for Judy Garland. The project was unusual in that it was tied in with a commercial venture, the establishment of the Harvey House restaurant chain in the late 1800s, which was created to provide reputable eating places for train passengers traveling through the disreputable West. For Miss Garland, the film gave her the chance to follow *Meet Me in St. Louis* with another Americana musical. Set in Sandrock, New Mexico (though location shooting was near Chatsworth, in the San Fernando Valley), the movie centered its conflict upon the hostility felt by certain patrons and loose ladies of the Alhambra saloon toward the starched innocents employed by Harvey (who nevertheless get a rousing welcome upon their arrival on the Atchison, Topeka and Santa Fe Railroad). Romance for Miss Garland takes the form of saloon-keeper John Hodiak (vaguely recalling Clark Gable in *San Francisco*), and non-too-serious rivalry is provided by saloon singer Angela Lansbury (in a role first intended for Ann Sothern).

"Have You Got Any Castles, Baby?" Music by Richard A. Whiting; lyric by Johnny Mercer. Chivalrous offer to build castles and slay dragons introduced, oddly enough, by Priscilla Lane and a line of cuties in *Varsity Show* (Warner 1937). The number was offered as part of a collegiate revue presented in a New York theatre.

"Have Yourself a Merry Little Christmas" Music & lyric by Hugh Martin & Ralph Blane. Tender ballad sung by Judy Garland to Margaret O'Brien in *Meet Me in St. Louis* (MGM 1944) as the two sisters look out of a window in their home and sadly contemplate moving from St. Louis to New York. As originally written, the lyric painted an entirely hopeless picture with such lines as:

> Have yourself a merry little Christmas,
> It may be your last;
> Next year we may all be living in the past.

When she first heard the song, Miss Garland felt that singing so gloomy a threnody to a little girl would make her seem like a monster, and she insisted that the songwriters change the mood from pessimism to optimism. Two of the lines proved especially adaptable. "Faithful friends who were dear to us/ Will be near to us no more" had no trouble at all turning into "Faithful friends who are dear to us/ Will be near to us once more."

Haver, June (née June Stovenour), actress, singer, dancer; b. Rock Island, Ill., June 10, 1926. One of Fox's blonde multi-talented musical stars, originally signed as an alternative to either Alice Faye or Betty Grable. Miss Haver introduced "On the Boardwalk at Atlantic City" in *Three Little Girls in Blue* and "Give Me the Simple Life" in *Wake Up and Dream*. Appeared opposite Dick Haymes, Fred MacMurray (whom she married after retirement in 1953), John Payne, Ray Bolger, Gordon MacRae, Dan Dailey.

1943   The Gang's All Here (*Maybelle*)
1944   Irish Eyes Are Smiling (*Mary "Irish" O'Neill*)
1945   Where Do We Go from Here? (*Lucilla*)
        The Dolly Sisters (*Rosie Dolly*)
1946   Three Little Girls in Blue (*Pam*)
        Wake Up and Dream (*Jenny*)
1947   I Wonder Who's Kissing Her Now (*Katie*)
1949   Oh, You Beautiful Doll (*Doris Breitenbach*)
        Look for the Silver Lining (*Marilyn Miller*)
1950   The Daughter of Rosie O'Grady (*Patricia O'Grady*)
        I'll Get By (*Liza Martin*)
1953   The Girl Next Door (*Jeannie*)

Havoc, June (née Ellen Evangeline Hovick), actress; b. Seattle, Wash., Nov. 8, 1916. Slim blonde former vaudeville performer who has played sharp-tongued, flashy showbiz types on both stage and screen. Miss Havoc is the sister of the late Gypsy Rose Lee. Bib: *Early Havoc* (1960) and *More Havoc* (1980), both by Miss Havoc.

1941   Four Jacks and a Jill (*June Havoc*)
1942   Sing Your Worries Away (*Rocksey Rochelle*)
1943   Hello, Frisco, Hello (*Beulah Clancy*)
1944   Casanova in Burlesque (*Lillian Colman*)
1948   When My Baby Smiles at Me (*Gussie*)
1949   Red, Hot and Blue (*Sandra*)
1980   Can't Stop the Music (*Helen Morell*)

Hawks, Howard, director; b. Goshen, Ind., May 30, 1896; d. Palm Springs, Dec. 29, 1977. Veteran director of dramas (*Scarface*), comedies (*His Girl Friday*), and adventure tales (*Sergeant York*), whose first musical film was a remake of his *Ball of Fire*. Bib: *Howard Hawks* by Robin Wood (1968).

1948	A Song Is Born
1953	Gentlemen Prefer Blondes

Haymes, (Richard Benjamin) Dick, actor, singer; b. Buenos Aires, Sept. 13, 1916 (English father, Irish mother); d. Los Angeles, March 28, 1980. Pug-nosed singer with rich, creamy baritone who followed Frank Sinatra's path of first singing with orchestras of Harry James and Tommy Dorsey, then going on to screen career. Haymes appeared in Fox films from 1944 to 1947, acting opposite Betty Grable twice, and introduced "The More I See You," "It's a Grand Night for Singing," "For You, For Me, For Evermore." Also made records and sang in nightclubs. Among his seven wives were Joanne Dru, Rita Hayworth, and singer Fran Jeffries.

1943	DuBarry Was a Lady (band singer)
1944	Four Jills in a Jeep (*Lt. Dick Ryan*)
	Irish Eyes Are Smiling (*Ernest Ball*)
1945	Diamond Horseshoe (*Joe Davis Jr.*)
	State Fair (*Wayne Frake*)
1946	Do You Love Me? (*Jimmy Hale*)
1947	The Shocking Miss Pilgrim (*John Prichard*)
	Carnival in Costa Rica (*Jeff Stevens*)
1948	Up in Central Park (*John Matthews*)
	One Touch of Venus (*Joe Grant*)
1953	All Ashore (*Joe Carter*)
	Let's Do It Again (voice on record)
	Cruisin' Down the River (*Beauregard Clemment*)

Hayward, Susan (née Edythe Marrener), actress, singer; b. Brooklyn, June 30, 1918; d. Beverly Hills, March 14, 1975. Russet-haired, round-faced, intense actress who appeared in almost 60 films between 1937 and 1972. Remembered in musicals primarily for two biographical films, *With a Song in My Heart* (voice dubbed by Jane Froman) and *I'll Cry Tomorrow*. Bib: *Films of Susan Hayward* by Eduardo Moreno (1979); *Susan Hayward* by Beverly Linet (1980).

1937	Hollywood Hotel (bit)
1941	Sis Hopkins (*Carol Hopkins*)
1942	Star Spangled Rhythm (specialty)
1943	Hit Parade of 1943 (*Jill Wright*)
1947	Smash-Up (*Angie*)

1952	With a Song in My Heart (*Jane Froman*)
1955	I'll Cry Tomorrow (*Lillian Roth*)

Hayworth, Rita (née Margarita Carmen Cansino), actress, dancer; b. Brooklyn, Oct. 17, 1918. A statuesque dancing actress, Miss Hayworth projected a warm-blooded if controlled sensuality through a screen career of over 30 years. Her two musicals with Fred Astaire, *You'll Never Get Rich* and *You Were Never Lovelier,* and her one with Gene Kelly, *Cover Girl,* were the highlights of her years as Columbia's reigning star. Nan Wynn dubbed her singing of "I'm Old Fashioned," Martha Mears did it for "Long Ago and Far Away," and Anita Ellis provided a similar chore for "Put the Blame on Mame." Miss Hayworth, who began her dancing career in her father's family act, was known as Rita Cansino up to 1937. The second and fourth of her five husbands were Orson Welles and Dick Haymes. Bib: *Films of Rita Hayworth* by Gene Ringgold (1974); *Rita Hayworth* by John Kobal (1977). (Died New York, May 14, 1987.)

1935	Under the Pampas Moon (*Carmen*)
	Paddy O'Day (*Tamara Petrovitch*)
1940	Music in My Heart (*Patricia O'Malley*)
1941	You'll Never Get Rich (*Sheila Winthrop*)
1942	My Gal Sal (*Sally Elliott*)
	You Were Never Lovelier (*Maria Acuña*)
1944	Cover Girl (*Rusty Parker/Maribelle Hicks*)
1945	Tonight and Every Night (*Rosalind Bruce*)
1946	Gilda (*Gilda*)
1947	Down to Earth (*Terpsichore*)
1952	Affair in Trinidad (*Chris Emery*)
1953	Miss Sadie Thompson (*Sadie Thompson*)
1957	Pal Joey (*Vera Simpson*)

Healy, Mary, actress, singer; b. New Orleans, April 14, 1917. Dark-haired singing beauty, married to comedian Peter Lind Hayes, whose most important screen appearance was her first. Appeared with husband in nightclubs, theatres, and radio series.

1939	Second Fiddle (*Jean Varick*)
1940	Star Dust (*Mary*)
1941	Zis Boom Bah
1942	The Yanks Are Coming (*Rita Edwards*)
1943	Strictly in the Groove (*Sally Monroe*)
1953	The 5,000 Fingers of Dr. T (*Mrs. Collins*)

"Heigh-Ho" Music by Frank Churchill; lyric by Larry Morey. Jolly marching song for the elfin septet in the Walt Disney cartoon, *Snow White and the Seven Dwarfs* (1937). Also sung in *Having Wonderful Time* (RKO 1938).

Help! See Hard Day's Night, A.

"Help!" Music & lyric by John Lennon & Paul McCartney. Rhythmic cry for assistance ("Help me if you can I'm feelin' dow-ow-own"), sung by The Beatles (John Lennon, Paul McCartney, George Harrison, Ringo Starr) seen on television screen before credits of *Help!* (UA 1965).

Henderson, Ray (né Raymond Brost), composer; b. Buffalo, NY, Dec. 1, 1896; d. Greenwich, Conn., Dec. 31, 1970. With partners, co-lyricists B. G. DeSylva and Lew Brown, Henderson created a series of youthful, fast-moving Broadway musicals between 1925 and 1930; of these, *Good News* (filmed twice) and *Follow Thru* were brought to the screen with at least partially original scores. In Hollywood, the trio collaborated on songs for early talkies with Al Jolson ("Sonny Boy"), Janet Gaynor ("Sunny Side Up," "I'm a Dreamer, Aren't We All?," "If I Had a Talking Picture of You"), and Gloria Swanson. Other movie lyricists with whom Henderson worked were Irving Caesar and Ted Koehler ("Animal Crackers in My Soup"), and Jack Yellen. Among other singers who introduced his songs were Rudy Vallee, Alice Faye, and Shirley Temple. Film bio: *The Best Things in Life Are Free,* with Dan Dailey as Henderson.

Unless otherwise noted, the following had songs written with Messrs. DeSylva & Brown:
1928 The Singing Fool
1929 Say It with Songs
     Sunny Side Up
1930 Good News
     Follow Thru
     Just Imagine
1931 Indiscreet
1934 George White's Scandals (Yellen, Caesar)
1935 Curly Top (Caesar, Koehler)
1947 Good News
1956 The Best Things in Life Are Free

Henie, Sonja, actress, skater; b. Oslo, Norway, April 8, 1910; d. enroute to Oslo, Oct. 12, 1969. Three-time Olympic figure-skating champion, twinkly blonde Sonja Henie glided and twirled through a series of Fox musicals designed to show off her skills on the ice. Her romantic leads in two films each were Don Ameche, Tyrone Power, and John Payne. Following her screen career, Miss Henie starred in a series of ice shows that she also produced. Bib: *Wings on My Feet* by Miss Henie (1940).

1936 One in a Million (*Greta Muller*)
1937 Thin Ice (*Lili Heiser*)
1938 Happy Landing (*Trudy Ericksen*)
     My Lucky Star (*Kristina Nielsen*)
1939 Second Fiddle (*Trudi Hovland*)
1941 Sun Valley Serenade (*Karen Benson*)
1942 Iceland (*Katina Jonadottir*)
1943 Wintertime (*Nora*)
1945 It's a Pleasure (*Chris Linden*)
1948 The Countess of Monte Cristo (*Karen*)

Hepburn, Audrey (née Audrey Hepburn-Ruston), actress; b. Brussels, May 4, 1929. Delicate-featured, dark-haired beauty who has acted primarily in nonmusical films (though she did sing "Moon River" in *Breakfast at Tiffany's*). In the first of her two musicals she sang for herself, in the second Marni Nixon took over.

1957 Funny Face (*Jo Stockton*)
1964 My Fair Lady (*Eliza Doolittle*)

Herbert, Hugh, actor; b. Binghamton, NY, Aug. 10, 1887; d. Hollywood, March 13, 1952. Herbert was a sad-eyed, flat-nosed, thick-voiced character comedian with a bobbing head and an air of total befuddlement. Usually playing dimwitted professors or tycoons, his most distinctive mannerism was clapping his hands together and exclaiming "woo-woo." During the 30s he worked mostly at Warner. Early in his career he was a Broadway actor, playwright and screenwriter.

1929 The Great Gabbo (script only)
1933 Footlight Parade (*Charlie Bowers*)
     College Coach (*J. Marvin Barnett*)
1934 Fashions of 1934 (*Joe Ward*)
     Wonder Bar (*Corey Pratt*)
     Harold Teen
     Dames (*Ezra Ounce*)
1935 Sweet Adeline (*Rupert Rockingham*)
     Gold Diggers of 1935 (*T. Mosley Thorpe*)
     To Beat the Band (*Hugo Twist*)
1936 Colleen (*Cedric Ames*)
     Sing Me a Love Song (*Siegfried Hammerschlag*)
1937 Top o' the Town (*Hubert*)
     The Singing Marine (*Aeneas Phinney*)
     Hollywood Hotel (*Chester Marshall*)
1938 Gold Diggers in Paris (*Maurice Giraud*)
     The Great Waltz (*Hofbauer*)
1940 La Conga Nights (*Henry I. Dibble Jr./his 4 sisters & mother*)

        Hit Parade of 1941 (*Ferdinand Farraday*)
        Little Bit of Heaven (*Pop*)
1941   Hellzapoppin (*Detective Quimby*)
1942   Don't Get Personal (*Elmer Whippet*)
1943   Stage Door Canteen (guest bit)
1944   Ever Since Venus (*Col. P. G. Grimble*)
        Music for Millions (*Uncle Ferdinand*)
1948   One Touch of Venus (*Mercury*)
        A Song Is Born (*Prof. Twingle*)
1949   The Beautiful Blonde from Bashful Bend (*Doctor*)

Herbert, Victor, composer; b. Dublin, Feb. 1, 1859; d. New York, May 26, 1924. America's first major composer of operettas, Herbert wrote the scores for 43 Broadway productions, of which the following were filmed: *Babes in Toyland* (twice, with second adapted by George Bruns and Mel Leven); *Mlle. Modiste* (retitled *Kiss Me Again*); *Naughty Marietta* (Jeanette MacDonald and Nelson Eddy's first hit, with new lyrics by Gus Kahn); and *Sweethearts* (new lyrics by Robert Wright and George Forrest). His movie, *The Great Victor Herbert,* with Walter Connolly as Herbert, included many of his stage compositions. On screen, his songs were sung by, among others, Mary Martin, Allan Jones, Tommy Sands, and Annette Funicello. Herbert's one film score was to accompany the silent movie, *The Fall of a Nation* (1916). His most frequent lyricist collaborators were Glen MacDonough, Henry Blossom, Rida Johnson Young, Harry B. Smith, and Robert B. Smith. Bib: *Victor Herbert* by Edward N. Waters (1955).

1931   Kiss Me Again (Blossom)
1934   Babes in Toyland (MacDonough)
1935   Naughty Marietta (Young, Kahn)
1938   Sweethearts (Wright, Forrest)
1939   The Great Victor Herbert (misc.)
1961   Babes in Toyland (Bruns-Leven)

"(Lookie, Lookie, Lookie) Here Comes Cookie" Music & lyric by Mack Gordon. Chirpy song of expectation about one who is called Cookie " 'cause she takes the cake." Introduced by Gracie Allen in *Love in Bloom* (Par. 1935).

"Here Lies Love" Music by Ralph Rainger; lyric by Leo Robin. End-of-a-love-affair lament introduced in *The Big Broadcast* (Par. 1932). First sung in a speakeasy nightclub scene by Arthur Tracy as a musical commentary on the crushing news Bing Crosby receives—via a newspaper headline—that he has been jilted by the girl he was to marry the following day. Song then performed by Vincent Lopez's orchestra at another nightspot located in the same skyscraper where Crosby lives. In his apartment, Bing reprises the number as he burns all of his ex-fiancée's photographs.

"Here's What I'm Here For" Music by Harold Arlen; lyric by Ira Gershwin. Ballad of romantic tenacity sung by Judy Garland in *A Star Is Born* (Warner 1954), but cut from print after film was released.

Herman, (Gerald) Jerry, composer, lyricist; b. New York, July 10, 1932. Herman's first (long-run) Broadway musicals, *Hello, Dolly!* and *Mame,* were brought to the screen with, respectively, Barbra Streisand and Lucille Ball.

1969   Hello, Dolly!
1974   Mame

"Hey, Babe, Hey!" Music & lyric by Cole Porter. Jaunty song of affection ("I'm nuts about you!"), sung by James Stewart to Eleanor Powell on the patio of the Lonely Hearts Club in New York, in *Born To Dance* (MGM 1936). Song then reprised by Sid Silvers to Una Merkel, Buddy Ebsen and Frances Langford (their variation began, "Pret-ty ba-by, pret-ty ba-by"), and ended with the sextet tapping away.

Heyman, Edward, lyricist; b. New York, March 14, 1907; d. Guadalajara, Mexico, March 30, 1981. Heyman worked in Hollywood 1939–54. His songs include "I Cover the Waterfront" (music by Johnny Green), "Moonburn" (Hoagy Carmichael), and "Love Letters" (Victor Young). Other partners were composers Dana Suesse, Arthur Schwartz, Morton Gould, Rudolf Friml, and Nacio Herb Brown. Among those who sang his lyrics were Bing Crosby, Lily Pons, Jane Powell, Nelson Eddy, Kathryn Grayson, and Frank Sinatra.

1935   Sweet Surrender (Suesse)
1936   That Girl from Paris (Schwartz)
1945   Delightfully Dangerous (Gould)
1947   Northwest Outpost (Friml)
1948   On an Island with You (Brown)
        The Kissing Bandit (Brown)

"Hi-Diddle-Dee-Dee (An Actor's Life for Me)" Music by Leigh Harline; lyric by Ned Washington. In the cartoon *Pinocchio* (Disney 1940), a fox named J. Worthington Foulfellow (voice of Walter Catlett) sings this spirited ditty to our blockheaded hero (Dickie Jones) by way of convincing him to join a puppet show.

"High Hopes" Music by James Van Heusen; lyric by Sammy Cahn. In a nonmusical, *A Hole in the Head* (Par. 1959), Frank Sinatra and his son, Eddie Hodges, try to buck up each other's spirits by taking a lesson from two creatures with "high apple-pie-in-the-sky hopes"—the ant who tries to move a rubber tree plant and the ram who tries to punch a hole in a dam.

"High Noon" Music by Dimitri Tiomkin; lyric by Ned Washington. Rambling, doom-laden Western ballad sung by Tex Ritter over credits of film of same name (UA 1952), and used as recurring theme.

High Society (1956). Music & lyrics by Cole Porter; screenplay by John Patrick from Broadway play *The Philadelphia Story* by Philip Barry.

An MGM film produced by Sol C. Siegel; directed by Charles Walters; art directors, Cedric Gibbons, Hans Peters; costumes, Helen Rose; music director, Johnny Green; associate, Saul Chaplin; orchestrations, Conrad Salinger, Nelson Riddle; cameraman, Paul Vogel; editor, Ralph Winters; Technicolor; VistaVision.

Cast: Bing Crosby (*C. K. Dexter Haven*); Grace Kelly (*Tracy Samantha Lord*); Frank Sinatra (*Mike Connor*); Celeste Holm (*Liz Imbrie*); John Lund (*George Kittredge*); Louis Calhern (*Uncle Willie*); Sidney Blackmer (*Seth Lord*); Louis Armstrong (*Louis Armstrong*); Margalo Gilmore (*Mrs. Seth Lord*); Lydia Reed (*Caroline Lord*).

Songs: "High Society Calypso" - Armstrong/ "Little One" - Crosby, with Armstrong band; reprised in French by Reed/ "Who Wants To Be a Millionaire?" - Sinatra, Holm/ "True Love" - Crosby, with Kelly/ "You're Sensational" - Sinatra/ "I Love You, Samantha" Crosby, with Armstrong band/ "Now You Has Jazz" - Crosby, Armstrong/ "Well, Did You Evah?" - Crosby, Sinatra/ "Mind If I Make Love to You?" - Sinatra. Unused: "Caroline," "Hey, Sexy," "Let's Vocalize," "So What?," "A Step Montage."

The Philadelphia Story, Philip Barry's witty play about marital problems among the socially elite, was first produced on Broadway in 1939 with Katharine Hepburn, Joseph Cotten, Van Heflin, and Shirley Booth; the following year MGM filmed it with Miss Hepburn, Cary Grant, James Stewart, and Ruth Hussey. For the studio's musical version, called *High Society,* the locale was changed to Newport, Rhode Island, and the leading roles were taken by Grace Kelly (whose family is associated with Philadelphia), Bing Crosby, Frank Sinatra, and Celeste Holm. Though the plot was kept pretty much the same, Crosby is now a songwriter-promoter associated with the local jazz festival, which also becomes the excuse for some musical appearances by Louis Armstrong. In the story, Tracy's ex-husband Dexter shows up uninvited at her wedding and manages to woo her back. Mike and Liz appear as a writer and photographer for *Spy* magazine (called *Destiny* in the play) who have been sent to cover the nuptials and festivities. The musical highlight: Crosby and Sinatra singing and hoking "Well Did You Evah?," originally written for the 1939 Broadway musical *DuBarry Was a Lady. High Society* marked the final Hollywood appearance of soon-to-be Princess Grace of Monaco.

High, Wide and Handsome (1937). Music by Jerome Kern; lyrics by Oscar Hammerstein II; screenplay by Hammerstein & Rouben Mamoulian (uncredited).

A Paramount film produced by Arthur Hornblow, Jr.; directed by Rouben Mamoulian; choreography, LeRoy Prinz; art directors, Hans Dreier, John Goodman; costumes, Travis Banton; music director, Boris Morros; orchestrations, Robert Russell Bennett; cameramen, Victor Milner, Theodore Sparkuhl; editor, Archie Marshek.

Cast: Irene Dunne (*Sally Waterson*); Randolph Scott (*Peter Cortlandt*); Dorothy Lamour (*Molly*); Akim Tamiroff (*Joe Varesi*); Raymond Walburn (*Doc Waterson*); Charles Bickford (*Red Scanlon*); Ben Blue (*Samuel*); Elizabeth Patterson (*Grandma Cortlandt*); William Frawley (*Maurice*); Alan Hale (*Walter Bremman*); Irving Pichel (*Stark*); Lucien Littlefield (*Dr. Lippincott*); Helen Lowell (*Mrs. Lippincott*); Frank Sully (*Gabby Johnson*); Ed Gargan (*Foreman*); Roger Imhof (*Bowers*); Raymond Brown (*P. T. Barnum*).

Songs: "High, Wide and Handsome" - Dunne/ "Can I Forget You?" - Dunne/ "Will You Marry Me Tomorrow, Maria?" - Frawley, guests/ "The Folks Who Live on the Hill" - Dunne/ "The Things I Want" - Lamour/ "Allegheny Al" - Lamour, Dunne. Unused: "He Wore a Star," "Grandma's Song."

A brawling, sprawling panoramic view of Americana focusing on the discovery of oil in Pennsylvania in 1859, the film also included such picturesque areas of period musical entertainment as medicine shows, riverboats, saloons, circuses, and square dance socials. Based partly on historic fact, the melodramatic story was mostly concerned with the struggle between the oil-drilling farmers (led by Randolph Scott) and the railroad tycoon (Alan Hale) who wants to take over their land. The picture's climax, the laying of an oil pipeline over a hill to the refinery, involved a classic good-guys-vs-bad-guys encounter, and featured an entire circus troupe—complete with elephants—coming to the rescue. Most of the exterior shooting was done on location near Chino, California. Since Irene Dunne had starred in *Show Boat,* the previous slice of Kern and Hammerstein Americana, it seems likely that the character she played in *High, Wide and Handsome* was suggested by the previous role—also that the part of Molly was derived from Julie, Doc Waterson from Capt. Andy, and Grandma Cortlandt from Parthy Ann Hawks.

"Hi-Lili, Hi-Lo" Music by Bronislaw Kaper; lyric by Helen Deutsch. In *Lili* (MGM 1953), when Carrot Top (Mel Ferrer), a carnival puppet, asks her to sing, unhappy waif Leslie Caron replies, "It's just an old song but I used to sing it with my father." While a female puppet dances, Miss Caron sings the lilting waltz, with Carrot Top joining in. Later in the film, the music is used for a dream ballet as the waif dances with the now humanized puppets.

Hilliard, Harriet (née Peggy Lou Snyder), actress, singer; b. Des Moines, Iowa, July 18, 1914. Round-faced singing actress with small but expressive voice who introduced "Get Thee Behind Me Satan" in *Follow the Fleet* (her only major film) and "Says My Heart" in *Cocoanut Grove.* She began career as vocalist with Ozzie Nelson's orchestra, then married Nelson (who died in 1975) and appeared with him in four films plus long-running radio and television series (with sons David and Ricky).

Asterisk indicates appearance with Mr. Nelson:
1936 Follow the Fleet (*Connie Martin*)
1937 New Faces of 1937 (*Patricia*)
　　 Life of the Party (*Mitzi*)
1938 Cocoanut Grove (*Linda Rogers*)
1941 Sweetheart of the Campus* (*Harriet Hale*)
1942 Jukebox Jennie (*Genevieve Horton*)
1943 Hi, Buddy (*Gloria Bradley*)
　　 Gals, Incorporated (*Gwen*)
　　 Honeymoon Lodge* (*Lorraine Logan*)
1944 Swingtime Johnny (*Linda*)
　　 Hi, Good Lookin'* (*Kelly Clark*)
　　 Take It Big* (*Jerry Clinton*)

"Hit the Road to Dreamland" Music by Harold Arlen; lyric by Johnny Mercer. Rhythmic number in which a couple, having been out all night, hear the crowing of

the rooster and realize that it's time to get some sleep. Featured in a star-spangled show in *Star Spangled Rhythm* (Par. 1942), with Mary Martin and Dick Powell, accompanied by the Golden Gate Quartet as waiters, singing in the dining car of a train speeding through the night.

Hoffman, Al, composer; b. Minsk, Russia, Sept. 25, 1902; d. New York, July 21, 1960. To US 1908. Hoffman joined co-composer Al Goodhart and lyricist Maurice Sigler—later succeeded by Sammy Lerner—to write songs for British film musicals between 1935 and 1937. Among their screen contributions were Jack Hylton's "She Shall Have Music" and Jessie Matthews' "Everything's in Rhythm with My Heart," with others introduced by Jack Buchanan, Jack Hulbert, and Anna Neagle. In Hollywood, Hoffman wrote songs for Walt Disney's *Cinderella* (including "Bibbidi-Bobbidi Boo") with Jerry Livingston and Mack David.

Unless otherwise noted, following had songs written with Messrs. Goodhart & Sigler:
1935 Jack of All Trades
　　 She Shall Have Music
　　 Come Out of the Pantry
　　 First a Girl
1936 When Knights Were Bold
　　 Squibs
　　 This'll Make You Whistle
1937 Gangway (Goodhart-Lerner)
　　 London Melody (Goodhart-Lerner)
1949 Cinderella (US) (Livingston-David)

Holiday Inn (1942). Music & lyrics by Irving Berlin; screenplay by Claude Binyon from story by Elmer Rice.

A Paramount film produced and directed by Mark Sandrich; choreography, Fred Astaire, Danny Dare; art directors, Hans Dreier, Roland Anderson; costumes, Edith Head; music director, Robert Emmett Dolan; cameraman, David Abel; editor, Ellsworth Hoagland.

Cast: Bing Crosby (*Jim Hardy*); Fred Astaire (*Ted Hanover*); Marjorie Reynolds (vocals by Martha Mears) (*Linda Mason*); Virginia Dale (*Lila Dixon*); Walter Abel (*Danny Reed*); Louise Beavers (*Mamie*); Harry Barris (*bandleader*); Bob Crosby's Bob Cats.

Songs: "I'll Capture Your Heart Singing" - Crosby, Astaire, Dale/ "Lazy" - Crosby/ "You're Easy To Dance With" - Astaire, dance by Astaire, Dale; reprised as dance by Astaire, Reynolds/ "White Christmas" - Crosby, Reynolds (Mears)/ "Happy Holiday" - Crosby, Reynolds (Mears)/ "Holiday Inn" - Crosby,

Reynolds (Mears)/ "Let's Start the New Year Right" - Crosby/ "Abraham" - Crosby, Beavers, Reynolds (Mears)/ "Be Careful, It's My Heart" - Crosby; dance by Astaire, Reynolds/ "I Can't Tell a Lie" - Astaire; dance by Astaire, Reynolds/ "Easter Parade" - Crosby/ "Let's Say It with Firecrackers" - chorus; dance by Astaire/ "Song of Freedom" - Crosby, chorus/ "Plenty To Be Thankful For" - Crosby. Unused: "It's a Great Country."

The opportunity to team the screen's premier male singer with the screen's premier male dancer came about as a result of an idea Irving Berlin and Moss Hart had of doing a Broadway revue based on American holidays. When that didn't work out, Berlin convinced producer-director Mark Sandrich that the concept could work equally well as a movie—provided, of course, that the musical numbers were tied together with a suitable but unobtrusive plot. In said plot, which begins Christmas Eve and ends New Year's Eve two years later, easygoing Bing Crosby quits his nightclub act with Fred Astaire and Virginia Dale to settle down on a Connecticut farm. When he finds himself unsuited to the life of a farmer, Crosby decides to open his place as a nightclub, but only on holidays. The film's conflict arises when Bing and Fred become rivals for the affection of Marjorie Reynolds, Holiday Inn's featured female entertainer. Of the score, Berlin contributed nine songs suitable for eight holidays—Christmas, New Year, Lincoln's Birthday, Valentine's Day, Washington's Birthday, Easter, the Fourth of July, which got two, and Thanksgiving. Of these, "Easter Parade" was the only one from the trunk, and "White Christmas" was promptly on its way to become the most popular secular Christmas song of all time.

Four years later, Crosby and Astaire were again teamed in another Berlin catalogue musical, *Blue Skies,* also for Paramount. The performers were to have made a third similar outing for the same studio in 1954, but *White Christmas,* again full of Berlin tunes, found Crosby teamed with Danny Kaye because of Astaire's illness. Both these movies also used nightclubs as settings for the songs.

Hollander, Frederick (né Friedrich Holländer), composer; b. London, Oct. 18, 1896 (German parents); d, Munich, Jan, 18, 1976. Hollander was signed by Paramount as result of his work for the German film *Der Blaue Engel* (filmed simultaneously in English as *The Blue Angel*), in which Marlene Dietrich sang his most famous song, "Falling in Love Again," English lyric by Sammy Lerner. She was also identified with Hollander's Hollywood output, including "The Boys in the Backroom" and "I've Been in Love Before." Other songs: "Moonlight and Shadows" (sung by Dorothy Lamour), "My Heart and I" (Bing Crosby), "Whispers in the Dark" (Connie Boswell). In addition to writing his own lyrics, Hollander collaborated with Sam Coslow, Frank Loesser, and Leo Robin, and also scored nonmusical films. He returned to Germany in 1956.

1930	The Blue Angel (Ger.) (Lerner)	
1933	Heart Song (Ger.) (also dir.)	
1934	I Am Suzanne (also lyr.)	
1937	The Thrill of a Lifetime (Coslow)	
1938	Zaza (Loesser)	
1939	Man About Town (Loesser)	
	Destry Rides Again (Loesser)	
1940	Seven Sinners (Loesser)	
1948	A Foreign Affair (also lyr.)	
	That Lady in Ermine (Robin)	

Holliday, Judy (née Judith Tuvim), actress, singer; b. New York, June 21, 1921; d. New York, June 7, 1965. Beginning with the stage comedy *Born Yesterday* Miss Holliday excelled at playing smart dumb-blonde characters. Her only starring role in a screen musical, opposite Dean Martin, was in a part she had originated on Broadway.

1944	Greenwich Village (extra)
	Something for the Boys (bit)
1960	Bells Are Ringing (*Ella Peterson*)

Holloway, Stanley (Augustus), actor, singer; b. London, Oct. 1, 1890. A jolly, salt-of-the-earth, working-man-type comic actor and singer, Holloway appeared in London stage musicals (including *The Co-Optimists* series) and British films. His best-remembered stage role, which he repeated in the movie version, was in *My Fair Lady.* Bib: *Wiv a Little Bit o' Luck* by Holloway (1967). (Died Littlehampton, Eng., Jan. 30, 1982.)

1929	The Co-Optimists
1934	Lily of Killarney (*Father o'Flynn*)
	Road House (*Donovan*)
1935	D'Ye Ken John Peel? (*Sam Small*)
	In Town Tonight
1936	Squibs (*Charley Lee*)
1937	Song of the Forge (*Joel/ Sir William Barrett*)
1944	Champagne Charlie (*Alfred Vance*)
1948	One Night with You (*Tramp*)
1952	The Beggar's Opera (*Lockitt*)
1964	My Fair Lady (US) (*Alfred Doolittle*)

1968 Mrs. Brown You've Got a Lovely Daughter (*Mr. Brown*)

Holm, Celeste, actress, singer; b. New York, April 29, 1919. Versatile blonde, wide-eyed actress more associated with stage than with films.

1946 Three Little Girls in Blue (*Miriam*)
1947 Carnival in Costa Rica (*Celeste*)
1948 Road House (*Susie Smith*)
1956 High Society (*Liz Imbrey*)
1965 Cinderella (tv) (*Fairy Godmother*)

"Honeymoon Hotel" Music by Harry Warren; lyric by Al Dubin. Narrative musical number, created by Busby Berkeley for *Footlight Parade* (Warner 1933) as part of a stage "prologue" for talkie films. In the scene—something of a follow-up to the Warren-Dubin-Berkeley "Shuffle Off to Buffalo" in *42nd Street*—Dick Powell first proposes marriage to Ruby Keeler ("How about a little celebration/ To the jingle of a wedding bell?"), then quickly suggests a little reservation at the Honeymoon Hotel. With the knot tied, the newlyweds check into the Jersey City hostelry, where they are introduced to the bellhop (Sam McDaniel), desk clerk (Harry Seymour), waiter, detectives (Fred Kelsey is one), telephone operator, and washroom attendant. In their room, Keeler and Powell are surprised by the girl's family (including Jimmy Conlin and Billy Barty). Once the visitors leave, Powell and the other recent bridegrooms march to the bathroom, where they don pajamas, while some of the wives befriend the nervous Miss Keeler. By mistake, Powell enters the wrong room, then quickly emerges and accidentally puts his arm around a shapely honeymooner. Ruby sees this and threatens to call a lawyer, but she believes Dick's story, apologizes, and they're off to sleep. Final shot: a magazine ad showing the picture of a baby.

"Hooray for Hollywood" Music by Richard A. Whiting; lyric by Johnny Mercer. Energetic tribute to, and unofficial anthem of, the cinema capital—"where any office boy or young mechanic/ Can be a panic with just a good-looking pan." Introduced in the opening scene of *Hollywood Hotel* (Warner 1937) by Johnny "Scat" Davis and Frances Langford, accompanied by Benny Goodman's orchestra. All are shown riding in separate automobiles on their way to the St. Louis airport to bid farewell to Hollywood-bound Dick Powell.

"Hooray for Love" Music by Harold Arlen; lyric by Leo Robin. Bouncy cheer sung by Tony Martin and Yvonne DeCarlo in *Casbah* (Univ. 1948), while dancing in a tobacco shop.

Hope, (Leslie Townes) Bob, actor, singer; b. Eltham, Eng., May 29, 1903. Hope was the screen's leading portrayer of the likable but brash cowardly hero masking his insecurity with a string of wisecracks. One of Paramount's most durable stars, he appeared opposite Bing Crosby in seven "Road" pictures (six of them co-starring Dorothy Lamour), in which he was invariably the gullible victim of Crosby's machinations. In other comic adventure films, both with and without songs, his leading ladies included Shirley Ross, Betty Hutton, Jane Russell, Lucille Ball, and Marilyn Maxwell. He also introduced, both in duets and solos, "Thanks for the Memory," "Two Sleepy People," "The Lady's in Love with You," "Buttons and Bows," and "Silver Bells." Hope had his own radio program, has appeared frequently on television, and has made many trips abroad to entertain US servicemen. After beginning his career in vaudeville, he was seen on Broadway in nine musicals, among them *Roberta* and *Red, Hot and Blue!* Bib: *Have Tux Will Travel* (1954) and *The Road to Hollywood* (1977), both by Hope; *The Amazing Careers of Bob Hope* by Joe Morelli, Edward Epstein, and Eleanor Clarke (1973).

1938 Big Broadcast of 1938 (*Buzz Fielding*)
     College Swing (*Bud Brady*)
     Give Me a Sailor (*Jim Brewster*)
1939 Some Like It Hot (*Nicky Nelson*)
1940 Road to Singapore (*Ace Lanigan*)
1941 Road to Zanzibar (*Hubert "Fearless" Frazier*)
     Louisiana Purchase (*Jim Taylor*)
1942 Road to Morocco (*Turkey Jackson/ Aunt Lucy*)
     Star Spangled Rhythm (specialty)
1943 Let's Face It (*Jerry Walker*)
1945 Duffy's Tavern (specialty)
     Road to Utopia (*Chester Hooten*)
1947 Variety Girl (specialty)
     Road to Rio (*Hot-Lips Barton*)
1948 The Paleface (*Painless Peter Potter*)
1950 Fancy Pants (*Arthur Tyler*)
1951 The Lemon Drop Kid (*Sidney Milburn*)
1952 Son of Paleface (*Junior Potter*)
     Road to Bali (*Harold Gridley*)
1953 Here Come the Girls (*Stanley Snodgrass*)
     Scared Stiff (guest bit)

1955 The Seven Little Foys (*Eddie Foy*)
1956 That Certain Feeling (*Francis X. Dignan*)
1957 Beau James (*Jimmy Walker*)
1959 The Five Pennies (guest bit)
1962 Road to Hong Kong (*Chester Babcock*)
1967 I'll Take Sweden (*Bob Holcomb*)
1979 The Muppet Movie (guest bit)

Hornblow, Arthur, Jr., producer; b. New York, March 15, 1893; d. New York, July 17, 1976. Former Broadway producer and playwright who became production executive for Samuel Goldwyn in 1927, and film producer the following year. He was with Paramount between 1933 and 1944, then MGM. As an independent, he produced *Oklahoma!*, the first Todd-AO movie. Hornblow's second of three wives was Myrna Loy.

1935 Mississippi
1936 The Princess Comes Across
1937 Swing High, Swing Low
     High, Wide and Handsome
     Waikiki Wedding
1938 Artists and Models Abroad
     Tropic Holiday
1939 Man About Town
1952 Million Dollar Mermaid
1955 Oklahoma!

Horne, Lena (Calhoun), singer, actress; b. Brooklyn, June 30, 1917. Highly stylized song interpreter whose Hollywood career consisted primarily of specialty appearances in MGM musicals (presumably so that her frames could be easily removed in certain theatres in the South). Major acting roles were in *Cabin in the Sky* and *Stormy Weather*. Miss Horne introduced "Love" in *Ziegfeld Follies*, has sung mostly in nightclubs and on records, and was married to conductor-arranger Lennie Hayton (deceased). Bib: *In Person—Lena Horne* (1950) and *Lena* (1965), both by Miss Horne.

1938 The Duke Is Tops (*Ethel*)
1942 Panama Hattie (specialty)
1943 Cabin in the Sky (*Georgia Brown*)
     Stormy Weather (*Selena Rogers*)
     I Dood It (specialty)
     Swing Fever (specialty)
     Thousands Cheer (specialty)
1944 Broadway Rhythm (*Fernway de la Fer*)
     Two Girls and a Sailor (specialty)
1946 Ziegfeld Follies (specialty)
     Till the Clouds Roll By ("*Julie*")
1948 Words and Music (specialty)

1950 The Duchess of Idaho (specialty)
1956 Meet Me in Las Vegas (specialty)
1978 The Wiz (*Glinda*)

Horton, Edward Everett, actor; b. Brooklyn, March 18, 1886; d. Encino, Cal., Sept. 30, 1970. Prissy, pernickety Edward Everett Horton usually played the easily rattled man in charge, showing his irritation with pursed lips and double takes. He supported Fred Astaire and Ginger Rogers in three films, and Maurice Chevalier in three.

1931 Kiss Me Again (*René*)
1933 A Bedtime Story (*Victor*)
     The Way to Love (*Prof. Gaston Bibi*)
     Soldiers of the King (Eng.) (*Sebastian Marvello*)
1934 Sing and Like It (*Adam Frink*)
     Kiss and Make-Up (*Marcel Caron*)
     The Gay Divorcee (*Egbert Fitzgerald*)
     The Merry Widow (*Ambassador Popoff*)
1935 The Night Is Young (*Szereny*)
     All the King's Horses (*Peppi*)
     In Caliente (*Harold Brandon*)
     Top Hat (*Horace Hardwick*)
     Going Highbrow (*Augie*)
1936 The Singing Kid (*Davenport Rogers*)
     Hearts Divided (*John Hathaway*)
1937 The King and the Chorus Girl (*Count Humbert*)
     Shall We Dance (*Jeffrey Baird*)
     Hitting a New High (*Blynn*)
1938 College Swing (*Hubert Dash*)
1939 Paris Honeymoon (*Ernest Figg*)
     That's Right You're Wrong (*Tom Village*)
1941 You're the One (*Death Valley Joe Frink*)
     Ziegfeld Girl (*Noble Sage*)
     Sunny (*Henry Bates*)
1942 I Married an Angel (*Peter*)
     Springtime in the Rockies (*McTavish*)
1943 Thank Your Lucky Stars (*Farnsworth*)
     The Gang's All Here (*Peyton Potter*)
1944 Brazil (*Everett St. John Everett*)
1945 Lady on a Train (*Haskell*)
1946 Cinderella Jones (*Keating*)
     Earl Carroll Sketchbook (*Dr. Milo Edwards*)
1947 Down to Earth (*Messenger 7013*)

Hovick, Louise. *See* **Lee, Gypsy Rose.**

"How About You?" Music by Burton Lane; lyric by Ralph Freed. In *Babes on Broadway* (MGM 1941), Judy Garland and Mickey Rooney sang and danced their way through a "laundry-list" song of the small pleasures each wished to share with the other—New York in June, a Gershwin tune, a fireside in a storm, potato chips, moonlight, motor trips, good books, FDR's looks, hand-holding at the movies, Jack Benny's jokes, common folks, window shopping on Fifth Avenue, banana splits, late suppers at the Ritz, and—since they both have theatrical aspirations—dreaming of fame ("your name right beside mine").

"How Am I To Know?" Music by Jack King; lyric by Dorothy Parker. Romantic query if it's the real thing, first posed by Russ Columbo in *Dynamite* (MGM 1929), later by Ava Gardner in *Pandora and the Flying Dutchman* (MGM 1951).

"How Blue the Night" Music by Jimmy McHugh; lyric by Harold Adamson. Dick Haymes, in *Four Jills in a Jeep* (Fox 1944), sang of nights that are blue and days that are long while he is away from his beloved. The solo was followed by a choral rendition and a tap dance by Mitzi Mayfair.

"How Could You Believe Me When I Said I Love You When You Know I've Been a Liar All My Life?" Music by Burton Lane; lyric by Alan Jay Lerner. Squabbling duet—also called "The Liar Song"—performed by Fred Astaire and Jane Powell as a couple of street-corner toughs in a London revue in *Royal Wedding* (MGM 1951). The idea for the song came about one day when Lerner and Lane were riding to MGM, and Lerner remarked, "This picture is so damn charming it's going to delicate itself to death. What it needs is a real corny vaudeville number. How's this for a title?" On the spur of the moment he blurted out, "Howcouldyoubelieve mewhenIsaidIloveyouwhenyouknowI'vebeena liarallmylife"? Lane quickly came up with a suitable tune, and by the time they'd reached the studio gate they had almost completed the song. Originally conceived with Judy Garland in mind (she'd been the second actress signed for the female lead but dropped out before shooting began), the piece was something of a raucous follow-up to the Garland-Astaire "Couple of Swells" in *Easter Parade* and the Garland-Kelly "Be a Clown" in *The Pirate*. A further distinction is that the song's title is possibly the longest ever used in the movies.

"How Little We Know" Music by Hoagy Carmichael; lyric by Johnny Mercer. Though love may be as changeable as the weather, the singer still hopes this time it will last. The flowing, Latin-flavored melody was sung in *To Have and Have Not* (Warner 1944) first—partially—by Hoagy Carmichael at the piano of a Martinique nightspot, and later—entirely—by Lauren Bacall.

"How Lucky Can You Get?" Music by John Kander; lyric by Fred Ebb. In *Funny Lady* (Col. 1975), Fanny Brice (Barbra Streisand) has just given a dazzling opening-night performance, and—in an entirely fictitious scene—former husband Nick Arnstein (Omar Sharif) has come to her dressing room to offer congratulations. Nick quickly discovers that Fanny is still in love with him and Fanny quickly discovers that Nick has remarried. Once she's alone, in a mood of utter despair, she plays her recording of "How Lucky Can You Get?," with its carefree sentiment ("satin on my shoulder and a smile on my lips") ironically underscoring her grief. Glumly she tears the petals off a daisy, puffs on a cigarette, paces the floor, sips champagne, and occasionally sings along with her own voice. Upon leaving the room, her mood changes as the tempo of the music suddenly accelerates. In a frenzy, Fanny turns on all the spotlights, plants herself on the bare stage, proclaims her defiant self-satisfaction—and storms out of the theatre.

"How Sweet You Are" Music by Arthur Schwartz; lyric by Frank Loesser. Sugary enconium delivered by Dinah Shore in *Thank Your Lucky Stars* (Warner 1943). In the scene, part of a charity revue, Miss Shore introduced the ballad (later reprised by chorus), not, as one is first led to suspect, in a modern wartime setting, but at a party for Union officers in 1861.

Hughes, Howard (Robard), producer; b. Houston, Dec. 24, 1905; d. enroute to Houston, April 5, 1976. Eccentric billionaire industrialist and aviator who produced early sound-film classics *Hells Angels* and *Scarface*. Sponsored career of Jane Russell (he directed *The Outlaw*). Bib: *Howard Hughes* by John Keats (1966).

1951	Two Tickets to Broadway
	Double Dynamite
1952	The Las Vegas Story
1954	The French Line

Hulbert, Jack, actor, singer, director, screenwriter; b. Ely, Eng., April 24, 1892; d. London, March 25, 1978. A lantern-jawed comic actor with a half-moon smile, Hulbert often appeared with his wife, Cicely Courtneidge, in both London stage musicals and British films.

Bib: *The Little Woman's Always Right* by Hulbert (1975).

Asterisk indicates appearance with Miss Courtneidge:
1930 Elstree Calling* (specialty) (also dir.)
1931 Sunshine Susie (*Herr Hasel*)
1932 Love on Wheels (*Fred Hopkins*)
      Happily Ever After* (*Willie*) (also script)
1936 Jack of All Trades (*Jack Warrender*) (also dir., script)
1937 Take My Tip* (*Lord George Pilkington*)
1938 Gaiety Girls (*Martin*)
1940 Under Your Hat* (*Jack Millett*) (also prod.)

Humberstone, H. Bruce, director; b. Buffalo, Nov. 18, 1903. Former actor who directed all of Fox's singing and dancing (or skating) blondes with the exception of Shirley Temple.

1938 Rascals
1941 Tall, Dark and Handsome
      Sun Valley Serenade
1942 Iceland
1943 Hello, Frisco, Hello
1944 Pin-Up Girl
1945 Wonder Man
1946 Three Little Girls in Blue
1950 South Sea Sinner
1951 Happy Go Lovely (Eng.)
1952 She's Working Her Way Through College
1953 The Desert Song

Hunter, Ross (né Martin Fuss), actor, producer; b. Cleveland, May 6, 1916. Actor who turned Universal producer in 1953 and whose biggest musical successes were *Flower Drum Song* and *Thoroughly Modern Millie*.

Asterisk indicates Mr. Hunter was producer only:
1944 Louisiana Hayride (*Gordon Pearson*)
      Ever Since Venus (*Bradley Miller*)
      She's a Sweetheart (*Paul*)
1945 Hit the Hay (*Ted Barton*)
1946 Sweetheart of Sigma Chi (*Ted Sloan*)
1964 Flower Drum Song*
      I'd Rather Be Rich*
1967 Thoroughly Modern Millie*
1973 Lost Horizon*

Hutton, Betty (née Elizabeth June Thornburg), actress, singer; b. Battle Creek, Mich., Feb. 26, 1921. Animated, throaty-voiced blonde actress who, except for her loanout performance in MGM's *Annie Get Your Gun,* appeared exclusively in Paramount pictures. The sister of singer Marion Hutton, she introduced a fusillade of explosive numbers including "Arthur Murray Taught Me Dancing in a Hurry," "'Murder' He Says," "Doctor, Lawyer, Indian Chief," and "Poppa, Don't Preach to Me," yet was also adept at interpreting more poignant sentiments such as "I Wish I Didn't Love You So." Miss Hutton's co-stars included Bob Hope, Bing Crosby, Howard Keel, and Fred Astaire.

1942 The Fleet's In (*Bessie Dale*)
      Star-Spangled Rhythm (*Polly Judson*)
1943 Happy Go Lucky (*Bubbles Hennessey*)
      Let's Face It (*Winnie Potter*)
1944 And the Angels Sing (*Bobbie Angel*)
      Here Come the Waves (*Susie Allison/Rosemary Allison*)
1945 Incendiary Blonde (*Texas Guinan*)
      Duffy's Tavern (specialty)
      The Stork Club (*Judy Peabody*)
1946 Cross My Heart (*Peggy Harper*)
1947 The Perils of Pauline (*Pearl White*)
1949 Red, Hot and Blue (*Eleanor Collier*)
1950 Annie Get Your Gun (*Annie Oakley*)
      Let's Dance (*Kitty McNeil Everett*)
1951 Sailor Beware (guest bit)
1952 The Greatest Show on Earth (*Holly*)
      Somebody Loves Me (*Blossom Seeley*)
1954 Satins and Spurs (tv)

Hutton, Marion (née Marion Thornburg), singer, actress; b. 1919, Battle Creek, Mich. Older sister of Betty Hutton who appeared in first two films as band singer with Glenn Miller's orchestra, and who introduced "My Dreams Are Getting Better All the Time." (Died Kirkland, Wash., Jan. 9, 1987.)

1941 Sun Valley Serenade (band singer)
1942 Orchestra Wives (band singer)
1943 Crazy House (specialty)
1944 In Society (*Elsie*)
      Babes on Swing Street (specialty)
1949 Love Happy (*Bunny Dolan*)

I

"I Begged Her" Music by Jule Styne; lyric by Sammy Cahn. Gene Kelly and Frank Sinatra's account of an imagined romantic conquest related to their sailor buddies in *Anchors Aweigh* (MGM 1945). Followed by a tap dance that ends with the two of them exuberantly leaping over the beds in a dormitory.

"I Can Wiggle My Ears" Music by Al Hoffman & Al Goodhart; lyric by Maurice Sigler. Introduced by Donald Stewart in a nightclub in *First a Girl* (Gaumont-Brit. 1935), the song offers a breezy catalogue of unappreciated accomplishments—walking on one's fingers, piloting a plane, paddling a canoe across the Atlantic, shooting a 72 in golf, playing the trombone, dancing the rumba, excelling at Houdini-like tricks, etc. The idea of the song is similar to that of "I Can't Get Started" by Vernon Duke and Ira Gershwin, which Bob Hope sang to Eve Arden the following year in the Broadway revue *Ziegfeld Follies*.

"I Can't Be Bothered Now" Music by George Gershwin; lyric by Ira Gershwin. With London traffic swirling around him in *A Damsel in Distress* (RKO 1937), Fred Astaire entertained a street crowd by singing about—and demonstrating—his single-minded devotion to dancing.

"I Can't Begin To Tell You" Music by James V. Monaco; lyric by Mack Gordon. Ballad of a speechless lover introduced in *The Dolly Sisters* (Fox 1945) by John Payne as a song he's just written; later reprised by Payne and Betty Grable. Also sung by Ginger Rogers in *Dreamboat* (Fox 1952).

"I Can't Escape from You" Music by Richard A. Whiting; lyric by Leo Robin. Though the singer is free as a breeze or the birds in the trees, or even to wander the seven seas, he still can't get away from his beloved. Introduced by Bing Crosby in *Rhythm on the Range* (Par. 1936).

"I Concentrate on You" Music and lyric by Cole Porter. Thoughts about a loved one help banish the glooms. In *Broadway Melody of 1940* (MGM 1940), Douglas McPhail introduced the throbbing ballad in a scene during a Broadway revue in which it was danced by Eleanor Powell (as Columbine) and Fred Astaire (as Harlequin).

"I Couldn't Sleep a Wink Last Night" Music by Jimmy McHugh; lyric by Harold Adamson. Reconciliatory ballad sung in *Higher and Higher* (RKO 1943) by Frank Sinatra. In the film, the singer, playing a singer named Frank Sinatra, has come to call on his neighbor, Michelle Morgan, bearing a gift of roses and a brand-new song he sings just for her. Song was also sung by Philip Terry in *Beat the Band* (RKO 1947).

"I Don't Want To Cry Anymore" Music & lyric by Victor Schertzinger. Torchy lament of a lost love sung by Mary Martin as a nightclub singer in *Rhythm on the River* (Par. 1940).

"I Don't Want To Make History (I Just Want To Make Love)" Music by Ralph Rainger; lyric by Leo Robin. The expoits of Columbus, Napoleon, and Joan of Arc mean little to one who hears a different call to arms. Introduced by Frances Langford in *Palm Springs* (Par. 1936).

"I Don't Want To Walk Without You, Baby" Music by Jule Styne; lyric by Frank Loesser. An appeal for a lover's return ("or you'll break my heart for me"), sung by Johnny Johnston, then by Betty Jane Rhodes in

Sweater Girl (Par. 1942). Styne and Loesser wrote the song (their first collaboration) when they were under contract to Republic, and it was intended for a Judy Canova film, *Sis Hopkins*. Loesser, however, felt that the music was too good to waste on a minor effort for a minor studio. The song was put aside until the following year when, with the writers now at Paramount, it showed up in a minor effort for a major studio. Two years later, Styne wrote another popular "walk" ballad, "I'll Walk Alone," with lyric by Sammy Cahn.

"I Dream Too Much" Music by Jerome Kern; lyric by Dorothy Fields. Waltzing confession sung at the end of film of the same name (RKO 1935) by Lily Pons and chorus appearing in musical comedy supposedly written by Henry Fonda. The movie's title, originally *Love Song,* was changed because the producer expected this song to become a hit.

"I Fall in Love Too Easily" Music by Jule Styne; lyric by Sammy Cahn. Sailor Frank Sinatra's romantic admission in *Anchors Aweigh* (MGM 1945), sung as he played the piano in a deserted Hollywood Bowl.

"I Fall in Love with You Every Day" Music by Manning Sherwin; lyric by Frank Loesser. Ballad of romantic renewal introduced by John Payne and Florence George in *College Swing* (Par. 1938).

"I Feel a Song Comin' On" Music by Jimmy McHugh; lyric by Dorothy Fields & George Oppenheimer. Exultant declaration sung by harmonizing trio—Frances Langford, Alice Faye, and Patsy Kelly—in *Every Night at Eight* (Par. 1935); also done in a torchier version by Miss Faye. Oppenheimer got credit for the number because he supplied Miss Fields with the title.

"I Feel Like a Feather in the Breeze" Music by Harry Revel; lyric by Mack Gordon. Levitational sensation caused when the one you love loves you. Sung by the coeds in *Collegiate* (Par. 1936).

"I Get the Neck of the Chicken" Music by Jimmy McHugh; lyric by Frank Loesser. Comic lament of luckless Marcy McGuire introduced in *Seven Days' Leave* (RKO 1942).

"I Go for That" Music by Matty Malneck; lyric by Frank Loesser. Dorothy Lamour sang this song of romantic approval ("You play the uke, you're from Dubuque") in *St. Louis Blues* (Par. 1939).

"I Guess I'll Have To Change My Plan" Music by Arthur Schwartz; lyric by Howard Dietz. Elegant song-and-dance number performed by the screen's two most elegant song-and-dance men, Fred Astaire and Jack Buchanan (both in top hat, white tie, and tails and sporting canes), in *The Band Wagon* (MGM 1953). Clifton Webb first sang the piece—in which the singer blithely decides to terminate a romance because his beloved is married—in the 1929 Broadway revue, *The Little Show*.

"I Had the Craziest Dream" Music by Harry Warren; lyric by Mack Gordon. The dream was of being loved, and the plan is to make it come true. Introduced in *Springtime in the Rockies* (Fox 1942) by the Harry James orchestra, with Helen Forrest as vocalist.

"I Have Eyes" Music by Ralph Rainger; lyric by Leo Robin. In *Paris Honeymoon* (Par. 1939), Bing Crosby's eyes are only for Shirley Ross and Shirley's eyes are only for Bing as they sing to each other over the telephone.

"I Have the Room Above" Music by Jerome Kern; lyric by Oscar Hammerstein II. Ballad of romantic frustration of one who'd like to become better acquainted with the occupant of the room below. The song was written for the 1936 film version of *Show Boat* (Univ.), in which Allan Jones sang it about—and to—Irene Dunne, who then turned it into a duet.

"I Hear Music" Music by Burton Lane; lyric by Frank Loesser. In which music is heard in the everyday sounds of the morning breeze, the milkman climbing the stairs, the song of a sparrow, the coffee perking, and a telephone call from someone you love. Introduced in *Dancing on a Dime* (Par. 1941) by Peter Lind Hayes, Eddie Quillan, Frank Jenks, and Robert Paige.

"I Know Why (and So Do You)" Music by Harry Warren; lyric by Mack Gordon. The reason for all sorts of unnatural phenomena—robins singing in December, violets growing in the snow, etc.—may not be revealed in the lyric but it's obviously love. Ballad was performed by Glenn Miller's orchestra in *Sun Valley Serenade* (Fox 1941) at an audition for the Sun Valley Lodge, with vocals by Lynn Bari (with Pat Friday's voice), The Modernaires, and John Payne. Song is later reprised by Payne and Sonja Henie dancing to a phonograph record in a ski hut. The Miller orchestra, led by James Stewart, also played the music in *The Glenn Miller Story* (Univ. 1954).

"I Like Myself" Music by André Previn; lyric by Betty Comden & Adolph Green. Gene Kelly sang this song of personal contentment in *It's Always Fair Weather* (MGM 1955), then blissfully danced down the streets of New York on roller skates. The number took twelve days to rehearse and four days to shoot. Previously, Fred Astaire and Ginger Rogers had performed a roller-skating dance to "Let's Call the Whole Thing Off" in *Shall We Dance* (RKO 1937).

"I Love a New Yorker" Music by Harold Arlen; lyric by Ralph Blane & Arlen. Tribute to a "bold, breezy and bright" city slicker, performed as a high-strutting song-and-dance number by Betty Grable and Dan Dailey in *My Blue Heaven* (Fox 1950).

"I Love To Dance Like They Used To Dance" Music by Billy Goldenberg; lyric by Marilyn & Alan Bergman. Fond memories of ballroom dancing ("Not hide and seek/ Just cheek to cheek"), introduced by Martha Tilton from dance-hall bandstand in television's *Queen of the Stardust Ballroom* (CBS 1975). Lyric was changed for Broadway musical *Ballroom* based on the same story, with title shortened to "I Love To Dance."

"I Love You, Samantha" Music & lyric by Cole Porter. Sung by C. K. Dexter Haven (Bing Crosby) as he thinks of Tracy Samantha Lord (Grace Kelly) while dressing for a formal bash in *High Society* (MGM 1956). The singer was accompanied by Louis Armstrong on trumpet, playing in a room below.

"I Love You So Much" Music by Harry Ruby; lyric by Bert Kalmar. Perky forthright declaration ("It's a wonder you don't feel it") introduced by Bert Wheeler and Dorothy Lee in *The Cuckoos* (RKO 1930).

"I Nearly Let Love Go Slipping Through My Fingers" Music & lyric by Harry Woods. Romantic carelessness gaily revealed by Jessie Matthews in *It's Love Again* (Gaumont-Brit. 1936).

"I Never Knew Heaven Could Speak" Music by Harry Revel; lyric by Mack Gordon. Heaven personified as a speaking, dancing, embracing lover. Alice Faye introduced the romantic notion at a backstage party in *Rose of Washington Square* (Fox 1939).

"I Only Have Eyes for You" Music by Harry Warren; lyric by Al Dubin. With the stars twinkling above and the island of Manhattan aglow in the distance, poor young songwriter Dick Powell and his girl, Ruby Keeler, snuggle against the rail of a Staten Island ferryboat. Oblivious to everything but Ruby, Dick expresses his feelings in song, which so delights his beloved that, when he's finished, the misty-eyed heroine bats her eyes and murmurs sweetly, "Gee, Jimmy, that's swell." The song was introduced in *Dames* (Warner 1934), in which it was later reprised as a Busby Berkeley spectacular in a Broadway revue. In it, Powell is seen as a ticket-seller of a Broadway theatre who meets Miss Keeler after work. As they stroll down the busy streets, he sings of his unwavering ocular concentration and—presto!—everyone else disappears. The couple duck into a crowded subway, where again he sings, and again the same thing happens. Even the assorted advertising posters now bear Ruby's likeness. In a dream sequence, Ruby is joined by an array of girls all wearing Ruby Keeler hairdos as they move up, down and around various levels and bridges. There's even a jigsaw puzzle of Ruby's face. The number ends with the twosome brought back to reality at the end of the subway line, and Dick carefully carrying Ruby over the tracks. Song was also sung in *The Girl from Jones Beach* (Warner 1949); by Gordon MacRae in *Tea for Two* (Warner 1950), and by Al Jolson (dubbed for Larry Parks) in *Jolson Sings Again* (Col. 1949).

"I Poured My Heart into a Song" Music & lyric by Irving Berlin. Possibly the one piece that best reveals Berlin's songwriting credo: sincerity, not smartness or cleverness or Hit Parade standing, is the most important element. Song was introduced by Tyrone Power and reprised by Rudy Vallee in *Second Fiddle* (Fox 1939).

"I Promise You" Music by Harold Arlen; lyric by Johnny Mercer. Poetic pledges exchanged by Bing Crosby and Betty Hutton on a flower-filled stage in a Navy show in *Here Come the Waves* (Par. 1944).

"I Remember" Music & lyric by Stephen Sondheim. Wistful recollections of the outside world sung by Charmian Carr as an inmate of a department store in the television fantasy, *Evening Primrose* (ABC 1966).

"I Remember It Well" Music by Frederick Loewe; lyric by Alan Jay Lerner. In *Gigi* (MG 1958), former lovers Hermione Gingold and Maurice Chevalier accidentally meet at a French resort and nostalgically reminisce about a romantic rendezvous—though Chevalier's memory has become rather hazy as to details.

"I Remember You" Music by Victor Schertzinger; lyric by Johnny Mercer. In a nighttime beach scene in *The Fleet's In* (Par. 1942), Dorothy Lamour leads Bob Eberly, Helen O'Connell and sailors, accompanied by Jimmy Dorsey's orchestra, as they languidly serenade "the one who made my dreams come true."

"I Said No" Music by Jule Styne; lyric by Frank Loesser. A girl tries to decline but eventually her resistance is broken and she willingly submits—to subscribing to *Liberty* magazine. Betty Jane Rhodes sang this bit of double-entendre in *Sweater Girl* (Par. 1942).

"I Should Care" Music by Paul Weston & Axel Stordahl; lyric by Sammy Cahn. Ballad of feigned romantic indifference interpolated in *Thrill of a Romance* (MGM 1945), in which it was sung by Esther Williams and reprised by Robert Allen.

"I Still Suits Me." *See* **"Ah Still Suits Me"**

"I Used To Be Color Blind" Music & lyric by Irving Berlin. Sung by Fred Astaire to Ginger Rogers in a dream sequence in *Carefree* (RKO 1938). Fred then led Ginger through a languorous slow-motion dance over a bed of giant-size lily pads which culminated in the first real clinch the team ever had on screen. The song was written because the sequence was initially to have been shot in color.

"I Wanna Be a Dancin' Man" Music by Harry Warren; lyric by Johnny Mercer. Personal avowal which Fred Astaire—in white suit and straw boater—sang and danced to on a beer-hall stage in *The Belle of New York* (MGM 1952).

"I Want To Be a Minstrel Man." *See* **"You're All The World to Me"**

"I Was Doing All Right" Music by George Gershwin; lyric by Ira Gershwin. Now that she's got her man, Ella Logan revealed in *Goldwyn Follies* (Goldwyn 1938), life may be miserable when he's away but she's doing better than ever when he's near.

"I Was Lucky" Music by Jack Stern; lyric by Jack Meskill. Maurice Chevalier, in *Folies Bergère* (UA 1935), exulted in his good fortune at finding the right girl.

"I Wish I Didn't Love You So" Music & lyric by Frank Loesser. The romance has broken up but Betty Hutton still carries the torch in *The Perils of Pauline* (Par. 1947).

"I Wish I Knew" Music by Harry Warren; lyric by Mack Gordon. In *Diamond Horseshoe* (Fox 1945), Betty Grable is seen onstage (accompanied by Carmen Cavallero at the piano) as she expresses the romantic dilemma of one unsure that the one she loves loves her.

"I Wished on the Moon" Music by Ralph Rainger; lyric by Dorothy Parker. In a "radio eye"—or television—sequence in *Big Broadcast of 1936* (Par. 1935), Bing Crosby sang of his lunar desires that all came true when he found the right girl.

"I Won't Dance" Music by Jerome Kern; lyric by Dorothy Fields based on a lyric by Oscar Hammerstein II. Staccato refusal motivated by fear that dancing will lead to romancing. Sung by Fred Astaire and Ginger Rogers in a Paris nightclub in *Roberta* (RKO 1935), then performed—against his will—by Fred as a tap solo. As an "in" joke, the lyric contains reference to dancing "The Continental," which Astaire and Rogers had danced in the previous year's *The Gay Divorcee*. Originally, with a partly different melody, "I Won't Dance" had words by Oscar Hammerstein II when it was introduced in *Three Sisters,* a 1934 musical staged in London. Miss Fields retained the general idea and the lines, "I won't dance/ Don't ask me," for her version, one of the two songs ("Lovely To Look At" was the other) that marked her initial collaboration with Jerome Kern. Although neither Otto Harbach nor Jimmy McHugh had a hand in the new lyric, both were officially credited along with Fields and Hammerstein. The reason: Harbach because he had been the lyricist of the stage musical on which the film was based; McHugh because he had heretofore been Miss Fields' regular songwriting partner and this was done as a pacifying gesture. The following year, Kern and Fields came up with a far more unwieldy refusal, "Never Gonna Dance," performed by Fred and Ginger in *Swing Time*. "I Won't Dance" was also sung by Van Johnson and Lucille Bremer in *Till the Clouds Roll By* (MGM 1946), and Marge and Gower Champion in *Lovely to Look At* (MGM 1952), a remake of *Roberta*.

"I Yi Yi Yi Yi (I Like You Very Much)" Music by Harry Warren; lyric by Mack Gordon. The most popular Carmen Miranda samba written by a Hollywood team, this sprightly number was performed by Miss Miranda at a lavish outdoor party in *That Night in Rio* (Fox 1941). Miss Miranda also sang it in *Four Jills in a Jeep* (Fox 1944).

"I'd Know You Anywhere" Music by Jimmy McHugh; lyric by Johnny Mercer. Ballad of romantic recognition (she knows him because she's dreamed about him), sung by Ginny Simms, with Kay Kyser's orchestra, in *You'll Find Out* (RKO 1940). The setting was a formal party in a haunted mansion.

"I'd Rather Be Blue over You (Than Be Happy with Somebody Else)" Music by Fred Fisher; lyric by Billy Rose. The "outcha-m'goucha" song about absence and abstinence making the heart grow fonder. Sung by Fanny Brice in *My Man* (Warner 1928) and by Barbra Streisand (as Miss Brice) in *Funny Girl* (Col. 1968).

"I'd Rather Lead a Band" Music & lyric by Irving Berlin. In *Follow the Fleet* (RKO 1936), Fred Astaire, as a sailor called on to entertain a visiting admiral on his ship, sings of his unequaled joy waving a stick in front of a dance orchestra. Fred further obliges with a tap solo, after which the entire ship's complement bounds on deck for some nifty close-order drill dancing with nothing but Fred's tapping toes to provide the orders. As staged, the routine was something of a nautical follow-up to the "Top Hat, White Tie and Tails" number (also written by Berlin) that Astaire and a male chorus had performed in *Top Hat* the previous year.

"If I Had a Million Dollars" Music by Matty Malneck; lyric by Johnny Mercer. The Boswell Sisters sang this monetary expression of affection in *Transatlantic Merry-Go-Round* (UA 1934).

"If I Had a Talking Picture of You" Music by Ray Henderson; lyric by B. G. DeSylva & Lew Brown. The first use of the talkies in a romantic ballad ("I would give ten shows a day/ And a midnight matinee") was introduced in *Sunny Side Up* (Fox 1929) by Janet Gaynor and Charles Farrell as part of an elaborate charity entertainment in Southampton. Despite the production possibilities indicated in the song's lyric, the piece was presented in a simple garden setting framed by a trellis, first by the formally clad leads and then by a group of formally clad children. Later in the film, Farrell reprised the number to a photograph of Miss Gaynor.

"If I Only Had a Brain" Music by Harold Arlen; lyric by E. Y. Harburg. In *The Wizard of Oz* (MGM 1939), Dorothy's three new friends sing of the things they lack that they think can be granted to them only by the all-powerful Wizard: the Scarecrow (Ray Bolger) wants a brain; the Tin Woodman (Jack Haley) wants a heart; the Cowardly Lion (Bert Lahr) wants courage. ("But I could show my prowess/ Be a lion not a mowess/ If I only had da noive").

"If I Steal a Kiss" Music by Nacio Herb Brown; lyric by Edward Heyman. Stolen kisses, dreams, and moonlight are sure to be returned but a stolen heart is kept forever. Frank Sinatra introduced the languid ballad in *The Kissing Bandit* (MGM 1948).

"If You Can't Sing It . . ." *See* **"You'll Have to Swing It"**

"If You Feel Like Singing, Sing" Music by Harry Warren; lyric by Mack Gordon. Rollicking chase-the-blues number sung by Judy Garland while taking a shower in *Summer Stock* (MGM 1950). In England the song title's first five words were used as the title of the film.

"I'll Capture Your Heart Singing" Music & lyric by Irving Berlin. Bing Crosby and Fred Astaire, as a song-and-dance team in *Holiday Inn* (Par. 1942), kid about their respective specialties while wooing Virginia Dale in the opening nightclub routine.

"I'll Give You Three Guesses" Music by Henry Mancini; lyric by Johnny Mercer. In *Darling Lili* (Par. 1969), Julie Andrews, accompanied by a male quartet strumming banjos, performed the coquettish, old-fashioned number on the stage of a Paris music hall during World War I. Later in the film, the same song was used for Miss Andrews' torrid—and slightly incongruous—strip tease.

"I'll Never Let a Day Pass By" Music by Victor Schertzinger; lyric by Frank Loesser. Ardent declaration sung by Don Ameche and Mary Martin in *Kiss the Boys Goodbye* (Par. 1941). Ameche is said to have insisted that the lyricist change the song's original title phrase, "I'll never let a day go by," because it sounded like an ethnic slur.

"I'll Never Stop Loving You" Music by Nicholas Brodszky; lyric by Sammy Cahn. Ballad of eternal devotion, sung by Doris Day in *Love Me or Leave Me* (MGM 1955) during a film recording sequence.

"I'll Plant My Own Tree" Music by André Previn; lyric by Dory Previn. Emotional declaration of individuality affirmed by Margaret Whiting dubbing for Susan Hayward in *Valley of the Dolls* (1967). The song was written for Judy Garland who was originally to have played Miss Hayward's role.

"I'll Remember April" Music by Gene dePaul; lyric by Don Raye & Pat Johnson. Remembrance of a brief but intense love affair introduced by Dick Foran in *Ride 'Em Cowboy* (Univ. 1942); also sung by Kirby Grant and Gloria Jean in *I'll Remember April* (Univ. 1945).

"I'll Si Si Ya in Bahia" Music by Harry Warren; lyric by Leo Robin. Bing Crosby, as a Broadway producer-director in *Just for You* (Par. 1952), demonstrates the right way to do the number during rehearsals for a show. The scene depicts a crowded airport and the spirited samba expresses a young man's desire to fly down to Bahia, Brazil, on a DC-6 to find his Maria and take her back to the U.S.A.

"I'll Sing You a Thousand Love Songs" Music by Harry Warren; lyric by Al Dubin. Romantic offer of a tireless vocalist. Ballad was introduced in *Cain and Mabel* (Warner 1936) by Robert Paige (then known as David Carlyle) and chorus serenading Marion Davies in an elaborate production number partly set on a Venetian canal. Four other songs were interpolated during the eight-minute presentation because, as composer Warren once explained, "Al Dubin and I had become weary of these elongated versions of our songs in the Busby Berkeley productions, so we thought we would give this melody a little relief."

"I'll String Along with You" Music by Harry Warren; lyric by Al Dubin. In *Twenty Million Sweethearts* (Warner 1934), though radio singer Dick Powell reveals he's been looking for an angel to sing his love songs to, he realistically admits that he's quite happy with his all too mortal sweetheart. And Ginger Rogers echoes the jaunty sentiment when she joins him on the air. The song was also sung by Joan Leslie and Jack Carson in *The Hard Way* (Warner 1942); Doris Day in *My Dream Is Yours* (Warner 1949); and Danny Thomas in *The Jazz Singer* (Warner 1953).

"I'll Take Romance" Music by Ben Oakland; lyric by Oscar Hammerstein II. Romantic yearnings ("While my heart is young and eager and gay,/ I'll give my heart away") expressed by Grace Moore in *I'll Take Romance* (Col. 1937). Also by Gloria Jean in *Manhattan Angel* (Col. 1949).

"I'll Walk Alone" Music by Jule Styne; lyric by Sammy Cahn. Wartime sentiment of lonely one waiting for her lover to return, sung by Dinah Shore in *Follow the Boys* (Univ. 1944). Also sung by Jane Froman (for Susan Hayward) in *With a Song in My Heart* (Fox 1952). In 1942, with Frank Loesser's lyric, Styne wrote his first "walk" ballad, "I Don't Want To Walk Without You, Baby."

"Illusions" Music & lyric by Frederick Hollander. Marlene Dietrich sang this dirge of disillusionment as a Berlin café entertainer in *A Foreign Affair* (Par. 1948).

"I'm a Dreamer, Aren't We All?" Music by Ray Henderson; lyric by B. G. DeSylva & Lew Brown. Seated in a wing chair in a modest tenement apartment (in *Sunny Side Up,* Fox 1929), romantic Janet Gaynor tells her friend, Marjorie White, "You know, there's a song that expresses my feelings perfectly." And then, strumming a handy zither, she sings wistfully of her dream romance. Later in the movie, she sings the piece alone on stage in a Southampton charity show.

"I'm an Old Cowhand" Music & lyric by Johnny Mercer. A satirical look at home-on-the-range cowboys, this was Mercer's first Hollywood song hit. Bing Crosby and most of the cast introduced it in *Rhythm on the Range* (Par. 1936). Also sung by Roy Rogers in *King of the Cowboys* (Rep. 1943).

"I'm Bubbling Over" Music by Harry Warren; lyric by Mack Gordon. Efferverscent piece sung by Grace Bradley and the Brewster Twins during a radio broadcast in *Wake Up and Live* (Fox 1937). Number later used in film for Condos Brothers' dance, accompanied by Ben Bernie's orchestra during broadcast from the High Hat Club.

"I'm Easy" Music & lyric by Keith Carradine. Carradine introduced the rueful piece in *Nashville* (ABC 1975). As performed in a nightclub scene, the song about a man who reluctantly agrees to "play the game" with a woman who's not free becomes a signal to a married woman (Lily Tomlin) seated in the audience.

"I'm Glad I'm Not Young Anymore" Music by Frederick Loewe; lyric by Alan Jay Lerner. Seated at a Parisian outdoor restaurant, Maurice Chevalier ruminates about the advantages of romantically uncomplicated old age in *Gigi* (MGM 1958). Lyricist Lerner claims that the idea for the song was sparked by a comment Chevalier made to him: "At 72, I'm too old for women, too old for that extra glass of wine, too old for sports. All I have left is the audience but I have found it is quite enough."

"I'm Going Shopping with You" Music by Harry Warren; lyric by Al Dubin. Sung by Dick Powell to Gloria Stuart on a shopping spree in *Gold Diggers of 1935* (Warner 1935).

"I'm in the Mood for Love" Music by Jimmy McHugh; lyric by Dorothy Fields. Propinquity causes romantic desires in this soulful ballad that Frances Langford introduced in *Every Night at Eight* (Par. 1935). Also sung by Miss Langford (over credits) in *Palm Springs* (Par. 1936); Gloria DeHaven in *Between Two Women* (MGM 1944); and Dean Martin in *That's My Boy* (Par. 1951).

"I'm Late" Music by Sammy Fain; lyric by Bob Hilliard. Scurrying song for the White Rabbit (voice of Bill Thompson) in *Alice in Wonderland* (Disney 1951), as he rushes to keep a very important date down the rabbit hole.

"I'm Like a Fish out of Water" Music by Richard A. Whiting; lyric by Johnny Mercer. In *Hollywood Hotel* (Warner 1937), Dick Powell and Rosemary Lane take off their shoes and go wading in a hotel fountain. Their mutual attraction, however, finds them ill-at-ease in the other's presence which prompts them—in song—to compare their awkwardness to a series of unlikely situations: J. P. Morgan swinging on the organ, Marion Talley singing like Rudy Vallee, Ginger Rogers in charge of the Brooklyn Dodgers, etc.

"I'm Old-Fashioned" Music by Jerome Kern; lyric by Johnny Mercer. In which Rita Hayworth (with Nan Wynn's dubbed voice) explains to Fred Astaire in *You Were Never Lovelier* (Col. 1942) exactly the kind of girl she is. Then, after revealing her preference for such outdated pleasures as moonlight, the sound of raindrops on a window pane, and "the starry song that April sings," the couple dance ardently around the enormous gardens surrounding her home. Johnny Mercer once said that this lyric expressed his personal philosophy more closely than any he ever wrote.

"I'm Putting All My Eggs in One Basket" Music & lyric by Irving Berlin. In *Follow the Fleet* (RKO 1936), sailor Fred Astaire and former vaudeville partner Ginger Rogers rehearse the number aboard an old ship where they plan to offer a benefit show. Fred first plays the tune on an upright piano, then sings the words with Ginger, and they both end up doing a carefree, hokey, seemingly spontaneous dance. Note that in the music, the line, "Saved up in my love account," goes back to the same seven-note phrase that Irving Berlin used for "Would I exchange that first kiss" in the previously written "Not for All the Rice in China" from *As Thousands Cheer* (NY 1933). Also noteworthy is that the song, which pledges an end to philandering and offers a vow to concentrate on only one, takes its title from a line in Cervantes' *Don Quixote*—" 'Tis the part of a wise man to keep himself today for tomorrow, and not venture all his eggs in one basket."

"I'm Shooting High" Music by Jimmy McHugh; lyric by Ted Koehler. "I'm on a rainbow rafter/ Climbing up to where you are," sang Alice Faye in *King of Burlesque* (Fox 1935), as she vowed to win a special starry someone. Spirited piece was introduced in a production number in which Miss Faye danced with Nick Long, Jr.

"I'm Sorry for Myself" Music & lyric by Irving Berlin. Mary Healy, in *Second Fiddle* (Fox 1939), introduced this number whose bouncy rhythm prevents its self-pitying lyric from being taken seriously.

"I'm Wishing" Music by Frank Churchill; lyric by Larry Morey. Forced into a life of drudgery (even though she's a princess), the heroine of *Snow White and the Seven Dwarfs* (Disney 1937) goes to a well to fill her wash pail, and expresses—with accompanying well echoes—her longing for a man to find her and carry her away. Then, just as she finishes, darned if a handsome prince doesn't arrive to join her in the song's last line. The voices in the cartoon feature were those of Adriana Caselotti and Harry Stockwell.

"Impatient Years, The" Music by James Van Heusen; lyric by Sammy Cahn. Tender song of young love sung by Paul Newman and Eva Marie Saint in the television production of *Our Town* (NBC 1955).

"In Acapulco" Music by Harry Warren; lyric by Mack Gordon. Lively song-and-dance tribute to the Mexican resort performed by Betty Grable and company at the nightclub featured in *Diamond Horseshoe* (Fox 1945). The number was originally intended for Carmen Miranda but Carmen wasn't available.

"In Love in Vain" Music by Jerome Kern; lyric by Leo Robin. Ballad of unrequited love sung by Jeanne Crain (with Louanne Hogan's dubbed voice) and, briefly, by William Eythe in *Centennial Summer* (Fox 1946).

In Old Chicago. See San Francisco.

"In Old Chicago" Music by Harry Revel; lyric by Mack Gordon. Rousing anthem sung in film of the same name (Fox 1938) by Alice Faye and chorus in a boisterous beer hall. Another popular movie song about Chicago was James Van Heusen and Sammy Cahn's "My Kind of Town" in *Robin and the Seven Hoods* (Warner 1964).

"In Our United State" Music by Burton Lane; lyric by Ira Gershwin. In *Give a Girl a Break* (MGM 1953), Debbie Reynolds and Bob Fosse stroll in a riverfront park (presumably in Queens) and, with the United Nations buildings behind them, begin discussing the troubled state of the world. Their thoughts, however, quickly turn to "the wonderful status of us," which they describe in political terms ("Fooling around will be unconstitutional"). The number ends with a dance and Fosse falling into the East River.

"In the Cool Cool Cool of the Evening" Music by Hoagy Carmichael; lyric by Johnny Mercer. Partygoers Bing Crosby and Jane Wyman joyfully prepare for a fun-filled bash—"Well, you can tell 'em we'll be there"—in *Here Comes the Groom* (Par. 1951).

"In the Middle of a Kiss" Music & lyric by Sam Coslow. Johnny Downs and Arline Judge introduced the song of romantic revelation in *College Scandal* (Par. 1935). Composer Coslow claims that the number was written at a party as a result of a bet. Boasting that he could write a song within an hour, he accepted the challenge and finished it in 35 minutes.

"In the Still of the Night" Music & lyric by Cole Porter. In *Rosalie* (MGM 1937), Nelson Eddy poured out his heart to Eleanor Powell while standing beneath a tree in a romantic garden in the Kingdom of Romanza. Song was also sung by Dorothy Malone (Cary Grant at the piano) in *Night and Day* (Warner 1946).

"In Your Own Quiet Way" Music by Harold Arlen; lyric by E. Y. Harburg. In which, according to Dick Powell in *Stage Struck* (Warner 1936), the unaggressive type wins in matters of the heart.

"Inch Worm, The" Music & lyric by Frank Loesser. Gentle, brief (16 bars) plea to appreciate beauty sung by Danny Kaye in *Hans Christian Andersen* (Goldwyn 1952). The song was based on an Andersen fairy tale.

International House. See Big Broadcast of 1938.

Invitation to the Dance. See Ziegfeld Follies.

"Isn't It Kinda Fun?" Music by Richard Rodgers; lyric by Oscar Hammerstein II. Casual love song in which boy and girl acknowledge that while their romance may be just a fling they have a hunch it may turn out to be the real thing. Sung by Dick Haymes and Vivian Blaine in *State Fair* (Fox 1945); also by Ann-Margret and David Street in the film's remake (Fox 1962). The sentiment expressed in the song's lyric is similar to that of the previous "All in Fun," which Hammerstein had written with Jerome Kern for the Broadway musical, *Very Warm for May* (1939).

"Isn't It Romantic?" Music by Richard Rodgers; lyric by Lorenz Hart. As performed in *Love Me Tonight* (Par. 1932), the ballad was extended beyond its normal length and outfitted with special lines so that it might provide the means through which the film changed locales. It is first heard in a tailor shop in Paris, where the tailor (Maurice Chevalier) and his bridegroom-to-be customer (Bert Roach) extol the workmanship in the customer's new morning suit, and it continues through a refrain in which the tailor imagines marriage to an adoring and subservient wife who will scrub both the floors and his back, cook him onion soup, and make sure to provide him with a large family. The customer picks up the song and sings it in the street where it is overheard by a taxi driver (Rolfe Sedan), who whistles the melody as his fare, a composer (Tyler Brooke), jots down notes on a pad. In a railway car, the composer now adds words to the music which is sung by a platoon of French soldiers who continue singing while marching through the countryside. Hearing the tune, a Gypsy violinist plays it around a campfire and he, in turn, is heard by a lovesick princess (Jeanette MacDonald) leaning out of a window in her chateau. Now it is she who sings the melody but with new words that reveal her longing for a prince in armour who will kiss her hand, bend his knee, and be her slave. Thus, even though they are miles away and have not met as yet, the tailor and the princess are linked by the same music and their desire for the same kind of worshipful mate.

In its more commercial form, "Isn't It Romantic?" was sung in *Isn't It Romantic?* (Par. 1948); in *Sabrina* (Par. 1954); and by Mae Questel in *It's Only Money* (Par. 1962).

"Isn't This a Lovely Day (To Be Caught in the Rain)?" Music & lyric by Irving Berlin. In *Top Hat* (RKO 1935), Fred Astaire and Ginger Rogers, both in riding habits, dash into a London park bandstand during a sudden thunderstorm. Fred tries to allay Ginger's fears by explaining what thunder really is: "When a clumsy cloud from here meets a fluffy little white cloud from there, he billows toward her. She scurries away and he scuds right up to her. She cries a little. And there you

have your shower. He comforts her. They spark. That's the lightning. They kiss. Thunder!" Then, on cue, a thunderclap sends Ginger into Fred's arms, and Fred sings of their fortuitous meeting caused by the unfortunate weather. The song is followed by a challenge tap dance with Ginger ably following Fred's steps around the bandstand, and it ends with a burst of mutual exhilaration.

"Isn't This Better?" Music by John Kander; lyric by Fred Ebb. Though the trip actually occurred some seven years later and was made by Billy Rose alone, in *Funny Lady* (Col. 1975), Fanny Brice (Barbra Streisand) and Rose (James Caan) are in a train compartment speeding to Fort Worth the day after their wedding. As Billy sleeps, Fanny cradles his head in her lap and expresses her contentment with a relationship based on friendship rather than passion.

"It Could Happen to You" Music by James Van Heusen; lyric by Johnny Burke. Though Dorothy Lamour—in *And the Angels Sing* (Par. 1944)—is warning others to beware of romantic temptation, she admits that she hasn't taken her own advice.

"It Don't Worry Me" Music & lyric by Keith Carradine. Loping song of total indifference to the world's problems ("You may say that I ain't free/ But it don't worry me"), first heard on a tape recording by Keith Carradine in a motel-room scene in *Nashville* (ABC 1975). Also used for film's climax when Barbara Harris leads the crowd at a political rally following an assassination.

"It Happened in Monterey" Music by Mabel Wayne; lyric by Billy Rose. Recollection of an unforgettable love affair in old Mexico, sung by John Boles and Jeanette Loff, accompanied by Paul Whiteman's orchestra, in *King of Jazz* (Univ. 1930).

"It Happened in Sun Valley" Music by Harry Warren; lyric by Mack Gordon. Careening number recalling a happy skiing accident "when you slipped and fell and so did I." Introduced at the beginning of *Sun Valley Serenade* (Fox 1941) by Lynn Bari (voice dubbed by Pat Friday) auditioning for the Sun Valley Lodge. A bit later, the song (including its verse) was gaily sung by members of Glenn Miller's orchestra riding in sleighs to the lodge.

"It Happens Every Spring" Music by Josef Myrow; lyric by Mack Gordon. Celebrating—in the film of the same name (Fox 1949)—all the small pleasures of that time of year when the world is young again and "we're children in an upsydaisy swing."

"It Might as Well Be Spring" Music by Richard Rodgers; lyric by Oscar Hammerstein II. In which a teenage girl expresses the "starry-eyed and vaguely discontented" feeling of adolescence. Sung in two versions of *State Fair* (Fox): by Jeanne Crain (with Louanne Hogan's dubbed voice) in 1945, and by Pamela Tiffin (with Anita Gordon's dubbed voice) in 1962. Originally, Hammerstein had wanted to write a lyric about a girl with spring fever, but since state fairs are held in the fall he decided to write about a girl who feels all the feverish symptoms even though it's the wrong season. In the music, Rodgers purposely matched the restless, jumpy quality expressed in lines about being "as restless as a willow in a windstorm" and "as jumpy as a puppet on a string." Moreover, as the composer wrote in his autobiography, *Musical Stages,* "Since the song is sung by a young girl who can't quite understand why she feels the way she does, I deliberately ended the main phrase on the uncertain sound of the F natural (on the word 'string') rather than on the more positive F sharp."

"It Only Happens When I Dance with You" Music & lyric by Irving Berlin. Concerned that his dancing partner, Ann Miller, is planning to quit the act, Fred Astaire—in *Easter Parade* (MGM 1948)—tries wooing her back by expressing, in song, how much dancing with her means to him. He further demonstrates his feelings by twirling Ann around the cramped quarters of her apartment. Later in the film the song is sung by Judy Garland to Astaire; still later, it is again used for an Astaire-Miller dance, this time on the New Amsterdam Roof during a performance of the *Ziegfeld Midnight Frolic* (incorrectly called the *Ziegfeld Follies* in the movie).

"It Was Written in the Stars" Music by Harold Arlen; lyric by Leo Robin. In *Casbah* (Univ. 1948), Tony Martin (as Pepe Le Moko) and Marta Toren attend a street festival in Morocco and hear a native song. When Marta wants to know its meaning, Tony sings the supposed English version dealing with fate ruling their romantic destiny. Following the vocal, Katherine Dunham and her dancers interpret the music.

"It's a Grand Night for Singing" Music by Richard Rodgers; lyric by Oscar Hammerstein II. Swooping, waltzing ode to the pleasures of vocalizing on a beautiful autumn evening. Introduced in *State Fair* (Fox 1945) at an outdoor dance at the Iowa State Fair by William Marshall, Dick Haymes, Jeanne Crain (Louanne Hogan's voice), Dana Andrews, and chorus; reprised by Vivian Blaine, Marshall, and chorus. Also sung in film remake (1962) at the Texas State Fair by Pat Boone, Bobby Darin, Pamela Tiffin (Anita Gordon's voice), and Bob Smart.

"It's a Great Big World" Music by Harry Warren; lyric by Johnny Mercer. In *The Harvey Girls* (MGM 1946), Judy Garland, Virginia O'Brien, and Cyd Charisse played three waitresses at Harvey House who live above the restaurant. At night on the balcony outside their bedroom, clad in nightgowns and robes, they wistfully expressed their romantic yearnings in song and dance. Miss Charisse's singing was done by Marion Doenges.

"It's a Great Day for the Irish" Music & lyric by Roger Edens. Rousing tribute to St. Patrick's Day in New York, sung by Judy Garland and Douglas McPhail in *Little Nellie Kelly* (MGM 1940).

"It's a Most Unusual Day" Music by Jimmy McHugh; lyric by Harold Adamson. Lilting waltz expressing the effect of a sunny, cloudless spring day. Sung in *A Date with Judy* (MGM 1948) by Jane Powell then Elizabeth Taylor (with her voice dubbed) while rehearsing for a high-school prom. Reprised at end of the film by Miss Powell and the movie's principals at a formal outdoor party.

"It's a New World" Music by Harold Arlen; lyric by Ira Gershwin. No more sorrow or fear now that love has come. In *A Star Is Born* (Warner 1954), the touching affirmation is first heard as a recording by Judy Garland (as Vicki Lester); after hearing her own voice, Miss Garland then sings the piece (without orchestra accompaniment) to James Mason.

It's Always Fair Weather (1955). Music by André Previn; lyrics & screenplay by Betty Comden & Adolph Green.

An MGM film produced by Arthur Freed; directed by Gene Kelly & Stanley Donen; choreography, Kelly & Donen; art directors, Cedric Gibbons, Arthur Lonergan;

costumes, Helen Rose; music director, André Previn; orchestrations, Previn; vocal arrangements, Robert Tucker, Jeff Alexander; cameraman, Robert Bronner; editor, Adrienne Fazan; Eastman Color; CinemaScope.

Cast: Gene Kelly (*Ted Riley*); Dan Dailey (*Doug Hallerton*); Cyd Charisse (vocals by Carole Richards) (*Jackie Leighton*); Dolores Gray (*Madeline Bradbille*); Michael Kidd (vocals by Jud Conlin) (*Angie Valentine*); David Burns (*Tim*); Jay C. Flippen (*Charles Culloran*); Hal March (*Rocky Heldon*); Lou Lubin (*fight manager*).

Songs: "March, March" - Kelly, Dailey, Kidd (Conlin)/ "The Time for Parting" - Kelly, Dailey, Kidd (Conlin)/ "Once Upon a Time" - Kelly, Dailey, Kidd (Conlin)/ "Thanks a Lot but No Thanks - Gray/ "Blue Danube" ("Why Are We Here?") (music, Johann Strauss) - Kelly, Dailey, Kidd (Conlin)/ "Music Is Better Than Words" (lyric, Roger Edens) - Gray/ "Situation-Wise" - Dailey/ "I Like Myself" - Kelly/ "Stillman's Gym" - Lubin, gym users/ "Baby, You Knock Me Out" - Charisse (Richards), gym users. Unused: "I Thought They'd Never Leave," "Love Is Nothing but a Racket," "I Said Good Mornin'," "Jack and the Space Giants" (ballet).

Gene Kelly and the writing team of Comden and Green had the same idea: a musical built around the three sailor characters in *On the Town* that would show what Gabey, Ozzie, and Chip might be like ten years later. When MGM balked at signing Jules Munshin and Frank Sinatra to re-create their earlier roles, the characters were changed to three ex-soldiers, and Dan Dailey and Michael Kidd were cast to appear with Kelly. The third screen musical co-directed by Kelly and Stanley Donen with a screenplay by Comden and Green, *It's Always Fair Weather* also marked the first with songs written by composer André Previn.

In the film, the youthful exuberance of *On the Town* made way for a more cynical and satirical approach. Meeting at a Third Avenue bar for their tenth reunion, Kelly (a smalltime fight manager), Dailey (a pompous advertising executive), and Kidd (who runs a diner in Schenectady) find they have little in common and don't like each other anymore. Through the efforts of television coordinator Cyd Charisse, the three become involved in a *This Is Your Life*-type program presided over by unctuous Dolores Gray, which somehow helps them get a better understanding of themselves and each other. Taking full advantage of the dancing skills of its stars, *It's Always Fair Weather* was notable for two street dances, one by the trio with garbage-can lids attached to

their feet and the other by Kelly alone on roller skates, and also for Cyd Charisse's routine with the boxers at Stillman's gym. The film used CinemaScope to good effect, particularly in a scene showing the three men soliloquizing in three separate panels.

"It's Always You" Music by James Van Heusen; lyric by Johnny Burke. Ballad sung by Bing Crosby to Dorothy Lamour in *Road to Zanzibar* (Par. 1941), in which her closeness is apparent whenever he sees a star, or touches a rose, or feels a breeze, or hears a melody. In the scene, Crosby and Lamour are in a canoe on an African lake. Dorothy recalls a similar situation in a movie in which a boy sings and is miraculously accompanied by a full orchestra. Bing recalls another film in which a boy merely runs his hand through the water and the sound of a harp is heard. He tries it, and it works.

"It's Anybody's Spring" Music by James Van Heusen; lyric by Johnny Burke. Philosophical ballad about the unimportance of money and material possessions ("And if you flash a bankroll/ Do you suppose the brook would care?"). Bing Crosby introduced the song (with Bob Hope on accordion) in *Road to Utopia* (Par. 1945) during an amateur talent contest on deck of a ship heading for Alaska. Crosby lost.

"It's Easy To Remember" Music by Richard Rodgers; lyric by Lorenz Hart. Bing Crosby, in *Mississippi* (Par. 1935), sings of a lost love at an outdoor celebration in the old South. The song was written after the other numbers for the movie had been completed and Rodgers and Hart were already back in New York. To satisfy the need for an additional song, the songwriters wrote it in the East, made a recording, and mailed it to the producer.

"It's Love Again" Music & lyric by Sam Coslow. Reversing—in the verse—her previously held low opinion of love (during which the writer managed to rhyme "chop suey," "hooey," "do we?," and "screwy"), Jessie Matthews joyously proclaimed her new romance and offered to shout her discovery from the housetops. Announcement was first made in the British film *It's Love Again* (Gaumont-Brit. 1936).

"It's Love I'm After" Music by Lew Pollack; lyric by Sidney Mitchell. Powerhouse number of romantic single-mindedness introduced by Judy Garland in *Pigskin Parade* (Fox 1936).

"It's Magic" Music by Jule Styne; lyric by Sammy Cahn. Romantic phenomena—his sigh becomes a song, he speaks and violins are heard—revealed by Doris Day in *Romance on the High Seas* (Warner 1948). Also performed by Gene Nelson and Janice Rule in *Starlift* (Warner 1951). According to lyricist Cahn's autobiography, *I Should Care*, "Jule and I started going through the script of the picture, and as I was reading he was fooling around at the piano with this tango he always warmed up with. We needed a song for a scene in which Jack Carson is to take Doris Day to a nightclub in Cuba. Suddenly, I began to listen to the tango and I said, 'What's that?' and Jule said: 'Just something I've been playing for two years,' and I said: 'Play it again, *slowly.*' And he did. 'Once more, *slower.*' He did, and we wrote 'It's Magic.' " The song became so popular that when the film was released in England its title was changed to *It's Magic*.

"It's Mine, It's Yours" Music by Harold Arlen; lyric by Ira Gershwin. Jaunty cure-all to ensure happiness: appreciate the wonders of life and have a cheerful disposition. Introduced in *The Country Girl* (Par. 1954) by Bing Crosby.

"It's Swell of You" Music by Harry Revel; lyric by Mack Gordon. Lilting appreciation of one who "showed me the way to love," performed in *Wake Up and Live* (Fox 1937) by 1) Ben Bernie's orchestra with the tapping Condos Brothers during a radio broadcast, and 2) Jack Haley (with the dubbed voice of Buddy Clark) as a mike-fright victim singing into an assumed dead microphone.

"It's the Animal in Me" Music by Harry Revel; lyric by Mack Gordon. In a jungle setting—supposedly part of a "radio-eye," or television, program—Ethel Merman belted out this assertion of female aggressiveness in *Big Broadcast of 1936* (Par. 1935). Curiously, the number had been filmed the previous year for Paramount's *We're Not Dressing*, but the scene was cut, then simply inserted as a specialty in the new movie.

"It's the Natural Thing To Do" Music by Arthur Johnston; lyric by Johnny Burke. If it's normal for birds, cats, doves, and rabbits to fall in love then it's certainly all right for this boy and girl. The song, something of variation on Cole Porter's "Let's Do It," was intro-

duced by Bing Crosby in *Double or Nothing* (Par. 1937).

"It's the Same Old Dream" Music by Jule Styne; lyric by Sammy Cahn. Introduced by Frank Sinatra in *It Happened in Brooklyn* (MGM 1947). Requested by a group of teenagers to sing the song, Sinatra, as a salesman in a music store, performs it as an appropriately slow-tempo ballad. The kids then jazz it up but, undaunted, Sinatra reprises the song with even more feeling.

Iturbi, José, pianist, conductor, actor; b. Valencia, Spain, Nov. 28, 1895; d. Hollywood, June 28, 1980. Iturbi added cultural uplift to MGM musicals, in which he always appeared under his own name (even when he played the romantic lead opposite Jeanette MacDonald), and he was seen as Kathryn Grayson's musical mentor in three films. He began his career in 1923 as a concert pianist, made his US debut in 1928, and became a symphony conductor in 1936.

1943	Thousands Cheer
1944	Two Girls and a Sailor
	Music for Millions
1945	A Song To Remember (piano for Cornel Wilde)
	Anchors Aweigh
1946	Holiday in Mexico
1948	Three Daring Daughters
1949	That Midnight Kiss

"I've Been in Love Before" Music by Frederick Hollander; lyric by Frank Loesser. In *Seven Sinners* (Univ. 1940), cabaret entertainer Marlene Dietrich revealed that she learned a lot from a past romance.

"I've Got a Feelin' You're Foolin' " Music by Nacio Herb Brown; lyric by Arthur Freed. Jaunty ballad of suspected romantic fickleness sung by Robert Taylor and June Knight in *Broadway Melody of 1936* (MGM 1935). In the setting, an elegant New York penthouse, the piano, tables, and chairs pop up from the floor at appropriately timed moments in the song, which is then danced to by Miss Knight and Nick Long, Jr. Later, the number is reprised by Frances Langford. It was also sung by Jane Froman for Susan Hayward in *With a Song in My Heart* (Fox 1952) and by a chorus in *Singin' in the Rain* (MGM 1952).

"I've Got a Gal in Kalamazoo" Music by Harry Warren; lyric by Mack Gordon. A successor to the same writers' "Chattanooga Choo-Choo," this insistent number was performed in *Orchestra Wives* (Fox 1942) by Tex Beneke, Marion Hutton and the Modernaires, backed by Glenn Miller's orchestra, then followed by the singing and dancing Nicholas Brothers. Warren had originally written the tune as a rhythmic exercise; it was Gordon who saw its possibilities as a real song and came up with the alphabet-opening lyric about the singer's expected reunion with his "real pipperoo" schooldays' sweetheart.

"I've Got a Pocketful of Dreams" Music by James V. Monaco; lyric by Johnny Burke. Carefree confession of an impecunious dreamer. Introduced in *Sing You Sinners* (Par. 1938) at a party by a trio of brothers: Bing Crosby (on guitar), Fred MacMurray (clarinet), and Donald O'Connor (accordian). Hollywood's other "Pocketful" song, "Pocketful of Miracles," was written by James Van Heusen and Sammy Cahn for the film of the same name.

"I've Got Beginner's Luck." *See* **Beginner's Luck"**

"I've Got My Eyes on You" Music & lyric by Cole Porter. Ballad of romantic surveillance introduced by Fred Astaire in *Broadway Melody of 1940* (MGM 1940). In the scene, which takes place on the deserted stage of a Broadway theatre after a rehearsal, Astaire notices Eleanor Powell's picture on the cover of the sheet music on an upright piano. He plays the melody and sings to the photograph, then dances with the sheet music as if he were holding Miss Powell in his arms. The real Miss Powell, who has been watching all along, bursts into applause at the end as she exclaims, "That was swell, Johnny, swell!" Song was also sung by Kathryn Grayson in *Andy Hardy's Private Secretary* (MGM 1941).

"I've Got My Love To Keep Me Warm" Music & lyric by Irving Berlin. Despite the snowing snow and the blowing wind the singer's burning love provides so much heat that overcoat and gloves are unnecessary. As presented in *On the Avenue* (Fox 1937), the ballad is sung by Dick Powell in a Broadway revue as he changes

to a summer dinner jacket and straw hat to welcome an array of show girls in fur coats. Alice Faye, whose frilly evening gown shows that her body temperature is similar to Dick's, joins him in a brief duet. Here, however, the song's presentation is interrupted by Powell's angrily whispered admonition to Miss Faye regarding changes she'd made in the previous sketch, and by her scream when Powell squeezes her arm too tightly.

"I've Got To Sing a Torch Song" Music by Harry Warren; lyric by Al Dubin. In *Gold Diggers of 1933* (Warner 1933), composer-lyricist-singer Dick Powell's audition song for Broadway producer Ned Sparks so impressed Sparks that his first reaction was, "Fire Dubin and Warren!"

"I've Got You Under My Skin" Music & lyric by Cole Porter. Tegumentary predicament of one who's fallen in love despite premonition that it won't last. The ballad was first heard in *Born To Dance* (MGM 1936) as accompaniment to nightclub dance by Georges and Jalna; it was then sung by Virginia Bruce to James Stewart on a huge penthouse terrace. Porter originally wrote the song for a different scene but it was found inappropriate and dropped. Later, it was put back in the score for Frances Langford, but she was replaced by Miss Bruce. Song was also sung by Ginny Simms in *Night and Day* (Warner 1946), and Marina Koshetz in *Luxury Liner* (MGM 1948).

"I've Heard That Song Before" Music by Jule Styne; lyric by Sammy Cahn. In *Youth on Parade* (Rep. 1942), Martha O'Driscoll (with Margaret Whiting's voice) hears a melody that makes her recall a lost romance. The song was the first collaboration between Styne and Cahn. When the lyricist heard the tune, the first thing he said was, "I've heard that song before." The composer took this as a criticism of his originality until Cahn quickly convinced him he was just trying out a title. Two years later, they wrote the similarly titled "There Goes That Song Again," which Harry Babbitt introduced in *Carolina Blues*.

J

James, Harry (Hagg), bandleader, trumpeter; b. Albany, Ga., March 15, 1916. Slim, mustached musician who first won notice as trumpeter in Benny Goodman orchestra (with whom he appeared in first film), and who fronted his own band beginning in 1939. James introduced "I Had the Craziest Dream" in *Springtime in the Rockies,* which starred Betty Grable (whom he married and divorced). (Died Las Vegas, July 5, 1983.)

Unless otherwise noted, Mr. James was featured with his orchestra under his own name in following:
1937 Hollywood Hotel (with Goodman band)
1942 Private Buckaroo
      Springtime in the Rockies
      Syncopation
1943 Swing Fever
      Best Foot Forward
1944 Two Girls and a Sailor
      Bathing Beauty
1946 Do You Love Me? (*Barry Clayton*)
      If I'm Lucky (*Earl Gordon*)
1950 Young Man with a Horn (trumpet for Kirk Douglas)
      I'll Get By
      Carnegie Hall
1955 The Benny Goodman Story (*Harry James*)
1956 The Opposite Sex
1957 The Big Beat
1961 Ladies Man

Jazz Singer, The (1927). Screenplay by Alfred A. Cohn from short story "The Day of Atonement" and the Broadway play *The Jazz Singer,* both by Samson Raphaelson.

A Warner Bros. film produced by Darryl F. Zanuck; directed by Alan Crosland; music director, Louis Silvers; cameraman, Hal Mohr; editor, Harold McCord; titles, Jack Jarmuth.

Cast: Al Jolson (*Jack Robin né Jakie Rabinowitz*); May McAvoy (*Mary Dale*); Warner Oland (vocal by Joseph Diskay) (*Cantor Rabinowitz*); Eugenie Besserer (*Sarah Rabinowitz*); Otto Lederer (*Moisha Yudelson*); Bobby Gordon (*Jakie Rabinowitz at 13*); Roscoe Karns (*agent*): Cantor Josef Rosenblatt; William Demarest (*Buster Billings*); Richard Tucker (*Harry Lee*); Myrna Loy, Audrey Ferris (*chorus girls*).

Songs: "My Gal Sal" (Paul Dresser) – Gordon/ "Waiting for the Robert E. Lee" (Lewis Muir-L. Wolfe Gilbert) – Gordon/ "Kol Nidre" (trad.) – Oland (Diskay); reprised by Jolson/ "Dirty Hands, Dirty Face" (James Monaco-Edgar Leslie, Grant Clarke) – Jolson/ "Toot, Toot, Tootsie! (Goo'bye)" (Ted FioRito, Robert King-Gus Kahn) – Jolson/ "Kaddish" (trad.) – Rosenblatt/ "Blue Skies" (Irving Berlin) – Jolson/ "Mother of Mine, I Still Have You" (Louis Silvers-Clarke) – Jolson/ "My Mammy" (Walter Donaldson-Sam Lewis, Joe Young) – Jolson. Unused: "It All Depends on You."

Though Edison had experimented with combining film and sound, and talking pictures had been unveiled as early as 1900 at the Paris Exposition, movies with soundtracks were only sporadically attempted—and only as short subjects—until 1926. That year, Warner Bros., after securing the Vitaphone sound process from Western Electric, offered the silent feature *Don Juan* with an orchestra soundtrack on the same program with an assortment of musical shorts. A second program the same year included separate singing appearances by Al Jolson and George Jessel.

Under Sam Warner's leadership, the studio chose *The Jazz Singer,* a successful Broadway play, as its first feature-length release with audible songs and bits of dialogue. The play, which had been based on a story with a main character modeled after Al Jolson, starred George Jessel, who was signed by Warner to re-create his role before the decision was made to add sound. When that decision was made, Jessel withdrew because he wanted more money, and Jolson replaced him in the part of Jakie Rabinowitz, the cantor's son who runs away from home to become jazz singer Jack Robin. After his father dies, however, the singer gives up his big chance on Broadway and returns to take over the cantor's duties in the synagogue. For the screen version, a new ending was tacked on showing Jack, some time later, in a Broadway musical called *The Jazz Singer* belting out a mammy number to his beaming mammy.

The first spoken words heard in the film occur when Jolson, after singing "Dirty Hands, Dirty Face," tells his audience, "Wait a minute, wait a minute. You ain't heard nothin' yet . . ." and introduces his next number, "Toot, Toot, Tootsie!" The movie's only spoken dialogue takes place between the singer and his mother when he returns home briefly and tells her all the things he will do for her after he becomes a success. The historic opening of *The Jazz Singer* was on October 6, 1927, at the Warners Theatre in New York.

About a year and a half after the film's release, Jessel appeared in *Lucky Boy,* his own part-sound variation on the jazz-singer theme. In 1945, Warner had to abandon a planned remake of *The Jazz Singer* because there would be too many similarities with Columbia's forthcoming biography *The Jolson Story.* The Warner studio finally did make the second screen version seven years later with Danny Thomas, Peggy Lee, and Eduard Franz (as the cantor). A third version, in 1980, co-starred Neil Diamond and Cantor Laurence Olivier. Bib: *The Jazz Singer* ed. Robert L. Carringer (1979).

Jean, Gloria (née Gloria Jean Schoonover), actress, singer; b. Buffalo, April 14, 1928. Universal's teenage singing backup for Deanna Durbin was a cheery, kid-next-door type who appeared in support of Bing Crosby (in *If I Had My Way*) and W. C. Fields (in nonmusical *Never Give a Sucker an Even Break*).

1939	The Underpup (*Pip-Emma*)
1940	If I Had My Way (*Patricia Johnson*)
	A Little Bit of Heaven (*Midge*)
1942	What's Cookin'? (*Sue*)
	Get Hep to Love (*Doris Stanley*)
	When Johnny Comes Marching Home (*Marilyn*)
1943	Cinderella Swings It
	Mr. Big (*Patricia*)
	Moonlight in Vermont (*Gwen Harding*)
1944	Follow the Boys (specialty)

	Pardon My Rhythm (*Jinx Page*)
	The Ghost Catchers (*Melinda*)
	The Reckless Age (*Linda Wadsworth*)
1945	I'll Remember April (*April*)
	Easy to Look At (*Judy*)
1947	Copacabana (*Anne*)
1948	I Surrender, Dear
1949	Manhattan Angel
	There's a Girl in My Heart (*Ruth Kroner*)
	An Old-Fashioned Girl (*Polly Milton*)

"Jeepers Creepers" Music by Harry Warren; lyric by Johnny Mercer. Louis Armstrong introduced this rhythmic tribute to ophthalmic appeal in *Going Places* (Warner 1938). In the film, Jeepers Creepers was the name of a race horse who won the big race only when Armstrong and his band rode in a wagon alongside the track and serenaded the animal with its favorite song. It was also sung by Charles Smith in *Yankee Doodle Dandy* (Warner 1942); and by a group of diners in *The Cheap Detective* (Col. 1978).

Jessel, George (Albert), actor, singer, producer, lyricist; b. New York, April 3, 1898; d. May 24, 1981. Cigar-chomping raconteur and actor, Jessel won Broadway fame for his performance in *The Jazz Singer.* In Hollywood he was a producer at Fox between 1945 and 1953, overseeing musicals starring Betty Grable, June Haver, and Mitzi Gaynor. Also wrote songs with composer Ben Oakland. Bib: *So Help Me* (1943) and *The World I Lived In* (1976), both by Jessel.

Asterisk indicates Mr. Jessel was producer:

1929	Lucky Boy (*Georgie Jessel*)
	Love, Live and Laugh (*Luigi*)
1930	Happy Days (*minstrel chorus*)
1943	Stage Door Canteen (guest bit)
1944	Four Jills in a Jeep (*M.C.*)
1945	The Dolly Sisters *
1946	Do You Love Me? *
1947	I Wonder Who's Kissing Her Now *
1948	When My Baby Smiles at Me *
1949	Oh, You Beautiful Doll *
	Dancing in the Dark *
1951	Meet Me After the Show *
	The Golden Girl *
1952	Wait Till the Sun Shines, Nellie *
	Bloodhounds of Broadway *
1953	Tonight We Sing *
	The "I Don't Care" Girl * (also narrator)
1957	Beau James (*George Jessel*)
1959	Juke Box Rhythm (guest bit)

"Jingle Jangle Jingle" Music by Joseph Lilley; lyric by Frank Loesser. Rollicking number—the title refers to the sound of spurs—sung by rangers, led by Fred MacMurray, in nonmusical *The Forest Rangers* (Par. 1942).

"Jockey on the Carrousel, The" Music by Jerome Kern; lyric by Dorothy Fields. In *I Dream Too Much* (RKO 1935), while whirling about on a merry-go-round, Lily Pons grants the request of a jolly male quartet by relating "a story that my *maman* used to tell": all about a jockey figure on a carrousel horse who dies while reaching for a ring for his beloved dancing doll.

Johnson, (Charles) Van, actor; b. Newport, RI, Aug. 25, 1916. Sandy-haired, freckled actor who projected youthful sincerity in MGM nonmusicals and musicals. Co-starred with Esther Williams in four films, others with Judy Garland (*In the Good Old Summertime*), June Allyson, Kathryn Grayson.

1940   Too Many Girls (*student*)
1944   Two Girls and a Sailor (*John Dyckman III*)
1945   Thrill of a Romance (*Thomas Milvaine*)
1946   Easy To Wed (*Bill Chandler*)
       No Leave, No Love (*Sgt. Michael Hanlon*)
       Till the Clouds Roll By (specialty)
1949   In the Good Old Summertime (*Andy Larkin*)
1950   The Duchess of Idaho (*Dick Layn*)
       Grounds for Marriage (*Dr. Lincoln Bartlett*)
1953   Easy To Love (*Ray Lloyd*)
1955   Brigadoon (*Jeff Douglass*)
1957   The Pied Piper of Hamlin (tv) (*Pied Piper*)
       Kelly and Me (*Len Carmody*)

Johnston, Arthur (James), composer; b. New York, Jan. 10, 1898; d. Corona del Mar, Cal., May 1, 1954. Former theatre pianist and amanuensis for Irving Berlin, whose Hollywood songs were sung by Bing Crosby ("The Day You Came Along," "Down the Old Ox Road," "Learn To Croon," "Thanks," "One, Two, Button Your Shoe," "Pennies from Heaven," "All You Want To Do Is Dance," "The Moon Got in My Eyes"); Kate Smith ("Moon Song"); Carl Brisson and Kitty Carlisle ("Cocktails for Two"); Mae West ("My Old Flame"); and Dick Powell ("Thanks a Million"). Johnston, who worked mostly at Paramount with lyricist Sam Coslow, also wrote songs with Gus Kahn and Johnny Burke.

1933   Hello, Everybody (Coslow)
       College Humor (Coslow)
       Too Much Harmony (Coslow)
1934   Murder at the Vanities (Coslow)
       Many Happy Returns (Coslow)
       Belle of the Nineties (Coslow)
1935   The Girl Friend (Kahn)
       Thanks a Million (Kahn)
1936   Go West Young Man (Burke)
       Pennies from Heaven (Burke)
1937   Double or Nothing (Burke)

Johnston, Johnny, actor, singer; b. St. Louis, Dec. 1, 1915. Former radio and band singer who introduced "That Old Black Magic" in *Star Spangled Rhythm*. Has also appeared on Broadway (*A Tree Grows in Brooklyn*) and in nightclubs; was once married to Kathryn Grayson.

1942   Sweater Girl (*Johnny Arnold*)
       Priorities on Parade (*Johnny Draper*)
       Star Spangled Rhythm (specialty)
1944   You Can't Ration Love (*John*)
1946   This Time for Keeps (*Dick Johnson*)
1956   Rock Around the Clock (*Steve Hollis*)

"Joint Is Really Jumpin' in Carnegie Hall, The" Music & lyric by Roger Edens, Ralph Blane, and Hugh Martin. Bouncing account of the invasion of the venerable concert hall by swing bands. Introduced as part of an all-star variety show in *Thousands Cheer* (MGM 1943) by Judy Garland, accompanied by José Iturbi.

"Jolly Holiday" Music & lyric by Richard M. Sherman & Robert B. Sherman. Jolly number used as theme for fantasy section in *Mary Poppins* (Disney 1964), combining live actors with animated cartoons. As Mary Poppins, Julie Andrews, escorting her two charges, Karin Dotrice and Matthew Garber, comes upon her friend Bert, played by Dick Van Dyke, a sidewalk chalk artist. After the children have expressed admiration for a picture of an English countryside, Julie and Dick sing of the jolly holiday they will have there. Then, miraculously, the foursome go right through the picture and into the country where they sing with cartoon butterflies and farm animals. Julie and Dick perform a song-and-dance number, then find an outdoor tea restaurant where Dick dances with and imitates four penguin waiters.

"Jolly Tar and the Milkmaid, The" Music by George Gershwin; lyric by Ira Gershwin. A mock 18th-century

English ballad about a British sailor whose marriage proposal is declined by a maid since she's already married and the mother of three. The sailor then admits that he already has three wives, in Kerry, Spain, and Timbuktu. Introduced by Fred Astaire, Jan Duggan, Mary Dean, Pearl Amatore, Betty Rome, and Madrigal Singers at Totleigh Castle in *A Damsel in Distress* (RKO 1937).

Jolson, Al (né Asa Yoelson), actor, singer; b. Srednik, Russia, May 26, 1886 (?); d. San Francisco, Oct. 23, 1950. Jolson was a propulsive, compulsive entertainer who'd been one of Broadway's most celebrated attractions when he starred in Warner's first full-length part-talkie, *The Jazz Singer*. He also appeared in two screen versions of his stage hits (*Big Boy* and *The Wonder Bar*), the offbeat *Hallelujah, I'm a Bum*, and co-starred with Ruby Keeler, the third of his four wives, in *Go Into Your Dance*. Among the songs he sang in films were "There's a Rainbow 'Round My Shoulder," "Sonny Boy," "Let Me Sing and I'm Happy," "You Are Too Beautiful," "About a Quarter to Nine," "She's a Latin from Manhattan," and "Anniversary Song." His singing voice was used on the soundtrack of two movie bios, *The Jolson Story* and *Jolson Sings Again*, both with Larry Parks as Jolson. Bib: *The Immortal Jolson* by Pearl Seiben (1962); *Jolson* by Michael Freedland (1972); *Al Jolson* by Robert Oberfirst (1980).

Asterisk indicates brief appearance by Mr. Jolson:

1927 The Jazz Singer (*Jack Robin*)
1928 The Singing Fool (*Al Stone*)
1929 Say It with Songs (*Joe Lane*)
1930 Mammy (*Al Fuller*)/
     Show Girl in Hollywood*
     Big Boy (*Gus*)
1933 Hallelujah, I'm a Bum (*Bumper*)
1934 Wonder Bar (*Al Wonder*)
1935 Go Into Your Dance (*Al Howard*)
1936 The Singing Kid (*Al Jackson*)
1939 Rose of Washington Square (*Ted Cotter*)
     Swanee River (*E. P. Christy*)
1945 Rhapsody in Blue (*Al Jolson*)
1946 The Jolson Story* (vocals for Larry Parks)
1949 Jolson Sings Again (vocals for Larry Parks)

Jolson Story, The (1946). Screenplay by Sidney Buchman (uncredited), Stephen Longstreet, based on life of Al Jolson.

A Columbia film produced by Sidney Skolsky; directed by Alfred E. Green; choreography, Jack Cole, Joseph Lewis; art directors, Stephen Gooson, Walter Holscher; costumes, Jean Louis; music director, Morris Stoloff; associate music director, Saul Chaplin; orchestrations, Martin Fried; cameraman, Joseph Walker; editor, William Lyons; Technicolor.

Cast: Larry Parks (vocals by Al Jolson) (*Al Jolson né Asa Yoelson*); Evelyn Keyes (*Julie Benson*); William Demarest (*Steven Martin*); Ludwig Donath (*Cantor Yoelson*); Tamara Shayne (*Mrs. Yoelson*); Bill Goodwin (*Tom Baron*); Ernest Cossart (*Father McGee*); John Alexander (*Lew Dockstader*); Jo-Carroll Dennison (*Anne Murray*); Scotty Beckett (*Al Jolson as a boy*); Ann E. Todd (*Anne Murray as a girl*); Edwin Maxwell (*Oscar Hammerstein*); Eddie Kane (*Florenz Ziegfeld*); Robert Mitchell Boychoir.

Songs: "Let Me Sing and I'm Happy" (Irving Berlin) - Jolson/ "On the Banks of the Wabash" (Paul Dresser) - Beckett/ "Sabbath Prayer" - Beckett, Boychoir/ "Ave Maria" (Schubert-Scott) - Beckett, Boychoir/ "When You Were Sweet Sixteen" (James Thornton) - Beckett/ "After the Ball" (Charles Harris) - Beckett/ "By the Light of the Silvery Moon" (Gus Edwards-Edward Madden) - Beckett/ "Goodbye, My Blue Bell" - Beckett/ "Ma Blushin' Rosie" (John Stromberg-Edgar Smith)*/ "I Want a Girl Just Like the Girl That Married Dear Old Dad" (Harry Von Tilzer-Will Dillon)*, chorus/ "My Mammy" (Walter Donaldson-Sam Lewis, Joe Young)*/ "I'm Sittin' on Top of the World" (Ray Henderson-Lewis, Young)*/ "You Made Me Love You" (James V. Monaco-Joseph McCarthy)*/ "Swanee" (George Gershwin-Irving Caesar) - Jolson/ "Toot, Toot, Tootsie! (Goo'bye)" (Ted Fio Rito, Robert King, Gus Kahn)*/ "The Spaniard That Blighted My Life" (Billy Merson)*, chorus/ "April Showers" (Louis Silvers-B. G. DeSylva)*/ "California, Here I Come" (Joseph Meyer-DeSylva)*/ "Liza" (Gershwin-Gershwin, Kahn)*, dance by Keyes, chorus/ "There's a Rainbow 'Round My Shoulder" (Dave Dreyer-Billy Rose) - Jolson/ "She's a Latin form Manhattan" (Harry Warren-Al Dubin) - chorus, dance by Keyes/ "Avalon" (Vincent Rose-Jolson) - Jolson/ "About a Quarter to Nine" (Warren-Dubin)*/ "Anniversary Song" (Ion Ivanovici-Chaplin, Jolson)*/ "Waiting for the Robert E. Lee" (Lewis Muir-Wolfe Gilbert)*/ "Rockabye Your Baby with a Dixie Melody" (Jean Schwartz-Lewis, Young)*. Unused: "Who Paid the Rent for Mrs. Rip Van Winkle?," "Carolina in the Morning," "Sonny Boy." (*Indicates Parks on screen with Jolson's dubbed voice.)

For many years, Sidney Skolsky, a Hollywood columnist, tried in vain to interest the major studios in a film based on the life of Al Jolson. Eventually, Columbia's Harry Cohn, a Jolson fan, agreed to do it, with Larry Parks as Jolson (after Richard Conte, Danny Thomas, and José Ferrer had been among those tested) and Jolson dubbing the songs on the soundtrack (though in a long shot he is shown onscreen doing "Swanee"). *The Jolson Story* was a fictionalized, sentimental account of the entertainer's life (Ruby Keeler, here called Julie Benson, was his third not his first wife), with songs frequently presented out of sequence, but it became an immensely popular attraction and was directly responsible for the resurgence of Jolson's career.

Primarily in the early sequences there are similarities between this film and the 1927 *The Jazz Singer,* which had starred Jolson in a role suggested by his own life. In both films, a young Jewish boy is reprimanded by his father, a cantor, for singing secular songs in public. The boy then runs away from home to become an entertainer, sings such numbers as "My Mammy" and "Toot, Toot, Tootsie," falls in love with a dancer not of his faith, and becomes a success. But in the first movie, the father never becomes reconciled to his son's career and, when he dies, is replaced by his son in the synagogue. In the second, Papa Yoelson (contrary to Jolson's real father) basks in Al's success and, at the end of the picture, happily celebrates his 50th wedding anniversary.

A sequel to *The Jolson Story,* titled *Jolson Sings Again,* was released by Columbia in 1949, with Parks again as Jolson and Jolson again as his own singing voice. Written and produced by Sidney Buchman and directed by Henry Levin, the film covered Jolson's career entertaining troops during World War II, his remarriage to a nurse (played by Barbara Hale), and the making of *The Jolson Story* (which included a scene of Larry Parks as Jolson meeting Larry Parks as the actor who will portray him on the screen). William Demarest, Ludwig Donath, Tamara Shayne, and Bill Goodwin repeated their original roles in the picture. Al Jolson was also played on the screen by Norman Brooks in *The Best Things in Life Are Free* (Fox 1956), the story of De-Sylva, Brown, and Henderson.

Jones, Allan, actor, singer; b. Scranton, Pa., 1907. Round-faced, wavy-haired tenor—something of an alternate to Nelson Eddy—he appeared opposite Irene Dunne (*Show Boat*), Kitty Carlisle (*A Night at the Opera*), Jeanette MacDonald (*The Firefly*), and Mary Martin (*The Great Victor Herbert*). Jones was under contract to MGM through 1938; beginning in 1940 he was with Universal. The former husband of actress Irene Hervey and father of singer Jack Jones, he introduced "Alone," "Cosi-Cosa," and "The Donkey Serenade." After his film career, he became a nightclub singer.

1935 Reckless (*Allan*)
     A Night at the Opera (*Ricardo Baroni*)
1936 Rose Marie (opera singer)
     The Great Ziegfeld (vocal for Dennis Morgan)
     Show Boat (*Gaylord Ravenal*)
1937 A Day at the Races (*Gil Stewart*)
     The Firefly (*Don Diego Manrique de Lara*)
1938 Everybody Sing (*Ricky Saboni*)
1939 The Great Victor Herbert (*John Ramsey*)
     Honeymoon in Bali (*Eric Sinclair*)
1940 The Boys from Syracuse (*Antipholus of Ephesus/Antipholus of Syracuse*)
     One Night in the Tropics (*Jim Moore*)
1941 There's Magic in Music (*Michael Maddy*)
1942 True to the Army (*Pvt. Bill Chandler*)
     Moonlight in Havana (*Whizzer Norton*)
     When Johnny Comes Marching Home (*Johnny Kovacs*)
1943 Rhythm of the Islands (*Tommy*)
     You're a Lucky Fellow, Mr. Smith (*Tony*)
     Larceny with Music (*Ken Daniels*)
     Crazy House (specialty)
1944 Sing a Jingle (*Ray King*)
1945 Senorita from the West (*Phil Bradley*)
     Honeymoon Ahead (*Orpheus*)
1965 A Swingin' Summer (*Johnson*)

Jones, Shirley (Mae), actress, singer; b. Smithton, Pa., March 31, 1934. Miss Jones went to Hollywood to star as the demure heroine of two Rodgers and Hammerstein films, *Oklahoma!* and *Carousel,* both opposite Gordon MacRae; later she turned to more dramatic work in films and television. Once married to the late actor Jack Cassidy, she is the stepmother of singer David Cassidy and the mother of Shaun Cassidy.

1955 Oklahoma! (*Laurey Williams*)
1956 Carousel (*Julie Jordan Bigelow*)
1957 April Love (*Liz Templeton*)
1959 Never Steal Anything Small (*Linda Cabot*)
1960 Pepe (*Suzie Murphy*)
1962 The Music Man (*Marian Paroo*)

"Joobalai" Music by Ralph Rainger; lyric by Leo Robin. Jumpy gypsy melody ("straight from Romany") sung in *Paris Honeymoon* (Par. 1939) by Bing Crosby and Franciska Gaal.

"Journey to a Star, A" Music by Harry Warren; lyric by Leo Robin. Ballad of romantic propinquity offered in *The Gang's All Here* (Fox 1943) on three occasions: 1) on the deck of a Staten Island ferry by Alice Faye to James Ellison as a song she will introduce in a new nightclub revue; 2) as part of a benefit show at a country estate, again sung by Miss Faye, this time accompanied by Benny Goodman's orchestra and danced by Tony DeMarco and Sheila Ryan; 3) as the film's Busby Berkeley finale, with the heads of the movie's leading actors poking through colored screens as each sings a line of the song.

"June Comes Around Every Year" Music by Harold Arlen; lyric by Johnny Mercer. Bing Crosby's voice (dubbed for Eddie Bracken's) sang of the annual rekindling of the romantic spark in *Out of This World* (Par. 1945).

"June in January" Music by Ralph Rainger; lyric by Leo Robin. When you're in love, sang Bing Crosby in *Here Is My Heart* (Par. 1934), the snow is just white blossoms and there's always spring in your heart.

Jurmann, Walter, composer; b. Austria, Oct. 12, 1903; d. Budapest, June 24, 1971. Jurmann scored many films and, with co-composer Bronislaw Kaper, wrote the music to "Cosi-Cosa" (in *A Night at the Opera*), "Someone To Care for Me," and "All God's Chillun Got Rhythm." Lyrics to his songs were supplied by Al Dubin, Ned Washington, Gus Kahn, and Paul Francis Webster.

1931	Her Majesty Love (Dubin)	
1937	Three Smart Girls (Kaper-Kahn)	
	A Day at the Races (Kaper-Kahn)	
1938	Everybody Sing (Kaper-Kahn)	
1943	Presenting Lily Mars (Webster)	

"Just Let Me Look at You" Music by Jerome Kern; lyric by Dorothy Fields. Ballad of speechless adulation introduced in *Joy of Living* (RKO 1938) by Irene Dunne, who sang it in three different scenes: 1) at home, where it's being rehearsed as a new number slated to go into a Broadway musical *after* it had already opened; 2) in a limousine, where it's overheard by madcap Douglas Fairbanks, Jr., who's hitched a ride on the automobile's baggage rack; 3) in court, where it's seductively sung to the judge. Melodically, the song is reminiscent of Tchaikowsky's "None but the Lonely Heart." The third Kern-Fields "look" song, "Just Let Me Look at You" followed "Lovely to Look At" (*Roberta*) and "The Way You Look Tonight" (*Swing Time*).

"Just You, Just Me" Music by Jesse Greer; lyric by Raymond Klages. Bouncy invitation to cuddle and coo offered by Marion Davies and Lawrence Grey in *Marianne* (MGM 1929). Also sung by Liza Minnelli in *New York, New York* (UA 1977).

K

Kahal, Irving, lyricist; b. Houtzdale, Pa., March 5, 1903; d. New York, July 2, 1942. Kahal teamed with composer Sammy Fain for such hits as "You Brought a New Kind of Love to Me" (Pierre Norman was the co-composer) in *The Big Pond,* and "By a Waterfall" in *Footlight Parade.* Maurice Chevalier, Dick Powell, and Rudy Vallee introduced his songs in movies.

1930　Young Man of Manhattan (Fain, Norman)
1933　Footlight Parade (Fain)
　　　College Coach (Fain)
1934　Harold Teen (Fain)
1935　Sweet Music (Fain)

Kahn, Gus, lyricist; b. Coblenz, Germany, Nov. 6, 1886; d. Beverly Hills, Oct. 8, 1941. Also active in Tin Pan Alley, vaudeville, and Broadway musicals (his most successful, *Whoopee,* was the only one transferred to the screen), Kahn wrote lyrics in Hollywood to the music of a wide array of composers: Walter Donaldson ("My Baby Just Cares for Me"); Vincent Youmans ("Flying Down to Rio," "The Carioca," "Orchids in the Moonlight," all with Edward Eliscu as co-lyricist); Victor Schertzinger ("One Night of Love"); Werner Heymann; Arthur Johnston ("Thanks a Million"); Victor Herbert; Bronislaw Kaper and Walter Jurmann ("Someone To Care for Me," "All God's Chillun Got Rhythm"); Kaper alone ("San Francisco"); Sigmund Romberg; Harry Warren; Tchaikovsky; Robert Stolz; Earl Brent; Nacio Herb Brown ("You Stepped Out of a Dream"); Noël Coward. Eddie Cantor, Fred Astaire, Ethel Merman, Dick Powell, Allan Jones, Deanna Durbin, Jeanette MacDonald, Judy Garland, Nelson Eddy, Tony Martin, and Doris Day were among those who sang Kahn lyrics on the screen. Film bio: *I'll See You in My Dreams,* with Danny Thomas as Kahn.

1930　Whoopee (Donaldson)
1933　Flying Down to Rio (Youmans-Eliscu)

1934　Caravan (Heymann)
　　　Kid Millions (Donaldson)
　　　Operator 13 (Donaldson)
1935　Naughty Marietta (Herbert)
　　　The Girl Friend (Johnston)
　　　Thanks a Million (Johnston)
1937　Three Smart Girls (Kaper, Jurmann)
　　　A Day at the Races (Kaper, Jurmann)
1938　Everybody Sing (Kaper, Jurmann)
　　　The Girl of the Golden West (Romberg)
1939　Honolulu (Warren)
　　　Broadway Serenade (Tchaikovsky; Romberg; Donaldson)
1940　Spring Parade (Stolz, etc.)
　　　Go West (Brent; Kaper)
1941　Bitter Sweet (Coward)
1951　I'll See You in My Dreams (Donaldson, etc.)

Kalmar, Bert, lyricist, screen writer; b. New York, Feb. 16, 1884; d. Los Angeles, Sept. 18, 1947. Kalmar and his lifetime partner, composer Harry Ruby, wrote the scores for nine Broadway musicals, including three that were filmed: *The Ramblers* (retitled *The Cuckoos*), *Animal Crackers* (starring the Marx Brothers), and *Top Speed.* They also wrote two other Marx Brothers movies, *Horse Feathers* and *Duck Soup,* and their songs were sung on the screen by Bert Wheeler ("I Love You So Much"), Bing Crosby ("Three Little Words"), Eddie Cantor, Judy Garland, and Louis Armstrong ("A Kiss To Build a Dream On," written with Oscar Hammerstein II). Film bio: *Three Little Words,* with Fred Astaire as Kalmar.

All songs for the following were written with Mr. Ruby; asterisk indicates partners also wrote script:
1930　The Cuckoos
　　　Animal Crackers
　　　Top Speed
　　　Check and Double Check

1932	Horse Feathers*
	The Kid from Spain*
1933	Duck Soup*
1934	Hips Hips Hooray*
1936	Walking on Air*
1938	Everybody Sing
1950	Three Little Words

Kander and Ebb. John (Harold) Kander, composer; b. Kansas City, Mo., March 18, 1927. Fred Ebb, lyricist; b. New York, April 8, 1932. So-far inseparable songwriting team whose only Broadway musical transferred to the screen to date has been *Cabaret*. They have also created film songs for Barbra Streisand ("How Lucky Can You Get?") and Liza Minnelli ("New York, New York").

1972	Cabaret
1975	Funny Lady
1976	A Matter of Time
1977	New York, New York

Kane, Helen (née Helen Schroeder), actress, singer; b. New York, Aug. 4, 1904; d. Queens, NY, Sept. 26, 1966. Round-faced, "boop-boop-a-doop"-squealing vaudeville and Broadway headliner who was seen in early talkies; later played by Debbie Reynolds in *Three Little Words*.

1929	Sweetie (*Helen Fry*)
	Pointed Heels (*Dot Nixon*)
1930	Paramount on Parade (specialty)
	Heads Up (*Betty Trumbull*)
	Dangerous Nan McGrew (*Nan McGrew*)
1950	Three Little Words (vocal for Debbie Reynolds)

Kaper, Bronislaw, composer; b. Warsaw, Feb. 5, 1902. Scored many nonmusical films (*Gaslight, Mutiny on the Bounty,* etc.) and films with extended ballets (*Lili, The Glass Slipper*), mostly at MGM. With co-composer Walter Jurmann he wrote music for "Cosi-Cosa" (lyric by Ned Washington) in *A Night at the Opera*, "Someone To Care for Me" (Gus Kahn) in *Three Smart Girls,* and "All God's Chillun Got Rhythm" (Kahn) in *A Day at the Races.* Alone, Kaper composed "San Francisco" (Kahn) for *San Francisco,* and "Hi Lili, Hi-Lo" (Helen Deutsch) in *Lili.* (Died Los Angeles, April 25, 1983.)

1937	Three Smart Girls (Jurmann-Kahn)
	A Day at the Races (Jurmann-Kahn)
1938	Everybody Sing (Jurmann-Kahn)
1953	Lili (Deutsch)
1955	The Glass Slipper (Deutsch)

Kasznar, Kurt (né Kurt Serwicher), actor; b. Vienna, Aug. 12, 1913; d. Santa Monica, Aug. 6, 1979. Dark-haired, rotund actor with ability to project both worldliness and warmth in appearances on screen and stage. Kasznar, who came to the US in the mid-30s with director Max Reinhardt, was also a producer and playwright.

1952	Lovely To Look At (*Max Foglesby*)
	Glory Alley (*Gus Evans*)
1953	Lili (*Jacquot*)
	Sombrero (*Father Zacaya*)
	Kiss Me, Kate ("*Baptista*")
	Give a Girl a Break (*Leo Belney*)
1955	My Sister Eileen (*Appopolous*)
1956	Anything Goes (*Victor*)
1959	For the First Time (*Ladislas Tabori*)
1967	Androcles and the Lion (tv) (*manager of gladiators*)

Kaye, Danny (né David Daniel Kominsky), actor, singer, dancer; b. Brooklyn, Jan. 18, 1913. A slim, gracefully awkward comic actor, Kaye usually played the meek hero who eventually triumphs after a series of misadventures. To take advantage of his experience as a nightclub performer, he was often seen as an entertainer; to take advantage of his range, he frequently portrayed dual roles or dichotomous characters. Samuel Goldwyn produced six of his films, and Virginia Mayo and Vera-Ellen were his most frequent co-stars. Kaye introduced "Anywhere I Wander," "Thumbelina," and "No Two People" in *Hans Christian Andersen.* Bib: *The Danny Kaye Story* by Kurt Singer (1958). (Died Los Angeles, March 3, 1987.)

1944	Up in Arms (*Danny Weems*)
1945	Wonder Man (*Buster Dingle/ Buzzy Bellew*)
1946	The Kid from Brooklyn (*Burleigh Sullivan*)
1947	The Secret Life of Walter Mitty (*Walter Mitty*)
1948	A Song Is Born (*Prof. Hobart Frisbee*)
1949	It's a Great Feeling (guest bit)
	The Inspector General (*Georgi*)
1951	On the Riviera (*Jack Martin/Henri Duran*)
1952	Hans Christian Andersen (*Hans Christian Andersen*)
1954	Knock on Wood (*Jerry Morgan*)
	White Christmas (*Phil Davis*)
1956	The Court Jester (*Hubert Hawkins*)
1958	Merry Andrew (*Andrew Larrabee*)
1959	The Five Pennies (*Red Nichols*)
1961	On the Double (*Ernie Williams/ Gen. Mackenzie-Smith*)
1976	Peter Pan (tv) (*Capt, Hook/ Mr. Darling*)

Keel, (Harold Clifford) Howard, actor, singer; b. Gillespie, Ohio, April 13, 1917. After appearing on Broadway in *Carousel* and in London in *Oklahoma!,* Keel became MGM's major male singing star, appearing in remade Broadway hits opposite Betty Hutton, Kathryn Grayson, and Ann Blyth, and in original screen musicals opposite Esther Williams, Jane Powell (*Seven Brides for Seven Brothers*), and, in a loanout to Warner, Doris Day.

1950   Annie Get Your Gun (*Frank Butler*)
          Pagan Love Song (*Hazard Endicott*)
1951   Show Boat (*Gaylord Ravenal*)
          Texas Carnival (*Slim Shelby*)
1952   Lovely to Look At (*Tony Naylor*)
          I Love Melvin (guest bit)
1953   Calamity Jane (*Bill Hickock*)
          Kiss Me, Kate (*Fred Graham*)
1954   Rose Marie (*Sgt. Mike Malone*)
          Seven Brides for Seven Brothers (*Adam Pontipee*)
          Deep in My Heart (specialty)
1955   Jupiter's Darling (*Hannibal*)
          Kismet (*Hajj*)

Keeler, (Ethel Hilda) Ruby, actress, dancer, singer; b. Halifax, Nova Scotia, Aug. 25, 1909. Innocent-looking, blank-faced, buck-and-winging Ruby Keeler became a Warner attraction in nine musicals, seven of them with Dick Powell (including *42nd Street, Gold Diggers of 1933, Footlight Parade*). She also appeared with Al Jolson, to whom she was married at the time, in *Go Into Your Dance.* Either singing or tapping, she introduced such numbers as "Shuffle Off to Buffalo," "Forty-Second Street," "Honeymoon Hotel," "She's a Latin from Manhattan," and "Too Marvelous for Words." In 1971, Miss Keeler emerged from retirement to appear on the stage in *No, No, Nanette,* after a Broadway absence of 41 years.

Asterisk indicates appearance with Mr. Powell:
1930   Show Girl in Hollywood (guest bit)
1933   42nd Street* (*Peggy Sawyer*)
          Gold Diggers of 1933* (*Polly Parker*)
          Footlight Parade* (*Bea Thorn*)
1934   Dames* (*Barbara Hemingway*)
          Flirtation Walk* (*Kit Fits*)
1935   Go Into Your Dance (*Dorothy Wayne*)
          Shipmates Forever* (*June Blackburn*)
1936   Colleen* (*Colleen Reilly*)
1937   Ready, Willing and Able (*Jane*)
1941   Sweetheart of the Campus (*Betty Blake*)

"Keep Young and Beautiful" Music by Harry Warren; lyric by Al Dubin. In *Roman Scandals* (Goldwyn 1933), Eddie Cantor, dreaming he's in ancient Rome, lectures the ladies of the emperor's court on the importance of calisthenics and cosmetics ("If you're wise exercise all the fat off/ Take it off offa here offa there"). During the extended Busby Berkeley production number, the girls go through the prescribed instructions to ensure their allure.

"Keeping Myself for You" Music by Vincent Youmans; lyric by Sidney Clare. Ballad of romantic frustration written for the first film version of *Hit the Deck* (RKO 1930), in which it was sung by Polly Walker and Jack Oakie. Also sung in second film version (MGM 1955) by Ann Miller and girls chorus, and by Tony Martin.

Kelly, (Eugene Curran) Gene, actor, dancer, singer, choreographer, director; b. Pittsburgh, Aug. 23, 1912. Next to Fred Astaire, Gene Kelly was Hollywood's most innovative and influential dancer-choreographer, using an earthy, athletic style combining tap, acrobatics, and ballet. Some of his most inventive cinematic work was seen in *Cover Girl* (in which he danced with his alter ego), and in the 12 musicals he made for Arthur Freed's unit at MGM, including *Anchors Aweigh* (dancing in the cartoon sequence with a mouse), *The Pirate, On the Town* (using on-location scenes in New York for the first time), *An American in Paris* (the climactic ballet with its French Impressionist settings), *Singin' in the Rain* (doing and dancing just that), and *It's Always Fair Weather* (the skate dance). On six of these Kelly was associated with co-choreographer and/or co-director Stanley Donen; he also introduced such songs as "Long Ago and Far Away" and "Be a Clown." His romantic and dancing partners included Judy Garland (three films), Cyd Charisse (three), Kathryn Grayson (two), Vera-Ellen (two), Rita Hayworth, Esther Williams, Leslie Caron, Debbie Reynolds, Mitzi Gaynor, and Shirley MacLaine. He also hoofed with Frank Sinatra in three movies, Fred Astaire in two, and Donald O'Connor. Kelly's Hollywood career was launched after winning notice on Broadway acting in *Pal Joey* and choreographing *Best Foot Forward.* Bib: *Films of Gene Kelly* by Tony Thomas (1974); *Gene Kelly* by Clive Hirschhorn (1975).

Asterisk indicates Mr. Kelly was also choreographer or co-choreographer; dagger indicates he was also director or co-director:
1942   For Me and My Gal (*Harry Palmer*)*
1943   DuBarry Was a Lady (*Alec Howe*)
          Thousands Cheer (*Eddie Marsh*)

1944 Cover Girl (*Danny McGuire*)*
1945 Anchors Aweigh (*Joe Brady*)*
1946 Ziegfeld Follies (specialty)
1947 Living in a Big Way (*Leo Gogarty*)*
1948 The Pirate (*Serafin*)*
Words and Music (specialty)*
1949 Take Me Out to the Ball Game (*Eddie O'Brien*) (also script)*
On the Town (*Gabey*)*†
1950 Summer Stock (*Joe Ross*)*
1951 An American in Paris (*Jerry Mulligan*)*
1952 Singin' in the Rain (*Don Lockwood*)*†
1954 Brigadoon (*Tommy Albright*)*
Deep in My Heart (specialty)*
1955 It's Always Fair Weather (*Ted Riley*)*†
1956 Invitation to the Dance (various)*†
1957 Les Girls (*Barry Nichols*)
1960 Let's Make Love (*Gene Kelly*)
1964 What a Way To Go (*Pinky Benson*)*
1967 The Young Girls of Rochefort (*Andy Miller*)
1969 Hello, Dolly! (dir. only)
1974 That's Entertainment (narrator)
1976 That's Entertainment Part 2 (narrator)†
1980 Xanadu (*Danny McGuire*)
1985 That's Dancing! (narrator)

Kelly, (Sarah Veronica Rose) Patsy, actress; b. Brooklyn, Jan. 12, 1910. Disenchanted wisecracking comedienne, usually seen as a domestic or secretary who made successful Broadway comeback in *No, No, Nanette* (1971) and *Irene* (1973). (Died Sept. 25, 1981.)

1933 Going Hollywood (*Jill Barker*)
1935 Go Into Your Dance (*Irma*)
Every Night at Eight (*Daphne O'Connor*)
Thanks a Million (*Phoebe Mason*)
1936 Sing, Baby, Sing (*Fitz*)
Pigskin Parade (*Bessie Winters*)
1937 Nobody's Baby (*Kitty*)
Wake Up and Live (*Patsy Kane*)
Ever Since Eve (*Nellie Moore*)
1940 Hit Parade of 1941 (*Judy Abbott*)
1941 Road Show (*Jinx*)
Playmates (*Lulu Monahan*)
1942 Sing Your Worries Away (*Bebe*)

Kern, Jerome (David), composer; b. New York, Jan. 27, 1885; d. New York, Nov. 11, 1945. Kern was a master melodist whose stage scores influenced George Gershwin and Richard Rodgers, among others, and whose productions, beginning in the mid-1910s, helped pioneer the modern musical theatre. Eight of the composer's 38 Broadway musicals were filmed: *Sally; Sunny* (twice); *Show Boat* (three times); *Sweet Adeline; The Cat and the Fiddle; Music in the Air; Roberta* (twice, the second retitled *Lovely To Look At*); and *Very Warm for May* (retitled *Broadway Rhythm*, with only one Kern song retained). In Hollywood, Kern's major original musicals were *Swing Time*, with lyricist Dorothy Fields ("A Fine Romance," "The Way You Look Tonight"); *High, Wide and Handsome*, with Oscar Hammerstein II ("The Folks Who Live on the Hill," "Can I Forget You?"); *You Were Never Lovelier*, with Johnny Mercer ("You Were Never Lovelier," "Dearly Beloved," "I'm Old-Fashioned"); *Cover Girl*, with Ira Gershwin ("Long Ago and Far Away"). Kern also wrote "Lovely To Look At" and "I Won't Dance" with Miss Fields, and "All Through the Day" with Hammerstein. Other movie collaborators were E. Y. Harburg ("Can't Help Singing," "More and More") and Leo Robin ("In Love in Vain").

Film stars who were associated with Kern songs include Jeanette MacDonald, Gloria Swanson, John Boles, Irene Dunne, Fred Astaire, Ginger Rogers, Lily Pons, Allan Jones, Paul Robeson, Helen Morgan, Anna Neagle, Ginny Simms, Gene Kelly, Rita Hayworth, Deanna Durbin, Howard Keel, and Kathryn Grayson. Film bio: *Till the Clouds Roll By*, with Robert Walker as Kern. Bib: *The Jerome Kern Song Book* (1955); *Jerome Kern: His Life and Music* by Gerald Bordman (1980).

1929 Show Boat (Hammerstein)
Sally (DeSylva; Grey)
1930 Sunny (Harbach, Hammerstein)
1934 The Cat and the Fiddle (Harbach)
Music in the Air (Hammerstein)
1935 Sweet Adeline (Hammerstein)
Roberta (Harbach; Fields)
I Dream Too Much (Fields)
1936 Show Boat (Hammerstein)
Swing Time (Fields)
1937 High, Wide and Handsome (Hammerstein)
1938 Joy of Living (Fields)
1940 One Night in the Tropics (Fields)
1941 Sunny (Harbach, Hammerstein)
1942 You Were Never Lovelier (Mercer)
1944 Cover Girl (Gershwin)
Can't Help Singing (Harburg)
1946 Centennial Summer (Robin, etc.)
Till the Clouds Roll By (misc.)
1951 Show Boat (Hammerstein)
1952 Lovely To Look At (Harbach; Fields)

Kidd, Michael (né Milton Greenwald), choreographer, director, actor, dancer; b. New York, Aug. 12, 1919. After dancing with the Ballet Theatre, Kidd became a

Broadway choreographer in 1947 with *Finian's Rainbow*. In Hollywood, his major work was staging the dances for *The Band Wagon, Seven Brides for Seven Brothers,* and *Guys and Dolls* (which he had choreographed for the stage).

Unless otherwise noted, Mr. Kidd was choreographer of the following:

1952 Where's Charley?
1953 The Girl Next Door
     The Band Wagon
1954 Knock on Wood
     Seven Brides for Seven Brothers
1955 It's Always Fair Weather (*Angie Valentine* only)
     Guys and Dolls
1958 Merry Andrew (also dir.)
1968 Star!
1969 Hello, Dolly!
1976 Peter Pan (tv) (also dir.)
1978 Movie Movie

King, Charles, actor, singer; b. New York, Oct. 31, 1889; d. London, Jan. 11, 1944. A breezy, song-and-dance man with a lengthy Broadway career, King made his major film appearance in *The Broadway Melody,* introducing the title song and "You Were Meant for Me." He also sang "Happy Days Are Here Again" in *Chasing Rainbows.*

1929 The Broadway Melody (*Eddie Kerns*)
     Hollywood Revue of 1929 (specialty)
1930 Chasing Rainbows (*Terry*)
     Oh, Sailor Behave (*Charlie Carroll*)

King, Henry, director; b. Christiansburg, Va., Jan. 24, 1892. Veteran Fox director who began his career in 1915, he covered a wide variety of themes and locales in his 49 feature-length sound films. (Died June 29, 1983.)

1933 I Love You Wednesday
1934 Marie Galante
1936 Ramona
1938 In Old Chicago
     Alexander's Ragtime Band
1946 Margie
1952 Wait Till the Sun Shines, Nellie
1956 Carousel

King and I, The (1956). Music by Richard Rodgers; lyrics by Oscar Hammerstein II; screenplay by Ernest Lehman from Broadway musical by Rodgers & Hammerstein based on *Anna and the King of Siam* by Margaret Landon and nonmusical film screenplay by Talbot

Jennings and Sally Benson, both derived from published diary of Anna Leonowens, *The English Governess at the Siamese Court.*

A 20th Century-Fox film produced by Charles Brackett; directed by Walter Lang; choreography, Jerome Robbins; art directors, Lyle Wheeler, John DeCuir; costumes, Irene Sharaff; music director, Alfred Newman; orchestrations, Edward Powell, Gus Levene, Bernard Mayers, Robert Russell Bennett; cameraman, Leon Shamroy; editor, Robert Simpson; DeLuxe Color; CinemaScope 55.

Cast: Deborah Kerr (vocals by Marni Nixon) (*Anna Leonowens*); Yul Brynner (*King Somdetch P'hra Paaremndr Maha Mongkut*); Rita Moreno (*Tuptim*); Terry Saunders (*Lady Thiang*); Carlos Rivas (vocals by Reuben Fuentes) (*Lun Tha*); Martin Benson (*Kralahome*); Rex Thompson (*Louis Leonowens*); Patrick Adiarte (*Prince Chulalongkorn*); Alan Mowbray (*Sir John Haig*); Geoffrey Toone (*Sir Edward Ramsay*); Yuriko ("*Eliza*"); Gemze deLappe ("*Simon of Legree*"); Dusty Worrall ("*Uncle Thomas*"); Michiko ("*Angel*").

Songs: "I Whistle a Happy Tune" - Kerr, Thompson/ "March of the Siamese Children" - orchestra/ "Hello, Young Lovers" - Kerr (Nixon)/ "A Puzzlement" - Brynner/ "Getting To Know You" - Kerr (Nixon), children/ "We Kiss in a Shadow" - Moreno, Rivas (Fuentes)/ "Shall I Tell You What I Think of You? - Kerr/ "Something Wonderful" - Saunders/ "The Small House of Uncle Thomas" (ballet) - Moreno; dance by Yuriko, Michiko, deLappe, Worrall, dancers/ "Song of the King" - Brynner/ "I Have Dreamed" - Moreno, Rivas (Fuentes)/ "Shall We Dance?" - Kerr (Nixon), Brynner. Unused: "My Lord and Master." "Western People Funny."

First the story was told as a diary by an English schoolteacher. Then it became a novel called *Anna and the King of Siam.* Then it was a movie version of the novel with Irene Dunne and Rex Harrison. Then it was a stage musical by Rodgers and Hammerstein starring Gertrude Lawrence and Yul Brynner. Finally, it was a movie version of the Broadway musical starring Deborah Kerr and with Brynner repeating his original—and most closely identified—role. (Other repeaters were choreographer Robbins, costumer Sharaff, and dancers Yuriko, Michiko, de Lappe, and Worrall.) The original diary contained many characters and situations also found in subsequent versions. Primarily there was the love-hate relationship between Anna Leonowens—the Victorian teacher, whose ideal was Abraham Lincoln and who was unafraid to speak out against slavery and repression—and the semi-barbaric monarch who became increasingly dependent upon her. During her stay at the royal palace Mrs. Leonowens even helped one of the king's wives translate *Uncle Tom's Cabin,* and she was influential in having the crown prince abolish slavery once he ascended the throne.

As a stage work, *The King and I* ranks among the five most durable Rodgers and Hammerstein musicals, and its screen version—along with *The Sound of Music*—is considered the most successfully realized of all their shows. Apart from its fidelity to source, the movie utilized the opulent sets to give it the right touch of exotic stylization in the musical sequences, including the visually stunning ballet "The Small House of Uncle Thomas."

Kiss Me, Kate (1953). Music & lyrics by Cole Porter; screenplay by Dorothy Kingsley from Broadway musical by Samuel and Bella Spewack & Porter based (in part) on Shakespeare's *The Taming of the Shrew.*

An MGM film produced by Jack Cummings; directed by George Sidney; choreography, Hermes Pan, Bob Fosse; art directors, Cedric Gibbons, Urie McLeary; costumes, Walter Plunkett; music directors, André Previn, Saul Chaplin; orchestrations, Conrad Salinger, Skip Martin; vocal supervisor, Robert Tucker; cameraman, Charles Rosher; editor, Ralph Winters; Ansco Color.

Cast: Kathryn Grayson (*Lilli Vanessi*); Howard Keel (*Fred Graham*); Ann Miller (*Lois Lane*); Tommy Rall (*Bill Calhoun*); Keenan Wynn (*Lippy*); James Whitmore (*Slug*); Bobby Van (*"Gremio"*); Bob Fosse (*"Hortensio"*); Kurt Kasznar (*"Baptista"*); Ron Randall (*Cole Porter*); Willard Parker (*Tex Calloway*); Carol Haney (*dancer*); Claud Allister (*Paul*).

Songs: "So in Love" - Grayson, Keel/ "Too Darn Hot" - Miller/ "Why Can't You Behave?" - Miller; dance by Miller, Rall/ "Wunderbar" - Keel, Grayson/ "We Open in Venice" - Keel, Grayson, Miller, Rall/ "Tom, Dick or Harry" - Miller, Fosse, Rall, Van/ "I've Come To Wive It Wealthily in Padua" - Keel/ "I Hate Men" - Grayson/ "Were Thine That Special Face" - Keel/ "Where Is the Life That Late I Led?" - Keel/ "Always True to You (in My Fashion)" - Miller, Rall/ "Brush Up Your Shakespeare" - Wynn, Whitmore/ "From This Moment On" - Miller, Rall, Fosse, Van, Haney/ "Kiss Me, Kate" - Keel, Grayson. Unused: "Another Op'nin', Another Show," "I Am Ashamed That Women Are So Simple."

Cole Porter's most celebrated stage musical starred Alfred Drake and Patricia Morison as a recently divorced couple appearing in a musical production of Shakespeare's *The Taming of the Shrew,* with their offstage sparring complementing the onstage performance. On screen, the musical brought Kathryn Grayson and Howard Keel together for the third and last time in a movie version of a Broadway musical (the previous two: *Show Boat* and *Lovely To Look At,* another name for *Roberta*). One of few musicals to be shot in 3-D (that's why Keel sings "Where Is the Life That Late I Led?" on a runway jutting into the theatre audience), *Kiss Me, Kate* was the first screen adaptation of a Cole Porter show to be a more-or-less faithful reproduction—even though the censors changed "stuck a pig" to "met a bore" in one song and "virgin" to "maiden" in another. Among the film's highlights were the dancing sequences featuring Tommy Rall, Bobby Van, and Bob Fosse, who made his choreographic debut with a segment of the routine to "From This Moment On," a Porter song added to the score. One odd Hollywood touch was having an impersonated Cole Porter show up early in the film to help induce a reluctant Miss Grayson to appear in Keel's production.

Other film musicals based on stage musicals derived from Shakespearean plays were *The Boys from Syracuse* (1940) from *The Comedy of Errors* (1593), and *West Side Story* (1961) from *Romeo and Juliet* (1595).

"Kiss the Boys Goodbye" Music by Victor Schertzinger; lyric by Frank Loesser. A deliberate follow-up to Cole Porter's "My Heart Belongs to Daddy," which had helped Mary Martin make an auspicious debut in the Broadway musical, *Leave It to Me,* "Kiss the Boys Goodbye" was sung by Miss Martin in the 1941 Paramount film of the same name. Here the lady begs her "daddy" for permission for one final fling before their wedding in order to warn her beaux "that my heart belongs to you." Song was also sung by Shirley Booth in *About Mrs. Leslie* (Par. 1954).

"Kiss To Build a Dream On, A" Music by Harry Ruby; lyric by Bert Kalmar & Oscar Hammerstein II. A farewell kiss prompts the dream of a lasting romance in this ballad sung by Kay Brown and Louis Armstrong in *The Strip* (MGM 1951). The song had originally been written by Kalmar and Ruby alone under the title "Moonlight on the Meadow"; with Hammerstein's help they rewrote it for the Marx Brothers' film *A Night at the Opera,* but the piece was never used.

Koehler, Ted, lyricist; b. Washington, DC, July 14, 1894; d. Santa Monica, Jan. 17, 1973. Koehler wrote lyrics—to Harold Arlen's music—for three editions of the Cotton Club revues before settling in Hollywood. With partners Arlen, Ray Henderson, Irving Caesar, Jimmy McHugh, Sammy Stept, Burton Lane, and M. K. Jerome, he supplied songs for, among others, Ann Sothern (''Let's Fall in Love''), Shirley Temple (''Animal Crackers in My Soup''), Alice Faye (''I'm Shooting High''), and Dinah Shore (''Now I Know'').

1934   Let's Fall in Love (Arlen)
1935   Curly Top (Henderson-Caesar)
       King of Burlesque (McHugh)
1936   Dimples (McHugh)
1937   23½ Hours' Leave (Stept)
       Artists and Models (Lane; Arlen)
1943   Stormy Weather (script)
1944   Up in Arms (Arlen)
       Rainbow Island (Lane)
1947   My Wild Irish Rose (Jerome)

Kohlmar, Fred, producer; b. New York, Aug. 10, 1905; d. Hollywood, Oct. 13, 1969. Producer at Paramount, Fox, and Columbia who worked with Bing Crosby, Alice Faye, Betty Grable, Frank Sinatra, Rita Hayworth, and Ann-Margret among others.

1943   Let's Face It
       Riding High
1945   That Night in Rio
1948   You Were Meant for Me
1951   Call Me Mister
1953   Down Among the Sheltering Palms
1955   My Sister Eileen
1957   Pal Joey
1963   Bye Bye Birdie

''Kokomo, Indiana'' Music by Josef Myrow; lyric by Mack Gordon. Perky hymn to the simple life, introduced by vaudeville team Betty Grable and Dan Dailey—both wearing top hats and tails—in *Mother Wore Tights* (Fox 1947).

Korngold, Erich Wolfgang, composer; b. Brno, Austria, May 29, 1897; d. Hollywood, Nov. 29, 1957. Musical prodigy who won early fame with opera, *Die tote Stadt.* To Hollywood in 1935 to compose background music for Max Reinhardt's screen version of *A Midsummer Night's Dream;* remained to create lush scores for Warner epics such as *Anthony Adverse, Adventures of Robin Hood,* and *The Sea Hawk.* Joined lyricist Oscar Hammerstein II to write songs for a Paramount musical starring Gladys Swarthout.

1936   Give Us This Night (Hammerstein)

Koster, Henry (né Hermann Kosterlitz), director; b. Berlin, May 1, 1905. At Universal, he worked on six Deanna Durbin films, all of them for producer Joe Pasternak (for whom he also directed three other musicals). Koster also directed at MGM and Fox.

1937   Three Smart Girls
       100 Men and a Girl
1939   Three Smart Girls Grow Up
       First Love
1940   Spring Parade
1941   It Started with Eve
1944   Music for Millions
1946   Two Sisters from Boston
1947   The Unfinished Dance
1949   The Inspector General
1950   Wabash Avenue
       My Blue Heaven
1952   The Stars and Stripes Forever
1961   Flower Drum Song
1966   The Singing Nun

Krupa, Gene, bandleader, drummer; b. Chicago, Jan. 15, 1909; d. Yonkers, NY, Oct. 6, 1973. Flashy, gum-chewing drummer with Benny Goodman's orchestra who formed his own band in 1938 and made specialty appearances in movies. Film bio: *The Gene Krupa Story,* with Sal Mineo as Krupa (and Krupa dubbing his drumming).

1936   Big Broadcast of 1937
1937   Hollywood Hotel
1939   Some Like It Hot
1941   Ball of Fire
1942   Syncopation
1945   George White's Scandals
1946   Beat the Band
1948   Glamour Girl
1949   Make Believe Ballroom
1954   The Glenn Miller Story
1955   The Benny Goodman Story
1960   The Gene Krupa Story (drums for Sal Mineo)

Kyser, (James Kern) Kay, bandleader, actor; b. Rocky Mount, NC, June 18, 1897. Kyser's *College of Musical Knowledge* (''C'mon, chillun, le's dance!'') was a popular radio attraction when RKO cast the hawknosed, bespectacled bandleader in a series of comic adventure films that also involved his musicians and vocalists. The latter included Ginny Simms (succeeded by Georgia Carroll, who became Kyser's wife), Harry Babbitt, and Ish Kabibble (né Merwyn Bogue). (Died Chapel Hill, NC, July 25, 1985.)

Unless otherwise noted, Mr. Kyser used his own name in the following:

1939	That's Right, You're Wrong
1940	You'll Find Out
1941	Playmates
1942	My Favorite Spy
1943	Stage Door Canteen (specialty)
	Thousands Cheer (specialty)
	Swing Fever (*Lowell Blackford*)
	Around the World
1944	Carolina Blues

L

"Lady in Red, The" Music by Allie Wrubel; lyric by Mort Dixon. Rhythmic paean to the slightly gaudy (but proper) lady whose personality, originality, and vitality have made her the toast of the town. Introduced in a nightclub floorshow in Caliente in *In Caliente* (Warner 1935). The song was first sung in a darkened room by the chorus girls (each one singing a line as she lit a candle on a table), then by the bartenders, then by featured soloist Wini Shaw, and, finally, by Judy Canova to Edward Everett Horton.

"Lady in the Tutti-Frutti Hat, The" Music by Harry Warren; lyric by Mack Gordon. Introduced by Carmen Miranda in *The Gang's All Here* (Fox 1943) in a lavish Busby Berkeley nightclub sequence set on a banana plantation. As the curtain rises, the female banana pickers languidly loll under the trees, then rouse themselves to welcome Miss Miranda arriving in an ox cart. After singing the animated self-descriptive number, she beats out the tempo on a circular marimba made of bananas. The girls now hold aloft huge bananas in formation, the scene dissolves into kaleidoscopic patterns, and the number ends with the girls waving goodbye to the departing singer, then again lying down under the trees. The final shot is of Miss Miranda in front of a painted backdrop of hundreds of bananas made to look as if they were sprouting out of her headdress, as huge strawberries appear on her right and left. Let Freudians make of this what they will.

"Lady's in Love with You, The" Music by Burton Lane; lyric by Frank Loesser. How to know if it's the real thing: the gleam in her eye when she straightens your tie, her speed in getting dressed when you have a date, and her thoughtfulness in picking a secluded spot in a restaurant. Shirley Ross and Bob Hope, backed by Gene Krupa's orchestra, first enumerated the symptoms in *Some Like It Hot* (Par. 1939).

Lahr, Bert (né Irving Lahrheim), actor; b. New York, Aug. 13, 1895; d. New York, Dec. 4, 1967. Raucous clown with rubbery face and pouched beady eyes, noted for his satirical putdown of the manners and accents of the socially elite. After headlining in burlesque, Lahr became a major Broadway attraction in 13 musicals including *Flying High,* which he also filmed. His most enduring screen success was scored in *The Wizard of Oz* (singing "If I Only Had the Nerve" and "If I Were King of the Forest"). Bib: *Notes on a Cowardly Lion* by John Lahr (his son) (1969).

1931	Flying High (*Rusty Krause*)
1937	Merry-Go-Round (*Bert*)
	Love and Hisses (*Sugar Boles*)
1938	Josette (*Barney Barnaby*)
	Just Around the Corner (*Gus*)
1939	Zaza (*Cascart*)
	The Wizard of Oz (*Zeke/ Cowardly Lion*)
1942	Sing Your Worries Away (*Chow Brewster*)
	Ship Ahoy (*Skip Owens*)
1944	Meet the People (*Commander*)
1949	Always Leave Them Laughing (*Eddie Eagan*)
1954	Rose Marie (*Barney McCorkle*)
1955	The Second Greatest Sex (*Job McClure*)
1968	The Night They Raided Minsky's (*Prof. Spats*)

Laine, Frankie (né Frank Paul LoVecchio), singer, actor; b. Chicago, March 30, 1913. Leathery song belter who made many records, appeared in nightclubs, on television, and in low budget Columbia musicals.

1949	Make Believe Ballroom (specialty)
1950	When You're Smiling (*Frankie Laine*)
1951	On the Sunny Side of the Street
1952	Rainbow 'Round My Shoulder (*Frankie Laine*)

1955 Bring Your Smile Along (*Jerry Dennis*)
1956 Meet Me in Las Vegas (specialty)
      He Laughed Last

Lake, Veronica (née Constance Frances Marie Ockelman), actress, singer; b. Brooklyn, Nov. 14, 1919; d. Burlington, Vt., July 7, 1973. Tiny, seductive Veronica Lake was noted for her long blonde eye-covering hairdo and purring voice seen and heard in Paramount films. Bib: *Veronica* by Miss Lake (1968).

1942 Star-Spangled Rhythm (specialty)
1945 Bring on the Girls (*Teddy Collins*)
      Out of This World (*Dorothy Dodge*)
      Duffy's Tavern (specialty)
1947 Variety Girl (guest bit)
1948 Isn't It Romantic? (*Candy*)

Lamas, Fernando (Alvaro), actor, singer; b. Buenos Aires, Jan. 9, 1915. Muscular, romantic leading man appearing mostly in MGM films; married to Arlene Dahl then Esther Williams. (Died Oct. 8, 1982.)

1951 Rich, Young and Pretty (*Paul Sarnac*)
1952 The Merry Widow (*Prince Danilo*)
1953 Dangerous When Wet (*André Lanet*)
1954 Rose Marie (*James Duval*)
1955 The Girl Rush (*Victor Monte*)

Lamb, Gil, actor, dancer; b. Minneapolis, 1906. Sad-faced, spidery dancing actor who performed in wartime Paramount musicals.

1942 The Fleet's In (*Spike*)
      Star Spangled Rhythm (*High Pockets*)
1943 Riding High (*Foggy Day*)
1944 Rainbow Island (*Pete Jenkins*)
1946 Hit Parade of 1947 (*Eddie Page*)
1963 Bye Bye Birdie (*Shriner*)

Lamour, Dorothy (née Dorothy Mary Leta Slaton), actress, singer; b. New Orleans, Dec. 10, 1914. Sultry, nasal-voiced Dorothy Lamour, Paramount's most durable singing star, was the sarong-wearing jungle princess in a number of tropical-island epics, a genre she helped satirize as the romantic lead in six "Road" pictures with Bing Crosby and Bob Hope. She was also cast opposite Dick Powell, Fred MacMurray, and Don Ameche in musicals and introduced such songs as "Moonlight and Shadows," "I Remember You," "It Could Happen to You," and "Personality." Bib: *My Side of the Road* by Miss Lamour (1980).

1933 Footlight Parade (chorus)
1936 College Holiday (coed)

1937 Swing High, Swing Low (*Anita Alvarez*)
      High, Wide and Handsome (*Molly*)
      Thrill of a Lifetime (specialty)
1938 Big Broadcast of 1938 (*Dorothy Wyndham*)
      Her Jungle Love (*Tura*)
      Tropic Holiday (*Manuela*)
1939 St. Louis Blues (*Norma Malone*)
      Man About Town (*Diana Wilson*)
1940 Road to Singapore (*Mima*)
      Johnny Apollo (*Lucky Dubarry*)
      Moon Over Burma (*Aria Dean*)
1941 Road to Zanzibar (*Donna Latour*)
1942 The Fleet's In (*Countess*)
      Beyond the Blue Horizon (*Tama*)
      Road to Morocco (*Princess Shalmar*)
      Star Spangled Rhythm (specialty)
1943 Dixie (*Millie Cook*)
      Riding High (*Ann Castle*)
1944 And the Angels Sing (*Nancy Angel*)
      Rainbow Island (*Lona*)
1945 Duffy's Tavern (specialty)
      Masquerade in Mexico (*Angel O'Reilly*)
      Road to Utopia (*Sal Van Hoyden*)
1947 Variety Girl (specialty)
      Road to Rio (*Lucia Maria de Andrade*)
1948 Lulu Belle (*Lulu Belle*)
1949 Slightly French (*Mary O'Leary*)
1951 Here Comes the Groom (specialty)
1952 The Greatest Show on Earth (*Phyllis*)
      Road to Bali (*Lelah*)
1962 Road to Hong Kong (*Dorothy Lamour*)

Landis, Carole (née Frances Lillian Mary Ridste), actress, singer; b. Fairchild, Wisc., Jan. 1, 1919; d. Brentwood Hts., Cal., July 5, 1948. Well-proportioned blonde actress who usually played second leads in Fox films. Bib: *Four Jills in a Jeep* by Miss Landis (1944).

1937 A Day at the Races (extra)
      Broadway Melody of 1938 (bit)
      Varsity Show (bit)
      Hollywood Hotel (bit)
1938 Gold Diggers in Paris (bit)
1941 Road Show (*Penguin Moore*)
      Moon Over Miami (*Barbara Latimer*)
      Cadet Girl (*Gene Baxter*)
1942 My Gal Sal (*Mae Collins*)
      Orchestra Wives (*Natalie*)
      The Powers Girl (*Kay Evans*)
1943 Wintertime (*Flossie Fouchere*)
1944 Four Jills in a Jeep (*Carole Landis*)

Lane, Burton (né Burton Levy), composer; b. New York, Feb. 2, 1912. Lane's best-known film songs were written with lyricists Harold Adamson (''Everything I Have Is Yours''); Frank Loesser (''Moments Like This,'' ''Says My Heart,'' ''The Lady's in Love with You,'' ''I Hear Music''); Ralph Freed (''How About You?''); Alan Jay Lerner (''Too Late Now,'' ''You're All the World to Me''). Other collaborators: E. Y. Harburg, Ted Koehler, Dorothy Fields. Lane has also written six Broadway scores, of which *Finian's Rainbow* and *On a Clear Day You Can See Forever* were adapted to the screen. Singers identified with his songs include Bob Hope, Shirley Ross, Mickey Rooney, Judy Garland, Fred Astaire, Jane Powell, Petula Clark, and Barbra Streisand.

1933	Dancing Lady (Adamson)
1934	Bottoms Up (Adamson)
1938	College Swing (Loesser)
	Cocoanut Grove (Loesser, etc.)
1939	St. Louis Blues (Loesser)
	She Married a Cop (Freed)
1941	Dancing on a Dime (Loesser)
	Babes on Broadway (Freed; Harburg)
1942	Ship Ahoy (Harburg)
1944	Rainbow Island (Koehler)
1951	Royal Wedding (Lerner)
1953	Junior Miss (tv) (Fields)
	Give a Girl a Break (Gershwin)
1955	Jupiter's Darling (Adamson)
1968	Finian's Rainbow (Harburg)
1969	On a Clear Day You Can See Forever (Lerner)
1982	Heidi's Song (Cahn)

Lane, Lola (née Lola Mullican), actress, singer; b. Macy, Ind., May 21, 1909. Dark-haired actress, best remembered for nonmusical *Four Daughters* films she made with sisters Priscilla Lane and Rosemary Lane. Among five husbands were actor Lew Ayres and director Alexander Hall. (Died June 22, 1981.)

1929	Fox Movietone Follies (*Lila Beaumont*)
1930	Let's Go Places (*Marjorie Lorraine*)
	Good News (*Pat*)
1937	Hollywood Hotel (*Mona Marshall*)

Lane, Lupino (né Henry George Lupino), actor, singer, dancer; b. London, June 16, 1892; d. London, Nov. 10, 1959. Acrobatic dancer-actor of slight build who had lengthy career on the London musical stage. Lane's biggest hit was *Me and My Girl,* which he filmed as *The Lambeth Walk;* also made four feature musicals in Hollywood. He was the uncle of Ida Lupino. Bib: *Born To Star* by James Dillon White (1957).

1929	The Love Parade (US) (*Jacques*)
1930	The Show of Shows (US) (specialty)

	Golden Dawn (US) (*Pigeon*)
	Bride of the Regiment (US) (*Sprotti*)
	The Yellow Mask (*Sam Slipper*)
1932	Maid of the Mountains (dir., script only)
1933	A Southern Maid (*Antonio Lopez*)
1935	The Deputy Drummer (*Adolphus Miggs*)
1939	The Lambeth Walk (*Bill Snibson*)

Lane, Priscilla (née Priscilla Mullican), actress, singer; b. Indianola, Iowa, June 12, 1917. Blonde actress who began career singing with Fred Waring's orchestra and is best remembered for nonmusical *Four Daughters* films she made with sisters Lola Lane and Rosemary Lane. Introduced ''This Time the Dream's on Me'' in *Blues in the Night.*

1937	Varsity Show (*Betty Bradley*)
1938	Cowboy from Brooklyn (*Jane Hardy*)
1939	The Roaring Twenties (*Jean Sherman*)
1941	Blues in the Night (*Character*)

Lane, Rosemary (née Rosemary Mullican), actress, singer; b. Indianola, Iowa, April 14, 1914; d. Woodland Hills, Cal., Nov. 25, 1974. Dark-haired actress who began career singing with Fred Waring's orchestra and is best remembered for nonmusical *Four Daughters* films she made with sisters Lola Lane and Priscilla Lane. Also appeared in Broadway musical, *Best Foot Forward.*

1937	Varsity Show (*Barbara Steward*)
	Hollywood Hotel (*Virginia*)
1938	Gold Diggers in Paris (*Kay Morrow*)
1940	The Boys from Syracuse (*Phyllis*)
1941	Time Out for Rhythm (*Frances Lewis*)
1943	Chatterbox (*Carol Forrest*)
	Harvest Melody (*Gilda Parker*)
1944	Trocadero (*Judy*)

Lanfield, Sidney, director; b. Chicago, April 20, 1899. Director of Fox musicals in the 1930s, then mostly comedies for Paramount and MGM. Lanfield worked on three musicals each with Alice Faye and Sonja Henie, two each with Don Ameche, Tyrone Power, and Bob Hope. His most highly regarded musical was *You'll Never Get Rich,* starring Fred Astaire and Rita Hayworth. (Died Marina del Rey, Cal., June 30, 1972.)

1930	Cheer Up and Smile
1934	Moulin Rouge
1935	King of Burlesque
1936	Sing, Baby, Sing
	One in a Million
1937	Wake Up and Live
	Thin Ice
	Love and Hisses

1939 Second Fiddle
      Swanee River
1941 You'll Never Get Rich
1943 Let's Face It
1945 Bring on the Girls
1951 The Lemon Drop Kid
1952 Skirts Ahoy

Lang, Walter, director; b. Memphis, Tenn., Aug. 10, 1896; d. Palm Springs, Feb. 7, 1972. Fox director who guided Betty Grable in six musicals (including *Mother Wore Tights*) and had major successes with Rodgers and Hammerstein's *State Fair* and *The King and I* and Irving Berlin's *Call Me Madam* and *There's No Business Like Show Business*. Other stars he worked with included Dan Dailey, Alice Faye, Don Ameche, Ethel Merman, Donald O'Connor, and Susan Hayward.

1935 Hooray for Love
1940 The Blue Bird
      Star Dust
      Tin Pan Alley
1941 Moon Over Miami
      Weekend in Havana
1942 Song of the Islands
1943 Coney Island
1944 Greenwich Village
1945 State Fair
1947 Mother Wore Tights
1948 When My Baby Smiles at Me
1949 You're My Everything
1951 On the Riviera
1952 With a Song in My Heart
1953 Call Me Madam
1954 There's No Business Like Show Business
1956 The King and I
1960 Can-Can
1961 Snow White and the Three Stooges

Langford, Frances (née Frances Newbern), singer, actress; b. Lakeland, Fla., April 4, 1913. Tiny, round-faced singer with Southern-Comfort voice who won fame on radio, primarily with Bob Hope, recordings, and in movies. Though her starring roles were mostly in minor musicals, Miss Langford introduced such major songs as "I'm in the Mood for Love," "I Feel a Song Comin' On," "You Are My Lucky Star," "Broadway Rhythm," "You Hit the Spot," "I Don't Want To Make History," and "Hooray for Hollywood."

1935 Every Night at Eight (*Susan Moore*)
      Broadway Melody of 1936 (specialty)
1936 Collegiate (*Miss Hay*)
      Palm Springs (*Joan Smyth*)

Born to Dance (*Peggy Turner*)
1937 Hit Parade of 1937 (*Ruth Allison*)
      Hollywood Hotel (*Alice*)
1940 Too Many Girls (*Eileen Eilers*)
      Hit Parade of 1941 (*Pat Abbott*)
1941 All-American Coed (*Virginia Collinge*)
      Swing It Soldier (*Patricia*)
1942 Mississippi Gambler (*Beth*)
      Yankee Doodle Dandy (specialty)
1943 Follow the Band (specialty)
      This Is the Army (specialty)
      Cowboy in Manhattan (*Babs Lee*)
      Never a Dull Moment (*Julie Russell*)
      Career Girl (*Joan Terry*)
1944 The Girl Rush (*Flo*)
      Dixie Jamboree (*Susan Jackson*)
      Radio Stars on Parade (*Sally Baker*)
1946 People Are Funny (specialty)
      Bamboo Blonde (*Louise Anderson*)
1947 Beat the Band (*Ann*)
1948 Melody Time (voice only)
1951 Purple Heart Diary (*Frances Langford*)
1954 The Glenn Miller Story (specialty)

Lansbury, Angela (Brigid), actress, singer; b. London, Oct. 16, 1925. Versatile actress, often given bitchy roles in films, whose abilities as a musical star were first appreciated on Broadway (*Mame, Sweeney Todd*) after her years as a Hollywood contractee.

1946 The Harvey Girls (*Em*)
      Till the Clouds Roll By (specialty)
1956 The Court Jester (*Princess Gwendolyn*)
1961 Blue Hawaii (*Sarah Lee Gates*)
1971 Bedknobs and Broomsticks (*Eglantine*)
1982 The Last Unicorn (voice of *Mama Fortun*)
1983 The Pirates of Penzance (*Ruth*)

Lanza, Mario (né Alfredo Arnold Cocozza), actor, singer; b. Philadelphia, Jan. 31, 1921; d. Rome, Oct. 7, 1959. Robust, curly-haired tenor who sang in opera and concerts before scoring success in first MGM film. Lanza acted opposite Kathryn Grayson twice, introduced "Be My Love" and "Because You're Mine" and did more to popularize opera—particularly with his portrayal of Enrico Caruso—than any other singer. Bib: *Mario Lanza: His Tragic Life* by Raymond Strait & Terry Robinson (1980).

1949 That Midnight Kiss (*Johnny Donnetti*)
1950 The Toast of New Orleans (*Pepe Duvalle*)
1951 The Great Caruso (*Enrico Caruso*)
1952 Because You're Mine (*Renaldo Rossano*)
1954 The Student Prince (vocals for Edmund Purdom)
1956 Serenade (Damon Vincenti)

1958 The Seven Hills of Rome (*Marc Revere*)
1959 For the First Time (*Tonio Costa*)

"Last Dance, The" Music & lyric by Paul Jabara. Introduced by Donna Summer in *Thank God It's Friday* (Col. 1978).

"Latin Quarter, The" Music by Harry Warren; lyric by Al Dubin. Spirited Left Bank tour in *Gold Diggers in Paris* (Warner 1938), performed as a production number featuring Rudy Vallee, Rosemary Lane, Allen Jenkins, and Mabel Todd.

Laurel and Hardy, actors. Stan Laurel (né Arthur Stanley Jefferson), b. Ulverston, Eng., June 16, 1890; d. Santa Monica, Feb. 23, 1965. Oliver (Norvell) Hardy, b. Atlanta, Jan. 18, 1892; d. Hollywood, Aug. 7, 1957. Classic slapstick comedy team of blank-faced, weepy, easily duped Laurel and blimpish, overbearing Hardy. The partners made their first of 103 shorts and feature-length films in 1926, their last in 1951. Bib: *Mr. Laurel and Mr. Hardy* by John McCabe (1961); *Films of Laurel and Hardy* by William K. Everson (1967); *A Fine Mess* ed. Richard Anobile (1975).

1929 Hollywood Revue of 1929 (specialty)
1930 The Rogue Song
1933 The Devil's Brother
1934 Hollywood Party
     Babes in Toyland
1936 The Bohemian Girl
1938 Swiss Miss
1943 Jitterbugs
1950 Riding High (Hardy only as *Horse Player*)

"Lavender Blue (Dilly Dilly)" Music by Eliot Daniel; lyric by Larry Morey. Folkish marriage proposal—with no less than ten "dilly dillys"—sung by Burl Ives as he calls on Beulah Bondi in *So Dear to My Heart* (Disney 1948). Daniel and Morey adapted the piece from a bawdy 17th-century English folksong known in two versions, "Diddle-Diddle" and "The Kind Country Lovers."

Lawford, Peter (Aylen), actor, singer; b. London, Sept. 7, 1923. Lawford's nasal British accent and tweedy, unassuming air almost invariably cast him as a member of the social elite. His Hollywood musicals found him acting opposite June Allyson twice, and he also wooed and won Kathryn Grayson, Esther Williams, and Jane Powell. Under contract to MGM between 1938 and 1952, Lawford appeared mostly in dramatic roles. (Died Beverly Hills, Dec. 24, 1984.)

1943 Girl Crazy (*student*)
1945 Two Sisters from Boston (*Lawrence Patterson Jr.*)
1946 It Happened in Brooklyn (*Jamie Shelgrove*)
1947 Good News (*Tommy Marlowe*)
1948 On an Island with You (*Lt. Lawrence Kingslee*)
     Easter Parade (*Jonny Harrow*)
1951 Royal Wedding (*Lord John Brindale*)
1957 Ruggles of Red Gap (tv) (*Lord Brinstead*)
1960 Pepe (guest bit)
1966 A Man Called Adam (*Manny*)

Lawrence, Gertrude (née Gertrud Alexandra Dagmar Lawrence Klasen), actress, singer, dancer; b. London, July 4, 1898; d. New York, Sept. 6, 1952. Stylish, stylized London and Broadway stage actress who made six films, only one of which was a musical. Film bio: *Star!*, with Julie Andrews as Miss Lawrence. Bib: *A Star Danced* by Miss Lawrence (1945); *Gertrude Lawrence* by Sheridan Morley (1980).

1929 Battle of Paris (*Georgie*)

Laye, Evelyn, actress, singer; b. London, July 10, 1900. Her well-trained voice, fragile beauty, and natural elegance helped make Evelyn Laye the most popular star of the London light-opera stage. Apart from British films, she starred in two Hollywood musicals and introduced "When I Grow Too Old To Dream." Her husbands have been actors Sonnie Hale (divorced) and Frank Lawton. Bib: *Boo, to My Friends* by Miss Laye (1958).

1931 One Heavenly Night (US) (*Lilli*)
1933 Waltz Time (*Rosalinde Eisenstein*)
1934 Princess Charming (*Princess Elaine*)
     Evensong (*Irela*)
1935 The Night Is Young (US) (*Lisl*)

"Learn To Croon" Music by Arthur Johnston; lyric by Sam Coslow. How to win your heart's desire, as prescribed by Bing Crosby in *College Humor* (Par. 1933). This was Crosby's first use of his "boo-boo-boo" trademark in the movies. The song was also heard in *Jolson Sings Again* (Col. 1949) on a Crosby radio broadcast.

LeBaron, William, producer; b. Elgin, Ill., Feb. 16, 1883; d. Santa Monica, Feb. 9, 1958. After a career as a Broadway librettist and lyricist, LeBaron became a Hollywood producer in 1924. He was primarily with Paramount (1933–41) and Fox (1941–46), in charge of musicals starring John Boles, Bebe Daniels, Mae West (four), Bing Crosby, George Raft, Gladys Swarthout, W. C. Fields, Mary Martin, Alice Faye, Carmen Miranda, Betty Grable (four), Glenn Miller, Sonja Henie, Lena Horne.

1929	Street Girl
	Rio Rita
1933	She Done Him Wrong
	College Humor
	I'm No Angel
1934	Bolero
1935	All the King's Horses
	Rumba
	Here Comes Cookie
	Coronado
	Goin' to Town
1936	Rose of the Rancho
	Klondike Annie
	Give Us This Night
1940	Rhythm on the River
1941	Las Vegas Nights
	Kiss the Boys Goodbye
	Weekend in Havana
1942	Song of the Islands
	Orchestra Wives
	Springtime in the Rockies
	Iceland
	Footlight Serenade
1943	Stormy Weather
	Wintertime
	The Gang's All Here
1944	Pin-Up Girl
	Sweet and Low Down
	Greenwich Village
1946	Three Little Girls in Blue
1947	Carnegie Hall

Lee, Gypsy Rose (née Louise Hovick), actress; b. Seattle, Jan. 9, 1914; d. Los Angeles, April 26, 1970. Tongue-in-cheeky burlesque stripper who also appeared on Broadway. The sister of June Havoc, she was known as Louise Hovick in her first four movie musicals. Bib: *Gypsy* by Miss Lee (1957), the basis for the 1959 stage musical and its 1963 film version, with Natalie Wood as Miss Lee.

1937	Sally, Irene and Mary (*Joyce Taylor*)
	Ali Baba Goes to Town (*Sultana*)
	You Can't Have Everything (*Lulu Reilly*)
1938	My Lucky Star (*Marcelle*)
1943	Stage Door Canteen (guest bit)
1944	Belle of the Yukon (*Belle DeValle*)

Lee, Peggy (née Norma Egstrom), singer, actress, lyricist; b. Jamestown, ND, May 26, 1920. Beginning as a vocalist with Benny Goodman's orchestra, Miss Lee developed into a major nightclub, concert, and recording artist, famed for her husky whisper and rhythmic precision. She won praise for her performance in *Pete Kelly's Blues* and her songs (with composer Sonny Burke) for *Lady and the Tramp*.

1942	The Powers Girl (band singer)
1943	Stage Door Canteen (band singer)
1950	Mr. Music (specialty)
1953	The Jazz Singer (*Judy Lane*)
1955	Lady and the Tramp (voice only) (also lyr.) (Burke)
	Pete Kelly's Blues (*Rose Hopkins*)

Lee, Sammy (né Samuel Levy), choreographer; b. New York, May 26, 1890; d. Woodland Hills, Cal., March 30, 1968. Broadway dance director of the 1920s who worked in Hollywood with such performers as Lilian Harvey, Joan Crawford, Alice Faye, Shirley Temple, Eleanor Powell, and June Allyson.

1929	It's a Great Life
	Hollywood Revue of 1929
1933	It's Great To Be Alive
	Adorable
	Jimmy and Sally
	My Lips Betray
	Dancing Lady
1934	365 Nights in Hollywood
1935	King of Burlesque
1937	New Faces of 1937
	Life of the Party
	Heidi
	Ali Baba Goes to Town
1939	Honolulu
1940	Hullabaloo
1943	Hit the Ice
1944	Meet the People
	Two Girls and a Sailor
	Carolina Blues
1945	Earl Carroll Vanities

Leigh, Janet (née Jeanette Helen Morrison), actress, singer, dancer; b. Merced, Cal., July 6, 1927. Pert, fresh-scrubbed ingenue usually in nonmusicals who made lasting impression in Alfred Hitchcock's *Psycho*. Formerly married to actor Tony Curtis.

1948	Words and Music (*Dorothy Rodgers*)
1951	Two Tickets to Broadway (*Nancy Peterson*)
	Strictly Dishonorable (*Isabelle Dempsey*)
1953	Walking My Baby Back Home (*Chris Hall*)

1954 Living It Up (*Wally Cook*)
1955 Pete Kelly's Blues (*Ivy Conrad*)
     My Sister Eileen (*Eileen Sherwood*)
1960 Pepe (*Janet Leigh*)
1963 Bye Bye Birdie (*Rosie DeLeon*)

Leisen, Mitchell, director; b. Menominee, Wisc., Oct. 6, 1897; d. Woodland Hills, Cal., Oct. 27, 1972. Beginning as a costume and set designer, Leisen became identified with Paramount comedies between 1933 and 1951. Among those he directed in musicals were Carl Brisson, Jack Benny, Bob Hope, Dorothy Lamour, Ginger Rogers, and Betty Hutton.

1934 Murder at the Vanities (also *bandleader*)
1935 Four Hours To Kill
1936 Big Broadcast of 1937
1937 Swing High, Swing Low
1938 Big Broadcast of 1938
     Artists and Models Abroad
1944 Lady in the Dark (also script)
1945 Masquerade in Mexico
1947 Variety Girl (guest bit only)
1953 Tonight We Sing
1957 The Girl Most Likely

Lemmon, (John Uhler) Jack, actor; b. Boston, Feb. 8, 1925. Bland-looking actor who moved easily from comic (*The Apartment*) to dramatic roles (*Days of Wine and Roses*), and whose best-remembered musical was *Some Like It Hot*. Bib: *Films of Jack Lemmon* by Joe Baltake (1977); *Lemmon* by Don Widener (1975).

1955 Three for the Show (*Marty Stewart*)
     My Sister Eileen (*Robert Baker*)
1956 You Can't Run Away from It (*Peter Warner*)
1959 Some Like It Hot (*Jerry*)
1960 Pepe (guest bit)
1976 The Entertainer (tv) (*Archie Rice*)

Lennon, John. *See* **Beatles, The.**

Leonard, Robert Z(igler), director, producer; b. Denver, Ill., Oct. 7, 1889; d. Beverly Hills, Aug. 27, 1968. Beginning his career in 1910 as an actor, Leonard became a major MGM director, with *The Great Ziegfeld* and *Maytime* his most popular musicals. He worked with Jeanette MacDonald on five films, three of them with Nelson Eddy. Other stars in his musicals were Marion Davies, Clark Gable, Joan Crawford, Myrna Loy, Judy Garland, Van Johnson, Jane Powell, and Esther Williams.

1929 Marianne (also *doughboy*)
1930 In Gay Madrid
1933 Dancing Lady
1936 The Great Ziegfeld
1937 Maytime
     The Firefly
1938 Girl of the Golden West
1939 Broadway Serenade (also prod.)
1940 New Moon (also prod.)
1941 Ziegfeld Girl
1945 Abbott & Costello in Hollywood (guest bit only)
1949 In the Good Old Summertime
1950 Nancy Goes to Rio
     Duchess of Idaho
1952 Everything I Have Is Yours
1957 Kelly and Me

Lerner, Alan Jay, lyricist, screen writer; b. New York, Aug. 31, 1918. Major Broadway lyricist-librettist with five out of eleven stage productions (*Brigadoon, Paint Your Wagon, My Fair Lady, Camelot, On a Clear Day You Can See Forever*) transferred to the screen, and one screen production (*Gigi*) transferred to the stage. *Gigi*, Lerner's best realized film work, was written with his most frequent collaborator, composer Frederick Loewe, and yielded such songs as "Gigi," "I Remember It Well," "Thank Heaven for Little Girls," and "The Night They Invented Champagne." In Hollywood, where he wrote screenplays for all his movies, Lerner also teamed with Burton Lane ("Too Late Now," "You're All the World to Me") and André Previn (added songs for *Paint Your Wagon*). Fred Astaire, Jane Powell, Gene Kelly, Maurice Chevalier, Rex Harrison, and Barbra Streisand were among those who sang Lerner songs on the screen. Bib: *The Lerner & Loewe Song Book* (1962); *The Street Where I Live* by Lerner (1978). (Died New York, June 14, 1986.)

Asterisk indicates Mr. Lerner was also producer:
1951 Royal Wedding (Lane)
     An American in Paris (script only)
1954 Brigadoon (Loewe)
1958 Gigi (Loewe)
1964 My Fair Lady (Loewe)
1967 Camelot (Loewe)
1969 Paint Your Wagon (Loewe; Previn) *
1970 On a Clear Day You Can See Forever (Lane) *
1974 The Little Prince (Loewe)

Le Roy, Mervyn, director, producer; b. San Francisco, Oct. 16, 1900. Equally proficient at directing social dramas (*Little Caesar, I Am a Fugitive from a Chain Gang*) and musicals (*Gold Diggers of 1933*), LeRoy was with Warner from 1927 to 1938, MGM from 1938 to 1954. As producer only, his most notable achievement was *The Wizard of Oz*. Joan Blondell, Dick Powell, Ruby Keeler, Irene Dunne, Howard Keel, Esther Williams, and Rosalind Russell were among the actors LeRoy directed in musicals. (Died Beverly Hills, Sept. 13, 1987.)

Asterisk indicates Mr. LeRoy was also producer:
1929 Broadway Babies
1930 Little Johnny Jones
      Playing Around
      Show Girl in Hollywood
      Top Speed
1933 Gold Diggers of 1933
1934 Happiness Ahead
1935 Sweet Adeline
1937 The King and the Chorus Girl*
      Mr. Dodd Takes the Air (prod. only)
1938 Fools for Scandal*
1939 The Wizard of Oz (prod. only)
      At the Circus (prod. only)
1952 Lovely to Look At
      Million Dollar Mermaid
1953 Latin Lovers
1954 Rose Marie*
1962 Gypsy*

Leslie, Joan (née Joan Agnes Theresa Sadie Brodel), actress; b. Detroit, Jan. 26, 1925. Miss Leslie projected a well-scrubbed, trusting screen image that caught the fancy of two composers, George M. Cohan (*Yankee Doodle Dandy*) and George Gershwin (*Rhapsody in Blue*). She also danced with Fred Astaire and introduced "My Shining Hour (with Sally Sweetland's singing voice). She was known as Joan Brodel in films between 1936 and 1940.

1940 Star Dust (*coed*)
1942 Yankee Doodle Dandy (*Mary Cohan*)
      The Hard Way (*Katherine Chernin*)
1943 The Sky's the Limit (*Joan Manion*)
      This Is the Army (*Eileen Dibble*)
      Thank Your Lucky Stars (*Pat Dixon*)
1944 Hollywood Canteen (guest bit)
1945 Where Do We Go from Here? (*Sally*)
      Rhapsody in Blue (*Julie Adams*)
1946 Cinderella Jones (*Judy Jones*)
      Two Guys from Milwaukee (*Connie Read*)

Lester, Richard, director; b. Philadelphia, 1932. Lester's trademark use of fragmented scenes to enhance the comic effect of his films was particularly effective in his first two musicals, both with The Beatles.

1964 A Hard Day's Night
1965 Help!
1966 A Funny Thing Happened on the Way to the Forum

"Let Me Sing and I'm Happy" Music & lyric by Irving Berlin. Exuberant plea by Al Jolson in minstrel show in *Mammy* (Warner 1930); also sung by Jolson over credits in *The Jolson Story* (Col. 1946). The songwriter's very personal expression was developed from a poem he had written that began: "Let me sing a simple song/ That helps to jog the world along/ Along its weary way/ And I'll be glad today." For the song's verse, in which indifference was expressed about those who make the nation's laws, Berlin drew on the apothegm quoted in 1704 by Andrew Fletcher, a Scottish political leader: "If a man were permitted to make all the ballads, he need not care who should make the laws of a nation."

"Let Yourself Go" Music & lyric by Irving Berlin. Rhythmic invitation to lose all restraints on the dance floor. Sung in *Follow the Fleet* (RKO 1936) by Ginger Rogers, as an entertainer in a dime-a-dance ballroom, accompanied by Betty Grable, Joy Hodges, and Jennie Gray; followed by an elimination dance contest in which, not surprisingly, Ginger and Fred Astaire won first prize.

"Let's Call the Whole Thing Off" Music by George Gershwin; lyric by Ira Gershwin. Musical logomachy ("You say ee-ther and I say eye-ther") for Fred Astaire and Ginger Rogers in *Shall We Dance* (RKO 1937). After the lighthearted bickering, which takes place on New York's Central Park Mall, the team performs a gliding, tapping dance on roller skates that builds to a round-and-round chase and ends with Fred and Ginger falling headlong onto the grass.

"Let's Face the Music and Dance" Music & lyric by Irving Berlin. Performed in *Follow the Fleet* (RKO 1936) by Fred Astaire and Ginger Rogers as part of a revue being staged on a remodeled ship. In the number, Fred first appears in white tie and tails at a gambling table at the Monte Carlo Casino. Deserted by admiring ladies (including Lucille Ball) once his winning streak is over, he ambles onto the terrace, where he is further snubbed. Dejected, he takes out a pistol to end it all, then suddenly discovers a girl (Ginger) about to commit suicide by jumping off the ledge. He pulls her back, throws away both his gun and empty wallet, then tries to buck up both their spirits by singing and leading the girl in a dance. At first she stiffly rejects the gambler's advances, but eventually she succumbs to the sweep and passion of the music, and the two dance courageously in the face of the troubles that lie ahead.

"Let's Fall in Love" Music by Harold Arlen; lyric by Ted Koehler. Ardent proposal sung in *Let's Fall in Love* (Col. 1934) by Art Jarrett and reprised by Ann Sothern. The song, Arlen and Koehler's first for the movies, was also sung by Don Ameche and Dorothy Lamour in *Slightly French* (Col. 1949); Robert Cummings in *Tell It to the Judge* (Col. 1949); Judy Holliday and Jack Lemmon in *It Should Happen to You* (Col. 1954); and was played by pianist Carmen Cavallero (for Tyrone Power) in *The Eddy Duchin Story* (Col. 1956).

"Let's Get Lost" Music by Jimmy McHugh; lyric by Frank Loesser. Mary Martin sang this invitation to romantic solitude in *Happy Go Lucky* (Par. 1943).

"Let's Take the Long Way Home" Music by Harold Arlen; lyric by Johnny Mercer. Romantic desire to prolong the blissful night expressed by Bing Crosby to Betty Hutton in *Here Come the Waves* (Par. 1944).

Levant, Oscar, composer, actor, pianist; b. Pittsburgh, Dec. 27, 1906; d. Beverly Hills, Aug. 14, 1972. Levant was active in Hollywood both as composer (collaborating with lyricists Sidney Clare, Dorothy Fields, and William Kernell) and onscreen as the cynical, cigarette-puffing confidant of, among others, Bing Crosby, Dan Dailey, Doris Day, Fred Astaire, and Gene Kelly. Occasionally, as in *An American in Paris,* he was featured as pianist. Bib: *A Smattering of Ignorance* (1942), *Memoirs of an Amnesiac* (1965), *The Unimportance of Being Oscar* (1968), all by Levant.

Names in italics are parts Mr. Levant played; others in parentheses are his collaborators:

1929 Street Girl (Clare)
The Dance of Life (*Jerry*)
Tanned Legs (Clare)
1930 Love Comes Along (Clare)
1935 Music Is Magic (Clare)
In Person (Fields)
1936 Charlie Chan at the Opera (Kernell)
1940 Rhythm on the River (*Billy Starbuck*)
1941 Kiss the Boys Goodbye (*Oscar Rayburn*)

1945 Rhapsody in Blue (*Oscar Levant*)
1946 Humoresque (*Sid Jeffers*)
1948 You Were Meant for Me (*Oscar Hoffman*)
Romance on the High Seas (*Oscar Farrar*)
1949 The Barkleys of Broadway (*Ezra Miller*)
1951 An American in Paris (*Adam Cook*)
1953 The "I Don't Care" Girl (*Bennett*)
The Band Wagon (*Lester Marton*)

Levin, Henry, director; b. Trenton, NJ, June 5, 1909; d. Glendale, Cal., May 1, 1980. After experience as stage director, went to Hollywood in 1943 and directed a total of 52 films. Among actors Levin worked with in musicals were Larry Parks, Betty Grable, Tony Martin, Pat Boone, and Connie Francis. Also active in television.

1949 Jolson Sings Again
1950 The Petty Girl
1953 The Farmer Takes a Wife
1956 Let's Be Happy (Eng.)
1957 Bernardine
April Love
1960 Where the Boys Are
1962 Wonderful World of the Brothers Grimm

Lewis, Jerry (né Joseph Levitch), actor; b. Newark, NJ, March 16, 1926. A headliner in nightclubs, theatres, and television, Lewis was the loose limbed juvenile cutup whose spastic clowning contrasted with his self-assured, casual singing partner, Dean Martin. The team starred in 17 Paramount films between 1949 and 1956, in which the emphasis was usually more on the antic Lewis than the romantic Martin. After the partnership ended, Lewis continued as his own writer, director, and producer. Bib: *Everybody Loves Somebody* by Arthur Marx (1974).

1949 My Friend Irma (*Seymour*)
1950 My Friend Irma Goes West (*Seymour*)
At War with the Army (*PFC Korwin*)
1951 That's My Boy (*Junior Jackson*)
Sailor Beware (*Melvin Jones*)
1952 Jumping Jacks (*Hap Smith*)
Road to Bali (guest bit)
The Stooge (*Ted Rogers*)
1953 Scared Stiff (*Myron Mertz*)
The Caddy (*Harvey*)
Money from Home (*Virgil Yokum*)
1954 Living It Up (*Homer Flagg*)
Three Ring Circus (*Jerry Hotchkiss*)
1955 You're Never Too Young (*Wilbur Hoolick*)
Artists and Models (*Eugene Fullstack*)

1956 Pardners (*Wade Kingsley Sr./Wade Kingsley Jr.*)
Hollywood or Bust (*Malcolm Smith*)
1958 Rock-a-Bye Baby (*Clayton Poole*) (also prod.)
1960 Cinderfella (*Fella*) (also prod., script)
1961 The Ladies' Man (*Hubert J. Heebert*) (also dir., prod., script)
1963 The Nutty Professor (*Julius Kelp*) (also dir., script)

Lewis, Monica, singer, actress; b. 1925. Blonde nightclub and recording artist who made three musicals at MGM; married to producer Jennings Lang.

1951 Excuse My Dust (*Daisy Lou Schultzer*)
The Strip (*Monica Lewis*)
1952 Everything I Have Is Yours (*Sybil Meriden*)

Lewis, Ted (né Theodore Leopold Friedman), bandleader, singer, clarinetist, actor; b. Circleville, Ohio, June 6, 1891; d. New York, Aug. 25, 1971. Hammy bandleader-entertainer (''Is everybody happy?'') who wore a battered top hat and played an occasional clarinet. Lewis began in vaudeville in 1910, was featured in nightclubs and made many records. In films, appeared both in major roles and in specialty numbers with orchestra.

1929 Is Everybody Happy? (*Ted Todd*)
The Show of Shows (specialty)
1935 Here Comes the Band
1937 Manhattan Merry-Go-Round (specialty)
1941 Hold That Ghost (specialty)
1943 Is Everybody Happy? (*Ted Lewis*)
1944 Follow the Boys (specialty)

Liberace (Wladziu Valentino), pianist, actor; b. West Allis, Wisc., May 16, 1919. Glossy, flossy concert pianist with dimpled grin who appears mostly in concerts and nightclubs. Bib: *Liberace, An Autobiography* (1973). (Died Palm Springs, Feb. 4, 1987.)

1950 South Sea Sinner (*Maestro*)
1951 Footlight Varieties (specialty)
1955 Sincerely Yours (*Anthony Warren*)
1965 When the Boys Meet the Girls (specialty)

Lightner, Winnie (née Winifred Hanson), actress, singer, dancer; b. Greenport, NY, Sept. 17, 1899; d. Sherman Oaks, Cal., March 5, 1971. Energetic blonde performer in vaudeville and six Broadway revues before Hollywood career. Her second husband was director Roy Del Ruth.

1929 Gold Diggers of Broadway (*Mable*)
The Show of Shows (specialty)
1930 Hold Everything (*Toots Breen*)

Life of the Party (*Flo*)
She Couldn't Say No (*Winnie Harper*)
1933 Dancing Lady (*Rosette LaRue*)

''Like Someone in Love'' Music by James Van Heusen; lyric by Johnny Burke. Dinah Shore first displayed the symptoms—star gazing, hearing guitars, walking on air, etc.—in *Belle of the Yukon* (Par. 1944).

Lillie, Beatrice (Gladys), actress, singer; b. Toronto, May 29, 1894. Sly, mischievous, madcap comedienne whose antics made her a stage favorite for 50 years in both London and New York. Bib: *Every Other Inch a Lady* by Miss Lillie (1972).

1929 The Show of Shows (specialty)
1930 Are You There? (*Shirley Travers*)
1938 Doctor Rhythm (*Lorelei Dodge-Blodgett*)
1967 Thoroughly Modern Millie (*Mrs. Meers*)

''Little Drops of Rain'' Music by Harold Arlen; lyric by E. Y. Harburg. Poignant ballad showing how the important things of life start small. Sung by Judy Garland on the soundtrack of the cartoon *Gay Purr-ee* (Warner 1962), then reprised by Robert Goulet.

''Little Kiss Each Morning (A Little Kiss Each Night), A'' Music & lyric by Harry Woods. Rudy Vallee's prescription for happiness in *The Vagabond Lover* (RKO 1929).

''Little Prince'' Music by Frederick Loewe; lyric by Alan Jay Lerner. Tender song of affection sung by pilot Richard Kiley in—and to—*The Little Prince* (Par. 1974).

''Little Things You Used To Do, The'' Music by Harry Warren; lyric by Al Dubin. In *Go Into Your Dance* (Warner 1935), Al Jolson, at a nightclub audition, urged Helen Morgan, ''Come on, baby, chirp like a canary.'' Which she did by singing this torchy lament enumerating such once familiar sights and sounds as her lover's cigarette ashes on the floor, the way he slammed the door, the spot on his tie, and the way that he'd lie.

''Little White Gardenia, A'' Music & lyric by Sam Coslow. Floral love token offered by Carl Brisson in *All the King's Horses* (Par. 1935) and reprised by Mary Ellis. Songwriter Coslow claims that he got the idea from a story related by Brisson about an unknown woman who left him a white gardenia once a week during his London appearance in *The Merry Widow*.

"Living in the Sunlight—Loving in the Moonlight"
Music by Al Sherman; lyric by Al Lewis. Recommendation for a wonderful time, brightly sung by Maurice Chevalier to entertain a group of businessmen in *The Big Pond* (Par. 1930).

Livingston, Jerry (né Jerome Levinson), composer; b. Denver, March 25, 1909. Former bandleader, principally associated in Hollywood with lyricist Mack David, with whom he wrote "Bibbidi-Bobbidi-Boo" (Al Hoffman, co-composer) for Walt Disney's *Cinderella,* plus four Martin and Lewis comedies. Also worked with Helen Deutsch. (Died July 1, 1987.)

1949 Cinderella (David-Hoffman)
1950 At War with the Army (David)
1951 Sailor Beware (David)
1952 Jumping Jacks (David)
1953 Scared Stiff (David)
1956 Jack and the Beanstalk (tv) (Deutsch)

Livingston and Evans, composers, lyricists. Jay Livingston (né Jacob Harold Levison), b. McDonald, Pa., March 28, 1915. (Raymond B.) Ray Evans, b. Salamanca, NY, Feb. 4, 1915. Teamed early in careers to write for Olsen and Johnson; under contract to Paramount 1945–55. Many of their best-known numbers were theme songs for nonmusicals: "To Each His Own," "Golden Earrings" (music by Victor Young), "Mona Lisa," "Que Sera Sera," "Tammy," "Dear Heart" (music by Henry Mancini). Those who introduced Livingston-Evans songs include Bob Hope ("Buttons and Bows," "Silver Bells"), Marlene Dietrich, Dean Martin, Dinah Shore, Bing Crosby, Doris Day, Debbie Reynolds, and Rosemary Clooney. Partners also wrote scores for first original color television musical, *Satins and Spurs,* and two Broadway shows.

1943 Footlight Glamour
1944 Swing Hostess
1945 Why Girls Leave Home
1948 Isn't It Romantic?
      The Paleface
1949 My Friend Irma
1950 My Friend Irma Goes West
      Fancy Pants
1951 Aaron Slick from Punkin Crick
      The Lemon Drop Kid
      Here Comes the Groom
1952 Son of Paleface

1953 The Stars Are Singing
      Those Redheads from Seattle
      Here Come the Girls
1954 Red Garters
      Satins and Spurs (tv)
1958 The Big Beat
1959 A Private's Affair
1961 All Hands on Deck

Loesser, Frank (Henry), composer, lyricist; b. New York, June 29, 1910; d. New York, July 26, 1969. Though he won his greatest fame as composer-lyricist of such Broadway musicals as *Where's Charley?, Guys and Dolls,* and *How To Succeed in Business Without Really Trying* (all filmed), Loesser began his career as a Hollywood lyricist exclusively, mostly at Paramount. His collaborators included composers Burton Lane ("Says My Heart," "The Lady's in Love with You"); Manning Sherwin; Frederick Hollander ("The Boys in the Backroom"); Hoagy Carmichael ("Small Fry," "Two Sleepy People"); Matty Malneck; Jimmy McHugh ("Can't Get Out of This Mood," "Let's Get Lost," " 'Murder' He Says"); Victor Schertzinger ("Kiss the Boys Goodbye"); Louis Alter ("Dolores"); Harold Spina; Joseph Lilley ("Jingle, Jangle, Jingle"); Jule Styne ("I Don't Want To Walk Without You"); and Arthur Schwartz ("They're Either Too Young or Too Old"). After Loesser became a composer, his screen songs included "Spring Will Be a Little Late This Year," "Poppa, Don't Preach to Me," "Baby, It's Cold Outside," and, from *Hans Christian Andersen,* "Anywhere I Wander," "No Two People," and "Thumbelina." Among those who sang Loesser songs were Dorothy Lamour, Bob Hope, Shirley Ross, Bing Crosby, Marlene Dietrich, Mary Martin, Betty Hutton, Dick Powell, Fred Astaire, Deanna Durbin, Danny Kaye, Ray Bolger, Marlon Brando, and Frank Sinatra. Bib: *The Frank Loesser Song Book* (1972).

From 1947 on, Mr. Loesser was both composer and lyricist:
1938 College Swing (Lane; Sherwin)
1939 Zaza (Hollander)
      St. Louis Blues (Lane)
      Some Like It Hot (Lane; Carmichael)
      Man About Town (Hollander)
      Hawaiian Nights (Malneck)
      Destry Rides Again (Hollander)
1940 Buck Benny Rides Again (McHugh)
      Seven Sinners (Hollander)
1941 Dancing on a Dime (Lane)
      Las Vegas Nights (Lane; Alter)

Sis Hopkins (Styne)
Kiss the Boys Goodbye (Schertzinger)
Glamour Boy (Schertzinger)
Mr. Bug Goes to Town (Carmichael)
1942   True to the Army (Spina)
Sweater Girl (Styne)
Seven Days' Leave (McHugh)
1943   Happy Go Lucky (McHugh)
Thank Your Lucky Stars (Schwartz)
1947   The Perils of Pauline
Variety Girl
1949   Neptune's Daughter
Red, Hot and Blue (also *Hairdo Lempke*)
1950   Let's Dance
1952   Where's Charley?
Hans Christian Andersen
1955   Guys and Dolls
1966   How To Succeed in Business Without Really Trying

Loewe, Frederick, composer; b. Berlin, June 10, 1904 (Austrian parents). Four out of six stage musicals written by Loewe with lyricist Alan Jay Lerner (*Brigadoon, Paint Your Wagon, My Fair Lady, Camelot*) were transferred to the screen, and one Lerner-Loewe screen musical, *Gigi*, was transferred to the stage. Among its songs were "Gigi," "I Remember It Well," "Thank Heaven for Little Girls," and "The Night They Invented Champagne." Those movie performers identified with Loewe's music included Gene Kelly, Maurice Chevalier, and Rex Harrison. Bib: *The Lerner & Loewe Song Book* (1962).

1954   Brigadoon
1958   Gigi
1964   My Fair Lady
1967   Camelot
1969   Paint Your Wagon
1974   The Little Prince

Logan, Ella, actress, singer; b. Glasgow, March 6, 1913; d. Burlingame, Cal., May 1, 1969. Diminutive, vivacious singer whose most famous role was in the Broadway musical, *Finian's Rainbow*. In Hollywood, she introduced "I Was Doing All Right" in *The Goldwyn Follies*.

1937   Top of the Town (*Dorine*)
52nd Street (*Betty Malina*)
1938   The Goldwyn Follies (*Glory Wood*)

Logan, Joshua (Lockwood), director; b. Texarkana, Texas, Oct. 5, 1908. Broadway veteran who also directed two of his stage musicals, *South Pacific* and *Fanny,* in their screen versions (latter was filmed without songs). Bib: *Josh* (1976) and *Movie Stars, Real People and Me* (1978), both by Logan.

1958   South Pacific
1967   Camelot
1969   Paint Your Wagon

Lombard, Carole (née Jane Alice Peters), actress; b. Fort Wayne, Ind., Oct. 6, 1908; d. plane crash near Las Vegas, Jan. 16, 1942. The screen's most stylish comedienne of the 1930s was the nonsinging heroine of musicals, mostly at Paramount, co-starring Charles "Buddy" Rogers, Bing Crosby, George Raft, Fred MacMurray, and Fernand Gravet. She was married to William Powell (divorced) and Clark Gable. Bib: *Films of Carole Lombard* by Frederick Ott (1972); *Screwball* by Larry Swindell (1975).

1930   Safety in Numbers (*Pauline*)
1934   We're Not Dressing (*Doris Worthington*)
Bolero (*Helen Hathaway*)
1935   Rumba (*Diana Harrison*)
1937   Swing High, Swing Low (*Maggie King*)
1938   Fools for Scandal (*Kay Winters*)

Lombardo, (Gaetano) Guy, bandleader; b. London, Ontario, Canada, June 19, 1902; d. Houston, Texas, Nov. 5, 1977. Durable orchestra leader whose syrupy musical style became a fixture of New Year's Eve celebrations. Bib: *Auld Acquaintance* by Lombardo (1976).

1934   Many Happy Returns (*Guy Lombardo*)
1943   Stage Door Canteen (specialty)
1946   No Leave, No Love (specialty)

"Lonesome Polecat" Music by Gene de Paul; lyric by Johnny Mercer; Achingly deliberate song of romantic frustration sung in *Seven Brides for Seven Brothers* (MGM 1954) by brothers Matt Mattox (voice dubbed by Bill Lee), Russ Tamblyn, Tommy Rall, Jeff Richards, Marc Platt, and Jacques D'Amboise, and danced by Mattox. In the film, the boys are seen chopping wood and sawing a tree in winter; as they sing, their words are timed to the swinging axes and the back-and-forth movement of the saw.

"Long Ago (and Far Away)" Music by Jerome Kern; lyric by Ira Gershwin. In *Cover Girl* (Col. 1944), the scene is a deserted nightclub in Brooklyn where Phil Silvers is picking out the song's melody on the piano while proprietor Gene Kelly cleans up. Rita Hayworth enters and—with Martha Mears' voice—sings of the materialized love she had longed for long ago in a dream. Gene returns the sentiment, they kiss, and enjoy a brief, languorous dance. Ira Gershwin has related that he had tried four or five sets of lyrics before settling on the one that was used. One of the abandoned lyrics, when the song was called "Midnight Music," ended with an alliterative line the composer especially liked: "Darkened streets began to shine/ The moment midnight music made you mine." "Long Ago (and Far Away)" was also sung by Kathryn Grayson in *Till the Clouds Roll By* (MGM 1946).

"Look of Love, The" Music by Burt Bacharach; lyric by Hal David. Romantic declaration introduced on soundtrack of the James Bond spoof, *Casino Royale* (Col. 1967) by Dusty Springfield. Bacharach has claimed that he got the idea for the melody from looking at Ursula Andress ("very sexy in an elegant way").

"Lookie, Lookie, Lookie, Here Comes Cookie." *See* **"Here Comes Cookie"**

Loring, Eugene (né Leroy Kerpestein), choreographer, dancer; b. Milwaukee, 1914. Formerly with the Ballet Theatre (his most celebrated work was *Billy the Kid*), Loring was associated with Fred Astaire on four screen musicals. (Died Kingston, NY, Aug. 30, 1982.)

1945	Yolanda and the Thief
1946	Ziegfeld Follies
	Fiesta
1947	Something in the Wind (also dancer)
1948	Mexican Hayride
1949	The Inspector General
1950	The Toast of New Orleans
1953	The 5000 Fingers of Dr. T
	Torch Song (also *Gene*)
1954	Deep in My Heart
1956	Meet Me in Las Vegas
1957	Funny Face
	Silk Stockings
1960	Pepe

"Lose That Long Face" Music by Harold Arlen; lyric by Ira Gershwin. "Like Peter Pan, the sweeter pan wins the day," sang Judy Garland as a cheerful freckled newsboy in a production number in *A Star Is Born* (Warner 1954). Unfortunately, the song was cut soon after the film's release.

"Lost Horizon" Music by Burt Bacharach; lyric by Hal David. Mystical invitation to escape life's cares sung by Shawn Phillips over credits of *Lost Horizon* (Col. 1973).

"Louise" Music by Richard A. Whiting; lyric by Leo Robin. Maurice Chevalier's closely identified song ("Ev'ry little breeze seems to whisper Louise") which he used to serenade a girl (Sylvia Beecher) while sitting on a garden wall in *Innocents of Paris* (Par. 1929). The song was also sung by Johnny Johnston in *You Can't Ration Love* (Par. 1944); Jerry Lewis in *The Stooge* (Par. 1952); and Chevalier again in *New Kind of Love* (Par. 1963).

"Love" Music & lyric by Hugh Martin & Ralph Blane. Set to a pulsating beat, the many faces thereof were enumerated by Lena Horne in a tropical barroom scene in *Ziegfeld Follies* (MGM 1946).

"Love and Learn Blues." *See* **"Dissertation on the State of Bliss"**

"Love and Marriage" Music by James Van Heusen; lyric by Sammy Cahn. In the television adaptation of Thornton Wilder's *Our Town* (NBC 1955), stage manager Frank Sinatra introduced Act II (called "Love and Marriage") by singing about the combination that goes together like a horse and carriage.

Love, Bessie (née Juanita Horton), actress, singer, dancer; b. Midland, Texas, Sept. 10, 1898. The diminutive blonde heroine of *The Broadway Melody* began in films in 1915 and acted on the screen for some 60 years. (Died London, April 26, 1986.)

1929	The Broadway Melody (*Hank Mahoney*)
	Hollywood Revue of 1929 (specialty)
1930	They Learned About Women (*Mary*)
	Chasing Rainbows (*Carlie*)
	Good News (*Babe*)
1936	Live Again (Eng.) (*Cathleen Vernon*)

"Love Him" Music & lyric by Jay Livingston & Ray Evans. Bubbly announcement which Betty Hutton (as Blossom Seeley), accompanied by Ralph Meeker (Benny Fields), proclaimed during a benefit show in *Somebody Loves Me* (Par. 1952).

"Love in Bloom" Music by Ralph Rainger; lyric by Leo Robin. No, it isn't the trees or the spring or a dream, it's the real thing at last. Introduced by Bing Crosby and Kitty Carlisle in *She Loves Me Not* (Par. 1934). Also sung by Lynne Overman in *New York Town* (Par. 1941), and Judy Canova in *True to the Army* (Par. 1942). Best known as theme song of Jack Benny, who played it on the violin in *Man About Town* (Par. 1939).

"Love Is a Many-Splendored Thing" Music by Sammy Fain; lyric by Paul Francis Webster. Emotional tribute to romance, sung by the Four Aces over closing credits of film of same name (Fox 1955).

"Love Is Here To Stay" Music by George Gershwin; lyric by Ira Gershwin. The radio, telephone, and movies may be just passing fancies and even the Rockies and Gibraltar may not last forever, but, sang Kenny Baker in *The Goldwyn Follies* (Goldwyn 1938), the one thing that's permanent is our love. The song was also sung by Gene Kelly, then danced by him and Leslie Caron in *An American in Paris* (MGM 1951). The creation of the melody was the subject of some dispute between composer Vernon Duke and lyricist Ira Gershwin. Duke, who had taken over the *Follies'* remaining composing chores after George Gershwin's death, claimed in his book *Passport to Paris,* "All that could be found of 'Love Is Here To Stay' was a 20-bar incompleted lead sheet; fortunately, Oscar Levant remembered the harmonies from George's frequent piano performances of the song and I was able faithfully to reconstruct it." But according to Ira in *Lyrics on Several Occasions,* "George and I managed to finish five songs the first six weeks of our contract. (Vernon Duke and I fixed up a couple of missing verses later.) 'Love Is Here To Stay,' one of the five, was the last song George composed."

"Love Is Just Around the Corner" Music by Lewis Gensler; lyric by Leo Robin. Bouncy invitation to cuddle in a corner, extended by Bing Crosby in *Here Is My Heart* (Par. 1934) to Marian Mansfield, a girl who's even cuter than Venus ("And what's more you've got arms"). Song also sung by Robert Cummings in *Millions in the Air* (Par. 1935).

"Love Is On the Air Tonight" Music by Richard A. Whiting; lyric by Johnny Mercer. For the finale of *Varsity Show* (Warner 1937), a college revue on Broadway called *Varsity Show,* the cast marches in military formation down a flight of steps as Priscilla and Rosemary Lane sing about love being on a heart-to-heart hookup over the radio. Following a baton-twirling specialty, director Busby Berkeley had bandleader Fred Waring lead his Pennsylvanians in tossing footballs to the actors, who then heave them into the midst of the students. Seen in overhead shots they form the names of major colleges on cards while they sing songs appropriate to each school.

"Love Is the Tender Trap." *See* **"Tender Trap, The"**

"Love Is Where You Find It" Music by Nacio Herb Brown; lyric by Earl Brent. Rousing advice to take love while you may, offered by Jane Powell in *A Date with Judy* and by Kathryn Grayson in *The Kissing Bandit* (both MGM 1948).

"Love Isn't Born" Music by Arthur Schwartz; lyric by Frank Loesser. The premise that love won't come to the shy and demure but must be stimulated by feminine charms. Advice offered as part of an all-star charity revue in *Thank Your Lucky Stars* (Warner 1943) by Ann Sheridan singing to a dormitory of coeds.

Love Me Or Leave Me (1955). Screenplay by Daniel Fuchs and Isobel Lennart from story by Fuchs based on life of Ruth Etting.

An MGM film produced by Joe Pasternak; directed by Charles Vidor; choreography, Alex Romero; art directors, Cedric Gibbons, Urie McCleary; costumes, Helen Rose; music director, George Stoll; cameraman, Arthur Arling; editor, Ralph Winters; Eastman Color; CinemaScope.

Cast: Doris Day (*Ruth Etting Snyder*); James Cagney (*Martin "Gimp" Snyder*); Cameron Mitchell (*Johnny Alderman*); Robert Keith (*Bernard Loomis*); Tom Tully (*Frobisher*); Claude Stroud (*Eddie Fulton*); Harry Bellaver (*Georgie*); Richard Gaines (*Paul Hunter*); Veda Ann Borg (*hostess*).

Songs: "I'm Sitting on Top of the World" (Ray Henderson-Sam Lewis, Joe Young) - Stroud/ "It All Depends on You" (Henderson-B. G. DeSylva, Lew Brown) - / "You Made Me Love You" (James V. Monaco-Joe McCarthy) - / "Stay on the Right Side, Sister" (Rube Bloom-Ted Koehler) - / "Everybody Loves My Baby" (Spencer Williams-Jack Palmer) - / "Mean to Me" (Fred Ahlert-Roy Turk) - / "Sam, the Old Accordion Man" (Walter Donaldson) - / "Shaking the Blues Away" (Irving Berlin) - / "Ten Cents a Dance" (Richard Rodgers-Lorenz Hart) - / "I'll Never Stop Loving You" (Nicholas Brodszky-Sammy Cahn) - / "Never Look Back" (Brodszky-Cahn) - / "At Sundown'' (Donaldson) - / ''Love Me or Leave Me'' (Donaldson-Gus Kahn). All songs except first one sung by Day. Unused: ''Shine On Harvest Moon,'' ''Back in Your Own Back Yard.''

Hollywood's first showbiz biography to offer an unglamorized, mostly unsentimentalized account of a performer's life traced the career of ambitious torch-singer Ruth Etting from dime-a-dance hostess to nightclub, Broadway, and Hollywood star (though the real Ruth Etting was never a success in movies). As the movie's heroine, Doris Day was cast against her accustomed ginger-peachy apple-pie type to give her most impressive screen performance. But what gave the film its special distinction was James Cagney's performance as Gimp Snyder, a bullying but oddly sympathetic mobster who adored the singer, married her, and strongarmed her way to the top. At the end of the movie, as in real life, Snyder shoots (but only wounds) his wife's lover, which somehow leads to a happy fadeout for all three.

The success of *Love Me or Leave Me* helped pave the way for the public acceptance of such other more-or-less realistic musical biographies as MGM's *I'll Cry Tomorrow* (Susan Hayward as Lillian Roth), Paramount's *The Joker Is Wild* (Frank Sinatra as Joe E. Lewis), and Warner's *The Helen Morgan Story* (Ann Blyth, with Gogi Grant's voice, as Helen Morgan).

''Love Me Tender'' Music by George R. Poulton; lyric by Elvis Presley & Vera Matson. Plaintive, folkish ballad introduced by Elvis Presley in film of the same name (Fox 1956). The melody dates from 1861 when it had a lyric by William W. Fosdick called ''Aura Lea'' (later spelled ''Aura Lee''); also sung at West Point as ''Army Blue'' beginning in 1865.

Love Me Tonight (1932). Music by Richard Rodgers; lyrics by Lorenz Hart; screenplay by Samuel Hoffenstein, Waldemar Young, and George Marion, Jr., from play, *Tailor in the Chateau,* by Leopold Marchand & Paul Armont.

A Paramount film produced & directed by Rouben Mamoulian; art director, Hans Dreier; costumes, Travis Banton; music director, Nathaniel Finston; cameraman, Victor Milner; editor, William Shea.

Cast: Maurice Chevalier (*Maurice Courtelin*); Jeanette MacDonald (*Princess Jeanette*); Charlie Ruggles (*Vicomte Gilbert de Vareze*); Charles Butterworth (*Count de Savignac*); Myrna Loy (*Countess Valentine*); C. Aubrey Smith (*Duke*); Elizabeth Patterson, Ethel Griffies, Blanche Friderici (*aunts*); Joseph Cawthorn

(*doctor*); Robert Greig (*major-domo*); Marion ''Peanuts'' Byron (*Bakery Girl*); Bert Roach (*Emile*); George ''Gabby'' Hayes (*grocer*); Rolfe Sedan (*taxi driver*); Tyler Brooke (*composer*); Edgar Norton (*valet*); Herbert Mundin (*groom*); Rita Owin (*chambermaid*); Cecil Cunningham (*laundress*); Mel Calish (*chef*).

Songs: ''That's the Song of Paree'' - Chevalier, with Byron, Hayes, Parisians/ ''Isn't It Romantic?'' - Chevalier, Roach, Sedan, Brooke, French soldiers, gypsy violinist, MacDonald/ ''Lover'' - MacDonald/ ''Mimi'' - Chevalier; reprised by Smith, Ruggles, Patterson, Griffies, Friderici, Butterworth/ ''A Woman Needs Something Like That'' - Cawthorn, MacDonald/ ''Deer Hunt'' sequence - orchestra/ ''The Poor Apache'' - Chevalier/ ''Love Me Tonight'' - Chevalier, MacDonald/ ''The Son of a Gun Is Nothing but a Tailor'' - Smith, Patterson, Griffies, Friderici, Loy, Greig, Norton, Cunningham, Owin, Calish. Unused: ''The Man for Me'' (''The Letter Song'').

Though owing some of its satirical touches to such directors as René Clair and Ernst Lubitsch, *Love Me Tonight* remains one of the screen's most innovative and imaginative musicals. By its close integration of story, dialogue, song, scoring, and locale, and its sweeping use of the camera and skilful editing, it set the standards in the creation of a purely cinematic form of musical comedy. Because of the conceptual approach of director Rouben Mamoulian (who succeeded George Cukor before shooting began) and the composer-lyricist team of Richard Rodgers and Lorenz Hart, the film had a number of stylish, stylized musical sequences. There is the opening on an early-morning Paris with street workers drilling, brooms swishing, knives grinding, doors slamming, horns blaring, whistles tooting, and chimneys belching smoke, all synchronized into a symphony of sound (a device Mamoulian had first used in the 1927 play *Porgy* and which would be reused in Otto Preminger's 1959 film *Porgy and Bess*). Also, for the first time on screen, one song, ''Isn't It Romantic?,'' is the means through which the action is moved from one location to another—in this case, from a Paris tailor shop to a chateau in the country. Other imaginative sequences include the deer hunt ballet, in which slow motion is made to enhance the pastoral quality of the chase, and the quick cutting to various parts of the chateau to register musical reactions once it is discovered that Maurice Chevalier is not really a baron but only a lowly tailor come to collect a debt. Despite the deception, however, Maurice ends up with Princess Jeanette MacDonald after she has bravely stood in front of the oncoming train that is taking Maurice back to Paris.

Of the four films Chevalier and MacDonald made together, *Love Me Tonight* was the only one not directed by Ernst Lubitsch. It also marked the first time Myrna Loy was given a chance to show her ability as a light comedienne.

"Love Me Tonight" Music by Richard Rodgers; lyric by Lorenz Hart. Plea to avoid romantic delay introduced in *Love Me Tonight* (Par. 1932), as Maurice Chevalier dreams that he is singing with Jeanette MacDonald. The melody of Jule Styne's "Diamonds Are a Girl's Best Friend" (in the 1949 Broadway musical, *Gentlemen Prefer Blondes*) is reminiscent of this song.

"Love of My Life" Music & lyric by Cole Porter. Judy Garland sang to Gene Kelly of the fulfillment of her romantic dreams just before his scheduled hanging in *The Pirate* (MGM 1948).

Love Parade, The (1929). Music by Victor Schertzinger; lyrics by Clifford Grey; screenplay by Ernest Vajda & Guy Bolton from play, *Le Prince Consort,* by Leon Xanrof & Jules Chancel.

A Paramount film produced & directed by Ernst Lubitsch; art director, Hans Dreier; costumes, Travis Banton; music director, Victor Schertzinger; cameraman, Victor Milner; editor, Merrill White.

Cast: Maurice Chevalier (*Count Alfred Renard*); Jeanette MacDonald (*Queen Louise*); Lupino Lane (*Jacques*); Lillian Roth (*Lulu*); Edgar Norton (*Master of Ceremonies*); Lionel Belmore (*Prime Minister*); Eugene Pallette (*Minister of War*); Virginia Bruce (*Lady in Waiting*); Ben Turpin (*lackey*); Jean Harlow (*extra in theatre*).

Songs: "Champagne" - Lane/ "Paris, Stay the Same" - Chevalier, Lane/ "Dream Lover" - MacDonald/ "Anything To Please the Queen" - MacDonald, Chevalier/ "My Love Parade" - Chevalier, MacDonald/ "Let's Be Common" - Lane, Roth/ "March of the Grenadiers" - MacDonald, Grenadiers/ "Nobody's Using It Now" - Chevalier/ "The Queen Is Always Right" - Lane, Roth, servants.

The Love Parade, Ernst Lubitsch's first sound film, was also the first screen musical with a romantically sophisticated point of view as well as one in which the camera was used with some flexibility in the musical scenes, whether informally intimate ("My Love Parade") or formally remote ("March of the Grenadiers"). Moreover, it marked the director's first

opportunity—of three—to work with Maurice Chevalier and Jeanette MacDonald as a team. Set in Paris and in the mythical queendom of Sylvania, *The Love Parade* was a frothy boudoir operetta very much in the style of such other Lubitsch-Chevalier endeavors as *The Smiling Lieutenant* and *The Merry Widow* (which also co-starred Miss MacDonald). Though, unlike the other two, it was not adapted from a Viennese operetta, the film could almost be a sequel to *The Merry Widow* as it revealed what might have happened if Danilo had been recalled from Paris before meeting Sonia. In *The Love Parade,* Count Alfred has been summoned home from his diplomatic post by Sylvania's Queen Louise because of his numerous escapades. The queen, however, falls in love with Alfred and they marry. Bored at being a figurehead, the prince consort threatens to return to Paris, but he is persuaded to remain when Louise promises to treat him like a king.

"Love Theme from 'A Star Is Born'." *See* **"Evergreen"**

"Love Thy Neighbor" Music by Harry Revel; lyric by Mack Gordon. Building a hut on a tropical island in *We're Not Dressing* (Par. 1934), sailor Bing Crosby offers biblical advice (Leviticus XIX, 18) that might just possibly lead to romance.

"Love Walked In" Music by George Gershwin; lyric by Ira Gershwin. Welcome appearance revealed by Kenny Baker as a lunch-counter waiter in *The Goldwyn Follies* (Goldwyn 1938). The lyric to the song never completely satisfied Ira Gershwin, who felt it was padded (the word "right," for example, in the line, "Love walked right in") and pompous ("wallowing in a swamp of vague generalities"). Song was also sung by Mark Stevens (with Bill Days's voice) in *Rhapsody in Blue* (Warner 1945).

"Love, You Didn't Do Right By Me" Music & lyric by Irving Berlin. Affecting torch ballad, sung by Rosemary Clooney as a nightclub singer in *White Christmas* (Par. 1954).

"Love, Your Magic Spell Is Everywhere" Music by Edmund Goulding; lyric by Elsie Janis. In which Gloria Swanson, in the *Trespasser* (UA 1929), emotionally revealed her inability to resist romance.

"Loveliest Night of the Year, The" Music by Juventino Rosas, adapted by Irving Aaronson; lyric by Paul Francis Webster. Sung by Ann Blyth (her only song in the film) as Mrs. Enrico Caruso in *The Great Caruso* (MGM 1951), while waltzing with her husband (Mario Lanza) during his birthday party at an Italian restaurant in New York. The melody was adapted from Rosas' *"Obre las Olas"* (*"Over the Waves"*), a Mexican waltz published in 1888, which has somehow become associated with performing seals.

"Lovely Lady" Music by Jimmy McHugh; lyric by Ted Koehler. Kenny Baker's ardent, waltzing serenade introduced in a production number in *King of Burlesque* (Fox 1935).

Lovely To Look At. See Roberta.

"Lovely To Look At" Music by Jerome Kern; lyric by Dorothy Fields. Cascading ballad introduced at a fashion show in *Roberta* (RKO 1935) by Irene Dunne, then reprised and danced in same scene by Fred Astaire and Ginger Rogers. Also sung by Howard Keel in *Lovely To Look At* (MGM 1952), a remake of *Roberta*. Upon hearing the music for the first time, producer Pandro S. Berman commented to Kern, "Isn't it kind of short?" To which the composer replied, "That's all I had to say"— and he wouldn't add a note to the 16-bar refrain. Since this was the first song Kern and Fields wrote together, Miss Fields agreed to allow Jimmy McHugh, previously her regular partner, to share lyric-writing credit. Also the first of the team's "Look" songs, "Lovely To Look At" was followed by "The Way You Look Tonight" (*Swing Time*) and "Just Let Me Look At You" (*Joy of Living*).

"Lovely Way To Spend an Evening, A" Music by Jimmy McHugh; lyric by Harold Adamson. In *Higher and Higher* (RKO 1943), Frank Sinatra (as Frank Sinatra) sings to Michelle Morgan of his delight in being with her as they sit on a park bench in New York's Central Park. Conveniently, he is accompanied by a symphony orchestra giving an outdoor concert.

"Lover" Music by Richard Rodgers; lyric by Lorenz Hart. As presented in *Love Me Tonight* (Par. 1932), the lilting ballad was sung by Jeanette MacDonald while riding in a buggy, with certain words also used to give instructions to her horse (i.e., "woe" became "Whoa!" and "hay" became "Hey!"). Song later outfitted with

more commercial lyric and sung by Deanna Durbin in *Because of Him* (Univ. 1946); Peggy Lee in *The Jazz Singer* (Warner 1953); Fred Astaire in *The Pleasure of His Company* (Par. 1961); and Jerry Lewis in *The Errand Boy* (Par. 1962).

Loy, Myrna (née Myrna Williams), actress, dancer; b. Raidersburg, Mont., Aug. 2, 1905. Sloe-eyed early screen vamp whose comic ability was first revealed in *Love Me Tonight* and who later became celebrated as the flippant, worldly Nora Charles in *The Thin Man* series. First and third of four husbands were producers Arthur Hornblow, Jr., and Gene Markey.

1927 The Jazz Singer (*chorus girl*)
1929 The Desert Song (*Azuri*)
     The Show of Shows (specialty)
1930 Cameo Kirby (*Lea*)
     Bride of the Regiment (*Sophie*)
1932 Love Me Tonight (*Countess Valentine*)
1936 The Great Ziegfeld (*Billie Burke*)

Lubitsch, Ernst, director, producer; b. Berlin, Jan. 28, 1892; d. Los Angeles, Nov. 30, 1947. Celebrated for his distinctive "Lubitsch touch" that enlivened a series of Hollywood comedies, both silent and sound, with music and without. Usually set in Europe, his films offered a stylized world of gaiety, charm, and wit usually inhabited by Maurice Chevalier (in five musicals) and Jeanette MacDonald (in four, three of them with Chevalier and one with Jack Buchanan). Bib: *The Lubitsch Touch* by Herman G. Weinberg (1977); *Cinema of Ernst Lubitsch* by Leland Poague (1977).

Asterisk indicates Mr. Lubitsch was also producer:
1929 The Love Parade*
1930 Paramount on Parade (part dir.)
     Monte Carlo*
1931 The Smiling Lieutenant*
1932 One Hour with You*
1934 The Merry Widow (also assoc. prod.)
1947 That Lady in Ermine* (part dir.)

"Lullaby of Broadway" Music by Harry Warren; lyric by Al Dubin. Driving number used for a celebrated Busby Berkeley creation in *Gold Diggers of 1935* (Warner 1935). In the scene, offered as part of the entertainment at a resort hotel, we first see the tiny disembodied face of singer Wini Shaw becoming larger and larger until it takes up the entire screen. First she paints the picture of pell-mell Broadway life with its hip-hooray and ballyhoo, then, on the words, "Good night, baby," the tempo slows as she sings a lullaby to a Manhattan lady going home to her flat at dawn. Suddenly, Miss Shaw's face turns upside down to become a section of Manhattan's skyline. It is 6:45 a.m., everyone is waking up and scurrying off to work. But this is the time that Wini, in an evening gown, comes home with top-hatted Dick Powell, who gallantly leaves her with a kiss. She pours milk for her cat and sleeps until 6:45 p.m., when she dresses and is whisked off to all the night spots. At one cavernous, high-in-the-sky pleasure dome, she and Powell are the only customers as half the city's population dances on a number of levels while being shot from a number of angles (including directly beneath a male trio's tapping feet). Playfully, Wini rushes past the door leading to the balcony, with Dick and the dancers in pursuit. As Powell pushes out the door, it hits the girl and she falls over the ledge to her death. Again it is 6:45 a.m., and again we are back at her apartment, but this time there is no one to give the cat its milk. Once more we see the city's skyline, then Wini Shaw's face singing the "Lullaby" as it reverses the opening scene and recedes into darkness. The song was also sung by Doris Day in *Lullaby of Broadway* (Warner 1951).

"Lulu's Back in Town" Music by Harry Warren; lyric by Al Dubin. The reason—in *Broadway Gondolier* (Warner 1935)—why Dick Powell, with the Mills Brothers, sings of the necessity for getting his tuxedo pressed, sewing a button on his vest, having his shoes shined, and slicking his hair.

Lupino, Ida, actress; b. London, Jan. 1, 1914. Husky-voiced, slim blonde actress whose roles turned increasingly dramatic; later became director and producer. Most of her singing in films was done by Peg LaCentra. Miss Lupino is the daughter of British comedian Stanley Lupino and the niece of British comedian Lupino Lane.

1934	Prince of Arcadia (Eng.)	(*Princess*)
1935	Paris in Spring	(*Mignon de Charelle*)
1936	Anything Goes	(*Hope Harcourt*)
1937	Artists and Models	(*Paula Sewell*)
1942	The Hard Way	(*Helen Chernin*)
1943	Thank Your Lucky Stars	(specialty)
1944	Hollywood Canteen	(guest bit)
1946	The Man I Love	(*Petey Brown*)
1948	Road House	(*Lily Stevens*)

"Lydia, the Tattooed Lady" Music by Harold Arlen; lyric by E. Y. Harburg. Raucous description of the art work found on the lady's body ("Here is Captain Spald-

ing exploring the Amazon/ Here's Lady Godiva but with her pajamas on"). Delivered by leering cicerone Groucho Marx, accompanied on piano by brother Chico, as he entertains train passengers in *At the Circus* (MGM 1939). Song was also sung by Virginia Weidler in *The Philadelphia Story* (MGM 1940).

Lynn, Diana (née Dolores Loehr), actress, pianist; b. Los Angeles, Oct. 7, 1926; d. Los Angeles, Dec. 18, 1971. A versatile actress on both screen and stage, pert, round-faced Diana Lynn was also a concert pianist. In Hollywood, where she used the name Dolly Loehr for her first film, she initially won recognition in bratty kid-sister parts.

1941	There's Magic in Music	(*Dolly Loehr*)
1942	Star Spangled Rhythm	(specialty)
1944	And the Angels Sing	(*Josie Angel*)
1945	Out of This World	(*Betty Miller*)
	Duffy's Tavern	(specialty)
1947	Variety Girl	(guest bit)
1949	My Friend Irma	(*Jane Stacy*)
1950	My Friend Irma Goes West	(*Jane Stacy*)
1952	Meet Me at the Fair	(*Zerelda Wing*)
1955	You're Never Too Young	(*Nancy Collins*)
1957	Junior Miss (tv)	(*Ellen Curtis*)

Lynn, Vera, (née Vera Margaret Welch), singer, actress; b. London, March 20, 1917. Dame of the British Empire 1975. England's most popular vocalist during World War II made a few British films and was most closely associated with song, "We'll Meet Again." Bib: *Vocal Refrain* by Miss Lynn (1976).

1942	We'll Meet Again	(*Peggy Brown*)
1943	Rhythm Serenade	(*Ann Martin*)
1944	One Exciting Night	(*Vera Baker*)

Lyon, Ben, actor, singer; b. Atlanta, Feb. 16, 1901; d. aboard Queen Elizabeth II, March 22, 1979. Became film actor in 1923 and is best remembered for dramatic roles (e.g., *Hell's Angels*). Moved to England with wife Bebe Daniels, where they were popular radio team; later was casting director for Fox. Bib: *Life with the Lyons* by Miss Daniels & Lyon (1953); *Bebe and Ben* by Jill Allgood (1975).

1931	The Hot Heiress	(*Hap Harrigan*)
	Indiscreet	(*Tony Blake*)
	Her Majesty Love	(*Fred Von Wellingen*)
1936	Dancing Feet	(*Peyton*)
1937	Stardust (Eng.)	(*Roy Harley*)
1941	Hi, Gang! (Eng.)	(*Ben Lyon*)

M

MacDonald, Jeanette (Anna), actress, singer; b. Philadelphia, June 18, 1903; d. Houston, Jan. 14, 1965. Former Broadway leading lady who became the slim, trilling, patrician heroine of screen operetta, first with Maurice Chevalier (*The Love Parade, One Hour with You, Love Me Tonight, The Merry Widow*), then even more successfully with Nelson Eddy (including *Naughty Marietta, Rose Marie, Maytime, Sweethearts*). She also appeared opposite Jack Buchanan (*Monte Carlo*), Ramon Novarro (*The Cat and the Fiddle*), Clark Gable (*San Francisco*), and Allan Jones (*The Firefly*). Among the songs she introduced were ''Beyond the Blue Horizon,'' ''Isn't It Romantic?,'' ''Lover,'' ''San Francisco,'' and ''Would You?'' Miss MacDonald, who was married to Gene Raymond, made many recordings. Bib: *Films of Jeanette MacDonald and Nelson Eddy* by Eleanor Knowles (1975).

Asterisk indicates appearance with Mr. Eddy:
1929 The Love Parade (*Queen Louise*)
1930 The Vagabond King (*Katherine de Vaucelles*)
   Monte Carlo (*Countess Helene Mara*)
   Let's Go Native (*Joan Wood*)
   The Lottery Bride (*Jennie Swanson*)
   Oh, for a Man! (*Carlotta Manson*)
1932 One Hour with You (*Colette Bertier*)
   Love Me Tonight (*Princess Jeanette*)
1934 The Cat and the Fiddle (*Shirley Sheridan*)
   The Merry Widow (*Sonia*)
1935 Naughty Marietta* (*Princess Marie*)
1936 Rose Marie* (*Marie de Flor*)
   San Francisco (*Mary Blake*)
1937 Maytime* (*Marcia Mornay*)
   The Firefly (*Nina Maria Azara*)
1938 The Girl of the Golden West* (*Mary Robbins*)
   Sweethearts* (*Gwen Marlowe*)
1939 Broadway Serenade (*Mary Hale*)
1940 New Moon* (*Marianne de Beaumanoir*)
   Bitter Sweet* (*Sari Linden*)
1941 Smilin' Through (*Kathleen/Moonyean Clare*)
1942 I Married an Angel* (*Brigitta*)
   Cairo (*Marcia Warren*)
1944 Follow the Boys (specialty)
1948 Three Daring Daughters (*Louise Morgan*)
1949 The Sun Comes Up (*Helen Lorfield Winter*)

''Mack the Black'' Music & lyric by Cole Porter. Galvanic number about the exploits of a daring pirate who sailed ''round the Carib*bé*-an—or in case you're not agreein'—the C*a*rib*-*bean Sea.'' Introduced by Judy Garland in *The Pirate* (MGM 1948), in a scene in which she wanders into a tent where Gene Kelly and his troupe of strolling players are putting on a show. Succumbing to the revolving mirror Kelly uses in his hypnotism act, Miss Garland confesses her love for the notorious pirate, Macoco—and then sings all about him. Though in the play from which the film was adapted the pirate's name was Estramundo, Cole Porter suggested it be changed to Macoco since he had a friend of that name who was known as Mack the Black.

MacLaine, Shirley (née Shirley MacLean Beatty), actress, singer, dancer; b. Richmond, Va., April 24, 1934. Though she went to Hollywood after being discovered in the Broadway musical *The Pajama Game*, Miss MacLaine has starred primarily in nonmusical films. The sister of actor Warren Beatty, she has also appeared on television and in one-woman concerts. Bib: *Films of Shirley MacLaine* by Patricia Erens (1978).

1955 Artists and Models (*Bessie Sparrowbush*)
1960 Can-Can (*Simone Pistache*)
1964 What a Way To Go (*Louisa May Benson*)
1968 Sweet Charity (*Charity Hope Valentine*)

MacMurray, (Frederick Martin) Fred, actor, singer; b. Kankakee, Ill., Aug. 30, 1907. Personable, down-to-earth leading man who appeared mostly in Paramount films, both musical and nonmusical. In former, often played the part of a musician (he had been a saxophonist before his acting debut) and introduced "Small Fry" and "Jingle Jangle Jingle." Appeared opposite such ladies as Carole Lombard (twice), Gladys Swarthout, Dorothy Lamour, Mary Martin, and June Haver (later his wife). Also acted in television series and in Walt Disney films.

1935   To Beat the Band (musician)
1937   Champagne Waltz (*Buzzy Bellew*)
       Swing High, Swing Low (*Skid Johnson*)
1938   Cocoanut Grove (*Johnny Prentice*)
       Sing You Sinners (*David Beebe*)
1939   Café Society (*Chick O'Bannon*)
1942   Star Spangled Rhythm (specialty)
1944   And the Angels Sing (*Happy Morgan*)
1945   Where Do We Go from Here? (*Bill*)
1950   Never a Dull Moment (*Chris Heyward*)
1967   The Happiest Millionaire (*Anthony J. Drexel Biddle*)

MacRae, Gordon, actor, singer; b. East Orange, NJ, March 12, 1921. Robust leading man with matching baritone who starred in Warner musicals between 1949 and 1953. In mid-50s he appeared with Shirley Jones in film versions of two Rodgers and Hammerstein classics, *Oklahoma!* and *Carousel.* Acted opposite Doris Day in four movies, June Haver in two. Made records and appeared in nightclubs and on television. (Died Lincoln, Neb., Jan. 24, 1986.)

1949   Look for the Silver Lining (*Frank Carter*)
1950   The Daughter of Rosie O'Grady (*Tony Pastor*)
       Tea for Two (*Jimmy Smith*)
       The West Point Story (*Tom Fletcher*)
1951   On Moonlight Bay (*Bill Sherman*)
       Starlift (*Gordon MacRae*)
1952   About Face (*Tony Williams*)
1953   By the Light of the Silvery Moon (*Bill Sherman*)
       The Desert Song (*Paul Bonnard*)
       Three Sailors and a Girl (*Choirboy Jones*)
1955   Oklahoma! (*Curly McLain*)
1956   Carousel (*Billy Bigelow*)
       The Best Things in Life Are Free (*Buddy DeSylva*)
1958   The Gift of the Magi (tv) (*Jim Young*)

Magidson, Herb, lyricist; b. Braddock, Pa., Jan. 7, 1906. Magidson's most noted Hollywood songs were both written with composer Con Conrad: "The Continental" (*The Gay Divorcee*) and "Midnight in Paris" (*Here's to Romance*). He also wrote with Michael Cleary, Ned Washington, Joe Meyer, Jack Yellen, Ben Oakland, Allie Wrubel, Jule Styne, and Lew Pollack. His songs were associated with Fred Astaire, Ginger Rogers, Nino Martini, Alice Faye, Harriet Hilliard, and Kenny Baker. (Died Beverly Hills, Jan. 2, 1986.)

1929   The Forward Pass (Cleary-Washington)
1930   Little Johnny Jones (Cleary-Washington)
1931   Bright Lights (Cleary-Washington)
1934   The Gift of Gab (Conrad)
       The Gay Divorcee (Conrad)
1935   George White's Scandals (Meyer-Yellen)
1936   Hats Off (Oakland)
1937   Life of the Party (Wrubel)
1938   Radio City Revels (Wrubel)
1942   Priorities on Parade (Styne)
       Sleepy-Time Gal (Styne)
1944   Music in Manhattan (Pollack)
1945   Sing Your Way Home (Wrubel)

"Main Street" Music by Roger Edens; lyric by Betty Comden & Adolph Green; Jaunty celebration of small-town America, sung and danced by Gene Kelly and Vera-Ellen at a rehearsal hall in *On the Town* (MGM 1949).

"Make 'Em Laugh" Music by Nacio Herb Brown; lyric by Arthur Freed. Donald O'Connor's big number in *Singin' in the Rain* (MGM 1952), in which he goes through a series of sight gags to cheer up Gene Kelly. The idea of the song was pirated from *The Pirate's* "Be a Clown" by Cole Porter.

"Make Way for Tomorrow" Music by Jerome Kern; lyric by Ira Gershwin & E. Y. Harburg. Joyously optimistic march for Gene Kelly, Rita Hayworth (Martha Mears' voice), and Phil Silvers in *Cover Girl* (Col. 1944). In the scene, the three celebrants improvise an assortment of handy props—bread sticks for batons, garbage-can tops for shields, a mailbox for a tom-tom, assorted buckets and paddles—as they dance merrily through a Brooklyn street and up and down brownstone steps. They have an encounter with a policeman, tap dance with a milkman, narrowly avoid being hit by a flower pot, and do their best to straighten out a drunk (Jack Norton).

Mamoulian, Rouben, director; b. Tiflis, Russia, Oct. 8, 1898. Highly imaginative, versatile director responsible for such major screen musicals as *Love Me Tonight* and *High, Wide and Handsome,* as well as such major stage musicals as *Porgy and Bess, Oklahoma!,* and *Car-*

ousel. Among actors he directed: Helen Morgan, Maurice Chevalier, Jeanette MacDonald, Nino Martini, Irene Dunne, Mickey Rooney, Fred Astaire, and Cyd Charisse. Bib: *Mamoulian* by Tom Milne (1969). (Died Woodland Hills, Cal., Dec. 4, 1987.)

1929	Applause
1932	Love Me Tonight (also prod.)
1936	The Gay Desperado
1937	High, Wide and Handsome (also co-script)
1948	Summer Holiday
1957	Silk Stockings

"Man and His Dream, A" Music by James V. Monaco; lyric by Johnny Burke. Nocturnal romantic fantasizing by Bing Crosby in *The Star Maker* (Par. 1939).

"Man That Got Away, The" Music by Harold Arlen; lyric by Ira Gershwin. Compelling torch song about the end of an affair that runs the emotional gamut from feigned relief ("Good riddance, goodbye") to a vain hope for reconciliation. Introduced in *A Star Is Born* (Warner 1954) by Judy Garland accompanied by musicians at a deserted Los Angeles nightclub in the wee hours of the morning.

Mancini, Henry, composer; b. Cleveland, April 16, 1924. Prolific creator of film and television background scores who began career as dance-band pianist and arranger, then became conductor at Universal (1951–57). Songs from nonmusical films scored by Mancini include "Moon River" and "Days of Wine and Roses" (both lyrics by Johnny Mercer) and "Dear Heart" (Jay Livingston and Ray Evans). He also wrote "Whistling Away the Dark" for *Darling Lili*. Mancini has made many records and concert appearances.

1969	Darling Lili (Mercer)
1982	Victor/Victoria (Bricusse)

"Marie" Music & lyric by Irving Berlin. Romantic serenade introduced by unidentified singer in *The Awakening* (UA 1928). Also sung by chorus in *Alexander's Ragtime Band* (Fox 1938).

Marshall, George, director; b. Chicago, Dec. 29, 1891; d. Los Angeles, Feb. 17, 1975. Marshall began directing films in 1917. He was at Fox during the 30s, with Paramount between 1942 and 1954, though his most famous movie with music was Universal's *Destry Rides Again*. Alice Faye, Dick Powell, Bob Hope, Dorothy Lamour, Betty Hutton, Mary Martin, Dean Martin, and Jerry Lewis all were in at least two films directed by Marshall, who continued to be active through 1969.

1934	She Learned About Sailors
	365 Nights in Hollywood
1935	Music Is Magic
1936	Can This Be Dixie?
1938	The Goldwyn Follies
	Hold That Coed
1939	Destry Rides Again
1941	Pot o' Gold
1942	Star-Spangled Rhythm
1943	True to Life
	Riding High
1944	And the Angels Sing
1945	Incendiary Blonde
1947	The Perils of Pauline
	Variety Girl (also guest bit)
1949	My Friend Irma
1950	Fancy Pants
	Never a Dull Moment
1953	Scared Stiff
	Money from Home
1954	Red Garters
1955	The Second Greatest Sex

Martin, Dean (né Dino Paul Crocetti), actor, singer; b. Steubenville, Ohio, June 17, 1917. Martin rose to fame in theatres, nightclubs, and on television as the pococurante crooning partner of the juvenile spastic clown, Jerry Lewis. The team starred in 17 Paramount films between 1949 and 1956; after the breakup, Martin continued on his own in both musical and dramatic films. He also starred in a television series and has made many records. His most popular movie song was "That's Amore," introduced in *The Caddy*. Bib: *Everybody Loves Somebody* by Arthur Marx (1974).

1949	My Friend Irma (*Steve Laird*)
1950	My Friend Irma Goes West (*Steve Laird*)
	At War with the Army (*Sgt. Vic Puccinelli*)
1951	That's My Boy (*Bill Baker*)
	Sailor Beware (*Al Crothers*)
1952	Jumping Jacks (*Chick Allen*)
	Road to Bali (guest bit)
	The Stooge (*Bill Miller*)
1953	Scared Stiff (*Larry Todd*)
	The Caddy (*Joe Anthony*)
	Money from Home ("*Honey-Talk*" *Nelson*)
1954	Living It Up (*Steve Harris*)
	Three Ring Circus (*Pete Nelson*)
1955	You're Never Too Young (*Bob Miles*)
	Artists and Models (*Rick Todd*)

1956 Pardners (*Slim Moseley Sr./Slim Moseley Jr.*)
      Hollywood or Bust (*Steve Wiley*)
1957 10,000 Bedrooms (*Ray Hunter*)
1960 Bells Are Ringing (*Jeff Moss*)
1962 Road to Hong Kong (guest bit)
1964 Robin and the Seven Hoods (*Little John*)
1965 Kiss Me Stupid (*Dino*)

Martin, Hugh, composer, lyricist; b. Birmingham, Ala., Aug. 11, 1914. After beginning as singer with Ralph Blane in vocal quartet in Broadway musicals, Martin joined Blane to write the score of *Best Foot Forward,* later filmed. In Hollywood, the team's most notable achievement was *Meet Me in St. Louis,* whence came "The Boy Next Door," "The Trolley Song," and "Have Yourself a Merry Little Christmas." Other Martin-Blane songs include "Love" (*Ziegfeld Follies*) and "Pass That Peace Pipe" with Roger Edens (*Good News*). June Allyson, Judy Garland, Lena Horne, Jane Powell, and Vic Damone all sang film songs by Hugh Martin.

1943 Best Foot Forward (Blane)
1944 Meet Me in St. Louis (Blane)
1945 Abbott and Costello in Hollywood (Blane)
1954 Athena (Blane)
1955 The Girl Rush (Blane)
1957 The Girl Most Likely (Blane)
1958 Hans Brinker (tv) (alone)

Martin, Mary (Virginia), actress, singer; b. Weatherford, Texas, Dec. 1, 1913. Major star of Broadway musicals (eight, including *South Pacific, Peter Pan,* and *The Sound of Music*), Miss Martin combined naïve charm and buoyant enthusiasm with a warm and rangy soprano. In Hollywood she sang opposite Dick Powell in three films, Bing Crosby in two; others were with Allan Jones, Jack Benny, Don Ameche, and Fred MacMurray. Among songs she introduced on the screen were "Ain't It a Shame About Mame?," "I Don't Want To Cry Anymore," "Kiss the Boys Goodbye," "Hit the Road to Dreamland," and "Let's Get Lost." Bib: *My Heart Belongs* by Miss Martin (1976).

1938 Shopworn Angel (vocal for Margaret Sullavan)
1939 The Great Victor Herbert (*Louise Hall*)
1940 Rhythm on the River (*Cherry Lane*)
      Love Thy Neighbor (*Mary Allen*)
1941 Kiss the Boys Goodbye (*Cindy Lou Bethany*)
      Birth of the Blues (*Betty Lou Cobb*)
1942 Star Spangled Rhythm (specialty)
1943 Happy Go Lucky (*Marjorie Stuart*)
      True to Life (*Bonnie Porter*)

1946 Night and Day (*Mary Martin*)
1953 Main Street to Broadway (*Mary Martin*)

Martin, Tony (né Alvin Morris), actor, singer; b. Oakland, Cal., Dec. 25, 1912. Emotional singer with romantic vibrato who projected an air of self-conscious confidence. Active in Fox films in the late 30s, then mostly at MGM. "When Did You Leave Heaven?," "You Stepped Out of a Dream," "For Every Man There's a Woman," and "Hooray for Love" were among the songs Martin introduced. Known as Anthony Martin in his first six films, the singer has acted opposite Alice Faye (his first wife), Rita Hayworth, Janet Leigh, Ann Miller, and Vera-Ellen. He is married to Cyd Charisse, with whom he appears in nightclubs and theatres. Bib: *The Two of Us* by Miss Charisse & Martin (1976).

1936 Follow the Fleet (*sailor*)
      Poor Little Rich Girl (*radio singer*)
      Sing, Baby, Sing (*Tony Renald*)
      Pigskin Parade (*Tommy Baker*)
      Banjo on My Knee (*Chick Bean*)
1937 The Holy Terror (*Danny Walker*)
      Sing and Be Happy (*Buzz Mason*)
      You Can't Have Everything (*Bobby Walker*)
      Life Begins in College (*bandleader*)
      Ali Baba Goes to Town (*Yusuf*)
1938 Sally, Irene and Mary (*Tommy Reynolds*)
      Kentucky Moonshine (*Jerry Wade*)
      Thanks for Everything (*Tommy Davis*)
1940 Music in My Heart (*Bob Gregory*)
1941 Ziegfeld Girl (*Frank Merton*)
      The Big Store (*Tommy Rogers*)
1946 Till the Clouds Roll By ("*Ravenal*")
1948 Casbah (*Pepe LeMoko*)
1951 Two Tickets to Broadway (*Danny Carter*)
1953 Here Come the Girls (*Allen Trent*)
      Easy To Love (*Barry Gordon*)
1954 Deep in My Heart (specialty)
1955 Hit the Deck (*Bilge Clark*)
1956 Meet Me in Las Vegas (guest bit)
1957 Let's Be Happy (Eng) (*Stanley Smith*)

Martini, Nino, actor, singer; b. Verona, Italy, Aug. 8, 1904; d. Verona, Dec. 9, 1976. Metropolitan opera tenor of slight build whose screen career is recalled for introducing the song "Midnight in Paris" and playing the lead in Rouben Mamoulian's *The Gay Desperado.*

1930 Paramount on Parade (specialty)
1935 Here's to Romance (*Nino Donelli*)
1936 The Gay Desperado (*Chivo*)
1937 Music for Madame (*Tonio*)
1949 One Night with You (Eng.) (*Giuilo Moris*)

Marx Brothers, actors. Groucho (né Julius Henry), b. New York, Oct. 2, 1890; d. Los Angeles, Aug. 19, 1977. Harpo (né Adolph Arthur), b. New York, Nov. 23, 1888; d. Hollywood, Sept. 28, 1964. Chico (né Leonard), b. New York, March 22, 1887; d. Hollywood, Oct. 11, 1961. Zeppo (né Herbert), b. New York, Feb. 25, 1901; d. Palm Springs, Nov. 30, 1979. Surrealistic clowns who began in vaudeville (1917–24), then appeared in three Broadway musicals, of which two, *The Cocoanuts* and *Animal Crackers,* were filmed. Groucho, the acknowledged leader, was the insulting, wise-cracking con man with a painted-on thick mustache and a long cigar, who leered at the pretty girls and walked in a crouch; the impish, mute Harpo sported a top hat and curly blond wig and played the harp; Chico spoke with a supposed Italian accent, wore a cone-shaped hat, played piano, and was usually the thick-headed foil; Zeppo was the bland juvenile and singer. The foursome appeared in four Paramount films with songs; with the retirement of Zeppo in 1933, the remaining Groucho, Harpo, and Chico acted in five MGM musicals, of which *A Night at the Opera* and *A Day at the Races* were the acknowledged best. The act broke up in 1949, with Groucho continuing alone in films and as host of a television quiz show.

Bib: *The Marx Brothers* by Kyle Crichton (1950); *Groucho and Me* by Groucho (1959); *Harpo Speaks* by Harpo (1961); *The Marx Brothers: Their World of Comedy* by Allen Eyles (1966); *The Marx Brothers at the Movies* by Paul Zimmerman (1968); *Why a Duck?* ed. Richard Anobile (1971); *The Marx Brothers Scrapbook* (1973); *Groucho, Harpo, Chico and Sometimes Zeppo* by Joe Adamson (1973).

1929   The Cocoanuts (Groucho: *Mr. Hammer;* Harpo: *Harpo;* Chico: *Chico;* Zeppo: *Jamison*).

1930   Animal Crackers (Groucho: *Capt. Jeffrey T. Spalding;* Harpo: *Professor;* Chico: *Emanuel Ravelli;* Zeppo: *Horatio Jamison*)

1932   Horse Feathers (Groucho: *Prof. Quincy Adams Wagstaff;* Harpo: *Pinky;* Chico: *Barovelli;* Zeppo: *Frank Wagstaff*)

1933   Duck Soup (Groucho: *Rufus T. Firefly;* Harpo: *Pinky;* Chico: *Chicolini;* Zeppo: *Bob Rolland*)

1935   A Night at the Opera (Groucho: *Otis B. Driftwood;* Harpo: *Tomasso;* Chico: *Fiorello*)

1937   A Day at the Races (Groucho: *Dr. Hugo Z. Hackenbush;* Harpo: *Stuffy;* Chico: *Tony*)

1939   At the Circus (Groucho: *J. Cheever Loophole;* Harpo: *Punchy;* Chico: *Antonio Pirelli*)

1940   Go West (Groucho: *S. Quentin Quayle;* Harpo: *Rusty Panello;* Chico: *Joseph Panello*)

1941   The Big Store (Groucho: *Wolf J. Flywheel;* Harpo: *Wacky;* Chico: *Ravelli*)

1943   Stage Door Canteen (Harpo only: guest bit)

1947   Copacabana (Groucho only: *Lionel Q. Devereaux*)

1949   Love Happy (Groucho: *Sam Grunion;* Harpo: *Harpo;* Chico: *Faustino the Great*) (Harpo also script)

1950   Mr. Music (Groucho only: guest bit)

1951   Double Dynamite (Groucho only: *Emil J. Kech*)

Mary Poppins (1964). Music & lyrics by Richard M. Sherman & Robert B. Sherman; screenplay by Bill Walsh & Don DaGradi from books by P. L. Travers.

A Buena Vista film produced by Walt Disney; directed by Robert Stevenson; choreography, Marc Breaux & DeeDee Wood; art directors, Carroll Clark, William Tuntke, Tony Walton; costumes, Walton, Bill Thomas; music director, Irwin Kostal; orchestrations, Kostal; cameraman, Edward Colman; editor, Cotton Warburton; Technicolor.

Cast: Julie Andrews (*Mary Poppins*); Dick Van Dyke (*Bert/ Mr. Dawes*); David Tomlinson (*George W. Banks*); Glynis Johns (*Winifred Banks*); Hermione Baddeley (*Ellen*); Reta Shaw (*Mrs. Brill*); Karen Dotrice (*Jane Banks*); Matthew Garber (*Michael Banks*); Ed Wynn (*Uncle Albert*); Elsa Lanchester (*Katie Nanna*); Arthur Treacher (*Constable Jones*); Reginald Owen (*Admiral Boom*); Jane Darwell (*bird woman*).

Songs: "The Perfect Nanny" - Dotrice, Garber/ "Sister Suffragette" - Johns/ "The Life I Lead" - Tomlinson/ "A Spoonful of Sugar" - Andrews/ "Jolly Holiday" - Van Dyke, Andrews/ "Supercalifragilisticexpialidocious" - Andrews, Van Dyke, Pearlies/ "Stay Awake" - Andrews/ "I Love To Laugh" - Wynn, Andrews, Van Dyke/ "Feed the Birds" - Andrews/ "Fidelity Fiduciary Bank" - Van Dyke, Tomlinson/ "Chim-Chim-Cheree" - Van Dyke, Andrews, Dotrice, Garber/ "Step in Time" - Van Dyke, chimney sweeps/ "Let's Go Fly a Kite" - Tomlinson, Van Dyke, Londoners.

A fantasy combining live action with animated cartoon characters, *Mary Poppins,* based on the children's classic, was Walt Disney's most popular and highly acclaimed production. It gave Julie Andrews her first screen role (because Warner had passed her over for the lead in *My Fair Lady,* which she had originated on the stage), and it gave Dick Van Dyke the rare opportunity of playing two unrelated characters in one film (Bert, the street entertainer / sidewalk artist / chimney sweep / kite salesman, and Mr. Dawes, the president of the bank). In London 1910, stuffy Mr. Banks, a banker, places an ad for a governess for his two children, which is answered by Mary Poppins, who flies off a cloud and into the Banks home at 17 Cherry Tree Lane. Mary Poppins soon takes the children on a series of adventures, the most memorable being the one that finds them jumping right through Bert's sidewalk chalk drawing and into an idyllic countryside full of singing cartoon farm animals and dancing cartoon penguins. Mary even wins a horse race riding a merry-go-round horse. Papa Banks objects that his offsprings are having too much fun, so he takes them to the place where he works, which inadvertently causes a run on the bank. When Banks is dismissed, it only succeeds in turning him into a more understanding father, and he even manages to get his job back. Her mission accomplished, Mary Poppins flies off into the sky.

Seven years later the Disney studio offered another London-based fantasy, *Bedknobs and Broomsticks,* which again contained a flying heroine (played by Angela Lansbury). Also along were such *Mary Poppins* alumni as writers Walsh and DaGradi, producer Walsh, director Stevenson, the songwriting Sherman brothers, music director Kostal, and actor David Tomlinson.

Massey, Ilona (née Ilona Hajmassy), actress, singer; b. Budapest, July 5, 1912; d. Bethesda, Md., Aug. 10, 1974. Frosty blonde former opera singer who appeared with Nelson Eddy in three films.

1937 Rosalie (*Countess Brenda*)
1939 Balalaika (*Lydia Pavlovna Marakova*)
1942 New Wine (*Anna*)
1945 Holiday in Mexico (*Toni Countess Karpathy*)
1947 Northwest Outpost (*Natalia Alanova*)
1949 Love Happy (*Mme. Egilichi*)

Matthews, Jessie (Margaret), actress, singer, dancer; b. London, March 11, 1907. Good Queen Jess reigned between 1934 and 1937 as the undisputed monarch of British screen musicals. Wide-eyed and doll-faced, projecting both innocence and sex appeal, she sang in a tremulous voice and danced her way with spritelike grace through a series of gossamer tales that, almost invariably, cast her in a role requiring her to masquerade as another character. Among the film songs with which she was associated were "When You've Got a Little Springtime in Your Heart," "Over My Shoulder" (both from *Evergreen,* adapted from her biggest London stage hit), "Everything's in Rhythm with my Heart," "It's Love Again," and "May I Have the Next Romance with

You?" Beginning her career as understudy to Gertrude Lawrence, Miss Matthews became a favorite in London revues and musical comedies before making her talkie debut in 1931. Ten of her 17 films were musicals, with Victor Saville directing four, and Sonnie Hale three. Hale, the second of Miss Matthews' three husbands, also appeared with her in three movies. Bib: *Over My Shoulder* by Miss Matthews (1974); *Jessie Matthews* by Michael Thornton (1974). (Died Aug. 20, 1981.)

1931 Out of the Blue (*Tommy Tucker*)
1933 The Good Companions (*Susie Dean*)
1934 Waltzes from Vienna (*Resi*)
       Evergreen (*Harriet Green/Harriet Green Jr.*)
1935 First a Girl (*Elizabeth*)
1936 It's Love Again (*Elaine Bradford*)
1937 Head Over Heels (*Jeanne*)
       Gangway (*Pat Wayne*)
       Sailing Along (*Kay Martin*)
1958 Tom Thumb (US) (*Anna*)

Mature, Victor, actor; b. Louisville, Jan. 19, 1915. Mature cut a dashing figure in adventure films and a few musicals, in which he played opposite Betty Grable, Rita Hayworth, Lucille Ball, Betty Hutton, Jane Russell, and Esther Williams.

1942 Song of the Islands (*Jeff Harper*)
       My Gal Sal (*Paul Dresser*)
       Footlight Serenade (*Tommy Lundy*)
       Seven Days' Leave (*Johnny Grey*)
1949 Red, Hot and Blue (*Danny James*)
1950 Wabash Avenue (*Andy Clark*)
1952 Las Vegas Story (*Dave Andrews*)
       Million Dollar Mermaid (*James Sullivan*)

Maxwell, (Marvel) Marilyn, actress, singer; b. Clarinda, Iowa, Aug. 3, 1921; d. Beverly Hills, March 20, 1972. Miss Maxwell was a former band vocalist who became featured singer on Bob Hope's radio program and appeared mostly in MGM and Paramount films. Introduced "Silver Bells" with Hope.

1943 Presenting Lily Mars (bit)
       DuBarry Was a Lady (*"Miss February"*)
       Best Foot Forward (bit)
       Thousands Cheer (specialty)
       Swing Fever (*Ginger Gray*)
1944 Lost in a Harem (*Hazel Moon*)
1948 Summer Holiday (*Belle*)
1951 The Lemon Drop Kid (*Brainey Baxter*)
1958 Rock-a-Bye Baby (*Carla Naples*)
1964 The Lively Set (*Marge Owens*)

"May I?" Music by Harry Revel; lyric by Mack Gordon. In which a bashful suitor, after revealing that he stutters and stammers whenever he's near the girl he loves, confesses that his one ambition is to share a love affair with her and *then* marry her. Sung in *We're Not Dressing* (Par. 1934) by Bing Crosby as a sailor entertaining guests on a yacht.

"May I Have the Next Romance with You?" Music by Harry Revel; lyric by Mack Gordon. Lilting amatory request sung by Jessie Matthews in *Head Over Heels* (Gaumont-Brit. 1937).

"Maybe This Time" Music by John Kander; lyric by Fred Ebb. Propulsive number of hoped-for romantic satisfaction, performed by Liza Minnelli in cabaret sequence in *Cabaret* (Allied 1972). The song was written about seven years before Miss Minnelli sang it in the film.

Mayo, (Archibald L.) Archie, director; b. New York, 1891; d. Guadalajara, Dec. 4, 1968. Mayo directed such diverse personalities as Fanny Brice, Al Jolson, Ruby Keeler, Jascha Heifetz, Alice Faye, Glenn Miller, Jack Oakie, and Benny Goodman in musical films mostly at Warner and Fox.

1928	My Man
1929	Is Everybody Happy?
1931	Oh Sailor Behave
1935	Go Into Your Dance
1939	They Shall Have Music
1941	The Great American Broadcast
1942	Orchestra Wives
1944	Sweet and Low Down

Mayo, Virginia (née Virginia Jones), actress, dancer; b. St. Louis, Nov. 20, 1920. Blank-faced blonde beauty who rose from the Broadway chorus to become Danny Kaye's leading lady in four Goldwyn musicals. Also in Warner movies with James Cagney, Dennis Morgan, and Gene Nelson.

1944	Up in Arms (chorus)
	Seven Days Ashore (*Carol*)
1945	Wonder Man (*Ellen Shanley*)
1946	The Kid from Brooklyn (*Polly Pringle*)
1947	The Secret Life of Walter Mitty (*Rosalind Van Hooren*)
1948	A Song Is Born (*Honey Swanson*)
1949	Always Leave Them Laughing (*Nancy Eagan*)
1950	The West Point Story (*Eve Dillon*)
1951	Painting the Clouds with Sunshine (*Carol*)
	Starlift (guest bit)
1952	She's Working Her Way Through College (*Angela Gardner*)
1953	She's Back on Broadway (*Catherine Terris*)

Maytime (1937). Screenplay by Noel Langley.

An MGM film produced by Hunt Stromberg; directed by Robert Z. Leonard; opera sequences directed by William von Wymetal; art directors, Frederic Hope, Edwin B. Willis; costumes, Adrian; music director, Herbert Stothart; musical adaptation, Stothart; cameraman, Oliver T. Marsh; editor, Conrad Nervig.

Cast: Jeanette MacDonald (*Marcia Mornay* aka *Miss Morrison*); Nelson Eddy (*Paul Allison*); John Barrymore (*Nicolai Nazaroff*); Herman Bing (*August Archipenko*); Tom Brown (*Kip*); Lynne Carver (*Barbara Roberts*); Rafaela Ottiano (*Ellen*); Charles Judels (*cabby*); Paul Porcasi (*Trentini*); Sig Rumann (*Fanchon*); Walter Kingsford (*Rudyard*); Guy Bates Post (*Emperor Napoleon III*); Harry Davenport (*opera director*); Billy Gilbert (*drunk*); Leonid Kinskey (*student*); Don Cossack Choir.

Songs: "Now Is the Month of Maying" (trad.) - children/ "Will You Remember?" (Sigmund Romberg-Rida Johnson Young) - Eddy; reprised by Eddy, MacDonald/ "Les Filles de Cadix" (Delibes-deMusset) - MacDonald/ "Le Regiment de Sambre et Meuse" (Planquette) - MacDonald, Don Cossacks/ "Plantons da Vigne" (trad.) - Eddy/ "Vive l'Opera" (trad.-Robert Wright, George Forrest) - Eddy, chorus/ "Ham and Eggs" (Herbert Stothart-Wright, Forrest) - Eddy, chorus/ "Carry Me Back to Old Virginny" (James Bland) - Eddy, MacDonald/ "Nobles Seigneurs, Salut" and "Une Dame Noble et Sage" (Meyerbeer-Scribe, Deschamps, *Les Huguenots*) - MacDonald chorus/ "Santa Lucia" (trad.) - uncredited singer, Eddy, MacDonald/ "Czaritza" (Tchaikovsky-Giles Guilbert) - MacDonald, Eddy, chorus. Unused: "Farewell to Dreams" (Romberg-Gus Kahn).

Though ostensibly adapted from a 1917 Broadway operetta by Sigmund Romberg and Rida Johnson Young, *Maytime* retained only one song from the production and, except for the romantic influence of the titular month, told a story without any points of similarity. The third film made together by Jeanette MacDonald and Nelson Eddy, the sentimental tale was originally to have been personally produced by MGM's production chief, Irving Thalberg, and directed by Edmund Goulding. When Thalberg died after the film was in production,

Hunt Stromberg and Robert Z. Leonard, the new producer and director, decided to scrap the original screenplay—which also had nothing in common with the Romberg-Young operetta—and come up with a third story. In this version, it is May Day 1905, in a small American town. Giving romantic advice to a young girl, an old woman relates in flashback the story of her own Maytime of happiness when, as an opera star known as Marcia Mornay, she had fallen in love with singer Paul Allison in Paris. Because she was ambitious, she gave up Paul, married her manager, Nicolai Nazaroff, and had a successful career. Paul, however, was engaged to appear with her at her debut at the Metropolitan Opera, and they both realized they were still in love. Nazaroff realized it, too, and one snowy night took out his revolver and killed Paul. Which is all the young girl needs to know to make her appreciate that marrying for love is preferable to a career. Though the screenplay was not based directly on anything previously written, the device of having an old woman advise a girl by relating her life through flashback, the killing of the hero, and the romantic moral of the story being told all indicate writer Noel Langley's familiarity with Noël Coward's 1929 operetta *Bitter Sweet*. In fact, three years later, in a vain attempt to recapture the ardent *Maytime* mood, MacDonald and Eddy were co-starred in their own version of *Bitter Sweet*.

McCarey, Leo, director, screenwriter, producer; b. Los Angeles, Oct. 3, 1898; d. Santa Monica, July 5, 1969. As director, McCarey was noted for comedies (*The Awful Truth*) and sentimental tales (*Love Affair*), as well as for musicals ranging from the raucous (*Duck Soup*) to the religious (*Going My Way*). He also wrote songs with Harry Warren and Harold Adamson (including "An Affair To Remember"). Among stars he directed in musicals were Jeanette MacDonald, Gloria Swanson, Eddie Cantor, the Marx Brothers, Mae West, Bing Crosby (twice), and Cary Grant.

Asterisk indicates Mr. McCarey was also screenwriter & producer:
1929	Red Hot Rhythm
1930	Let's Go Native
1931	Indiscreet
1932	The Kid from Spain (also script)
1933	Duck Soup
1934	Belle of the Nineties
1939	Love Affair
1944	Going My Way*
1945	The Bells of St. Mary's*
1957	An Affair To Remember* (Warren-Adamson)

McCartney, Paul. *See* **Beatles, The.**

McDonald, Grace, actress, dancer, singer; b. Boston, 1919. Peppy, round-faced song-and-dancer who first appeared with brother Ray McDonald in vaudeville. Acted mostly in wartime musicals at Universal; introduced "Mister Five by Five."

1941	Dancing on a Dime (*Lorie Fenton*)
	Behind the Eight Ball (*Babs*)
1942	What's Cooking? (*Angela*)
	Give Out Sisters (*Gracie Waverly*)
1943	Strictly in the Groove (*Dixie*)
	How's About It?
	It Ain't Hay (*Kitty McCloin*)
	Get Going (*Judy King*)
	Gals Inc. (*Molly*)
	Always a Bridesmaid (*Linda Marlowe*)
	Crazy House (specialty)
1944	Hat Check Honey (*Susan Brent*)
	Follow the Boys (*Kitty West*)
	Murder in the Blue Room (*Peggy*)
	My Gal Loves Music (*Judy Mason*)
1945	Honeymoon Ahead (*Evelyn*)
	See My Lawyer (*Betty*)

McDonald, Ray, actor, dancer, singer; b. Boston, 1920; d. New York, Feb. 20, 1959. Slight, boyish-looking Ray McDonald first appeared in vaudeville with sister Grace in a song-and-dance act. In Hollywood mostly at MGM, he is remembered particularly for introducing "Pass That Peace Pipe" with Joan McCracken in *Good News*. Last two films were with Peggy Ryan, whom he married and divorced.

1941	Babes on Broadway (*Ray Lambert*)
1942	Born To Sing (*Steve*)
1943	Presenting Lily Mars (*Charlie Potter*)
1946	Till the Clouds Roll By (specialty)
1947	Good News (*Bobby Turner*)
1949	There's a Girl in My Heart (*Danny Kroner*)
1952	All Ashore (*Skip Edwards*)

McGuire, (Marilyn) Marcy, actress, singer; b. 1925 Red-headed, hoydenish bobby-soxer type who played the kid who flipped over Frank Sinatra in *Higher and Higher*.

1942	Seven Days' Leave (*Marcy*)
	Around the World (*Marcy*)

1943 Higher and Higher (*Mickey*)
  Follies Girl (*Trixie*)
1944 Seven Days Ashore (*Dot*)
1945 Sing Your Way Home (*Bridget*)
1952 Jumping Jacks (*Julia Loring*)

McHugh, (Francis Curran) Frank, actor; b. Homestead, Pa., May 23, 1899. Comic actor usually seen as amiable, naïve chum of film's leads. A Warner contract player for 12 years, McHugh appeared in many nonmusicals through the late 1960s. (Died Sept. 11, 1981.)

1930 Top Speed (*Tad Jordan*)
1931 Kiss Me Again (*Francois*)
  Bright Lights (*reporter*)
  College Lovers (*Speed Haskins*)
1932 Blessed Event (*Reilly*)
1933 Footlight Parade (*Francis*)
1934 Fashions of 1934 (*Snap*)
  Happiness Ahead (*Tom Bradley*)
1935 Gold Diggers of 1935 (*Humbolt Prentiss*)
  Stars Over Broadway (*"Offkey" Cramer*)
1936 Stage Struck (*Sid*)
1937 Ever Since Eve (*"Mabel" DeCraven*)
  Mr. Dodd Takes the Air (*"Sniffer" Hurst*)
1938 Swing Your Lady (*Popeye*)
1944 Going My Way (*Father Timothy O'Dowd*)
  Bowery to Broadway (*Joe Kirby*)
1945 State Fair (*McGee*)
1947 Carnegie Hall (*John Donovan*)
1954 There's No Business Like Show Business (*Eddie Duggan*)
1959 Say One for Me (*Father Jim Dugan*)
1967 Easy Come, Easy Go (*Capt. Jack*)

McHugh, (James Francis) Jimmy, composer; b. Boston, July 10, 1892; d. Beverly Hills, May 23, 1969. With lyricist Dorothy Fields, McHugh began by writing scores for Cotton Club revues and three Broadway musicals before embarking on his fruitful career in Hollywood. His early movie hits, all with Miss Fields, included "Cuban Love Song," "I Feel a Song Comin' On," and "I'm in the Mood for Love." He then wrote "I'm Shooting High" (with Ted Koehler); "You're a Sweetheart," "I Couldn't Sleep a Wink Last Night," "A Lovely Way To Spend an Evening," and "The Music Stopped" (all with Harold Adamson, with whom he worked on 19 films); "Can't Get Out of This Mood," "Let's Get Lost," and " 'Murder' He Says" (all with Frank Loesser); and "You've Got Me This Way" (with Johnny Mercer). Among those who introduced McHugh songs were Lawrence Tibbett, Alice Faye, Frances

Langford, Shirley Temple, Tony Martin, Lily Pons, Deanna Durbin, Ginny Simms, Mary Martin, Dick Powell, Frank Sinatra, Vivian Blaine, and Perry Como.

1930 Love in the Rough (Fields)
1935 Hooray for Love (Fields)
  Every Night at Eight (Fields)
  King of Burlesque (Koehler)
1936 Dimples (Koehler)
  Banjo on My Knee (Adamson)
1937 Merry-Go-Round of 1938 (Adamson)
  Hitting a New High (Adamson)
  You're a Sweetheart (Adamson)
  Top of the Town (Adamson)
1938 Mad About Music (Adamson)
  Road to Reno (Adamson)
  That Certain Age (Adamson)
1940 Buck Benny Rides Again (Loesser)
  You'll Find Out (Mercer)
1941 You're the One (Mercer)
1942 Seven Days' Leave (Loesser)
1943 Happy Go Lucky (Loesser)
  Around the World (Adamson)
  Higher and Higher (Adamson)
1944 Four Jills in a Jeep (Adamson)
  Something for the Boys (Adamson; Loesser)
1945 Bring on the Girls (Adamson)
  Nob Hill (Adamson)
  Doll Face (Adamson)
1947 Calendar Girl (Adamson)
  Hit Parade of 1947 (Adamson)
  Smash Up (Adamson)
1948 If You Knew Susie (Adamson)
1957 The Helen Morgan Story (guest bit)

McLeod, Norman Z(enos), director; b. Grayling, Mich., Sept. 30, 1898; d. Hollywood, Jan. 26, 1964. Former cartoon animator and script writer who directed films mostly at Paramount. Worked with the Marx Brothers, Ann Sothern, Bing Crosby, Red Skelton, Danny Kaye, Bob Hope, Fred Astaire, Betty Hutton.

1932 Horse Feathers
1934 Melody in Spring
  Many Happy Returns
1935 Redheads on Parade
  Coronado
1936 Pennies from Heaven
1941 Lady, Be Good
1942 Panama Hattie
  The Powers Girl
1946 The Kid from Brooklyn
1947 The Secret Life of Walter Mitty
  Road to Rio

1948   Isn't It Romantic?
       The Paleface
1950   Let's Dance

McPhail, Douglas, singer, actor; b. Los Angeles, April 16, 1910; d. Los Angeles, Dec. 7, 1944. Chubby, youthful-looking tenor who appeared in MGM musicals. Introduced ''I Concentrate on You.''

1938   Sweethearts (*Harvey Horton*)
1939   Babes in Arms (*Don Brice*)
1940   Little Nellie Kelly (*Dennis Fogarty*)
       Broadway Melody of 1940 (*masked singer*)
1942   Born To Sing (*Murray Saunders*)

Meet Me in St. Louis (1944). Music & lyrics mostly by Hugh Martin & Ralph Blane; screenplay by Irving Brecher & Fred F. Finklehoffe from *The New Yorker* stories and novel by Sally Benson.

An MGM film produced by Arthur Freed; directed by Vincente Minnelli; choreography, Charles Walters; art directors, Cedric Gibbons, Lemuel Ayers; costumes, Irene Sharaff; music director, George Stoll; orchestrations, Roger Edens, Conrad Salinger; cameraman, George Folsey; editor, Albert Akst; Technicolor.

Cast: Judy Garland (*Esther Smith*); Margaret O'Brien (*''Tootie'' Smith*); Mary Astor (*Anne Smith*); Lucille Bremer (*Rose Smith*); Leon Ames (vocal by Arthur Freed) (*Alonzo Smith*); Tom Drake (*John Truett*); Marjorie Main (*Katie*); Harry Davenport (*Grandpa Smith*); June Lockhart (*Lucille Ballard*); Henry H. Daniels, Jr. (*Alonzo Smith, Jr.*); Joan Carroll (*Agnes Smith*); Hugh Marlowe (*Col. Darly*); Chill Wills (*Mr. Neeley*); Darryl Hickman (*Johnny Tevis*).

Songs: ''Meet Me in St. Louis, Louis'' (Kerry Mills-Andrew Sterling) - Daniels, Carroll, Davenport, Garland, Bremer/ ''The Boy Next Door'' - Garland/ ''Skip to My Lou'' (trad.) - Garland/ ''Under the Bamboo Tree'' (J. Rosamond Johnson-Bob Cole) - Garland, O'Brien/ ''Over the Bannister - Garland/ ''The Trolley Song'' - chorus, Garland/ ''You and I'' (Nacio Herb Brown-Arthur Freed) - Ames (Freed)/ ''Have Yourself a Merry Little Christmas'' - Garland. Unused: ''Boys and Girls Like You and Me'' (Richard Rodgers-Oscar Hammerstein II).

A placid, sentimental tale of turn-of-the-century America, *Meet Me in St. Louis* re-created a color-drenched, picture-postcard view of stability and close family ties. The film, which was Arthur Freed's favorite of all his productions, focused on a brief period in the lives of members of the Smith family of 5135 Kensington Ave., St. Louis, beginning in the summer of 1903 and ending in the spring of the following year. This enabled the movie to be divided into four segments, each covering a season and each introduced by a filigreed photograph of the American Gothic house in which the family lived. In the narrative, teenage Esther (Judy Garland) falls in love with the boy next door (a role originally intended for Van Johnson but played by Tom Drake); seven-year-old ''Tootie'' (Margaret O'Brien) gets involved in mischief on a frightening Halloween (a sequence that was almost cut); there is a dilemma concerning who will escort who to a dance; and Papa Smith (Leon Ames) is offered a better position in his bank's New York office. This last incident provokes the film's major crisis, which is easily resolved when Mr. Smith decides to remain in St. Louis so that his family can attend the opening of the Louisiana Purchase Exposition.

The first Technicolor film directed by Vincente Minnelli, the movie was also the first original screen musical with a score by Hugh Martin and Ralph Blane. In addition to their flavorsome, well-integrated pieces—including ''The Boy Next Door,'' ''The Trolley Song,'' and ''Have Yourself a Merry Little Christmas''—the movie even had room for a show-stopping cakewalk, ''Under the Bamboo Tree,'' performed with artless grace by Misses Garland and O'Brien. Though the studio heads were initially opposed to making a film with so little action and conflict, Freed's persuasiveness won them over. The producer also had to win over Judy Garland, then 20, who was anxious to concentrate on more mature roles. And then she almost had the picture stolen from her by the lachrymose Miss O'Brien.

By offering the image of a strife-free, contented world, *Meet Me in St. Louis* was especially reassuring to filmgoers during World War II. Of the other films with Americana themes that followed in its wake, the one that came closest in atmosphere was Fox's *Centennial Summer* (1946), about a family living at the time of the Philadelphia Centennial Exposition of 1876. Prominent members of the Rogers household were Walter Brennan, Dorothy Gish, Linda Darnell, and Jeanne Crain, with Constance Bennett as their flirtatious aunt from Paris. Otto Preminger directed, Jerome Kern composed the music (his last score), and Leo Robin wrote most of the lyrics.

Melchior, Lauritz (né Lebricht Hommel), singer, actor; b. Copenhagen, March 20, 1890; d. Santa Monica,

March 18, 1973. Wagnerian heldentenor of ample girth who made his Metropolitan Opera debut in 1926, and was on hand to provide cultural uplift to the MGM musicals that José Iturbi didn't appear in.

1945 Thrill of a Romance (*Nils Knudsen*)
1946 Two Sisters from Boston (*Ostrom*)
1947 This Time for Keeps (*Richard Herald*)
1948 Luxury Liner (*Olaf Eriksen*)
1953 The Stars Are Singing (*Poldi*)

"Melody from the Sky, A" Music by Louis Alter; lyric by Sidney Mitchell. The mating of music and nature lovingly described by Fuzzy Knight in *Trail of the Lonesome Pine* (Par. 1936).

Melton, James, actor, singer; b. Moultrie, Ga., Jan. 2, 1904; d. New York, April 21, 1961. Operatic tenor with pudgy, boyish face who joined the Metropolitan five years after appearing in three Warner musicals. Introduced "September in the Rain."

1935 Stars Over Broadway (*Jan King*)
1936 Sing Me a Love Song (*Jerry Haines*)
1937 Melody for Two (*Tod Weaver*)
1946 Ziegfeld Follies (specialty)

"Memphis in June" Music by Hoagy Carmichael; lyric by Paul Francis Webster. Evocative picture of a perfumed lazy summer day when "everything is peacefully dandy." Introduced by Hoagy Carmichael in nonmusical film *Johnny Angel* (RKO 1945).

Menjou, Adolphe (Jean), actor; b. Pittsburgh, Feb. 18, 1890; d. Beverly Hills, Oct. 29, 1963. Menjou was a nonsinging actor with a prominent nose and a military mustache, often cast as a dapper, irascible man of authority. Career spanned 1916–60. Bib: *It Took Nine Tailors* by Menjou (1948).

1929 Fashions in Love (*Paul de Remy*)
1930 Morocco (*La Bessière*)
       New Moon (*Gov. Boris Brusiloff*)
1934 Little Miss Marker (*Sorrowful Jones*)
1935 Gold Diggers of 1935 (*Nicolai Nicoleff*)
       Broadway Gondolier (*Prof. De Vinci*)
1936 Sing, Baby, Sing (*Farraday*)
       One in a Million (*Thaddeus Spencer*)
1937 100 Men and a Girl (*John Cardwell*)
1938 The Goldwyn Follies (*Oliver Merlin*)
       Thanks for Everything (*J. B. Harcourt*)
1939 That's Right, You're Wrong (*Stacey Delmore*)
1941 Road Show (*Col. Carleton Carroway*)

1942 Syncopation (*George Latimer*)
       You Were Never Lovelier (*Edouardo Acuña*)
1943 Sweet Rosie O'Grady (*Tom Moran*)
1944 Step Lively (*Wagner*)
1946 The Bachelor's Daughters (*Moody*)
1947 I'll Be Yours (*J. Conrad Nelson*)
1949 My Dream Is Yours (*Thomas Hutchins*)
       Dancing in the Dark (*Crossman*)
1955 Timberjack (*Swiftwater Tilton*)
1956 Bundle of Joy (*B. J. Merlin*)

Mercer, (John Herndon) Johnny, lyricist, composer; b. Savannah, Ga., Nov. 18, 1909; d. Los Angeles, June 25, 1976. Though also a composer ("I'm an Old Cowhand," "Something's Gotta Give"), Mercer won fame primarily as a versatile lyricist with a talent for colloquial expressions and poetic imagery. Among his most successful Hollywood collaborations were with Richard A. Whiting ("Too Marvelous for Words," "I'm Like a Fish out of Water," "Hooray for Hollywood"); Harry Warren ("You Must Have Been a Beautiful Baby," "Jeepers Creepers," "On the Atchison, Topeka and the Santa Fe"); Harold Arlen ("Blues in the Night," "This Time the Dream's on Me," "That Old Black Magic," "Hit the Road to Dreamland," "My Shining Hour," "One for My Baby," "Ac-Cent-Tchu-Ate the Positive," "Let's Take the Long Way Home"); Victor Schertzinger ("Arthur Murray Taught Me Dancing in a Hurry," "Tangerine," "I Remember You"); Jerome Kern ("Dearly Beloved," "I'm Old Fashioned," "You Were Never Lovelier"); Hoagy Carmichael ("How Little We Know," "In the Cool Cool Cool of the Evening"); Gene dePaul (the *Seven Brides for Seven Brothers* score); Henry Mancini ("Moon River," "The Days of Wine and Roses," "Whistling Away the Dark"). Other song-writing partners were Lewis Gensler, Matty Malneck, Hal Borne, Artie Shaw, Jimmy McHugh, Arthur Schwartz, and Saul Chaplin.

Some of the singers who introduced Mercer numbers were Priscilla Lane, Rosemary Lane, Dick Powell, Louis Armstrong, Fred Astaire, Dorothy Lamour, Betty Hutton, Bing Crosby, Judy Garland, Jane Powell, Howard Keel, June Allyson, Danny Kaye, and Julie Andrews. Mercer also wrote scores for two Broadway musicals, *Top Banana* and *Li'l Abner,* both filmed, sang on radio and television, and was a co-founder (plus recording artist) of Capitol Records.

1935 Old Man Rhythm (Gensler) (also *Colonel*)
       To Beat the Band (Malneck) (also specialty)
1937 Ready, Willing and Able (Whiting)

Varsity Show (Whiting)
Hollywood Hotel (Whiting)
1938   Cowboy from Brooklyn (Whiting)
Garden of the Moon (Warren)
Going Places (Warren)
1939   Naughty but Nice (Warren)
1940   You'll Find Out (McHugh)
Second Chorus (Borne; Shaw)
1941   You're the One (McHugh)
Navy Blues (Schwartz)
Blues in the Night (Arlen)
1942   The Fleet's In (Schertzinger)
You Were Never Lovelier (Kern)
Star Spangled Rhythm (Arlen)
1943   The Sky's the Limit (Arlen)
True to Life (Carmichael)
1944   Here Come the Waves (Arlen)
1946   The Harvey Girls (Warren)
1953   Dangerous When Wet (Schwartz)
1954   Top Banana (alone)
Seven Brides for Seven Brothers (dePaul)
1955   Daddy Long Legs (alone)
1956   You Can't Run Away from It (dePaul)
1958   Merry Andrew (Chaplin)
1959   Li'l Abner (dePaul)
1969   Darling Lili (Mancini)

Merkel, Una, actress; b. Covington, Ky., Dec. 10, 1903. Blonde, chirpy-voiced Una Merkel usually played the heroine's no-nonsense friend in a career that began in 1930 and continued through almost 100 films. (Died Los Angeles, Jan. 2, 1986.)

1933   42nd Street (*Lorraine Fleming*)
Broadway to Hollywood (*flirt*)
1934   The Merry Widow (*Queen Dolores*)
1935   The Night Is Young (*Fanni*)
Broadway Melody of 1936 (*Kitty Corbett*)
1936   Born To Dance (*Jenny Saks*)
1939   Some Like It Hot (*Flo Saunders*)
Destry Rides Again (*Lily Belle Callahan*)
1941   Road to Zanzibar (*Julia Quimby*)
1943   This Is the Army (*Rose Dibble*)
1944   Sweethearts of the USA (*Patsy*)
1950   My Blue Heaven (*Miss Gilbert*)
1951   Rich, Young and Pretty (*Glynnie*)
Golden Girl (*Mrs. Crabtree*)
1952   With a Song in My Heart (*Sister Marie*)
The Merry Widow (*Kitty Riley*)
1953   I Love Melvin (*Mom Schneider*)
1956   Bundle of Joy (*Mrs. Dugan*)
1957   The Girl Most Likely (*Mom*)
1958   Aladdin (tv) (*Aladdin's Mother*)
1966   Spinout (*Violet Ranley*)

Merman, Ethel (née Ethel Zimmermann), actress, singer; b. Astoria, Queens, NY, Jan. 16, 1909. Broadway's indomitable musical-comedy star, clarion-voiced Ethel Merman repeated only two roles, those in *Anything Goes* and *Call Me Madam,* in screen versions of her stage hits. In Hollywood, she appeared in two films each with Eddie Cantor, Bing Crosby, and Donald O'Connor; also with Sonja Henie, Tyrone Power, Alice Faye, and Dan Dailey. Bib: *Who Could Ask for Anything More?* (1955) and *Merman—An Autobiography* (1978), both by Miss Merman. (Died Feb. 15, 1984.)

1930   Follow the Leader (*Helen King*)
1934   We're Not Dressing (*Edith*)
Kid Millions (*Dot*)
1935   Big Broadcast of 1936 (specialty)
1936   Strike Me Pink (*Joyce Lennox*)
Anything Goes (*Reno Sweeney*)
1938   Happy Landing (*Flo Kelly*)
Alexander's Ragtime Band (*Jerry Allen*)
Straight, Place and Show (*Linda*)
1943   Stage Door Canteen (specialty)
1953   Call Me Madam (*Sally Adams*)
1954   There's No Business Like Show Business (*Molly Donahue*)
1972   Journey Back to Oz (voice of *Wicked Witch*)

Merrill, Bob (né Henry Robert Merrill Lavan), composer, lyricist; b. Atlantic City, May 17, 1921. Pop songwriter turned theatre composer-lyricist who supplied songs for one screen musical. Also wrote words to music by Jule Styne for two Broadway musicals (*Funny Girl* was filmed with Barbra Streisand) and one for television with Liza Minnelli.

1962   Wonderful World of the Brothers Grimm (alone)
1965   Dangerous Christmas of Red Riding Hood (tv) (Styne)
1968   Funny Girl (Styne)

Merry Widow, The (1934). Music by Franz Lehar; lyrics by Lorenz Hart; screenplay by Samson Raphaelson & Ernest Vajda from Viennese operetta *Die lustige Witwe* by Viktor Leon, Leon Stein, and Lehar adapted from French play *L'Attaché d'ambassade* by Henri Meilhac.

An MGM film produced by Irving Thalberg; directed by Ernst Lubitsch; choreography, Albertina Rasch; art directors, Cedric Gibbons, Gabriel Scognamillo, Frederick Hope; costumes, Ali Hubert, Adrian; music director, Herbert Stothart ; musical adaptation, Stothart; cameraman, Oliver T. Marsh; editor, Frances Marsh.

THE MERRY WIDOW

Cast: Maurice Chevalier (*Captain Danilo*); Jeanette MacDonald (*Sonia*); Edward Everett Horton (*Ambassador Popoff*); Una Merkel (*Queen Dolores*); George Barbier (*King Achmed*); Minna Gombell (*Marcelle*); Sterling Holloway (*Mischka*); Donald Meek (*valet*); Henry Armetta (*Turk*); Akim Tamiroff (*Maxim's manager*); Herman Bing (*Zizipoff*); Ruth Channing (*Lulu*); Shirley Chambers (Shirley Ross) (*girl at Maxim's*); Leonid Kinskey (*shepherd*); Richard Carle (*attorney*); Billy Gilbert (*lackey*); Katherine Burke (Virginia Field) (*prisoner*).

Songs: "Girls, Girls, Girls" - soldiers, Chevalier/ "Vilia" - MacDonald, chorus/ "Tonight Will Teach Me To Forget" (lyric, Gus Kahn) - MacDonald/ "Maxim's - Chevalier/ "Melody of Laughter" - MacDonald, suitors/ "The Merry Widow Waltz" - MacDonald; dance by Chevalier, MacDonald/ "If Widows Are Rich" - MacDonald.

The Merry Widow swirled into Vienna in 1905, and soon became a worldwide phenomenon. English-language versions opened in 1907 in London (with Lily Elsie and Joseph Coyne) and in New York (Ethel Jackson and Donald Brian), and the work has been continually revived ever since. The bubbly confection of a story takes place in Paris where the Marsovian ambassador, fearful that his country's wealthiest citizen, Sonia Sadoya, will marry a foreigner, plots to have her wed Count Danilo of his staff. Danilo woos Sonia with a waltz or two, but his pride prevents him from marrying for money. At a party in her home outside Paris, which she has decorated to resemble Maxim's, Sonia smooths the marital path by confessing that she will lose all her fortune if she marries again. When a relieved Danilo proposes, she further reveals that her late husband's will specifies that the money will go to her new husband, which somehow makes everything all right.

There have been four English-language screen versions of *The Merry Widow*, beginning in 1912 when Wallace Reid and Alma Rubens appeared in a two-reeler. A second silent version, this time of feature length, was released by MGM in 1925. Drastically rewritten by director Erich von Stroheim, the film starred John Gilbert as Prince Danilo Petrovitch of Monteblanco and Mae Murray as Sally O'Hara, an American dancer touring the prince's country. When the king forbids Danilo to marry a commoner, Sally weds the wealthy Baron Sixtus Sadoja (Tully Marshall), a drooling foot fetishist, who conveniently dies on their wedding night. Sally then takes off to Paris and meets Danilo again at Maxim's, where their romance is rekindled to the strains

of "The Merry Widow Waltz" performed by the movie-theatre pianist. After Danilo is slightly wounded in a duel with smirking Crown Prince Mirko (Roy D'Arcy), the king dies, Mirko is assassinated, and Danilo and Sally are crowned king and queen.

In 1929, MGM production chief Irving Thalberg began negotiating for the talkie rights to the operetta, which took almost five years to clear. Directed by the master of Continental froth, Ernst Lubitsch, and starring Maurice Chevalier (in a character resembling the ones he had played in Lubitsch's *The Love Parade* and *The Smiling Lieutenant*), the movie united the actor for the fourth time with Jeanette MacDonald (winning the role over Grace Moore and Joan Crawford). It also united the melodies of Franz Lehar with the lyrics of Lorenz Hart, thus marking the only occasion Hart ever put words to the music of anyone other than Richard Rodgers. In this adaptation, the story begins in the mythical kingdom of Marshovia (with an "h"), where roguish Captain Danilo is thwarted in his wooing of the heavily veiled Sonia, still in mourning for her late husband. Sonia, however, finds herself attracted to the officer and suddenly decides to rid herself of her widow's weeds and dash off to Paris. Fearful that his country's richest woman may marry a foreigner and never return, Marshovia's king selects Danilo—who happens to be the queen's lover—to propose marriage to Sonia. The two meet again at Maxim's (later to be an important locale in another MGM musical, *Gigi*), where Danilo, not recognizing Sonia without her veil, mistakes her for a cabaret girl. Danilo soon realizes who she is when they again meet at the Marshovian Embassy ball and join hundreds of dancers elegantly gliding through mirrored halls. Though their ardor is flamed by the insinuating waltz, count and widow call the whole thing off when Ambassador Popoff (Edward Everett Horton) impulsively announces the couple's engagement. Taken home to stand trial for failing his duty, Danilo has a reconciliation with Sonia and, while the waltz is again being played, they become man and wife in his prison cell. The 1934 *Merry Widow* was also shot at the same time in a French version (*La Veuve joyeuse*), with Marcel Vallee substituted for Horton, Daniele Parola for Una Merkel, André Berley for George Barbier, Fifi D'Orsay for Minna Gombell, and Akim Tamiroff for Henry Armetta.

MGM filmed *The Merry Widow* a third time in 1952, with Lana Turner as a rich American widow, Crystal Radek, who visits her husband's homeland (Marshovia with an "h" again), where she is wooed by Fernando

Lamas, as Count Danilo. Produced by Joe Pasternak and directed by Curtis Bernhardt, this Technicolor version retained six Lehar melodies outfitted with new lyrics by Paul Francis Webster. Lamas, who took over a role originally announced for Ricardo Montalban, did most of the singing.

"Midnight in Paris" Music by Con Conrad; lyric by Herb Magidson. Full-throated invitation to share its pleasures, introduced by Nino Martini in *Here's to Romance* (Par. 1935).

Milestone, Lewis (né Lewis Milstein), director; b. Odessa, Sept. 30, 1895; d. Los Angeles, Sept. 25, 1980. Milestone, who began his Hollywood career in 1918, was also credited with such diverse nonmusical films as *All Quiet on the Western Front, The Front Page,* and *The General Died at Dawn.*

1933 Hallelujah, I'm a Bum
1935 Paris in Spring
1936 Anything Goes
1953 Melba

"Milkman, Keep Those Bottles Quiet" Music by Gene dePaul; lyric by Don Raye. Raucous complaint of a wartime defense worker who needs her sleep. Introduced by Nancy Walker in a summer-theatre revue in *Broadway Rhythm* (MGM 1944).

Miller, Ann (née Johnnie Lucille Collier), actress, dancer, singer; b. Chireno, Texas, April 12, 1919. Apple-cheeked, lacquer-haired Ann Miller was second only to Eleanor Powell as Hollywood's leading lady with the tap. She made largely low-budget films between 1937 and 1946, then graduated to a series of major MGM musicals including *Easter Parade* ("It Only Happens When I Dance with You"), *On the Town,* and *Kiss Me, Kate.* After her screen career, Miss Miller danced in nightclubs, and in 1979 opened on Broadway in *Sugar Babies.* Bib: *Miller's High Life* by Miss Miller (1972).

1937 New Faces of 1937 (specialty)
      Life of the Party (*Betty*)
1938 Radio City Revels (*Billie*)
      Having Wonderful Time (*Vivian*)
1940 Too Many Girls (*Pepe*)
      Hit Parade of 1941 (*Annabelle Potter*)
      Melody Ranch (*Julie*)
1941 Time Out for Rhythm (*Kitty Brown*)
      Go West Young Lady (*Lola*)

1942 True to the Army (*Vicki Marlow*)
      Priorities on Parade (*Donna D'Arcy*)
1943 Reveille with Beverly (*Beverly Ross*)
      What's Buzzin', Cousin? (*Anna Crawford*)
1944 Jam Session (*Terry Baxter*)
      Hey, Rookie (*Winnie Clark*)
      Carolina Blues (*Julie Carver*)
1945 Eadie Was a Lady (*Eadie*)
      Eve Knew Her Apples (*Eve Porter*)
1946 The Thrill of Brazil (*Linda Lorens*)
1948 Easter Parade (*Nadine Hale*)
      The Kissing Bandit (specialty)
1949 On the Town (*Claire Hudeson*)
1951 Texas Carnival (*Sunshine Jackson*)
      Two Tickets to Broadway (*Joyce Campbell*)
1952 Lovely To Look At (*Bubbles Cassidy*)
1953 Small Town Girl (*Lisa Belmont*)
      Kiss Me, Kate (*Lois Lane*)
1954 Deep in My Heart (specialty)
1955 Hit the Deck (*Ginger*)
1956 The Opposite Sex (*Gloria*)

Miller, (Alton) Glenn, bandleader, trombonist; b. Clarinda, Iowa, March 1, 1904; d. plane crash English Channel, Dec. 15, 1944. Led popular orchestra with reed-dominated sound from 1939 until army induction three and one-half years later. Appeared with band in two Fox films in which they introduced "Chattanooga Choo-Choo," "I Know Why," "I've Got a Gal in Kalamazoo," "At Last," and "Serenade in Blue." Film bio: *The Glenn Miller Story,* with James Stewart as Miller (and Joe Yukl playing trombone). Bib: *Glenn Miller and His Orchestra* by George T. Simon (1980).

1941 Sun Valley Serenade (*Phil Carey*)
1942 Orchestra Wives (*Gene Morrison*)

Miller, Marilyn (née Marilynn Reynolds), actress, dancer, singer; b. Evansville, Ind., Sept. 1, 1898; d. New York, April 7, 1936. Radiant Broadway musical-comedy star who re-created her two most famous roles, *Sally* and *Sunny,* in the movies. Film bio: *Look for the Silver Lining,* with June Haver as Miss Miller.

1929 Sally (*Sally*)
1930 Sunny (*Sunny*)
1931 Her Majesty Love (*Lia Toerreck*)

Mills Brothers, singers. Herbert, b. Piqua, Ohio, April 2, 1912. Harry, b. Piqua, Aug. 19, 1913. Donald, b. Piqua, April 29, 1915. Close harmony singing trio with distinctive mellow sound. Became a quartet when joined by their older brother, John, Jr.; after his death in 1936 he was replaced by their father, John, Sr. Upon father's retirement in 1956, group became a trio again. Popular in radio and in concerts; also made many records. Introduced "Lulu's Back in Town" in *Broadway Gondolier*.

1932   The Big Broadcast
1934   Twenty Million Sweethearts
       Operator 13
       Strictly Dynamite
1935   Broadway Gondolier
1936   Sky's the Limit (Eng.)
1942   Rhythm Parade
1943   He's My Guy
       Chatterbox
       Reveille with Beverly
1950   When You're Smiling
1957   The Big Beat

"Mimi" Music by Richard Rodgers; lyric by Lorenz Hart. Suddenly smitten by the alluring sight of Jeanette MacDonald in *Love Me Tonight* (Par. 1932), Maurice Chevalier expresses his confused romantic feelings in a saucy tribute that ends with the once daring line, "You know I'd like to have a little son of a Mimi bye and bye." (Jeanette's name in the film, incidentally, was Jeanette). Song reprised in separate early-morning scenes by C. Aubrey Smith, Charlie Ruggles, the triad of Elizabeth Patterson, Ethel Griffies and Blanche Friderici, and Charles Butterworth. (Myrna Loy's rendition was cut when the film was rereleased in 1950 because her navel showed through her nightgown.) Chevalier again sang the number in two subsequent films: *Pepe* (Col. 1960) and *A New Kind of Love* (Par. 1963).

"Mind If I Make Love to You?" Music & lyric by Cole Porter. Casual romantic invitation proffered by Frank Sinatra to Grace Kelly in *High Society* (MGM 1956), as they danced by the side of a pool.

Minnelli, Liza (May), actress, singer, dancer; b. Los Angeles, March 12, 1946. Supercharged performer, the daughter of Judy Garland and Vincente Minnelli, who made it on her own on Broadway, recordings, in television, nightclubs, concerts, and films (most notably *Cabaret*). On screen, she sang "Maybe This Time" and introduced "New York, New York."

1949   In the Good Old Summertime (*Baby Larkin*)
1965   Dangerous Christmas of Red Riding Hood (tv) (*Red Riding Hood*)
1972   Cabaret (*Sally Bowles*)
       Journey Back to Oz (voice of *Dorothy*)
1974   That's Entertainment (narrator)

1976   A Matter of Time (*Nina*)
1977   New York, New York (*Francine Evans*)
1985   That's Dancing! (narrator)

Minnelli, Vincente, director; b. Chicago, Feb. 28, 1903. MGM's leading director of musicals, celebrated for his imaginative use of camera and color in such films as *Meet Me in St. Louis, The Pirate, An American in Paris, The Band Wagon,* and *Gigi*. Minnelli, who began as a designer and director on Broadway, was brought to Hollywood by Arthur Freed, who produced 12 of his 16 musical films. He directed Judy Garland (to whom he was once married) in four musicals, Gene Kelly and Fred Astaire in three each; also Ethel Waters, Lena Horne, Eleanor Powell, Red Skelton, Cyd Charisse, Howard Keel, Leslie Caron, Maurice Chevalier, Judy Holliday, Dean Martin, Barbra Streisand, and Liza Minnelli (his and Miss Garland's daughter). Bib: *I Remember It Well* by Minnelli (1974); *Vincente Minnelli and the Hollywood Musical* by Joseph Casper (1977). (Died Los Angeles, July 25, 1986.)

1943   Cabin in the Sky
       I Dood It
1944   Meet Me in St. Louis
1945   Yolanda and the Thief
1946   Ziegfeld Follies
       Till the Clouds Roll By (part dir.)
1948   The Pirate
1951   An American in Paris
       Lovely To Look At (part dir.)
1953   The Band Wagon
1954   Brigadoon
1955   Kismet
1958   Gigi
1960   Bells Are Ringing
1970   On a Clear Day You Can See Forever
1976   A Matter of Time

"Minnie from Trinidad" Music & lyric by Roger Edens. Rhythmic self-description ("I'm not so good but I'm not so bad") introduced by Judy Garland in a tropical production number in *Ziegfeld Girl* (MGM 1941), and danced by Sergio Orta. "Minnie" seems to have been a relative of Cole Porter's Haiti-visiting "Katie."

Miranda, Carmen (née Maria do Carmo Miranda da Cunha), singer, actress; b. Marco de Canavezes, Portugal, Feb. 9, 1909; d. Hollywood, Aug. 5, 1955. Diminutive, highly animated performer of samba tongue-twisters, whose six-inch heels, fruited headdresses, flashing eyes, and expressive hand movements made her a unique and much imitated entertainer. Between 1940 and 1946, all her films were at Fox, usually playing comic roles requiring someone with a fiery temperament. She was most often in musicals with Don Ameche, Alice Faye, Betty Grable, John Payne, Vivian Blaine, and Perry Como; her best-known Hollywood song was "I Yi Yi Yi Yi" in *That Night in Rio*. Miss Miranda, who first became an entertainer in Brazil, went to Hollywood after scoring in Broadway revue *The Streets of Paris*.

1940	Down Argentine Way (specialty)
1941	That Night in Rio (*Carmen*)
	Weekend in Havana (*Rosita Rivas*)
1942	Springtime in the Rockies (*Rosita*)
1943	The Gang's All Here (*Rosita*)
1944	Four Jills in a Jeep (specialty)
	Greenwich Village (*Princess Querida*)
	Something for the Boys (*Chiquita Hart*)
1945	Doll Face (*Chita*)
1946	If I'm Lucky (*Michele O'Toole*)
1947	Copacabana (*Carmen Novarro*)
1948	A Date with Judy (*Rosita Conchellas*)
1950	Nancy Goes to Rio (*Marina Rodriguez*)
1953	Scared Stiff (*Carmelita Castinha*)

"Miss Brown to You" Music by Ralph Rainger & Richard A. Whiting; lyric by Leo Robin. Tennessee's "lovable, huggable Emily Brown" is coming north just to be with the lucky fellow. Performed on radio in *Big Broadcast of 1936* (Par. 1935) by the Nicholas Brothers and Ray Noble's orchestra, the song is heard by Bill Robinson who then taps down a Harlem street.

"Mister Five by Five" Music by Gene dePaul; lyric by Don Raye. Bouncy number about a mellow cat who's as wide as he's tall, introduced by Grace McDonald with Sonny Dunham's orchestra in *Behind the Eight Ball* (Univ. 1942). Song is said to have been inspired by blues-singer James Rushing.

"Misto Cristofo Columbo" Music & lyric by Jay Livingston & Ray Evans. Cheery salute to the man who "proved to all the squares that the world was round." Introduced by Bing Crosby, with Dorothy Lamour, Cass Daley, Phil Harris, and Louis Armstrong aboard an airplane in *Here Comes the Groom* (Par. 1951).

Mitchell, Sidney, lyricist; b. Baltimore, June 15, 1888; d. Los Angeles, Feb. 25, 1942. Mitchell, who wrote mostly at Fox, teamed with composer Louis Alter to write "You Turned the Tables on Me," "Twilight on

the Trail," and "A Melody from the Sky"; with Lew Pollack for "One in a Million" and "It's Love I'm After." Other collaborators were Archie Gottler, Con Conrad, George Meyer, and Sammy Stept. Among those who sang songs with Mitchell lyrics: Alice Faye, Shirley Temple, Betty Grable, Tony Martin, Don Ameche, Jack Haley.

1929	Fox Movietone Follies (Gottler, Conrad)
	Broadway (Gottler, Conrad)
	The Cockeyed World (Gottler, Conrad)
1930	Let's Go Places (Gottler, Conrad)
	Maybe It's Love (Gottler, Meyer)
1934	I Like It That Way (Gottler)
1936	Dancing Feet (Stept)
	Trail of the Lonesome Pine (Alter)
	Laughing Irish Eyes (Stept)
	Captain January (Pollack)
	Sitting on the Moon (Stept)
	Pigskin Parade (Pollack)
	One in a Million (Pollack)
1937	Thin Ice (Pollack)
	Life Begins in College (Pollack)
1938	In Old Chicago (Pollack)
	Rebecca of Sunnybrook Farm (Pollack)
	Kentucky Moonshine (Pollack)

"Moments Like This" Music by Burton Lane; lyric by Frank Loesser. Though she's not the only one in his life, the singer—Florence George in *College Swing* (Par. 1938)—is determined to make the most of her moments with the man she loves.

"Mona Lisa" Music & lyric by Jay Livingston & Ray Evans. In which the serenader wonders aloud about a beautiful but aloof Italian girl with "a Mona Lisa strangeness" in her smile. Introduced in nonmusical war film *Captain Carey, U.S.A.* (Par. 1950). According to co-writer Ray Evans, "The song was sung by an unknown actor (undoubtably dubbed), who played the part of a blind street singer and accordionist. The raison d'être was that Alan Ladd, an O.S.S. officer, was working with the Italian underground, the Partisans, against the Nazis. The song, heard only in Italian and in fragments, was designed to be a warning to Ladd and the underground when the Nazis were coming. When Jay and I were given the assignment, instead of doing the obvious—something 'misterioso' and menacing—we decided to write against the plot by coming up with a song as Italianate and pretty as we could. However, we didn't write the Italian lyric, a restatement of our own, which the director demanded for the sake of realism. It was done by an Italian professor at UCLA for a fee.''

Monaco, James V. (Jimmy), composer; b. Fornia, Italy, Jan. 13, 1885; d. Beverly Hills, Oct. 16, 1945. Former nightclub pianist who wrote songs for seven Bing Crosby movies (including the first ''Road'' show) with lyricist Johnny Burke (''I've Got a Pocketful of Dreams,'' ''On the Sentimental Side,'' ''East Side of Heaven,'' ''An Apple for the Teacher,'' ''Ain't It a Shame About Mame?,'' ''Only Forever,'' ''April Played the Fiddle,'' ''Too Romantic''). Monaco also wrote with Al Dubin and Mack Gordon (''I Can't Begin To Tell You''), and his songs were also sung by Dorothy Lamour, Mary Martin, Betty Grable, and Dick Haymes.

1938	Doctor Rhythm (Burke)
	Sing You Sinners (Burke)
1939	East Side of Heaven (Burke)
	The Star Maker (Burke)
1940	Road to Singapore (Burke)
	If I Had My Way (Burke)
	Rhythm on the River (Burke)
1943	Stage Door Canteen (Dubin)
1944	Pin-Up Girl (Gordon)
	Sweet and Low Down (Gordon)
	Irish Eyes Are Smiling (Gordon)

Monroe, Marilyn (née Norma Jean Mortenson), actress, singer; b. Los Angeles, June 1, 1926; d. Brentwood, Cal., Aug. 5, 1962. Purring blonde kitten whose vulnerable sensuality made her a legendary figure during her brief career. Major musicals: *Gentlemen Prefer Blondes* (introducing ''When Love Goes Wrong''), *Some Like It Hot*. Bib: *Marilyn Monroe* by Maurice Zolotow (1960); *Films of Marilyn Monroe* by Michael Conway & Mark Ricci (1964).

1949	Ladies of the Chorus (*Peggy*)
	Love Happy (*client*)
1953	Gentlemen Prefer Blondes (*Lorelei Lee*)
1954	River of No Return (*Kay*)
	There's No Business Like Show Business (*Vicky*)
1959	Some Like It Hot (*Sugar Kane*)
1960	Let's Make Love (*Amanda Dell*)

Montalban, Ricardo, actor, singer, dancer; b. Mexico City, Nov. 25, 1920. Virile romantic lead at MGM who danced with Cyd Charisse in three movies. Introduced ''Baby, It's Cold Outside'' with Esther Williams. Later scored success in television series, *Fantasy Island*. Bib: *Reflections* by Montalban (1980).

1947	Fiesta (*Pepe Morales*)
1948	On an Island with You (*Ricardo Montez*)
	The Kissing Bandit (specialty)
1949	Neptune's Daughter (*José O'Rourke*)
1950	Two Weeks with Love (*Desi Armendez*)
1953	Sombrero (*Pepe Gonzales*)
1953	Latin Lovers (*Roberto Santos*)
1966	The Singing Nun (*Father Clementi*)
	Alice Through the Looking Glass (tv) (*White King*)
1968	Sweet Charity (*The Actor*)

Monte Carlo (1930). Music by Richard A. Whiting & W. Franke Harling; lyrics by Leo Robin; screenplay by Ernest Vajda & Vincent Lawrence from German play *Die Blaue Küste* by Hans Müller.

A Paramount film produced & directed by Ernst Lubitsch; art director, Hans Dreier; music director, W. Franke Harling; cameraman, Victor Milner; editor, Merrill White.

Cast: Jack Buchanan (*Count Rudolph Farriere*); Jeanette MacDonald (*Countess Helene Mara*); ZaSu Pitts (*Berthe*); Claud Allister (*Duke Otto von Liebenheim*); Tyler Brooke (*Armand*); Lionel Belmore (*Count Gustav von Liebenheim*); Donald Novis (*''Monsieur Beaucaire''*); Frances Dee (*receptionist*); John Carroll (*wedding guest*); John Roche (*Paul*); Helen Garden (*''Lady Mary''*); David Percy (*''herald''*); Erik Bye (*''Lord Winterset''*).

Songs: ''She'll Love Me and Like It'' - Allister/ ''Beyond the Blue Horizon'' - MacDonald, peasants; reprised by MacDonald, Buchanan/ ''Give Me a Moment, Please'' - Buchanan, MacDonald/ ''Trimmin' the Women'' - Buchanan, Brooke, Roche/ ''Whatever It Is, It's Grand'' - McDonald, Buchanan/ ''Always in All Ways'' - Buchanan, MacDonald/ *''Monsieur Beaucaire''* excerpts - Percy, Garden, Bye, Novis, chorus. Unused: ''A Job with a Future.''

As did all six of his film musicals, *Monte Carlo* found director Ernst Lubitsch poking sly, satirical fun at the romantic antics of affluent and aristocratic Europeans. Again his heroine was played by the mischievous coquette Jeanette MacDonald (who was in four Lubitsch movies), this time acting opposite dapper British song-and-dance man Jack Buchanan (whose next Hollywood film was *The Band Wagon* 23 years later). As always during her Lubitsch period, Miss MacDonald had at least one scene in which she appeared in revealing lingerie or nightgown. In fact, in *Monte Carlo* she played a Countess who is first seen dashing for a train with nothing on under her coat but her underwear. The reason is that Countess Helene has impulsively run away from her wedding to a wealthy silly-ass nobleman, and she's happy to go wherever the train will take her. The destination turns out to be Monte Carlo, where the mercenary lady is unlucky at the gambling tables. Her fortunes change, however, upon meeting Buchanan, as Count Rudolph, who passes himself off as a hairdresser just to be near her. She is attracted to him but social differences make proud Helene spurn Rudolph's advances until, at the local opera house, she attends a performance of *Monsieur Beaucaire*. Its libretto, based on Booth Tarkington's story, is about an aristocratic lady who sends her lover away when she discovers that he's a hairdresser. But he's really a nobleman and now it's his turn to denounce her. When Rudolph confesses to Helene that he too is of noble birth, he makes sure that their romance has a happier ending.

Lubitsch took full advantage of the camera in *Monte Carlo,* especially in his fusion of sight and sound in the musical sequences. In addition to the celebrated "Beyond the Blue Horizon," which Miss MacDonald sang to the accompaniment of chugging railroad wheels, there were the duets, "Give Me a Moment, Please," sung over the telephone, and "Always in All Ways," in which the camera followed the couple gaily setting off for the Casino.

"Moon and the Willow Tree, The" Music by Victor Schertzinger; lyric by Johnny Burke. Ballad sung by Dorothy Lamour in *Road to Singapore* (Par. 1940) in which the singer's two friends—one gay and lighthearted, the other sad—offer conflicting views on the imminence of romance.

"Moon Got in My Eyes, The" Music by Arthur Johnston; lyric by Johnny Burke. Dazzled by the romantic moon, Bing Crosby—in *Double or Nothing* (Par. 1937)—thought he'd found true love at last.

"Moon River" Music by Henry Mancini; lyric by Johnny Mercer. Sung by Audrey Hepburn in *Breakfast at Tiffany's* (Par. 1961), while sitting on a New York City fire escape playing her guitar as she thinks of her lazy, youthful days in the South. Lyricist Mercer once told author Max Wilk that the term "huckleberry friend" was something he probably heard in his childhood "when we'd go into the fields and pick wild berries. I was just free-associating about the South." Mercer also revealed that originally he had called the song

"Red River," because of the muddy rivers in his native Georgia, but he dropped the title because of its possible confusion with "Red River Valley." The song itself was in danger of being dropped from the film when some studio executives complained that the picture ran too long.

"Moon Song" Music by Arthur Johnston; lyric by Sam Coslow. Ballad of a romance that wasn't meant to be, sung by Kate Smith in *Hello, Everybody* (Par. 1933).

"Moonburn" Music by Hoagy Carmichael; lyric by Edward Heyman. In which it is revealed that an appearance of good health has resulted not from a sunburn but from a combination of moonlight and a girl's sweetness. Introduced by Bing Crosby in *Anything Goes* (Par. 1935) singing through a ship's porthole to Ida Lupino. Crosby had the song interpolated in the film after hearing Carmichael sing it at a party.

"Moonlight and Shadows" Music by Frederick Hollander; lyric by Leo Robin. Languid romantic piece sung by Dorothy Lamour—first in native jargon, then in English—in *Jungle Princess* (Par. 1936).

"Moonlight Becomes You" Music by James Van Heusen; lyric by Johnny Burke. "You certainly know the right thing to wear," crooned Bing Crosby to Dorothy Lamour while serenading her in a garden beneath her window. The film was *Road to Morocco* (Par. 1942).

"Moonstruck" Music by Arthur Johnston; lyric by Sam Coslow. In *College Humor* (Par. 1933), Bing Crosby found himself rhyming "kiss me" with "bliss be" as he wondered whether his romantic feelings could be the real thing.

Moore, Constance, actress, singer; b. Sioux City, Iowa, Jan. 18, 1919. Blonde singing beauty who began career as radio vocalist and appeared in succession of low-budget musicals, mostly at Universal and Republic. Also appeared with Ray Bolger in Broadway musical, *By Jupiter*.

1938 Swing That Cheer (*Marian Stuart*)
      The Freshman Year (*Marian*)
1939 Hawaiian Nights (*Connie Lane*)
      Laugh It Off (*Ruth Spencer*)
      Charlie McCarthy, Detective (*Sheila*)
1940 Argentine Nights (*Bonnie Brooks*)

I'm Nobody's Sweetheart Now (*Betty Gilbert*)
La Conga Nights (*Helen Curtiss*)
1941 Las Vegas Nights (*Norma Jennings*)
1944 Show Business (*Constance Ford*)
Atlantic City (*Marilyn Whitaker*)
1945 Delightfully Dangerous (*Josephine Williams*)
Earl Carroll Vanities (*Princess Drina*)
Mexicana (*Alison Calvert*)
1946 Earl Carroll Sketch Book (*Pamela Thayer*)
In Old Sacramento (*Belle Malone*)
1947 Hit Parade of 1947 (*Ellen Baker*)

Moore, Grace, actress, singer; b. Slabtown, Tenn., Dec. 5, 1901; d. plane crash, Copenhagen, Jan. 26, 1947. Blonde, slightly glacial soprano who sang in Broadway musicals (including two *Music Box Revues*) and at the Metropolitan Opera (1928–31) before scoring major screen success in Columbia's *One Night of Love*. The film's title song plus "Stars in My Eyes" and "I'll Take Romance" were among the pieces she introduced in Hollywood. Miss Moore's leading men included Lawrence Tibbett, Tullio Carminati, Franchot Tone, and Cary Grant. Film bio: *So This Is Love,* with Kathryn Grayson as Miss Moore. Bib: *You're Only Human Once* by Miss Moore (1944).

1930 A Lady's Morals (*Jenny Lind*)
New Moon (*Princess Tanya Strogoff*)
1934 One Night of Love (*Mary Barrett*)
1935 Love Me Forever (*Margaret Howard*)
1936 The King Steps Out (*Princess Elizabeth*)
1937 When You're in Love (*Louise Fuller*)
I'll Take Romance (*Elsa Terry*)

Moore, Victor (Frederick), actor; b. Hammonton, NJ, Feb. 24, 1876; d. East Islip, NY, July 23, 1962. Bumbling, wambling, bleating, dumpling-shaped Victor Moore was Broadway's most endearing clown during the 30s and early 40s. He re-created his stage roles in the film versions of *Heads Up* and *Louisiana Purchase,* though he is best remembered on screen as Fred Astaire's sidekick in *Swing Time.*

1930 Dangerous Nan McGrew (*Doc Froster*)
Heads Up (*Skippy Dugan*)
1934 Romance in the Rain (*J. Franklyn Blank*)
The Gift of Gab (*Col. Trivers*)
1936 Swing Time (*Pop Cardetti*)
Gold Diggers of 1937 (*J. J. Hobart*)
1937 Life of the Party (*Oliver*)
1938 Radio City Revels (*Plummer*)
1941 Louisiana Purchase (*Sen. Oliver P. Loganberry*)
1942 Star Spangled Rhythm (*Pop Webster*)

1943 True to Life (*Pop*)
Riding High (*Mortimer J. Slocum*)
The Heat's On (*Hubert Bainbridge*)
1944 Carolina Blues (*Phineas/ his 3 brothers, 2 aunts*)
1945 Duffy's Tavern (*Michael O'Malley*)
1946 Ziegfeld Follies (specialty)

"More and More" Music by Jerome Kern; lyric by E. Y. Harburg. Ballad through which Denna Durbin expressed her increasingly romantic feelings in *Can't Help Singing* (Univ. 1944). Lyricist Harburg originally ended the song with "More and more I'm less and less unwilling/ To give up wanting more and more of you," but then realized the the double negative reversed the meaning. The solution: removing the "un" from "unwilling."

"More I See You, The" Music by Harry Warren; lyric by Mack Gordon. Song of accelerating romantic desire introduced by Dick Haymes in *Diamond Horseshoe* (Fox 1945).

Moreno, Rita, (née Rosita Dolores Alverio), actress, dancer; b. Humacao, Puerto Rico, Dec. 11, 1931. Fiery actress whose most notable performance in a screen musical was her last. Active in television and theatre.

1950 The Toast of New Orleans (*Tina*)
Pagan Love Song (*Teuru*)
1952 Singin' in the Rain (*Zelda Zanders*)
1953 Latin Lovers (*Christina*)
1956 The King and I (*Tuptim*)
The Vagabond King (*Huguette*)
1961 West Side Story (*Anita*)

Morey, Larry, lyricist; b. Los Angeles, March 26, 1905; d. Los Angeles, May 8, 1971. Writer for Walt Disney films who collaborated with Frank Churchill on "Heigh Ho," "Whistle While You Work," and "Some Day My Prince Will Come"; with Eliot Daniel on "Lavender Blue."

1937 Snow White and the Seven Dwarfs (Churchill)
1948 So Dear to My Heart (Daniel)

Morgan, Dennis (né Stanley Morner), actor, singer; b. Prentice, Wisc., Dec. 20, 1910. Wavy-haired, square-jawed Dennis Morgan played romantic heroes in Warner musicals opposite such stars as Ann Sheridan, Janis Paige, and Virginia Mayo; also teamed with Jack Carson in four films. Though Morgan possessed an operatic tenor, it was, incredulously, Allan Jones' voice that emerged from his mouth singing "A Pretty Girl Is Like a Melody" in *The Great Ziegfeld*. He did, however, get to introduce "A Gal in Calico."

1936 The Great Ziegfeld (*"singer"*)
1942 The Hard Way (*Paul Collins*)
1943 The Desert Song (*Paul Hudson*)
       Thank Your Lucky Stars (*Tommy Randolph*)
1944 Shine On, Harvest Moon (*Jack Norworth*)
       Hollywood Canteen (specialty)
1946 Two Guys from Milwaukee (*Prince Henry*)
       The Time, the Place and the Girl (*Steve Ross*)
1947 My Wild Irish Rose (*Chauncey Olcott*)
1948 Two Guys from Texas (*Steve Carroll*)
       One Sunday Afternoon (*Biff Grimes*)
1949 It's a Great Feeling (*Dennis Morgan*)
1951 Painting the Clouds with Sunshine (*Vince Nichols*)

Morgan, Frank (né Francis Phillip Wuppermann), actor; b. New York, June 1, 1890; d. Hollywood, Sept. 18, 1949. An amiable character comedian, Morgan was noted for his sputtering delivery punctuated by nervous chuckles. Appearing in over 70 films, mostly at MGM, he usually played either a dapper but hapless man in charge (kings, governors, Broadway producers) or a seedy con man. In musicals, he is best remembered for his roles in *Naughty Marietta* and *The Wizard of Oz*.

1930 Queen High (*Nettleton*)
       Dangerous Nan McGrew (*Muldoon*)
1933 Hallelujah, I'm a Bum (*Mayor John Hastings*)
       Best of Enemies (*William Hartman*)
       Broadway to Hollywood (*Ted Hackett*)
1934 The Cat and the Fiddle (*Jules Daudet*)
1935 Naughty Marietta (*Gov. Gaspard d' Annard*)
       A Perfect Gentleman (*Major*)
1936 The Great Ziegfeld (*Jack Billings*)
       Dancing Pirate (*Alcalde*)
       Dimples (*Prof. Eustace Appleby*)
1937 Rosalie (*King Frederick*)
1938 Sweethearts (*Felix Lehman*)
1939 Broadway Serenade (*Cornelius Collier*)
       The Wizard of Oz (*Prof. Marvel/ The Wizard*)
       Balalaika (*Ivan Danchenoff*)
1940 Broadway Melody of 1940 (*Bob Casey*)
       Hullabaloo (*Frank Merriweather*)
1943 Thousands Cheer (specialty)
1945 Yolanda and the Thief (*Victor Trout*)
1948 Summer Holiday (*Uncle Sid*)

Morgan, Helen, actress, singer; b. Danville, Ohio, 1900; d. Chicago, Oct. 8, 1941. Nightclub torch singer with delicate, tear-stained voice whose specialty was playing tragic heroines (e.g., *Show Boat*, both on stage and screen). Film bio: *The Helen Morgan Story*, with Ann Blyth acting Miss Morgan and Gogi Grant singing her songs. Bib: *Helen Morgan* by Gilbert Maxwell (1974).

1929 Show Boat (specialty)
       Applause (*Kitty Darling*)
       Glorifying the American Girl (specialty)
1930 Roadhouse Nights (*Lola Fagan*)
1934 You Belong to Me (*Mme. Alva*)
       Marie Galante (*Tapia*)
1935 Sweet Music (*Helen Morgan*)
       Go Into Your Dance (*Luana Bell*)
       Frankie and Johnnie (*Frankie*)
1936 Show Boat (*Julie LaVerne*)

Mother Wore Tights (1947). Music mostly by Josef Myrow; lyrics mostly by Mack Gordon; screenplay by Lamar Trotti from book by Miriam Young.

A 20th Century-Fox film produced by Lamar Trotti; directed by Walter Lang; choreography, Seymour Felix, Kenny Williams; art directors, Richard Day, Joseph Wright; costumes, Orry-Kelly; music director, Alfred Newman; orchestrations, Gene Rose; cameraman, Harry Jackson; editor, J. Watson Webb, Jr.; Technicolor.

Cast: Betty Grable (*Myrtle McKinley Burt*); Dan Dailey (*Frank Burt*); Mona Freeman (*Iris Burt*); Vanessa Brown (*Bessie*); Connie Marshall (*Mickie Burt*); Robert Arthur (*Bob Clarkman*); Sara Allgood (*Grandma McKinley*); William Frawley (*Schneider*); Sig Rumann (*Papa*); Lee Patrick (*Lil*); Chick Chandler (*Ed*); Anne Baxter (narrator).

Songs: "You Do" - Dailey; reprised by Grable, Freeman/ "Burlington Bertie from Bow" (William Hargreaves) - Dailey; reprised by Grable/ "This Is My Favorite City" - Grable, Dailey/ "Kokomo, Indiana" - Grable, Dailey/ "Tra-la-la" (music, Harry Warren) - Grable, Dailey, Freeman/ "Swingin' Down the Lane" (Isham Jones-Gus Kahn) - Freeman, friends/ "Stumbling" (Zez Confrey) - Freeman, Patrick, Chandler/ "There's Nothing Like a Song" - Grable, Dailey/ "Rolling Down to Bowling Green" - Grable, Dailey/ "Fare-thee-well, Dear Alma Mater" - students.

Mother Wore Tights was Betty Grable's biggest box-office hit. The first of her four musicals in which she co-starred with Dan Dailey, it told a sentimental, nostalgic show-business tale from the team's first meeting in 1900 at Schneider's Opera House in San Francisco (when Dailey sings "You Do"), through their days touring in vaudeville (when Grable sings "You Do"), and ends with their daughter's graduation from an exclusive school (when she sings "You Do").

"Mr. and Mrs. Is the Name" Music by Allie Wrubel; lyric by Mort Dixon. Joyful announcement for Dick Powell and Ruby Keeler in *Flirtation Walk* (Warner 1934).

"Mr. Paganini." *See* **"You'll Have To Swing It"**

"Mrs. Robinson" Music & lyric by Paul Simon. Folkish recollection of yesterday's magic ("Where have you gone, Joe DiMaggio?"), sung on soundtrack by Simon and Garfunkel to a leading character (played by Ann Bancroft) in *The Graduate* (Embassy 1967).

Munshin, Jules, actor, singer; b. New York, 1916; d. New York, Feb. 19, 1970. Actor with nasal voice and comic haughtiness who first won notice in Broadway revue, *Call Me Mister*. He supported co-stars Gene Kelly and Frank Sinatra in two films, and Fred Astaire in two.

1948 Easter Parade (*François*)
1949 Take Me Out to the Ball Game (*Nat Goldberg*)
   That Midnight Kiss (*Michael Pemberton*)
   On the Town (*Ozzie*)
1957 Silk Stockings (*Bibinsky*)
   Ten Thousand Bedrooms (*Arthur*)

" 'Murder' He Says" Music by Jimmy McHugh; lyric by Frank Loesser. A highly animated complaint about a hepcat's romantic vocabulary, first registered by Betty Hutton in *Happy Go Lucky* (Par. 1943).

Murphy, George (Lloyd), actor, dancer, singer; b. New Haven, Conn., July 4, 1902. Dependable song-and-dance man with crinkly grin who didn't always win the girl but at least got his chance to whirl her around the dancefloor. Among his partners were Alice Faye (with whom he introduced "You're a Sweetheart"), Eleanor Powell, Shirley Temple, and Judy Garland. Murphy began his career in vaudeville and nightclubs with his wife, Julie Johnson, and appeared in Broadway musicals before going to Hollywood; he later served as US Senator from California. Bib: *Say, Didn't You Used to Be George Murphy?* by Murphy (1970).

1934 Kid Millions (*Jerry Lane*)
1935 After the Dance (*Jerry Davis*)
1937 Top of the Town (*Ted Lane*)
   Broadway Melody of 1938 (*Sonny Ledford*)
   You're a Sweetheart (*Hal Adams*)

1938 Little Miss Broadway (*Roger Wendling*)
   Hold That Coed (*Rusty*)
1940 Broadway Melody of 1940 (*King Shaw*)
   Two Girls on Broadway (*Eddie Kerns*)
   Little Nellie Kelly (*Jerry Kelly*)
1941 Rise and Shine (*Jimmy McGonigle*)
1942 For Me and My Gal (*Jimmy Metcalfe*)
   The Powers Girl (*Jerry Hendricks*)
1943 The Mayor of 44th Street (*Joe Jonathan*)
   This Is the Army (*Jerry Jones*)
1944 Broadway Rhythm (*Johnnie Demming*)
   Show Business (*George Doane*)
   Step Lively (*Gordon Miller*)
1948 Big City (*Pat O'Donnell*)

"Music Is Better Than Words" Music by André Previn; lyric by Roger Edens. At least in creating the proper romantic atmosphere. Belted out by Dolores Gray on a television program in *It's Always Fair Weather* (MGM 1955); also sung by her in *Designing Woman* (MGM 1957). The number was added to the score of *It's Always Fair Weather* after the film's regular lyricists, Betty Comden and Adolph Green, had returned to New York.

"Music Makes Me" Music by Vincent Youmans; lyric by Gus Kahn & Edward Eliscu. Music's influence on romance rhythmically explained by Ginger Rogers as the vocalist with Gene Raymond's band in *Flying Down to Rio* (RKO 1933). The scene was the Date Room of Miami's Hotel Hibiscus.

Music Man, The (1962). Music & lyrics by Meredith Willson; screenplay by Marion Hargrove from Broadway musical by Willson based on story by Willson & Franklin Lacey.

A Warner Bros. film produced & directed by Morton Da Costa; choreography, Onna White, Tom Panko; art director, Paul Groesse; costumes, Dorothy Jeakins; music director, Ray Heindorf; orchestrations, Heindorf, Frank Comstock, Gus Levene; cameraman, Robert Burks; editor, William Ziegler; Technicolor; Technirama.

Cast: Robert Preston (*Prof. Harold Hill*); Shirley Jones (*Marian Paroo*); Buddy Hackett (*Marcellus Washburn*); Hermione Gingold (*Eulalie Mackechnie Shinn*); Paul Ford (*Mayor Shinn*); Pert Kelton (*Mrs. Paroo*); Ronny Howard (*Winthrop Paroo*); Buffalo Bills (*Jacey Squires, Olin Britt, Ewart Dunlap, Oliver Hix*);

Timmy Everett (*Tommy Djilas*); Susan Luckey (*Zaneeta Shinn*); Mary Wickes (*Mrs. Squires*).

Songs: "Rock Island" - traveling salesmen/ "Iowa Stubborn" - townspeople/ "Trouble" - Preston, townspeople/ "Piano Lesson" - Jones, Kelton/ "Goodnight, My Someone" - Jones/ "Seventy-Six Trombones" - Preston, townspeople/ "Sincere" - Buffalo Bills/ "The Sadder-but-Wiser Girl" - Preston/ "Pick-a-Little, Talk-a-Little" - Gingold, biddies/ "Marian the Librarian" - Preston/ "Being in Love" - Jones/ "Gary, Indiana" - Preston; reprised by Howard/ "Wells Fargo Wagon" - townspeople/ "Lida Rose" & "Will I Ever Tell You?" - Buffalo Bills, Jones/ "Shipoopi" - Hackett, townspeople/ "Till There Was You" - Jones. Unused: "My White Knight."

Produced and directed by its original Broadway director, Morton Da Costa, the screen version of *The Music Man* was a faithful re-creation of the successful stage musical of 1957. It had all Meredith Willson's songs except for the replacement of "My White Knight" by "Being in Love." Its dances were again by Onna White. It retained the services of cast principals Pert Kelton, Paul Ford (who had replaced David Burns on Broadway), and the Buffalo Bills (though Shirley Jones was substituted for Barbara Cook). But most important, it preserved the dynamic stage performance of Robert Preston as the fast-talking music man who hoodwinks the citizens of River City, Iowa, into believing that he can teach the town's youth how to play instruments in a marching band. And thanks to the love of Marian the Librarian, at the end of the story he does just that as the screen is jammed with thousands of colorfully uniformed musicians blaring away as they gaily march down the street.

"Music Stopped, The" Music by Jimmy McHugh; lyric by Harold Adamson. Recollection of a romantic evening when the singer and his lady, oblivious to the fact that the orchestra had already left and they were the only ones on the dance floor, kept on dancing "because the lights were low and we were in love." Sung in *Higher and Higher* (RKO 1943) by Frank Sinatra first at a New York social event as he serenaded—and danced with—both Michele Morgan and Barbara Hale. At the end of the film, as a literal interpretation of the line, "Dancing on a cloud way up in the blue," Jack Haley and Miss Morgan danced off into the blue, and Sinatra reprised the song as he grew bigger and bigger on the cloud-filled screen.

"My Baby Just Cares for Me" Music by Walter Donaldson; lyric by Gus Kahn. In *Whoopee* (Goldwyn 1930) Eddie Cantor, as a black-faced singing waiter, exultantly brags that his girl prefers him to the likes of Ronald Colman, Lawrence Tibbett ("she'd rather have me around to kibitz") Buddy Rogers, and Maurice Chevalier.

"My Dreams Are Getting Better All the Time" Music by Vic Mizzy; lyric by Mann Curtis. Tripping number in which dreams lend romantic encouragement, introduced by Marion Hutton in *In Society* (Univ. 1944).

My Fair Lady (1964). Music by Frederick Loewe; lyrics by Alan Jay Lerner; screenplay by Lerner from Broadway musical by Lerner & Loewe based on play, *Pygmalion* by George Bernard Shaw.

A Warner Bros. film produced by Jack L. Warner; directed by George Cukor; choreography, Hermes Pan; production design, Cecil Beaton; art director, Gene Allen; costumes, Beaton; music director, André Previn; orchestrations, Alexander Courage, Robert Franklyn, Al Woodbury; cameraman, Harry Stradling; editor, William Ziegler; Technicolor; Super PanaVision 70.

Cast: Audrey Hepburn (vocals by Marni Nixon) (*Eliza Doolittle*); Rex Harrison (*Prof. Henry Higgins*); Stanley Holloway (*Alfred P. Doolittle*); Wilfred Hyde-White (*Col. Hugh Pickering*); Gladys Cooper (*Mrs. Higgins*); Jeremy Brett (vocals by Bill Shirley) (*Freddie Eynsford-Hill*); Theodore Bikel (*Zoltan Karpathy*); Mona Washbourne (*Mrs. Pearce*); Isobel Elsom (*Mrs. Eynsford-Hill*); John Alderson (*Jamie*); John McLiam (*Harry*); John Holland (*butler*); Henry Daniell (*Prince Gregor of Transylvania*); Bina Rothschild (*Queen of Transylvania*); Grady Sutton (*guest at ball*); Charles Fredericks (*imaginary king*).

Songs: "Why Can't the English?" - Harrison/ "Wouldn't It Be Loverly?" - Hepburn (Nixon), Cockneys/ "I'm an Ordinary Man" - Harrison/ "With a Little Bit of Luck" - Holloway, Alderson, McLiam, Cockneys/ "Just You Wait" - Hepburn (Nixon)/ "The Rain in Spain" - Harrison, Hepburn (Nixon), Hyde-White/ "I Could Have Danced All Night" - Hepburn (Nixon), with Washbourne, chambermaids/ "Ascot Gavotte" - spectators/ "On the Street Where You Live" - Brett (Shirley)/ "Embassy Waltz" - orchestra/ "You Did It" - Harrison, Hyde-White/ "Show Me" - Hepburn (Nixon), Brett (Shirley)/ "Get Me to the Church on Time" - Holloway, Cockneys/ "A Hymn to Him" - Harrison, Hyde-White/ "Without You" - Hepburn

(Nixon)/ ''I've Grown Accustomed to Her Face'' - Harrison.

In turning Bernard Shaw's classic play *Pygmalion* into the classic musical *My Fair Lady,* Lerner and Loewe retained most of the playwright's dialogue, added scenes in Tottenham Court Road, the Ascot Racetrack, and the Embassy Ball, and—contrary to the play—ended the story on a romantic note by having Eliza Doolittle, the Cockney flower-seller who has learned to speak like a lady, return to her autocratic linguistics professor, Henry Higgins. Though the leads in the original 1956 Broadway production, Rex Harrison and Julie Andrews, had won high praise, when producer Jack L. Warner paid a record $5.5 million (plus other emoluments) for the screen rights he wanted the insurance of established boxoffice names. Harrison was signed for Higgins only after Cary Grant turned down the part, but Warner bypassed Miss Andrews completely (which left her free to make *Mary Poppins*) and tapped Audrey Hepburn as Eliza (though her singing was dubbed). The producer, however, did keep the services of the original librettist (Lerner) and costume designer (Cecil Beaton, who was also production designer), plus the stage's Alfred P. Doolittle (Stanley Holloway).

On screen the story remained basically as it had been, except for some ''opening-up'' of such scenes as Covent Garden and the black-and-white Ascot. *My Fair Lady* became the first movie musical based on a Shaw play. When Oscar Straus' *The Chocolate Soldier,* adapted from Shaw's *Arms and the Man,* was filmed in 1941 (with Nelson Eddy and Risë Stevens), the plot was jettisoned in favor of Ferenc Molnar's *The Guardsman* because Shaw wanted too much money. The nonmusical *Pygmalion* was filmed three times: in Germany (1935), with Gustaf Grundgens and Jenny Jugo; in The Netherlands (1937), with Johan de Meester and Lily Bouwmeester; and in England (1938), with Leslie Howard and Wendy Hiller. Bib: *Cecil Beaton's ''Fair Lady''* (1964).

"My Future Just Passed" Music by Richard A. Whiting; lyric by George Marion, Jr. One look was enough to convince Charles ''Buddy'' Rogers—in *Safety in Numbers* (Par. 1930)—that he's found the girl he'd been dreaming about.

"My Heart and I" Music by Frederick Hollander; lyric by Leo Robin. Both are in love with her—as Bing Crosby explained to Ida Lupino while seated in a lifeboat on a ship's deck in *Anything Goes* (Par. 1936).

"My Heart Is a Hobo" Music by James Van Heusen; lyric by Johnny Burke. Chipper number in praise of the carefree life, sung by Bing Crosby to Barry Fitzgerald in *Welcome Stranger* (Par. 1947) while they enjoy an afternoon of fishing.

"My Heart Is an Open Book" Music & lyric by Mack Gordon. Joe Morrison sang this romantic avowal in *Love in Bloom* (Par. 1935).

"My Heart Is Taking Lessons" Music by James V. Monaco; lyric by Johnny Burke. Singing lessons, that is, prompted by infatuation, according to Bing Crosby in *Doctor Rhythm* (Par. 1938).

"My Heart Tells Me" Music by Harry Warren; lyric by Mack Gordon. Cardiac warning to be romantically on guard, introduced by Phil Regan in *Sweet Rosie O'Grady* (Fox 1943), then sung by Betty Grable, first in a bathtub later on stage in a beerhall.

"My Ideal" Music by Richard A. Whiting & Newell Chase; lyric by Leo Robin. In *Playboy of Paris* (Par. 1930) Maurice Chevalier wondered aloud if he would ever find her.

"My Kind of Town" Music by James Van Heusen; lyric by Sammy Cahn. Frank Sinatra introduced this breezy anthem celebrating Chicago, the ''one town that won't let you down,'' in *Robin and the Seven Hoods* (Warner 1964). The scene took place on the steps of a courthouse after Robin (Sinatra) was acquitted of killing a sheriff.

"My Love Parade" Music by Victor Schertzinger; lyric by Clifford Grey. In which a new inamorata is praised for being a composite of all the attractive features of former conquests (''Eyes of Lisette, smile of Mignonette . . .''). Maurice Chevalier first used this odd technique of wooing in *The Love Parade* (Par. 1929), when he sang the piece to Jeanette MacDonald in her boudoir. Even odder, she joined in the song.

"My Old Flame" Music by Arthur Johnston; lyric by Sam Coslow. Torch ballad dimly recalling a lost love (''I can't even remember his name'') sung by Mae West in *Belle of the Nineties* (Par. 1934), accompanied by Duke Ellington's orchestra. In the scene Miss West renders the piece after a group of male admirers have asked to hear her favorite song.

"My One and Only Highland Fling" Music by Harry Warren; lyric by Ira Gershwin. Performed as a routine in a Broadway revue in the *The Barkleys of Broadway* (MGM 1949). In the scene Fred Astaire and Ginger Rogers, with suitably dour expressions and burry accents, appear in tam-o-shanters and tartan kilts to confess previous highland flings and affirm their decision to settle down to "the fling of a husband-and-wifetime."

"My Personal Property" Music by Cy Coleman; lyric by Dorothy Fields. Because she's in love, Shirley McLaine—in *Sweet Charity* (Univ. 1969)—feels that all New York belongs to her as she bounds joyously through Central Park. The song, which replaced "You Should See Yourself," was the only new number added to the screen version of the Broadway musical.

"My Resistance Is Low" Music by Hoagy Carmichael; lyric by Harold Adamson. Romantic vulnerability admitted by Jane Russell and Hoagy Carmichael as gambling-den entertainers in *The Las Vegas Story* (RKO 1952).

"My Shining Hour" Music by Harold Arlen; lyric by Johnny Mercer. Wartime song of leave-taking introduced by Joan Leslie (but with Sally Sweetland's voice), backed by Freddie Slack's orchestra, in *The Sky's the Limit* (RKO 1943). Fred Astaire later sang the number to Miss Leslie with a more lighthearted beat and a supposedly improvised lyric ("Like the face of Mischa Auer on the Music Hall marquee"); still later, the couple danced to the music on a penthouse terrace.

"My Walking Stick" Music & lyric by Irving Berlin. Rhythmic appreciation of an important adjunct to masculine attire ("Can't look by best, feel undressed without my cane"). In *Alexander's Ragtime Band* (Fox 1938) it was belted out by Ethel Merman—in top hat, cutaway, and striped pants—accompanied by cane-twirling chorus girls and an orchestra led by Tyrone Power.

Myrow, Josef, composer; b. Russia, Feb. 28, 1910. Former concert pianist and radio conductor who wrote songs mostly at Fox and mostly with lyricist Mack Gordon ("On the Boardwalk at Atlantic City," "You Make Me Feel So Young," "You Do," "It Happens Every Spring"). Other collaborators were Eddie DeLange, Ralph Blane, and Robert Wells. Perry Como, Vivian Blaine, June Haver, Betty Grable, Dan Dailey, Debbie Reynolds, and Donald O'Connor all introduced Myrow songs.

1946	If I'm Lucky (DeLange)
	Three Little Girls in Blue (Gordon)
1947	Mother Wore Tights (Gordon)
1950	Wabash Avenue (Gordon)
1953	I Love Melvin (Gordon)
	The Girl Next Door (Gordon)
1954	The French Line (Blane, Wells)
1956	Bundle of Joy (Gordon)

N

Nashville (1975). Music & lyrics by Richard Baskin, Henry Gibson, Ronee Blakely, and Keith Carradine; screenplay by Joan Tewkesbury.

An ABC Entertainment film produced by Jerry Weintraub & Robert Altman; directed by Altman; costumes, Jules Melillo; music director, Richard Baskin; cameraman, Paul Lohmann; editors, Sid Levin, Dennis Hill; MGM Film Lab. color.

Cast: Barbara Baxley (*Lady Pearl*); Ned Beatty (*Delbert Reese*); Karen Black (*Connie White*); Ronee Blakely (*Barbara Jean*); Timothy Brown (*Tommy Brown*); Keith Carradine (*Tom Frank*); Geraldine Chaplin (*Opal*); Shelley Duvall (*L. A. Joan*); Allen Garfield (*Burnett*), Henry Gibson (*Haven Hamilton*), Jeff Goldblum (*tricycle man*); Barbara Harris (*Albuquerque*); Michael Murphy (*John Triplette*); Allan Nicholls (*Bill*); Dave Peel (*Bud Hamilton*); Cristina Raines (*Mary*); Lily Tomlin (*Linnea Reese*); Gwen Welles (*Sueleen Gay*); Keenan Wynn (*Green*); Misty Mountain Boys; Sheila Bailey, Patti Bryant (Smokey Mountain Laurel); Elliott Gould, Julie Christie (guest bits); Johnny Barnett (singer).

Songs: "200 Years" (Baskin-Gibson) - Gibson/ "Do You Believe in Jesus?" - Tomlin, gospel singers/ "I Never Get Enough" - Welles/ "Mississippi River" - Misty Mountain Boys/ "Troubled Times" - Bailey, Bryant/ "Let Me Be the One" - Welles/ "It Don't Worry Me" (Carradine) - Carradine; reprised by Harris, chorus/ "Gentle Woman" - Peel/ "Bluebird" (Blakely) - Brown/ "For the Sake of the Children" (Baskin) - Gibson/ "Keep a-Goin' " (Baskin-Gibson) - Gibson/ "Memphis" (Black) - Black/ "Rolling Stone" (Black) - Black/"Honey, Won't You Let Me Try Again?" - Carradine/ "Tapedeck in His Tractor" (Blakely) - Blakely/ "Dues" (Blakely) - Blakely/ "Sad but True" - Barnett/ "Since You've Gone" - Carradine, Nicholls, Raines/ "I'm Easy" (Carradine) - Carradine/ "Love You from a Distance" - Carradine/ "There's Trouble in the USA" - uncredited singer/ "One, I Love You" (Baskin) - Blakely, Gibson/ "My Idaho Home" (Blakely) - Blakely.

Director Robert Altmann's use of hand-held cameras, quick cutting, and overlapping dialogue created an artful mosaic focusing on various characters involved in the country-music scene. With Nashville serving as a microcosm of the United States, the film dealt with such themes as fame, ambition, idolatry, vanity, rivalry, jealousy, political power, and slippin' around. Landmarks of the locale—recording studios, country fairs, honkytonks, and of course the Grand Ol' Opry—are shown, and there are thinly veiled portraits of two of Nashville's stellar attractions, Loretta Lynn (called Barbara Jean) and Hank Snow (Haven Hamilton). The 1980 film *Coal Miner's Daughter,* in which Sissy Spacek plays Miss Lynn, contained scenes and situations that recalled *Nashville.*

"Nasty Man" Music by Ray Henderson; lyric by Jack Yellen & Irving Caesar. Lighthearted admonition to a philanderer, introduced by Alice Faye and Scan-Dolls in production number at beginning of *George White's Scandals* (Fox 1934). More commonly known as "Oh You Nasty Man," the song was prompted by an expression made popular by comic Joe Penner.

Naughty Marietta (1935). Music by Victor Herbert; lyrics by Rida Johnson Young & Gus Kahn; screenplay by John Lee Mahin, Frances Goodrich, and Albert Hackett from Broadway musical by Mrs. Young & Herbert.

An MGM film produced by Hunt Stromberg; directed by W. S. VanDyke; art director, Cedric Gibbons; costumes, Adrian; music director, Herbert Stothart; adaptation, Stothart; cameraman, William Daniels; editor, Blanche Sewell.

Cast: Jeanette MacDonald (*Princess Marie de Namours de la Bonfain* aka *Marietta Frannini*); Nelson Eddy (*Capt. Dick Warrington*); Frank Morgan (*Gov. Gaspard d'Annard*); Elsa Lanchester (*Mme. d'Annard*); Douglass Dumbrille (*Prince de Namours de la Bonfain*); Joseph Cawthorn (*"Schumie" Schumann*); Cecilia Parker (*Julie*); Walter Kingsford (*Don Carlos de Braganza*); Akim Tamiroff (*Rudolpho*); Edward Brophy (*Ezekiel Kramer*); Harold Huber (*Abraham*); Marjorie Main (*casquette girl*); Dr. Edouard Lippé (*landlord*); Cora Sue Collins (*Felice*); Stanley Fields (*pirate*); Charles Bruins (*ship singer*); Delos Jewkes (*priest*); Zarubi Elmassian (*Suzette*); M. Sankar, Countess Sonia, Alexander Bokefi, William Sabot (*marionette voices*).

Songs: "Chansonette" (Kahn) - MacDonald, students/ "Antoinette and Anatole" (Kahn) - Bruins, girls/ "Live for Today" (Kahn) - Jewkes, girls/ "Tramp, Tramp, Tramp" (Young, Kahn) - Eddy, scouts/ "The Owl and the Polecat" (Kahn) - Eddy/ " 'Neath the Southern Moon" (Young) - Eddy/ "Italian Street Song" (Young) - Elmassian, Eddy, MacDonald/ "Ship Ahoy" (Kahn) - Sankar, Sonia, Bokefi, Sabot, MacDonald/ "I'm Falling in Love with Someone" (Young) - Eddy/ "Ah, Sweet Mystery of Life" (Young) - MacDonald, Eddy.

Naughty Marietta flourishingly ushered in the great age of Hollywood operetta. It did so by pairing Jeanette MacDonald, whom many considered washed up in films, with Nelson Eddy, a concert baritone with limited acting experience, in a comic opera that MGM had originally bought five years before as a vehicle for Marion Davies. (So enthusiastically was the new team received that they co-starred in a total of eight musicals—one more than Dick and Ruby, two less than Fred and Ginger.) Though the period and locale of *Naughty Marietta* were still late 18th-century New Orleans, the original libretto of one of Victor Herbert's most acclaimed works underwent a number of major changes. Now our heroine, formerly a Neapolitan, is a French princess in disguise who runs away from a loveless marriage by joining a shipload of casquette girls on their way to the New World to marry planters and trappers. Possibly because the original story was too close to *The Desert Song*, Capt. Dick Warrington is no longer pursuing the notorious pirate who turns out to be the French Lieutenant Governor's son, and whose identity is revealed by the quadroon slave who loves him. Now the pirates are dispatched by Capt. Dick's men early in the movie, and the main conflict centers on the problem of Marietta's identity and how—between solos and duets—Dick manages to keep the lady from sailing back to France.

Five years later, MGM co-starred MacDonald and Eddy in *New Moon,* a leaden attempt to recapture the flavor of their first success. Based on a 1928 Romberg and Hammerstein operetta, the Robert Z. Leonard production had the same setting as *Naughty Marietta,* only this time it's Nelson, as a duke in disguise, who is brought to New Orleans to work as a bondsman on the plantation of aristocratic Jeanette. Other things in common include the fussy French governor, the brocaded nobility, the snarling pirates, the shipload of brides (though these are bound for Martinique), the elaborate formal balls—and the same historical error of making New Orleans a French possession when, at the time, it belonged to Spain.

Neagle, Anna (née Florence Marjorie Robertson), actress, dancer, singer, producer; b. London, Oct. 20, 1904. Dame of the British Empire 1970. A reigning star of both the London stage and the British screen, Miss Neagle is best known for her film portrayals of influential women of history. All her movies—including three Hollywood musicals—were produced by her husband, Herbert Wilcox. Among actors with whom she appeared were Jack Buchanan, Fernand Gravet (Graavey), Tullio Carminati, and Ray Bolger. Bib: *There's Always Tomorrow* by Miss Neagle (1974). (Died June 3, 1986.)

1932 Goodnight Vienna (*Vicki*)
1933 The Little Damozel (*Julie Alardy*)
Bitter Sweet (*Sari Linden*)
1934 The Queen's Affair (*Queen Nadina*)
1936 Lime Light (*Marjorie Kaye*)
1937 London Melody (*Jacqueline*)
1940 Irene (US) (*Irene O'Dare*)
1941 No, No, Nanette (US) (*Nanette*)
Sunny (US) (*Sunny Sullivan*)
Spring in Park Lane (*Judy Howard*)
1947 The Courtneys of Curzon Street (*Cathy Courtney*)
1954 Lilacs in the Spring (*Carole Lillian/ Nell Gwyn/ Queen Victoria*)
1956 King's Rhapsody (*Marta Karillos*)
These Dangerous Years (prod. only)
1958 Wonderful Things (prod. only)
1959 The Lady Is a Square (*Frances Baring*) (also prod.)
The Heart of a Man (prod. only)

Nelson, Gene (né Eugene Berg), actor, dancer, singer, director; b. Seattle, March 24, 1920. Affable, easygoing dancing actor who began career in Sonja Henie's ice show, and who appeared mostly in Warner musicals with Gordon MacRae, Doris Day, and Virginia Mayo. Becoming a director in the early 60s, he was responsible for two Elvis Presley films.

Asterisk indicates Mr. Nelson was director only:
1947   I Wonder Who's Kissing Her Now (*Tommy Yale*)
1950   The Daughter of Rosie O'Grady (*Doug Martin*)
       Tea for Two (*Tommy Trainor*)
       The West Point Story (*Hal Cortland*)
1951   Lullaby of Broadway (*Tom Farnham*)
       Painting the Clouds with Sunshine (*Ted Lansing*)
       Starlift (specialty)
1952   She's Working Her Way Through College (*Don Weston*)
1953   She's Back on Broadway (*Gordon Evans*)
       Three Sailors and a Girl (*Twitch*)
1954   So This Is Paris (*Al Howard*) (also chor.)
1955   Oklahoma! (*Will Parker*)
1963   Hootenanny Hoot*
1964   Kissin' Cousins*
1965   Harum Scarum*
       Your Cheatin' Heart*

Nelson, (Oswald George) Ozzie, actor, singer, bandleader; b. Jersey City, NJ, March 20, 1906; d. Hollywood, June 3, 1975. Nelson first won success as a collegiate-looking singing bandleader during the 1930s. He married his vocalist and singing partner, Harriet Hilliard, and appeared with her in five films and on a successful radio and television series (along with sons David and Ricky). Bib: *Ozzie* by Nelson (1973).

Asterisk indicates appearance with Miss Hilliard:
1941   Sweetheart of the Campus* (*Ozzie Norton*)
1942   Strictly in the Groove (*Ozzie*)
1943   Honeymoon Lodge* (specialty)
1944   Hi, Good Lookin'* (specialty)
       Take It Big* (specialty)
1946   People Are Funny (*Leroy Brinker*)

"Never Gonna Dance" Music by Jerome Kern; lyric by Dorothy Fields. A rejected, dejected Fred Astaire made this emotional avowal—presumably about never going to dance again if he can't dance with her—to Ginger Rogers in *Swing Time* (RKO 1936). The rendition, which takes place in a deserted, elegant nightclub, is followed by a dance in which the formally garbed twosome at first try to keep their feelings in check, then reveal their love as they cling desperately together, twirling and gliding on two levels of the dance floor. One unusual aspect of the complicated and barely intel-

ligible lyric is that even the commercially published version contains the line, "Though I'm left without my Penny," a reference to the character Miss Rogers played in the film. A year before the song was written, Kern and Fields had collaborated on a more buoyant farewell to dancing, "I Won't Dance," which Astaire and Rogers introduced in *Roberta*.

"Never in a Million Years" Music by Harry Revel; lyric by Mack Gordon. In *Wake Up and Live* (Fox 1937), this ballad of eternal romantic devotion is first performed by Ben Bernie's orchestra during a broadcast from the High Hat Club. Unknown to anyone, Jack Haley, as a singer suffering from mike fright, enters an empty control room at the radio station where he works as a guide, and sings with the band under false assumption that the microphone is dead. With his identity unknown, Haley is promptly hailed as the Phantom Troubador—though it was actually Buddy Clark's phantom voice that was dubbed on the soundtrack.

New Moon. See Naughty Marietta.

"New York, New York." *See* **"Theme from New York, New York"**

Newley, Anthony, actor, singer, composer, lyricist; b. London, Sept. 24, 1931. Stylized performer with distinctive reedy voice who collaborated with Leslie Bricusse on London and New York stage hit *Stop the World—I Want to Get Off*, filmed in both 1966 and 1978. "Candy Man" was the most popular movie song they wrote together. Between 1957 and 1960, Newley acted in British films.

Asterisk indicates collaboration with Mr. Bricusse:
1957   The Good Companions (*Mibrau*)
1959   The Lady Is a Square (*Freddie*)
       Idol on Parade (*Jeep Jackson*)
       Johnny Ten Percent (*Johnny*)
1960   Jazz Boat (*Bert Harris*)
1966   Stop the World—I Want to Get Off*
1967   Doctor Dolittle (*Matthew Mugg*)
1971   Willy Wonka and the Chocolate Factory*
1975   Mr. Quilp (*Daniel Quilp*) (also comp., lyr.)
1976   Peter Pan (tv)*
1978   Sammy Stops the World*

Newman, Alfred, composer; b. New Haven, Conn., March 17, 1901; d. Hollywood, Feb. 17, 1970. Newman's Hollywood career was divided between conducting and arranging scores for musicals, and composing, conducting, and arranging scores for nonmusicals. Of the more than 200 films he worked on, first for Goldwyn but mostly for Fox, only a Shirley Temple vehicle actually had a collection of Newman-composed songs (lyrics by Walter Bullock). His main theme from *Robinson Crusoe, Jr.*, then reused in *The Hurricane,* later served as the basis for the song "The Moon of Manakoora."

1940   The Blue Bird (Bullock)

Newton-John, Olivia, actress, singer; b. Cambridge, Eng., Sept. 26, 1948. Blonde latter-day Sandra Dee type who has enjoyed highly successful career as country-influenced pop singer.

1970   Tomorrow (Eng.) (*Olivia*)
1978   Grease (*Sandy Allison*)
1980   Xanadu (*Kira*)
1983   Two of a Kind (*Debbie Wylder*)

"Nice Work If You Can Get It" Music by George Gershwin; lyric by Ira Gershwin. Introduced by Fred Astaire, Jan Duggan, Mary Dean, and Pearl Amatore as singers in Totleigh Castle in *A Damsel in Distress* (RKO 1937); reprised at end of film for Astaire's drum solo and dance. The melody of the song was developed from an unused nine-bar theme, "There's No Stopping Us Now," intended for the 1930 Broadway musical *Girl Crazy,* and the lyric was developed from the caption of a cartoon by *Punch*'s George Belcher. It showed two Cockney charwomen discussing a mutual friend "who 'ad become a 'ore," and one of them remarking, "'At's nice work if you can get it." Note that one line, "Who could ask for anything more?," echoes a line from another *Girl Crazy* song, "I Got Rhythm." "Nice Work If You Can Get It" was also sung, briefly, by Georges Guetary in *An American in Paris* (MGM 1951).

Nicholas Brothers, dancers, singers; b. New York. Harold and Fayard's fulgurous footwork was much in view in specialty numbers mostly in Fox musicals. The brothers began as a team in vaudeville in 1930, and have also appeared in Broadway and London musicals, nightclubs, and concerts.

1934   Kid Millions
1935   Big Broadcast of 1936 (*Dot; Dash*)
1940   Down Argentine Way
        Tin Pan Alley
1941   The Great American Broadcast
        Sun Valley Serenade
1942   Orchestra Wives

1943   Stormy Weather
1944   The Reckless Age (Harold only)
        Carolina Blues (Harold only)
1948   The Pirate

Niesen, Gertrude, actress, singer; b. at sea, July 8, 1910 (Swedish father, Russian mother); d. Glendale, Cal., March 27, 1975. Tiny, foggy-voiced blonde singer of vaudeville, radio, and nightclubs, who made a success in the Broadway musical *Follow the Girls* and acted mostly in low-budget films.

1937   Top of the Town (*Gilda Norman*)
1938   Start Cheering (*Sarah*)
1940   A Night at Earl Carroll's (specialty)
1941   Rookies on Parade (*Marilyn Fenton*)
1943   He's My Guy (specialty)
        Thumbs Up (*Gertrude Niesen*)
        This Is the Army (specialty)

"Night Fever" Music & lyric by Barry, Maurice, and Robin Gibb. Disco number sung by the The BeeGees on soundtrack of *Saturday Night Fever* (Par. 1977) as John Travolta leads the unison dancing at the 2001 Oddyssey.

"Night Over Shanghai" Music by Harry Warren; lyric by Johnny Mercer. Atmospheric piece ("Moon on the rise/ Pale yellow faces with sad old eyes") used for production number in *The Singing Marine* (Warner 1937). Staged as part of a musical show in a nightclub, this Oriental companion to "Lullaby of Broadway" opens with a pin spot on Larry Adler's hands playing the theme on his mouth organ. Dick Powell, as a Marine, picks up the song as he wanders off the street and into a basement cabaret where melodramatic doings result in a Chinese girl (Doris Weston) getting killed. "Night Over Shanghai" was the first collaboration between Warren and Mercer. Warren's previous "Shanghai" song, "Shanghai Lil," with lyric by Al Dubin, was sung in *Footlight Parade*.

"Night They Invented Champagne, The" Music by Frederick Loewe; lyric by Alan Jay Lerner. Suitably bubbly tribute to an historic occasion and the joys that it begat. In *Gigi* (MGM 1958), Gaston (Louis Jourdan) has promised Gigi (Leslie Caron) and her grandmother (Hermione Gingold) that he will take them to Trouville if they beat him at cards. When they do, the three (with Betty Wand's voice dubbed for Miss Caron's) have themselves an arm-flinging, leg-kicking, champagne-sipping celebration in anticipation of the forthcoming trip. The number was written by Lerner and Loewe to convey much the same kind of spontaneous exhilaration as in *My Fair Lady*'s "The Rain in Spain."

"Niña" Music & lyric by Cole Porter. In *The Pirate* (MGM 1948), Gene Kelly as an itinerant actor, struts through a sleepy Caribbean town where he greets every pretty girl as "Niña." "Why Niña?," he is asked. "Why not?," he replies—though why any local should question his use of the name is a bit odd since "Niña" is a term of endearment in South America. Kelly then sings to the ladies of the effect they have upon him as he leaps fleetingly and twirls flirtingly from one beauty to another. During the course of the dance, he climbs balconies, slides down a pole, stomps out a flamenco, takes a cigarette out of a girl's mouth, sucks it into his, closes his mouth, kisses her, and blows out the smoke. Lyricist Porter, incidentally, managed to rhyme "Niña" with "mean ya," "seen ya," "neurasthenia," "gardenia," and "schizophrenia."

"Nina, the Pinta, the Santa Maria, The" Music by Kurt Weill; lyric by Ira Gershwin. Lengthy narrative—actually a mini-musical—about Columbus's discovery of America. In *Where Do We Go from Here?* (Fox 1945), Fred MacMurray, anxious to join the Navy in World War II despite his 4F classification, receives help from a friendly genie. The genie, however, gets his dates mixed up and takes MacMurray back to 1492, when he becomes a sailor aboard Columbus's flagship, the *Santa Maria*. In the number, the sailors, led by Carlos Ramirez, express the belief that the world is flat and, homesick for macaroni and minestrone, stage a mutiny. The men are about to take over the ship when MacMurray quells the uprising by painting a multicolored, multirhymed picture of the brave new world they are all about to discover.

"No, Love, No Nothin' " Music by Harry Warren; lyric by Leo Robin. Lament of loneliness, fidelity, and romantic frustration sung by Alice Faye in *The Gang's All Here* (Fox 1943) during rehearsal of a nightclub revue. The ballad is performed in a small apartment setting as a girl restlessly goes through the humdrum routine of her day—ironing, draping wet stockings on a radiator, gazing at the picture of her soldier husband, leaning against a window frame, pacing the floor, sitting in an easy chair, holding a pipe, closing the window, putting out the empty milk bottles, picking up a man's pair of slippers, opening the bedroom door to reveal the shadow of a bedpost, turning out the table light, and, finally, sinking into the easy chair at the song's end.

"No Strings" Music & lyric by Irving Berlin. "I'm fancy free and free for anything fancy," sang Fred Astaire jauntily to Edward Everett Horton in *Top Hat* (RKO 1935). Then, to emphasize his carefree, unattached condition, Astaire tap dances all around Horton's hotel suite—and wakes up Ginger Rogers in the room below.

"No Two People" Music & lyric by Frank Loesser. In which Danny Kaye and Jeanmaire, both clad in green, revealed their unsurpassed romantic bliss as they pranced about in a wedding dream sequence in *Hans Christian Andersen* (Goldwyn 1952).

Noble, (Raymond) Ray, composer, pianist, bandleader; b. Brighton, Eng., Dec. 17, 1903; d. London, April 4, 1978. Originally leader of English recording orchestra (1929–34), then to US where he led band with many celebrated jazzmen. In films and radio he was featured pianist with his group and occasionally played the role of a sillyass uppercrust Englishman. As composer, he wrote with lyricst Max Kester.

1935	Princess Charming (Eng.) (comp. only) (Kester)	
	Big Broadcast of 1936 (specialty)	
1937	A Damsel in Distress (*Reggie*)	
1942	Here We Go Again (specialty)	
1945	Lake Placid Serenade (specialty)	
	Out of This World (specialty)	

"Nobody" Music & lyric by Roger Edens. In this name-dropping number, sung by Judy Garland in *Strike Up the Band* (MGM 1940), the singer's loveless lot is contrasted with that of some of the legendary couples of history—Romeo and Juliet, Louis XVI and Marie Antoinette, Pelléas and Mélisande, Isabella and Ferdinand, Launcelot and Elaine, Lunt and Fontanne, Chopin and George Sand, plus such tongue-in-cheek combinations as Minneapolis and St. Paul, Abercrombie and Fitch, Dr. Jekyll and Mr. Hyde, Alexander and his Ragtime Band, and Metro Goldwyn and Mayer.

"Nobody Does It Better" Music by Marvin Hamlisch; lyric by Carole Bayer Sager. Willowy, seductive theme from the James Bond film, *The Spy Who Loved Me* (UA 1977), sung over credits by Carly Simon. Also known as "Theme from The Spy Who Loved Me."

North, Sheree (née Dawn Bethel), actress, singer, dancer; b. Hollywood, Jan. 17, 1933. Vivacious blonde actress-dancer, originally groomed as possible successor to Marilyn Monroe; later turned to dramatic roles.

1951 Excuse My Dust (club member)
1953 Here Come the Girls (chorus girl)
1954 Living It Up (dancer)
1956 The Best Things in Life Are Free (*Kitty*)
1958 Mardi Gras (*Eadie West*)
1969 The Trouble with Girls (*Nita Bix*)

"Not Mine" Music by Victor Schertzinger; lyric by Johnny Mercer. Accompanied by Jimmy Dorsey's orchestra, Dorothy Lamour introduced this ballad of resigned loneliness on the porch of her house in *The Fleet's In* (Par. 1942). The number was then reprised with different words by Betty Hutton.

Novarro, Ramon (né Ramon Samaniegoes), actor, singer; b. Durango, Mexico, Feb. 6, 1899; d. Hollywood, Oct. 31, 1968 (murdered). Latin lover type who entered films in 1923 and appeared in silent version of *The Student Prince*. Novarro introduced "Pagan Love Song" in *The Pagan* and "When I Grow Too Old To Dream" in *The Night Is Young*.

1929 Devil May Care (*Armand*)
1930 In Gay Madrid (*Ricardo*)
     Call of the Flesh (*Juan*)
1934 The Cat and the Fiddle (*Victor Florescu*)
1935 The Night Is Young (*Archduke Paul Gustave*)

"Now I Know" Music by Harold Arlen; lyric by Ted Koehler. In *Up in Arms* (Goldwyn 1944), Pvt. Danny Kaye is too shy to cut a record at a fair, so Nurse Dinah Shore obliges with this insinuating revelation of sudden love.

"Now It Can Be Told" Music & lyric by Irving Berlin. In the deserted ballroom of San Francisco's Cliff Hotel—in *Alexander's Ragtime Band* (Fox 1938)—band pianist Don Ameche is playing the song's melody as band vocalist Alice Faye comes over to ask what it is. "Oh, just a little hit tune I've been working on," Don replies, then sings it and asks Alice if she likes it. "Like it?" she exclaims. "Why, it's great! It's got everything. Imagine you having that in you. Why, it'll make you famous." Don lowers his eyes. "I wrote it for you, Stella," he says. "If it's any good, that's why." That very night Alice officially introduces the sentimental ballad with Tyrone Power's orchestra. By the time she has finished, and with Don looking on in misery, Alice and Ty know they're in love.

"(Where Are You) Now That I Need You?" Music & lyric by Frank Loesser. Heartbroken note from one who loves so madly she could die. Betty Hutton introduced the torchy ballad in *Red, Hot and Blue* (Par. 1949).

Nugent, Elliott, director, actor; b. Dover, Ohio, Sept. 20, 1896; d. New York, Aug. 9, 1980. Primarily known for his appearances in such Broadway plays as *The Male Animal* (which he also co-authored) and *The Voice of the Turtle,* Nugent acted in early sound films and later turned to directing (including three Bing Crosby musicals).

Unless otherwise noted, Mr. Nugent directed the following:
1929 So This Is College (*Eddie* only)
1934 She Loves Me Not
     Strictly Dynamite
1935 Love in Bloom
1938 Give Me a Sailor
1943 Stage Door Canteen (guest bit only)
1944 Up in Arms
1947 Welcome Stranger (also bit)
1952 Just for You

O

Oakie, Jack (né Lewis Delaney Offield), actor, singer; b. Sedalia, Mo., Nov. 12, 1903; d. Northridge, Cal., Jan. 23, 1978. Outgoing roly-poly comic actor who usually played cheerful collegians, sailors, vaudevillians or wheeler-dealers. A master of the surprise double-take, Oakie acted in some 80 films through 1962, with most of his musicals at Paramount and Fox. Among songs he introduced: "Keeping Myself for You," "With My Eyes Wide Open I'm Dreaming," "You Hit the Spot."

1929	Close Harmony (*Ben Barney*)
	Street Girl (*Joe Spring*)
	Sweetie (*Tap-Tap Thompson*)
1930	Paramount on Parade (specialty)
	Hit the Deck (*Bilge Smith*)
	Let's Go Native (*Voltaire McGinnis*)
1931	June Moon (*Fred Stevens*)
1932	Dancers in the Dark (*Duke Taylor*)
1933	College Humor (*Barney Shirrel*)
	Too Much Harmony (*Benny Day*)
	Sitting Pretty (*Chick Parker*)
1934	Murder at the Vanities (*Jack Ellery*)
	Shoot the Works (*Nicky*)
	College Rhythm (*Finnegan*)
1935	Big Broadcast of 1936 (*Spud Miller*)
	King of Burlesque (*Joe Cooney*)
1936	Collegiate (*Jerry Craig*)
	Colleen (*Joe Cork*)
	That Girl from Paris (*Whammo*)
1937	Champagne Waltz (*Happy Gallagher*)
	Hitting a New High (*Corny*)
1938	Radio City Revels (*Harry*)
	Thanks for Everything (*Bates*)
1940	Young People (*Joe Ballantine*)
	Tin Pan Alley (*Harry Calhoun*)
1941	The Great American Broadcast (*Chuck Hadley*)
	Navy Blues (*Cake O'Hara*)
	Rise and Shine (*Boley Bolenciewicz*)
1942	Iceland (*Slip Riggs*)
	Song of the Islands (*Rusty*)
1943	Hello, Frisco, Hello (*Dan Daley*)

	Wintertime (*Skip Hutton*)
	Something To Shout About (*Larry Martin*)
1944	Sweet and Low Down (*Popsy*)
	The Merry Monahans (*Pete Monahan*)
	Bowery to Broadway (*Mike O'Rourke*)
1945	That's the Spirit (*Steve*)
	On Stage Everybody (*Mike Sullivan*)
1948	When My Baby Smiles at Me (*Bozo*)

Oakland, Ben, composer; b. Brooklyn, Sept. 24, 1907; d. Los Angeles, Aug. 26, 1979. In Hollywood, Oakland collaborated with lyricists Herb Magidson, Milton Drake, Oscar Hammerstein II ("I'll Take Romance"), and Sammy Lerner.

1936	Hats Off (Magidson)
1938	All American Sweetheart (Drake)
	The Lady Objects (Hammerstein; Drake)
1939	Laugh It Off (Lerner)

O'Brien, (Angela Maxine) Margaret, actress; b. San Diego, Jan. 15, 1937. Teary child actress whose most fondly remembered musical was *Meet Me in St. Louis.*

1941	Babes on Broadway (bit)
1943	Thousands Cheer (specialty)
1944	Meet Me in St. Louis ("*Tootie*" *Smith*)
	Music for Millions ("*Mike*")
1947	The Unfinished Dance (*Meg Merlin*)
1948	Big City (*Midge*)

O'Brien, (William Joseph Patrick) Pat, actor; b. Milwaukee, Nov. 11, 1899. Warner's beefy, dependable coach-sergeant-reporter-detective-priest appeared in close to 90 movies, most of them nonmusicals. Bib: *The Wind at My Back* by O'Brien (1963). (Died Oct. 15, 1983.)

1931	Flying High (*Sport*)
1933	College Coach (*Coach Gore*)
1934	Twenty Million Sweeethearts (*Rush Blake*)
	Flirtation Walk (*Sgt. Scrappy Thornhill*)

1935   In Caliente (*Larry McArthur*)
          Stars Over Broadway (*Al McGillevray*)
1938   Cowboy from Brooklyn (*Roy Chadwick*)
          Garden of the Moon (*John Quinn*)
1942   Broadway (*Dan McCorn*)
1943   His Butler's Sister (*Martin Murphy*)
1959   Some Like It Hot (*Mulligan*)

O'Brien, Virginia, actress, singer; b. Los Angeles, April 18, 1921. Wide-eyed, blank-faced comedienne in MGM musicals noted for scat-singing in a flat, expressionless voice.

1940   Hullabaloo (*Virginia*)
1941   The Big Store (*Kitty*)
          Lady, Be Good (*Lull*)
1942   Ship Ahoy (*Fran Evans*)
          Panama Hattie (*Flo Foster*)
1943   DuBarry Was a Lady (*Ginny*)
          Thousands Cheer (specialty)
1944   Meet the People (*Woodpecker Peg*)
          Two Girls and a Sailor (specialty)
1945   The Harvey Girls (*Alma*)
1946   Till the Clouds Roll By (*"Ellie"*)
          Ziegfeld Follies (specialty)

"Occasional Man, An" Music & lyric by Hugh Martin & Ralph Blane. Provocative description, set to an undulating rhythm, of an idyllic Pacific island where a girl has everything she wants—the sun to tan her, palms to fan her, papayas, peaches, sandy beaches, plus an occasional man. Introduced by Gloria De Haven in *The Girl Rush* (Par. 1955).

O'Connor, Donald (David Dixon Ronald), actor, singer, dancer; b. Chicago, Aug. 30, 1925. Energetic, brashly engaging song-and-dance man who spent the 1940s in low budget Universal musicals, in 12 of which opposite Peggy Ryan. Others with whom he appeared more than once: Andrews Sisters, Gloria Jean, Susanna Foster, Ann Blyth. He first attracted notice in his early teens in *Sing You Sinners* with Bing Crosby (introducing "Small Fry"); later scored in such major musicals as *Singin' in the Rain* and *Call Me Madam*. He has also had his own television series and has appeared in nightclubs.

1937   Melody for Two (bit)
1938   Sing You Sinners (*Mike Beebe*)
1939   On Your Toes (*Phil as a boy*)
1942   Private Buckaroo (*Donny*)
          Give Out Sisters (*Don*)

          Get Hep to Love (*Jimmy Arnold*)
          When Johnny Comes Marching Home (*Frankie*)
1943   Mr. Big (*Donald*)
          Top Man (*Don Warren*)
          It Comes Up Love (*Ricky*)
1944   Chip Off the Old Block (*Donald Corrigan*)
          Follow the Boys (specialty)
          This Is the Life (*Jimmy Plum*)
          The Merry Monahans (*Jimmy Monahan*)
          Bowery to Broadway (specialty)
1945   Patrick the Great (*Pat Donahue Jr.*)
1947   Something in the Wind (*Charlie Read*)
1948   Are You with It? (*Milton Haskins*)
          Feudin', Fussin' and a-Fightin' (*Wilbur McMurtry*)
1949   Yes, Sir, That's My Baby (*William Winfield*)
1950   The Milkman (*Roger Bradley*)
1952   Singin' in the Rain (*Cosmo Brown*)
          I Love Melvin (*Melvin Hoover*)
1953   Call Me Madam (*Kenneth Gibson*)
          Walking My Baby Back Home (*Jigger Millard*)
1954   There's No Business Like Show Business (*Tim Donahue*)
1956   Anything Goes (*Ted Adams*)
1966   Olympus 7-0000 (tv) (*Hermes*)
1974   That's Entertainment (narrator)

"Oh, But I Do" Music by Arthur Schwartz; lyric by Leo Robin. Dennis Morgan sang this ballad of romantic affirmation to Martha Vickers as they danced in a nightclub in *The Time, the Place and the Girl* (Warner 1946).

"Oh You Nasty Man." *See* **"Nasty Man"**

Oklahoma! (1955). Music by Richard Rodgers; lyrics by Oscar Hammerstein II; screenplay by Sonya Levien & William Ludwig from Broadway musical by Rodgers & Hammerstein based on play *Green Grow the Lilacs* by Lynn Riggs.

A Magna film produced by Arthur Hornblow Jr.; directed by Fred Zinnemann; choreography, Agnes de Mille; production design, Oliver Smith; costumes, Orry Kelly, Motley; music director, Jay Blackton; orchestrations, Robert Russell Bennett; music adaptation, Adolph Deutsch; cameraman, Robert Surtees; editor, Gene Ruggiero; Eastman Color; Todd-AO.

Cast: Gordon MacRae (danced by James Mitchell) (*Curly McLain*); Shirley Jones (danced by Bambi Linn) (*Laurey Williams*); Gloria Grahame (*Ado Annie Carnes*); Charlotte Greenwood (*Aunt Eller Murphy*);

Eddie Albert (*Ali Hakim*); Gene Nelson (*Will Parker*); James Whitmore (*Andrew Carnes*); Rod Steiger (*Jud Fry*); J. C. Flippen (*Ike Skidmore*); Barbara Lawrence (*Gertie Cummings*); Marc Platt (*dancer*).

Songs: "Oh, What a Beautiful Mornin' " - MacRae/ "The Surrey with the Fringe on Top" - MacRae, Jones, Greenwood/ "Kansas City" - Nelson, Greenwood, farmers/ "I Cain't Say No" - Grahame/ "Many a New Day" - Jones, girls/ "People Will Say We're in Love" - MacRae, Jones/ "Pore Jud Is Daid" - MacRae, Steiger/ "Out of My Dreams" - Jones, girls/ "The Farmer and the Cowman" - MacRae, Greenwood, Nelson, Flippen, Whitmore, Grahame, chorus/ "All er Nothin" - Grahame, Nelson/ "Oklahoma" - MacRae, Greenwood, Nelson, Whitmore, Jones, Flippen, chorus. Unused: "It's a Scandal, It's a Outrage," "Lonely Room."

When it opened on stage in 1943, *Oklahoma!* was notable for its breakthrough in fusing the elements of story, song, and dance, for its folksy Americana quality, and for accelerating the careers of Alfred Drake (Curly), Celeste Holm (Ado Annie), and Howard DaSilva (Jud). On the screen 12 years later, *Oklahoma!* was notable for emphasizing the fresh-air spirit of the original (Curly now makes his entrance through the cornfields on a horse), for the introduction of a wide-screen process known as Todd-AO, and for launching the career of Shirley Jones. Though none of the major actors of the stage production repeated their roles in the movie, dancers Bambi Linn and Marc Platt were in it (though in different parts), and choreographer de Mille, conductor Blackton, and arranger Bennett were again on hand.

Following the show's highly successful Broadway opening, movie offers were quickly made and quickly rejected, since Rodgers and Hammerstein, whose first collaboration it was, were unwilling to jeopardize the run with a rival version. In 1953, however, they agreed to become associated with a company set up to produce films in Todd-AO (though a year after it had been out, *Oklahoma!* was re-released by 20th Century-Fox in CinemaScope), with themselves as executive producers. Among those tested for the leads were Paul Newman and James Dean (Curly), Joanne Woodward (Laurey), and Eli Wallach (Jud); Charlotte Greenwood, who had to turn down the part of Aunt Eller on the stage, finally got her chance to play it in the picture. Most of the exterior location shooting was done near Nogales, Arizona, because its terrain was considered more like turn-of-the-century Oklahoma than Oklahoma's.

"Old Music Master" Music by Hoagy Carmichael; lyric by Johnny Mercer. In which a "little Memphis boy" persuades a classical composer one long-ago night to get with it by switching to "swing, boogie-woogie and jive." Introduced by Dick Powell in *True to Life* (Par. 1943).

"Ole Buttermilk Sky" Music by Hoagy Carmichael; lyric by Jack Brooks. Loping song of anticipated reunion with a bride-to-be. Hoagy Carmichael sang the number at the end of the nonmusical film *Canyon Passage* (Univ. 1946) while wearing a stovepipe hat and riding a mule through the mountains of California.

Oliver! (1968). Music & lyrics by Lionel Bart; screenplay by Vernon Harris from Bart's London musical based on Charles Dickens' novel *Oliver Twist*.

A Columbia film produced by John Woolf; directed by Carol Reed; choreography, Onna White; production design, John Box; art director, Terence Marsh; costumes, Phyllis Dalton; music director, John Green; orchestrations, Green, Eric Rogers; cameraman, Oswald Morris; editor, Ralph Kemplen; Technicolor; Pana-Vision.

Cast: Ron Moody (*Fagin*); Oliver Reed (*Bill Sikes*); Harry Secombe (*Mr. Bumble*); Shani Wallis (*Nancy*); Mark Lester (*Oliver Twist*); Jack Wild (*Artful Dodger*); Peggy Mount (*Widow Corney*); Hugh Griffith (*Magistrate*); Sheila White (*Bet*); James Hayter (*Jessop*); Fred Emney (*Governor*); Leonard Rossiter (*Sowerberry*).

Songs: "Food, Glorious Food" - Lester, boys/ "Oliver!" - Secombe, Mount, boys/ "Boy for Sale" - Secombe/ "Where Is Love?" - Lester/ "You've Got To Pick a Pocket or Two" - Moody/ "Consider Yourself" - Wild, Lester, chorus/ "I'd Do Anything" - Wild, Wallis, White, Lester, Moody, boys/ "Be Back Soon" - Moody, boys/ "As Long as He Needs Me" - Wallis/ "Who Will Buy?" - Lester, Londoners/ "It's a Fine Life" - Wallis, White, crowd/ "Reviewing the Situation" - Moody/ "Oom-Pah-Pah" - Wallis, crowd. Unused: "I Shall Scream," "That's Your Funeral," "My Name."

Charles Dickens' melodramatic novel *Oliver Twist* helped expose the hidden misery of London's seamier side and did much to bring about reforms in Britain's child labor laws. As a musical in London in 1960 (where it held the long-run record for 12 years) and in New York in 1963, the story of the orphan's adventures as a member of Fagin's band of pickpockets became a more

sentimentalized and sanitized view of colorful, picturesque London in 1830, with even the fiendish Fagin
made likable. On screen, director Carol Reed emphasized the period atmosphere by showing the grimy back
alleys, the bustling markets, and the joyful, orderly
world of a residential crescent in Bloomsbury. Ron
Moody re-created his original role of Fagin (Clive Revill
had played it in New York), and Mark Lester won the
part of Oliver after some 2000 boys had been auditioned.

Previous film adaptations of *Oliver Twist* were made
in 1909, 1910, 1912 (Nat C. Goodwin as Fagin), 1916
(Tully Marshall as Fagin and Marie Doro as Oliver),
1922 (Lon Chaney and Jackie Coogan), 1933 (Irving Pichel and Dickie Moore), and 1948 (Alec Guinness and
John Howard Davies). Other screen musicals adapted
from Dickens' novels were *Scrooge* (*A Christmas
Carol*) with Albert Finney in 1970, and *Mr. Quilp* (*The
Old Curiosity Shop*) with Anthony Newley in 1975.

Olivier, Laurence, actor, singer; b. Dorking, Eng.,
May 22, 1907. Peerless life peer (created baron in 1970)
who has excelled in classical and modern roles on stage
and screen. Made London stage debut in 1924, New
York debut in 1929, first film in 1930. Bib: *Laurence
Olivier* by John Cottrell (1975); *Olivier* ed. Margaret
Morley (1978).

1952   The Beggar's Opera (*Macheath*)
1960   The Entertainer (*Archie Rice*)
1969   Oh! What a Lovely War (*Sir John French*)
1980   The Jazz Singer (*Cantor Rabinovitch*)

Olsen and Johnson, actors. (John Siguard) Ole Olsen,
b. Peru, Ind., Nov. 6, 1892; d. Albuquerque, NM, Jan.
26, 1963. (Harold) Chic Johnson, b. Chicago, March
5, 1891; d. Las Vegas, Nev., Feb. 25, 1962. Vaudeville
slapstick team whose specialty was sadistic mayhem.
They scored unexpected success on Broadway in *Hellzapoppin*, which they adapted to the screen.

Unless noted, the team was known as Olsen & Johnson in
following:
1931   Oh, Sailor Behave! (*Simon; Peter*)
1941   Hellzapoppin
1943   Crazy House
1944   The Ghost Catchers
1945   See My Lawyer

"On the Atchison, Topeka and the Santa Fe" Music
by Harry Warren; lyric by Johnny Mercer. Propulsive
number in *The Harvey Girls* (MGM 1946) welcoming
Engine No. 49 from Philadel-phi-ay to Sandrock, New

Mexico. While still down the line, the train is first heard
and heralded by Ben Carter, the porter at the Alhambra
saloon, then serenaded by cowboys waiting on the station platform. Train engineer Vernon Dent and fireman
Jack Clifford add their musical comments, as do passenger Marjorie Main and conductor Ray Teal, and passengers Ray Bolger and Virginia O'Brien. As the train
comes to a halt, the Harvey girls alight and—in a section
written by Roger Edens and Kay Thompson—introduce
themselves in song. The girls quickly make friends with
the singing cowboys, and rope-twirler Sam Garrett adds
his specialty to the occasion. Judy Garland, the last to
get off, does her own version of the song ("Back in
O'hio where I was born") as she describes the pleasures
of the trip; then, with Ray Bolger, leads the high-stepping, hat-tossing celebrants alongside the train now
heading for Californ-i-ay. Later in the film the music
was reprised for a tap-dancing specialty by Ray Bolger.
Other locomotive numbers by composer Warren: "Shuffle Off to Buffalo" (with Al Dubin) in *42nd Street* (Warner 1933), and "Chattanooga Choo-Choo" (with Mack
Gordon) in *Sun Valley Serenade* (Fox 1941).

On the Avenue (1937). Music & lyrics by Irving Berlin;
screenplay by Gene Markey & William Conselman.

A 20th Century-Fox film produced by Gene Markey;
directed by Roy Del Ruth; choreography, Seymour Felix; art director, Mark Lee Kirk; costumes, Gwen Wakeling; music director, Arthur Lange; cameraman, Lucien
Andriot; editor, Allen McNeil.

Cast: Dick Powell (*Gary Blake*); Madeleine Carroll
(*Mimi Caraway*); Alice Faye (*Mona Merrick*); Ritz
Brothers (specialty); George Barbier (*Commodore Car-
away*); Alan Mowbray (*Frederick Sims*); Cora Wither-
spoon (*Aunt Fritz*); Walter Catlett (*Jake Dibble*); Joan
Davis (*Miss Katz*); Stepin Fetchit (*Step*); Sig Rumann
(*Hanfstangel*); Billy Gilbert (*Joe Papalopoulos*); E. E.
Clive (*cabby*); Lynn Bari (*chorus girl*).

Songs: "He Ain't Got Rhythm" - Faye, Ritz Bros./
"The Girl on the Police Gazette" - Powell, quartet/
"You're Laughing at Me" - Powell/ "This Year's
Kisses" - Faye/ "I've Got My Love To Keep Me
Warm" - Powell, Faye/ "Slumming on Park Avenue" -
Faye, chorus, Ritz Bros. Unused: "On the Avenue,"
"On the Steps of Grant's Tomb," "Swing Sister."

In 1933, *As Thousands Cheer*, with a score by Irving
Berlin, was a satirical Broadway revue created in the
form of a newspaper, with its songs, dances, and
sketches poking fun at real people who were headline

news at the time. In 1937, the film musical, *On the Avenue,* also with a Berlin score, told the story of what might have happened had one of the revue's targets taken exception to the way he or she was depicted in the show. Thus this was a backstage tale with a slight twist, since it was not concerned with the trials of putting on a musical. Here the show—called *On the Avenue*—is established as a hit from the outset, and the trials have to do with the steps taken by Madeleine Carroll, as the richest girl in the world, to stop Dick Powell, the show's star and author, from making her and her family look ridiculous in one of the sketches. Along the way, of course, Madeleine and Dick fall in love and manage to surmount all obstacles, including those placed in their path by Dick's jilted sweetheart, Alice Faye.

"On the Boardwalk at Atlantic City" Music by Josef Myrow; lyric by Mack Gordon. On their way to "romantic, enchantic" Atlantic City, Vera-Ellen, June Haver, and Vivian Blaine—in *Three Little Girls in Blue* (Fox 1946)—sing this rollicking ode to the seaside resort.

"On the Good Ship Lollipop" Music by Richard A. Whiting; lyric by Sidney Clare. Shirley Temple's most closely identified song, which she introduced in *Bright Eyes* (Fox 1934), describes a child's vision of a candy shop full of bonbons, lemonade stands, and crackerjack bands. Number was also sung by Dan Dailey and Shari Robinson in *You're My Everything* (Fox 1949) and by Helen Mirren in *The Fiendish Plot of Dr. Fu Manchu* (Orion-Warner 1980).

"On the Sentimental Side" Music by James V. Monaco; lyric by Johnny Burke. Even though his girl has ditched him, sentimentally inclined Bing Crosby—in *Doctor Rhythm* (Par. 1938)—hopes she'll reconsider.

On the Town (1949). Music by Leonard Bernstein, Roger Edens; lyrics & screenplay by Betty Comden & Adolph Green from Broadway musical by Bernstein, Comden & Green, suggested by Jerome Robbins' ballet, *Fancy Free.*

An MGM film produced by Arthur Freed; directed & choreographed by Gene Kelly & Stanley Donen; associate producer, Roger Edens; art directors, Cedric Gibbons, Jack Martin Smith; costumes, Helen Rose; music director, Lennie Hayton; orchestrations Edens, Hayton;

vocal arrangements, Saul Chaplin; cameraman, Harold Rosson; editor, Ralph Winters; Technicolor.

Cast: Gene Kelly (*Gabey*); Frank Sinatra (*Chip*); Betty Garrett (*Hildy Esterhazy*); Ann Miller (*Claire Huddesen*); Jules Munshin (*Ozzie*); Vera-Ellen (*Ivy Smith*); Florence Bates (*Mme. Dilvovska*); Alice Pearce (*Lucy Schmeeler*); George Meader (*professor*); Bern Hoffman (*dock worker*); Bea Benaderet (*subway rider*); Hans Conried (*François*); Carol Haney (*dancer*).

Songs: "I Feel Like I'm Not Out of Bed Yet" (Bernstein) - Hoffman/ "New York, New York" (Bernstein) - Kelly, Sinatra, Munshin/ "Miss Turnstiles Ballet" (Bernstein) - dance by Ellen, admirers/ "Prehistoric Man" (Edens) - Miller; dance by Miller, Munshin, Kelly, Sinatra, Garrett/ "Come Up to My Place" (Bernstein) - Garrett, Sinatra/ "Main Street" (Edens) - Kelly; dance by Kelly, Ellen/ "You're Awful" (Edens) - Sinatra, Garrett/ "On the Town" (Edens) - Kelly, Sinatra, Munshin, Miller, Garrett, Ellen/ "Count on Me" (Edens) - Sinatra, Garrett, Munshin, Miller, Pearce, Kelly/ "A Day in New York Ballet" (Bernstein) - dance by Kelly, Ellen, Haney, dancers.

The 1944 Broadway musical was transferred to the screen with three of its original songs by Bernstein, Comden and Green, five new ones by Edens, Comden and Green (because producer Freed was not fond of Bernstein's music), a cast whose three male leads had just been in *Take Me Out to the Ball Game,* a script by original librettists Comden and Green, and the debut of the directing-choreographing team of Gene Kelly and Stanley Donen. It was also the first film ever to have musical sequences shot on location at familiar landmarks in New York City (major exception: the Empire State Building, whose observation roof was reconstructed in Culver City). Among choreographic highlights were the "Miss Turnstiles Ballet," showing Vera-Ellen in various activities (two years later, Kelly would create a similar dance for Leslie Caron in *An American in Paris*) and the "Day in New York Ballet," which redundantly encapsulated the plot of the movie. Of the cast, only Alice Pearce re-created the role she had originated on stage; otherwise, John Battles was replaced by Gene Kelly, Cris Alexander by Frank Sinatra, Adolph Green by Jules Munshin, Sono Osato by Vera-Ellen, Nancy Walker by Betty Garrett, and Betty Comden by Ann Miller.

On the Town tells the story of three sailors, Gabey, Chip, and Ozzie, on an adventure-crammed shore leave, from the moment they bound out of the Brooklyn Navy

Yard at 6 a.m. to their return 24 hours later when they must bid fond farewells to the three girls they have met and lost their hearts to. Other screen musicals have also used the sailors-on-leave theme. In 1936 Fred Astaire and Randolph Scott found romance in a San Francisco dance hall in RKO's *Follow the Fleet,* and in 1942 so did William Holden and Eddie Bracken in Paramount's *The Fleet's In.* Three years later, Kelly and Sinatra first donned sailor suits to visit Los Angeles in MGM's *Anchors Aweigh.* In the early 50s the duos became trios in Columbia's *All Ashore* (Mickey Rooney, Dick Haymes, and Ray McDonald on Catalina Island); in Warner's *Three Sailors and a Girl* (Gordon MacRae, Gene Nelson, and Jack E. Leonard in New York); in Universal's *So This Is Paris* (Tony Curtis, Gene Nelson, and Paul Gilbert in the French capital); and in MGM's *Hit the Deck* (Tony Martin, Vic Damone, and Russ Tamblyn in San Francisco). Something of a sequel to *On the Town,* MGM's *It's Always Fair Weather* (1955) was about the New York reunion of army buddies Gene Kelly, Dan Dailey, and Michael Kidd.

On with the Show (1929). Music by Harry Akst; lyrics by Grant Clarke; screenplay by Robert Lord from story by Humphrey Pearson.

A Warner Bros. film produced by Darryl F. Zanuck; directed by Alan Crosland; choreography, Larry Ceballos; music director, Louis Silvers; cameraman, Tony Gaudio; editor, Jack Killifer; Technicolor.

Cast: Betty Compson (vocals by Josephine Houston) (*Nita French*); Arthur Lake (*Harold Astor*); Sally O'Neil (vocals by Josephine Houston) (*Kitty*); Joe E. Brown (*Ike Beaton*); Louis Fazenda (*Sarah Fogarty*); Ethel Waters (*Ethel Waters*); William Bakewell (*Jimmy*); Fairbanks Twins (*Dorsey Twins*); Sam Hardy (*Jerry*); Lee Moran (*Pete*); Wheeler Oakman (*Bob Wallace*); Thomas Jefferson (*Dad*); Purnell Pratt (*Sam Bloom*); Henry Fink (*father in show*); Josephine Houston (*Bert*); Four Covans (dancers); Harmony Four Quartet.

Songs: "Welcome Home" - Fink, chorus/ "Let Me Have My Dreams" - Compson (Houston); reprised by O'Neil (Houston)/ "Am I Blue?" - Waters, Harmony Four/ "Lift the Juleps to Your Two Lips" - Fink, Houston, chorus; dance by Covans/ "In the Land of Let's Pretend" - Mildred Carroll, chorus/ "Don't It Mean a Thing to You?" - Houston, Lake/ "Birmingham Bertha" - Waters/ "Wedding Day" - Fink, Lake, Houston, chorus.

On with the Show was something of a forerunner of *42nd Street* since it was the first backstage movie in which a young girl takes over the leading role from the aging star of a Broadway-bound musical comedy. The film was also a precursor of *Wonder Bar* and *Murder at the Vanities* because its running time covered the same length of time as the story it told, and it also anticipated *Kiss Me, Kate* not only by having its show-within-a-show run parallel to the main story but because its plot, though seen only in excerpts, can easily be followed by the movie audience. The first completely all-color talkie, *On with the Show* captures the look and feel both of backstage life and of the kind of Broadway musical comedies that were being presented in the late 20s. It also offers the opportunity of seeing the young Ethel Waters, as part of the show, singing "Am I Blue?" and "Birmingham Bertha."

The film covers the out-of-town tryout of a musical called *The Phantom Sweetheart* from the arrival of the audience at the Wallace Theatre to the curtain calls (which even include the stage hands). Most of the time it is concerned with the myriad problems weighing on harried producer Sam Hardy: a creditor who threatens to stop the show; a backer who wants to take his money out because the hatcheck girl (Sally O'Neil) won't give him a tumble; a company of squabbling actors (including Arthur Lake, Joe E. Brown, Louise Fazenda, and the Fairbanks Twins); a boxoffice robbery; an old actor who faints in the wings thus forcing the producer himself to take over the part; and a star (Betty Compson) who quits during the performance.

"Once and for Always" Music by James Van Heusen; lyric by Johnny Burke. Romantic pledge made by Bing Crosby and Rhonda Fleming in *A Connecticut Yankee in King Arthur's Court* (Par. 1949).

"Once in a Blue Moon" Music by Harry Revel; lyric by Mack Gordon. While strolling on a tropical island beach in *We're Not Dressing* (Par. 1934), Bing Crosby admitted to Carole Lombard how happy he was that a rare someone like her just happened to come along.

"One for My Baby (and One More for the Road)" Music by Harold Arlen; lyric by Johnny Mercer. It's 2:45 a.m. in a bar where the only people are Joe, the bartender, and a customer who's determined to get smashed. Requesting music that's "dreamy and sad" on the jukebox, the unhappy imbiber confides that he is about to relate the story of his recently terminated romance. Being true to his code, however, he refuses to reveal the details that caused "the end of a brief episode"—but he apologizes anyway for bending the bartender's ear and keeping him from closing the place. The torchy ballad was introduced by Fred Astaire in *The Sky's the Limit* (RKO 1943), followed by Astaire's drunken dance atop the bar of a hotel cocktail lounge. Also sung by Ida Lupino in *Road House* (RKO 1948); Jane Russell in *Macao* (RKO 1952); and Frank Sinatra in *Young at Heart* (Warner 1954).

One Hour with You (1932). Music by Oscar Straus, Richard A. Whiting; lyrics by Leo Robin; screenplay by Samson Raphaelson from film *The Marriage Circle* adapted from play *Nur ein Traum* by Lothar Schmidt.

A Paramount film produced by Ernst Lubitsch; directed by Lubitsch, George Cukor; art director, Hans Dreier; costumes, Travis Banton; music director, Nathaniel Finston; cameraman, Victor Milner; editor, William Shea.

Cast: Maurice Chevalier (*Dr. André Bertier*); Jeanette MacDonald (*Colette Bertier*); Genevieve Tobin (*Mitzi Olivier*); Roland Young (*Prof. Olivier*); Charles Ruggles (*Adolph*); George Barbier (*police chief*); Josephine Dunn (*Mlle. Martel*); Richard Carle (*detective*); Charles Judels (*policeman*); Donald Novis (*singer*).

Songs: "What a Little Thing Like a Wedding Ring Can Do." (Straus) - Chevalier, MacDonald/ "We Will Always Be Sweethearts" (Straus) - MacDonald; reprised by MacDonald, Chevalier/ "Three Times a Day" (Whiting) - Chevalier, Tobin/ "One Hour with You" (Whiting) - Novis, Tobin, Chevalier, Ruggles, MacDonald/ "Oh, That Mitzi!" (Straus) - Chevalier/ "What Would You Do?" (Whiting) - Chevalier.

Though George Cukor's name appears on the film's credits as co-director, his association lasted only two weeks and was only as a result of Ernst Lubitsch's need to finish work on another movie. The release is, in fact, *echt* Lubitsch, since its frothy Parisian fable tells of a wealthy doctor whose loving wife suddenly suspects him of infidelity with her best friend, and it unreels with the kind of buoyant sophistication associated with the German director's output. Moreover, it was a remake of a Lubitsch-directed 1924 silent film, *The Marriage Circle,* in which the leads had been played by Florence Vidor, Monte Blue, Marie Prevost, and Adolphe Menjou, and its cast was headed by such Lubitsch-directed veterans as Chevalier and MacDonald (though Carole Lombard had initially been slated for her role). *Une Heure près*

toi, a French version of *One Hour with You,* was also filmed at the same time, with Geneviève Tobin replaced by Lily Damita, Roland Young by Ernest Ferny, and Charles Ruggles by Pierre Etchepare.

"One Hour with You" Music by Richard A. Whiting; lyric by Leo Robin. Romantic if durationally limited proposal sung by danceband vocalist Donald Novis during a dinner party at the palatial home of Maurice Chevalier and Jeanette MacDonald in *One Hour with You* (Par. 1932). The number, with its lyric altered to suit the characters and situation in the story, is then picked up by Genevieve Tobin and Chevalier, by Charlie Ruggles and Miss MacDonald, and, finally, by Chevalier and Miss MacDonald. Eddie Cantor, who made "One Hour with You" his radio theme song, sang it on the soundtrack of *The Eddie Cantor Story* (Warner 1954), with his voice dubbed for Keefe Brasselle.

One Hundred Men and a Girl (1937). Screenplay by Bruce Manning, Charles Kenyon, and James Mulhauser from idea by Hans Kraly.

A Universal film produced by Charles R. Rogers, Joe Pasternak; directed by Henry Koster; production design, John Harkrider; costumes, Vera West; music director, Leopold Stokowski; associate music director, Charles Previn; orchestrations, Previn; cameraman, Joseph Valentine; editor, Bernard Burton.

Cast: Deanna Durbin (*Patricia Cardwell*); Leopold Stokowski (*Leopold Stokowski*); Adolphe Menjou (*John Cardwell*); Alice Brady (*Mrs. Frost*); Eugene Pallette (*John Frost*); Mischa Auer (*Michael Borodoff*); Billy Gilbert (*garage owner*); Frank Jenks (*cab driver*); Alma Kruger (*Mrs. Tyler*); Jack Smart (J. Scott Smart) (*Marshall*); Jed Prouty (*Tommy Bitters*); Leonid Kinskey (*party pianist*); Edwin Maxwell (*Ira Westing*).

Music: Symphony No. 5, 4th Movement (Tchaikovsky) - Stokowski, symphony orch./ "It's Raining Sunbeams" (Frederick Hollander-Sam Coslow) - Durbin/ "Rakoczy March" (Berlioz) - Stokowski, symphony orch./ "A Heart That's Free" (Alfred Robyn-T. Reiley) - Durbin/ "Prelude to Act III" (Wagner, *Lohengrin*) - Stokowski, symphony orch./ "Alleluja" (Mozart) - Durbin; Stokowski, symphony orch./ "Second Hungarian Rhapsody" (Liszt) - Stokowski, symphony orch./ "Libiamo ne' lieti calici" (Verdi-Piave, *La Traviata*) - Durbin; Stokowski, symphony orch.

After scoring impressively as an affluent Little Miss Fixit in her first feature film, *Three Smart Girls* (1936),

14-year-old Deanna Durbin won even greater popularity as an indigent Little Miss Fixit in *100 Men and a Girl*. Combining an ingenuous charm with a classically trained singing voice she made such a hit that her first two films were credited with saving Universal Pictures from bankruptcy. They were also credited with helping to launch the screen careers of such other teenage sopranos as Gloria Jean (also at Universal), Susanna Foster, Ann Blyth, and Jane Powell.

The mass appeal of *100 Men and a Girl* was especially noteworthy since it dealt with the world of symphonic music. As the daughter of an unemployed trombonist (Adolphe Menjou), Deanna toils ceaselessly throughout the film to establish a symphony orchestra that would give jobs to her father and his fellow out-of-work musicians. Eventually she succeeds with the financial help of an initially reluctant millionaire (Eugene Pallette) and the artistic—and promotional—help of an initially reluctant Leopold Stokowski. At the concert that crowns her efforts, Deanna is called onstage to acknowledge the applause and to sing. Asked by Maestro Stokowski which selection she has chosen, the young lady unhesitatingly furnishes him with the only information needed: *"Traviata."*

"One I Love, The" Music by Bronislaw Kaper, Walter Jurmann; lyric by Gus Kahn. Ballad of romantic expectancy introduced by Allan Jones in *Everybody Sing* (MGM 1938). The song, first intended to be sung by Jeanette MacDonald during a rehearsal scene in *San Francisco* (MGM 1936), was replaced by "Would You?"

"One in a Million" Music by Lew Pollack; lyric by Sidney Mitchell. In *One in a Million* (Fox 1936), Leah Ray sang the title song as featured vocalist of Adolphe Menjou's all-girl orchestra during a rehearsal on a train heading for a Swiss hotel. Number was later reprised by Borrah Minevitch's Harmonica Rascals, and by the soundtrack chorus singing during Sonja Henie's ice show at New York's Madison Square Garden.

One Night of Love (1934). Screenplay by S. K. Lauren, James Gow, and Edmund North from story by Dorothy Speare & Charles Beahan.

A Columbia film produced by Everett Riskin; directed by Victor Schertzinger; art director, Stephen Gooson; costumes, Robert Kalloch; music directors, Morris Stoloff, Louis Silvers; cameraman, Joseph Walker; editor, Gene Milford.

Cast: Grace Moore (*Mary Barrett*); Tullio Carminati (*Monteverdi*); Lyle Talbot (*Bill Houston*); Mona Barrie (*Lally*); Jessie Ralph (*Angelina*); Nydia Westman (*Lydia*); Jane Darwell (*Mrs. Barrett*); Henry Armetta (*café owner*); Herman Bing (*vegetable man*).

Songs & Arias: "One Night of Love" (Victor Schertzinger-Gus Kahn)/ "Sempre libera" (Verdi-Piave, *La Traviata*)/ "Sextet" (Donizetti-Cammarano, *Lucia di Lammermoor*)/ "Ciribiribin" (Pestalozza-Tiochet)/ "Habanera" (Bizet-Meilhac, Halevy, *Carmen*)/ "Love duet" (Puccini-Illica, Giacosa, *Madama Butterfly*)/ "Un bel di" (*Madama Butterfly*)/ "None but the Lonely Heart" (Tchaikovsky-Mey, Goethe)/ "Indian Love Call" (Rudolf Friml-Otto Harbach, Oscar Hammerstein II). All selections sung by Miss Moore.

Although she had signed with Columbia only after being turned down as Maurice Chevalier's co-star in MGM's *The Merry Widow*, Grace Moore scored such a personal success in *One Night of Love* that her film became a far greater popular attraction. In fact, it was the first successful Hollywood musical featuring a genuine prima donna, and it paved the way for the brief screen vogue of such other comely divas as RKO's Lily Pons and Paramount's Gladys Swarthout. Miss Moore's vehicle told a conveniently unobtrusive tale of an American soprano who studies in Italy and eventually wins fame at the Met, an outline that could also have applied to the star's own career. Among the many demands the singer made during the preparation of the film was that Adolphe Menjou be replaced by Tullio Carminati as the Italian maestro.

"One Night of Love" Music by Victor Schertzinger; lyric by Gus Kahn. In the film of the same name (Col. 1934), Grace Moore yearned for a starlight romantic night "when two hearts are one." The song's melody was deliberately based on the love duet from Puccini's *Madama Butterfly*.

"One Song" Music by Frank Churchill; lyric by Larry Morey. The Prince (Harry Stockwell) in *Snow White and the Seven Dwarfs* (Disney 1937) sees the girl he loves and pours out his heart.

"One, Two, Button Your Shoe" Music by Arthur Johnston; lyric by Johnny Burke. Dressed in clown costume, Bing Crosby—in *Pennies from Heaven* (Col. 1936)—sang a variation on the nursery rhyme while entertaining children in an orphanage.

"Only Forever" Music by James V. Monaco; lyric by Johnny Burke. In *Rhythm on the River* (Par. 1940), lyricist Mary Martin, inspired by Bing Crosby's music, writes a lyric consisting of four self-posed questions, with all of them answered by the song's title phrase. Bing first sang the song to Mary on a run-aground ferryboat; later, at the film's conclusion, the two sang it as a duet during a radio broadcast from a glittering New York nightclub.

"Open Your Eyes" Music by Burton Lane; lyric by Alan Jay Lerner. Jane Powell trilled brightly about enjoying the wonders of life as she entertained fellow passengers on a transatlantic ocean voyage in *Royal Wedding* (MGM 1951). Following the rendition, she and brother Fred Astaire attempt to dance but the rolling ship soon sends them sprawling. (This episode was based on an actual situation involving Fred and his real sister, Adele, during their first Atlantic crossing.)

"Orchids in the Moonlight" Music by Vincent Youmans; lyric by Edward Eliscu & Gus Kahn. In *Flying Down to Rio* (RKO 1933), Raul Roulien sang the ardent tango to Dolores Del Rio, while enlarged photographs of the prescribed flower kept changing in the background. The piece then served for a tango by Miss Del Rio and Fred Astaire.

"Our Big Love Scene" Music by Nacio Herb Brown; lyric by Arthur Freed. Though the lyric is about *acting* a love scene ("We'll rehearse it ev'ry day/ Faithfully we'll learn our play"), by the time the song is ended we know that the feeling isn't just make-believe. In *Going Hollywood* (MGM 1933), Bing Crosby was heard singing the ballad over the radio by lovesick schoolteacher Marion Davies.

"Our Love Affair" Music by Roger Edens; lyric by Arthur Freed. In *Strike Up the Band* (MGM 1940), high school bandleader Mickey Rooney and aspiring singing star Judy Garland rehearse the number in Judy's home. Judy finds personal meaning in the song, but Mickey is only interested in explaining how he plans to stage it in a benefit show. To demonstrate his idea, he uses the fruit on a kitchen table to represent members of a symphony orchestra; as the music is played, the fruit comes to animated "life" as the musicians' heads and their instruments. This staging concept was suggested to the film's director, Busby Berkeley, by Vincente Minnelli.

"Our Song" Music by Jerome Kern; lyric by Dorothy Fields. Grace Moore, in *When You're in Love* (Col. 1937), ardently sang of music and words divinely inspired.

"Out of This World" Music by Harold Arlen; lyric by Johnny Mercer. Romantic notion, set to an outer-spacey, long-line melody, expressed by Eddie Bracken (with Bing Crosby's dubbed voice) in *Out of This World* (Par. 1945). In the song, the singer confesses to his girl that he's clear out of this world whenever he looks at her, that he even hears strange out-of-this world music, that she is out of a fairy tale, and that no armored knight was ever more enchanted by a Lorelei than he. According to legend, however, no armored knight was ever enchanted by a Lorelei at all since she only went for sailors.

"Over My Shoulder" Music & lyric by Harry Woods. Bright, breezy farewell-to-troubles number introduced by uncredited singer-dancer leading the chorus in a London stage revue in *Evergreen* (Gaumont-Brit. 1934). In the scene, Jessie Matthews, the star of the show who has tricked the public into believing she is her own mother, interrupts the performance with a frantic dance during which she throws over her shoulder the dress and gray wig that were used in the deception. Later, in the film's finale, Miss Matthews gets her chance to sing the song.

"Over the Rainbow" Music by Harold Arlen; lyric by E. Y. Harburg. According to Arlen, "We had just finished all the songs for *The Wizard of Oz* [MGM 1939] except for the one for Judy Garland to sing in Kansas. I felt we needed something with sweep, a melody with a broad, long line, but it was hard for me to come up with an idea. After a couple of days I wanted to forget about it, and I went for a drive with my wife. As we drove by Schwab's Drugstore on Sunset, an idea suddenly came to me. We stopped the car and I jotted down the main theme of what became 'Over the Rainbow.'" The next day Arlen finished the music and asked Harburg to hear it. "At first, I thought it was too symphonic for a little girl in Kansas," the lyricist later recalled. "I told Harold, 'This is something for Nelson Eddy.'" Harburg, who was won over when the composer obligingly played the melody with a lighter touch, has also explained, "Kansas is an arid, colorless place without many flowers. In the scene early in the movie, Dorothy was having trouble at home and, naturally, she had the impulse to run away. Since the only colorful thing she'd ever seen was the rainbow, I thought it would be fitting for her to want to go to the other end of the rainbow because that would be full of bright colors. I began writing, 'On the other side of the rainbow . . .' but that didn't fit the melody. Finally, I thought of 'Over the rainbow.' "

Following the film's first preview, the MGM brass felt that the song slowed down the action and ordered it cut from the picture. It was, in fact, cut three times, each time over the protests of associate producer Arthur Freed, who eventually got it reinstated permanently. Other initial opposition to the song came from the music publisher who felt the leap of an octave on the opening word "Somewhere" was too difficult to sing. He also felt that the middle section ("Someday I'll wish upon a star . . .") sounded too much like a child's piano exercise.

"Over the Rainbow" became the song most closely associated with Judy Garland, who once commented, "It is so symbolic of everybody's dream and wish that I am sure that's why people sometimes get tears in their eyes when they hear it. It's the song that's closest to my heart." James Stewart was associated with "Over the Rainbow" in two films: he sang it in *The Philadelphia Story* (MGM 1940) and led an orchestra playing it in *The Glenn Miller Story* (Univ. 1954). The song was also dubbed for Eleanor Parker by Eileen Farrell on the soundtrack of *Interrupted Melody* (MGM 1955).

P

"Pagan Love Song" Music by Nacio Herb Brown; lyric by Arthur Freed. "Come with me where moonbeams light Tahitian skies," serenaded Ramon Novarro in *The Pagan* (MGM 1929) and Howard Keel in *Pagan Love Song* (MGM 1950).

Paige, Janis (née Donna Mae Tjaden), actress, singer; b. Tacoma, Wash., Sept. 16, 1922. Leggy blonde comedienne who appeared chiefly in Warner Bros. musicals with Dennis Morgan and Jack Carson. Also acted on Broadway, most notably in *The Pajama Game*.

    1944 Bathing Beauty (bit)
          Hollywood Canteen (*Angela*)
    1946 The Time, the Place and the Girl (*Sue Jackson*)
    1947 Love and Learn (*Jackie*)
    1948 Romance on the High Seas (*Elvira Kent*)
          One Sunday Afternoon (*Virginia Brush*)
    1951 Two Gals and a Guy (*Della Oliver*)
    1956 Silk Stockings (*Peggy Dayton*)
    1963 Follow the Boys (*Liz Bradville*)

Paige, Robert (né John Arthur Page), actor, singer; b. Indianapolis, Dec. 21, 1910. Teamed with Jane Frazee in seven Universal musicals, Paige was best served musically when he joined Deanna Durbin to introduce "Can't Help Singing" and "Californ-i-ay." Actor was known as David Carlyle 1931–36.

    1936 Cain and Mabel (*Ronny Cauldwell*)
    1938 The Lady Objects (*Ken Harper*)
    1941 Dancing on a Dime (*Ted Brooks*)
          San Antonio Rose (*Con Conway*)
          Melody Lane (*Gabe Morgan*)
          Hellzapoppin (*Jeff*)
    1942 What's Cookin'? (*Bob*)
          Almost Married (*James Manning III*)
          Pardon My Sarong (*Tommy Layton*)
          Get Hep to Love (*Steve Winters*)

          Don't Get Personal (*Paul Stevens*)
    1943 How's About It
          Hi' Ya Chum (*Tommy Craig*)
          Hi Buddy (*Johnny Blake*)
          Cowboy in Manhattan (*Bob Allen*)
          Mr. Big (*Johnny Hanley*)
          Get Going (*Bob Carlton*)
          Crazy House (guest bit)
    1944 Follow the Boys (guest bit)
          Can't Help Singing (*Johnny Lawlor*)
    1945 Shady Lady (*Bob Wendell*)
    1963 Bye Bye Birdie (*Bob Precht*)

Painting the Clouds with Sunshine. See Gold Diggers of 1933.

"Painting the Clouds with Sunshine" Music by Joe Burke; lyric by Al Dubin. What the singer is always doing to hide the fact that he feels miserable. Introduced by Nick Lucas in *Gold Diggers of Broadway* (Warner 1929); also sung by Dennis Morgan and Lucille Norman in *Painting the Clouds with Sunshine* (Warner 1951).

Pajama Game, The (1957). Music & lyrics by Richard Adler & Jerry Ross; screenplay by George Abbott & Richard Bissell from Broadway musical by Adler, Ross, Abbott, Bissell based on Bissell's novel *7½ Cents*.

A Warner Bros. film produced & directed by George Abbott & Stanley Donen; choreography, Bob Fosse; art director, Malcolm Bert; costumes by William & Jean Eckart; music director, Ray Heindorf; orchestrations, Nelson Riddle, Buddy Bregman; cameraman, Harry Stradling; editor, William Ziegler; WarnerColor.

Cast: Doris Day (*Babe Williams*); John Raitt (*Sid Sorokin*); Carol Haney (*Gladys Hotchkiss*); Eddie Foy, Jr. (*Vernon Hines*); Reta Shaw (*Mabel*); Barbara Nichols (*Poopsie*); Thelma Pelish (*Mae*); Jack Straw (*Prez*);

Ralph Dunn (*Hassler*); Ralph Chambers (*Charlie*); Jack Waldron (*salesman*); Jackie Kelk (*first helper*); Buzz Miller, Kenneth LeRoy, Peter Gennaro (*dancers*).

Songs: "The Pajama Game" - Foy/ "Racing with the Clock" - Foy, workers/ "I'm Not at All in Love" - Day, with Nichols, Pelish, girls/ "I'll Never Be Jealous Again" - Foy, Shaw/ "Hey, There" - Raitt; reprised by Day/ "Once-a-Year Day" - Raitt, Day; dance by Haney, Gennaro, Miller, LeRoy, workers/ "Small Talk" - Raitt, Day/ "There Once Was a Man" - Raitt, Day/ "Steam Heat" - Haney, Miller, LeRoy/ "Hernando's Hideaway" - Haney, workers/ "7½ Cents" - Straw, Day, Nichols, workers. Unused: "A New Town Is a Blue Town," "Her Is," "Think of the Time I Save," "The Man Who Invented Love" (Adler alone).

Though, in 1954, it had an unlikely subject for a musical comedy—union workers' demands for a wage increase in a pajama factory—*The Pajama Game* became one of Broadway's longest running hits. It was veteran director-librettist George Abbott's greatest success and was the first book musical to unveil the talents of songwriters Adler and Ross and choreographer Bob Fosse. In transferring the work to the screen, Abbott and Fosse were again on hand, this time with the added expertise of film director Stanley Donen. Retained from the original cast were John Raitt (as the factory superintendent), Eddie Foy, Jr. (the time-study man), Carol Haney, Reta Shaw, Thelma Pelish, Ralph Dunn, Ralph Chambers, Jack Waldron, Buzz Miller, Kenneth LeRoy, and Peter Gennaro, with Janis Paige replaced as the female lead by the better boxoffice draw Doris Day (though the part had originally been intended for Patti Page). As a film *The Pajama Game* remained close to the original stage concept, yet managed to liberate the action by opening up such scenes as the workers' picnic, with its joyous "Once-a-Year Day" dance, and the union rally. There was also effective use made of the camera during the "Racing with the Clock" number, first speeded up to show feverish activity and later slowed down when the workers cut their productivity to help win their salary demands.

Damn Yankees, a second Broadway musical involving Abbott, Fosse, Adler, and Ross, was also brought to the screen by Warner. The 1958 release again had Abbott and Donen to co-produce and co-direct, Abbott to write the screenplay, Fosse to choreograph, and Ray Heindorf as music director. The plot, about a baseball fan selling his soul to the devil in exchange for a year playing with the Washington Senators, starred Gwen Verdon and Ray Walston, from the stage, augmented by Tab Hunter.

Pan, Hermes (né Hermes Panagiotopulos), choreographer, dancer; b. Nashville, Tenn., 1905. Closely associated with Fred Astaire (they worked on 17 films together), Pan also was responsible for the dance routines in 10 Betty Grable musicals. He was under contract to RKO (1933–39), Fox (1941–48), and MGM (1949–56).

Asterisk indicates association with Mr. Astaire:
1933 Flying Down to Rio*
1934 The Gay Divorcee*
1935 Roberta*
     Old Man Rhythm
     Top Hat*
     In Person
     I Dream Too Much
1936 Follow the Fleet*
     Swing Time*
1937 Shall We Dance*
     A Damsel in Distress*
1938 Radio City Revels
     Carefree*
1939 The Story of Vernon and Irene Castle*
1940 Second Chorus*
1941 That Night in Rio
     Moon Over Miami (also dancer)
     Sun Valley Serenade
     A Weekend in Havana
     Rise and Shine
1942 Song of the Islands
     My Gal Sal (also dancer)
     Footlight Serenade
     Springtime in the Rockies
1943 Coney Island (also dancer)
     Sweet Rosie O'Grady (also dancer)
1944 Pin-Up Girl (also dancer)
     Irish Eyes Are Smiling
1945 Diamond Horseshoe
1946 Blue Skies*
1947 The Shocking Miss Pilgrim
     I Wonder Who's Kissing Her Now
1948 That Lady in Ermine
1949 The Barkleys of Broadway*
1950 Three Little Words*
     Let's Dance*
1951 Excuse My Dust
     Texas Carnival
1952 Lovely To Look At
1953 Kiss Me, Kate
1954 The Student Prince
1955 Jupiter's Darling
     Hit the Deck
1956 Meet Me in Las Vegas
     Silk Stockings*
1957 Pal Joey (also dancer)

1959 Never Steal Anything Small
      Porgy and Bess
1960 Can-Can
1961 Flower Drum Song
1964 My Fair Lady
1968 Finian's Rainbow*
1969 Darling Lili
1973 Lost Horizon

"Paradise" Music by Nacio Herb Brown; lyric by Gordon Clifford. Seductive ballad ("His eyes afire with one desire") recalling a lover who now comes only in dreams. Pola Negri—with appropriate humming and whistling—introduced the number in a cabaret scene in *A Woman Commands* (RKO 1932).

"Paree" Music by Sigmund Romberg; lyric by Oscar Hammerstein II. In *New Moon* (MGM 1940), Jeanette MacDonald entertained a shipload of aristocrats by singing this coloratura aria, which had been dropped from the original 1928 Broadway operetta. Despite its intended French flavor, the song's melody bears a resemblance to "El Relicario" by the Spanish composer José Padilla.

"Paris in the Spring" Music by Harry Revel; lyric by Mack Gordon. The place and the time for romance, as shared by Mary Ellis and Tullio Carminati in *Paris in Spring* (Par. 1935).

"Paris Is a Lonely Town" Music by Harold Arlen; lyric by E. Y. Harburg. Even Paris can be a dreary town "when love's a laugh and you're the clown." Introduced on soundtrack of cartoon film *Gay Purr-ee* (Warner 1961) by Judy Garland.

"Paris, Stay the Same" Music by Victor Schertzinger; lyric by Clifford Grey. Affectionate farewell sung by Maurice Chevalier on a Parisian balcony in *The Love Parade* (Par. 1929), then reprised by Lupino Lane and a yelping dog named Jiggs.

Parks, Larry (né Samuel Klausman), actor, singer; b. Olathe, Kansas, Dec. 3, 1914; d. Studio City, Cal., April 13, 1975. Parks will be forever associated with the two films he made impersonating Al Jolson (though Jolson did the singing). All of his movies were at Columbia. He was married to actress Betty Garrett.

1941 Sing for Your Supper (*Mickey*)
1942 You Were Never Lovelier (*Tony*)

1943 Is Everybody Happy? (*Jerry*)
      Reveille with Beverly (*Eddie Ross*)
1944 She's a Sweetheart (*Rocky Hill*)
      Stars on Parade (*Danny Davis*)
      Hey, Rookie (*Jim Lighter*)
1946 The Jolson Story (*Al Jolson*)
1947 Down to Earth (*Danny Miller*)
1949 Jolson Sings Again (*Al Jolson/ Larry Parks*)

"Pass Me By" Music by Cy Coleman; lyric by Carolyn Leigh. Lighthearted march sung by Digby Wolfe over credits of nonmusical film *Father Goose* (Univ. 1964).

"Pass That Peace Pipe" Music & lyric by Roger Edens, Hugh Martin, and Ralph Blane. Joan McCracken introduced this spirited "Indian" number in *Good News* (MGM 1947) as she led a tribe of collegians (including Ray McDonald) in a dance routine all around an ice-cream parlor. The song, written in 1943, had been originally intended for a Fred Astaire-Gene Kelly spot in *Ziegfeld Follies*.

Pasternak, (Josef) Joe, producer; b. Szilagy Somlyo, Transylvania, Sept. 19, 1901. Primarily identified with wholesome, family entertainment (major exceptions: *Destry Rides Again* and *Love Me or Leave Me*), first at Universal (1936–41), then at MGM (1942–66). Pasternak, who is credited with discovering Deanna Durbin and who produced her first ten films, was also associated with Jane Powell (eight films), Kathryn Grayson (six), Esther Williams (six), Mario Lanza (five), June Allyson (four), and Judy Garland (three). Directors he worked with most frequently were Henry Koster, Norman Taurog, and Richard Thorpe. Bib: *Easy the Hard Way* by Pasternak (1956).

Asterisk indicates Deanna Durbin film:
1937 Three Smart Girls*
      One Hundred Men and a Girl*
1938 Mad About Music*
      That Certain Age*
1939 Three Smart Girls Grow Up*
      The Underpup
      First Love*
      Destry Rides Again
1940 It's a Date*
      Spring Parade*
      A Little Bit of Heaven
      Seven Sinners
1941 Nice Girl?*
      It Started with Eve*
1942 Seven Sweethearts

1943 Presenting Lily Mars
Thousands Cheer
1944 Two Girls and a Sailor
Music for Millions
1945 Thrill of a Romance
Anchors Aweigh
1946 Two Sisters from Boston
Holiday in Mexico
No Leave No Love
1947 The Unfinished Dance
This Time for Keeps
1948 Three Daring Daughters
Big City
On an Island with You
A Date with Judy
Luxury Liner
The Kissing Bandit
1949 In the Good Old Summertime
That Midnight Kiss
1950 Nancy Goes to Rio
The Duchess of Idaho
Summer Stock
The Toast of New Orleans
1951 The Great Caruso
Rich, Young and Pretty
The Strip
1952 Skirts Ahoy
The Merry Widow
Because You're Mine
1953 Small Town Girl
Latin Lovers
Easy To Love
1954 The Student Prince
Athena
1955 Hit the Deck
Love Me or Leave Me (also guest bit)
1956 Meet Me in Las Vegas
The Opposite Sex
1957 10,000 Bedrooms
This Could Be the Night
1960 Where the Boys Are
1962 Jumbo
1964 Looking for Love
1965 Girl Happy
1966 Spinout

Payne, John, actor, singer; b. Roanoke, Va., May 23, 1912. Payne was Fox's dependable, virile leading man in its musicals of the 1940s, acting opposite all the studio's major blonde attractions—Alice Faye, Betty Grable, Sonja Henie, and June Haver. He introduced "You Say the Sweetest Things, Baby" and "Give Me the Simple Life." The first two of his three wives were Ann Shirley and Gloria De Haven.

1936 Hats Off (*Jimmy Maxwell*)
1938 Love on Toast (*Bill Adams*)
College Swing (*Martin Bates*)
Garden of the Moon (*Don Vincente*)
1940 Star Dust (*Bud Borden*)
Tin Pan Alley (*Skeets Harrigan*)
1941 The Great American Broadcast (*Rix Martin*)
Weekend in Havana (*Jay Williams*)
Sun Valley Serenade (*Ted Scott*)
1942 Footlight Serenade (*Bill Smith*)
Iceland (*Cpl. Jimmy Murfin*)
Springtime in the Rockies (*Dan*)
1943 Hello, Frisco, Hello (*Johnny Cornell*)
1945 The Dolly Sisters (*Harry Fox*)
1946 Wake Up and Dream (*Jeff*)

Penner, Joe (né Josef Pinter), actor; b. Nagechkereck, Hungary, Nov. 11, 1905; d. Philadelphia, Pa., Jan. 10, 1941. Childlike comic who won fame on radio, responsible for introducing catch phrases "You wanna buy a duck" and "Oh, you nasty man!"

1934 College Rhythm (*Joe*)
1936 Collegiate (*Joe*)
1937 New Faces of 1937 (*Seymore Seymore*)
Life of the Party (*Joe Penner*)
1938 Go Chase Yourself (*Wilbur P. Meely*)
1940 The Boys from Syracuse (*Dromio of Ephesus/ Dromio of Syracuse*)

"Pennies from Heaven" Music by Arthur Johnston; lyric by Johnny Burke. What it rains everytime it rains, according to this philosophical piece that advises, "If you want the things you love, you must have showers." Introduced by Bing Crosby in *Pennies from Heaven* (Col. 1936); also sung by Dick Haymes in *Cruisin' Down the River* (Col. 1953).

"Pennsylvania Polka" Music & lyric by Zeke Manners & Lester Lee. "Ev'rybody's got the mania to do the polka from Pennsylvania," gave out the Andrews Sisters in *Give Out Sisters* (Univ. 1942).

"People Like You and Me" Music by Harry Warren; lyric by Mack Gordon. Jump tune dedicated to "Best-things-in-life-are-free"-type pleasures, performed in *Orchestra Wives* (Fox 1942) by Glenn Miller's orchestra. In the first vocal rendition it is sung by Marion Hutton and the Modernaires, then in a patriotic variation ("Get a load of those guys, high in the skies, winging to victory") they are joined by Tex Beneke.

"Pepe" Music by Hans Wittstatt; lyric by Dory Langdon. Perky number introduced by Shirley Jones in *Pepe* (Col. 1960). The scene was the town square in Acapulco, Mexico, where Miss Jones, holding up a doll called Pepe, sang the song to a group of children. Then, joined by Cantinflas, they all danced gaily down the street. The song was originally a German piece known as "Andalusian Girl."

Perlberg, William, producer; b. New York, Oct. 22, 1896; d. Los Angeles, Oct. 31, 1968. Beginning in 1943, Perlberg was associated with writer-director (and ultimately co-producer) George Seaton, with whom he worked on many musicals—including *The Country Girl*—and nonmusicals. Among stars who appeared in Perlberg films were Betty Grable in five (two of them with Dick Haymes) and Bing Crosby in two.

1936	The King Steps Out
1938	The Lady Objects
1943	Hello, Frisco, Hello
	Coney Island
	Sweet Rosie O'Grady
1945	Diamond Horseshoe
	Where Do We Go from Here?
1947	The Shocking Miss Pilgrim
1950	Wabash Avenue
	I'll Get By
1951	Aaron Slick from Punkin Crick
1952	Somebody Loves Me
1953	Little Boy Lost
1954	The Country Girl

"Personality" Music by James Van Heusen; lyric by Johnny Burke. In which it is revealed that Mme. Pompadour, DuBarry, Juliet, Pierrette, Juno, and Salome all got ahead because they knew how to use it. Sung by Dorothy Lamour at the Golden Rail Saloon, Skagway, Alaska, in *Road to Utopia* (Par. 1945).

"Pettin' in the Park" Music by Harry Warren; lyric by Al Dubin. Cutesy number sung by Dick Powell and Ruby Keeler in a Broadway revue in *Gold Diggers of 1933* (Warner). Following Ruby's tap routine, the scene opens to depict a Busby Berkeley Freudian world in Central Park, where monkeys cuddle in a cage and various couples pet on park benches. Ruby and Dick drive up in a taxi. Because he's obviously made a pass at her, she angrily gets out of the cab and is directed by policewoman Aline MacMahon to the roller-skating service "For Little Girls Who Have To Walk Home." Apparently there's a lot of them, as a flock of girls are seen skating out of the shop. Now the policemen are on roller skates, too, and after naughty little Billy Barty wings one with a spit ball he manages to elude their grasp by skating between their legs. The season changes to winter so that the girls can now play with huge snowballs and form kaleidoscopic patterns that are shot from above. Summertime in the park finds the girls petting with their straw-hatted beaux, but a sudden downpour sends the girls scurrying to a two-level dressing room. There they take off their wet dresses and are seen in silhouette—until Billy Barty raises the dressing room shade to reveal the girls in metallic bathing suits. Dick can't cuddle with Ruby in such an outfit, so Billy obligingly gives him a can opener. With the Hays Office apparently looking the other way, Dick is last seen prying open the back of Ruby's tin suit.

"Piccolino, The" Music & lyric by Irving Berlin. The song was written as the final number performed by Fred Astaire and Ginger Rogers in *Top Hat* (RKO 1935) and was intended as the successor to two previous numbers about new dances: "The Carioca" in *Flying Down to Rio* and "The Continental" in *The Gay Divorcee*. Using a melody he had written for a dance sequence in *Music Box Revue of 1921*, Berlin recounted the tale of a displaced Latin in Brooklyn, who composed this catchy bit that Venetians have been "humming and strumming upon their guitars." In the film the song was performed at an early morning (or late night) Carnival on the Lido by local revelers. Miss Rogers then sings it to Astaire, who escorts her onto the floor where they lead the other celebrants in the dance.

"Pick Yourself Up" Music by Jerome Kern; lyric by Dorothy Fields. In *Swing Time* (RKO 1936), Fred Astaire, though a professional dancer, convinces dancing teacher Ginger Rogers that he can't dance a step as they sing this bubbly polka. When Ginger is fired by the studio manager (Eric Blore), Fred gets her job back by demonstrating how much he's really learned after just one lesson. Kern's melody was based on a Bohemian motif that Bedrich Smetana and Jaromir Weinberger had used.

Pidgeon, Walter (Davis), actor, singer; b. East St. John, New Brunswick, Canada, Sept. 23, 1897. Unflappable paterfamilias of Mrs. Miniver dramas, Pidgeon began his screen career as a romantic singing lead. Later musicals found him playing the understanding father or father-figure of Judy Garland, Deanna Durbin, Jane Powell, Esther Williams, and Barbra Streisand. (Died Santa Monica, Sept. 25, 1984.)

1928	Melody of Love (*Jack Clark*)
1930	Show Girl in Hollywood (guest bit)
	Bride of the Regiment (*Col. Vultow*)
	Viennese Nights (*Franz*)
	Sweet Kitty Bellairs (*Lord Verney*)
1931	Kiss Me Again (*Lt. Paul de St. Cyr*)
	The Hot Heiress (*Ollie Clay*)
1938	The Girl of the Golden West (*Jack Rance*)
	Listen, Darling (*Richard Thurlow*)
1940	It's a Date (*John Arlen*)
1946	Holiday in Mexico (*Amb. Jeffrey Adams*)
1952	Million Dollar Mermaid (*Frederick Kellerman*)
1954	Deep in My Heart (*J. J. Shubert*)
1955	Hit the Deck (*Adm. Daniel Smith*)
1965	Cinderella (tv) (*king*)
1968	Funny Girl (*Florenz Ziegfeld*)

Pinocchio (1940). Music by Leigh Harline; lyrics by Ned Washington; background score by Paul J. Smith; adapted from Carlo Lorenzini's story by Ted Sears, Otto Englander, Webb Smith, William Cottrell, Joseph Sabo, Erdman Penner, Aurelius Battaglia.

A Walt Disney film released by RKO-Radio; directed by Ben Sharpsteen, Hamilton Luske, Bill Roberts, Norman Ferguson, Jack Kenney, Wilfred Jackson, T. Hee; supervising animators, Fred Moore, Franklin Thomas, Milton Kahl, Vladimir Tytla, Ward Kimball, Arthur Babbitt, Eric Larson, Wolfgang Reitherman; art directors, Charles Philippi, Hugh Hennesy, Kenneth Anderson, Dick Kelsey, Kendall O'Connor, Terrell Stapp, Thor Putnam, John Hubley, Al Zinnen; music directors, Leigh Harline, Paul J. Smith; Technicolor.

Voices: Dickie Jones (*Pinocchio*); Christian Rub (*Gepetto*); Cliff Edwards (*Jiminy Cricket*); Evelyn Venable (*Blue Fairy*); Walter Catlett (*J. Worthington Foulfellow*); Frankie Darro (*Lampwick*); Charles Judels (*Stromboli*); Don Brodie (*Barker*).

Songs: "When You Wish Upon a Star" - Edwards/ "Little Woodenhead" - Rub/ "Give a Little Whistle" - Edwards, Jones/ "Turn on the Old Music Box" - Rub/ "Hi Diddle Dee Dee (An Actor's Life for Me)" - Catlett, Jones/ "I've Got No Strings" - Jones/ "Give a Little Whistle" - Edwards, Jones. Unused: "Three Cheers for Anything," "Honest John," "Figaro and Cleo," "Monstro the Whale," "I'm a Happy-Go-Lucky Fellow," "As I Was Sayin' to the Duchess."

Walt Disney's second full-length animated cartoon feature proved no letdown after *Snow White and the Seven Dwarfs*. Again based on a familiar children's story, this was a highly imaginative treatment that was far more episodic in nature than its predecessor. Narrated by Jiminy Cricket (with Cliff Edwards' voice), it tells of a wood-carving Pygmalion named Gepetto who carves a boy out of wood that comes to life with the help of the Blue Fairy (modeled on Marjorie Belcher, later Marge Champion, who had served a similar function for Snow White). Pinocchio has three harrowing adventures: first he becomes a member of a marionette troupe run by the cruel Stromboli; next he gets into bad habits on Pleasure Island and almost turns into a donkey; finally he rescues Gepetto from the belly of Monstro the Whale. This last act is enough to persuade the Blue Fairy to turn Pinocchio into a real boy, and Jiminy, who had been Pinocchio's conscience, is awarded a gold medal. The character of Jiminy Cricket (again with Cliff Edwards' voice) also showed up in 1947 in the Disney feature *Fun and Fancy Free,* as well as in various Disney shorts. In 1957, CBS-TV offered a new non-cartoon musical version with a score by Alec Wilder and William Engvick. Mickey Rooney played Pinocchio, and other roles were taken by Fran Allyson (Blue Fairy), Martyn Green (Fox), Stubby Kaye (Town Crier), and Jerry Colonna (Ringmaster). Jiminy Cricket, being a Disney creation, was not included.

Pinza, (Fortunato) Ezio, singer, actor; b. Rome, May 18, 1892; d. Stamford, Conn., May 9, 1957. The Metropolitan's star basso enjoyed far greater success in his Broadway musicals *South Pacific* and *Fanny* than he did in his Hollywood appearances. Bib: *Ezio Pinza: An Autobiography* (1959).

1947	Carnegie Hall (specialty)
1950	Mr. Imperium (*Mr. Imperium*)
1951	Strictly Dishonorable (*Augustino Caraffa*)
1953	Tonight We Sing (*Feodor Chaliapin*)

Pirate, The (1948). Music & lyrics by Cole Porter; screenplay by Frances Goodrich & Albert Hackett from Broadway play by S. N. Behrman based on German play *Der Seeräuber* by Ludwig Fulda.

An MGM film produced by Arthur Freed; directed by Vincente Minnelli; associate producer, Roger Edens; choreography, Robert Alton, Gene Kelly; music director, Lennie Hayton; orchestrations, Conrad Salinger; cameraman, Harry Stradling; editor, Blanche Sewell; Technicolor.

Cast: Judy Garland (*Manuela*); Gene Kelly (*Serafin*);

Walter Slezak (*Don Pedro*); Gladys Cooper (*Aunt Ines*); Reginald Owen (*Advocate*); George Zucco (*Viceroy*); Nicholas Brothers (*dancers*); Lester Allen (*Uncle Capucho*); Cully Richards (*Trillo*); Ben Lessy (*Gumbo*); Lola Albright (bit).

Songs: "Niña" - Kelly/ "Mack the Black" - Garland; dance by Kelly/ "You Can Do No Wrong" - Garland/ "Be a Clown" - Kelly, Nicholas Bros.; reprised by Kelly, Garland/ "Love of My Life" - Garland. Unused: "Voodoo," "Manuela."

As a Broadway play in 1942, *The Pirate* told the tale of Serafin (played by Alfred Lunt), the leader of a band of strolling players, who recognizes the stuffy mayor of a West Indies village as Estramundo, a reformed pirate. The mayor's wife, Manuela (Lynn Fontanne), not knowing her husband's true identity, daydreams about the romantic desperado, and Serafin, to help in his wooing, pretends to be Estramundo. When his deception is revealed, the lady will have none of him, but she changes her mind after learning who Estramundo really is. For the musical film, the basic story was retained, except that the mayor was now Manuela's suitor not her husband and the name of the pirate became—at Cole Porter's request—Macoco. The movie allowed director Minnelli the opportunity to create a colorful, satirical fantasy world, Gene Kelly the opportunity to base his bravura interpretation on the personalities of his childhood heroes, Douglas Fairbanks and John Barrymore, and Judy Garland (though she was in frail health) the opportunity to show her comic range in a sophisticated, highly charged performance.

"Please" Music by Ralph Rainger; lyric by Leo Robin. Plea of a frustrated lover sung in *The Big Broadcast* (Par. 1932) by Bing Crosby, with Eddie Lang on guitar, as they rehearse in a radio studio. Ballad later sung by Stuart Erwin, also with Lang, on the Big Broadcast radio show in an awkward attempt to cover for the absent Crosby. Suddenly, the singer shows up to reprise the song on the air with altered lyrics suitable for tying up the movie's plot. Number was also sung by an uncredited Chinese in *Stowaway* (Fox 1936).

"Please Don't Say No, Say Maybe" Music by Sammy Fain; lyric by Ralph Freed. Introduced in *Thrill of a Romance* (MGM 1945) by the King Sisters, accompanied by Tommy Dorsey and his orchestra. Also used in a "Cyrano" scene in which Lauritz Melchior, hiding in the bushes sings for Van Johnson as he supposedly serenades Esther Williams.

"Pocketful of Miracles" Music by James Van Heusen; lyric by Sammy Cahn. Optimistic, uptempo theme of nonmusical *Pocketful of Miracles* (UA 1961), sung by Frank Sinatra as a voice-over during credits. It was only after the film had been completed that director Frank Capra approached Cahn about writing the title song. At first the lyricist refused because, as he wrote in his autobiography, *I Should Care*, "Jimmy Van Heusen and Johnny Burke had written a song entitled 'Pocketful of Dreams,'" which was still well known. When Cahn told Van Heusen the reason for his objection, the composer, according to the lyricist's book, changed Cahn's mind by telling him, "If I wrote that song with Burke, I can also give you permission to write another with me." "I've Got a Pocketful of Dreams," however, was composed by Jimmy Monaco not Jimmy Van Heusen.

Pollack, Lew, composer; b. New York, June 16, 1895; d. Hollywood, Jan. 18, 1946. Pollack's best-known film songs are "Sing, Baby, Sing," with lyricist Jack Yellen, and "One in a Million" and "It's Love I'm After," both with Sidney Mitchell. Others with whom he collaborated were Walter Bullock, Sidney Clare, Herman Ruby, Charles Newman, Harry Harris, Herb Magidson, and Mort Greene. Mostly featured in Fox musicals, his songs were sung by Shirley Temple, Alice Faye, Tony Martin, and Judy Garland.

1936	Song and Dance Man (Clare)
	Captain January (Mitchell; Yellen)
	Pigskin Parade (Mitchell)
	One in a Million (Mitchell)
1937	Thin Ice (Mitchell)
	Life Begins in College (Mitchell)
1938	In Old Chicago (Mitchell)
	Rebecca of Sunnybrook Farm (Mitchell)
	Kentucky Moonshine (Mitchell)
1942	The Yanks Are Coming (Ruby)
1943	Tahiti Honey (Newman)
	Jitterbugs (Newman)
1944	Sweethearts of the USA (Newman)
	Seven Days Ashore (Greene)
	Music in Manhattan (Magidson)
	The Girl Rush (Harris)
1946	Bamboo Blonde (Greene)

Pons, (Alice Josephine) Lily, singer, actress; b. Cannes, France, April 12, 1904; d. Dallas, Feb. 13,

1976. Slight, dark-haired coloratura soprano who made her Metropolitan debut in 1931 and scored a success in her first Hollywood film. She was married to and divorced from conductor André Kostelanetz.

1935 I Dream Too Much (*Annette*)
1936 That Girl from Paris (*Nikki Monet*)
1937 Hitting a New High (*Suzette*)
1947 Carnegie Hall (specialty)

"Pop! Goes Your Heart" Music by Allie Wrubel; lyric by Mort Dixon. Sprightly disclosure of the immediate good fortune that comes your way when you suddenly fall in love, introduced by Dick Powell in *Happiness Ahead* (Warner 1934).

"Poppa, Don't Preach to Me" Music & lyric by Frank Loesser. The postcard message of an American tourist in Paris who, despite her feared parental admonition, has decided not to return home. Introduced by Betty Hutton in *The Perils of Pauline* (Par. 1947).

Porgy and Bess (1959). Music by George Gershwin; lyrics by DuBose Heyward & Ira Gershwin; screenplay by N. Richard Nash from Broadway musical by Gershwin, Heyward, and Gershwin based on play *Porgy* by Dorothy & DuBose Heyward and novel by DuBose Heyward.

A Samuel Goldwyn film released by Columbia; directed by Otto Preminger; choreography, Hermes Pan; production design, Oliver Smith; art directors, Serge Krizman, Joseph Wright; costumes, Irene Sharaff; music director, André Previn, associate music director, Ken Darby; cameraman, Leon Shamroy; editor, Daniel Mandell; Technicolor; Todd-AO.

Cast: Sidney Poitier (vocals by Robert McFerrin) (*Porgy*); Dorothy Dandridge (vocals by Adele Addison) (*Bess*); Sammy Davis, Jr. (*Sportin' Life*); Pearl Bailey (*Maria*); Brock Peters (*Crown*); Diahann Carroll (vocals by Loulie Jean Norman) (*Clara*); Ruth Attaway (vocals by Inez Matthews) (*Serena*); Leslie Scott (*Jake*); Clarence Muse (*Peter*); Helen Thigpen (*Strawberry Woman*); Merritt Smith (*Crab Man*); Joel Fluellen (*Robbins*).

Songs: "Summertime" (Heyward) - Carroll (Norman)/ "A Woman Is a Sometime Thing" (Heyward) - Scott/ "Gone, Gone, Gone" (Heyward) - chorus/ "Porgy's Prayer" (Heyward) - Poitier (McFerrin)/ "My Man's Gone Now" (Heyward) - Attaway (Matthews)/ "I Got Plenty o' Nuthin' " - Poitier (McFerrin)/ "Bess, You Is My Woman Now" - Poitier (McFerrin), Dandridge (Addison)/ "Oh, I Can't Sit Down" (Gershwin) - Bailey, chorus/ "It Ain't Necessarily So" - Davis/ "I Ain't Got No Shame" - Davis/ "What You Want with Bess?" (Heyward) - Dandridge (Addison)/ "I Loves You, Porgy" - Dandridge (Addison), Poitier (McFerrin)/ "A Red-Headed Woman" (Gershwin) - Peters/ "There's a Boat Dat's Leavin' Soon for New York" (Gershwin) - Davis/ "Oh, Bess, Where's My Bess?" (Gershwin) - Poitier (McFerrin)/ "I'm on My Way" (Heyward) - Poitier (McFerrin).

Producer Samuel Goldwyn had to wait ten years before securing the screen rights to *Porgy and Bess*. Then actors refused to appear in the film because of alleged Negro stereotypes (Sidney Poitier was signed for the lead, then withdrew, then agreed to do it anyway), a fire totally destroyed the soundstage plus sets and costumes the day before shooting was to begin which resulted in a delay of almost three months, and differences with director Rouben Mamoulian (he had staged both the 1927 play *Porgy* and the 1935 Gershwin opera) caused Goldwyn to replace him with Otto Preminger (with whom the producer's relations were only slightly less stormy). The wide-screen film was faithful to the source, retaining virtually all the music, though it was careful to establish the time period as 1912, lest audiences accept the movie as a reflection of current Negro life. To "cinematize" the story, the camera showed stevedores and fishermen working on a wharf and also the residents of Catfish Row enjoying themselves both on an excursion steamer and at a picnic on Kittiwah Island (actually Venice Island, near Stockton, Cal.).

The plot concerns a crippled beggar, who rides around Charleston, South Carolina, in a goat-drawn cart, and his love for Crown's woman. When the brutal Crown flees Catfish Row after murdering Robbins in a crap game, Porgy and Bess enjoy temporary happiness together. But Bess succumbs to Crown on the island after the picnic, and Porgy kills him in a fight after he has come back to Catfish Row. Bess, fearful that Porgy will be put in jail and never come back, goes off to New York with the happy-dust dealer, Sportin' Life. At the film's end, Porgy is released and heads north in his cart to find his Bess. On stage, *Porgy and Bess* was seen in New York in 1935 (with Todd Duncan and Anne Brown), 1942 (same leads), 1953, and 1976.

Porter, Cole (Albert), composer, lyricist; b. Peru, Ind., June 9, 1891; d. Santa Monica, Oct. 15, 1964. Pantheon creator of throbbing, minor-key melodies and ingeniously rhymed, topically smart lyrics. Of Porter's 23 Broadway musicals, the following were transformed into movies of widely varying quality usually with little regard for the original scores: *Paris; Fifty Million Frenchmen* (background only); *Gay Divorce* (now *The Gay Divorcee* with only Porter's "Night and Day" retained); *Anything Goes* (among things that went in the two versions were a number of Porter songs); *DuBarry Was a Lady* (three Porter songs retained); *Panama Hattie* (four Porter songs); *Let's Face It* (two Porter songs); *Something for the Boys* (no Porter songs); *Mexican Hayride* (no Porter songs); *Kiss Me, Kate* (the first screen version of a Porter musical with a basically complete score, this one also added the composer's "From This Moment On"); *Can-Can; Silk Stockings*. In addition, *Night and Day*, Porter's film bio with Cary Grant as the composer, and *At Long Last Love* had scores consisting primarily of Porter's theatre songs.

Among his best known pieces coming out of Hollywood are "Easy To Love" and "I've Got You Under My Skin" (both in *Born To Dance*); "Rosalie" and "In the Still of the Night" (*Rosalie*); "I've Got My Eyes on You" and "I Concentrate on You" (*Broadway Melody of 1940*); "You'd Be So Nice To Come Home To" (*Something To Shout About*); "Don't Fence Me In" (added to *Hollywood Canteen*); "Be a Clown" (*The Pirate*); and "True Love" (*High Society*). Bing Crosby, Eleanor Powell, Fred Astaire, and Gene Kelly starred in three films each with Porter scores; Mitzi Gaynor and Frank Sinatra in two each. Others identified with his songs on the screen were Gertrude Lawrence (she sang "They All Fall in Love" in *The Battle of Paris*), Ethel Merman, James Stewart, Nelson Eddy, Rita Hayworth, Ann Sothern, Lena Horne, Don Ameche, Roy Rogers, Ginny Simms, Judy Garland, Howard Keel, Kathryn Grayson, Louis Armstrong, Cyd Charisse, and Maurice Chevalier.

Bib: *103 Lyrics of Cole Porter* ed. Fred Lounsberry (1954); *The Cole Porter Song Book* (1959); *Cole Porter: The Life That Late He Led* by George Eells (1967); *Cole* by Brendan Gill & Robert Kimball (1971).

1929	The Battle of Paris
1936	Anything Goes
	Born To Dance
1937	Rosalie
1940	Broadway Melody of 1940
1941	You'll Never Get Rich
1942	Panama Hattie
1943	DuBarry Was a Lady
	Let's Face It
	Something To Shout About
1946	Night and Day
1948	The Pirate
1953	Kiss Me, Kate
1956	Anything Goes
	High Society
1957	Silk Stockings
	Les Girls
1958	Aladdin (tv)
1960	Can-Can
1975	At Long Last Love

Potter, H(enry) C(odman), director; b. New York, Nov. 13, 1904; d. New York, Aug. 31, 1977. Stage and screen director whose film musicals ran the gamut from Astaire and Rogers to Olsen and Johnson.

1938	Romance in the Dark
1939	The Story of Vernon and Irene Castle
1940	Second Chorus
1941	Hellzapoppin
1955	Three for the Show

Powell, (Richard Ewing) Dick, actor, singer; b. Mountain View, Ark., Nov. 14, 1904; d. Hollywood, Jan. 3, 1963. Powell was the wavy-haired, apple-cheeked premier juvenile lead of Warner Bros. backstage musicals (plus a few at Fox, Paramount, and MGM). He played the romantic interest opposite Ruby Keeler in seven films (including their major efforts, *42nd Street, Gold Diggers of 1933,* and *Footlight Parade*), and also acted with Joan Blondell (his second wife), Ann Dvorak, Ginger Rogers, Alice Faye (in Fox's *On the Avenue*), Priscilla Lane, Rosemary Lane, Ann Sheridan, Mary Martin, Dorothy Lamour, and June Allyson (his third wife). Among songs he introduced were "Young and Healthy," "By a Waterfall," "Honeymoon Hotel," "Fair and Warmer," "Flirtation Walk," "I Only Have Eyes for You," "I'll String Along with You," "Don't Give Up the Ship," "Thanks a Million," "With Plenty of Money and You," "'Cause My Baby Says It's So," "I've Got My Love To Keep Me Warm," "You're Laughing at Me," "I'm Like a Fish Out of Water," "You Must Have Been a Beautiful Baby," and "Hit the Road to Dreamland." After his career in musicals he turned to private-eye roles, then became a director and producer both in films and television.

Asterisk indicates appearance with Miss Keeler:

1932	Blessed Event
1933	42nd Street* (*Billy Lawler*)

227

Gold Diggers of 1933* (*Brad Roberts*)
Footlight Parade* (*Scotty Blair*)
College Coach (*Phil Sargeant*)
1934 Dames* (*Jimmy Higgins*)
Wonder Bar (*Tommy*)
Twenty Million Sweethearts (*Buddy Clayton*)
Happiness Ahead (*Bob Lane*)
Flirtation Walk* (*Dick "Canary" Dorcy*)
1935 Gold Diggers of 1935 (*Dick Curtis*)
Broadway Gondolier (*Dick Purcell*)
Shipmates Forever* (*Dick Melville*)
Thanks a Million (*Eric Land*)
1936 Colleen* (*Don Adams*)
Hearts Divided (*Jerome Bonaparte*)
Stage Struck (*George Randall*)
Gold Diggers of 1937 (*Rosmer Peek*)
1937 On the Avenue (*Gary Blake*)
The Singing Marine (*Bob Brent*)
Varsity Show (*Chuck Daly*)
Hollywood Hotel (*Ronny Bowers*)
1938 Cowboy from Brooklyn (*Elly Jordan*)
Hard To Get (*Bill*)
Going Places (*Pete Mason*)
1939 Naughty but Nice (*Prof. Hardwick*)
1941 In the Navy (*Tommy Halstead*)
1942 Star Spangled Rhythm (specialty)
1943 Happy Go Lucky (*Pete Hamilton*)
True to Life (*Link Ferris*)
Riding High (*Steve Baird*)
1944 Meet the People (*Swanee Swanson*)
1956 You Can't Run Away from It (prod., dir. only)

Powell, Eleanor (Torrey), actress, dancer, singer; b. Springfield, Mass., Nov. 21, 1910. After winning Broadway success, Miss Powell brought her machine-gun footwork to Hollywood, where a succession of MGM musicals established her as Queen of Ra-Ta-Taps. Though basically a solo performer, she danced with Fred Astaire and George Murphy in *Broadway Melody of 1940;* among the songs she introduced—with feet and occasionally voice—were "Broadway Rhythm," "You Are My Lucky Star," "Easy To Love," and "I Concentrate on You." Miss Powell continued dancing in nightclubs following her film career. (Died Beverly Hills, Feb. 11, 1982.)

1935 George White's Scandals (*Marilyn Collins*)
Broadway Melody of 1936 (*Irene Foster*)
1936 Born To Dance (*Nora Paige*)
1937 Broadway Melody of 1938 (*Sally Lee*)
Rosalie (*Princess Rosalie*)
1939 Honolulu (*Dorothy March*)
1940 Broadway Melody of 1940 (*Clare Bennett*)

1941 Lady, Be Good (*Marilyn Marsh*)
1942 Ship Ahoy (*Tallulah Winters*)
1943 I Dood It (*Constance Shaw*)
Thousands Cheer (specialty)
1944 Sensations (*Ginny Walker*)
1950 Duchess of Idaho (specialty)

Powell, Jane (née Suzanne Burce), actress, singer; b. Portland, Oregon, April 1, 1929. Petite, blonde Jane Powell starred mostly in MGM musicals in which she was usually seen as a winsome, wealthy, adolescent Miss Fixit. Her well-endowed lydian soprano introduced such songs as "It's a Most Unusual Day," "Too Late Now," "Wonder Why," "When You're in Love" (in her best-regarded film, *Seven Brides for Seven Brothers*), and "Ride on a Rainbow" (in television's *Ruggles of Red Gap*). Among her co-stars: Fred Astaire, Vic Damone, Gordon MacRae, Howard Keel.

1944 Song of the Open Road (*Jane Powell*)
1945 Delightfully Dangerous (*Cheryl Williams*)
1946 Holiday in Mexico (*Christine Evans*)
1948 Three Daring Daughters (*Tess Morgan*)
Luxury Liner (*Polly Bradford*)
A Date with Judy (*Judy Foster*)
1950 Nancy Goes to Rio (*Nancy Barklay*)
Two Weeks with Love (*Patti Robinson*)
1951 Royal Wedding (*Ellen Bowen*)
Rich, Young and Pretty (*Liz Robinson*)
1953 Small Town Girl (*Cindy Kimball*)
Three Sailors and a Girl (*Penny Weston*)
1954 Deep in My Heart (specialty)
Athena (*Athena Mulvain*)
Seven Brides for Seven Brothers (*Millie Pontipee*)
1955 Hit the Deck (*Susan Smith*)
1957 The Girl Most Likely (*Dodie*)
Ruggles of Red Gap (tv) (*Clementine*)

Powell, William (Horatio), actor; b. Pittsburgh, July 29, 1892. Suave, heavy-lidded, well-groomed nonsinging actor who has become the public image of Broadway producer Florenz Ziegfeld. Powell's Hollywood career began in 1922; among his 95 films were *The Thin Man, My Man Godfrey,* and *Life with Father.* His first wife was Carole Lombard. (Died March 5, 1984.)

1929 Pointed Heels (*Robert Courtland*)
1930 Paramount on Parade (specialty)
1934 Fashions of 1934 (*Sherwood Nash*)
1935 Reckless (*Ned Riley*)
1936 The Great Ziegfeld (*Florenz Ziegfeld*)
1946 Ziegfeld Follies (*Florenz Ziegfeld*)
1949 Dancing in the Dark (*Emery Slade*)

Power, Tyrone (Edmund), actor; b. Cincinnati, May 5, 1913; d. Madrid, Nov. 15, 1958. A delicately featured actor, adept at both classical and modern roles, Power played the nonsinging male lead opposite Sonja Henie (twice) and Alice Faye (thrice) in Fox musicals. Bib: *Tyrone Power: The Last Idol* by Fred Lawrence Guiles (1979), *Films of Tyrone Power* by Dennis Belafonte (1979).

1934 Flirtation Walk (*cadet*)
1937 Thin Ice (*Prince Rudolph*)
1938 In Old Chicago (*Dion O'Leary*)
     Alexander's Ragtime Band (*Roger Grant*)
1939 Rose of Washington Square (*Bart Clinton*)
     Second Fiddle (*Jimmy Sutton*)
1956 The Eddy Duchin Story (*Eddy Duchin*)

Preisser, June, actress, dancer; b. New Orleans, 1920. Button-nosed, blonde contortionistic dancer who began with sister Cherry in vaudeville and Broadway revues. In Hollywood, she first appeared in MGM musicals, later was in five at Monogram opposite Freddie Stewart. (Died Boca Raton, Fla., Sept. 19, 1984 (auto crash).)

1939 Babes in Arms (*Rosalie Essex*)
     Dancing Coed (*Ticky James*)
1940 Strike Up the Band (*Barbara Morgan*)
1942 Sweater Girl (*Susan Lawson*)
1944 Babes on Swing Street (*Fern Wallace*)
     Murder in the Blue Room (*Jerry*)
1945 Let's Go Steady (*Mitzi Stack*)
     I'll Tell the World (*Marge Bailey*)
1946 Junior Prom (*Dodie*)
     Freddie Steps Out (*Dodie*)
     High School Hero (*Dodie*)
1947 Sarge Goes to College (*Dodie*)
     Vacation Days (*Dodie*)
     Two Blondes and a Redhead
1948 Campus Sleuth
     Music Man (*June Larkin*)

Preminger, Otto, director, producer, actor; b. Vienna, Dec. 5, 1906. Versatile director, in Hollywood since 1936, whose major films include *Laura, The Man with the Golden Arm,* and *Exodus.* Also played menacing, bald-domed, Teutonic heavies. Bib: *The Cinema of Otto Preminger* by Gerald Pratley (1971); *Preminger* by Preminger (1978). (Died New York, April 23, 1986.)

1936 Under Your Spell
1945 Where Do We Go from Here? (*Gen. Rahl* only)
1946 Centennial Summer (also prod.)
1948 That Lady in Ermine

1954 Carmen Jones (also prod.)
1959 Porgy and Bess

Presley, Elvis (Aron), singer, actor; b. Tupelo, Miss., Jan. 8, 1935; d. Memphis, Tenn., Aug. 16, 1977. Legendary rock singing idol whose screen image was usually that of an ambling free spirit who enjoyed outdoor life and was irresistible to every girl who heard him sing. Presley's throaty baritone and uninhibited singing gyrations won him a wide following, and his records were among the biggest sellers of the 1950s and 1960s. The best remembered songs he introduced in movies were "Love Me Tender" and "Can't Help Falling in Love." Bib: *Elvis in Hollywood* by Paul Lichter (1975); *Films and Career of Elvis Presley* by Steven & Boris Zmijewsky (1976); *Starring Elvis* by James Bowser (1977).

1956 Love Me Tender (*Clint*)
1957 Loving You (*Deke Rivers*)
     Jailhouse Rock (*Vince Everett*)
1958 King Creole (*Danny Fisher*)
1960 GI Blues (*Tulsa McCauley*)
1961 Wild in the Country (*Glenn Tyler*)
     Blue Hawaii (*Chad Gates*)
1962 Follow That Dream (*Toby Kwimper*)
     Kid Galahad (*Walter Gulick*)
     Girls! Girls! Girls! (*Ross Carpenter*)
1963 It Happened at the World's Fair (*Mike Edwards*)
     Fun in Acapulco (*Mike Windgren*)
1964 Kissin' Cousins (*Josh Morgan/ Jodie Tatum*)
     Viva Las Vegas (*Lucky Jackson*)
     Roustabout (*Charlie Rogers*)
1965 Girl Happy (*Rusty Wells*)
     Tickle Me (*Lonnie Beale*)
     Harum Scarum (*Johnny Tyrone*)
1966 Frankie and Johnny (*Johnny*)
     Paradise Hawaiian Style (*Rick Richards*)
     Spinout (*Mike McCoy*)
1967 Easy Come Easy Go (*Ted Johnson*)
     Double Trouble (*Guy Lambert*)
1968 Speedway (*Steve Grayson*)
     Stay Away Joe (*Joe Lightcloud*)
     Clambake (*Scott Heywood*)
     Live a Little Love a Little (*Greg Nolan*)
1969 Charro (*Jesse Wade*)
1970 The Trouble with Girls (*Walter Hale*)
     Change of Habit (*Dr. John Carpenter*)

Presnell, Harve, actor, singer; b. Modesto, Cal., Sept. 14, 1933. Heavy-set baritone who repeated his stage role in the movie version of *The Unsinkable Molly Brown.* Has appeared in concerts and in the touring company of the Broadway musical *Annie.*

1964 The Unsinkable Molly Brown (*Johnny Brown*)
1965 When the Boys Meet the Girls (*Danny Churchill*)
1969 Paint Your Wagon (*Rotten Luck Willie*)

Preston, Robert (né Robert Preston Meservey), actor, singer; b. Newton Highlands, Mass., June 8, 1918. Rugged, light-footed actor, who had to appear on Broadway in *The Music Man* (in which he later acted on the screen) before his musical talents were appreciated. (Died Santa Barbara, March 21, 1987.)

1940 Moon Over Burma (*Chuck Lane*)
1947 Variety Girl (guest bit)
1948 Big City (*Rev. Philip Andrews*)
1962 The Music Man (*Prof. Harold Hill*)
1974 Mame (*Beauregard Burnside*)
1982 Victor/Victoria (*Clare Todd*)

Previn, André, composer, pianist; b. Berlin, April 6, 1929. Began in Hollywood as an arranger, then became MGM music director and composer. Previn has also been a jazz pianist, music director of both the London Symphony Orchestra and the Pittsburgh Symphony, and musical-theatre composer (*Coco, The Good Companions*). His best-known movie songs are "The Faraway Part of Town" and "You're Gonna Hear from Me," both with lyrics by Dory Langdon (Previn's second wife). Other collaborators were Betty Comden and Adolph Green, and Alan Jay Lerner.

1947 It Happened in Brooklyn (soundtrack pianist only)
1955 It's Always Fair Weather (Comden, Green)
1960 Pepe (Langdon) (also *pianist*)
1969 Paint Your Wagon (Lerner)

Prinz, Le Roy, choreographer; b. St. Joseph, Mo., July 14, 1895. Hollywood's most prolific dance director worked primarily at Paramount (1933–41) and Warner (1942–57). Among his major assignments were *Show Boat, Yankee Doodle Dandy,* and *This Is the Army.* (Died Wadsworth, Cal., Sept. 13, 1983.)

1930 Madam Satan
1933 Too Much Harmony
1934 Bolero
1935 All the King's Horses
Stolen Harmony
Big Broadcast of 1936
1936 Show Boat (also *dance director*)
1937 Waikiki Wedding
Turn Off the Moon
High, Wide and Handsome
This Way Please
The Thrill of a Lifetime

Every Day's a Holiday
1938 Big Broadcast of 1938
Give Me a Sailor
Artists and Models Abroad
1940 Road to Singapore
Buck Benny Rides Again
Too Many Girls
1941 Road to Zanzibar
Time Out for Rhythm
All-American Coed (also dir., prod.)
1942 Fiesta (also dir., prod.)
Yankee Doodle Dandy
1943 This Is the Army
Thank Your Lucky Stars
The Desert Song
1944 Shine on Harvest Moon
Hollywood Canteen
1945 Rhapsody in Blue
1946 Night and Day
The Time, the Place and the Girl
1947 My Wild Irish Rose
Escape Me Never
1948 April Showers
Two Guys from Texas
1949 Look for the Silver Lining
It's a Great Feeling
Always Leave Them Laughing
My Dream Is Yours
1950 The Daughter of Rosie O'Grady
Tea for Two
The West Point Story
1951 Lullaby of Broadway
On Moonlight Bay
Painting the Clouds with Sunshine
Starlift
I'll See You in My Dreams
1952 April in Paris
About Face
She's Working Her Way Through College
1953 The Jazz Singer
She's Back on Broadway
By the Light of the Silvery Moon
The Desert Song
Calamity Jane
Three Sailors and a Girl
The Eddie Cantor Story
1954 Lucky Me
1957 The Helen Morgan Story
1958 South Pacific

Pryor, Roger, actor, singer; b. Asbury Park, NJ, Aug. 27, 1901; d. Puerta Vallarta, Mexico, Jan. 31, 1974. Former danceband singer who generally appeared in B musicals. His father was bandleader Arthur Pryor; his first wife was Ann Sothern. Later became advertising executive.

1933 Moonlight and Pretzels (*George Dwight*)
1934 I Like It That Way (*Jack Anderson*)
      Belle of the Nineties (*Tiger Kid*)
      Romance in the Rain (*Charlie Denton*)
      Gift of Gab (specialty)
      Wake Up and Dream (*Charlie Sullivan*)
1935 The Girl Friend (*George*)
      To Beat the Band (*Larry Barry*)
1936 Sitting on the Moon (*Danny West*)

"Pure Imagination" Music & lyric by Anthony Newley & Leslie Bricusse. The song with which Willy Wonka (Gene Wilder) welcomes his guests to the wonders of his factory in *Willy Wonka and the Chocolate Factory* (Par. 1971).

"Put 'Em in a Box (Tie 'Em with a Ribbon and Throw 'Em in the Deep Blue Sea)" Music by Jule Styne; lyric by Sammy Cahn. In which stars, robins, flowers, sentimental poetry, wedding bells, hansom cabs, kisses, and songs sung by "Frankie boy" or "Mister C" are all given the heave-ho " 'cause love and I, we don't agree." Doris Day introduced the jaunty number—accompanied by the Page Cavanaugh Trio—in *Romance on the High Seas* (Warner 1948), while singing in the bar of a ship docked in Havana.

"Put Me to the Test" Music by Jerome Kern; lyric by Ira Gershwin. Introduced by Gene Kelly in *Cover Girl* (Col. 1944) as part of the floorshow in a small Brooklyn nightclub. In the routine, Kelly appeared as a dresser in a department store window and sang the song to—and then danced with—come-alive mannequin Rita Hayworth. The song's lyric enumerates the comic macho proposals of a would-be modern knight who, to win his lady's favor, offers to climb the highest mountain, swim Radio City fountain, ride a Derby winner, pilot a plane to Paris, jump off the Eiffel Tower, and go over Niagara Falls in a barrel. Furthermore, he pledges to present her with a pyramid, a mountain puma, Montezuma's trea-sures, a snowball from Popocatepetl, a movie contract, and a blossom from Fujiyama. Ira Gershwin had originally written the lyric to a melody by his brother George for the 1937 film *A Damsel in Distress*. Because only the music of that song was used for a dance sequence featuring Fred Astaire and Burns and Allen, the lyricist retained the same words for his song with Kern. Not surprisingly, since it was influenced by the already-written lyric, Kern's tune sounded a lot like George's.

"Put the Blame on Mame" Music & lyric by Allan Roberts & Doris Fisher. Introduced in *Gilda* (Col. 1946) in a Rio de Janeiro casino by Rita Hayworth (with Anita Ellis' voice) wearing a black strapless gown, followed by a tipsily seductive—though unrevealing—striptease. Later Miss Hayworth (again dubbed) sang a slower version while strumming a guitar. The number discloses that the devastating Mame was the real cause of the Chicago fire, the blizzard of 1886, the San Francisco earthquake, and the shooting of Dan McGrew in the Klondike. Historical note: contrary to the lyric, the blizzard that buried Manhattan took place in 1888 not 1886.

"Puttin' on the Ritz" Music & lyric by Irving Berlin. Brightly syncopated number introduced by Harry Richman and chorus in a Broadway theatre in *Puttin' on the Ritz* (UA 1930). Song also sung by Clark Gable and "Les Blondes" in *Idiot's Delight* (MGM 1939); Fred Astaire in *Blue Skies* (Par. 1946), followed by a blazing tap dance backed by a row of seemingly miniature tapping Astaires; and Peter Boyle (Monster) and Gene Wilder (Dr. Frankenstein) in *Young Frankenstein* (Fox 1974). Originally, the piece had been an invitation to view the Harlem well-to-do on Lenox Avenue, where "a bevy of high browns from down the levee" and Lulu Belles with their swell beaux rub elbows and "spend their last two bits." By the time Astaire sang the piece, however, the revised lyric had moved the locale to Park Avenue, where millionaires such as Rockefellers walk with sticks or "um-ber-el-las in their mitts."

Q

"Que Sera, Sera (Whatever Will Be, Will Be)" Music & lyric by Jay Livingston & Ray Evans. Fatalistic piece sung by Doris Day as a lullaby to her son (Christopher Olsen) in nonmusical film, *The Man Who Knew Too Much* (Par. 1956). Though at first Miss Day felt that it was just a "kiddie song," without broad appeal, the number turned out to be the biggest hit she ever recorded.

Quine, Richard, actor, director; b. Detroit, Nov. 12, 1920. Vaudeville and Broadway actor-dancer who started his film career as an MGM juvenile, then, in the early 50s, became a Columbia director.

1941 Babes on Broadway (*Morton Hammond*)
1942 For Me and My Gal (*Danny*)
1948 Words and Music (*Ben Feiner*)
1951 On the Sunny Side of the Street
     Purple Heart Diary
1952 Sound Off
     Rainbow 'Round My Shoulder
1953 All Ashore
     Cruisin' Down the River
1954 So This Is Paris
1955 My Sister Eileen

R

Raft, George (né George Ranft), actor, dancer; b. New York, Sept. 24, 1895; d. Hollywood, Nov. 24, 1980. Swarthy, somewhat menacing actor, adept at depicting hoods, gamblers, and nightclub habitués. His two major dancing films were *Bolero* and *Rumba*, both opposite Carole Lombard. Film bio: *The George Raft Story*, with Ray Danton as Raft. Bib: *The George Raft File* by James Robert Parish (1973).

1929	Queen of the Night Clubs (*Gigolo*)
1931	Palmy Days (*Joe the Frog*)
1932	Dancers in the Dark (*Louie Brooks*)
1934	Bolero (*Raoul de Baere*)
1935	Rumba (*Joe Martin*)
	Stolen Harmony (*Ray Angelo*)
	Every Night at Eight (*Tops Cardona*)
1942	Broadway (*George Raft*)
1943	Stage Door Canteen (guest bit)
1944	Follow the Boys (*Tony West*)
1945	Nob Hill (*Tony Angelo*)
1959	Some Like It Hot (*Spats Columbo*)
1961	The Ladies Man (*George Raft*)

"Rainbow Connection, The" Music & lyric by Paul Williams & Kenny Ascher. Seated on his favorite cypress log deep in the swamps, Kermit the Frog (with Jim Henson's voice) opened *The Muppet Movie* (1979) by singing and plunking this lilting, latter-day "Over the Rainbow."

"Rainbow on the River" Music by Louis Alter; lyric by Paul Francis Webster. Cheery song of optimism chirped by little Bobby Breen in film of the same name (RKO 1936).

"Raindrops Keep Fallin' on My Head" Music by Burt Bacharach; lyric by Hal David. Perky number sung on soundtrack of *Butch Cassidy and the Sundance Kid* (Fox 1969) by B. J. Thomas, while Paul Newman shows off on a bicycle and Katharine Ross gets undressed.

Rainer, Luise, actress; b. Vienna, Jan. 12, 1909. Dramatic actress who made limited number of Hollywood films; remembered for emotional telephone scene in *The Great Ziegfeld*.

1936	The Great Ziegfeld (*Anna Held*)
1938	The Great Waltz (*Poldi Vogelhuber*)

Rainger, Ralph (né Ralph Reichenthal), composer; b. New York, Oct. 7, 1901; d. Beverly Hills, Oct. 23, 1942. Except for early songs with lyricist Sam Coslow then as his own lyricist, and one number with Dorothy Parker ("I Wished on the Moon"), Rainger worked exclusively in Hollywood with Leo Robin. At Paramount, the team wrote such Bing Crosby hits as "Please," "June in January," "Love in Bloom," "With Every Breath I Take," "My Heart and I," "Blue Hawaii," "I Have Eyes," and "The Funny Old Hills." For other singers: "I Don't Want To Make History" (Frances Langford), "Thanks for the Memory" (Bob Hope and Shirley Ross), "Whispers in the Dark" (Connie Boswell), "What Have You Got That Gets Me?" (Yacht Club Boys), and "Faithful Forever" (Jessica Dragonette and Lanny Ross). Their songs were also sung on the screen by Maurice Chevalier, Shirley Temple, Ethel Merman, Gladys Swarthout, John Boles, Dorothy Lamour, Betty Grable, and Dick Powell. Rainger's early career was as a composer and pianist for Broadway musicals.

Unless otherwise noted, following all had songs written with Mr. Robin:

1932	This Is the Night (Coslow)
	Blonde Venus (Coslow)

The Big Broadcast
1933   She Done Him Wrong (also 1yr.)
A Bedtime Story
International House
Torch Singer
The Way to Love
1934   Little Miss Marker
Shoot the Works
Here Is My Heart
1935   Rumba
Four Hours to Kill
Big Broadcast of 1936
Millions in the Air
1936   Rose of the Rancho
Palm Springs
Three Cheers for Love
Big Broadcast of 1937
College Holiday
1937   Waikiki Wedding
1938   Big Broadcast of 1938
Give Me a Sailor
Artists and Models Abroad
1939   Paris Honeymoon
Gulliver's Travels
1941   Tall, Dark and Handsome
Moon Over Miami
Rise and Shine
Cadet Girl
1942   My Gal Sal
Footlight Serenade
1943   Coney Island
Riding High

"Rainy Night in Rio, A" Music by Arthur Schwartz; lyric by Leo Robin. Sung in *The Time, the Place and the Girl* (Warner 1946) by Jack Carson, Dennis Morgan, Janis Paige, and Martha Vickers in the finale of a Broadway revue on opening night. In the scene, a sudden downpour in a Rio square forces the quartet to duck indoors to a convenient nightclub, where Carmen Cavallero plays piano and Cariocas dance the samba. The number ends with everyone out in the square again splashing about under umbrellas.

Rall, Tommy, actor, dancer, singer; b. Kansas City, Mo., Dec. 27, 1929. Lithe, versatile performer, also in Broadway musicals, whose best film role was in *Kiss Me, Kate* opposite Ann Miller.

1953   Kiss Me, Kate (*Bill Calhoun*)
1954   Seven Brides for Seven Brothers (*Frank Pontipee*)
1955   My Sister Eileen (*Chick Clark*)
1956   Invitation to the Dance (*Hoofer*)

1958   Merry Andrew (*Giacomo Gallini*)
1968   Funny Girl (dancer)
1981   Pennies from Heaven (*Ed*)

Ramirez, Carlos, singer; b. Bogota, Col. Round-faced singer of romantic Latin songs who appeared mostly in specialty numbers in MGM musicals. (Died 1986.)

1944   Two Girls and a Sailor
Bathing Beauty
1945   Where Do We Go from Here? (*Benito*)
Anchors Aweigh
1946   Easy To Wed
Night and Day
1953   Latin Lovers (vocals for Ricardo Montalban only)

"Rap Tap on Wood" Music & lyric by Cole Porter. In *Born To Dance* (MGM 1936), Eleanor Powell, newly arrived in New York, finds lodging at the Lonely Hearts Club, where she confides to manager Una Merkel that she's a dancer looking for work. "Would you be embarrassed to get up in front of all these people and do your stuff?" asks Una confidentially. No indeed, and Eleanor, then and there, sings and rap taps and makes everyone happy.

Rasch, Albertina, choreographer; b. Vienna, 1896; d. Woodland Hills, Cal., Oct. 2, 1967. A balletic choreographer on Broadway between 1925 and 1945, Miss Rasch did most of her film work at MGM. She was married to composer Dimitri Tiomkin.

1929   Hollywood Revue of 1929
Devil May Care
1930   Lord Byron of Broadway
1933   Broadway to Hollywood
Going Hollywood
1934   The Cat and the Fiddle
1935   Broadway Melody of 1936
After the Dance
1936   The King Steps Out
1937   The Firefly (also guest bit)
Rosalie
1938   The Girl of the Golden West
Sweethearts
The Great Waltz

Ratoff, Gregory (né Eugene Leontovitch), actor, director; b. Samara, Russia, April 20, 1897; d. Solothurn, Switzerland, Dec. 14, 1960. Portly character actor with thick accent who played anything from peddler to explosive tycoon. Associated primarily with Fox, where he later became a director.

Asterisk indicates Mr. Ratoff was director:

1933	I'm No Angel (*Benny Pinkowitz*)
	Broadway Through a Keyhole (*Max Mefoofsky*)
	Sitting Pretty (*Tannenbaum*)
	Girl Without a Room (*General*)
1934	Let's Fall in Love (*Max*)
	George White's Scandals (*Nicholas Mitwoch*)
1935	Hello, Sweetheart (Eng.) (*Joseph Lewis*)
	King of Burlesque (*Kolpolpeck*)
1936	Sing, Baby, Sing (*Nicky*)
	Under Your Spell (*Petroff*)
1937	Top of the Town (*J. J. Stone*)
1938	Sally, Irene and Mary (*Baron Zorka*)
1939	Rose of Washington Square*
1942	Footlight Serenade*
1943	The Heat's On* (also prod.)
	Something to Shout About* (also prod.)
1944	Irish Eyes Are Smiling*
1945	Where Do We Go from Here?*
1946	Do You Love Me*
1947	Carnival in Costa Rica*

Ray, Leah (née Leah Ray Hubbard), singer, actress; b. Norfolk, Va., Feb. 16, 1915. Dark-haired singing beauty, formerly vocalist with Phil Harris' orchestra, who introduced title song in *One in a Million*. Retired in 1938 after marriage to sports promoter Sonny Werblin.

1933	A Bedtime Story (*Gabrielle*)
1936	One in a Million (*Leah*)
1937	The Holy Terror (*Marjorie Dean*)
	Wake Up and Live (*café singer*)
	Sing and Be Happy (*Ann Lane*)
	Thin Ice (*band singer*)
1938	Happy Landing (*band singer*)
	Walking Down Broadway (*Linda Martin*)

Raye, Don (né Donald MacRae Wilhoite, Jr.), lyricist; b. Washington, DC, March 16, 1909. Raye's Hollywood output—heard mostly in Universal films—resulted from collaborations with composers Hughie Prince ("Boogie Woogie Bugle Boy") and Gene dePaul, his most frequent partner ("I'll Remember April," "Mister Five by Five," "Milkman, Keep Those Bottles Quiet"). The Andrews Sisters, Dick Foran, Grace McDonald, and Nancy Walker were among those who first sang Don Raye songs.

1941	Buck Privates (*Prince*)
	In the Navy (*dePaul*)
	Moonlight in Hawaii (*dePaul*)
	Keep 'Em Flying (*dePaul*)
	Behind the Eight Ball (*dePaul*)
	San Antonio Rose (*Prince; dePaul*)

Hellzapoppin (*dePaul*)

1942	Ride 'Em Cowboy (*dePaul*)
	Pardon My Sarong (*dePaul*)
1943	Hi'Ya Chum (*dePaul*)
	Larceny with Music (*dePaul*
1944	Broadway Rhythm (*dePaul*)
1948	A Song Is Born (*dePaul*)
1949	Ichabod and Mr. Toad (*dePaul*)

Raye, Martha (née Margaret Theresa Yvonne Reed), actress, singer; b. Butte, Mont., Aug. 27, 1908. A wide-mouthed clown with an aggressive comic and singing style, Miss Raye appeared in many Paramount films during the latter half of the 30s. She was teamed in five musicals with Bob Burns, and introduced "(If You Can't Sing It) You'll Have to Swing It." Her second and fourth (of six) husbands were composer David Rose and dancer Nick Condos. Also had own television series.

1936	Rhythm on the Range (*Emma Mazda*)
	Big Broadcast of 1937 (*Patsy*)
	College Holiday (*Daisy Schloggenheimer*)
1937	Hideaway Girl (*Helen Flint*)
	Waikiki Wedding (*Myrtle Finch*)
	Mountain Music (*Mary Beamish*)
	Artists and Models (specialty)
	Double or Nothing (*Liza Lou Lane*)
1938	Big Broadcast of 1938 (*Martha Bellows*)
	College Swing (*Mabel*)
	Give Me a Sailor (*Letty Larkin*)
	Tropic Holiday (*Midge Miller*)
1940	The Boys from Syracuse (*Luce*)
1941	Navy Blues (*Lillibelle Bolton*)
	Keep 'Em Flying (*Barbara Phelps/ Gloria Phelps*)
	Hellzapoppin (*Betty Johnson*)
1944	Four Jills in a Jeep (*Martha Raye*)
	Pin-Up Girl (*Marian*)
1962	Jumbo (*Lulu*)
1970	Pufnstuf (*Boss Witch*)

Raymond, Gene (né Raymond Guion), actor, singer; b. New York, Aug. 13, 1908. Blond, bland leading man who appeared in musicals opposite Dolores Del Rio, Lilian Harvey, Joan Crawford, Ann Sothern, Lily Pons, Harriet Hilliard, and Jeanette MacDonald (his wife). Raymond introduced "All I Do Is Dream of You" in *Sadie McKee*.

1933	Flying Down to Rio (*Roger Bond*)
1934	I Am Suzanne (*Tony*)
	Sadie McKee (*Tommy*)
	Transatlantic Merry-Go-Round (*Jimmy Brett*)
1935	Hooray for Love (*Doug*)

1936 Walking on Air (*Pete Quinlan*)
That Girl from Paris (*Windy McLean*)
1937 The Life of the Party (*Barry*)
1941 Smilin' Through (*Kenneth Wayne/Jeremy Wayne*)
1955 Hit the Deck (*Wendell Craig*)
1964 I'd Rather Be Rich (*Martin Wood*)

Reagan, Ronald (Wilson), actor; b. Tampico, Ill., Feb. 6, 1911. Affable, sincere nonsinging leading man with a 27-year Hollywood career, mostly at Warner. Married actresses Jane Wyman (divorced) and Nancy Davis. Served as governor of California, 1966–74. 40th President of the United States.

1937 Hollywood Hotel (bit)
1938 Going Places (*Jack Withering*)
1939 Naughty but Nice (*Ed Clark*)
1942 Juke Girl (*Steve Talbot*)
1943 This Is the Army (*Johnny Jones*)
1949 It's a Great Feeling (guest bit)
1952 She's Working Her Way Through College (*Johnny Palmer*)

Regan, Phil, actor, singer; b. Brooklyn, May 28, 1906. Regan's Irish tenor was heard in some major musicals, but he played leads mostly at Republic and Monogram. He introduced "My Heart Tells Me" in *Sweet Rosie O'Grady*.

1934 Student Tour (*Bobby*)
Dames (*Johnny Harris*)
1935 Sweet Adeline (*singer*)
Go Into Your Dance (*Eddie Rio*)
In Caliente (*singer*)
Broadway Hostess (*Tommy Blake*)
1936 Laughing Irish Eyes (*Danny O'Keefe*)
Happy-Go-Lucky (*Hap Cole*)
1937 Hit Parade of 1937 (*Pete Garland*)
Manhattan Merry-Go-Round (*Jerry Hart*)
1938 Outside of Paradise (*Danny O'Toole*)
1939 She Married a Cop (*Jimmy*)
1941 Las Vegas Nights (*Bill Stevens*)
1943 Sweet Rosie O'Grady (*singer*)
1945 Sunbonnet Sue (*Danny Dooley*)
1946 Swing Parade of 1946 (*Danny Warren*)
Sweetheart of Sigma Chi (*Lucky Ryan*)
1950 Three Little Words (*radio host*)

"Remember Me" Music by Harry Warren; lyric by Al Dubin. After apologetically revealing that he's the composer of the song, a husband trippingly recalls to his wife such pleasures as their September wedding, their honeymoon, and their small hillside cottage. Introduced by Kenny Baker in *Mr. Dodd Takes the Air* (Warner 1937).

"Remember My Forgotten Man" Music by Harry Warren; lyric by Al Dubin. Throbbing threnody of social consciousness introduced in *Gold Diggers of 1933* (Warner) as the Busby Berkeley finale of both a Broadway revue and of the picture itself. The scene opens with Joan Blondell, as a streetwalker, lighting the cigarette of a scruffy-looking drifter, and singing of the forgotten men who once were war heroes. Following the song's reprise by Etta Moten (leaning out of a window above), a policeman is about to arrest the bum for loitering when Miss Blondell shows him the man's medal. With the music taking on a martial beat, a flashback reveals hundreds of soldiers marching in formation on their way to their transport ship, the faces of the men as they trudge through the rain, and, finally, their moving on to battle as the wounded stumble in the opposite direction. Again the scene is back in the Depression, with the former soldiers lining up in a different kind of formation to await their turns at a soup kitchen. Backed by a huge semicircular arch made up of doughboys marching in silhouette on three levels, Miss Blondell (with dubbed voice) leads the forgotten men and women as they end the scene on a stirring revivalistic pitch.

"Remind Me" Music by Jerome Kern; lyric by Dorothy Fields. Musically involved ballad set to a compelling rumba beat in which the singer pleads to be warned against falling in love. Introduced by Peggy Moran in a New York nightclub scene in *One Night in the Tropics* (Univ. 1940). The song was actually written four years earlier for an unproduced film titled *Riviera*.

Revel, Harry, composer; b. London, Dec. 21, 1905; d. New York, Nov. 3, 1958. Writer of songs for London and Broadway musicals before major Hollywood assignments at Paramount (1933–36) and Fox (1936–38). Revel's most popular pieces, all written with his most frequent partner, lyricist Mack Gordon, include "Did You Ever See a Dream Walking?," "Love Thy Neighbor," "Once in a Blue Moon," "Stay as Sweet as You Are," "May I?," "With My Eyes Wide Open I'm Dreaming," "Take a Number from One to Ten," "Without a Word of Warning," "Here Comes Cookie," "Paris in the Spring," "Goodnight, My Love," "I Feel Like a Feather in the Breeze," "May I Have the Next Romance with You?," "You Hit the Spot," "Afraid to Dream," "Never in a Million Years," "There's a Lull in My Life," "You Can't Have Everything," and "You Say the Sweetest Things, Baby." Revel also worked with lyricists Mort Greene and Paul Francis Webster. His songs were associated mostly with Bing Crosby, Jack Haley, Lanny Ross, Jack Oakie, Lyda Roberti, Gracie Allen, Shirley Temple, Alice Faye, Jessie Matthews, Judy Garland, and Don Ameche.

1933 Broadway Through a Keyhole (Gordon)
     Sitting Pretty (Gordon) (also *pianist*)
1934 We're Not Dressing (Gordon)
     Shoot the Works (Gordon)
     She Loves Me Not (Gordon)
     College Rhythm (Gordon)
1935 Love in Bloom (Gordon)
     Stolen Harmony (Gordon)
     Paris in Spring (Gordon)
     Two for Tonight (Gordon)
     Collegiate (Gordon) (also *song coach*)
1936 Poor Little Rich Girl (Gordon)
     Stowaway (Gordon)
1937 Head Over Heels (Eng.) (Gordon)
     Everybody Dance (Eng.) (Gordon)
     Wake Up and Live (Gordon)
     This Is My Affair (Gordon)
     You Can't Have Everything (Gordon)
     Ali Baba Goes to Town (Gordon)
     Love and Hisses (Gordon)
1938 Josette (Gordon)
     Love Finds Andy Hardy (Gordon)
     My Lucky Star (Gordon)
     Thanks for Everything (Gordon)
1941 Four Jacks and a Jill (Greene)
1942 Call Out the Marines (Greene)
     Sing Your Worries Away (Greene)
     The Mayor of 44th Street (Greene)
     Moonlight Masquerade (Greene)
1943 It Ain't Hay (Webster)
     Hit the Ice (Webster)
1944 The Ghost Catchers (Webster)
     Minstrel Man (Webster)

Reynolds, (Mary Frances) Debbie, actress, singer, dancer; b. El Paso, Texas, April 1, 1932. During the early 50s, Miss Reynolds was one of MGM's eternally adolescent musical stars, projecting a hoydenish, button-cute personality that helped win her the major female role in *Singin' in the Rain* opposite Gene Kelly and Donald O'Connor. Other leading men were Carleton Carpenter (with whom she revived "Aba Daba Honeymoon"), Bob Fosse, Vic Damone, and Eddie Fisher (her first husband). "Tammy" was the best-known song she introduced in movies.

1950 The Daughter of Rosie O'Grady (*Maureen O'Grady*)
     Three Little Words (*Helen Kane*)
     Two Weeks with Love (*Melba Robinson*)

1951 Mr. Imperium (*Gwen*)
1952 Singin' in the Rain (*Kathy Selden*)
     Skirts Ahoy (guest bit)
     The Affairs of Dobie Gillis (*Pansy Hammer*)
     Give a Girl a Break (*Suzy Doolittle*)
     I Love Melvin (*Judy Leroy*)
1954 Athena (*Minerva Mulvain*)
1955 Hit the Deck (*Carol Pace*)
1956 Meet Me in Las Vegas (guest bit)
     Bundle of Joy (*Polly Parrish*)
1959 Say One for Me (*Holly*)
1960 Pepe (*Debbie Reynolds*)
1964 The Unsinkable Molly Brown (*Molly Brown*)
1966 The Singing Nun (*Sister Ann*)
1972 Charlotte's Web (voice of *Charlotte*)
1974 That's Entertainment (narrator)

Reynolds, Marjorie (née Marjorie Goodspeed), actress; b. Buhl, Idaho, Aug. 12, 1921. Blonde leading lady of Paramount films whose best role in a musical was that of the girl Bing Crosby and Fred Astaire fought over in *Holiday Inn*. Miss Reynolds was child actress Marjorie Moore until 1936.

1933 Wine, Women and Song (bit)
1935 Collegiate (bit)
1942 Holiday Inn (*Linda Mason*)
     Star-Spangled Rhythm (specialty)
1943 Dixie (*Jean Mason*)
1945 Bring on the Girls (*Sue Thomas*)
     Meet Me on Broadway
     Duffy's Tavern (*Peggy O'Malley*)
1949 That Midnight Kiss (*Mary*)
1959 Juke Box Rhythm (*Martha Manton*)

Rhodes, Betty Jane, actress, singer; b. Rockford, Ill., April 21, 1921. Radio and nightclub singer who began in movies in her mid-teens.

1937 The Life of the Party (*Susan*)
1940 Oh, Johnny (*Betty*)
1942 The Fleet's In (*Diana Golden*)
     Priorities on Parade (*Lee Davis*)
     Sweater Girl (*Louise Menard*)
     Star-Spangled Rhythm (specialty)
1943 Salute for Three (*Judy Ames*)
1944 You Can't Ration Love (*Betty*)

Rhodes, Erik, actor, singer; b. El Reno, Okla., Feb. 10, 1906. Forever associated with the Italianate, explosive characters he played in support of Fred Astaire and Ginger Rogers in two musicals. In one, *The Gay Divorcee,* he even got to sing "The Continental."

1934 Give Her a Ring (Eng.) (*Otto Brune*)
     The Gay Divorcee (*Rodolfo Tonetti*)

1935 Top Hat (*Alberto Beddini*)
      Old Man Rhythm (*Frank Rochet*)
1937 Music for Madame (*Spaghetti*)
1939 On Your Toes (*Constantine Morrosine*)

"Rhythm of the Rain" Music by Jack Meskill; lyric by Jack Stern. Pluvial production number in *Folies Bergère* (UA 1935), in which Maurice Chevalier and Ann Sothern sang of and demonstrated their fondness for the pitter-patter rhythm of the raindrops.

Richman, Harry (né Harry Reichmann), actor, singer; b. Cincinnati, Aug. 10, 1895; d. Hollywood, Nov. 3, 1972. Exuberant, much-imitated song stylist who scored his greatest successes in nightclubs and Broadway revues. Introduced "Puttin' on the Ritz" and "There's Danger in Your Eyes, Cherie" in his first film. Bib: *A Hell of a Life* by Richman (1966).

1930 Puttin' on the Ritz (*Harry Raymond*)
1936 The Music Goes Round (*Harry Wallace*)
1938 Kicking the Moon Around (Eng.) (*Harry*)

"Ride on a Rainbow" Music by Jule Styne; lyric by Leo Robin. Introduced by Jane Powell in television musical, *Ruggles of Red Gap* (NBC 1957), as she recalled the sensation of falling in love. The song's chief melodic strain is reminiscent of the verse to Kern and Hammerstein's "All the Things You Are."

"Right Girl for Me, The" Music by Roger Edens; lyric by Betty Comden & Adolph Green. In which Frank Sinatra, in *Take Me Out to the Ball Game* (MGM 1949), dreamily enumerates the ways he will know when she comes along.

"Right Romance, The" Music by Jerome Kern; lyric by Leo Robin. Amatory yearnings revealed by Jeanne Crain (voice dubbed by Louanne Hogan) in *Centennial Summer* (Fox 1946).

"Right Somebody To Love, The" Music by Lew Pollack; lyric by Jack Yellen. Affectionate sentiment sung by Shirley Temple to her guardian, Guy Kibbee, in *Captain January* (Fox 1936). In the grotesque imaginary sequence that followed, Kibbee became a tiny baby in an enormous highchair with Miss Temple his equally tiny nurse.

Rio Rita (1929). Music by Harry Tierney; lyrics by Joseph McCarthy; screenplay by Russell Mack and Luther Reed from Broadway musical by Tierney, McCarthy, Guy Bolton, and Fred Thompson.

An RKO-Radio film produced by William LeBaron; directed by Luther Reed; choreography, Pearl Eaton; art director, Max Rée; music director, Victor Baravalle; associate musical director, Max Steiner; cameraman, Robert Kurrle; editor, William Hamilton; part Technicolor.

Cast: Bebe Daniels (*Rita Ferguson*); John Boles (*Capt. James Stewart*); Bert Wheeler (*Chick Bean*); Robert Woolsey (*Ed Lovett*); Dorothy Lee (*Dolly Bean*); Don Alvarado (*Roberto Ferguson*); George Renavent (*Gen. Ravenoff*); Eva Rosita (*Carmen*); Helen Kaiser (*Katie Bean*).

Songs: "Jumping Bean" - Lee, girls/ "The Kinkajou" - Lee, girls/ "Sweethearts" - Daniels/ "River Song" - Daniels/ "Rio Rita" - Boles, Daniels/ "Siesta Time" - townspeople/ "Espanola" - Woolsey, girls/ "Are You There?" - Lee, Wheeler/ "The Rangers' Song" - Boles, Rangers/ "You're Always in My Arms" - Boles, Daniels/ "The Spanish Shawl" - Rosita/ "If You're in Love You'll Waltz" - Daniels/ "Out on the Loose" - Wheeler, girls/ "Poor Fool" - Daniels/ "Over the Boundary Line" - party guests/ "Sweetheart, We Need Each Other" - Wheeler, Lee. Unused: "The Best Little Lover in Town," "Following the Sun Around."

Rio Rita was the second all-talkie adaptation of a Broadway musical (the first had been *The Desert Song*) and the first one to enjoy boxoffice success. Based on Ziegfeld's celebrated 1927 production, it marked Bebe Daniels' sound-film debut and the screen debut of comedians Bert Wheeler and Robert Woolsey re-creating their original stage roles. In the story, Capt. James Stewart of the Texas Rangers pursues the notorious bandit, the Kinkajou, into Mexico, where he falls in love with the suspected outlaw's sister, Rita Ferguson (who is never called Rio Rita except in song). The lovers are torn between duty and devotion until the villainous Gen. Ravenoff is unmasked as the real Kinkajou during a festive barge party on the Rio Grande. (A variation on this plot turned up in the 1936 film, *Rose Marie*, in which James Stewart played the hunted brother.)

Though it used outdoor settings, the film was structured like a two-act stage musical, with the second half, aboard the barge, shot entirely in color. Except for changing the villain's name from Esteban to Ravenoff (presumably to avoid offending Latin American neighbors), the screen version stuck closely to its stage model. All but two of the songs were retained, with two added, though others have since been dropped to keep the running time well under the 2 hours 20 minutes of the original print.

Ritz Brothers (né Joachim), actors, singers. Al, b. Newark, NJ, Aug. 27, 1901; d. New Orleans, Dec. 22, 1965. Harry, b. Newark, May 22, 1906. Jimmy, b. Newark, Oct. 5, 1903. Led by Harry Ritz, the manic team of hawkfaced brothers provided slapstick screen entertainment primarily in Fox films of the late 30s. They were also headliners in vaudeville, Broadway revues, and nightclubs. (Harry died San Diego, March 30, 1986; Jimmy died Los Angeles, Nov. 17, 1985.)

1936	Sing, Baby, Sing
	One in a Million
1937	On the Avenue
	You Can't Have Everything
	Life Begins in College
1938	The Goldwyn Follies
	Kentucky Moonshine
	Straight, Place and Show
1939	The Three Musketeers
1940	Argentine Nights
1942	Behind the Eight Ball
1943	Hi' Ya Chum
	Never a Dull Moment

"Road to Morocco" Music by James Van Heusen; lyric by Johnny Burke. "Like Webster's Dictionary, we're Morocco bound," sang Bing Crosby and Bob Hope while perched on the back of a camel early in the Paramount film of the same name (1942).

Road to Singapore (1940). Music by James Monaco, Victor Schertzinger; lyrics by Johnny Burke; screenplay by Frank Butler & Don Hartman from story *Beach of Dreams* by Harry Hersey.

A Paramount film produced by Harlan Thompson; directed by Victor Schertzinger; choreography, LeRoy Prinz; art directors, Hans Dreier, Richard Odell; costumes, Edith Head; music director, Victor Young; cameraman, William Mellor; editor, Paul Weatherwax.

Cast: Bing Crosby (*Josh Mallon*); Dorothy Lamour (*Mima*); Bob Hope (*Ace Lanningan*); Charles Coburn (*Joshua Mallon IV*); Anthony Quinn (*Caesar*); Jerry Colonna (*Achilles Bombanassa*); Judith Barrett (*Gloria Wycott*); Pierre Watkin (*Morgan Wycott*); Johnny Arthur (*Timothy Willow*); Miles Mander (*Sir Malcolm Drake*).

Songs: "Captain Custard" (Schertzinger) -Crosby, Hope/ "Sweet Potato Piper" (Monaco) - Crosby, Lamour, Hope/ "Too Romantic" (Monaco) - Crosby, La-mour/ "Kaigoon" (Monaco) -chorus/ "The Moon and the Willow Tree" (Schertzinger) - Lamour.

The first Crosby-Lamour-Hope "Road" picture set the pattern for the entire series: buddies Bing and Bob find themselves in a faraway land, where they feud over Dorothy and fall into—and clown out of—a number of improbable scrapes. The lighthearted tone always treated the material as the Hollywood hokum it was, with the principals making supposedly ad-lib wisecracks both to each other and to the audience. Originally, Paramount planned to co-star Fred MacMurray and Jack Oakie in an adventure yarn to be called *Road to Mandalay,* but someone got the better idea of teaming Crosby and Hope, who had already begun a friendly feud over the radio, and somehow Mandalay was rerouted to Singapore. The success of the first journey prompted the five subsequent Paramount releases, which took the trio to Zanzibar (1941), Morocco (1942), Utopia (actually the Klondike) (1945), Rio (1947), and Bali (1952). Ten years later, Crosby and Hope were reunited in UA's *Road to Hong Kong,* with Joan Collins co-starred and Miss Lamour relegated to a guest bit. After *Singapore,* in which Bing played a wealthy adventurer and Bob his ne'er-do-well sidekick, the boys were usually cast as vaudevillians or carnival entertainers, with Crosby the con man and Hope the patsy. Increasingly, the escapades became more outlandish and the sight gags more incongruous.

In addition to Victor Schertzinger, who also directed *Road to Zanzibar,* the directors for the series were David Butler (*Morocco*), Hal Walker (*Utopia, Bali*), Norman McLeod (*Rio*), and Norman Panama (*Hong Kong*). Jimmy Van Heusen wrote the music for all but the first film, and Johnny Burke the lyrics for all but the last, which were written by Sammy Cahn. Among songs from various *Road* pictures were "It's Always You," "Constantly," "Moonlight Becomes You," "Road to Morocco," "It's Anybody's Spring," "Personality," and "But Beautiful." Paramount's *Rainbow Island* (1944), with Dorothy Lamour, Eddie Bracken, and Gil Lamb, was a spinoff from the *Road* series.

Roberta (1935). Music by Jerome Kern; lyrics mostly by Otto Harbach, Dorothy Fields; screenplay by Jane Murfin, Sam Mintz, Glenn Tryon, and Allan Scott from Broadway musical by Harbach & Kern based on novel *Gowns by Roberta* by Alice Duer Miller.

An RKO-Radio film produced by Pandro S. Berman; directed by William A. Seiter; choreography, Fred Astaire, Hermes Pan; art directors, Van Nest Polglase,

Carroll Clark; costumes, Bernard Newman; music director, Max Steiner; cameraman, Edward Cronjager; editor, William Hamilton.

Cast: Irene Dunne (*Stephanie*); Fred Astaire (*Huckleberry "Huck" Haines*); Ginger Rogers (*Lizzie Gatz* aka *Countess Tanka Scharwenka*); Randolph Scott (*John Kent*); Helen Westley (*Aunt Minnie*); Victor Varconi (*Ladislaw*); Claire Dodd (*Sophie Teale*); Luis Alberni (*Alexander Voyda*); Ferdinand Munier (*Lord Henry Delves*); Lucille Ball (*mannequin*); Candy Candido, Muzzy Marcellino, Gene Sheldon, Hal Borne, Howard Lally (*Wabash Indianians*)

Songs: "Indiana" (James Hanley-Ballard Macdonald) - Indianians/ "Let's Begin" (Harbach) -Astaire, Candido; dance by Astaire, Candido, Sheldon/ "Russian Song" (trad.) - Dunne/ "I'll Be Hard To Handle" (lyric, Bernard Dougall) -Rogers; dance by Astaire, Rogers/ "Yesterdays" (Harbach) - Dunne/ "I Won't Dance" (Fields, Oscar Hammerstein II) - Astaire, Rogers; dance by Astaire/ "Smoke Gets in Your Eyes" (Harbach) -Dunne; reprised as dance by Astaire, Rogers/ "Fashion Show" (Fields) - Astaire/ "Lovely To Look At" (Fields) - Dunne, male chorus; reprised by Astaire, Rogers.

Since Fred and Ginger's first starring vehicle, *The Gay Divorcee,* had been based on a popular Broadway musical, the RKO brass decided they should follow it up with another adaptation of a Broadway hit. *Roberta* proved to be an equally felicitous choice, especially since there was also a major role for one of the studio's stellar attractions, Irene Dunne. None of the actors in the 1933 Kern-Harbach stage musical was in the screen version: Tamara's role was played by Miss Dunne, Bob Hope's and George Murphy's were combined to fit Astaire, Lyda Roberti's was played by Miss Rogers (with a Lyda Roberti accent), Ray Middleton's by Randolph Scott, Fay Templeton's by Helen Westley, and Sydney Greenstreet's by Ferdinand Munier. The story kept close to the original, as it told of what happens when former All-American halfback John Kent inherits his Aunt Minnie's elegant dress salon in Paris—called Roberta—and falls in love with exiled Russian Princess Stephanie, his aunt's assistant. The main departure in the plot was to provide a secondary, somewhat casual romance for John's friend, bandleader Huck Haines, and Lizzie Gatz, alias Countess Tanka Scharwenka, a nightclub singer (on stage she had been a vamp who momentarily distracted the play's hero). As did the stage production, the film ends up as a combination fashion show and musical entertainment. Four of the ten original songs

were retained in the movie, some with altered lyrics, to which were added two new pieces by Kern and lyricist Dorothy Fields, "I Won't Dance" and "Lovely To Look At."

In 1952 MGM offered a completely altered version of *Roberta* titled *Lovely To Look At,* which was directed by Mervyn LeRoy. In this release, three Broadway producers (Howard Keel, Red Skelton, and Gower Champion) go to Paris, where Skelton has inherited half of Madame Roberta's dress salon. Business and romantic complications involve Kathryn Grayson and Marge Champion, two sisters who own the other half of the salon, and Ann Miller, an American dancer. This edition retained five of the original Kern-Harbach songs, the two added in 1935, plus two pieces cut from the Broadway production, "Clementina" and "An Armful of Trouble," which with new Fields lyrics, became "Lafayette" and "The Most Exciting Night."

Roberti, Lyda, actress, singer; b. Warsaw, May 20, 1909; d. Los Angeles, March 12, 1938. Excessively energetic blonde dynamo whose piquant Polish accent lent itself to frequent imitation. Miss Roberti, who also appeared in vaudeville and on Broadway, introduced "Take a Number from One to Ten."

1932	Dancers in the Dark (*Fanny Zabowolsky*)
	The Kid from Spain (*Rosalie*)
1933	Torch Singer (*Dora*)
1934	College Rhythm (*Mimi*)
1935	George White's Scandals (*Manya*)
	Big Broadcast of 1936 (*Countess Ysobel de Nargila*)
1937	Nobody's Baby (*Lena*)

Roberts, Alan, composer, lyricist; b. Brooklyn, March 12, 1905; d. Hollywood, Jan. 14, 1966. Roberts wrote songs for Columbia films with composer-lyricists Doris Fisher ("Put the Blame on Mame" for Rita Hayworth in *Gilda*) and Lester Lee.

1946	Gilda (Fisher)
	The Thrill of Brazil (Fisher)
	Singin' in the Corn (Fisher)
	Talk About a Lady (Fisher)
1947	Cigarette Girl (Fisher)
	Down to Earth (Fisher)
	When a Girl's Beautiful (Lee)
1949	Ladies of the Chorus (Lee)
	Slightly French (Lee)

Robeson, Paul (Leroy Bustill), actor, singer; b. Princeton, NJ, April 9, 1898; d. Philadelphia, Jan. 23, 1976. Actor of commanding presence and great intensity, with rich, resonant bass voice, who sang in film dramas made in both the US and Britain. In his one true musical, *Show Boat,* he re-created the role he had played in London and the first NY revival. Also concert and recording artist. Bib: *Paul Robeson, the American Othello* by Edwin Hoyt (1967); *Paul Robeson, All American* by Dorothy Gilliam (1976).

1933	The Emperor Jones (*Brutus Jones*)
1935	Sanders of the River (Eng.) (*Bosambo*)
	Song of Freedom (Eng.) (*John Zinga*)
	Show Boat (*Joe*)
1937	King Solomon's Mines (Eng.) (*Umbopa*)
1941	Proud Valley (Eng.) (*David Goliath*)

Robin, Leo, lyricist; b. Pittsburgh, April 6, 1900. Under contract to Paramount, Robin and his most frequent partner, composer Ralph Rainger, were responsible for such early Bing Crosby hits as "Please," "June in January," "Love in Bloom," "With Every Breath I Take," "My Heart and I," "Blue Hawaii," "I Have Eyes," and "The Funny Old Hills." The team also wrote "I Don't Want To Make History," "Thanks for the Memory," "Whispers in the Dark," "What Have You Got That Gets Me?," and "Faithful Forever." Other composers with whom Robin worked in Hollywod were Richard A. Whiting ("Louise," "My Ideal," "One Hour with You"); Whiting and W. Franke Harling ("Beyond the Blue Horizon"); Victor Schertzinger; Newell Chase; Oscar Straus ("We Will Always Be Sweethearts"); Frederick Hollander ("Moonlight and Shadows"); Lewis Gensler ("Love Is Just Around the Corner"); Nacio Herb Brown; Harry Warren ("A Journey to a Star," "No Love, No Nothin'," "Zing a Little Zong"); Jerome Kern ("In Love in Vain"); Arthur Schwartz ("A Gal in Calico," "Oh But I Do"); Johnny Green; Harold Arlen ("For Every Man There's a Woman," "Hooray for Love"); Jule Styne; and Nicholas Brodszky. Robin also worked with co-lyricists Sam Coslow and B. G. DeSylva.

Among singers who introduced songs with Robin lyrics were Maurice Chevalier, Jeanette MacDonald, Shirley Temple, Dorothy Lamour, Gladys Swarthout, Ethel Merman, John Boles, Alice Faye, Dennis Morgan, Tony Martin, Deanna Durbin, Dick Powell, and Betty Grable. Robin also wrote lyrics for seven Broadway musicals, of which *Hit the Deck* (with Vincent Youmans and Clifford Grey) and *Gentlemen Prefer Blondes* (Jule Styne) were filmed. (Died Los Angeles, Dec. 29, 1984.)

1929	Innocents of Paris (Whiting)
	Fashions in Love (Schertzinger)
	The Dance of Life (Whiting-Coslow)
1930	Hit the Deck (Youmans-Grey)
	The Vagabond King (Chase-Coslow)
	Monte Carlo (Whiting, Harling)
	Playboy of Paris (Whiting, Chase)
1932	One Hour with You (Whiting; Straus)
1933	A Bedtime Story (Rainger)
	International House (Rainger)
	My Weakness (Whiting-DeSylva)
	Torch Singer (Rainger)
	The Way to Love (Rainger)
1934	Little Miss Marker (Rainger)
	Here Is My Heart (Rainger; Gensler)
1935	Rumba (Rainger)
	Four Hours To Kill (Rainger)
	Big Broadcast of 1936 (Rainger)
	Millions in the Air (Rainger)
1936	Rose of the Rancho (Rainger)
	Palm Springs (Rainger)
	Three Cheers for Love (Rainger)
	Big Broadcast of 1937 (Rainger; Whiting)
	College Holiday (Rainger)
1937	Waikiki Wedding (Rainger)
1938	Big Broadcast of 1938 (Rainger)
	Give Me a Sailor (Rainger)
	Artists and Models Abroad (Rainger)
1939	Paris Honeymoon (Rainger)
	Gulliver's Travels (Rainger)
1941	Tall, Dark and Handsome (Rainger)
	Moon Over Miami (Rainger)
	Rise and Shine (Rainger)
	Cadet Girl (Rainger)
1942	My Gal Sal (Rainger)
	Footlight Serenade (Rainger)
1943	Coney Island (Rainger)
	Riding High (Rainger)
	Wintertime (Brown)
	The Gang's All Here (Warren)
1944	Greenwich Village (Brown)
1946	Centennial Summer (Kern)
	The Time, the Place and the Girl (Schwartz)
1947	Something in the Wind (Green)
1948	Casbah (Arlen)
	That Lady in Ermine (Hollander)
1951	Meet Me After the Show (Styne)
	Two Tickets to Broadway (Styne)
1952	Just for You (Warren)
1953	Gentlemen Prefer Blondes (Styne)
	Small Town Girl (Brodszky)
	Latin Lovers (Brodszky)
1955	Hit the Deck (Youmans-Grey)
	My Sister Eileen (Styne)
1957	Ruggles of Red Gap (tv) (Styne)

Robinson, (William Luther) Bill ("Bojangles"), dancer, actor, choreographer; b. Richmond, Va., May

25, 1878; d. New York, Nov. 25, 1949. Robinson's distinctive, deceptively easy-going tapping made him a vaudeville and Broadway headliner before he became Shirley Temple's dancing partner in four Fox movies (in a fifth, he was her choreographer). He also appeared opposite Lena Horne in *Stormy Weather*.

1930 Dixiana (specialty)
1935 The Little Colonel (*Walker*)
Hooray for Love (*Bill*)
The Littlest Rebel (*Uncle Billy*)
Big Broadcast of 1936 (specialty)
1936 Dimples (chor. only)
1938 Rebecca of Sunnybrook Farm (*Aloysius*)
Just Around the Corner (*Corporal Jones*)
1943 Stormy Weather (*Bill Williamson*)

Rodgers, Richard (Charles), composer; b. New York, June 28, 1902; d. New York, Dec. 30, 1979. Rodgers was the stage's most influential and durable composer, with a boundless flow of melody heard throughout a career spanning almost 60 years. Beginning in 1919, his music was mated to the witty, incisive lyrics of Lorenz Hart, with whom he wrote the scores for 26 musicals in New York and three in London; from 1943 to 1959, his second successful partnership, with the more sentimental and idiomatic Oscar Hammerstein II, resulted in nine Broadway shows. Of Rodgers' total theatre output, the following musicals were transferred to the screen (and often transformed entirely): *Present Arms* (retitled *Leathernecking*, with augmented songs); *Spring Is Here; Heads Up!; Ever Green* (augmented songs); *Jumbo; On Your Toes* (ballet and background music only); *Babes in Arms* (augmented songs); *I Married an Angel* (some lyrics by Robert Wright and George Forrest); *The Boys from Syracuse; Higher and Higher* (non-Rodgers & Hart score); *Pal Joey* (added Rodgers & Hart songs); *Oklahoma!; Carousel; South Pacific; The King and I; Flower Drum Song;* and *The Sound of Music* (plus two new Rodgers songs).

With Hart, Rodgers wrote the scores for three innovative screen musicals: *Love Me Tonight* ("Isn't It Romantic?," "Lover," "Mimi"); *The Phantom President* ("Give Her a Kiss"); and *Hallelujah, I'm a Bum* ("You Are Too Beautiful"). The partners also wrote "Down by the River," "Soon," and "It's Easy To Remember" for *Mississippi. Words and Music,* with Tom Drake as Rodgers, was a film bio of the team. With Hammerstein, Rodgers was responsible for the songs in *State Fair* ("It's a Grand Night for Singing," "It Might as Well

Be Spring"), and, by himself, provided added songs for the 1962 version. Rodgers and Hammerstein also collaborated on the television musical *Cinderella* ("Do I Love You Because You're Beautiful?"), which was subsequently remade. Among those who have sung Rodgers music in films and television are Maurice Chevalier, Jeanette MacDonald, George M. Cohan, Al Jolson, Bing Crosby, Jessie Matthews, Judy Garland, Allan Jones, Ann Miller, Nelson Eddy, Dick Haymes, Vivian Blaine, Mickey Rooney, Perry Como, Lena Horne, Gordon MacRae, Shirley Jones, Julie Andrews, Frank Sinatra, Mitzi Gaynor, Alice Faye, Pat Boone, and Bobby Darin. Bib: *The Rodgers and Hart Song Book* (1951); *The Rodgers and Hammerstein Song Book* (1958); *Musical Stages* by Rodgers (1975); *Rodgers and Hart* by Samuel Marx & Jan Clayton (1976); *The Sound of Their Music* by Frederick Nolan (1978); *Rodgers and Hammerstein Fact Book* ed. Stanley Green (1980); *The Rodgers and Hammerstein Story* by Green (1980).

1930 Spring Is Here (Hart)
Leathernecking (Hart)
Heads Up (Hart)
1931 The Hot Heiress (Hart)
1932 Love Me Tonight (Hart)
The Phantom President (Hart)
1933 Hallelujah, I'm a Bum (Hart) (also *photographer*)
1934 Hollywood Party (Hart)
Evergreen (Eng.) (Hart)
1935 Mississippi (Hart)
1936 Dancing Pirate (Hart)
1938 Fools for Scandal (Hart)
1939 Babes in Arms (Hart)
On Your Toes
1940 The Boys from Syracuse (Hart)
Too Many Girls (Hart)
1941 They Met in Argentina (Hart)
1942 I Married an Angel (Hart; Wright, Forrest)
1945 State Fair (Hammerstein)
1948 Words and Music (Hart)
1955 Oklahoma! (Hammerstein)
1956 Carousel (Hammerstein)
The King and I (Hammerstein)
1957 Pal Joey (Hart)
Cinderella (tv) (Hammerstein)
1958 South Pacific (Hammerstein)
1961 Flower Drum Song (Hammerstein)
1962 State Fair (Hammerstein; also lyr.)
Jumbo (Hart)
1965 The Sound of Music (Hammerstein; also lyr.)
Cinderella (tv) (Hammerstein)
1967 Androcles and the Lion (tv) (also lyr.)

Rogers, Charles "Buddy," actor, singer; b. Olathe, Kansas, Aug. 13, 1904. Clean-cut, wavy-haired leading man of early Paramount talkies, often teamed with Nancy Carroll. Rogers, who also led a dance band, introduced "My Future Just Passed." He was married to Mary Pickford.

1929	Close Harmony (*Al West*)
1930	Paramount on Parade (specialty)
	Safety in Numbers (*Bill Reynolds*)
	Follow Thru (*Jerry Downs*)
	Heads Up (*Jack Mason*)
1933	Best of Enemies (*Jimmy Hartman*)
	Take a Chance (*Kenneth Raleigh*)
1935	Old Man Rhythm (*Johnny Roberts*)
	Dance Band (Eng.) (*Buddy Morgan*)
1937	This Way Please (*Brad Morgan*)
	Let's Make a Night of It (Eng.) (*Jack Kent*)

Rogers, Ginger (née Virginia Katherine McMath), actress, singer, dancer; b. Independence, Mo., July 16, 1911. Former Charleston dancer and Broadway ingenue who appeared in Paramount and Warner musicals before winning eternal glory at RKO as Fred Astaire's lithesome dancing lady in nine films (plus one at MGM). Miss Rogers, who also had a successful career in nonmusicals (*Kitty Foyle, Roxie Hart*), helped introduce—as singer and/or dancer—such songs as "Shuffle Off to Buffalo" (*42nd Street*); "We're in the Money" (*Gold Diggers of 1933*); "Did You Ever See a Dream Walking?" (*Sitting Pretty*); "The Carioca" (*Flying Down to Rio*); "The Continental" (*The Gay Divorcee*); "I Won't Dance," "Lovely To Look At" (*Roberta*); "Isn't This a Lovely Day?," "Cheek to Cheek," "The Piccolino" (*Top Hat*); "Let Yourself Go," "I'm Putting All My Eggs in One Basket," "Let's Face the Music and Dance" (*Follow the Fleet*); "A Fine Romance," "Never Gonna Dance" (*Swing Time*); "Let's Call the Whole Thing Off," "They All Laughed," "Shall We Dance?" (*Shall We Dance*); "Change Partners," "I Used to Be Color Blind" (*Carefree*); and "Suddenly It's Spring" (*Lady in the Dark*). Miss Rogers has continued to perform in nightclubs and in theatres. Bib: *Ginger* by Dick Richards (1969); *The Fred Astaire and Ginger Rogers Book* by Arlene Croce (1972); *Films of Ginger Rogers* by Homer Dickens (1975).

Asterisk indicates appearance with Mr. Astaire:

1930	Young Man of Manhattan (*Puff Randolph*)
	Queen High (*Polly Rockwell*)
	The Sap from Syracuse (*Ellen Saunders*)
	Follow the Leader (*Mary Brennan*)

1933	42nd Street (*"Anytime" Annie Lowell*)
	Gold Diggers of 1933 (*Fay Fortune*)
	Sitting Pretty (*Dorothy*)
	Flying Down to Rio* (*Honey Hale*)
1934	Twenty Million Sweethearts (*Peggy Cornell*)
	The Gay Divorcee* (*Mimi Glossop*)
1935	Roberta* (*"Countess" Tanka Scharwenka*)
	Top Hat* (*Dale Tremont*)
	In Person (*Carol Corliss*)
1936	Follow the Fleet* (*Sherry Martin*)
	Swing Time* (*Penny Carrol*)
1937	Shall We Dance* (*Linda Keene*)
1938	Having Wonderful Time (*Teddy Shaw*)
	Carefree* (*Amanda Cooper*)
1939	The Story of Vernon and Irene Castle* (*Irene Castle*)
1944	Lady in the Dark (*Liza Elliott*)
1949	The Barkleys of Broadway* (*Dinah Barkley*)
1965	Cinderella (tv) (*Queen*)

Romberg, Sigmund, composer; b. Nagy Kaniza, Hungary, July 29, 1887; d. New York, Nov. 10, 1951. Romberg's name was synonymous with the florid, sentimental, heroic operettas that flourished on Broadway during the 1920s. His five most successful works were all adapted—and adjusted—for the screen: *Maytime* (new story, with only one Romberg song retained); *The Student Prince* (two versions, the first silent); *The Desert Song* (three versions); *The New Moon* (two versions, the first with different story); and *Up in Central Park*. Among Romberg's theatre collaborators were lyricists Rida Johnson Young, Dorothy Donnelly, Otto Harbach, Oscar Hammerstein II, and Dorothy Fields. In Hollywood, where he wrote mostly with Hammerstein ("You Will Remember Vienna," "When I Grow Too Old To Dream"), Romberg also was associated with Gus Kahn and Paul Francis Webster. Those who sang his songs on the screen included John Boles, Grace Moore, Lawrence Tibbett, Evelyn Laye, Ramon Novarro, Jeanette MacDonald, Nelson Eddy, Dennis Morgan, Deanna Durbin, Kathryn Grayson, Gordon MacRae, and Mario Lanza (voice only). Film bio: *Deep in My Heart,* with José Ferrer as Romberg. Bib: *Deep in My Heart* by Elliott Arnold (1949).

1929	The Desert Song (Harbach, Hammerstein)
1930	Viennese Nights (Hammerstein)
	New Moon (Hammerstein)
1931	Children of Dreams (Hammerstein)
1935	The Night Is Young (Hammerstein)
1938	The Girl of the Golden West (Kahn)
1940	New Moon (Hammerstein)

1943 The Desert Song (Harbach, Hammerstein)
1948 Up in Central Park (Fields)
1953 The Desert Song (Harbach, Hammerstein)
1954 The Student Prince (Donnelly; Webster)
 Deep in My Heart (misc.)

Romero, Cesar (Julius), actor, dancer; b. New York, Feb. 15, 1907. Romero played the suave Latin—or Latin type—in Fox musicals with Sonja Henie, Alice Faye, Carmen Miranda, Betty Grable, and Vera-Ellen. In all, he appeared in over 80 films.

1935 Metropolitan (*Niki Baroni*)
1938 Happy Landing (*Duke Sargent*)
 My Lucky Star (*George Cabot Jr.*)
1941 Tall, Dark and Handsome (*Shep Morrison*)
 The Great American Broadcast (*Bruce Chadwick*)
 Weekend in Havana (*Monty Blanco*)
1942 Orchestra Wives (*Sinjin*)
 Springtime in the Rockies (*Victor*)
1943 Coney Island (*Joe Rocco*)
 Wintertime (*Brad Barton*)
1947 Carnival in Costa Rica (*Pepe Castro*)
1948 That Lady in Ermine (*Mario*)
1949 The Beautiful Blonde from Bashful Bend (*Blackie Jobero*)
1951 Happy Go Lovely (*John Frost*)
1960 Pepe (guest bit)

Rooney, Mickey (né Joseph Yule, Jr.), actor, singer, dancer; b. Brooklyn, Sept. 23, 1920. Energetic, diminutive actor and entertainer often seen in film musicals as a youthful, pugnacious, irrepressible, multitalented theatrical aspirant. He co-starred with Judy Garland in a series of "barnyard musicals," including *Babes in Arms* (singing "Good Morning"), *Strike Up the Band* ("Our Love Affair"), and *Babes on Broadway* ("How About You?"), and he also introduced "The Stanley Steamer" in *Summer Holiday.* His screen image will forever be associated with that of Andy Hardy, a role he played in 14 films, some of them with songs. In 1979, Rooney made a successful Broadway debut in *Sugar Babies.* Ava Gardner was the first and Martha Vickers the third of his eight wives. Bib: *I.E.* by Rooney & Roger Kahn (1965).

1933 Broadway to Hollywood (*Ted Hackett III*)
1934 I Like It That Way (bit)
1935 Reckless (bit)
1938 Love Finds Andy Hardy (*Andy Hardy*)
1939 Babes in Arms (*Micky Moran*)
1940 Andy Hardy Meets Debutante (*Andy Hardy*)
 Strike Up the Band (*Jimmy Connors*)

1941 Babes on Broadway (*Tommy Williams*)
1943 Girl Crazy (*Danny Churchill*)
 Thousands Cheer (specialty)
1948 Summer Holiday (*Richard Miller*)
 Words and Music (*Larry Hart*)
1951 The Strip (*Stanley Maxton*)
1952 Sound Off (*Mike Donnelly*)
1957 Pinocchio (tv) (*Pinocchio*)
1958 All Ashore (*Moby Dickerson*)
1965 How to Stuff a Wild Bikini (*Peachy Keane*)
1977 Pete's Dragon (*Lampie*)
1978 The Magic of Lassie (*wrestling manager*)

"Rosalie" Music & lyric by Cole Porter. West Point cadet Nelson Eddy's romantic pitch to Vassar student Eleanor Powell, as he serenaded her beneath her dormitory window in *Rosalie* (MGM 1937); later sung in film by chorus as Miss Powell danced before a cast of thousands. In a letter to orchestra leader Paul Whiteman regarding this song, Cole Porter once wrote, "It was very important that the title song should be good. I wrote six before I handed one in, but I was very proud of No. 6. Louis B. Mayer asked me to play the score for him and when I was finished, he said to me, 'I like everything in the score except that song "Rosalie." It's too highbrow. Forget you are writing for Nelson Eddy and simply give us a good popular song.' So I took 'Rosalie No. 6' home and in hate wrote 'Rosalie No. 7.' Mayer was delighted with it, but I still resented my No. 6 having been thrown out, which to me seemed so much better. Six months later when the song became a hit, I saw Irving Berlin and he congratulated me on it. I said to him, 'Thanks a lot but I wrote that song in hate and I still hate it.' To which Irving replied, 'Listen, kid, take my advice. Never hate a song that's sold a half million copies.'" "Rosalie" was also sung by street singers in *Night and Day* (Warner 1946).

Rose Marie (1936). Music mostly by Rudolf Friml & Herbert Stothart; lyrics mostly by Otto Harbach & Oscar Hammerstein II; screenplay by Frances Goodrich, Albert Hackett, and Alice Duer Miller, loosely based on Broadway musical by Friml, Stothart, Harbach, and Hammerstein.

 An MGM film produced by Hunt Stromberg; directed by W. S. Van Dyke; opera sequences staged by William Von Wymetal; choreography, Chester Hale; art director, Cedric Gibbons; costumes, Adrian; music director, Herbert Stothart; music adaptation, Stothart; cameraman, William Daniels; editor, Blanche Sewell.

 Cast: Jeanette MacDonald (*Marie De Flor*); Nelson

Eddy (*Sgt. Bruce*); James Stewart (*John Flower*); Reginald Owen (*Myerson*); Allan Jones (*opera singer*); Alan Mowbray (*Premier*); David Niven (*Teddy*); Gilda Gray (*Belle*); George Regas (*Boniface*); Una O'Connor (*Anna*); Herman Bing (*Daniels*); Halliwell Hobbes (*Gordon*); Paul Porcasi (*Emil*).

Songs & Arias: "Juliette's Waltz" (Gounod-Barbier, Carré, from *Roméo et Juliette*) - MacDonald/ Opera montage - MacDonald, Jones/ "Pardon, Me, Madame" (Stothart-Gus Kahn) - MacDonald/ "The Mounties" (music with Stothart) - Eddy, Mounties/ "Dinah" (Harry Akst-Sam Lewis, Joe Young) - MacDonald/ "Some of These Days" (Shelton Brooks) - MacDonald, Gray/ "Rose Marie" - Eddy/ "Totem Tom-Tom" (music with Stothart) - Indians/ "Just for You" (music with Stothart-Kahn) - Eddy/ "Indian Love Call" - Eddy, MacDonald.

Since *Naughty Marietta* had proved profitable in 1935, MGM naturally decided to mine other Broadway operetta lodes using much the same creative staff. For *Rose Marie,* based on the 1924 hit starring Mary Ellis and Dennis King, there were the same producer, director, writers (two out of four anyway), new lyricist, art director, costume designer, music director and adapter, cameraman, and editor. But instead of being conceived as a vehicle for the previous film's Jeanette MacDonald and Nelson Eddy, the movie was initially planned with Grace Moore in the female lead. It was only when she proved unavailable that Miss MacDonald was signed to to appear with Eddy.

As a film, *Rose Marie* bore only a tenuous relationship to the original stage production. On Broadway, it told of the romance between singer Rose-Marie La Flamme, who entertains in a backwoods Saskatchewan hotel, and fur trapper Jim Kenyon. After being accused of a murder, Jim is eventually cleared when Sgt. Malone of the Mounties gets his man—who turns out to be Wanda the Indian maid. In the 1936 screen adaptation, Marie De Flor is a Canadian prima donna who assumes the name of Rose Marie after journeying incognito to the Canadian Rockies (the actual shooting was near Lake Tahoe, Nevada) in search of her errant brother, John Flower (played by James Stewart), who is wanted for murder. The diva meets Sgt. Bruce of the Mounties, they fall in love, then have a tearful parting—but not for long—when the stalwart officer does his duty and arrests Flower. (An earlier variation on this plot was seen in the 1929 film, *Rio Rita,* in which John Boles played Capt. James Stewart of the Texas Rangers.) Only four songs were retained from the 14 written for the Broadway op-

eretta, with the new score augmented by opera arias, pop standards, and two numbers written for the film.

The MacDonald-Eddy movie was the second of three MGM releases based on the same source. In 1928 Joan Crawford and James Murray were in a silent version directed by Lucien Hubbard; in 1954 Ann Blyth, Fernando Lamas, and Howard Keel co-starred in a CinemaScope color version (the first musical in that process), directed by Mervyn LeRoy. Both these films were more faithful to the 1924 Harbach-Hammerstein libretto than the one made in 1936. The LeRoy *Rose Marie* retained the same original four songs that MacDonald and Eddy sang, and added four new ones by Rudolf Friml and Paul Francis Webster, plus a comic number for Bert Lahr. Though the operetta's title was hyphenated on stage it went unhyphenated in all three screen editions.

***Rose of Washington Square*. See *Funny Girl*.**

Ross, Diana, singer, actress; b. Detroit, March 26, 1944. Slim, statuesque singer who has scored successes on records, in nightclubs, and in theatres.

1972   Lady Sings the Blues (*Billie Holiday*)
1978   The Wiz (*Dorothy*)

Ross, Herbert, director, choreographer; b. Brooklyn, May 13, 1927. Former Broadway dancer and choreographer who became Hollywood director of musicals and comedies.

Mr. Ross was choreographer of the following; asterisk indicates he was also director:
1954   Carmen Jones
1967   Doctor Dolittle
1968   Funny Girl (also co-dir.)
1969   Goodbye, Mr. Chips*
1975   Funny Lady*
1981   Pennies from Heaven* (also co-prod.)
1984   Footloose (dir. only)

Ross, Jerry (né Jerold Rosenberg), composer, lyricist; b. The Bronx, March 9, 1926; d. New York, Nov. 11, 1955. Ross and his co-composer-lyricist Richard Adler had two Broadway successes that were adapted to the screen.

1957   The Pajama Game
1958   Damn Yankees

Ross, (Lancelot) Lanny, actor, singer; b. Seattle, Jan. 19, 1906. Cleancut, blond leading man with flashing smile and near-operatic voice who introduced "Stay as

Sweet as You Are'' and ''Faithful Forever.'' Also starred on radio.

1934 Melody in Spring (*John Craddock*)
College Rhythm (*Larry Stacey*)
1938 The Lady Objects (*William Hayward*)
1939 Gulliver's Travels (voice of *Prince David*)
1943 Stage Door Canteen (guest bit)

Ross, Shirley (née Bernice Gaunt), actress, singer; b. Omaha, Jan. 7, 1909; d. Menlo Park, Cal., March 9, 1975. Red-headed romantic singing lead in Paramount films who, with Bob Hope, introduced ''Thanks for the Memory,'' ''Two Sleepy People,'' and ''The Lady's in Love with You.'' Other screen appearances were with Bing Crosby, Robert Cummings, and Fred MacMurray. Miss Ross was also in the Harlem nightclub scene in *Manhattan Melodrama* singing ''The Bad in Every Man'' (later known as ''Blue Moon'').

1934 Hollywood Party (*Shirley Ross*)
The Merry Widow (*girl at Maxim's*)
1936 San Francisco (*Trixie*)
Big Broadcast of 1937 (*Gwen Holmes*)
1937 Hideaway Girl (*Toni Ainsworth*)
Waikiki Wedding (*Georgia Smith*)
Blossoms on Broadway (*Sally Shea*)
1938 Big Broadcast of 1938 (*Cleo Fielding*)
1939 Paris Honeymoon (*Barbara Wayne*)
Some Like It Hot (*Lily Racquet*)
Café Society (*Bells Browne*)
1945 A Song for Miss Julie (*Valerie*)

Roth, Lillian (née Lillian Rutstein), actress, singer; b. Boston, Dec. 13, 1910; d. New York, May 12, 1980. Round-faced, dimpled, dark-haired song belter whose confessional autobiography *I'll Cry Tomorrow* (1945) became an MGM film starring Susan Hayward. A headliner in vaudeville and on Broadway, Miss Roth appeared in early Paramount talkies and introduced ''Sing You Sinners.''

1929 Illusion (singer)
The Love Parade (*Lulu*)
1930 The Vagabond King (*Huguette*)
Honey (*Cora Falkner*)
Paramount on Parade (specialty)
Animal Crackers (*Arabella Rittenhouse*)
Madam Satan (*Trixie*)
1933 Take a Chance (*Wanda Hale*)

Rubinstein, Artur, pianist; b. Lodz, Poland, Jan. 28, 1886. Renowned classical pianist whose US debut oc-

curred in 1906. Film appearances were limited to concerts. (Died Geneva, Dec. 20, 1982.)

1944 Follow the Boys
1946 I've Always Loved You (piano for Philip Dorn)
1947 Carnegie Hall
Song of Love (piano for Katharine Hepburn)
Night Song

Ruby, Harry (né Harry Rubinstein), composer, screenwriter; b. New York, Jan. 27, 1895; d. Los Angeles, Feb. 23, 1974. Ruby and his longtime partner, lyricist Bert Kalmar, wrote the scores for nine Broadway musicals, including three that were filmed: *The Ramblers* (retitled *The Cuckoos*), *Animal Crackers* (starring the Marx Brothers), and *Top Speed*. They wrote two other Marx Brothers movies, *Horse Feathers* and *Duck Soup*, and their songs were also sung on the screen by Bert Wheeler (''I Love You So Much''), Bing Crosby (''Three Little Words''), Eddie Cantor, Judy Garland, and Louis Armstrong (''A Kiss To Build a Dream On,'' written with Oscar Hammerstein II). In Hollywood, Ruby also wrote with Rube Bloom (''Give Me the Simple Life,'' introduced by June Haver and John Payne) and Ernesto Lecuona. Film bio: *Three Little Words*, with Red Skelton as Ruby.

Unless otherwise noted, all songs for following written with Mr. Kalmar; asterisk indicates partners also wrote script:
1930 The Cuckoos
Animal Crackers
Top Speed
Check and Double Check
1932 Horse Feathers *
The Kid from Spain *
1933 Duck Soup *
1934 Hips Hips Hooray *
1936 Walking on Air *
1938 Everybody Sing
1946 Wake Up and Dream (Bloom)
1947 Carnival in Costa Rica (Lecuona)
1950 Three Little Words (also *baseball player*)
1952 Lovely to Look At (script only)

Ruggles, (Charles Sherman) Charlie, actor; b. Los Angeles, Feb. 8, 1886; d. Santa Monica, Cal., Dec. 23, 1970. Slight, stammering, dapper Charlie Ruggles was often seen as Mary Boland's henpecked husband in Paramount comedies. The brother of director Wesley Ruggles, he made his stage debut in 1906 and appeared in over 80 films.

1929 Battle of Paris (*Zizi*)
1930 Roadhouse Nights (*Willie Bindbugel*)

Young Man of Manhattan (*Shorty Ross*)
Queen High (*T. Boggs Johns*)
1931 The Smiling Lieutenant (*Max*)
1932 One Hour with You (*Adolph*)
This Is the Night (*Bunny West*)
Love Me Tonight (*Vicomte Gilbert deVareze*)
1933 Melody Cruise (*Pete Wells*)
Girl Without a Room (*Vergil Crock*)
1934 Melody in Spring (*Warren Blodgett*)
1935 Big Broadcast of 1936 (specialty)
1936 Anything Goes (*Moon-Face Mooney*)
Hearts Divided (*Sen. Henry Ruggles*)
1937 Turn Off the Moon (*Elliott Dinwiddy*)
1938 Breaking the Ice (*Samuel Terwilliger*)
1939 Balalaika (*Nicki Popoff*)
1941 Go West, Young Lady (*Jim Pendergast*)
1945 Incendiary Blonde (*Cherokee Jim*)
1948 Give My Regards to Broadway (*Toby Helford*)
1949 Look for the Silver Lining (*Pop Miller*)
1964 I'd Rather Be Rich (*Dr. Crandall*)

Ruggles, Wesley, director; b. Los Angeles, June 11, 1889; d. Santa Monica, Jan. 8, 1972. Hollywood veteran who began as member of the Keystone Kops, went on to direct many Paramount films. He was the brother of actor Charlie Ruggles.

1929 Street Girl
1930 Honey
1933 College Humor
I'm No Angel
1934 Bolero
Shoot the Works
1938 Sing You Sinners (also prod.)
1946 London Town (Eng.) (Also script)

"Rumble Rumble Rumble" Music & lyric by Frank Loesser. Betty Hutton's spirited complaint—lodged in *The Perils of Pauline* (Par. 1947)—about the nerve-racking effects of a nonstop boogie-woogie pianist in the next apartment.

"Running Around in Circles Getting Nowhere." *See* **"Getting Nowhere"**

Russell, (Ernestine) Jane, actress; b. Bemidji, Minn., June 21, 1921. Excessively endowed, perpetually sneering actress who made much-publicized screen debut in Howard Hughes' *The Outlaw*. Major musicals were the two "Paleface" westerns with Bob Hope and *Gentlemen*

Prefer Blondes ("When Love Goes Wrong") with Marilyn Monroe.

1948 The Paleface (*Calamity Jane*)
1951 Double Dynamite (*Mildred Goodhue*)
1952 The Las Vegas Story (*Linda Rollins*)
Son of Paleface (*Mike Delroy*)
Road to Bali (guest bit)
1953 Gentlemen Prefer Blondes (*Dorothy Shaw*)
The French Line (*Mary Carson*)
1955 Gentlemen Marry Brunettes (*Bonnie Jones*)

Russell, Rosalind, actress; b. Waterbury, Conn., June 4, 1912; d. Beverly Hills, Nov. 28, 1976. Miss Russell's angular, well-tailored charms were much in evidence in such nonmusical films as *My Girl Friday, My Sister Eileen* (then repeating her role in its Broadway musical version called *Wonderful Town*), and *Auntie Mame*. Bib: *Life Is a Banquet* by Miss Russell (1977).

1934 The Night Is Young (*Countess Rafay*)
1935 Reckless (*Jo*)
1955 The Girl Rush (*Kay Holliday*)
1962 Gypsy (*Rose*)

Ryan, (Margaret Irene) Peggy, actress, dancer; b. Long Beach, Cal., Aug. 28, 1924. Former child performer in vaudeville who became Donald O'Connor's good-natured, unassuming dancing partner in 12 Universal musicals. Second of three husbands was Ray McDonald, her co-star in her last two films.

Asterisk indicates appearance with Mr. O'Connor:
1937 Top of the Town (*Peggy*)
1942 Private Buckaroo* (*Peggy*)
Give Out Sisters* (*Peggy*)
Get Hep to Love* (*Betty Blake*)
When Johnny Comes Marching Home* (*Dusty*)
1943 Mr. Big* (*Peggy*)
Top Man* (*Jane Warren*)
1944 Chip Off the Old Block* (*Peggy*)
Follow the Boys* (specialty)
This Is the Life* (*Sally McGuire*)
The Merry Monahans* (*Patsy Monahan*)
Babes on Swing Street (*Trudy Costello*)
Bowery to Broadway* (specialty)
1945 Here Come the Coeds (*Patty*)
Patrick the Great* (*Judy Watkins*)
That's the Spirit (*Sheila*)
On Stage Everybody (*Molly Sullivan*)
1949 There's a Girl in My Heart (*Sally Mullen*)
1952 All Ashore (*Gay Knight*)

S

Sakall, S. Z. (né Szoeke Szakall), actor; b. Budapest, Feb. 2, 1884; d. Hollywood, Feb. 12, 1955. Sakall was a tubby, nervous character comedian with an angelic smile who was nicknamed ''Cuddles'' because of his cuddly wattles that he slapped in moments of desperation. He acted in European films beginning in 1916, in Hollywood films beginning in 1940. Bib: *The Story of Cuddles* by Sakall (1953).

1930	Three Hearts in Waltz Time (Germany)
1940	The Lilac Domino (Eng.)
	It's a Date (*Carl Ober*)
	Spring Parade (*baker*)
1941	That Night in Rio (*Artur Penna*)
1942	Broadway (*Nick*)
	Yankee Doodle Dandy (*Schwab*)
	Seven Sweethearts (*Van Maaster*)
1943	Thank Your Lucky Stars (*Dr. Schlenna*)
	Wintertime (*Hjalmar Ostgaard*)
1944	Shine on Harvest Moon (*Poppa Karl*)
	Hollywood Canteen (guest bit)
1945	Wonder Man (*Schmidt*)
	The Dolly Sisters (*Uncle Latsie*)
1946	Cinderella Jones (*Gabriel Popik*)
	Two Guys from Milwaukee (*Count Oswald*)
	The Time, the Place and the Girl (*Ladislaus Cassel*)
1948	April Showers (*Curly*)
	Romance on the High Seas (*Laszlo Laszlo*)
1949	My Dream Is Yours (*Felix Hofer*)
	In the Good Old Summertime (*Otto Oberkugen*)
	Look for the Silver Lining (*Schendorff*)
	Oh You Beautiful Doll (*Fred Fisher*)
1950	The Daughter of Rosie O'Grady (*Miklos Toretzky*)
	Tea for Two (*J. Maxwell Blomhaus*)
1951	Lullaby of Broadway (*Adolph Hubbell*)
	Painting the Clouds with Sunshine (*Felix Hoff*)
1953	Small Town Girl (*Eric Schlemmer*)
1954	The Student Prince (*Josef Ruder*)

San Francisco (1936). Screenplay by Anita Loos & Robert Hopkins.

An MGM film produced by John Emerson & Bernard Hyman; directed by W. S. Van Dyke; choreography, Val Raset; art director, Cedric Gibbons; special effects, James Basevi; costumes, Adrian; music director, Herbert Stothart; orchestrations, Stothart; cameraman, Oliver T. Marsh; editor, Tom Held.

Cast: Clark Gable (*Blackie Norton*); Jeanette MacDonald (*Mary Blake*); Spencer Tracy (*Father Tim Mullin*); Jack Holt (*Jack Burley*); Ted Healy (*Matt*); Jessie Ralph (*Maisie Burley*); Margaret Irving (*Della Bailey*); Shirley Ross (*Trixie*); Harold Huber (*Babe*); Al Shean (''*Professor*'' *Herzen*); William Ricciardi (*Maestro Baldini*); Kenneth Harlan (*Chick*); Roger Imhof (*Alaska*); Charles Judels (*Tony*); Bert Roach (*Freddy Duane*); Warren Hymer (*Hazeltine*); Edgar Kennedy (*Sheriff*); Tandy MacKenzie (''*Faust*''); Tudor Williams (''*Mephistopheles*''); Vince Barnett (*drunk*).

Songs & Arias: ''Happy New Year'' (Bronislaw Kaper, Walter Jurmann-Gus Kahn) - Ross, chorus/ ''San Francisco'' (Kaper-Kahn) - MacDonald/ ''A Heart That's Free'' (Alfred Robyn-T. Reilley) - MacDonald/ ''The Holy City'' (F. E. Weatherly-Stephen Adams) -MacDonald, boys' choir/ ''Would You?'' (Nacio Herb Brown-Arthur Freed) - MacDonald/ ''Air des bijoux'' (Gounod-Barbier, Carré, *Faust*) - MacDonald/ ''Sempre libera'' (Verdi-Piave, *La Traviata*) - MacDonald, MacKenzie/ ''At a Georgia Camp Meeting'' (Kerry Mills) - dance by Negro minstrels/ ''Philippine Dance'' (Bob Carleton) - male trio/ ''Nearer My God to Thee'' (Lowell Mason-Sarah Adams) - MacDonald, quake victims/ ''The Battle Hymn of the Republic'' (William Steffe - Julia Ward Howe) - MacDonald, quake victims. Unused: ''The One I Love'' (Kaper, Jurmann-Kahn).

San Francisco, a prime example of that exceedingly limited film genre, the disaster musical, came into being primarily because co-authors Anita Loos and Robert Hopkins wanted to honor the brawling spirit of their native city. With the leading male character based on their friend, gambler and raconteur Wilson Mizner, they fashioned a tale, set in 1906, about Barbary Coast cabaret owner Blackie Norton and his love for prim prima donna Mary Blake. After alternating between singing rousing numbers at Blackie's Paradise Café and grand opera at the Tivoli Opera House, Mary—along with Blackie and their friend, Father Tim Mullin—is caught in the spectacularly reconstructed San Francisco earthquake. The three manage to survive the devastation which also serves to bring the irreverent Blackie back to God.

By teaming Jeanette MacDonald in the film with Clark Gable, MGM gave her the opportunity to prove she was a major star without the accustomed Nelson Eddy to sing with. Though the part of Blackie was written with Gable in mind, he was at first unavailable and another actor was scheduled. At the insistence of Miss MacDonald and director W. S. Van Dyke, however, production was delayed several months in order to accommodate Gable. Then, fearing his part subordinate to Miss MacDonald's, he insisted on additional scenes. But it was Spencer Tracy, in the supporting role of Father Tim, whose career got the biggest boost as a result of *San Francisco*.

So popular was *San Francisco* that Fox production head Darryl Zanuck wanted to borrow Gable and Jean Harlow from MGM to star in his own disaster epic, *In Old Chicago,* which would culminate in the fire of 1871. Miss Harlow's death put an end to negotiations, and Zanuck filmed his saga in 1937 with the studio's own Tyrone Power, Alice Faye, and Don Ameche. As did *San Francisco, In Old Chicago* combined a colorful period locale with political warfare, atmospheric songs (Miss Faye sang the stirring title number), and, as climax, an elaborately staged holocaust.

"San Francisco" Music by Bronislaw Kaper; lyric by Gus Kahn. Ringing tribute to the metropolis sung in *San Francisco* (MGM 1936) on four occasions: 1) by Jeanette MacDonald during a rehearsal at the Paradise cabaret, at first slowly then—ordered by Clark Gable— she sings with more spirit as the scene segues into a stage performance; 2) by the crowd (including Miss MacDonald, Shirley Ross, and Ted Healy) at an outdoor political rally; 3) by Miss MacDonald giving it the old razzmatazz in a competition—which she wins!—at the Chicken's Ball; and 4) by the survivors of the earthquake standing on a bluff overlooking the ruined city. Song was also sung by chorus in *Hello, Frisco, Hello* (Fox 1943).

San Juan, Olga, actress, singer, dancer; b. Brooklyn, March 16, 1927. Attractive performer, mostly in Paramount films, who also appeared on Broadway in *Paint Your Wagon.* Married actor Edmond O'Brien.

1944 Rainbow Island (*Moana*)
1945 Out of This World (specialty)
     Duffy's Tavern (specialty)
1946 Blue Skies (*Nita Nova*)
1947 Variety Girl (*Amber LaVonne*)
1948 The Countess of Monte Cristo (*Jenny*)
     One Touch of Venus (*Gloria*)
     Are You With It? (*Vivian Reilly*)
1949 The Beautiful Blonde from Bashful Bend (*Conchita*)

"Sand in My Shoes" Music by Victor Schertzinger; lyric by Frank Loesser. Connie Boswell, dreaming of Havana and a lost love, in *Kiss the Boys Goodbye* (Par. 1941).

Sandrich, Mark, director, producer; b. Brooklyn, 1900; d. Hollywood, March 5, 1945. Sandrich, who began his career in silent films, guided five of the Fred Astaire-Ginger Rogers musicals that Pandro S. Berman produced at RKO. At Paramount, where he was also a producer, he directed three films with Jack Benny and brought Astaire together with Bing Crosby in *Holiday Inn.*

One asterisk indicates film starring Astaire and Rogers; two asterisks indicate that Mr. Sandrich was also producer:
1933 Melody Cruise
1934 Hips Hips Hooray
     Cockeyed Cavaliers
     The Gay Divorcee*
1935 Top Hat*
1936 Follow the Fleet*
1937 Shall We Dance*
1938 Carefree*
1939 Man About Town
1940 Buck Benny Rides Again**
     Love Thy Neighbor**
1942 Holiday Inn**
1944 Here Come the Waves**

Sands, (Thomas Adrian) Tommy, actor, singer; b. Chicago, Aug. 27, 1937. Well-pompadoured, fleeting teenage singing rage, who married and divorced Nancy Sinatra.

1958 Sing, Boy, Sing (*Virgil Walker*)
     Mardi Gras (*Barry Denton*)
1961 Love in a Goldfish Bowl (*Gordon Slide*)
     Babes in Toyland (*Tom Piper*)

Santley, Joseph (né Joseph Mansfield), director; b. Salt Lake City, Jan. 10, 1889; d. W. Los Angeles, Aug. 8, 1971. Former leading man in Broadway musicals, Santley became a director mostly of low-budget Republic musicals. His best-remembered film was the Marx Brothers' *The Cocoanuts;* he also directed such performers as Ann Sothern, Judy Canova (four films), Gene Autry (three), Rita Hayworth, Tony Martin, and Bob Crosby.

1929 The Cocoanuts
1930 Swing High
1934 Loud Speaker
1936 Dancing Feet
       Laughing Irish Eyes
       Walking on Air
1938 Swing, Sister, Swing
1940 Music in My Heart
       Melody Ranch
       Melody and Moonlight
1941 Dancing on a Dime
       Sis Hopkins
       Rookies on Parade
       Puddin' Head
       Ice-Capades
1942 Yokel Boy
       Joan of Ozark
       Call of the Canyon
1943 Chatterbox
       Thumbs Up (also prod.)
       Sleepy Lagoon
       Here Comes Elmer
1944 Rosie the Riveter
       Three Little Sisters
       Brazil
1945 Earl Carroll Vanities
1949 Make Believe Ballroom
1950 When You're Smiling

Saville, Victor, director, producer; b. London, 1896; d. London, May 8, 1979. Saville had a 40-year career directing and producing films in Britain and the US. His most impressive musical was *Evergreen,* one of four with Jessie Matthews that he directed; in Hollywood he produced musicals with Jeanette MacDonald, Nelson Eddy, Risë Stevens, and Rita Hayworth.

Unless otherwise noted, Mr. Saville directed the following; asterisk indicates he was producer only:
1931 Sunshine Susie
1932 Love on Wheels (also script)
1933 The Good Companions
1934 Evergreen
       Evensong

1935 First a Girl
1936 It's Love Again
1940 Bitter Sweet (US)*
1941 Smilin' Through (US)*
       The Chocolate Soldier (US)*
1945 Tonight and Every Night (US) (also prod.)

"Say a Prayer for Me Tonight" Music by Frederick Loewe; lyric by Alan Jay Lerner. Nervous before her first grown-up date, Leslie Caron (with Betty Wand's voice) wistfully begged for divine help in *Gigi* (MGM 1958). The song was actually written two years before and intended for Julie Andrews to sing just before the ballroom scene in the Broadway musical *My Fair Lady,* but it was cut during the New Haven tryout.

"Say It" Music by Jimmy McHugh; lyric by Frank Loesser. Introduced in *Buck Benny Rides Again* (Par. 1940), by Ellen Drew, Virginia Dale, and Lillian Cornell as a singing trio in a nightclub.

"Says My Heart" Music by Burton Lane; lyric by Frank Loesser. In which the heart and the head offer conflicting romantic advice. Harriet Hilliard, accompanied by Harry Owens' orchestra, introduced the piece in the nightspot in *Cocoanut Grove* (Par. 1938). The song's melody bears a similarity to the Gershwin brothers' "Tell Me More" from the 1925 Broadway musical of the same name.

Schertzinger, Victor, director, composer, lyricist; b. Mahanoy City, Pa., April 8, 1890; d. Hollywood, Oct. 26, 1941. Schertzinger began his career as a composer by writing accompanying music for silent films beginning with *Civilization* in 1916. His first score for a sound film was *The Love Parade,* starring Maurice Chevalier and Jeanette MacDonald, with lyrics by Clifford Grey (including "My Love Parade"). Most of the musicals he directed—chiefly at Paramount and Columbia—featured his own songs, such as the title songs from Grace Moore's *One Night of Love* (with lyricist Gus Kahn) and Mary Martin's *Kiss the Boys Goodbye* (with Frank Loesser). Schertzinger also composed "Arthur Murray Taught Me Dancing in a Hurry," "Tangerine," and "I Remember You" (all with Johnny Mercer) for *The Fleet's In,* and wrote music and lyrics for "I Don't Want To Cry Anymore" for *Rhythm on the River.* Other lyric-writing partners were Leo Robin, Jack Scholl, Lew Brown, Johnny Burke, Walter Bullock, and Sidney Mitchell. As director, Schertzinger worked with Bing

Crosby on four musicals (including two "Road" journeys with Bob Hope and Dorothy Lamour); also Charles "Buddy" Rogers, Harry Richman, James Cagney, and Betty Hutton.

Unless otherwise noted, Mr. Schertzinger directed the following; a lyricist's name in parentheses indicates that Schertzinger was also the composer:

1929 The Love Parade (comp. only) (Grey)
      Fashions in Love (Robin)
1930 Paramount on Parade (co-dir.)
      Safety in Numbers
      Heads Up (also lyr.)
1934 One Night of Love (Kahn)
1935 Let's Live Tonight (Scholl)
      Love Me Forever (Kahn)
1936 The Music Goes Round (Brown)
      Follow Your Heart (Mitchell; Bullock)
1937 Something to Sing About (also lyr., script)
1939 The Mikado
1940 Road to Singapore (Burke)
      Rhythm on the River (also lyr.)
1941 Road to Zanzibar
      Kiss the Boys Goodbye (Loesser)
      Birth of the Blues
      Glamour Boy (comp. only) (Loesser)
1942 The Fleet's In (Mercer)

Schwartz, Arthur, composer, producer; b. Brooklyn, Nov. 25, 1900. Schwartz's minor-key melodies and bright up-tempo numbers, most often mated to poetic, witty lyrics by Howard Dietz, distinguished 18 stage musicals in New York and four in London. Though none of these was ever filmed, major Schwartz theatre songs were used in the movies *Dancing in the Dark* and *The Band Wagon*. Specifically written for the screen were such songs as "Love Isn't Born" and "They're Either Too Young or Too Old" (both with lyricist Frank Loesser); "Oh But I Do" and "A Gal in Calico" (both with Leo Robin); and "That's Entertainment" (with Dietz). Other film collaborators were Edward Heyman, Johnny Mercer, E. Y. Harburg, Dorothy Fields, Sammy Cahn, and, for television, Maxwell Anderson. Schwartz melodies were sung by, among others, Lawrence Tibbett, Lily Pons, Jeanette MacDonald, Bette Davis, Ann Sheridan, Dennis Morgan, Dean Martin, Bing Crosby, and Julie Andrews. (Died New York, Sept. 4, 1984.)

Asterisk indicates Mr. Schwartz was also producer:
1936 Under Your Spell (Dietz)
      That Girl from Paris (Heyman)
1941 Navy Blues (Mercer)
1942 Cairo (Harburg)

1943 Thank Your Lucky Stars (Loesser)
1944 Cover Girl (prod. only)
1946 Night and Day (prod. only)
      The Time, the Place and the Girl (Robin)
1949 Dancing in the Dark (Dietz)
1951 Excuse My Dust (Fields)
1953 Dangerous When Wet (Mercer)
      The Band Wagon (Dietz)
1955 You're Never Too Young (Cahn)
1956 High Tor (tv)* (Anderson)
1957 A Bell for Adano (tv)* (Dietz)

Scott, Hazel, pianist; b. Trinidad, WI, June 11, 1920. Nightclub pianist whose specialty was swinging the classics. (Died New York, Oct. 2, 1981.)

1943 Something To Shout About
      I Dood It
      The Heat's On
      Broadway Rhythm
1945 Rhapsody in Blue

"Search Is Through, The" Music by Harold Arlen; lyric by Ira Gershwin. Bing Crosby, in *The Country Girl* (Par. 1954), hears a phonograph record of a song he had recorded many years before and recalls, in a flashback, the day he cut the record and the tragedy that occurred right afterward. Later in the film, hearing the song again in a saloon, he drunkenly smashes his glass through the mirror behind the bar.

Seaton, George, director, producer, screenwriter; b. 1911; d. Beverly Hills, July 28, 1979. After his early career as radio's original Lone Ranger, Seaton became a Hollywood screenwriter with *A Day at the Races* in 1937. At Fox he was associated with producer William Perlberg for whom he wrote scripts and served as director; later the two became producing partners. Seaton directed Betty Grable and Bing Crosby in two musicals apiece.

Unless otherwise noted, Mr. Seaton was screenwriter of following; asterisk indicates he was also co-producer:
1937 A Day at the Races
1941 That Night in Rio
1943 Coney Island
1945 Diamond Horseshoe (also dir.)
1947 The Shocking Miss Pilgrim (also dir.)
1951 Aaron Slick from Punkin Crick *
1952 Somebody Loves Me (co-prod. only)
1953 Little Boy Lost * (also dir.)
1954 The Country Girl * (also dir.)

"Second Time Around, The" Music by James Van Heusen; lyric by Sammy Cahn. The advantages of mature romance revealed by Bing Crosby, as a widower in love with French teacher Nicole Maurey, in *High Time* (Par. 1960).

"Secret Love" Music by Sammy Fain; lyric by Paul Francis Webster. Introduced by Doris Day as the titular heroine of *Calamity Jane* (Warner 1953). In the scene, "Calám" (as she is called) joyously reveals her once hidden feelings toward Bill Hickock (Howard Keel) while leaning against a tree and then riding off on a horse.

"Seeing's Believing" Music by Harry Warren; lyric by Johnny Mercer. In *The Belle of New York* (MGM 1952), Fred Astaire, a rich New York playboy at the turn of the century, meets Salvation Army belle Vera-Ellen in Greenwich Village and immediately falls in love. Somehow this enables him to defy gravity and, once she leaves, he simply floats to the top of the Washington Square arch. There he sings of his newfound inamorata and dances merrily on and around the ledge.

Segal, Vivienne (Sonia), actress, singer; b. Philadelphia, April 19, 1897. Major Broadway singing star of operetta (*The Desert Song*) and musical comedy (*Pal Joey*) who made early Warner talkies.

1930	Song of the West (*Virginia Brown*)
	Bride of the Regiment (*Countess Anna Marie*)
	Golden Dawn (*Dawn*)
	Viennese Nights (*Elsa Hofner*)
1934	The Cat and the Fiddle (*Mlle. Odette*)

Seiter, William A., director; b. New York, June 10, 1891; d. Beverly Hills, July 26, 1964. Began as director of silent films, then worked at various studios with Irene Dunne, Fred Astaire and Ginger Rogers (*Roberta*), Astaire and Rita Hayworth (*You Were Never Lovelier*), Shirley Temple (two films), Alice Faye, Deanna Durbin (four), and Ava Gardner.

1929	Footlights and Fools
	Smiling Irish Eyes
1930	Sunny
	Kiss Me Again
1932	Girl Crazy
1933	Hello, Everybody
1935	Roberta
	In Person

1936	Dimples
	Stowaway
1937	This Is My Affair
	Life of the Party
	Life Begins in College
1938	Sally, Irene and Mary
	Thanks for Everything
1940	It's a Date
1941	Nice Girl?
1942	Broadway
	You Were Never Lovelier
1944	Four Jills in a Jeep
	Belle of the Yukon
1945	It's a Pleasure
	That Night with You
1947	I'll Be Yours
1948	Up in Central Park
	One Touch of Venus

"September in the Rain" Music by Harry Warren; lyric by Al Dubin. Recollection of a pluvial autumnal romance, written for *Stars Over Broadway* (Warner 1935) but used only for background. Two years later, however, James Melton sang it in Warner's *Melody for Two*.

"Serenade in Blue" Music by Harry Warren; lyric by Mack Gordon. In which a love affair is recalled everytime the "Serenade" is heard, with the hope that there still might be the possibility of a reconciliation. Introduced by Glenn Miller and his orchestra in *Orchestra Wives* (Fox 1942), with vocal by Lynn Bari (with Pat Friday's dubbed voice).

Seven Brides for Seven Brothers (1954). Music by Gene dePaul; lyrics by Johnny Mercer; screenplay by Frances Goodrich, Albert Hackett, and Dorothy Kingsley from story "The Sobbin' Women" by Stephen Vincent Benét suggested by Plutarch's *Lives*.

An MGM film produced by Jack Cummings; directed by Stanley Donen; choreography, Michael Kidd; art directors, Cedric Gibbons, Urie McCleary; costumes, Walter Plunkett; music director, Adolph Deutsch; orchestrations, Conrad Salinger, Alexander Courage, Leo Arnaud; cameraman, George Folsey; editor, Ralph Winters; Ansco Color; CinemaScope.

Cast: Jane Powell (*Milly Pontipee*); Howard Keel (*Adam Pontipee*); Jeff Richards (*Benjamin Pontipee*); Russ Tamblyn (*Gideon Pontipee*); Tommy Rall (*Frank Pontipee*); Marc Platt (*Daniel Pontipee*); Matt Mattox (vocals by Bill Lee) (*Caleb Pontipee*); Jacques d'Amboise (*Ephraim Pontipee*); Julie Newmeyer (Newmar) (*Dorcas Gaylin*); Virginia Gibson (*Liza*); Ruta Kilmonis (Lee) (*Ruth*); Kelly Brown (*Carl*); Nancy Kilgas (*Alice*); Betty Carr (*Sarah*); Norma Doggett (*Martha*).

Songs: ''Bless Your Beautiful Hide'' - Keel/ ''Wonderful, Wonderful Day'' - Powell/ ''When You're in Love'' - Powell, Keel/ ''Goin' Co'tin' '' - Powell, brothers/ ''House-Raising Dance'' - brothers, girls, city boys/ ''Lonesome Polecat'' - Mattox (Lee), brothers/ ''Sobbin' Women'' - Keel, brothers/ ''June Bride'' - Gibson, brides/ ''Spring, Spring, Spring'' - brothers, brides.

A hearty, outdoorsy (though filmed on the back lot) slice of Americana, *Seven Brides for Seven Brothers* reset Stephen Vincent Benét's folkish story—based on Plutarch—from the Tennessee Valley to the backwoods of Oregon in 1850. Adam Pontipee (Howard Keel) loses no time in persuading Milly (Jane Powell) to marry him and set up housekeeping in his rustic mountain home. Also living there are Adam's six love-starved but honorably intentioned brothers who take direct romantic action by kidnaping six city girls. Eventually, the girls—as did the Sabine women kidnaped by the ancient Romans—grow to love their captors, and the film ends with the six couples getting married at the same time. The movie highlighted the dancing of the brothers in two sequences created by Michael Kidd: the acrobatic barn-raising ballet that includes a choreographed donnybrook between the Pontipee boys and the city boys, and the ''Lonesome Polecat'' ballet in the snow. The score, originally planned to consist entirely of folk songs, was the first collaboration between Gene dePaul and Johnny Mercer.

''Shadow of Your Smile, The'' Music by Johnny Mandel; lyric by Paul Francis Webster. Delicate ballad of leave-taking sung by chorus over final credits of nonmusical film, *The Sandpiper* (Col. 1965).

''Shadow Waltz'' Music by Harry Warren; lyric by Al Dubin. Ardent serenade (with all those ''ing'' rhymes!), first sung in *Gold Diggers of 1933* (Warner) by struggling songwriter Dick Powell to Ruby Keeler in his apartment. Later, in an elaborate Broadway revue, Powell, now in all-white full dress, sings it again to Miss Keeler, now in a blonde wig and white gown. The vocal leads to a Busby Berkeley stageful of girls, all wearing identical blonde wigs and white dresses, playing electrified violins as they sweep and swirl over a series of plat-

forms and ramps. When the lights go out, only the illuminated violins can be seen glowing in the dark and, eventually, forming the outline of one huge violin. This was the first of Berkeley's three extravagant pageants featuring musical instruments: violins were followed by harps (''Spin a Little Web of Dreams'') in *Fashions of 1934* and by pianos (''The Words Are in My Heart'') in *Gold Diggers of 1935*.

Shall We Dance (1937). Music by George Gershwin; lyrics by Ira Gershwin; screenplay by Allan Scott & Ernest Pagano adapted by P. J. Wolfson from story ''Watch Your Step'' by Lee Loeb & Harold Buchman.

An RKO-Radio film produced by Pandro S. Berman; directed by Mark Sandrich; choreography, Fred Astaire, Hermes Pan, Harry Losee; art director, Van Nest Polglase; costumes, Irene; music director, Nathaniel Shilkret; orchestrations, Robert Russell Bennett; cameraman, David Abel; editor, William Hamilton.

Cast: Fred Astaire (*Peter P. ''Pete'' Peters* aka *Petrov*); Ginger Rogers (*Linda Keene* née *Linda Thompson*); Edward Everett Horton (*Jeffrey Baird*); Eric Blore (*Cecil Flintridge*); Jerome Cowan (*Arthur Miller*); Ketti Gallian (*Denise Lady Tarrington*); William Brisbane (*Jim Montgomery*); Harriet Hoctor (*specialty dancer*); Ann Shoemaker (*ship passenger*); Ben Alexander (*Evans*).

Songs: ''Slap That Bass'' - uncredited singer, Astaire/ ''Walking the Dog'' - orchestra/ ''(I've Got) Beginner's Luck'' - Astaire/ ''They All Laughed'' - Rogers; dance by Astaire, Rogers/ ''Let's Call the Whole Thing Off'' - Astaire, Rogers/ ''They Can't Take That Away from Me'' - Astaire; reprised as dance by Astaire, Hoctor/ ''Shall We Dance?'' - Astaire; dance by Astaire, Rogers, chorus. Unused: ''Hi-Ho!,'' ''Wake Up, Brother, and Dance.''

Shall We Dance (without a question mark) was the only Astaire-Rogers movie with a score by the Gershwin brothers and the last to surround the team with totally improbable luxury in the style inaugurated by *The Gay Divorcee* and *Top Hat*. With two veteran comedians of those films, Edward Everett Horton and Eric Blore, in similar roles, *Shall We Dance* was marked by a sophistication in ambience and song that contrasted with its naïveté in story and dialogue. The dancing twosome were first seen in Paris, then aboard a palatial ocean liner, and finally high in the Sky Room of a skyscraping, unnamed Manhattan hotel just like the Waldorf-Astoria. The plot finds ballet dancer Fred in love with musical-comedy star Ginger; somehow, the rumor gets out that they are married, which causes all sorts of misunderstanding until Fred gets the bright idea of their really getting married so that they can get a divorce. At the film's end, not surprisingly, they are happy to remain man and wife.

The idea of casting Fred Astaire as a ballet dancer whose ambition is to combine classic steps with modern taps had first occurred to the team of Richard Rodgers and Lorenz Hart. They submitted a scenario to Astaire, but he turned down their story because it did not give him the chance to don his trademark attire of top hat, white tie, and tails. The writers then refashioned the script into a 1936 Broadway musical called *On Your Toes,* with Ray Bolger in the lead. After its success, Astaire had a change of heart, and RKO tried to get the property for him and Miss Rogers; when that effort failed, the studio went ahead with its own movie about a ballet dancer that, at various times, was called *Stepping Toes, Stepping Stones, Watch Your Step,* and, ultimately *Shall We Dance.* (Warner's eventually filmed *On Your Toes* in 1939 with Eddie Albert and Vera Zorina, after a vain attempt to pair James Cagney with Ginger Rogers.)

"Shall We Dance?" Music by George Gershwin; lyric by Ira Gershwin. Rhythmically insistent invitation sung by Fred Astaire in *Shall We Dance* (RKO 1937). Performed in the movie's finale—in a revue staged atop a glittering New York hotel—the song is introduced as part of a production number in which ballet and modern ballroom and tap dancing are fused. Astaire, in white tie and tails sings and dances around a chorus of girls all wearing masks in Ginger Rogers' likeness. Seeing this, the real Ginger knows that Fred loves her, and she joins the masked girls on stage. After Fred has danced up to each girl, Ginger sends him a signal—"Otchi Tchornya"—which wheels him around and into her arms. Originally, another song, "Wake Up, Brother, and Dance," had been written for this sequence, but it was dropped when the producer prevailed upon the Gershwin brothers to come up with a title song for the film.

"Shanghai Lil" Music by Harry Warren; lyric by Al Dubin. Production number in *Footlight Parade* (Warner 1933), presented as the on-stage entertainment in a movie theatre. In the scene, James Cagney (an accidental last-minute substitution for a drunken actor) appears

in white tie and tails in a Shanghai dive and sings of his search for his Oriental inamorata ("The stars that hang high over Shanghai/ Bring back the mem'ry of a thrill"). No one has seen Lil (though one streetwalker complains that she's ruining her business), so Cagney continues his search in an opium den. Back in the saloon, he gets into a chair-and-table-throwing brawl, after which he somehow manages to change into a sailor uniform. Suddenly, Lil appears in the person of Ruby Keeler, and they celebrate their reunion by tap dancing on top of the bar. When sailor Cagney is called back to his ship, the now tenacious cocotte dons a sailor suit and goes along with him. Prior to their departure the audience is treated to a series of Busby Berkeley military drills, capped by the chorus holding aloft huge football-stadium cards forming our nation's emblem, the stars and stripes, and an applause-catching image of President Roosevelt. Composer Warren's second "Shanghai" song, "Night Over Shanghai," was written with Johnny Mercer for *The Singing Marine* (Warner 1937).

Shaw, Artie, (né Abraham Isaac Arshawsky), bandleader, clarinetist; b. New York, May 23, 1910. Leading swing-era bandleader with dour on-screen personality. Lana Turner was the second and Ava Gardner the fourth of his seven wives. Bib: *The Trouble with Cinderella* by Shaw (1979).

1939 Dancing Coed
1940 Second Chorus

Shaw, Winifred (also Wini) (née Winifred Lei Momi), singer, actress; b. San Francisco, Feb. 25, 1910. Torchy, dramatic, dark-haired singer noted for her renditions of "Lullaby of Broadway," "The Lady in Red," and "Too Marvelous for Words"; appeared mostly in Warner films. (Died May 2, 1982.)

1934 Million Dollar Ransom (*Babe*)
      Wake Up and Dream (*Mae LaRue*)
1935 Sweet Adeline (*Elysia*)
      Gold Diggers of 1935 (*singer*)
      In Caliente (*singer*)
      Broadway Hostess (*Winnie Wharton*)
1936 The Singing Kid (*singer*)
1937 Ready, Willing and Able (*Jane Clarke*)
      Melody for Two (*Lorna Wray*)

"She Is Not Thinking of Me" Music by Frederick Loewe; lyric by Alan Jay Lerner. As he contemplates his bubbly mistress, Eva Gabor, at Maxim's one night, Louis Jourdan—in *Gigi* (MGM 1958)—reveals (though with closed lips) his suspicion of her unfaithfulness. The number, also known as "Waltz at Maxim's," ends with Jourdan pouring champagne down Gabor's dress.

"She Reminds Me of You" Music by Harry Revel; lyric by Mack Gordon. In which Bing Crosby, in *We're Not Dressing* (Par. 1934), explains to an old flame that the reason he's fallen in love with someone new is because she reminds him of her. The new girl, in fact, doesn't mind the comparison at all, since she's let it be known that she'd be satisfied if he loved her only half as much as he had once loved the previous girl. Crosby, playing a sailor on a yacht, sang this rather confused romantic notion to his pet bear who, understandably, showed total incomprehension.

"She Shall Have Music" Music by Al Hoffman & Al Goodhart; lyric by Maurice Sigler. Romantic edict for continuous musical accompaniment (including songbirds and church bells) introduced by Jack Hylton's orchestra in British film of same name (1935). Song also adopted as Hylton's theme.

Sheridan, (Clara Lou) Ann, actress, singer; b. Denton, Texas, Feb. 21, 1915; d. Woodland Hills, Cal., Jan. 21, 1967. Striking-looking, slim beauty—something of a forerunner of Lauren Bacall—whose nimble comic timing made her adept at one-line put-downs. Miss Sheridan, known as Clara Lou Sheridan until early 1935, worked at Warner between 1936 and 1948. She introduced "Love Isn't Born" in *Thank Your Lucky Stars*.

1934	Bolero (bit)
	Murder at the Vanities (bit)
	Shoot the Works (bit)
	College Rhythm (bit)
1935	Rumba (bit)
	Mississippi (bit)
1936	Sing Me a Love Song (*Lola Parker*)
1938	Cowboy from Brooklyn (*Maxine Chadwick*)
1939	Naughty but Nice (*Zelda Manion*)
1941	Navy Blues (*Margo Jordan*)
1942	Juke Girl (*Lola Mears*)
1943	Thank Your Lucky Stars (specialty)
1944	Shine on Harvest Moon (*Nora Bayes*)
1956	The Opposite Sex (*Amanda*)

Sherman Brothers, composers, lyricists, screenwriters. Richard M., b. New York, June 12, 1928. Robert B., b. New York, Dec. 19, 1925. The screen's inseparable (so far) sibling partners are primarily known for their songs for Walt Disney productions and similar family-type entertainment. The sons of composer Al Sherman ("Living in the Sunlight—Loving in the Moonlight"), they enjoyed their biggest success with *Mary Poppins* ("Chim Chim Cheree," "A Spoonful of Sugar").

Asterisk indicates they also wrote screenplay:

1961	The Parent Trap
1962	In Search of the Castaways
1963	Summer Magic
	The Sword in the Stone
1964	Mary Poppins
1967	The Adventures of Bullwhip Griffin
	The Jungle Book
	The Happiest Millionaire
1968	The One and Only Genuine Original Family Band
	Bedknobs and Broomsticks
	Chitty Chitty Bang Bang
1970	The Aristocats
1972	Charlotte's Web
1973	Tom Sawyer*
1974	Huckleberry Finn*
1976	The Slipper and the Rose*
1978	The Magic of Lassie*

"She's a Latin from Manhattan" Music by Harry Warren; lyric by Al Dubin. All about a Latin dancing sensation known as Dolores whose background is considered to be either Cuban or Spanish, but who is really Susie Donahue from 10th Avenue and a 42nd Street chorus line. Introduced by Al Jolson in a nightclub production number in *Go Into Your Dance* (Warner 1935), with Ruby Keeler as the Senorita. Also sung by Jack Carson and Joan Leslie in *The Hard Way* (Warner 1942) and Evelyn Keyes and chorus in *The Jolson Story* (Col. 1946).

"Shoes with Wings On" Music by Harry Warren; lyric by Ira Gershwin. In his dancing shoes—more magical than Aladdin's lamp or Midas' golden touch—a young lad can transform his life by dancing the night away with his girl. Sung and danced by Fred Astaire in a Broadway revue in *The Barkleys of Broadway* (MGM 1949). In the scene, something of a variation on both Hans Christian Andersen's "The Red Shoes" and Goethe's "The Sorcerer's Apprentice," Fred plays a shoe repairman who is given a pair of white shoes by a dancing customer. As soon as the man leaves, the shoes miraculously begin dancing by themselves. Fred puts them on and suddenly *he's* dancing. Dozens of other pairs of shoes join in (their tapping also supplied by the disembodied Fred), and he is unable to stop them. Then, in a routine reminiscent of the legendary "Top Hat, White Tie and Tails" number—the dancing repairman tries shooting down the shoes, using a broom as his rifle. Eventually, he stops their dancing only by blazing away with two pistols—and all the shoes fall down on his head.

Shore, (Frances Rose) Dinah, singer, actress; b. Winchester, Tenn., March 1, 1917. First winning recognition on Eddie Cantor's radio program, this satin-voiced singer achieved her greatest fame on records and television. In films, she introduced "Like Someone in Love," "Now I Know," "I'll Walk Alone," and "Sleighride in July." Bib: *Dinah!* by Bruce Cassiday (1979).

1943   Thank Your Lucky Stars (*Dinah Shore*)
1944   Belle of the Yukon (*Lettie Candless*)
       Up in Arms (*Virginia Merrill*)
       Follow the Boys (specialty)
1946   Make Mine Music (voice only)
       Fun and Fancy Free (voice only)
       Till the Clouds Roll By (specialty)
1951   Aaron Slick from Punkin Crick (*Josie Berry*)

"Should I?" Music by Nacio Herb Brown; lyric by Arthur Freed. Dilemma of one unsure about revealing exactly how he (or she) feels, introduced in *Lord Byron of Broadway* (MGM 1930) by Charles Kaley and reprised by Ethelind Terry. Song also sung by Georgia Carroll with Kay Kyser's orchestra in *Thousands Cheer* (MGM 1943), and Wilson Wood in *Singin' in the Rain* (MGM 1952).

Show Boat (1936). Music by Jerome Kern; lyrics by Oscar Hammerstein II; screenplay by Hammerstein from Broadway musical by Kern & Hammerstein based on novel by Edna Ferber.

A Universal film produced by Carl Laemmle, Jr.; directed by James Whale; choreography, LeRoy Prinz; art director, Charles Hall; costumes, Doris Zinkeisen; music director, Victor Baravalle; orchestrations, Robert Russell Bennett; cameramen, John Mescall, John Fulton; editors, Ted Kent, Bernard Burton.

Cast: Irene Dunne (*Magnolia Hawks Ravenal*); Allan Jones (*Gaylord Ravenal*); Charles Winninger (*Capt. Andy Hawks*); Paul Robeson (*Joe*); Helen Morgan (*Julie LaVerne*); Helen Westley (*Parthy Ann Hawks*); Donald Cook (*Steve*); Queenie Smith (*Ellie May Schultz*); Sammy White (*Frank Schultz*); Hattie McDaniel

(*Queenie*); Clarence Muse (*Sam*); Eddie "Rochester" Anderson (*young Negro*); E. E. Clive (*Englishman*); Harry Barris (*Jake*).

Songs: "Cotton Blossom" - chorus/ "Where's the Mate for Me?" - Jones/ "Make Believe" - Dunne, Jones/ "Ol' Man River" - Robeson/ "Can't Help Lovin' Dat Man" - Morgan, McDaniel, Robeson, Dunne/ "I Have the Room Above Her" - Jones, Dunne/ "Gallivantin' Around" - Dunne/ "You Are Love" - Dunne, Jones/ "Ah Still Suits Me" - Robeson, McDaniel/ "Bill" (lyric with P. G. Wodehouse) - Morgan/ "Goodbye, Ma Lady Love" (Joe Howard) - Smith, White/ "After the Ball" (Charles K. Harris) - Dunne, revelers. Unused: "Why Do I Love You?," "Got My Eye on You."

Show Boat (1951). Music by Jerome Kern; lyrics by Oscar Hammerstein II; screenplay by John Lee Mahin.

An MGM film produced by Arthur Freed; directed by George Sidney; choreography by Robert Alton; art directors, Cedric Gibbons, Jack Martin Smith; costumes, Walter Plunkett; music director, Adolph Deutsch; orchestrations, Conrad Salinger; cameraman, Charles Rosher; editor, John Dunning; Technicolor.

Cast: Kathryn Grayson (*Magnolia Hawks Ravenal*); Ava Gardner (vocals by Annette Warren) (*Julie LaVerne*); Howard Keel (*Gaylord Ravenal*); Joe E. Brown (*Capt. Andy Hawks*); Marge Champion (*Ellie May Schultz*); Gower Champion (*Frank Schultz*); Robert Sterling (*Steve Baker*); Agnes Moorehead (*Parthy Ann Hawks*); Leif Erickson (*Pete*); William Warfield (*Joe*); Frances Williams (*Queenie*); Regis Toomey (*Sheriff Ike Vallon*); Fuzzy Knight (*Jake*); Adele Jergens (*Cameo McQueen*).

Songs: "Cotton Blossom" - chorus/ "Where's the Mate for Me?" - Keel/ "Make Believe" - Keel, Grayson/ "Can't Help Lovin' Dat Man" - Gardner (Warren), Grayson/ "I Might Fall Back on You" - Champions/ "Ol' Man River" - Warfield/ "You Are Love" - Grayson, Keel/ "Why Do I Love You?" - Grayson, Keel/ "Bill" (lyric with P. G. Wodehouse) - Gardner (Warren)/ "Life Upon the Wicked Stage" - Champions/ "After the Ball" (Charles K. Harris) - Grayson, revelers.

An acknowledged milestone in the history of the musical theatre, *Show Boat,* which Ziegfeld first presented in 1927, was brought to the screen on three occasions. Carl Laemmle produced the first version at Universal in 1929 (released even before the original Broadway run ended), which was actually adapted directly from Edna Ferber's novel. Originally shot without sound, the picture was then reshot with some audible dialogue and songs added (including "Ol' Man River" and "Can't Help Lovin' Dat Man" from the Kern-Hammerstein score). In leading roles were Laura La Plante (whose singing was dubbed by Eva Olivotti) as Magnolia, Joseph Schildkraut as Ravenal, Alma Rubens as Julie, Otis Harlan as Capt. Andy (who died in this version), and Stepin Fetchit as Joe. To capitalize on the fame of the Broadway musical, tacked onto the film was an 18-minute prologue featuring five selections by members of the original New York company: Helen Morgan (Julie), Jules Bledsoe (Joe), and Tess Gardella (Queenie).

In 1936 Laemmle's son, Carl, Jr., produced the second screen *Show Boat,* with Hammerstein adapting his own stage libretto and with a cast headed by veterans of various stage productions. Irene Dunne had toured in the part; Allan Jones had played Ravenal in summer theatre; Helen Morgan, Charles Winninger, and Sammy White had been in the original Ziegfeld production; and Paul Robeson had appeared as Joe both in London and in Ziegfeld's 1932 Broadway revival. Nine of the 18 songs were retained, and three new Kern and Hammerstein pieces were added. A major departure from the stage libretto was the ending. Instead of Magnolia and Ravenal being reunited on the deck of the showboat *Cotton Blossom* some 20 years after their separation, this time they get together again in the Broadway theatre where Ravenal works as a backstage doorman and where their daughter, Kim, is starring in a show.

MGM's 1951 edition stuck fairly close to the original during the early sequences, including the romantic meeting of riverboat gambler Ravenal and shy, demure Magnolia; the revelation that Julie, the showboat's chief attraction, is a Negro which forces her to leave the ship; and the marriage of Magnolia and Ravenal and their move to Chicago. The story is then considerably tightened and dramatically strengthened by having Ravenal leave his wife while she is pregnant and having Magnolia go back to the *Cotton Blossom* after singing at the Trocadero on New Year's Eve (in the original she had become a successful actress in New York). The film also reintroduces Julie and makes her the means through which Ravenal is reunited with his wife and child after a separation of only a few years. Though producer Arthur Freed had initially wanted Judy Garland for the expanded role of Julie—and studio boss Dore Schary had

promised the part to Dinah Shore—the character was played by Ava Gardner (with her singing dubbed on the film soundtrack but all hers on the "soundtrack" recording). The picture's chief historical inaccuracy, as pointed out in Miles Kreuger's book, *Show Boat: The Story of a Classic American Musical* (1977), was in turning the bargelike showboat into a steampowered paddle wheeler with two smokestacks—thereby leaving no room for an adequate theatre on the ship.

In addition to the three feature-length Hollywood *Show Boats,* a capsule version was part of MGM's 1946 Jerome Kern biography, *Till the Clouds Roll By,* also produced by Freed. Four selections were sung by Kathryn Grayson (Magnolia), Tony Martin (Ravenal), Virginia O'Brien (Ellie), Lena Horne (Julie), and Caleb Peterson (Joe).

"Shuffle Off to Buffalo" Music by Harry Warren; lyric by Al Dubin. Production number in Broadway-bound musical in *42nd Street* (Warner 1933). In this Busby Berkeley creation, newlyweds Ruby Keeler and Clarence Nordstrom take the Niagara Limited heading for their honeymoon at Niagara Falls and anticipate the pleasures of the journey ("To Niag'ra on a sleeper/ There's no honeymoon that's cheaper"). The train suddenly splits down the middle with both sides becoming one side of the car, Keeler and Nordstrom prance down the aisle, while Ginger Rogers and Una Merkel, sharing a berth, comment bitchily, "When she knows as much as we know/ She'll be on her way to Reno," and venture the opinion that the whole thing was a shotgun wedding. Other passengers join in the singing, the boys and girls undress in their respective undressing rooms, and everyone dances in pajamas. Final shot is of the snoring Pullman porter. Lyricist Dubin once told how he came to write the song: "There was a railroad station not far from the bungalow I was living in in California. Just as I was trying to think up a lyric to the melody, a train whistled. Then I got the idea. People going places. Why? On a honeymoon, of course. Where? To Niagara Falls. Wait a minute—you can't get Niagara Falls into a song title. We'll make it Buffalo. 'Shuffle Off to Buffalo'!" Song also sung by Jack Carson and Joan Leslie in *The Hard Way* (Warner 1942). For *Footlight Parade* (Warner 1933), Warren and Dubin wrote a follow-up number, "Honeymoon Hotel," which was also used for an elaborate Busby Berkeley routine. The composer's other railroad songs were "Chattanooga Choo-Choo" (lyric by Mack Gordon) in *Sun Valley Serenade* (Fox

1941) and ''On the Atchison, Topeka and the Santa Fe'' (lyric by Johnny Mercer) in *The Harvey Girls* (MGM 1946).

Sidney, George, director, producer; b. New York, Oct. 4, 1911. Between 1943 and 1955, Sidney directed major musicals at MGM, both originals (*Anchors Aweigh, The Harvey Girls*) and adaptations from the stage (*Annie Get Your Gun, Show Boat, Kiss Me, Kate*); between 1956 and 1964 he was at Columbia (*The Eddy Duchin Story*). He worked with Kathryn Grayson on four films (two of them with Gene Kelly, two with Howard Keel); also with Esther Williams, Frank Sinatra, Judy Garland, Jane Powell, Betty Hutton, Tyrone Power, Rita Hayworth, Ann-Margret, and Tommy Steele.

Asterisk indicates Mr. Sidney was also producer or co-producer:

1943 Thousands Cheer
1944 Bathing Beauty
1945 Anchors Aweigh
1946 The Harvey Girls
      Holiday in Mexico
1950 Annie Get Your Gun
1951 Show Boat
1953 Kiss Me, Kate
1955 Jupiter's Darling
1956 The Eddy Duchin Story
1957 Pal Joey
1960 Pepe*
1963 Bye Bye Birdie
1964 Viva Las Vegas*
1966 The Swinger*
1967 Half a Sixpence*

Siegel, Sol C., producer; b. New York, March 30, 1903. Produced films at Paramount (*Blue Skies*), Fox (*Call Me Madam, Gentlemen Prefer Blondes*), and MGM (*High Society, Les Girls*). Bing Crosby starred in four of his musicals; Ethel Merman, Donald O'Connor, Marilyn Monroe, Dan Dailey, Mitzi Gaynor, and Danny Kaye were all in more than one. (Died Dec. 29, 1982.)

1941 Glamour Boy
1942 Priorities on Parade
1946 Blue Skies
1947 Welcome Stranger
      The Perils of Pauline
1950 My Blue Heaven
1951 On the Riviera
1953 Call Me Madam
      Gentlemen Prefer Blondes
1954 There's No Business Like Show Business

1956 High Society
1957 Les Girls
1958 Merry Andrew

"Silhouetted in the Moonlight" Music by Richard A. Whiting; lyric by Johnny Mercer. In *Hollywood Hotel* (Warner 1939), Rosemary Lane and Dick Powell pay a nighttime visit to a deserted Hollywood Bowl. Miss Lane sings the song on stage to a moonlight-silhouetted Powell standing in the rear of the amphitheatre, and he sings it back to her. Ballad later reprised by Frances Langford and Jerry Cooper in the Orchid Room of the Hollywood Hotel, accompanied by Benny Goodman's orchestra.

"Silver Bells" Music & lyric by Jay Livingston & Ray Evans. Introduced by Marilyn Maxwell and Bob Hope (as a ragged sidewalk Santa Claus) while strolling through New York's snow-covered streets in *The Lemon Drop Kid* (Par. 1951). In writing the number, Livingston and Evans tried to make it as different as possible from all other yuletide songs. According to Livingston, ''Most Christmas songs are about Christmas at home or in the country, so we wrote ours about Christmas in the city. Of the standards we could think of, none was written in three-quarter time, so we chose that rhythm. To make it even more of a novelty, we wrote it so that the verse and the refrain could be sung simultaneously, and we even wrote a special fill-in for the refrain with words to match. Ray Evans had a little silver bell on his desk, a souvenir from a recent Paramount junket. I picked it up and rang it, and we started to write a song called 'Tinkle Bell.' That sounded silly so we changed it to 'Silver Bells.' ''

Silvers, Phil (né Philip Silver), actor; b. Brooklyn, May 11, 1911. Brash, bespectacled, nasal-voiced comic often seen in movies as the leading man's best friend. Had his best screen opportunity in *Cover Girl* with Rita Hayworth and Gene Kelly. Also acted on Broadway, including well-received performances in the two musicals that were filmed: *Top Banana* and *A Funny Thing Happened on the Way to the Forum* (a revival, in which he played Pseudolus). Perhaps best known for his Sergeant Bilko television series. Bib: *This Laugh Is on Me* by Silvers (1973). (Died Los Angeles, Nov. 1, 1985.)

1940 Hit Parade of 1941 (*Charlie Moore*)
1941 Lady, Be Good (*M.C.*)
      Ice-Capades (*Larry Herman*)

1942 My Gal Sal (*Wiley*)
       Footlight Serenade (*Slap*)
1943 Coney Island (*Frankie*)
1944 Cover Girl (*Genius*)
       Four Jills in a Jeep (*Eddie*)
       Something for the Boys (*Harry Hart*)
1945 Diamond Horseshoe (*Blinkie Walker*)
1946 If I'm Lucky (*Wally*)
1950 Summer Stock (*Herb Blake*)
1954 Top Banana (*Jerry Biffle*)
       Lucky Me (*Hap Snyder*)
1967 A Funny Thing Happened on the Way to the Forum
       (*Marcus Lycus*)

Silvers, Sid, actor, screenwriter; b. Brooklyn, Jan. 1, 1907. Silvers was a diminutive, roughhouse comic who also doubled as screenwriter of such films as *Broadway Melody* (two editions) and *Born To Dance*. (Died Santa Monica, Aug. 19, 1976.)

Asterisk indicates Mr. Silvers was also screenwriter or co-screenwriter:
1929 The Show of Shows (specialty)
1930 Dancing Sweeties (*Jerry Brown*)
       Follow the Leader (script only)
1933 My Weakness (*Maxie*)
1934 Bottoms Up (*Spud Mosco*)*
       Transatlantic Merry-Go-Round (*Shorty*)
1935 Broadway Melody of 1936 (*Snoop Blue*)*
1936 Born To Dance (*Gunny Sacks*)*
1937 Broadway Melody of 1938 (script only)
       52nd Street (*Sid*)
1942 The Fleet's In (script only)
       For Me and My Gal (script only)

Simms, (Virginia) Ginny, singer, actress; b. San Antonio, Texas, May 25, 1916. Round-cheeked, toothy vocalist with Kay Kyser's orchestra, who appeared with the bandleader in her first three films. On her own she introduced "Can't Get Out of This Mood."

1939 That's Right, You're Wrong (*Ginny*)
1940 You'll Find Out (*Ginny*)
1942 Playmates (*Ginny*)
       Here We Go Again (*Jean*)
       Seven Days' Leave (*Ginny*)
1943 Hit the Ice (*Marcia Manning*)
1944 Broadway Rhythm (*Helen Hoyt*)
1945 Shady Lady (*Lee*)
1946 Night and Day (*Carole Hill*)
1951 Disc Jockey (*Vickie Peters*)

Sinatra, (Francis Albert) Frank, actor, singer; b. Hoboken, NJ, Dec. 12, 1915. Former band singer with Tommy Dorsey's orchestra, Sinatra became, successively, a teenage singing idol, a star in film musicals (mostly at MGM), a dramatic actor (*From Here to Eternity*), and a pop culture legend. In his early musicals (*Anchors Aweigh, On the Town*) he was hollow-cheeked, boyish, and girl-shy; later efforts (*Guys and Dolls, High Society, Pal Joey*) found him more cynical and self-assured. Among songs he introduced in films or television were "Dolores," "I Couldn't Sleep a Wink Last Night," "A Lovely Way To Spend an Evening," "The Charm of You," "I Fall in Love Too Easily," "Time After Time," "Three Coins in the Fountain" (soundtrack only), "Love and Marriage," "The Tender Trap," "All the Way," "High Hopes," "Pocketful of Miracles," and "My Kind of Town." Kathryn Grayson, Betty Garrett, Jane Russell, Doris Day, Vivian Blaine, Rita Hayworth, and Shirley MacLaine were among the ladies he sang to on the screen. Sinatra has made many records and appeared frequently in concerts and nightclubs. He's been married four times (his second and third wives were Ava Gardner and Mia Farrow), and he is the father of singers Frank Sinatra, Jr., and Nancy Sinatra. Bib: *Sinatra: 20th Century Romantic* by Arnold Shaw (1968); *Films of Frank Sinatra* by Gene Ringgold & Clifford McCarty (1973); *Sinatra* by Earl Wilson (1976).

1941 Las Vegas Nights (*band singer*)
1942 Ship Ahoy (*band singer*)
1943 Reveille with Beverly (specialty)
       Higher and Higher (*Frank Sinatra*)
1944 Step Lively (*Glen Russell*)
1945 Anchors Aweigh (*Clarence Doolittle*)
1946 Till the Clouds Roll By (specialty)
1947 It Happened in Brooklyn (*Danny Miller*)
1948 The Kissing Bandit (*Ricardo*)
1949 Take Me Out to the Ball Game (*Dennis Ryan*)
       On the Town (*Chip*)
1951 Double Dynamite (*Johnny Dalton*)
1952 Meet Danny Wilson (*Danny Wilson*)
1954 Young at Heart (*Barney Sloane*)
1955 Guys and Dolls (*Nathan Detroit*)
       Meet Me in Las Vegas (guest bit)
       Our Town (tv) (*stage manager*)
1956 High Society (*Macaulay Connor*)
1957 The Joker Is Wild (*Joe E. Lewis*)
       Pal Joey (*Joey Evans*)
1960 Can-Can (*Francois Durnais*)
       Pepe (guest bit)
1962 Road to Hong Kong (guest bit)
1964 Robin and the Seven Hoods (*Robbo*) (also prod.)
1974 That's Entertainment (narrator)

"Since I Kissed My Baby Goodbye" Music & lyric by Cole Porter. Unsentimental attitude toward romantic fidelity confessed by the Delta Rhythm Boys and danced by Fred Astaire in an army guardhouse in *You'll Never Get Rich* (Col. 1941).

"Sing a Song of Sunbeams" Music by James V. Monaco; lyric by Johnny Burke. Optimistic credo buoyantly expressed by Bing Crosby in *East Side of Heaven* (Univ. 1939).

"Sing a Tropical Song" Music by Jimmy McHugh; lyric by Frank Loesser. Pseudo-calypso number about a tropical island's "national charac'-teristic" to "put the ac-cent' upon the wrong sylla'-ble." Demonstrated in *Happy Go Lucky* (Par. 1943) by Sir Lancelot, Dick Powell, and Eddie Bracken.

"Sing, Baby, Sing" Music by Lew Pollack; lyric by Jack Yellen. Rhythmic prescription for the blues introduced by Alice Faye in film of the same name (Fox 1936).

"Sing My Heart" Music by Harold Arlen; lyric by Ted Koehler. Buoyant advice to take love casually, sung by Irene Dunne in *Love Affair* (RKO 1939).

"Sing You Sinners" Music by W. Franke Harling; lyric by Sam Coslow. Leaning on a picket fence behind a Southern mansion in *Honey* (Par. 1930), Skeets Gallagher and a Northern visitor, Lillian Roth, notice a group of plantation workers rushing through the woods. "What on earth is that?" asks Lillian. "It's a celebration," Skeets tells her. "Once a year the darkies get together and have a festival. And, boy, is it hot!" And so the uninvited pair dash over to a clearing in the woods to observe the revelry, which at first consists of dozens of Negroes stomping about, waving their arms and wailing. Suddenly, a heavyset, bandannaed (and uncredited) singer cuts through the sounds with her revivalistic sermon on how to be saved—"Sing You Sinners." By this time, Lillian and Skeets are joined by other formally dressed residents of the mansion as they watch little Mitzi Green lead the black children in the song. No longer able to control herself, Lillian jumps up and belts it out, while the field hands sing and dance and Skeets mimics playing a banjo. The number ends on a frenzied, ecstatic note with a final reprise by the first singer.

Lyricist Coslow claims that the idea for the song came from a Sunday evening revival meeting that he had attended in a large tent outside San Diego. He thought of the title on the way back to Los Angeles, and the following morning he and composer Harling put the words and music together within an hour. Number was also sung by Billy Daniels in *Cruisin' Down the River* (Col. 1953) and Susan Hayward (as Lillian Roth) in *I'll Cry Tomorrow* (MGM 1955).

Singin' in the Rain (1952). Music by Nacio Herb Brown; lyrics by Arthur Freed; screenplay by Betty Comden & Adolph Green.

An MGM film produced by Arthur Freed; directed & choreographed by Gene Kelly & Stanley Donen; associate producer, Roger Edens; art directors, Cedric Gibbons, Randall Duell; costumes, Walter Plunkett; music director, Lennie Hayton; orchestrations, Conrad Salinger, Wally Heglin, Skip Martin; cameraman, Harold Rosson; editor, Adrienne Fazan; Technicolor.

Cast: Gene Kelly (*Don Lockwood*); Debbie Reynolds (vocal by Betty Royce) (*Kathy Selden*); Donald O'Connor (*Cosmo Brown*); Jean Hagen (*Lily Lamont*); Millard Mitchell (*R. F. Simpson*); Cyd Charisse (*dancer*); Douglas Fowley (*Roscoe Dexter*); Rita Moreno (*Zelda Zanders*); Jimmie Thompson (*singer*); Julius Tannen (*man on screen*); Wilson Wood (*singer*).

Songs: "Singin' in the Rain" - Kelly, Reynolds, O'Connor; reprised by Kelly/ "Fit as a Fiddle" (music, Al Hoffman, Al Goodhart) - Kelly, O'Connor/ "All I Do Is Dream of You" - Reynolds, chorus/ "Make 'Em Laugh" - O'Connor/ "I've Got a Feelin' You're Foolin' " - chorus/ "The Wedding of the Painted Doll" - chorus/ "Should I?" - Wood/ "Beautiful Girl" - Thompson/ "You Were Meant for Me" - Kelly; dance by Kelly, Reynolds/ "Moses" (Roger Edens-Betty Comden, Adolph Green) - Kelly, O'Connor/ "Good Morning" - Kelly, Reynolds, O'Connor/ "Would You?" - Reynolds (Royce)/ "Broadway Melody" - Kelly/ "Broadway Rhythm" - Kelly; dance by Kelly, Charisse/ "You Are My Luck Star" - Kelly, Reynolds.

Like his productions of *Easter Parade, An American in Paris,* and *The Band Wagon,* Arthur Freed's *Singin' in the Rain* was built around a song catalogue. Only in this case it belonged to Freed himself and the songs he wrote with composer Nacio Herb Brown. Since many of them dated from the earliest days of talkies, scriptwriters Comden and Green felt they could best be used in an original story dealing with the transition from silent to sound films. Initially, Howard Keel was penciled in for the male lead, which prompted the writers to try a story about a minor Western actor who becomes a star in talkies. That didn't work, so they began altering the character to that of a song-and-dance man who becomes a silent film star, then becomes even bigger in early sound musicals. This led to Gene Kelly. Debbie Reynolds, in her first major role, was cast as a talented but unheralded actress whose soundtrack lip-synching helps make a talkie star of a temperamental silent-screen star, played by Jean Hagen with an impenetrably squeaky voice. Though this spoofed the kind of behind-the-scene deception of the early sound period, *Singin' in the Rain* actually continued that deception. Because Miss Reynolds' speaking voice was considered too Texan, Miss Hagen, using her natural cultured voice, dubbed the lines that Miss Reynolds was supposed to be dubbing for her. As for Miss Reynolds' singing of "Would You?," that was dubbed by Betty Noyes.

Though its plot was entirely different, *Singin' in the Rain* continued the same kind of youthful high spirits that had previously distinguished Arthur Freed's production of *On the Town*. No accident, surely, since like its predecessor the film benefited from the services of the same directors, writers, associate producer, music director, cameraman, and star (Kelly). Among the highlights: Kelly's tour de force while singin' in the rain, which has since become his trademark number; the comic inventions of Donald O'Connor's "Make 'Em Laugh"; the joyful "Good Morning" performed by Kelly, Reynolds, and O'Connor; and the narrative "Broadway Ballet" featuring Kelly and Cyd Charisse. Bib: *Singin' in the Rain* by Betty Comden & Adolph Green (1972).

"Singin' in the Rain" Music by Nacio Herb Brown; lyric by Arthur Freed. That glorious feeling of singing and dancing during a downpour was first expressed by Cliff Edwards and chorus, all wearing slickers while being pelted by rain, in *Hollywood Revue of 1929* (MGM). Song also sung by Jimmy Durante in *Speak Easily* (MGM 1932); Judy Garland in *Little Nellie Kelly* (MGM 1940); Gene Kelly, Debbie Reynolds and Donald O'Connor—and also by Kelly alone—in *Singin' in the Rain* (MGM 1952); and Malcolm MacDowell in *A Clockwork Orange* (1972). This is a rare case in which a subsequent rendition of a song—Kelly's street-splashing, lamppost-climbing, umbrella-waving solo—has become more famous than the original.

"Singing a Vagabond Song" Music & lyric by Sam Messenheimer, Val Burton, and Harry Richman. Harry Richman sang and strutted through his theme song in a stage production in *Puttin' on the Ritz* (UA 1930). Song also sung by Ritz Brothers (as a parody) in *Sing, Baby, Sing* (Fox 1936), and Van Johnson in *Kelly and Me* (Univ. 1957).

"Sisters" Music & lyric by Irving Berlin. Waving huge fans, sisters Rosemary Clooney and Vera-Ellen (voice dubbed by Trudy Ewen) introduced the song of sibling devotion in *White Christmas* (Par. 1953). The scene took place in a Miami nightclub where, to a recording of the song made by the sisters, Bing Crosby and Danny Kaye reprised the number by mouthing the words and imitating the girls' gestures.

Skelton, (Richard Bernard) Red, actor; b. Vincennes, Ind., July 18, 1910. Chuckling, wide-mouthed, carrot-topped clownish comedian who appeared in vaudeville before screen debut (as Richard Skelton). In his films—all for MGM from 1941 on—he was usually cast as a grownup child pratfalling in and out of a variety of scrapes. Skelton, who appeared in musicals mostly with Ann Sothern, Eleanor Powell, and Esther Williams, made his last movie in 1965. He also had popular radio and television series. Bib: *Red Skelton* by Arthur Marx (1979).

1938	Having Wonderful Time (*Itchy*)
1941	Lady, Be Good (*Joe "Red" Willett*)
1942	Panama Hattie (*Red*)
	Ship Ahoy (*Merton K. Kibble*)
1943	DuBarry Was a Lady (*Louie Blore*)
	I Dood It (*Joseph Rivington Reynolds*)
	Thousands Cheer (specialty)
1944	Bathing Beauty (*Steve Elliott*)
1946	Ziegfeld Follies (specialty)
1949	Neptune's Daughter (*Jack Spratt*)
1950	The Duchess of Idaho (specialty)
	Three Little Words (*Harry Ruby*)
1951	Excuse My Dust (*Joe Belden*)
	Texas Carnival (*Connie Quinnell*)
1952	Lovely To Look At (*Al Marsh*)

"Slap That Bass" Music by George Gershwin; lyric by Ira Gershwin. Offering the unheeded advice that "dictators would be better off if they zoom-zoomed now and then," the song urges that the best way to fight the glooms is to slap a bass fiddle. Introduced in *Shall We Dance* (RKO 1937) first by an uncredited black singer, then by Fred Astaire in the engine room of a transatlantic ocean liner. The vocal was followed by Astaire's dancing all over the spanking-clean room, with his taps synchronized with the pounding pistons and chugging engines.

"Sleighride in July" Music by James Van Heusen; lyric by Johnny Burke. Rueful rumination of one who "didn't know enough to come in out of the moonlight," sung by Dinah Shore in *Belle of the Yukon* (RKO 1944).

"Slumming on Park Avenue" Music & lyric by Irving Berlin. Or putting down the swells. In *On the Avenue* (Fox 1937), a scene from a Broadway revue first offers the number sung by Alice Faye in a flashy outfit as she and her tenement neighbors tap their way to the fashionable thoroughfare and mingle with the rich. The number is then reprised by the Ritz Brothers (who interpolate a parodied "Cheek to Cheek"), with Harry made up as Miss Faye, and his two brothers, Al and Jimmy, wearing top hat and tails but no shoes. See "Puttin' on the Ritz" for another Berlin song about observing the affluent.

"Small Fry" Music by Hoagy Carmichael; lyric by Johnny Mercer. Stern lecture to a punk kid who skips school to hang around the poolroom, smoke cigarettes, dance in the streets for money, kiss the neighbor's daughter, and bet on the ponies. Introduced in *Sing You Sinners* (Par. 1938) as a bantering routine performed by a family act consisting of brothers Bing Crosby (in top hat and beard), Fred MacMurray (in wig and dress), and Donald O'Connor (as Small Fry).

"Smarty" Music by Burton Lane; lyric by Ralph Freed. Bouncy plea ("If you had a heart you could learn to be twice as smart"), sung by Bing Crosby at a lunch counter in *Double or Nothing* (Par. 1937).

Smith, (Gladys) Alexis, actress, singer, dancer; b. Penticton, BC, Canada, June 8, 1921. Sharp-featured beauty who loved George Gershwin in *Rhapsody in Blue* and Cole Porter in *Night and Day* but whose musical gifts went largely unrecognized until she appeared on Broadway in *Follies*. Most of her films were made at Warner.

1943 Thank Your Lucky Stars (specialty)
1944 Hollywood Canteen (guest bit)
1945 Rhapsody in Blue (*Christine Gilbert*)

1946 Night and Day (*Linda Lee Porter*)
1951 Here Comes the Groom (*Winifred Stanley*)
1957 Beau James (*Allie Walker*)

Smith, (Kathryn) Kate, singer, actress; b. Greenville, Va., May 1, 1906. Heavy-set, leather-lunged singer whose greatest success was achieved on radio. (Died Raleigh, NC, June 17, 1986.)

1932 The Big Broadcast (specialty)
1933 Hello, Everybody (*Kate Smith*)
1943 This Is the Army (specialty)

Snow White and the Seven Dwarfs (1937). Music by Frank Churchill; lyrics by Larry Morey; background score by Leigh Harline & Paul J. Smith; adapted from Jacob & Wilhelm Grimm's "Little Snow White" by Ted Sears, Otto Enlanger, Earl Hurd, Dorothy Ann Blank, Richard Creedon, Dick Richard, Merrill de Maris, Webb Smith.

A Walt Disney film released by RKO-Radio; directors, David Hand, Perce Pearce, Larry Morey, William Cottrell, Wilfred Jackson, Ben Sharpsteen; supervising animators, Hamilton Luske, Vladimir Tytla, Fred Moore, Norman Ferguson; art directors, Charles Philippi, Hugh Hennesy, Terrell Stapp, McLaren Stewart, Harold Miles, Tom Codrick, Gustaf Tenggren, Kenneth Anderson, Hazel Sewell; music directors, Frank Churchill, Paul J. Smith, Leigh Harline; Technicolor.

Voices: Adriana Caselotti (*Snow White*); Harry Stockwell (*Prince*); Lucille LaVerne (*Queen*); Roy Atwell (*Doc*); Pinto Colvig (*Grumpy, Sleepy*); Otis Harlan (*Happy*); Billy Gilbert (*Sneezy*); Scotty Mattraw (*Bashful*); Moroni Olsen (*Magic Mirror*).

Songs: "I'm Wishing" - Caselotti/ "One Song" - Stockwell/ "With a Smile and a Song" - Caselotti, animals, birds/ "Whistle While You Work" - Caselotti, animals, birds/ "Heigh-Ho" - Atwell, Colvig, Harlan, Gilbert, Mattraw/ "Bluddle-Uddle-Um-Dum" -Atwell, Colvig, Harlan, Gilbert, Mattraw/ "Isn't This a Silly Song?" - Caselotti, Atwell, Colvig, Harlan, Gilbert, Mattraw/ "Some Day My Prince Will Come" -Caselotti. Unused: "Music in Your Soup," "You're Never Too Old To Be Young."

Walt Disney's pioneering effort, the first feature-length animated cartoon, required the services of 750 artists working almost three years. The film marked the first time human figures were animated on the screen (Marjorie Belcher, later Marge Champion, was the model for Snow White), but its greatest achievement was in the humanizing of the dwarfs, the appeal of the songs and their integration in the story, and the vivid designs, especially for the forest sequences, which were enhanced by the realism of the ''multiplane'' camera. Certain liberties were taken with the Grimm fairytale on which the movie was based. In the fairytale, Snow White is all of seven when the jealous Queen first tries to have her killed; later the Queen makes three separate attempts to do her in, by strangling, paralyzing, and poisoning (Disney had her try only poisoning); Snow White is brought back to life when the poisoned apple is dislodged from her throat (in the movie she comes to when the Prince kisses her); and the Queen meets her end by dancing until she drops dead at the wedding of Snow White and the Prince (instead of falling to her death in a ravine during a rainstorm).

Following the success of *Snow White*, Paramount's Max Fleischer created the second feature-length cartoon, *Gulliver's Travels*, in 1939. Disney then offered such animated attractions as *Pinocchio* (1940), *Dumbo* (1941), *Bambi* (1942), *Cinderella* (1949), *Alice in Wonderland* (1951), *Peter Pan* (1953), and *Sleeping Beauty* (1959). In 1979, a stage production of *Snow White and the Seven Dwarfs* played New York's Radio City Music Hall and subsequently toured. Bib: *Walt Disney's Snow White and the Seven Dwarfs* (1979).

"So Do I" Music by Arthur Johnston; lyric by Johnny Burke. Ardent serenade (''The breeze runs after you when you're passing by''), sung by street singer Bing Crosby and danced by Edith Fellows in *Pennies from Heaven* (Col. 1936).

"So Near and Yet So Far" Music & lyric by Cole Porter. Rhythmic plaint of one whose beloved is uncooperative, sung by Fred Astaire and danced by Astaire and Rita Hayworth in a servicemen's show in *You'll Never Get Rich* (Col. 1941). The melody for the beguine-flavoured ballad was based on Porter's ''Kate the Great,'' which had been dropped from the Broadway musical *Anything Goes*.

"Somebody from Somewhere" Music by George Gershwin; lyric by Ira Gershwin. In *Delicious* (Fox 1930), Janet Gaynor, as a Scottish immigrant, is smuggled into a huge mansion in New York. She finds an empty bedroom, gets into bed, opens up a handy music box, and sings herself to sleep longing for the right man to appear some day.

"Someday My Prince Will Come" Music by Frank Churchill; lyric by Larry Morey. Hopeful ballad sung by Snow White (Adriana Caselotti) as she pines for her beloved in the cartoon feature *Snow White and the Seven Dwarfs* (Disney 1937).

"Someone To Care For Me" Music by Bronislaw Kaper & Walter Jurmann; lyric by Gus Kahn. Ballad of romantic longing, first sung in *Three Smart Girls* (Univ. 1937) by frosty, offkey Binnie Barnes during a formal dinner party. A bit later reprised by Deanna Durbin in her bedroom to show her father, Charles Winninger, how the song should be sung.

"Something's Gotta Give" Music & lyric by Johnny Mercer. Amatory application of a law of physics (the one about an irresistible force meeting an immovable object), sung by Fred Astaire to Leslie Caron in *Daddy Long Legs* (Fox 1955). Rendition then followed by an all-night dancing spree in Manhattan's fanciest nightspots. Song was also sung by Joanne Woodward in *The Stripper* (Fox 1963).

Sondheim, Stephen (Joshua), composer, lyricist; b. New York, March 22, 1930. Pre-eminent creator of Broadway scores, of which four—so far—have been brought to the screen. The first two, on which Sondheim served as lyricist only, had music by Leonard Bernstein and by Jule Styne. As composer, his only film score was the background music for *Stavisky* (1974). Bib: *Sondheim & Co.* by Craig Zadan (1974).

1961	West Side Story (Bernstein)
1962	Gypsy (Styne)
1966	Evening Primrose (tv) (alone)
1967	A Funny Thing Happened on the Way to the Forum (alone)
1978	A Little Night Music (alone)

"Song from 'Moulin Rouge,' The." *See* **"Where Is Your Heart?"**

"Song of the Marines" Music by Harry Warren; lyric by Al Dubin. Robust salute to the adventurous life provided by the corps (''We're shovin' right off, we're shovin' right off again''), sung by Dick Powell and fellow Leathernecks at the conclusion of *The Singing Marine* (Warner 1937). Song was something of a successor to ''Don't Give Up the Ship,'' sung by Powell in *Shipmates Forever* (Warner 1935).

"Soon" Music by Richard Rodgers; lyric by Lorenz Hart. Projection of romantic bliss (''Presently and pleasantly our hearts will beat in tune'') crooned by Bing Crosby in *Mississippi* (Par. 1935).

Sothern, Ann (née Harriette Lake), actress, singer; b. Valley City, ND, Jan. 22, 1909. Short, blonde actress with upturned nose and distinctive nasal voice who was known by her real name until she signed a Columbia contract in 1934. She introduced ''Let's Fall in Love,'' and appeared in musicals opposite Lanny Ross, George Murphy, Maurice Chevalier, Gene Raymond, Roger Pryor (her first husband), Robert Young, and Dan Dailey. Miss Sothern's comic gifts are particularly well remembered for the 10 ''Maisie'' films she made for MGM and for her television series.

1929	The Show of Shows (specialty)
1933	Broadway Through a Keyhole (*girl at beach*)
1934	Let's Fall in Love (*Jean*)
	Melody in Spring (*Jane Blodgett*)
	Kid Millions (*Joan Larrabee*)
1935	Folies Bergère (*Mimi*)
	Hooray for Love (*Pat*)
	The Girl Friend (*Linda*)
1936	Walking on Air (*Kit Bennett*)
1941	Lady, Be Good (*Dixie Donegan*)
1942	Panama Hattie (*Hattie Maloney*)
1943	Thousands Cheer (specialty)
1948	April Showers (*June Tyme*)
	Words and Music (*Joyce Harmon*)
1950	Nancy Goes to Rio (*Frances Elliott*)

Sound of Music, The (1965). Music by Richard Rodgers; lyrics by Oscar Hammerstein II; screenplay by Ernest Lehman from Broadway musical by Rodgers, Hammerstein, Howard Lindsay, and Russel Crouse suggested by *Story of the Trapp Family Singers* by Maria Augusta Von Trapp.

A 20th Century-Fox film produced & directed by Robert Wise; associate producer, Saul Chaplin; choreography, Marc Breaux & DeeDee Wood; production design, Boris Leven; costumes, Dorothy Jeakins; music director, Irwin Kostal; orchestrations, Kostal; cameraman, Ted McCord; editor, William Reynolds; DeLuxe Color; Todd-AO.

Cast: Julie Andrews (*Maria Rainer von Trapp*); Christopher Plummer (vocals by Bill Lee) (*Capt. Georg von Trapp*); Eleanor Parker (*Elsa Schraeder*); Richard Haydn (*Max Detweiler*); Peggy Wood (vocals by Margery McKay) (*Mother Abbess*); Charmian Carr (*Liesl von Trapp*); Heather Menzies (*Louisa von Trapp*); Nicolas Hammond (*Friedrich von Trapp*); Duane Chase (*Kurt von Trapp*); Angela Cartwright (*Brigitta von Trapp*); Debbie Turner (*Marta von Trapp*); Kym Karath (*Gretl von Trapp*); Anna Lee (*Sister Margaretta*); Portia Nelson (*Sister Berthe*); Daniel Truhite (*Rolfe*); Marni Nixon (*Sister Sophia*); Bil Baird Marionettes.

Songs: ''The Sound of Music'' - Andrews/ ''Preludium'' - nuns/ ''Maria'' - nuns/ ''I Have Confidence in Me'' (lyric, Richard Rodgers) - Andrews/ ''Sixteen Going on Seventeen'' - Truhitte, Carr/ ''My Favorite Things'' - Andrews/ ''Climb Ev'ry Mountain'' - Wood (McKay)/ ''The Lonely Goatherd'' - Andrews, children/ ''Do-Re-Mi'' - Andrews, children/ ''Something Good'' (lyric, Rodgers) - Andrews, Plummer (Lee)/ ''Processional'' - organ, orchestra/ ''Edelweiss'' - Plummer (Lee), Andrews, children/ ''So Long, Farewell'' - children. Unused: ''How Can Love Survive?,'' ''No Way To Stop It,'' ''An Ordinary Couple.''

According to the *Variety* survey, from 1966 through 1969 *The Sound of Music* was the all-time boxoffice champion in the US and Canada. Its great appeal— which still keeps it among the most popular films ever made—resulted from a melodious score, Julie Andrews' natural radiance, a wholesome subject involving seven children and a group of warmhearted nuns, plus authentic views of the Tyrolean Alps and a picture-postcard Salzburg (where most of the movie was shot). The film was based on the 1959 stage musical, Rodgers and Hammerstein's last collaboration, which had starred Mary Martin, and which in turn had been partly based on a German film *Die Trapp Familie,* starring Ruth Leuwerik. Both productions stemmed from the saga of Maria Rainer, a postulant at Nonnberg Abbey, who became governess to the seven children of the widowed Baron von Trapp. Baron and governess fell in love and married, then led their brood over the Alps to Italy (changed to Switzerland in the musical) to escape the Nazis who had invaded their homeland. (As the Trapp Family Singers, they gave professional concerts— mostly of folk music and light classics—throughout the US for 17 years.)

After buying the screen rights to the Broadway musical for a record $1,250,000, Fox cleared the way for *The Sound of Music* by releasing a dubbed German film, *The Trapp Family,* in 1961, made up by combining sections of *Die Trapp Familie* with its sequel, *Die Trapp Familie in Amerika.* The studio then gave the leading role to Miss Andrews even before her first film, *Mary Poppins,* had been released. Director Robert Wise, who took over after William Wyler bowed out, made effective use of the camera throughout. This was apparent right from the start when—as something of a fresh-air variation on the opening he'd used in *West Side Story*—Wise began the film with awesome views of the Alps, then zoomed in on a joyously singing Julie.

South Pacific (1958). Music by Richard Rodgers; lyrics by Oscar Hammerstein II; screenplay by Paul Osborn from Broadway musical by Rodgers, Hammerstein, and Joshua Logan, based on book *Tales of the South Pacific* by James Michener.

A Magna film released by 20th Century-Fox & produced by Buddy Adler; directed by Joshua Logan; choreography, LeRoy Prinz; art directors, Lyle R. Wheeler, John DeCuir; costumes, Dorothy Jeakins; music director, Alfred Newman, associate music director, Ken Darby; orchestrations, Edward Powell, Pete King, Bernard Mayers, Robert Russell Bennett; cameraman, Leon Shamroy; editor, Robert Simpson; Technicolor; Todd-AO.

Cast: Rossano Brazzi (vocals by Giorgio Tozzi) (*Emile de Becque*); Mitzi Gaynor (*Nellie Forbush*); John Kerr (vocals by Bill Lee) (*Lt. Joe Cable*); Ray Walston (*Luther Billis*); Juanita Hall (vocals by Muriel Smith) (*Bloody Mary*); France Nuycn (*Liat*); Russ Brown (*Capt. George Brackett*); Ken Clark (vocals by Thurl Ravenscroft) (*Stewpot*); Floyd Simmons (*Comdr. William Harbison*); Candace Lee (vocals by Marie Greene) (*Ngana*); Warren Hsieh (vocals by Betty Wand) (*Jerome*).

Songs: "Dites-moi" - Lee (Greene), Hsieh (Wand)/ "A Cockeyed Optimist" - Gaynor/ "Twin Soliloquies" - Gaynor, Brazzi (Tozzi)/ "Some Enchanted Evening" - Brazzi (Tozzi)/ "Bloody Mary" -sailors/ "My Girl Back Home" - Kerr (Lee)/ "There Is Nothin' Like a Dame" - sailors/ "Bali Ha'i" - Hall (Smith)/ "I'm Gonna Wash That Man Right Outa My Hair" - Gaynor/ "A Wonderful Guy" - Gaynor/ "Younger than Springtime" - Kerr (Lee)/ "Happy Talk" - Hall (Smith)/ "Honey Bun" - Gaynor/ "Carefully Taught" - Kerr (Lee)/ "This Nearly Was Mine" - Brazzi (Tozzi).

South Pacific was based on Rodgers and Hammerstein's Prize-winning Broadway adaptation of James Michener's Pulitzer Prize-winning book of wartime short stories. Two of the stories, "Our Heroine," about an unsophisticated Navy nurse and her love for a mature

French planter on a south sea island, and "Fo' Dolla," about a fleeting romance between a Navy lieutenant and a native girl, were combined to form the basic plot of the 1949 musical, which starred Mary Martin and Ezio Pinza. For the film, director Joshua Logan (he'd directed the stage production) wanted Elizabeth Taylor and composer Rodgers wanted Doris Day, but they settled for Mitzi Gaynor. Repeating their stage roles were Juanita Hall (though her singing was dubbed by Muriel Smith, who'd played her part in London), Ray Walston (from the touring and London companies), and Russ Brown (from the touring company). One song, "My Girl Back Home," cut before the Broadway opening was reinstated for the movie. The use of colored filters to establish various moods during the musical sequences was a not-too-successful attempt to break down the screen's inherent naturalism by helping audiences adjust to the artificiality of people singing their emotions. Backgrounds were shot in the Fiji Islands, with most location work on the Hawaiian island of Kauai.

"Spoonful of Sugar, A" Music & lyric by Richard M. Sherman & Robert B. Sherman. How to help make the medicine go down, as prescribed by governess Julie Andrews to charges Karen Dotrice and Matthew Garber in *Mary Poppins* (Disney 1964). As Julie sings, all she has to do is snap her fingers and the children's messy room rearranges itself in perfect order.

"Spring Again" Music by Vernon Duke; lyric by Ira Gershwin. With robins singing again and the moon a yellow balloon, Kenny Baker—in *The Goldwyn Follies* (Goldwyn 1938)—is convinced that there's no better time to fall in love. Because the song was added to the film after George Gershwin's death, it was the only one in the score not written by the composer.

"Spring, Spring, Spring" Music by Gene dePaul; lyric by Johnny Mercer. Perky view of the coming of the vernal season, introduced in *Seven Brides for Seven Brothers* (MGM 1954), by Matt Mattox (with Bill Lee's singing voice), Virginia Gibson, Jeff Richards, Julie Newmeyer (Newmar), Tommy Rall, Nancy Kilgas, Russ Tamblyn, Betty Carr, Marc Platt, Norma Doggett, Jacques d'Amboise, and Ruta Kilmonis (Lee).

"Spring Will Be a Little Late This Year" Music & lyric by Frank Loesser. Torchy lament sung by despondent Deanna Durbin in *Christmas Holiday* (Univ. 1944).

"Stanley Steamer, The" Music by Harry Warren; lyric by Ralph Blane. In *Summer Holiday* (MGM 1948), following a high school graduation in a Connecticut town in 1906, the Miller family (Mickey Rooney, Gloria DeHaven, Walter Huston, Selena Royle, Agnes Moorehead, and Butch Jenkins) get their veils, dusters, and goggles for a high-spirited, chugging ride in the family automobile. Both the song's composer and lyricist had previously written movie numbers about transportation. Warren wrote "Shuffle Off to Buffalo" (with Al Dubin), "Chattanooga Choo-Choo" (Mack Gordon), and "On the Atchison, Topeka and the Santa Fe" (Johnny Mercer); Blane wrote "The Trolley Song" (with Hugh Martin).

"Star!" Music by James Van Heusen; lyric by Sammy Cahn. Glossy theme song of film *Star!* (Fox 1968), sung over credits by Julie Andrews (who played Gertrude Lawrence in the movie). And how can you tell if the lady's a star? Well, for openers, she should be naughty but proper, chic-er than chic, brilliantly witty, and worshipped from afar.

Star Is Born, A (1954). Music by Harold Arlen; lyrics by Ira Gershwin; screenplay by Moss Hart based on screenplay of nonmusical film by Dorothy Parker, Alan Campbell, and Robert Carson from story by William A. Wellman & Carson suggested by film *What Price Hollywood* by Gene Fowler & Rowland Brown from story by Adela Rogers St. John.

A Warner Bros. film produced by Sidney Luft; directed by George Cukor; choreographer, Richard Barstow; art director, Malcolm Bert; costumes, Mary Ann Nyberg, Irene Sharaff; music director, Ray Heindorf; orchestrations, Skip Martin; vocal arrangements, Jack Cathcart; cameraman, Sam Leavitt; editor, Folmar Blangsted; Technicolor; CinemaScope.

Cast: Judy Garland (*Esther Blodgett Maine* aka *Vicki Lester*); James Mason (*Norman Maine* né *Ernest Sidney Gubbins*); Jack Carson (*Matt Libby*); Charles Bickford (*Oliver Niles*); Tom Noonan (*Danny McGuire*); Lucy Marlow (*Lola Lavery*); Irving Bacon (*Graves*); Hazel Shermet (*Miss Willer*); Don McKay, Jack Harmon (*band singers*); James Brown (*Glenn Williams*); Louis Jean Heidt (*director*); Grady Sutton (*Art Carver*); Laurindo Almeida (*guitarist*); Rex Evans (*M.C.*); Monty Montana Rodeo Troupe; Bobby Sailes (*dancer*).

Songs: "Gotta Have Me Go with You" - Garland, McKay, Harmon/ "The Man That Got Away" - Gar-

land/ "Born in a Trunk" (Edens - Gershe) - Garland/ "Swanee" (George Gershwin-Irving Caesar) - Garland/ "It's a New World" - Garland/ "Here's What I'm Here For" - Garland/ "Someone at Last" - Garland/ "Lose That Long Face" - Garland; dance by Garland, Sailes, chorus. Note: "Here's What I'm Here For" & "Lose That Long Face" cut after film's release. Unused: "Green Light Ahead," "I'm Off the Downbeat," "Dancing Partner."

Star Is Born, A (1976). Screenplay by John Gregory Dunne, Joan Didion, and Frank Pierson from story by William A. Wellman & Robert Carson.

A Warner Bros. film produced by Jon Peters, Barbra Streisand; directed by Frank Pierson; production design, Polly Pratt; costumes, Shirley Strahm, Seth Banks; music supervisor, Paul Williams; cameraman, Robert Surtees; editor, Peter Zinner; Metrocolor.

Cast: Barbra Streisand (*Esther Hoffman Howard*); Kris Kirstofferson (*John Norman Howard*); Paul Mazursky (*Brian*); Gary Busey (*Bobby Ritchie*); Oliver Clark (*Gary Danziger*); Vanetta Fields, Clydie King (*The Oreos*); M. G. Kelly (*Bebe Jesus*); Sally Kirkland (*photographer*); Marta Heflin (*Quentin*).

Songs: "Watch Closely Now" (Paul Williams, Kenny Ascher) - Kristofferson; reprised by Streisand/ "Queen Bee" (Rupert Holmes) - Streisand, Fields, King/ "Everything" (Holmes-Williams) - Streisand/ "Lost Inside of You" (Streisand, Leon Russell) - Kristofferson; reprised by Streisand/ "Evergreen" (Streisand-Williams) - Streisand with Kristofferson/ "The Woman in the Moon" (Williams, Ascher) - Streisand/ "I Believe in Love" (Kenny Loggins-Alan & Marilyn Bergman) - Streisand with Fields, King/ "Crippled Crow" (Donna Weiss) - Kristofferson/ "With One More Look at You" (Williams, Ascher) - Kristofferson; reprised by Streisand. Unused: "Hellacious Acres" (Williams, Ascher).

A Star Is Born is based on the legendary Hollywood saga of courage and heartbreak: the young female hopeful meets the mature, alcoholic male star, they fall in love, he helps her in her career, and they marry. Her career moves ahead as his falters; at the end he takes his own life and she nobly carries on. Supposedly suggested by the lives of silent screen actors, Marguerite de la Motte and John Bowers, the basic story was first brought to the screen in nonmusical form. In 1932, *What Price Hollywood*, produced by David O. Selznick and directed by George Cukor, gave us Constance Bennett as a waitress who becomes a movie star and Lowell Sherman as an alcoholic director who guides her career and then shoots himself when his own career goes on the skids. Five years later, Selznick produced a revised version of the film called *A Star Is Born,* which was co-authored and directed by William Wellman. Still unaccompanied by songs, the plot was strengthened by turning into the love story of rising star Esther Blodgett (Janet Gaynor) and fading star Norman Maine (Fredric March) who ends his life by drowning in the Pacific.

The 1954 *A Star Is Born,* the first with songs, stuck to the basic 1937 scenario except that it made Esther a band singer when Norman first meets her, and it provided her with a buddy-type friend (played by Tommy Noonan). The film marked the screen comeback of Judy Garland after a four-year absence; ironically, there were autobiographical elements not only in her own role but also in that of the self-destructive has-been actor. The producer was the inexperienced Sid Luft, then Miss Garland's husband, and Cary Grant, Ray Milland, and Humphrey Bogart were initially sought for the male lead before it went to James Mason. Because of Miss Garland's emotional problems, there were many production delays and firings and hirings, with shooting taking some ten months and costs well over $10 million (after the first eight days of filming, footage had to be reshot when it was decided to release the movie in Cinema-Scope). The 15-minute "Born in a Trunk" routine, added after director George Cukor had left, caused the final print to run about three hours. The studio then reduced the length by about a half-hour by cutting some pivotal scenes and two musical numbers—much to Cukor's widely quoted indignation.

There were certain behind-the-camera similarities between this production and the second musical version of *A Star Is Born* in 1976. Again the property was bought for a major screen personality (Barbra Streisand) who had a close relationship with its tyro producer (Miss Streisand's friend, Jon Peters). And again—as revealed in a magazine article by director Frank Pierson—there were confrontations and walk-outs that caused cost-mounting delays. In this go-round, which changed the principals from movie actors to rock singers, Esther Hoffman (Miss Streisand) is the nascent star while her mentor-husband, John Norman Howard (Kris Kristofferson), is the falling star ravaged by liquor and drugs who puts an end to his life by crashing his Ferrari. The film gave documentary reality to the rock-concert milieu, ably conveying the excitement of Esther's first ap-

pearance before a large crowd and the anguish of her performance after her husband's death.

Starr, Ringo. *See* **Beatles, The.**

"Stars in My Eyes" Music by Fritz Kreisler; lyric by Dorothy Fields. Airy romantic waltz sung by Grace Moore in *The King Steps Out* (Col. 1936). Kreisler's music dates from 1919 when it was known as "Who Can Tell?" (lyric by future film producer William LeBaron) in the Broadway operetta, *Apple Blossoms.*

State Fair (1945). Music by Richard Rodgers; lyrics by Oscar Hammerstein II; screenplay by Hammerstein based on screenplay of nonmusical film by Sonya Levien & Paul Green adapted from novel by Phil Stong.

A 20th Century-Fox film produced by William Perlberg; directed by Walter Lang; art directors, Lyle Wheeler, Lewis Creber; costumes, Rene Hubert; music directors, Alfred Newman, Charles Henderson; orchestrations, Edward Powell; cameraman, Leon Shamroy; editor, J. Watson Webb; Technicolor.

Cast: Jeanne Crain (vocals by Louanne Hogan) (*Margy Frake*); Dana Andrews (*Pat Gilbert*); Dick Haymes (*Wayne Frake*); Vivian Blaine (*Emily*); Charles Winninger (*Abel Frake*); Fay Bainter (*Melissa Frake*); Donald Meek (*Hippenstahl*); Frank McHugh (*McGee*); Percy Kilbride (*David Miller*); Henry Morgan (*barker*); William Marshall (*Marty*).

Songs: "Our State Fair" - Kilbride, Winninger, Bainter/ "It Might as Well Be Spring" - Crain (Hogan)/ "That's for Me" - Blaine; reprised by Crain (Hogan), Andrews/ "It's a Grand Night for Singing" - Marshall, Haymes, chorus; reprised by Blaine, Marshall, chorus/ "Isn't It Kinda Fun?" - Haymes, Blaine/ "All I Owe Ioway" - Marshall, Blaine, Winninger, Bainter, Meek, chorus. Unused: "We Will Be Together."

State Fair, the only film for which Rodgers and Hammerstein wrote an original score together, was the team's first collaboration after their initial stage hit *Oklahoma!* Continuing the bucolic Americana spirit of their maiden effort, the picture spun a simple tale of an Iowa farm family, the Frakes, and their adventures at the state fair. Daughter Margy falls for Pat, a newspaper reporter; son Wayne has a brief fling with Emily, a singer; Ma's mincemeat pie takes first prize; and Pa's hog, Blue Bell, wins the blue ribbon. A prior film version, without songs, was released by Fox in 1933, with Will Rogers, Louise Dresser, Janet Gaynor, and Norman Foster as the Frake family, and Lew Ayres and Sally Eilers as the people they meet.

Fox made a second musical version in 1962. Directed by José Ferrer, it moved its widescreen camera to Texas, where it all but overwhelmed the simple story. This time the Frakes were played by Tom Ewell, Alice Faye, Pamela Tiffin, and Pat Boone, with Bobby Darin and Ann-Margret as their fairground friends. All the 1945 film songs, except "All I Owe Ioway," were retained, and five new songs by Rodgers alone were added.

"Stay as Sweet as You Are" Music by Harry Revel; lyric by Mack Gordon. Romantic wish sung by Lanny Ross in *College Rhythm* (Par. 1934).

"Stayin' Alive" Music & lyric by Barry, Maurice, and Robin Gibb. Walking through Brooklyn streets during the credits of *Saturday Night Fever* (Par. 1977), John Travolta is accompanied on the soundtrack by this nervously rhythmic number sung by The BeeGees.

Steele, Tommy (né Thomas Hicks), actor, singer, dancer; b. London, Dec. 17, 1936. Blond rock and roll singer with toothy grin, who starred in the film version of his London and Broadway success, *Half a Sixpence*. All but two of Steele's movies were made in England.

1957 The Tommy Steele Story (*Tommy Steele*)
1958 The Duke Wore Jeans (*Tommy Hudson/Tony White-cliffe*)
1959 Tommy the Toreador (*Tommy Tompkins*)
1963 It's All Happening (*Billy Bowles*)
1964 The Dream Maker (*Billy Bowles*)
1967 The Happiest Millionaire (US) (*John Lawless*)
     Half a Sixpence (*Arthur Kipps*)
1968 Finian's Rainbow (US) (*Og*)

"Stepping Out with My Baby" Music & lyric by Irving Berlin. Cane-twirling, high-strutting number celebrating a night on the town. Introduced by Fred Astaire in *Easter Parade* (MGM 1948) as part of a Broadway revue; also featured dancers Dee Turnell (ballet), Pat Jackson (blues), and Bobbie Priest (jitterbug). At one point Astaire performed a series of slow-motion leaps as the dancers in the background continued their movements at the regular tempo, a technical feat that required four weeks to achieve proper synchronization between the slowed-up movement and the sound.

Stept, Sam. H, composer; b. Odessa, Russia, Sept. 18, 1897; d. Los Angeles, Dec. 1, 1964. Former bandleader

whose songwriting collaborators were Bud Green, Sidney Clare, Sidney Mitchell, Ted Koehler, Ned Washington, Charles Tobias, and Lew Brown.

1929 Lucky in Love (Green)
     Mother's Boy (Green)
1930 Playing Around (Green)
     Show Girl in Hollywood (Green)
1933 Shady Lady (Green)
1935 This Is the Life (Clare)
1936 Dancing Feet (Mitchell)
     Laughing Irish Eyes (Mitchell)
1937 23½ Hours' Leave (Koehler)
     Dodge City Trail (Washington)
1938 Having Wonderful Time (Tobias)
1942 Yokel Boy (Tobias, Brown)

Stevens, George, director; b. Oakland, Cal., Dec. 18, 1904; d. Lancaster, Cal., March 8, 1975. Former cameraman during silent-film era, Stevens became a director of feature films in 1933. Of his three musicals, all for RKO, the latter two starred Fred Astaire. Bib: *George Stevens: An American Romantic* by Donald Richie (1970).

1935 Nitwits
1936 Swing Time
1937 A Damsel in Distress

Stevens, Risë (née Risë Steenberg), actress, singer; b. New York, June 11, 1913. Metropolitan Opera mezzo-soprano who appeared on screen opposite Nelson Eddy and Bing Crosby.

1941 The Chocolate Soldier (*Maria Lanyi*)
1944 Going My Way (*Genevieve Linden*)
1949 Carnegie Hall (specialty)
1972 Journey Back to Oz (voice of *Good Witch*)

Stewart, James (Maitland), actor; b. Indiana, Pa., May 20, 1908. Laconic screen veteran whose co-stars in musicals included Eleanor Powell, Joan Crawford, Marlene Dietrich, Paulette Goddard, Lana Turner, and June Allyson. Stewart's musical accomplishments were almost exclusively confined to introducing "Easy To Love" in *Born To Dance*, and leading the orchestra in *The Glenn Miller Story*. Bib: *Films of James Stewart* by Kenneth Jones (1970).

1935 Rose Marie (*John Flower*)
1936 Born To Dance (*Ted Barker*)
1939 Ice Follies of 1939 (*Larry Hall*)
     Destry Rides Again (*Tom Destry*)
1941 Pot o' Gold (*Jimmy*)
     Ziegfeld Girl (*Gilbert Young*)
1952 The Greatest Show on Earth (*Buttons*)

1954 The Glenn Miller Story (*Glenn Miller*)
1978 The Magic of Lassie (*Clovis Mitchell*)

"Stiff Upper Lip" Music by George Gershwin; lyric by Ira Gershwin. Helpful advice cheerily offered by Gracie Allen in an amusement park in *A Damsel in Distress* (RKO 1937), followed by a fun-house dance by Gracie, George Burns, and Fred Astaire. Lyricist Ira built the song around what he took to be typically English expressions (i.e., "stout fella," "carry on, old fluff," "keep muddling through"); to his slight embarrassment he later discovered that "stiff upper lip" was actually first coined in Boston in 1815.

Stigwood, Robert, producer; b. Adelaide, Australia, 1934. West End and Broadway producer (*Hair, Jesus Christ Superstar, Evita*) with world-wide entertainment organization (established in 1967) responsible for concerts, records, and films.

1973 Jesus Christ Superstar
1975 Tommy
1976 Bugsy Malone
      The Entertainer (tv)
1977 Saturday Night Fever
1978 Grease
      Sgt. Pepper's Lonely Hearts Club Band
1980 Times Square
1982 Grease II
1983 Staying Alive

Stokowski, Leopold (Antoni Stanislaw Boleslawowicz), conductor; b. London, April 18, 1882 (Polish father, Irish mother); d. Hether Wallop, England, Sept. 13, 1977. Flamboyant conductor of symphony orchestras (he was music director of the Philadelphia Orchestra for 26 years), whose white locks and expressive hands made him particularly photogenic. Bib: *Leopold Stokowski* by Abram Chasins (1979).

1936 Big Broadcast of 1937 (specialty)
1937 One Hundred Men and a Girl (*Leopold Stokowski*)
1940 Fantasia (*Leopold Stokowski*)
1949 Carnegie Hall (specialty)

Story of Vernon and Irene Castle, The (1939). Screenplay by Richard Sherman adapted by Oscar Hammerstein II & Dorothy Yost from book *My Husband* by Irene Castle.

An RKO-Radio film produced by George Haight; directed by H. C. Potter; choreography, Fred Astaire, Hermes Pan; art director, Van Nest Polglase; costumes, Walter Plunkett, Irene Castle; music director, Victor Baravalle; orchestrations, Roy Webb, Robert Russell Bennett; cameraman, Robert de Grasse; editor, William Hamilton.

Cast: Fred Astaire (*Vernon Castle*); Ginger Rogers (*Irene Foote Castle*); Edna May Oliver (*Maggie Sutton*); Walter Brennan (*Walter*); Lew Fields (*Lew Fields*); Etienne Girardot (*Aubel*); Rolfe Sedan (*Emile Aubel*); Janet Beecher (*Annie Foote*); Leonid Kinskey (*artist*); Clarence Derwent (*Louis Barraya*); Victor Varconi (*Grand Duke*); Donald MacBride (*hotel manager*); Douglas Walton (*Peters*); Roy D'Arcy (*actor*); Marjorie Bell (Marge Champion) (*Irene's friend*).

Songs: "Oh, You Beautiful Doll" (Ayer-Brown) - male chorus/ "Glow-worm" (Lincke-Robinson) - female chorus/ "By the Beautiful Sea" (Carroll-Atteridge) - male chorus/ "Row, Row, Row" (Monaco-Jerome) - male chorus/ "Yama Yama Man" (Hoschna-Davis) - Rogers/ "Come Josephine in My Flying Machine" (Fisher-Bryan) - chorus/ "By the Light of the Silvery Moon" (Edwards-Madden) - dance by Astaire/ "Cuddle Up a Little Closer, Lovey Mine" (Hoschna-Harbach) - chorus/ "Only When You're in My Arms" (Con Conrad, Harry Ruby-Bert Kalmar) - Astaire/ "Waiting for the Robert E. Lee" (Muir) - dance by Astaire, Rogers/ "The Darktown Strutters' Ball" (Brooks) - uncredited French singer/ "Too Much Mustard" (Macklin) - dance by Astaire, Rogers/ "Rose Room" (Hickman) - dance by Astaire, Rogers/ "Très Jolie" (Waldteufel) - dance by Astaire, Rogers/ "When They Were Dancing Around" (Monaco) - dance by Astaire, Rogers/ "Little Brown Jug" (Winner) - dance by Astaire, Rogers/ "Dengozo" (Nazareth) - dance by Astaire, Rogers/ Medley: "You're Here and I'm Here," "Chicago," "Hello, Frisco, Hello," "Way Down Yonder in New Orleans," "Take Me Back to New York Town" - dance by Astaire, Rogers/ "It's a Long Way to Tipperary" (Williams-Judge) - soldiers, chorus/ "Hello, Hello, Who's Your Lady Friend?" (Lee-David) - Astaire, soldiers/ Medley: "Destiny Waltz," "Night of Gladness," "Missouri Waltz" - dance by Astaire, Rogers.

RKO's last co-starring assignment for Fred Astaire and Ginger Rogers was also the team's most uncharacteristic film. Forgoing customary comic backchat, sleek art-deco surroundings, and modern dance routines, they re-created the bygone world of Vernon and Irene Castle with the emphasis on romantic sentiment, period flavor, and early ballroom dances. (The Castles, be it noted, had acted in their own biographical film, *The Whirl of*

Life, in 1915.) The movie takes the legendary dancing couple—with some historical rearrangement—from their first meeting in New Rochelle in 1910, through their marriage and early setbacks, their initial success at the Café de Paris, their sensational American tour, Vernon's enlistment in the Royal Air Corps early in the first World War, and up to his death when, as a flight instructor, he crashes his plane to avoid hitting a student pilot. The movie ends with Vernon's shade appearing for a last waltz with Irene—just as in the 1936 film *Maytime,* the dead Nelson Eddy had returned for one last reprise with Jeanette MacDonald.

The Story of Vernon and Irene Castle was also the only Astaire-Rogers vehicle without an original score. Using authentic pre-World War songs, the couple revived such ancient dancefloor creations as the Texas Tommy (to "Waiting for the Robert E. Lee" performed as an audition for producer Lew Fields), the Castle Walk (introduced at the Café de Paris), and a medley of the tango, the polka, and the maxixe (as the team danced across a map of the United States followed by crowds of dancing couples). The single new song in the film, "Only When You're in My Arms," had a lyric by Bert Kalmar, who was later portrayed by Astaire in *Three Little Words.*

Stothart, Herbert, composer; b. Milwaukee, Sept. 11, 1885; d. Los Angeles, Feb. 1, 1949. Broadway composer-conductor-arranger who wrote scores with lyricists Otto Harbach and Oscar Hammerstein II for three operettas that were brought to the screen: *Rose-Marie* (co-composer, Rudolf Friml); *Song of the Flame* (co-composer, George Gershwin); and *Golden Dawn* (co-composer, Emmerich Kalman). In Hollywood as MGM's music director from 1929 to 1947, Stothart worked on all the Jeanette MacDonald-Nelson Eddy movies, arranging scores and rearranging music (e.g., Rudolf Friml's "Donkey Serenade" and George Posford's "At the Balalaika," both with lyrics by Robert Wright and George Forrest). Other collaborators were lyricists Clifford Grey and Gus Kahn.

Asterisk indicates lyrics by Messrs. Harbach & Hammerstein:
1929 Devil May Care (Grey)
1930 Golden Dawn* (Kalman)
      The Rogue Song (Grey)
      Song of the Flame* (Gershwin)
1936 Rose Marie* (Friml-Kahn)
1939 Balalaika (Wright, Forrest)
1942 I Married an Angel (Wright, Forrest)
1954 Rose Marie* (Friml)

"**Strangers**" Music & lyric by Richard Rodgers. Romantic duet for a couple's first meeting, sung by John Cullum and Inga Swenson in television production, *Androcles and the Lion* (NBC 1957).

Straus, Oscar, composer; b. Vienna, March 6, 1870; d. Bad Ischl, Austria, Jan. 11, 1954. Of Straus' 46 operas and operettas, most of which were first performed in Vienna, three received Hollywood screen treatments: *Ein Walzertraum* (retitled *The Smiling Lieutenant*); *Der tapfere Soldat* (*The Chocolate Soldier,* with a different story); and *Hochzeit in Hollywood* (*Married in Hollywood,* an early talkie operetta). The composer's most popular film song was "We Will Always Be Sweethearts" in *One Hour with You.* Those who wrote lyrics to Straus music heard on the screen were Harlan Thompson, Clifford Grey, Leo Robin, Paul Francis Webster, Stanislaus Stange, and Gus Kahn. His Hollywood interpreters included Grace Moore, Maurice Chevalier, Jeanette MacDonald, Nelson Eddy, Risë Stevens—and Bobby Breen. Bib: *Prince of Vienna* by Bernard Grun (1957).

1929 Married in Hollywood (Thompson)
1930 A Lady's Morals (Grey)
1931 The Smiling Lieutenant (Grey)
1932 One Hour with You (Robin)
1937 Make a Wish (Webster)
1941 The Chocolate Soldier (Stange; Kahn)

Streisand, Barbra (Joan), actress, singer; b. Brooklyn, April 24, 1942. Major singing and acting talent with wide-range, expressive voice, and unique persona. Miss Streisand became a Broadway star in *Funny Girl* and a film star in the movie version and has also appeared in nonsinging roles. On the screen she introduced "How Lucky Can You Get?," "The Way We Were," and "Evergreen" (which she wrote with Paul Williams). Bib: *Streisand* by René Jordan (1976); *Barbra* by James Spada (1974).

1968 Funny Girl (*Fanny Brice*)
1969 Hello, Dolly! (*Dolly Levi*)
      On a Clear Day You Can See Forever (*Daisy Gamble*)
1975 Funny Lady (*Fanny Brice*)
1976 A Star Is Born (*Esther Hoffman*) (also comp., co-prod.)
1983 Yentl (*Yentl*) (also dir., co-prod.)

Stromberg, Hunt, producer; b. Louisville, July 12, 1894; d. Santa Monica, Aug. 23, 1968. MGM producer (*The Thin Man, Pride and Prejudice*) responsible for five of the eight Jeanette MacDonald-Nelson Eddy musicals (plus one with MacDonald and Allan Jones).

1935 Naughty Marietta
1936 Rose Marie
       The Great Ziegfeld
1937 Maytime
       The Firefly
1938 Sweethearts
1942 I Married an Angel
1943 Lady of Burlesque

Strouse and Adams. Charles Strouse, composer; b. New York, June 7, 1928. Lee Adams, lyricist; b. Mansfield, Ohio, Aug. 14, 1924. The team first attracted notice with their songs for the Broadway musical *Bye Bye Birdie,* to date their only stage work to be filmed. Strouse also scored the film *Bonnie and Clyde* and wrote the music for *Annie.* (lyrics by Martin Charnin).

1963 Bye Bye Birdie (Adams)
1968 The Night They Raided Minsky's (Adams)
1982 Annie (Charnin)

"Style" Music by James Van Heusen; lyric by Sammy Cahn. What you've either got or you haven't got. Introduced in *Robin and the Seven Hoods* (Warner 1963) by the debonair, high-stepping trio, Frank Sinatra, Dean Martin, and Bing Crosby, all in tuxedoes, sporting canes and boutonnieres and wearing their straw hats at rakishly tilted angles.

Styne, Jule (né Jules Kerwin Stein), composer; b. London, Dec. 31, 1905. Before winning fame as a Broadway composer (*Gentlemen Prefer Blondes, Bells Are Ringing, Gypsy, Funny Girl,* all of which were filmed), Styne was a concert pianist, bandleader, vocal coach, and film composer, primarily in partnership with lyricist Sammy Cahn. Among their songs were "I've Heard That Song Before," "I'll Walk Alone," "There Goes That Song Again," "The Charm of You," "I Fall in Love Too Easily," "Time After Time," "It's Magic," "Three Coins in the Fountain." Styne also worked in Hollywood with George Brown, Walter Bullock, Sol Meyer, Eddie Cherkose, Frank Loesser ("I Don't Want To Walk Without You"), Herb Magidson, Kim Gannon, Harold Adamson, and Leo Robin; his stage and television collaborators were Robin, Betty Comden and Adolph Green, Stephen Sondheim, and Bob Merrill. Among singers identified with Styne songs on both big and little screens are Judy Canova, Frank Sinatra, Danny Kaye, Kathryn Grayson, Gene Kelly, Doris Day, Dennis Morgan, Gordon MacRae, Betty Grable, Tony Martin, Marilyn Monroe, Jane Powell, Judy Holliday, Dean Martin, Liza Minnelli, and Barbra Streisand. Bib: *Jule* by Theodore Taylor (1979).

1940 Sing, Dance, Plenty Hot (Brown)
       Hit Parade of 1941 (Bullock)
       Melody Ranch (Cherkose)
       Melody and Moonlight (Meyer)
1941 Sis Hopkins (Loesser)
       Angels with Broken Wings (Cherkose)
       Puddin' Head (Cherkose)
       Ridin' on a Rainbow (Meyer)
1942 Sleepy Time Gal (Magidson)
       Sweater Girl (Loesser)
       Priorities on Parade (Magidson)
       Youth on Parade (Cahn)
       The Powers Girl (Gannon)
       Johnny Doughboy (Cahn)
1943 Hit Parade of 1943 (Adamson)
       Thumbs Up (Cahn)
       Salute for Three (Gannon)
1944 Knickerbocker Holiday (Cahn)
       Step Lively (Cahn)
       Carolina Blues (Cahn)
1945 Tonight and Every Night (Cahn)
       Anchors Aweigh (Cahn)
1946 Tars and Spars (Cahn)
       Cinderella Jones (Cahn)
       The Kid from Brooklyn (Cahn)
       Earl Carroll Sketch Book (Cahn)
1947 Ladies' Man (Cahn)
       It Happened in Brooklyn (Cahn)
1948 Romance on the High Seas (Cahn)
       Two Guys from Texas (Cahn)
1949 It's a Great Feeling (Cahn)
1950 The West Point Story (Cahn)
1951 Meet Me After the Show (Robin)
       Two Tickets to Broadway (Robin)
       Double Dynamite (Cahn)
1953 Gentlemen Prefer Blondes (Robin)
1955 My Sister Eileen (Robin)
1957 Ruggles of Red Gap (tv) (Robin)
1960 Bells Are Ringing (Comden, Green)
1962 Gypsy (Sondheim)
1964 What a Way To Go (Comden, Green)
1965 Dangerous Christmas of Red Riding Hood (tv) (Merrill)
1967 I'm Getting Married (tv) (Comden, Green)
1968 Funny Girl (Merrill)

"Suddenly It's Spring" Music by James Van Heusen; lyric by Johnny Burke. The buoyant melody accompanied Ginger Rogers' cloud-filled dream dance with Don Loper in *Lady in the Dark* (Par. 1944), then was sung by chorus for the wedding procession that followed. Originally, Ginger did the singing but her vocal was cut.

"Summer Night" Music by Harry Warren; lyric by Al Dubin. Romantic sentiment addressed to the starry skies by James Melton in *Sing Me a Love Song* (Warner 1937).

Sun Valley Serenade (1941). Music by Harry Warren; lyrics by Mack Gordon; screenplay by Robert Ellis & Helen Logan from story by Art Arthur & Robert Harari from idea by Darryl Zanuck.

A 20th Century-Fox film produced by Milton Sperling; directed by H. Bruce Humberstone; choreography, Hermes Pan; art directors, Richard Day, Lewis Creber; music directors, Emil Newman, Glenn Miller; cameraman, Edward Cronjager; editor, James Clark.

Cast: Sonja Henie (*Karen Benson*); John Payne (*Ted Scott*); Glenn Miller (*Phil Carey*); Milton Berle (*Jerome K. "Nifty" Allen*); Lynn Bari (vocals by Pat Friday) (*Vivian Dawn*); Joan Davis (*Miss Carstairs*); Nicholas Brothers, Dorothy Dandridge (specialty); Tex Beneke, Paula Kelly & The Modernaires (band singers); Glenn Miller orchestra.

Songs: "It Happened in Sun Valley" - Bari (Friday); reprised by Berle, Henie, Payne, Bari (Friday), Miller orch./ "I Know Why (and So Do You)" - Bari (Friday), Modernaires, with Miller orch.; reprised by Henie, Payne/ "In the Mood" (Joe Garland) - Miller orch./ "At Last" - Miller orch./ "Chattanooga Choo Choo" - Beneke, Kelly, Modernaires, Nicholas Bros., Dandridge, Miller orch./ "The Kiss Polka" - uncredited girl trio.

Along with swimmer Esther Williams, skater Sonja Henie was the most popular athletic star in Hollywood musicals. *Sun Valley Serenade,* her seventh film, was based on a story idea supplied by Fox studio boss Darryl Zanuck, a frequent visitor to the ski resort in Sun Valley, Idaho. Buttressing the star was the Glenn Miller orchestra, then at the peak of its popularity, with "Chattanooga Choo Choo" the film's musical highlight. In the story, Miss Henie, as a war refugee adopted by the band, follows the group to Sun Valley to demonstrate her skating and skiing skills and to win pianist-arranger John Payne away from singer Lynn Bari.

Other skating stars did not fare as well on the screen. Neither Belita nor Vera Hruba Ralston, who both made their film debuts in Republic's *Ice Capades,* could ap-

proach Miss Henie's popularity (Miss Ralston even made a movie called *Lake Placid Serenade*). And in 1961, Fox's "new Sonja Henie," Carol Heiss, had the misfortune to be introduced to the movie public in *Snow White and the Three Stooges*.

"Sunday in New York." Music by Peter Nero; lyric by Carroll Coates. Finger-snapping ode ("Big city takin' a nap"), with a melody reminiscent of Cy Coleman's "I've Got Your Number." Introduced by Mel Tormé on soundtrack of film of the same name (MGM 1963).

"Sunday, Monday or Always" Music by James Van Heusen; lyric by Johnny Burke. Bing Crosby's romantic request for a permanent relationship, first expressed in *Dixie* (Par. 1943). Also sung by Crosby (off camera) in *Road to Utopia* (Par. 1945).

Sunny Side Up (1929). Music by Ray Henderson; lyrics by B. G. DeSylva & Lew Brown; screenplay by De-Sylva, Brown & Henderson, adapted by David Butler.

A Fox film directed by David Butler; choreography, Seymour Felix; art director, Harry Oliver; costumes, Sophie Wachner; music director, Howard Jackson; cameramen, Ernest Palmer, John Schmitz; editor, Irene Morra; part Multicolor.

Cast: Janet Gaynor (*Molly Carr*); Charles Farrell (*Jack Cromwell*); El Brendel (*Eric Swenson*); Marjorie White (*Bea Nichols*); Frank Richardson (*Eddie Rafferty*); Sharon Lynn (*Jane Worth*); Mary Forbes (*Mrs. Cromwell*); Jackie Cooper (*Jerry McGinnis*).

Songs: "I'm a Dreamer, Aren't We All?" - Gaynor/ "You Find the Time and I'll Find the Place" - Lynn/ "Pickin' Petals Off Daisies" - White, Richardson/ "Sunny Side Up" - Gaynor, street crowd; reprised by White, Richardson/ "Turn on the Heat" - Lynn; dance by chorus girls/ "If I Had a Talking Picture of You" - Gaynor, Farrell; reprised by little boy to little girl/ "Anytime You're Necht on a Broad Bricht Moonlicht Nicht" - White.

The first talkie made by Fox's popular young team, Janet Gaynor and Charles Farrell (they appeared together in 12 films, four of them musicals), *Sunny Side Up* was also the first movie with original songs by Broadway's De Sylva, Brown, and Henderson. Its Cinderella story—not too far removed from such musical-comedy sagas as *Irene* or *Sally*—deals with the romance between perky Mary Carr, who lives in a Yorkville tenement, and Waspy Jack Cromwell, who dwells in a Southampton mansion, and the climax occurs there at an elaborate outdoor charity show filmed in Multicolor. In one spectacular number, "Turn on the Heat," set in an Arctic locale, a blazing midnight sun melts the snow and igloos. As the dancing girls doff their Eskimo apparel in favor of brief tops and bottoms, grass and palm trees sprout, steam heat rises, and, finally, the whole stage goes up in flames as the girls dive into the water separating the performing area from the audience.

"Sunny Side Up" Music by Ray Henderson; lyric by B. G. DeSylva & Lew Brown. Chin-up exhortation ("Stand upon your legs/ Be like two fried eggs"), introduced by Janet Gaynor at a Fourth of July street fair in *Sunny Side Up* (Fox 1929). At the end of the number, Miss Gaynor cavorted about in an undertaker's top hat and cane, then got the whole block to sing along with her.

"Sunshine Cake" Music by James Van Heusen; lyric by Johnny Burke. How to be happy living on nothing. Gaily sung in *Riding High* (Par. 1950) by Bing Crosby, Clarence Muse, and Colleen Gray (probably dubbed), as they accompanied themselves by beating on a coffee pot, an egg beater, a frying pan, and a milk bottle.

"Supercalifragilisticexpialidocious" Music & lyric by Richard M. Sherman & Robert B. Sherman. In *Mary Poppins* (Disney 1964), in a fantasy section combining live actors with animated cartoons, Mary Poppins (Julie Andrews) wins a horse race riding on a merry-go-round horse. When a newspaper reporter comments, "There probably aren't words to describe your emotion at this moment," Mary briskly replies, "On the contrary, there's a perfect word for it. It's 'supercalifragilisticexpialidocìous'!'" Which naturally leads into the lively neologistic number, also performed by Mary's friend Bert (Dick Van Dyke) and a band of roistering, animated cartoon Pearlies.

"Sure Thing" Music by Jerome Kern; lyric by Ira Gershwin. Betting on a sentimental hunch, Rita Hayworth (Martha Mears's voice) revealed in *Cover Girl* (Col. 1944) that "somehow I'm sure I've found a sure thing in you." In the film the song was performed in flashback as a racetrack number—complete with young blades in striped blazers—on the stage of Tony Pastor's Music Hall. The idea behind the lyric recalls a previous Ira Gershwin song, "(I've Got) Beginner's Luck" (mu-

sic by brother George), which also dealt with a beginner becoming a winner.

Sutherland, A. Edward, director; b. London, Jan. 5, 1895; d. Palm Springs, Jan. 1, 1974. After acting in Keystone Kop movies, Sutherland became a Paramount director specializing in comedies and musicals. Among performers he directed were Nancy Carroll, Jack Oakie, Eddie Cantor, W. C. Fields, Bing Crosby, Gladys Swarthout, Mae West, Allan Jones, and Dorothy Lamour.

1929	Close Harmony
	The Dance of Life
	Pointed Heels
1930	Paramount on Parade (part)
	The Sap from Syracuse
1931	June Moon
	Palmy Days
1933	International House
	Too Much Harmony
1935	Mississippi
1937	Champagne Waltz
	Every Day's a Holiday
1940	The Boys from Syracuse
1942	Sing Your Worries Away
	One Night in the Tropics
1943	Dixie
1944	Follow the Boys

Swarthout, Gladys, actress, singer; b. Deepwater, Mo., Dec. 25, 1904; d. Florence, Italy, July 8, 1969. Strikingly attractive mezzo-soprano who sang at the Metropolitan Opera (1929–45), and who appeared in four Paramount films opposite John Boles (twice), Jan Kiepura, and Fred MacMurray.

1935	Rose of the Rancho (*Rosita Castro*)
1936	Give Us This Night (*Maria*)
1937	Champagne Waltz (*Elsa Strauss*)
1938	Romance in the Dark (*Ilona Boros*)

"Sweepin' the Clouds Away" Music & lyric by Sam Coslow. The finale of *Paramount on Parade* (Par. 1930) found chimney sweep Maurice Chevalier sweeping and singing on a Parisian rooftop. Presently, he is joined by a bevy of sweeperettes who prance about and form kaleidoscopic designs which are seen in some overhead shots. Maurice then climbs an ethereal ladder to a rainbow of girls and ends, literally, sweeping the clouds. Song was also sung by Helen Mack in *You Belong to Me* (Par. 1934).

273

"Sweet Is the Word for You" Music by Ralph Rainger; lyric by Leo Robin. Bing Crosby expressed amatory admiration in *Waikiki Wedding* (Par. 1937).

"Sweet Leilani" Music & lyric by Harry Owens. Mellifluous Hawaiian ballad introduced by Bing Crosby in *Waikiki Wedding* (Par. 1937).

"Sweet Music" Music by Harry Warren; lyric by Al Dubin. Paean to music's power, introduced by Rudy Vallee in film of same name (Warner 1935).

"Swing High, Swing Low" Music by Burton Lane; lyric by Ralph Freed. Rhythmic advice to take advantage of swing music as an adjunct to romance, proffered by chorus over credits of film of same name (Par. 1937).

Swing Time (1936). Music by Jerome Kern; lyrics by Dorothy Fields; screenplay by Howard Lindsay & Allan Scott, from story "Portrait of John Garnett" by Erwin Gelsey.

An RKO-Radio film produced by Pandro S. Berman; directed by George Stevens; choreography, Fred Astaire, Hermes Pan; art director, Van Nest Polglase; costumes, Bernard Newman; music director, Nathaniel Shilkret; orchestrations, Robert Russell Bennett; cameraman, David Abel; editor, Henry Berman.

Cast: Fred Astaire (*John "Lucky" Garnett*); Ginger Rogers (*Penelope "Penny" Carrol*); Victor Moore (*Pop Cardetti*); Helen Broderick (*Mabel Anderson*); Eric Blore (*Gordon*); Betty Furness (*Margaret Watson*); Georges Metaxa (*Ricardo Romero*); Landers Stevens (*Judge Watson*); Pierre Watkin (*Al Simpson*).

Songs: "It's Not in the Cards" - dance by Astaire, troupe/ "Pick Yourself Up" - Astaire, Rogers/ "The Way You Look Tonight" - Astaire/ "Waltz in Swing Time" - dance by Astaire, Rogers/ "A Fine Romance" - Astaire, Rogers/ "Bojangles of Harlem" - chorus; dance by Astaire, chorus/ "Never Gonna Dance" - Astaire; dance by Astaire, Rogers.

During production, it was first called *I Won't Dance*, then *Never Gonna Dance*, but such disavowals seemed unsuited as the name of the fifth Fred Astaire-Ginger Rogers vehicle and it was given the more buoyant appellation *Swing Time*. Though the title aimed at capitalizing on the burgeoning swing-music craze, the movie itself had nothing to do with the world of big bands or jitterbugs. In this one, Fred played a hoofer with a penchant for gambling (as he later did in *Let's Dance*) who teams with Ginger to win acclaim in two glittering nightclubs, the Club Raymond and the Silver Sandal. (Curiously, they dance the "Waltz in Swing Time" in the former as an audition for the latter, even though the Silver Sandal's owner is nowhere in sight.) Temporary romantic rivalry is provided by society bandleader Georges Metaxa (a menacing variation on Erik Rhodes' Latin-lover in *Top Hat*) who pursues Ginger, and socialite Betty Furness as Fred's fiancée.

Swing Time was the only Astaire-Rogers musical directed by George Stevens (he later directed Astaire without Rogers in *A Damsel in Distress*) and the only one with a complete score by Jerome Kern and Dorothy Fields (they had written two songs together for *Roberta*). The film also allowed Astaire to perform a number of uncharacteristic routines: he danced as awkwardly as he could at the beginning of "Pick Yourself Up"; he wore blackface for the only time in "Bojangles of Harlem"; and he failed to win Ginger over in their main romantic ballroom number, "Never Gonna Dance."

"Swingin' the Jinx Away" Music & lyric by Cole Porter. Breezy, optimistic number used for the spectacular finale of *Born To Dance* (MGM 1936). First sung by Frances Langford, in snappy white military uniform, accompanied by formally clad male chorus as part of a Broadway musical. Scene then opens up to become the deck of a battleship, with gangling Buddy Ebsen singing the song's verse followed by his dance solo, and a sailors' chorus and The Foursome vocal group doing the refrain. High up in the crow's nest, Captain Eleanor Powell, in shako, black cape, and spangled tights, flashes a smile and descends down a catwalk to the stage where she taps and turns cartwheels in front of dancing sailors and a brassy military band blaring away. Though the film's director and choreographer did not feel that the number was right for the finale, Cole Porter refused to change a word or a note. As he put it, "For weeks, I studied all of the American folk songs and tried to write a melody that would be essentially American, not fashionable jazz, but a spirited folk song such as 'The Arkansas Traveler.'" Arranger Roger Edens, however, has referred to the song as "a really jazzy kind of thing" and the production as "that really monstrous epitome of nonsense, the big half-million dollar battleship with several thousand dancers and singing sailors and sequined cannons."

"Swinging on a Star" Music by James Van Heusen; lyric by Johnny Burke. Sung by Bing Crosby and the Robert Mitchell Boychoir in *Going My Way* (Par. 1944). The formidable assignment given to songwriters Van Heusen and Burke was to come up with a number that would be the equivalent of teaching the Ten Commandments in a rhythmic, amusing manner. "It was some problem," Van Heusen once recalled, "and we struggled with it for days. In the end, it was Bing who supplied the inspiration. We were at his house for dinner and one of his boys was acting up. Bing chastised him by saying, 'What do you want to be—a mule?' That

sparked us off." In the film, the song was performed as an original composition by Father Chuck O'Malley (Crosby), who sings it with his church choir on the stage of the Metropolitan Opera House as part of an audition for a music publisher. Though the publisher (William Frawley) has supposedly already left the theatre, he hears the song and buys it on the spot. Crosby also sang the song in *Duffy's Tavern* (Par. 1945), accompanied by Dorothy Lamour, Betty Hutton, Sonny Tufts, Diana Lynn, and Arturo DeCordova.

Syncopation. *See* ***Birth of the Blues.***

T

"Take a Number from One to Ten" Music by Harry Revel; lyric by Mack Gordon. Rhythmic, hyperbolic assertion of love first offered by Lyda Roberti in *College Rhythm* (Par. 1934).

"Take Me to the World" Music & lyric by Stephen Sondheim. Confined to a department store in the television fantasy, *Evening Primrose* (ABC 1966), Anthony Perkins and Charmian Carr affirm their desire to rejoin the world outside.

"Takes Two To Make a Bargain" Music by Harry Revel; lyric by Mack Gordon. "Cupid as our pilot/ We can middle-aisle it," sang Bing Crosby in this jaunty proposal in *Two for Tonight* (Par. 1935).

"Talk to the Animals" Music & lyric by Leslie Bricusse. In which Rex Harrison as *Doctor Dolittle* (Fox 1967), prompted by Polynesia, his pet parrot, ruminates on the possibility of mastering animal conversation. At the end he is surrounded by his grunting, squeaking, squawking patients.

Tamblyn, Russ, actor, singer, dancer; b. Los Angeles, Dec. 30, 1934. Blond, boyish-looking performer who began as Rusty Tamblyn in radio.

1954	Seven Brides for Seven Brothers (*Gideon Pontipee*)
1955	Hit the Deck (*Danny Smith*)
1958	Tom Thumb (*Tom Thumb*)
1961	West Side Story (*Riff*)
1962	Wonderful World of the Brothers Grimm (*Woodsman*)
1963	Follow the Boys (*Lt. Smith*)

"Tammy" Music & lyric by Jay Livingston & Ray Evans. Bucolic expression of young love introduced in *Tammy and the Bachelor* (Univ. 1957) by the Ames Brothers on the soundtrack during credits, later by Debbie Reynolds, as Tammy, in her room. Because the song was not thought to have much potential, the commercial recording—contrary to the usual custom at the time—was taken directly from the soundtrack rather than have Miss Reynolds re-record the piece in a studio.

"Tangerine" Music by Victor Schertzinger; lyric by Johnny Mercer. Sultry number about self-centered Latin charmer, introduced in *The Fleet's In* (Par. 1942) by Bob Eberly (sweet) and Helen O'Connor (swing), with Jimmy Dorsey's orchestra. Scene was the Swingland Dance Hall in San Francisco.

Tauber, Richard (né Ernst Seifert), actor, singer; b. Linz, Austria, May 16, 1892; d. London, Jan. 8, 1948. An acclaimed lyric tenor, Tauber sang in opera and operetta mostly in Germany and London. All of his English-language films were made in Great Britain.

1934	Blossom Time (*Franz Schubert*)
1935	Heart's Desire (*Joseph Steidler*)
1936	Land Without Music (*Mario Carlini*)
	Pagliacci (*Canio Tonini*)
1946	Waltz Time (*Shepherd*)
	The Lisbon Story (*André Joubert*)

Taurog, Norman, director; b. Chicago, Feb. 23, 1899. Veteran director, whose film career began in 1917 as an actor, and who worked mostly at Paramount and MGM. Taurog directed Elvis Presley in nine musicals, Dean Martin and Jerry Lewis and Judy Garland in four each (including Garland's *Girl Crazy*), Bing Crosby in three; others include George Jessel, George M. Cohan, Maurice Chevalier, Eddie Cantor, Deanna Durbin, Fred Astaire and Eleanor Powell (*Broadway Melody of 1940*),

Mickey Rooney, Mario Lanza, Jane Powell, Debbie Reynolds, and Pat Boone. (Taurog died April 8, 1981, Palm Desert, Cal.)

1929 Lucky Boy
1930 Follow the Leader
1932 The Phantom President
1933 A Bedtime Story
     The Way to Love
1934 We're Not Dressing
     College Rhythm
1935 Big Broadcast of 1936
1936 Strike Me Pink
     Rhythm on the Range
1937 You Can't Have Everything
1938 Mad About Music
1940 Broadway Melody of 1940
     Little Nellie Kelly
1943 Presenting Lily Mars
     Girl Crazy
1948 Big City
     Words and Music
1949 That Midnight Kiss
1950 The Toast of New Orleans
1951 Rich, Young and Pretty
1952 Jumping Jacks
     The Stooge
1953 The Stars Are Singing
1954 Living It Up
1956 Pardners
     Bundle of Joy
1960 GI Blues
1961 All Hands on Deck
1962 Blue Hawaii
     Girls! Girls! Girls!
1963 Palm Springs Weekend
     It Happened at the World's Fair
1965 Tickle Me
1966 Spinout
1967 Double Trouble
1968 Speedway
     Love a Little Live a Little

Taylor, Elizabeth (Rosamond), actress; b. Hampstead Heath, London, Feb. 27, 1932. Screen beauty who has appeared in epics (*Cleopatra*), dramas (*Who's Afraid of Virginia Woolf?*), and a few musicals. Actors Michael Wilding, Eddie Fisher, and Richard Burton, and producer Michael Todd were among her husbands.

1948 A Date with Judy (*Carol Pringle*)
1954 Rhapsody (*Louise Durant*)
1974 That's Entertainment (narrator)
1976 The Blue Bird (*Mother/Maternal Love/Witch/Light*)
1978 A Little Night Music (*Desirée Armfeldt*)

Taylor, Robert (né Spangler Arlington Brough), actor; b. Filley, Neb., Aug. 5, 1911; d. Hollywood, June 8, 1969. Actor of classic good looks whose screen career lasted from 1934 to 1968. Chiefly in MGM films, Taylor appeared opposite Eleanor Powell in two musicals and introduced "I've Got a Feelin' You're Foolin.'" Barbara Stanwyck was his first wife. Bib: *Films of Robert Taylor* by Lawrence Quirk (1975).

1935 Broadway Melody of 1936 (*Bob Gordon*)
1937 Broadway Melody of 1938 (*Steve Raleigh*)
     This Is My Affair (*Lt. Richard Perry*)
1952 I Love Melvin (guest bit)

Temple, Shirley (Jane), actress, singer, dancer; b. Santa Monica, April 23, 1928. The screen's most adored child actress—celebrated for her Bright Eyes, her Curly Top, and her Dimples—showed a Depression-plagued nation how to conquer adversity through determination, optimism, and a cheery song or two (among them, "Baby, Take a Bow," "On the Good Ship Lollipop," and "Animal Crackers in My Soup"). Miss Temple made virtually all her musicals at Fox, where she was surrounded by such doting relatives and protectors as James Dunn, Bill Robinson (her dancing partner in four films), John Boles, Buddy Ebsen, Alice Faye, Jack Haley, Frank Morgan, George Murphy, Charles Farrell, Jack Oakie, and Charlotte Greenwood. In the 70s, Miss Temple was Ambassador to Ghana then US Chief of Protocol. Bib: *Films of Shirley Temple* by Robert Windeler (1978).

1934 Stand Up and Cheer (*Shirley Dugan*)
     Little Miss Marker (*Marky*)
     Baby Take a Bow (*Shirley*)
     Bright Eyes (*Shirley*)
1935 The Little Colonel (*Lloyd Sherman*)
     Curly Top (*Elizabeth "Curly" Blair*)
     The Littlest Rebel (*Virgie Cary*)
1936 Captain January (*Star*)
     Poor Little Rich Girl (*Barbara Barry*)
     Dimples (*Sylvia "Dimples" Appleby*)
     Stowaway (*Ching-Ching Stewart*)
1938 Rebecca of Sunnybrook Farm (*Rebecca Winstead*)
     Little Miss Broadway (*Betsy Brown*)
     Just Around the Corner (*Penny Hale*)
1939 The Little Princess (*Sara Crewe*)
1940 The Blue Bird (*Mytyl Tyl*)
     Young People (*Wendy Ballentine*)
1947 Honeymoon (*Barbara*)

"Temptation" Music by Nacio Herb Brown; lyric by Arthur Freed. Self-pitying dirge of amatory bondage sung by Bing Crosby in *Going Hollywood* (MGM 1933). The scene is a saloon in Tijuana where Bing, after being told off by Marion Davies, has gone on a bender with Fifi D'Orsay. As prismatically photographed couples sway on the crowded dance floor, Bing sits at the bar and pours his unhappy heart out to seductive Fifi.

"Ten Minutes Ago" Music by Richard Rodgers; lyric by Oscar Hammerstein II. Love at first sight revealed by Jon Cypher and Julie Andrews, as Prince and drudge, in the television musical *Cinderella* (CBS 1957). Eight years later it was sung by Stuart Damen and Leslie Ann Warren in the CBS remake.

"Tender Trap, The" Music by James Van Heusen; lyric by Sammy Cahn. How a bachelor suddenly gets hooked, cooked, and caught. Frank Sinatra explained it all on the soundtrack of the nonmusical film *The Tender Trap* (MGM 1955).

Terry, Ruth (née Ruth Mae McMahon), actress, singer; b. Benton Harbor, Mich., Oct. 21, 1920. Former band and nightclub singer who made major musical at Fox (*Alexander's Ragtime Band*), but spent most of her time at Republic (three oaters with Roy Rogers).

1937	Love and Hisses (specialty)	
1938	Alexander's Ragtime Band (*Ruby Lane*)	
	Hold That Coed (*Edie*)	
1940	Sing, Dance, Plenty Hot (*Irene*)	
1941	Blondie Goes Latin (*Lovey Nelson*)	
	Rookies on Parade (*Lois Rogers*)	
1942	Heart of the Golden West (*Mary Lou Popen*)	
1943	Hands Across the Border	
	Pistol Packin' Mama (*Vicki Norris/ Sally Benson*)	
	The Man from Music Mountain	
1944	My Buddy (*Lola*)	
	Lake Placid Serenade (*Susan*)	
	Jamboree (*Ruth Cortwright*)	

"Tess's Torch Song" Music by Harold Arlen; lyric by Ted Koehler. In *Up in Arms* (Goldwyn 1944), Dinah Shore as a WAC lieutenant entertained the troops on a Pacific Ocean transport ship by relating the torchy saga of one who lost both her man and her friend.

"Thank Heaven for Little Girls" Music by Frederick Loewe; lyric by Alan Jay Lerner. At the beginning of *Gigi* (MGM 1958), aging boulevardier Maurice Cheva-

lier expressed proper appreciation while eyeing the little girls in the Bois de Boulogne and imagining how they'd look when they grew up. The song, which was written while Loewe and Lerner were in Paris, was a hard one for the lyricist to complete. "I worked for three days on two lines for the song," he once told interviewer Pete Martin. " 'Those little eyes, so helpless and appealing,/ One day will flash and send you crashing through the ceiling.' In the beginning, I wrote those two lines in two hours. I wanted the 'flash' and the 'crash' because Maurice's accent would boom them over. But I wasn't completely satisfied, so I worked on them for three more days. Finally, one morning Fritz Loewe came home about six o'clock after a gay night on the town, and asked me, 'How's it coming?' I said, 'I know what I want to say but I can't find the words to say it. I must have at least a hundred versions so far.' I read my latest attempt to him and he said, 'Why that's perfect!' Then something struck in his memory, and he asked, 'Isn't that exactly the way it read three days ago?' He was right. I'd been going around in an incredible search for exactly the right words, and the right words were the first ones I'd thought of." Actually, Lerner revealed that he was never really totally satisfied. In his autobiography, *The Street Where I Live,* he wrote that the insoluble problem was the notion of someone crashing through a ceiling, which he maintained was a physical impossibility.

"Thank You Very Much" Music & lyric by Leslie Bricusse. Rollicking song of appreciation, sung in *Scrooge* (Nat. Gen. 1970) by Anton Rodgers and Londoners after they hear of Scrooge's death. Also joined in by Albert Finney as Scrooge.

"Thanks" Music by Arthur Johnston; lyric by Sam Coslow. Reasoning that "It's better to have loved and lost than never to have loved at all," Bing Crosby, in *Too Much Harmony* (Par. 1933), offered thanks for lovely delights and unforgettable nights that are no more. "Thanks" followed the previous year's "Please" (by Ralph Rainger and Leo Robin), which Crosby sang in *The Big Broadcast.*

"Thanks a Lot But No Thanks" Music by André Previn; lyric by Betty Comden & Adolph Green. Because she's a "faithful lassie waiting for her faithful lad," Dolores Gray—in a television show in *It's Always Fair Weather* (MGM 1955)—politely refuses such romantic offerings from wealthy admirers as a silver-blue mink, a plane, an ice-skating rink, a yacht, a solid-gold sink, a scrabble set with a platinum board, a factory once known as Ford, the lost chord, banks, the Santa Fe line, a darling uranium mine, champagne, the state of Maine, an autographed photo of John Wayne, a cruise, oil wells that ooze, Fred Astaire's shoes, and Ft. Knox sealed and signed.

"Thanks a Million" Music by Arthur Johnston; lyric by Gus Kahn. Appreciation expressed by Dick Powell in *Thanks a Million* (Fox 1935) to one who "made a million dreams come true."

"Thanks for the Memory" Music by Ralph Rainger; lyric by Leo Robin. Seated at the bar of the S. S. *Gigantic* in *Big Broadcast of 1938* (Par. 1938), Bob Hope and Shirley Ross, as a still-in-love divorced couple, ruefully reminisce about the varied things they once shared during their mercurial life together—rainy afternoons, swingy Harlem tunes, candlelight and wine, castles on the Rhine, the Parthenon, the Hudson River Line, crap games on the floor, nights in Singapore, China's funny walls, transatlantic calls, lunch from twelve to four, sunburns at the shore, gardens at Versailles, beef and kidney pie. All of which elicit Shirley's admiring comment, "You may have been a headache but you never were a bore." One line, "That weekend at Niag'ra when we never saw the Falls," was forbidden by the studio censor who made lyricist Robin change the word "never" to "hardly." Curiously, when Hope and Ross recorded the song for Decca, almost all the references in the original lyric were replaced. Hope, who made his feature debut in *Big Broadcast of 1938*, was so identified with the number that he made it his theme song. It also led to other conversational duets with Miss Ross, including "Two Sleepy People" (in *Thanks for the Memory*, 1938) and "The Lady's in Love with You" (in *Some Like It Hot*, 1939). Jack Strachey and Eric Maschwitz's "These Foolish Things," written for the 1936 London revue, *Spread It Abroad*, expressed a theme similar to that in "Thanks for the Memory."

"That Old Black Magic" Music by Harold Arlen; lyric by Johnny Mercer. Sung by Johnny Johnston as a GI and danced by Vera Zorina as his dream girl in an all-star show in *Star Spangled Rhythm* (Par. 1942). The lengthy, emotion-charged composition describes a romantic spell of such flaming intensity "that only your lips can put out the fire"—though one might argue that it is more likely for a kiss to start a fire than to stop one. Ballad also sung by Bing Crosby in *Here Come the Waves* (Par. 1944); Frank Sinatra in *Meet Danny Wilson* (Univ. 1952); Marilyn Monroe in *Bus Stop* (Fox 1956); Jerry Lewis in *The Nutty Professor* (Par. 1963), and Ann-Margret in *The Swinger* (Par. 1966). Lyricist Mercer once claimed that the idea for the lyric was sparked by the line, "Do do that voodoo that you do so well," in Cole Porter's "You Do Something to Me."

"That Old Feeling" Music by Sammy Fain; lyric by Lew Brown. Torchy ballad of one who feels the spark of love rekindled when she sees an old flame. Introduced by Virginia Verrill in *Vogues of 1938* (UA 1937).

"That's Amore" Music by Harry Warren; lyric by Jack Brooks. Sung by Dean Martin in *The Caddy* (Par. 1953), with his Italian-American family (Barbara Bates, Joseph Calleia, Argentina Brunetti) to entertain his friend, Jerry Lewis. Composer Warren once admitted that the rollicking, pseudo-Italian number would not have been in the picture had he not been a friend of the producer. "The script called for the character to sing either 'O Sole Mio' or 'Come Back to Sorrento.' I said to my friend, 'They've been done to death. How about letting me write a new song?' He said, 'Go ahead.' And I did."

"That's an Irish Lullaby." *See* **"Too-Ra-Loo-Ra-Loo-Ral"**

That's Entertainment. See Ziegfeld Follies.

"That's Entertainment" Music by Arthur Schwartz; lyric by Howard Dietz. The only song written specifically for *The Band Wagon* (MGM 1953), which otherwise had a score consisting of previously indited show tunes. In the film, after director Jack Buchanan explains that his new musical will be based on the *Faust* legend, song-and-dance man Fred Astaire asks, "Will that be entertaining?" Then, to illustrate the point that "the world is a stage, the stage is a world of entertainment," Buchanan, plus Nanette Fabray, Oscar Levant, and Astaire, proceed to sing about and act out a variety of situations—from a clown with his pants falling down, to a divorcée after her ex-husband's money, and from a clerk who's been thrown out of work, to a great Shakespearean scene ("Where a ghost and a prince meet/ And ev'ryone ends in mincemeat"). The song, which has become something of an unofficial show-business anthem, was used as the theme for *That's Entertainment* (MGM 1974) and sung by Gene Kelly and Fred Astaire in *That's Entertainment Part 2* (MGM 1976).

"That's for Me" Music by Richard Rodgers; lyric by Oscar Hammerstein II. Gracefully gliding ballad of love at first sight, introduced in *State Fair* (Fox 1945) by Vivian Blaine from the bandstand at the Iowa State Fair; reprised by Jeanne Crain (Louanne Hogan's voice) and Dana Andrews. In 1962 film version (also Fox) it was sung by Pat Boone.

"That's Love" Music by Richard Rodgers; lyric by Lorenz Hart. Minor-key lament introduced by Anna Sten in *Nana* (Goldwyn 1934). Composer Rodgers wrote in his autobiography, *Musical Stages,* "One day, he [Sam Goldwyn] asked me to play it for Frances Marion, a sweet, precious little woman who was one of Goldwyn's favorite screen writers. Al Newman [the music director] was also there. When I finished I looked up from the keyboard and was startled to see the lady standing with her eyes closed as if in a trance. When Sam asked her what she thought, she slowly opened her eyes and said, 'Sam, this song is the essence of Paris. I've never heard anything so Parisian in my life.' With that Goldwyn wheeled around to Newman and commanded, 'Newman, in the orchestra eight French horns!' "

"That's What I Want for Christmas" Music by Gerald Marks; lyric by Irving Caesar. Standing before a Christmas tree in the tacked-on final scene in *Stowaway* (Fox 1936), Shirley Temple wished for such altruistic gifts as foster mommy Alice Faye's life to be a song and foster daddy Robert Young to be kept safe and strong.

"Thee I Love." *See* **"Friendly Persuasion"**

"Theme from New York, New York" Music by John Kander; lyric by Fred Ebb. Rousing ode to the challenging metropolis ("If you can make it there,/ You'll make it anywhere"), sung in *New York, New York* (UA 1977) by Liza Minnelli as a song she's just written. The piece's somewhat awkward title was used to differentiate it from the previous "New York, New York," by Leonard Bernstein, Betty Comden, and Adolph Green.

"Theme from The Spy Who Loved Me." *See* **"Nobody Does It Better"**

"There Goes That Song Again" Music by Jule Styne; lyric by Sammy Cahn. Ballad of romantic recollection introduced by Harry Babbitt, with Kay Kyser's orchestra, in *Carolina Blues* (Col. 1944); also sung by Dick Haymes in *Cruisin' Down the River* (Col. 1953). In 1942 Styne and Cahn had written the similarly titled "I've Heard That Song Before," first sung in *Youth on Parade.*

"There Will Never Be Another You" Music by Harry Warren; lyric by Mack Gordon. Graceful rising-and-falling melody mated to a lyric of such regretful leave-taking that one wonders why the separation has to be so permanent. In *Iceland* (Fox 1942), it was introduced by band singer Joan Merrill, backed by Sammy Kaye's orchestra, in the dining room of an elegant Reykjavik hotel. During the reprise, Miss Merrill sang the ballad directly to ex-fiancé John Payne seated at a table with Sonja Henie. Song was also sung by Dennis Day in *I'll Get By* (Fox 1950).

"There's a Fellow Waiting in Poughkeepsie" Music by Harold Arlen; lyric by Johnny Mercer. A Navy show in *Here Come the Waves* (Par. 1944) offered a sketch titled "If Waves Acted Like Sailors," in which Betty Hutton happily boasted to her sister Waves of the boyfriends she had pining for her in cities throughout the United States.

"There's a Lull in My Life" Music by Harry Revel; lyric by Mack Gordon. In a radio broadcast in *Wake Up and Live* (Fox 1937), Alice Faye sings of the emptiness she feels when her lover goes away. Ben Bernie's orchestra provided the musical accompaniment.

"There's a Rainbow 'Round My Shoulder" Music & lyric by Dave Dreyer, Billy Rose, and Al Jolson. The feeling you get when you're in love, exuberantly expressed by Al Jolson in *The Singing Fool* (Warner 1928). Also sung by Jolson (dubbed for Larry Parks) in *The Jolson Story* (Col. 1946)

"There's Danger in Your Eyes, Cherie" Music by Pete Wendling; lyric by Jack Meskill. Romantic admission introduced by Harry Richman in *Puttin' on the Ritz* (UA 1930). Also sung by Danielle Darrieux in *Rich, Young and Pretty* (MGM 1951).

"There's Nothing Too Good for My Baby" Music by Harry Akst; lyric by Benny Davis. Depression-inspired uptempo love song for Eddie Cantor in *Palmy Days* (Goldwyn 1931). In it, the singer gaily proclaims that his beloved's wants are satisfied at the Five and Ten and that the closest she gets to limousines is in magazines.

"There's Something About a Soldier" Music & lyric by Noel Gay. Zippy tribute to the British army ("Oh, a military chest seems to suit the ladies best") sung by Cicely Courtneidge in *Soldiers of the King* (Gaumont-Brit. 1933).

"They All Fall in Love" Music & lyric by Cole Porter. "The young fall, the old fall,/ The red-hot mommas and the cold fall," sang Gertrude Lawrence in *The Battle of Paris* (Par. 1929). A successor to the songwriter's "Let's Do It," this "laundry-list" number was the first song Porter wrote for the screen.

"They All Laughed" Music by George Gershwin; lyric by Ira Gershwin. True love conquers despite the same kind of scoffing that had once greeted Columbus, Edison, the Wright brothers, Marconi, Whitney, Fulton, Hershey, Ford, and the construction of Rockefeller Center. The jaunty piece was introduced by Ginger Rogers in *Shall We Dance* (RKO 1937) in a glittering nightclub atop a New York hotel, then danced to by Miss Rogers and Fred Astaire.

"They Can't Take That Away from Me" Music by George Gershwin; lyric by Ira Gershwin. On a ferryboat after marrying Ginger Rogers in *Shall We Dance* (RKO 1937), Fred Astaire sadly anticipates their prearranged divorce and sings wistfully to her of the things he will always keep the memory of—the way she wears her hat, sips her tea, and holds her knife, as well as her beaming smile and offkey singing. Twelve years later, the ballad was again used in an Astaire-Rogers movie, MGM's *The Barkleys of Broadway*, in which, as part of a benefit show, it was sung by Fred to Ginger then used for their dance.

"They're Either Too Young or Too Old" Music by Arthur Schwartz; lyric by Frank Loesser. In which Bette Davis—in an all-star charity revue in *Thank Your Lucky Stars* (Warner 1943)—complained of the romantic frustrations caused by World War II ("What's good is in the army/ What's left will never harm me"). The setting in the show was a swank cocktail lounge where Bette sang to formally clad elders (including Jack Norton) and briefly jitterbugged with young Conrad Wiedell. Song also sung by Jane Froman (dubbing for Susan Hayward) in *With a Song in My Heart* (Fox 1952).

"Things Are Looking Up" Music by George Gershwin; lyric by Ira Gershwin. Happy as a pup because love has looked up at him, Fred Astaire sang of his newfound bliss in *A Damsel in Distress* (RKO 1937) while skipping with Joan Fontaine through the grounds of Totleigh Castle (located, according to lyricist Ira, in Upper Pelham-Grenville, Wodehouse, England).

"This Heart of Mine" Music by Harry Warren; lyric by Arthur Freed. In a self-contained scene from *Ziegfeld Follies* (MGM 1946), top-hatted and beribboned Fred Astaire, as a slick jewel thief, finds sudden romance when he meets intended victim Lucille Bremer at a formal embassy ball. Following his romantic musical confession, he continues to woo Miss Bremer as they dance ecstatically both inside and outside the ballroom. In fact, even after discovering Fred's occupation, the lady is only too happy to dance gaily off with the elegant, unrepentant thief.

"This Is the Beginning of the End" Music & lyric by Mack Gordon. Telltale signs ("You just give yourself away/ With ev'rything you say") signal the affair is over. Dorothy Lamour sang the torchy ballad in *Johnny Apollo* (Fox 1940) to an informal group at the Club Paradise.

"This Time the Dream's on Me" Music by Harold Arlen; lyric by Johnny Mercer. Romantic fantasies admitted by band singer Priscilla Lane in *Blues in the Night* (Warner 1941).

"This Year's Kisses" Music & lyric by Irving Berlin. She may have found a new romance but, admitted Alice Faye in *On the Avenue* (1937), she's "still wearing last year's love." The ballad was performed by Miss Faye leaning against the proscenium arch during the rehearsal of a Broadway revue.

Thomas, Danny (né Amos Jacobs), actor, singer; b. Deerfield, Mich., Jan. 6, 1914. Dark-haired, hawk-nosed actor-comedian who has also appeared in vaudeville, nightclubs, and television; later became a producer. Father of Marlo Thomas.

1947 The Unfinished Dance (*Paneros*)
1948 Big City (*Cantor David Feldman*)
1951 Call Me Mister (*Stanley*)
1952 I'll See You in My Dreams (*Gus Kahn*)
1953 The Jazz Singer (*Jerry Golding*)
1964 Looking for Love (guest bit)

Thompson, Kay, actress, singer, composer, lyricist; b. St. Louis, Nov. 9, 1913. A former concert pianist, dance band singer, and arranger, Miss Thompson was associated with producer Roger Edens at MGM, where she was noted for her stylized, hand-clapping vocal arrangements. She also had a successful nightclub act with the Williams Brothers (including Andy), wrote *Eloise,* gave a well-remembered performance in *Funny Face,* and collaborated on an occasional song.

1937 Manhattan Merry-Go-Round (specialty)
1946 The Kid from Brooklyn (*matron*)
1957 Funny Face (*Maggie Prescott*)

"Thoroughly Modern Millie" Music by James Van Heusen; lyric by Sammy Cahn. Razz-matazzy picture of the hedonistic Twenties—with its raised skirts, bobbed hair, rumble seats, and tango dances—sung in *Thoroughly Modern Millie* (Univ. 1967) by Julie Andrews.

Thorpe, (Rollo Smolt) Richard, director; b. Hutchinson, Kansas, Feb. 24, 1896. Silent film actor and director, whose musicals, mostly at MGM, found him directing such performers as Esther Williams (four times), Van Johnson, Jimmy Durante, Jane Powell, Ann Blyth, Mario Lanza (*The Great Caruso*), Fred Astaire, Red Skelton, and Elvis Presley.

1933 Rainbow Over Broadway
1944 Two Girls and a Sailor
1945 Thrill of a Romance
1947 Fiesta
     This Time for Keeps
1948 On an Island with You
     A Date with Judy
1949 The Sun Comes Up
1950 Three Little Words
1951 The Great Caruso
1954 The Student Prince
     Athena
1957 Ten Thousand Bedrooms
     Jailhouse Rock
1963 Follow the Boys
     Fun in Acapulco

"Three Coins in the Fountain" Music by Jule Styne; lyric by Sammy Cahn. Theme song of nonmusical film of the same name (Fox 1954), sung by Frank Sinatra on the soundtrack. Originally, the film was to have been titled *We Believe in Love,* but producer Sol C. Siegel changed it because of the commercial potentiality of the song.

Three Little Words (1950). Music by Harry Ruby; lyrics by Bert Kalmar; screenplay by George Wells based on lives of Kalmar and Ruby.

An MGM film produced by Jack Cummings; directed by Richard Thorpe; choreography, Fred Astaire, Hermes Pan; art directors, Cedric Gibbons, Urie McCleary; costumes, Helen Rose; music director, André Previn; orchestrations, Leo Arnaud; cameraman, Harry Jackson; editor, Ben Lewis; Technicolor.

Cast: Fred Astaire (*Bert Kalmar*); Red Skelton (*Harry Ruby*); Vera-Ellen (vocals by Anita Ellis) (*Jessie Brown Kalmar*); Arlene Dahl (*Eileen Percy Ruby*); Keenan Wynn (*Charlie Kope*); Gale Robbins (*Terry Lordel*); Gloria DeHaven (*Mrs. Carter DeHaven*); Phil Regan (*Phil Regan*); Harry Shannon (*Clanahan*); Debbie Reynolds (vocals by Helen Kane) (*Helen Kane*); Carleton Carpenter (*Dan Healy*); Paul Harvey (*Al Masters*); Pierre Watkin (*Philip Goodman*); Harry Barris (*pianist*); Harry Ruby (*baseball player*).

Songs: "Where Did You Get That Girl?" (music, Harry Puck) - Astaire, Ellen (Ellis)/ "She's Mine, All Mine" - barbershop quartet/ "Mr. and Mrs. Hoofer at Home" - dance by Astaire, Ellen/ "My Sunny Tennessee" - Astaire, Skelton/ "So Long, Oo-Long" - Astaire, Skelton/ "Who's Sorry Now?" (also music, Ted Snyder) - DeHaven/ "Come On, Papa" (lyric, Edgar Leslie) - Ellen (Ellis)/ "Nevertheless" - Astaire, Ellen (Ellis)/ "All Alone Monday" - Robbins/ "You Smiled at Me" - Dahl/ "I Wanna Be Loved by You" (also music, Herbert Stothart) - Astaire, Reynolds (Kane)/ "Up in the Clouds" - chorus/ "Thinking of You" Ellen (Ellis); dance by Astaire, Ellen; reprised by Dahl/ "Hooray for Captain Spalding" - Astaire, Skelton/ "I Love You So Much" - Dahl, male chorus/ "You Are My Lucky Star" (Nacio Herb Brown-Arthur Freed) - Regan/ "Three Little Words" - Astaire; reprised by Regan.

While lyricist Bert Kalmar and composer Harry Ruby are hardly among the household names of American popular song, the team's screen biography was among the most satisfying of Hollywood's attempts at dramatizing song catalogues. Eschewing lavish routines and dazzling guest stars, as in the same studio's salutes to Jerome Kern, Rodgers and Hart, and Sigmund Romberg, MGM's *Three Little Words* was a warm, unpretentious period musical that concentrated on the dancing skills of Fred Astaire (and new partner Vera-Ellen) and the restrained comic skills of Red Skelton. As was customary in musical biographies, there was little attempt at historical accuracy. (For one thing, Kalmar and Ruby didn't discover Helen Kane boop-boop-a-dooping in the street. She was already a Broadway headliner when she introduced "I Wanna Be Loved by You.") The main plot developments concern Kalmar's knee injury that forces the vaudeville hoofer to become a fulltime lyricist, his efforts to keep Ruby out of the clutches of predatory females, and the partners' estrangement that is ended when they accidentally write "Three Little Words."

"Three Little Words" Music by Harry Ruby; lyric by Bert Kalmar. "Eight little letters that simply mean 'I love you.'" Introduced in *Check and Double Check* (RKO 1930) by Duke Ellington's orchestra, with vocal by the Rhythm Boys (Bing Crosby, Harry Barris, and Al Rinker) heard on the soundtrack. Also sung by Fred Astaire (as Bert Kalmar) in *Three Little Words* (MGM 1950).

"Thumbelina" Music & lyric by Frank Loesser. Illustrating the aphorism, "When your heart is full of love you're nine feet tall," Danny Kaye sang the frisky number—based on a fairy tale—in *Hans Christian Andersen* (Goldwyn 1952). Song was sung to a little girl outside his cell window when Kaye, as Andersen, was briefly incarcerated.

Tibbett, Lawrence (Mervil), actor, singer; b. Bakersfield, Cal., Nov. 16, 1896; d. New York, July 15, 1960. Leading baritone with the Metropolitan Opera (1923–50), Tibbett became one of the earliest opera singers to win popularity in films. He introduced "Cuban Love Song," made records, and gave many recitals.

    1930   The Rogue Song (*Yegor*)
           New Moon (*Lt. Michael Petroff*)
    1931   The Prodigal (*Jeffrey*)
           Cuban Love Song (*Terry*)
    1935   Metropolitan (*Thomas Renwick*)
    1936   Under Your Spell (*Anthony Allen*)

"Ticket To Ride" Music & lyric by John Lennon & Paul McCartney. Sung on soundtrack of *Help!* (UA 1965) by the Beatles (John Lennon, Paul McCartney, George Harrison, Ringo Starr) as the foursome cavort in the snow.

"Time After Time" Music by Jule Styne; lyric by Sammy Cahn. Romantic self-satisfaction expressed by Frank Sinatra in *It Happened in Brooklyn* (MGM 1947); later reprised by Kathryn Grayson. The song was introduced in Jimmy Durante's apartment, with Sinatra singing it as a lyric he'd just written to music by Peter Lawford.

Tiomkin, Dimitri, composer; b. St. Petersburg, Russia, May 10, 1894; d. London, Nov. 11, 1979. A former concert pianist, Tiomkin went to Hollywood in 1930 and was credited with composing scores for 160 nonmusical films. Lyricist Ned Washington wrote words to his music for the title songs of *High Noon* and *Friendly Persuasion*. Tiomkin's first wife was choreographer Albertina Rasch. Bib: *Please Don't Hate Me* by Tiomkin (1960).

"Tip Toe Through the Tulips with Me" Music by Joseph Burke; lyric by Al Dubin. Nocturnal invitation to a sleeping girl to tip toe *out* of bed (!), sung by her amorous swain who's waiting at her window and wishes that she join him in a moonlit garden for a stroll and possible kiss beneath a willow tree. Nick Lucas introduced this naïve notion in *Gold Diggers of Broadway* (Warner 1929), and it was also sung by Gene Nelson, Lucille Norman, Virginia Mayo, and Virginia Gibson in *Painting the Clouds with Sunshine* (Warner 1951).

"Today I Love Ev'rybody" Music by Harold Arlen; lyric by Dorothy Fields. Exuberant song of indiscriminate affection, introduced in *The Farmer Takes a Wife* (Fox 1953) by Betty Grable.

"Tomorrow Is Another Day" Music by Bronislaw Kaper & Walter Jurmann; lyric by Gus Kahn. Optimistic philosophy (in which "trouble" handily rhymes with "bubble") prescribed by Allan Jones in *A Day at the Races* (MGM 1937).

Tone, (Stanislas Pascal) Franchot, actor; b. Niagara Falls, Feb. 27, 1905; d. New York, Sept. 18, 1968. Usually playing a moneyed playboy, Tone acted—but didn't sing—in musicals with Joan Crawford (his first wife), Grace Moore, Deanna Durbin (three films), Mary Martin, Susanna Foster, and Shirley Temple.

1933 Dancing Lady (*Todd Newton*)
1934 Moulin Rouge (*Douglas Hall*)
1935 Reckless (*Bob Harrison*)
1936 The King Steps Out (*Francis Joseph*)
1941 Nice Girl? (*Richard Calvert*)
1943 His Butler's Sister (*Charles Gerard*)
     True to Life (*Fletcher Marvin*)
1945 That Night with You (*Paul Renaud*)
1946 Because of Him (*Paul Taylor*)
1947 Honeymoon (*Flanner*)
1951 Here Comes the Groom (*Wilbur Stanley*)

"Too Late Now" Music by Burton Lane; lyric by Alan Jay Lerner. In *Royal Wedding* (MGM 1951), Jane Powell, at a party in London, reassures her timid suitor, Peter Lawford, that it's "too late now to forget and go on to someone new."

"Too Marvelous for Words" Music by Richard A. Whiting; lyric by Johnny Mercer. Featured in a Broadway revue in *Ready, Willing and Able* (Warner 1937), the song is first performed as a duet by boss Ross Alexander (dubbed by James Newill) and secretary Wini Shaw composing a letter—and a song—to Ross's sweetheart, Ruby Keeler. Ruby, upon receiving it, is so touched that she immediately telephones Ross and sings the letter right back to him. The stage is now occupied by a mammoth typewriter, with 16 girls lying on their backs so that their black-stockinged legs might somehow represent the typewriter ribbon. Ruby and Lee Dixon dance onto the typewriter to tap and type the message by bounding from key to key as the lyric to the song appears on a huge roll of paper. Said lyric deals with a lover's vain attempt to come up with the proper adjectives to describe his girl, rejecting as inadequate such encomia as "glamorous" and "amorous" (an odd choice anyway, old standby though it might be), and concluding that a satisfactory word simply cannot be found in Webster's Dictionary.

"Too Romantic" Music by James V. Monaco; lyric by Johnny Burke. Ballad of one fearful of the night ("moonlight and stars can make such a fool of me"), sung by Bing Crosby and Dorothy Lamour in *Road to Singapore* (Par. 1940).

"Too-Ra-Loo-Ra-Loo-Ral" Music & lyric by James Royce Shannon. Also known as "That's an Irish Lullaby," the piece won great popularity after Bing Crosby sang it to ailing Barry Fitzgerald in *Going My Way* (Par. 1944). Actually, the song dates from 1913 when it was introduced by Chauncey Olcott in the Broadway production *Shameen Dhu*.

Top Hat (1935). Music & lyrics by Irving Berlin; screenplay by Dwight Taylor & Allan Scott, adapted by Karl Noti from play *The Girl Who Dared* by Alexander Farago & Aladar Laszlo.

An RKO-Radio film produced by Pandro S. Berman; directed by Mark Sandrich; choreography, Fred Astaire, Hermes Pan; art director, Van Nest Polglase; costumes, Bernard Newman; music director, Max Steiner; cameraman, David Abel; editor, William Hamilton.

Cast: Fred Astaire (*Jerry Travers*); Ginger Rogers (*Dale Tremont*); Edward Everett Horton (*Horace Hardwick*); Helen Broderick (*Madge Hardwick*); Erik Rhodes (*Alberto Beddini*); Eric Blore (*Bates*); Leonard Mudie (*flower-shop owner*); Lucille Ball (*flower-shop clerk*).

Songs: "No Strings" - Astaire/ "Isn't This a Lovely Day?" - Astaire; dance by Astaire, Rogers/ "Top Hat, White Tie and Tails" - Astaire, male chorus/ "Cheek to Cheek" - Astaire; dance by Astaire, Rogers/ "The Piccolino" - Rogers; dance by Astaire, Rogers, Venetians. Unused: "Get Thee Behind Me Satan," "Wild About You," "You're the Cause."

Although *Top Hat* has come to be accepted as the quintessential Astaire-Rogers movie, its style, plot, characterizations, and musical sequences were all based on the team's previous success, *The Gay Divorcee* (which had the same co-author, director and producer). Like the former outing, the film was set in London and at a fashionable resort (in this case the Lido), and dealt with mistaken identity involving an American dancer (Astaire) who falls in love at first sight with another visiting American (Rogers). Romance is again expressed through song and dance, a new song about a new melody again becomes the extended production number at the resort, and, when last seen, the dancing duo is again nimbly scampering out of the hotel. Comedy is once more supplied by unctuous Eric Blore, volatile Erik Rhodes, and prissy Edward Everett Horton (who played Astaire's friend in both films), with sharp-tongued Helen Broderick the only new major cast member.

But the movie was raised to its Pantheon position in the world of Astaire and Rogers because of the remarkable interplay between the two stars, the imaginative, varied dance routines, the memorable Irving Berlin score, and the stylized, dazzlingly white art-deco decor, all of which established the tone and spirit of the subsequent movies the team did together. Mercifully, no one paid much heed to the elaborately illogical plot that kept the lovers spatting until almost the end because of Ginger's mistaken impression that Fred was really Broderick's spouse, Horton. Nor were too many concerned that in the course of just one night at the Venetian resort, the couple twirl around the dance floor during dinner, Fred proposes marriage to Ginger and she slaps him, Rhodes proposes marriage to Ginger and they wed immediately (though not by a real clergyman), Fred is moved out of the hotel bridal suite to make room for Ginger and Rhodes, Fred tap dances in the room above which disturbs Ginger and sends Rhodes racing upstairs to keell heem, Fred escapes and explains the mixup to Ginger in a gondola that drifts out to sea, and both end up at the hotel safe, dry, and happy to join the local Carnival in dancing to the strains of the catchy "Piccolino."

Top Hat broke all attendance records at New York's Radio City Music Hall and was equally successful throughout the country. It also proved a bonanza for Irving Berlin. His lawyer had asked for $100,000 for the score, but producer Pandro Berman wouldn't go any higher than a $75,000 advance against 10% of the gross—but only if the gross exceeded $1,250,000. The songwriter accepted reluctantly since few films at that time grossed over a million. *Top Hat,* however, grossed over $3,000,000, thus enabling Berlin to take home more than three times the amount that the studio had initially refused.

"Top Hat, White Tie and Tails" Music & lyric by Irving Berlin. "I've just got an invitation in the mail," sings an exultant top-hatted, white-tied and tailed Fred Astaire at the opening-night performance of a London revue in *Top Hat* (RKO 1935). In the scene, Fred dances alone and with similarly attired male dancers. At the end of the dance, he proceeds to shoot them down—one by one and for no apparent reason—with his cane simulating a rifle and his taps the sound of the shots (the hard-to-hit last remaining dancer is felled by a simulated bow and arrow). The lyric to the song expresses the pleasure of a young man who has just received an invitation to a formal party taking place that very evening (!), so, with no time to lose, he immediately dons the specified attire, making sure to dude up his short front, put in his studs, and polish his nails.

The melody to the song had been composed a few years prior to the making of the film and was first intended for an unproduced sequel to Irving Berlin's

Broadway revue, *As Thousands Cheer,* to be called *More Cheers.* Berlin's plan was to use it in a sketch about the Americanization of Russian leaders after President Roosevelt had granted diplomatic recognition to the Soviet Union (the original lyric went, in part, "Here we are beside a samovar/ Doin' the ha-cha-cha"). Another unfulfilled plan, after the song was called "Top Hat, White Tie and Tails," was to feature it in a different revue sketch in which a gentleman, invited to a formal bash, discovers all the other guests in dungarees.

The first time Fred Astaire ever danced with a top-hatted male chorus was in the number "High Hat" in the 1927 Broadway musical *Funny Face.* He initially did his cane shooting routine in "Say Young Man of Manhattan," performed in the 1930 musical *Smiles.*

Tormé, (Melvin Howard) Mel, singer, actor; b. Chicago, Sept. 13, 1925. Slightly built, sandy-haired singer who developed from mellow-voiced crooner to highly regarded jazz-influenced stylist. Tormé, who is also a songwriter, appears mostly in nightclubs and concerts.

1943 Higher and Higher (*Marty*)
1944 Pardon My Rhythm (*Ricky O'Bannon*)
     Ghost Catchers (drummer)
1945 Let's Go Steady (*Streak Edwards*) (also comp., lyr.)
1947 Good News (*Danny*)
1948 Words and Music (specialty)
1949 So Dear to My Heart (voice only)
1950 Duchess of Idaho (*Cyril*)
1960 A Man Called Adam (*Mel Tormé*)

Travolta, John, actor, singer, dancer; b. Englewood, NJ, Feb. 18, 1954. Dark-haired, intense actor with flashing smile whose first two musical films established his appeal as the screen's foremost street-smart dancing man.

1977 Saturday Night Fever (*Tony Manero*)
1978 Grease (*Danny Zuko*)
1980 Urban Cowboy (*Bud Davis*)
1983 Staying Alive (*Tony Manero*)

"Triplets" Music by Arthur Schwartz; lyric by Howard Dietz. Intricately rhymed, rapid-fire compilation of complaints by a sibling triad, the number was presented as part of a show in *The Band Wagon* (MGM 1953). To give the illusion of being infants, Fred Astaire, Nanette Fabray, and Jack Buchanan had specially made leather boots strapped over their knees with baby shoes attached. Since their legs and feet were covered with black stockings and their dancing was done on a black stage, the scampering threesome seemed to be performing on baby legs. After being dropped from the 1932 Broadway revue, *Flying Colors,* "Triplets" was first sung on the stage five years later by the Tune Twisters in *Between the Devil.*

"Trolley Song, The" Music & lyric by Hugh Martin & Ralph Blane. Rhythmic narrative, with its dramatic effect heightened by the use of vehicular sounds, describing how love came to a girl when she met a boy in a light brown derby and a bright green tie while riding in a turn-of-the-century streetcar. Introduced in *Meet Me in St. Louis* (MGM 1944) first by the passengers on the crowded trolley, then picked up by Judy Garland as she spies Tom Drake rushing to catch the moving car.

As related in Hugh Fordin's book, *The World of Entertainment,* the idea for the number was prompted by producer Arthur Freed's desire for an appropriate song to be sung during a trolley ride. Feeling that a song *about* a trolley would be too corny, writers Martin and Blane came up with one that could be sung *on* a trolley, "Know Where You're Goin' and You'll Get There." But Freed still wanted a song about the ride, and Blane went to the local library to do some research about St. Louis. There, in one volume, was a picture of a double-decker trolley car with the caption, "Clang, Clang, Clang, Went the Trolley." The rest came easy. Songs about transportation were later inserted in other MGM period musicals: "On the Atchison, Topeka and the Santa Fe" (by Harry Warren and Johnny Mercer) in *The Harvey Girls* (1946), and "The Stanley Steamer" (Warren and Blane) in *Summer Holiday* (1948).

"Tropical Magic" Music by Harry Warren; lyric by Mack Gordon. Languid ballad in *Weekend in Havana* (Fox 1941), first sung at the Casino Madrilena by a male trio (in Spanish as "Amor Tropical"), then by Alice Faye (in English) leaning against a pillar on the casino veranda. Later in the film the song serves as a duet for Miss Faye and John Payne as they ride in a donkey cart along a moonlit country road.

"True Blue Lou" Music by Richard A. Whiting; lyric by Sam Coslow & Leo Robin. Torchy tale about a girl whose devotion leaves her with a broken heart. Introduced by Hal Skelly in *The Dance of Life* (Par. 1929).

"True Love" Music & lyric by Cole Porter. In *High Society* (MGM 1956), ex-husband Bing Crosby gives socialite Grace Kelly a wedding gift of a model of their sailboat, *True Love.* As she recalls their honeymoon, a flashback reveals Crosby playing the concertina and singing the gently lapping ballad to Miss Kelly aboard the boat. Later in the film, she drunkenly sings it in the arms of writer Frank Sinatra after they've had a swim.

Tucker, Sophie (née Sonia Kalish), singer, actress; b. Russia, Jan. 13, 1884; d. New York, Feb. 9, 1966. Buxom, blonded Sophie Tucker, vaudeville's belting, self-styled "Last of the Red-Hot Mamas," spent most of her later years successfully talk-singing off-color ditties in nightclubs. Bib: *Some of These Days* by Miss Tucker (1945).

1929	Honky Tonk (*Sophie Leonard*)
1934	Gay Love (Eng.) (*Sophie Tucker*)
1937	Broadway Melody of 1938 (*Alice Clayton*)
1944	Follow the Boys (specialty)
	Sensations of 1945 (specialty)
1957	The Joker Is Wild (guest bit)

Tufts, (Bowen Charleton) Sonny, actor, singer; b. Boston, July 16, 1911; d. Santa Monica, June 4, 1970. Tufts was a beefy, crinkly-eyed actor with a diffident personality who appeared mostly in Paramount films. He introduced "Ac-Cent-Tchu-Ate the Positive" with Bing Crosby and was seen in two musical films with Betty Hutton.

1944	Bring on the Girls (*Phil North*)
	Here Come the Waves (*Windy Smith*)
1945	Duffy's Tavern (specialty)
1946	Cross My Heart (*Oliver Clark*)
1947	Variety Girl (guest bit)

Turner, (Julia Jean Mildred Frances) Lana, actress; b. Wallace, Idaho, Feb. 8, 1920. Blonde voluptuous beauty who acted mostly in MGM films, including musicals in which her singing was always dubbed. Leading men included James Stewart, George Murphy, Ezio Pinza, and Fernando Lamas. Bandleader Artie Shaw was the first of her seven husbands. Bib: *Lana* by Joe Morella & Edward Z. Epstein (1971); *Films of Lana Turner* by Lou Valentino (1976).

1938	Love Finds Andy Hardy (*Cynthia Potter*)
1939	Dancing Coed (*Patty Marlow*)
1940	Two Girls on Broadway (*Pat Mahoney*)
1941	Ziegfeld Girl (*Sheila Regan*)
1943	DuBarry Was a Lady (guest bit)
1951	Mr. Imperium (*Freddo Barlo*)
1952	The Merry Widow (*Crystal Radek*)
1953	Latin Lovers (*Nora Taylor*)

Tuttle, Frank, director; b. New York, Aug. 6, 1892; d. Hollywood, Jan. 6, 1963. Worked primarily at Paramount, where he began career as continuity writer. Tuttle directed six musicals with Bing Crosby, others with Nancy Carroll, Eddie Cantor, and Jack Benny.

1929	Sweetie
1930	Paramount on Parade (part)
	Love Among the Millionaires
	True to the Navy
1931	Dude Ranch
1932	The Big Broadcast
1933	Roman Scandals
1934	Here Is My Heart
1935	All the King's Horses
	Two for Tonight
1936	College Holiday
1937	Waikiki Wedding
1938	Doctor Rhythm
1939	Paris Honeymoon
	Charlie McCarthy, Detective

"Twilight on the Trail" Music by Louis Alter; lyric by Sidney Mitchell. Hymnlike theme of *Trail of the Lonesome Pine* (Par. 1936) sung by Fuzzy Knight.

"Two Blind Loves" Music by Harold Arlen; lyric by E. Y. Harburg. Musically based on "Three Blind Mice," the ballad was sung by Kenny Baker and Florence Rice as they sat at a lunch counter in *At the Circus* (MGM 1939).

"Two Dreams Met" Music by Harry Warren; lyric by Mack Gordon. Romantic ballad first sung in *Down Argentine Way* (Fox 1940) by Six Hits and a Miss in a New York nightclub. Later reprised in an Argentine hacienda by guitar-strumming Bando de Luna in Spanish, then by Betty Grable in English and by Don Ameche in Spanish.

Two Girls on Broadway. *See **Broadway Melody, The.***

"Two Hundred Years" Music by Richard Baskin; lyric by Henry Gibson. Quasi-country, slightly apologetic patriotic air ("We must be doin' somethin' right to last two hundred years") sung by Henry Gibson in a recording studio in *Nashville* (ABC 1975).

"Two Sleepy People" Music by Hoagy Carmichael; lyric by Frank Loesser. Drowsy duet sung by lovers Bob Hope and Shirley Ross in *Thanks for the Memory* (Par. 1938). The idea for the song supposedly occurred one night when Frank Loesser and his wife, Lynn, were visiting the Hoagy Carmichaels. Apologizing for their early leave taking, Lynn remarked, "We're two sleepy people"—which resulted in the songwriters making a dash for the piano and writing the song on the spot.

U

"**Ugly Duckling**" Music & lyric by Frank Loesser. Moralistic tale based on a fable by Hans Christian Andersen about a shunned ugly duckling who turns into a beautiful swan. Sung by Danny Kaye in the story-teller's biography (Goldwyn 1952) to a young boy (Peter Votrian) whose head had been shaved because of illness.

"**Up with the Lark**" Music by Jerome Kern; lyric by Leo Robin. Cheery good-morning song introduced at beginning of *Centennial Summer* (Fox 1946) by Jeanne Crain (with Louanne Hogan's voice), Linda Darnell, Buddy Swan, Constance Bennett, and Walter Brennan.

V

Vallee, (Hubert Prior) Rudy, actor, singer; b. Island Pond, Vt., July 28, 1901. Vallee began his career as a saxophone-playing, megaphone-holding bandleader whose slight, nasal voice helped make him a crooning sex symbol in the late 20s and early 30s. He had a popular radio series, made records, sang in theatres and nightclubs, and introduced such movie songs as "A Little Kiss Each Morning" and "I Poured My Heart Into a Song." After playing romantic leads in Hollywood, he switched to stuffy, pince-nez-wearing comic characters, such as the role he repeated in the filmed version of his Broadway hit, *How To Succeed in Business Without Really Trying.* Blb: *Vagabond Dreams Come True* (1930), *My Time Is Your Time* (1962), *Let the Chips Fall* (1976), all by Vallee. (Died July 3, 1986.)

1929	The Vagabond Lover (*Rudy*)
	Glorifying the American Girl (specialty)
1933	International House (specialty)
1934	George White's Scandals (*Jimmy Martin*)
1935	Sweet Music (*Skip Houston*)
1938	Gold Diggers in Paris (*Terry Moore*)
1939	Second Fiddle (*Roger Maxwell*)
1941	Time Out for Rhythm (*Daniel Collins*)
	Too Many Blondes (*Dick Kerrigan*)
1942	Happy Go Lucky (*Alfred Monroe*)
1946	People Are Funny (*Ormsby Jamison*)
1949	The Beautiful Blonde from Bashful Bend (*Charlie Hingleman*)
1955	Gentlemen Marry Brunettes (*Rudy Vallee*)
1957	The Helen Morgan Story (guest bit)
1958	Hansel and Gretel (tv) (*Poppa*)
1966	How to Succeed in Business Without Really Trying (*J. B. Biggley*)
1968	The Night They Raided Minsky's (narrator)
	Live a Little Love a Little (*Penlow*)

Van, Bobby (né Robert Jack Stein), actor, dancer, singer, choreographer; b. The Bronx, Dec. 6, 1930; d. Los Angeles, July 31, 1980. Spry, wiry song-and-dance man who also appeared on Broadway (including the 1971 revival of *No, No, Nanette*) and in nightclubs and television.

1952	Skirts Ahoy (bit)
	Because You're Mine (*Artie Pilcer*)
1953	Small Town Girl (*Ludwig Schlemmer*)
	The Affairs of Dobie Gillis (*Dobie Gillis*)
	Kiss Me, Kate (*"Gremio"*)
1961	The Ladies Man (chor. only)
1962	It's Only Money (chor. only)
1973	Lost Horizon (*Harry Lovett*)

Van Dyke, Dick, actor, singer; b. Danville, Ill., Dec. 13, 1925. Lanky, prognathous actor, adept at comic pratfalls, who had popular television series. Van Dyke appeared on Broadway in *Bye Bye Birdie* and repeated role on the screen; also introduced "Chim Chim Cheree" in *Mary Poppins.*

1963	Bye Bye Birdie (*Albert Peterson*)
1964	Mary Poppins (*Bert/ Mr. Dawes*)
1968	Chitty Chitty Bang Bang (*Caractacus Potts*)

Van Dyke, W(oodbridge) S(trong) II, director; b. San Diego, March 21, 1889; d. Los Angeles, Feb. 5, 1943. Beginning his career in 1918 and working exclusively at MGM from 1926 on, Van Dyke directed five of the eight Jeanette MacDonald-Nelson Eddy extravaganzas, plus two others with MacDonald and one other with Eddy. Nonmusicals included *Trader Horn, Tarzan of the Apes,* and *The Thin Man.*

1931	Cuban Love Song
1935	Naughty Marietta
1936	Rose Marie
	San Francisco
1937	Rosalie
1938	Sweethearts

1940 Bitter Sweet
1942 I Married an Angel
     Cairo

Van Heusen, James (né Edward Chester Babcock), composer; b. Syracuse, NY, Jan. 26, 1913. With his first partner, lyricist Johnny Burke, Van Heusen was primarily associated with songs introduced in Paramount movies by Bing Crosby—including six of the seven ''Road'' pictures—highlighted by ''Moonlight Becomes You,'' ''Road to Morocco,'' ''Sunday, Monday or Always,'' ''Swingin' on a Star,'' ''Aren't You Glad You're You?,'' and ''But Beautiful.'' After forming a partnership with Sammy Cahn in 1954, Van Heusen was responsible for such Frank Sinatra hits as ''Love and Marriage,'' ''The Tender Trap,'' ''All the Way,'' ''High Hopes,'' ''Pocketful of Miracles,'' and ''My Kind of Town.'' Others who introduced Van Heusen songs were Mary Martin, Dorothy Lamour (''It Could Happen to You,'' ''Personality''), Bob Hope, Betty Hutton, Dinah Shore (''Like Someone in Love''), Ginger Rogers (dancing to ''Suddenly It's Spring''), Dean Martin, Jackie Gleason (''Call Me Irresponsible''), Mitzi Gaynor, Marilyn Monroe, and Ann-Margret. Van Heusen has also written Broadway and nightclub scores.

1940 Love Thy Neighbor (Burke)
1941 Road to Zanzibar (Burke)
     Playmates (Burke)
1942 Road to Morocco (Burke)
1943 Dixie (Burke)
1944 Going My Way (Burke)
     And the Angels Sing (Burke)
     Belle of the Yukon (Burke)
1945 Road to Utopia (Burke)
1946 Cross My Heart (Burke)
     London Town (Eng.) (Burke)
1947 Welcome Stranger (Burke)
     Road to Bali (Burke)
1948 Mystery in Mexico (Burke)
1949 A Connecticut Yankee in King Arthur's Court
        (Burke)
     Top o' the Morning (Burke)
1950 Riding High (Burke)
     Mister Music (Burke)
1952 Road to Bali (Burke)
1953 Little Boy Lost (Burke)
1955 Our Town (tv) (Cahn)
1956 Anything Goes (Cahn)
     Pardners (Cahn)
1959 Say One for Me (Cahn)
1960 Let's Make Love (Cahn)
     High Time (Cahn)

1962 Road to Hong Kong (Cahn)
1964 Robin and the Seven Hoods (Cahn)
     The Pleasure Seekers (Cahn)
1967 Jack and the Beanstalk (Cahn)
1972 Journey Back to Oz (Cahn)

Velez, Lupe (née Guadalupe Velez de Villa Lobos), actress, singer, dancer; b. San Luis Potosi, Mexico, July 18, 1908; d. Beverly Hills, Dec. 14, 1944. Fiery Mexican Spitfire who appeared in medium-grade musicals and was teamed in late 30s with Leon Errol in series of slapstick comedies.

1929 Lady of the Pavements (*Nanon*)
     The Wolf Song (*Lola Salazar*)
1931 Cuban Love Song (*Nenita*)
1934 Hollywood Party (*Lupe*)
     Palooka (*Nina Madero*)
     Strictly Dynamite (*Vera*)
1936 Gypsy Melody (Eng.) (*Mila*)
1937 Stardust (Eng.) (*Carla de Huleva*)
1939 The Girl from Mexico (*Carmelita*)
1941 Redhead from Manhattan
     Playmates (*Carmen del Toro*)
     Six Lessons from Madam LaZonga (*Madam La-Zonga*)

Vera-Ellen (née Vera Ellen Westmeyr Rohe), actress, dancer; b. Cincinnati, Feb. 16, 1921. Blonde, round-faced, diminutive former Broadway ingenue, she danced in Hollywood musicals with Danny Kaye (three times), Gene Kelly (twice), Fred Astaire (twice), and Donald O'Connor. Introduced (with Carol Stewart's voice) ''You Make Me Feel So Young'' in Fox's *Three Little Girls in Blue*. (Died Los Angeles, Aug. 30, 1981.)

1945 Wonder Man (*Midge Mallon*)
1946 The Kid from Brooklyn (*Susie Sullivan*)
     Three Little Girls in Blue (*Myra*)
1947 Carnival in Costa Rica (*Luisa Molina*)
1948 Words and Music (specialty)
1949 Love Happy (*Maggie Phillips*)
     On the Town (*Ivy Smith*)
1950 Three Little Words (*Jessie Kalmar*)
1951 Happy Go Lovely (Eng.) (*Janet Jones*)
1952 The Belle of New York (*Angela Bonfils*)
1953 Call Me Madam (*Princess Maria*)
1954 White Christmas (*Judy Haynes*)
1957 Let's Be Happy (Eng.) (*Jeanne McLean*)

Verdon, (Gwyneth Evelyn) Gwen, actress, dancer, singer; b. Los Angeles, Jan. 13, 1926. One of Broadway's stellar attractions, Miss Verdon starred on screen only to re-create her stage role in *Damn Yankees*. Miss Verdon was once married to director Bob Fosse.

1951 On the Riviera (dancer)
     Meet Me After the Show (dancer)
1952 The Merry Widow (dancer)
1953 The Farmer Takes a Wife (*Abigail*)
1958 Damn Yankees (*Lola*)

"Very Precious Love, A" Music by Sammy Fain; lyric by Paul Francis Webster. Romantic pitch sung by Gene Kelly to Natalie Wood in nonmusical film *Marjorie Morningstar* (Warner 1958).

Vidor, Charles, director; b. Budapest, April 27, 1900; d. Vienna, June 4, 1959. After directing films in Germany, Vidor settled in Hollywood in 1932. His major screen musicals were *Cover Girl,* with Gene Kelly and Rita Hayworth, and *Love Me or Leave Me,* with Doris Day and James Cagney; also worked with Danny Kaye and Frank Sinatra.

1944 Cover Girl
1945 A Song To Remember
1946 Gilda
1952 Hans Christian Andersen
1954 Rhapsody
1955 Love Me or Leave Me
1957 The Joker Is Wild
1960 Song Without End (part)

W

"Waiter and the Porter and the Upstairs Maid, The"
Music & lyric by Johnny Mercer. Story related by Bing
Crosby, Jack Teagarden, and Mary Martin in *Birth of
the Blues* (Par. 1941) of a guest at a stuffy party who
sneaked into the kitchen and had himself a real ball with
a trio of domestics. Song was performed on the bandstand of a swank New Orleans restaurant.

"Waiting at the End of the Road" Music & lyric by
Irving Berlin. Spiritual-type chorale offering the promise of peace and contentment after one has traveled a
weary road. Sung by Daniel L. Haynes and Dixie Jubi-
lee Singers as plantation workers in *Hallelujah* (MGM
1929) as they line up for their cotton harvest to be
weighed.

"Wake Up and Live" Music by Harry Revel; lyric by
Mack Gordon. Uplifting piece sung by radio's "Wake-
Up-and-Live Girl" Alice Faye during a broadcast in film
of the same name (Fox 1937). Later in the film, supposedly as part of the cure for Jack Haley's mike fright,
Miss Faye persuades Haley to sing into a dead microphone during a broadcast by Ben Bernie's orchestra. But
the microphone isn't dead and Haley—or rather voice
dubber Buddy Clark—is heard over the air.

"Walk Through the World" Music & lyric by Leslie
Bricusse. Lyrical ballad about joys of spending their lives
together, sung by Petula Clark in *Goodbye, Mr. Chips*
(MGM 1969) to Peter O'Toole (Mr. Chips) during their
honeymoon.

Walker, (Harold) Hal, director; b. Ottumwa, Iowa,
March 20, 1896; d. Tracy, Cal., July 3, 1972. Director
all of whose films were Paramount musicals, including

two "Road" movies and four with Martin and Lewis.
Left films for television.

1945	Out of This World
	Duffy's Tavern
	The Stork Club
	Road to Utopia
1950	My Friend Irma Goes West
	At War with the Army
1951	That's My Boy
	Sailor Beware
1952	Road to Bali

Walker, Nancy (née Anna Myrtle Swoyer), actress,
singer; b. Philadelphia, May 10, 1922. Short, slack-
jawed comedienne, noted for her sourfaced, deadpan delivery. First won notice in Broadway musical, *Best Foot
Forward,* in role she repeated in film version. Introduced "Milkman, Keep Those Bottles Quiet"; later became television actress, then director.

1943	Best Foot Forward (*Blind Date*)
	Girl Crazy (*Polly Williams*)
1944	Broadway Rhythm (*Trixie Simpson*)
1954	Lucky Me (*Flo Neely*)
1980	Can't Stop the Music (dir. only)

"Walking the Dog" Music by George Gershwin. Perky
perambulatory instrumental accompanying Fred Astaire
as he literally dogs Ginger Rogers' footsteps on an ocean
liner's kennel deck in *Shall We Dance* (RKO 1937). The
piece, something of a variation on "Fascinating
Rhythm," was originally published under the title
"Promenade."

Waller, (Thomas Wright) Fats, singer, pianist, bandleader; b. New York, May 21, 1904; d. aboard train,
Kansas City, Mo., Dec. 15, 1943. Rotund jazz pianist
whose zestful singing and playing were featured in three

films. Made many records; also subject of retrospective Broadway revue, *Ain't Misbehavin'*.

1935 Hooray for Love
      King of Burlesque
1943 Stormy Weather

Wallis, (Harold) Hal B(rent), producer; b. Chicago, Sept. 14, 1898. Veteran studio executive—in films since 1922—who produced at Warner (1930–45), Paramount (1945–67), and independently, and whose most distinguished musical was *Yankee Doodle Dandy* starring James Cagney. Wallis worked with Dean Martin and Jerry Lewis on ten films (plus one with Lewis alone), Elvis Presley on nine, Dick Powell on seven; others with whom he was associated in musicals were Joan Blondell, Ruby Keeler, and Ann Sheridan. Among his major dramatic productions were *Little Caesar, Sergeant York,* and *Casablanca.* Bib: *Starmaker* by Wallis & Charles Higham (1980). (Died Rancho Mirage, Oct. 5, 1986.)

1933 Gold Diggers of 1933
      Footlight Parade
1936 The Green Pastures
      Gold Diggers of 1937
1937 Ready, Willing and Able
      The Singing Marine
      Hollywood Hotel
1938 Swing Your Lady
      Gold Diggers in Paris
      Cowboy from Brooklyn
      Hard To Get
      Going Places
1939 Naughty but Nice
      On Your Toes
1941 Navy Blues
      Blues in the Night
1942 Juke Girl
      Yankee Doodle Dandy
1943 This Is the Army
1949 My Friend Irma
1950 My Friend Irma Goes West
1951 That's My Boy
      Sailor Beware
1952 Jumping Jacks
      The Stooge
1953 Scared Stiff
      Money from Home
1954 Three-Ring Circus
1955 Artists and Models
1956 Hollywood or Bust
1957 Loving You
1958 King Creole
      Rock-a-Bye Baby

1960 GI Blues
1961 Blue Hawaii
1962 Girls! Girls! Girls!
1963 Fun in Acapulco
1964 Roustabout
1966 Paradise, Hawaiian Style
1967 Easy Come, Easy Go

Walsh, Raoul, director; b. New York, March 11, 1887; d. Simi, Cal., Dec. 31, 1980. Walsh began his career as an actor with D. W. Griffith; became a director after losing an eye in 1928. He worked at various studios with such actors as Bing Crosby, Alice Faye, Mae West, Jack Benny, Bob Hope, Dorothy Lamour, and Dennis Morgan. *High Sierra* and *White Heat* were among his many action films. Bib: *Each Man in His Time* by Walsh (1974).

1929 The Cock-Eyed World
      Hot for Paris
1933 Going Hollywood
1935 Under Pressure
      Every Night at Eight
1936 Klondike Annie
1937 Artists and Models
      Hitting a New High
1938 College Swing
1939 St. Louis Blues
1946 The Man I Love
1949 It's a Great Feeling (guest bit only)
1952 Glory Alley
1959 A Private's Affair

Walters, Charles ("Chuck"), director, choreographer; b. Pasadena, Nov. 17, 1911. A Broadway dancer turned choreographer who became an MGM choreographer turned director, Walters worked with Judy Garland on seven films (including *Meet Me in St. Louis, Easter Parade*), also with Mickey Rooney, June Allyson, Fred Astaire, Ginger Rogers, Ray Bolger, Gene Kelly, Esther Williams, Vera-Ellen, Leslie Caron, Bing Crosby, Frank Sinatra, Doris Day, and Debbie Reynolds. Later directed nonmusicals. (Died Malibu, Aug. 13, 1982.)

Unless otherwise noted, Mr. Walters was director of the following; asterisk indicates he was choreographer only:
1942 Seven Days' Leave*
1943 Presenting Lily Mars* (also dancer)
      DuBarry Was a Lady*
      Girl Crazy* (also dancer)
      Best Foot Forward*
      Meet the People*
      Broadway Rhythm*
1944 Meet Me in St. Louis*

1945 The Harvey Girls*
     Abbott and Costello in Hollywood* (also dancer)
1946 Ziegfeld Follies* (part)
1947 Good News (also chor.)
1948 Summer Holiday*
     Easter Parade (also co-chor.)
1949 The Barkleys of Broadway
1950 Summer Stock (also co-chor.)
1951 Texas Carnival
1952 The Belle of New York
1953 Easy To Love
     Lili (also chor., dancer)
     Torch Song (also chor., dancer)
     Dangerous When Wet (also chor.)
1955 The Glass Slipper (also co-chor., dancer)
1956 High Society
1962 Jumbo
1964 The Unsinkable Molly Brown

"Waltz at Maxim's." *See* **"She Is Not Thinking of Me"**

"Waltz in Swing Time" Music by Jerome Kern. An audition dance in *Swing Time* (RKO 1936) performed at the swank Club Raymond by Fred Astaire, sporting an unaccustomed floppy *La Bohème* bowtie, and Ginger Rogers in billowy white ruffles. In his biography of Jerome Kern, Gerald Bordman wrote that, according to arranger Robert Russell Bennett, "Kern provided some basic themes and then told me to put them together in any way that would satisfy Astaire."

Waring, (Frederick M.) Fred, bandleader, actor; b. Tyrone, Pa., June 9, 1900. Durable collegiate bandleader whose Pennsylvanians featured the singing Lane sisters—Priscilla and Rosemary—before their film debuts. Also featured Glee Club; made many records.

1929 Syncopation (specialty)
1937 Varsity Show (*Ernie Mason*)
1948 Melody Time (soundtrack only)

Warren, Harry (né Salvatore Guaragna), composer; b. Brooklyn, Dec. 24, 1893. The most prolific and durable of all Hollywood composers, Warren was the mainstay of the Warner musicals of the 30s and the Fox musicals of the early 40s. His first major screen partner was lyricist Al Dubin, with whom he worked on such enduring early efforts as *42nd Street, Footlight Parade,* and four *Gold Diggers* movies. Among their songs: "Forty-Second Street," "Shuffle Off to Buffalo," "You're Getting To Be a Habit with Me," "Young and Healthy," "Shadow Waltz," "We're in the Money,"

"Honeymoon Hotel," "Keep Young and Beautiful," "The Boulevard of Broken Dreams," "I Only Have Eyes for You," "I'll String Along with You," "Fair and Warmer," "About a Quarter to Nine," "She's a Latin from Manhattan," "Don't Give Up the Ship," "Lullaby of Broadway," "September in the Rain," "The Words Are in My Heart," "All's Fair in Love and War," "With Plenty of Money and You," "Am I in Love?," "'Cause My Baby Says It's So," "Remember Me," and "Song of the Marines." After Warren and Dubin broke up in 1938, the composer collaborated with such other lyricists as Johnny Mercer ("Jeepers Creepers," "You Must Have Been a Beautiful Baby," "On the Atchison, Topeka and the Santa Fe"); Mack Gordon ("Down Argentina Way," "Chattanooga Choo-Choo," "I Know Why," "I Yi Yi Yi Yi," "At Last," "I Had the Craziest Dream," "I've Got a Gal in Kalamazoo," "Serenade in Blue," "You'll Never Know," "My Heart Tells Me," "The More I See You"); Leo Robin ("No Love No Nothin'," "A Journey to a Star," "Zing a Little Zong"); Arthur Freed ("This Heart of Mine"); Ralph Blane ("The Stanley Steamer"); and Jack Brooks ("That's Amore"). Other lyricists with whom Warren worked in Hollywood were Sam Lewis, Joe Young, Gus Kahn, Ira Gershwin, Dorothy Fields, Sammy Cahn, Mack David, Harold Adamson, and Leo McCarey.

Warren songs were introduced by, among others, Dick Powell, Ruby Keeler, Joan Blondell, Eddie Cantor, Al Jolson, Ginger Rogers, Wini Shaw, Helen Morgan, James Melton, Kenny Baker, Rudy Vallee, Ann Sheridan, Shirley Temple, Betty Grable, Carmen Miranda, Alice Faye, Don Ameche, Glenn Miller's orchestra, Dick Haymes, Fred Astaire, Judy Garland, Mickey Rooney, Doris Day, Gene Kelly, Howard Keel, Esther Williams, Bing Crosby, and Dean Martin. Bib: *Harry Warren and the Hollywood Musical* by Tony Thomas (1975). (Died Los Angeles, Sept. 22, 1981.)

1930 Spring Is Here (Lewis, Young)
1933 42nd Street (Dubin) (also *songwriter*)
     Gold Diggers of 1933 (Dubin)
     Footlight Parade (Dubin)
     Roman Scandals (Dubin)
1934 Moulin Rouge (Dubin)
     Wonder Bar (Dubin)
     Twenty Million Sweethearts (Dubin)
     Dames (Dubin)
1935 Gold Diggers of 1935 (Dubin)
     Go Into Your Dance (Dubin)
     Broadway Gondolier (Dubin)
     Shipmates Forever (Dubin)
     Stars Over Broadway (Dubin)

1936 Colleen (Dubin)
     Hearts Divided (Dubin)
     Cain and Mabel (Dubin)
     Gold Diggers of 1937 (Dubin)
     Sing Me a Love Song (Dubin)
1937 Melody for Two (Dubin)
     Mr. Dodd Takes the Air (Dubin)
     The Singing Marine (Dubin)
1938 Gold Diggers in Paris (Dubin)
     Garden of the Moon (Dubin; Mercer)
     Going Places (Mercer)
1939 Naughty but Nice (Mercer)
     Honolulu (Kahn)
1940 Young People (Gordon)
     Down Argentine Way (Gordon)
1941 That Night in Rio (Gordon)
     The Great American Broadcast (Gordon)
     Sun Valley Serenade (Gordon)
     Weekend in Havana (Gordon)
1942 Orchestra Wives (Gordon)
     Iceland (Gordon)
     Springtime in the Rockies (Gordon)
1943 Sweet Rosie O'Grady (Gordon)
     The Gang's All Here (Robin)
1945 Diamond Horseshoe (Gordon)
     Yolanda and the Thief (Freed)
1946 Ziegfeld Follies (Freed)
     The Harvey Girls (Mercer)
1948 Summer Holiday (Blane)
1949 The Barkleys of Broadway (Gershwin)
     My Dream Is Yours (Blane)
1950 Summer Stock (Gordon)
     Pagan Love Song (Freed)
1951 Texas Carnival (Fields)
1952 The Belle of New York (Mercer)
     Skirts Ahoy (Blane)
     Just for You (Robin)
1953 The Caddy (Brooks)
1955 Artists and Models (Brooks)
1956 The Birds and the Bees (David)
1957 An Affair to Remember (Adamson, McCarey)
1958 Rock-a-Bye Baby (Cahn)
1960 Cinderfella (Brooks)
1961 The Ladies' Man (Brooks)

"Was It Rain?" Music by Lou Handman; lyric by Walter Hirsch. Romantic recollection of a tearful parting (in which "misty" rhymes with "kiss me"), introduced by Frances Langford and Phil Regan in *Hit Parade* (Rep. 1937).

Washington, Ned, lyricist; b. Scranton, Pa., Aug. 15, 1901; d. Los Angeles, Dec. 20, 1976. Wrote songs for Walt Disney's *Pinocchio* with Leigh Harline ("When You Wish Upon a Star") and *Dumbo* with Frank Churchill and Oliver Wallace; also collaborated on "Cosi-Cosa" (Bronislaw Kaper and Walter Jurmann), "Stella by Starlight" (Victor Young), "My Foolish Heart" (Young), and "High Noon" (Dimitri Tiomkin). Others with whom Washington worked were Michael Cleary, Herb Magidson, Sam H. Stept, Agustin Lara, Phil Ohman, Gabriel Ruiz, and Lester Lee.

1929 The Forward Pass (Cleary-Magidson)
1930 Little Johnny Jones (Cleary-Magidson)
1931 Bright Lights (Cleary-Magidson)
1937 Dodge City Trail (Stept)
1938 Tropic Holiday (Lara)
1940 Pinocchio (Harline)
1941 Dumbo (Churchill, Wallace)
1943 Sleepy Lagoon (Ohman)
     Hands Across the Border (Ohman)
1944 The Cowboy and the Senorita (Ohman)
1945 Mexicana (Ruiz)
1953 Miss Sadie Thompson (Lee)
     Let's Do It Again (Lee)

Waters, Ethel, actress, singer; b. Chester, Pa., Oct. 31, 1896; d. Chatsworth, Cal., Sept. 1, 1977. Singer of great range and emotion, famed for appearances in vaudeville, six Broadway musicals (including *Cabin in the Sky*, which she filmed), dramatic works (notably *The Member of the Wedding*), nightclubs, and concerts. Introduced "Am I Blue?" and "Happiness Is a Thing Called Joe" in movies; also made many records. Bib: *His Eye Is on the Sparrow* by Miss Waters (1951).

1929 On with the Show (specialty)
1934 Gift of Gab (specialty)
1942 Cairo (*Cleona Jones*)
1943 Cabin in the Sky (*Petunia Jackson*)
     Stage Door Canteen (specialty)

"Way We Were, The" Music by Marvin Hamlisch; lyric by Alan & Marilyn Bergman. Nostalgic theme of nonmusical film of same name (Col. 1973), sung on soundtrack by the movie's star, Barbra Streisand. According to composer Hamlisch, Miss Streisand had objected to the song as being too simple and agreed to sing it only after everyone connected with the production had voted in its favor.

"Way You Look Tonight, The" Music by Jerome Kern; lyric by Dorothy Fields. Song of total adoration sung by Fred Astaire in *Swing Time* (RKO 1936) while seated at the piano in Ginger Rogers' hotel apartment. In the scene, Miss Rogers, hearing the song while shampooing her hair in the bathroom, is so moved by the lyric about her warm smile, soft cheeks, tender words, and nose-wrinkling laugh, that she emerges from the room with her hair still lathered—then rushes right back in embarrassment. This was the second of the three Kern-Fields "look" songs, the others being "Lovely To Look At" in *Roberta* and "Just Let Me Look at You" in *Joy of Living*.

Wayne, David (né Wayne McMeekan), actor, singer; b. Traverse City, Mich., Jan. 30, 1914. A slightly built, protean actor primarily identified with the stage (*Finian's Rainbow, The Teahouse of the August Moon*) and television.

1950 My Blue Heaven (*Walter Pringle*)
1952 With a Song in My Heart (*Don Ross*)
Wait 'Til the Sun Shines Nellie (*Ben Halper*)
1953 The I Don't Care Girl (*Ed McCoy*)
Tonight We Sing (*Sol Hurok*)
Down Among the Sheltering Palms (*Lt. Carl Schmidt*)
1957 Ruggles of Red Gap (tv) (*Egbert Floud*)
Junior Miss (tv) (*Willis Reynolds*)
1974 Huckleberry Finn (*Dauphin*)

"We Saw the Sea" Music & lyric by Irving Berlin. The frustrated, unromantic life of a sailor, as described in the opening scene of *Follow the Fleet* (RKO 1936) by Fred Astaire and fellow seamen (including Tony Martin).

"We Will Always Be Sweethearts" Music by Oscar Straus; lyric by Leo Robin. In *One Hour with You* (Par. 1932), Jeanette MacDonald trillingly revealed to her friend, Genevieve Tobin—how much she was in love with spouse Maurice Chevalier. Waltz later reprised as duet by MacDonald and Chevalier.

Webster, Paul Francis, lyricist; b. New York, Dec. 20, 1907. All-purpose craftsman whose lyrics have been mated to melodies of Louis Alter ("Rainbow on the River"), Oscar Straus, Frank Churchill, Victor Young, Harry Revel, Hoagy Carmichael, Juventino Rosas ("The Loveliest Night of the Year"), Franz Lehar, Sammy Fain ("Secret Love," "Love Is a Many-Splendored Thing," "April Love," 'A Certain Smile"), Nicholas Brodszky, Rudolf Friml, Dimitri Tiomkin ("Friendly Persuasion"), and Johnny Mandel ("The Shadow of Your Smile"). Among those who have sung Webster lyrics: Bobby Breen, Ginny Simms, Betty Hut-

ton, Ann Blyth, Mario Lanza, Doris Day, Howard Keel, and Pat Boone. (Died Beverly Hills, March 23, 1984.)

1936 Rainbow on the River (Alter)
1937 Make a Wish (Alter, Straus)
1938 Breaking the Ice (Churchill; Young)
1943 Presenting Lily Mars (Jurmann)
It Ain't Hay (Revel)
Hit the Ice (Revel)
1944 Ghost Catchers (Revel)
Minstrel Man (Revel)
1945 The Stork Club (Revel; Carmichael)
1952 The Merry Widow (Lehar)
1953 Calamity Jane (Fain)
1954 Rose Marie (Friml)
Lucky Me (Fain)
The Student Prince (Brodszky)
1956 Hollywood or Bust (Fain)
1957 April Love (Fain)
Let's Be Happy (Eng.) (Brodszky)
1958 Mardi Gras (Fain)
1959 A Diamond for Carla (tv) (Fain)
The Big Circus (Fain)

"Wedding of the Painted Doll, The" Music by Nacio Herb Brown; lyric by Arthur Freed. Perky Toyland epithalamion sung by James Burrows and danced by Dolls in Technicolor production number in *The Broadway Melody* (MGM 1929). Also sung by chorus in *Singin' in the Rain* (MGM 1952).

Weill, Kurt, composer; b. Dessau, Germany, March 2, 1900; d. New York, April 3, 1950. Weill won early fame for his acerbic, cynical Berlin musical, *Die Dreigroschenoper* (*The Three Penny Opera*), performed in New York in three different English versions and filmed twice (the second time in both German and English). Settling in the US in 1935, the composer became a major force in the American musical theatre; of his eight Broadway musicals, *Knickerbocker Holiday, Lady in the Dark, One Touch of Venus,* and *Lost in the Stars* were all filmed, though the first three with considerably less than reverential treatment. He also wrote the score for the Hollywood musical, *Where Do We Go From Here?* On the screen Weill songs were sung by Lotte Lenya (his wife), Ginger Rogers, Nelson Eddy, June Haver, Fred MacMurray, and Sammy Davis, Jr. In Germany he worked mostly with lyricist-playwright Bertolt Brecht; in the US his songs had lyrics by Maxwell Anderson, Sam Coslow, Ira Gershwin, Ogden Nash, Marc Blitzstein, and Ann Ronell, among others. Bib: *The Days Grow Short* by Ronald Sanders (1980).

1930 Die Dreigroschenoper (Ger.) (Brecht)
1938 You and Me (Coslow)
1944 Lady in the Dark (Gershwin)
      Knickerbocker Holiday (Anderson)
1945 Where Do We Go from Here? (Gershwin)
1948 One Touch of Venus (Nash; Ronell)
1964 Die Dreigroschenoper (Three Penny Opera) (Ger.)
      (Brecht; Blitzstein)
1974 Lost in the Stars (Anderson)

"Well, Did You Evah?" Music & lyric by Cole Porter. Lighthearted put-down of high society's casual attitude toward disastrous news, performed in *High Society* (MGM 1956) by Bing Crosby and Frank Sinatra. Finding themselves alone at the bar during a formal social bash in Newport, Crosby and Sinatra get well fortified as they exchange gossipy information, then high kick their way back to the party. The number dates from 1939 when it was introduced in the Broadway musical *DuBarry Was a Lady* by Betty Grable and Charles Walters.

"We'll Make Hay While the Sun Shines" Music by Nacio Herb Brown; lyric by Arthur Freed. In a movie production number—dreamed by screen hopeful Marion Davies in *Going Hollywood* (MGM 1933)—Bing Crosby sings to Marion of the joys of country life as they stroll past fields of swaying daisies and into their cottage. Marion joins Bing in song while riding in a horse-and-buggy, then does a buck and wing with a scarecrow. After the couple bound about with farmers and farmerettes in a hay field, a sudden shower sends Marion and Bing indoors where they cuddle in heavy blankets before an open fireplace as Bing obliges with a final reprise.

"We're in the Money" Music by Harry Warren; lyric by Al Dubin. Excessively optimistic anthem ("You never see a headline 'bout a breadline today") introduced by Ginger Rogers at the beginning of *Gold Diggers of 1933* (Warner 1933). In this production number, part of a Broadway revue in rehearsal, Miss Rogers and the chorus girls are clad only in huge, strategically placed gold coins, and Ginger even gets to sing in pig Latin. Number is also known as "The Gold Digger's Song." Another Warren-Dubin "money" song, "With Plenty of Money and You," was in *Gold Diggers of 1937*.

"We're Off To See the Wizard" Music by Harold Arlen; lyric by E. Y. Harburg. Scampering number for the oddly assorted foursome in *The Wizard of Oz* (MGM 1939)—Dorothy (Judy Garland), the Scarecrow (Ray Bolger), the Tin Woodman (Jack Haley), and the Cowardly Lion (Bert Lahr).

"We're Working Our Way Through College" Music by Richard A. Whiting; lyric by Johnny Mercer. Cheeky view of college life, sung by Dick Powell and collegians parading through campus of Winfield College in *Varsity Show* (Warner 1937). Retitled "She's Working Her Way Through College," song was also sung in film of same name (Warner 1952) by Gene Nelson, Virginia Mayo, and collegians.

West, Mae, actress, singer, screenwriter; b. Brooklyn, Aug. 17, 1892; d. Los Angeles, Nov. 22, 1980. With her clenched-teeth delivery, hourglass figure and sashaying walk, Mae West managed both to personify and satirize female sexuality. Her unique, unvarying screen personality, displayed in a series of films she wrote herself, was credited with putting Paramount back on its feet during the Depression. Miss West, who made her Broadway debut in 1911, had her greatest stage success in *Diamond Lil,* which she adapted for the screen as *She Done Him Wrong.* Among movie songs she introduced was "My Old Flame" in *Belle of the Nineties.* Bib: *Goodness Had Nothing To Do With It* by Miss West (1956); *Films of Mae West* by Jon Tuska (1977).

1933 She Done Him Wrong (*Lady Lou*)
      I'm No Angel (*Tira*)
1934 Belle of the Nineties (*Ruby Carter*)
1935 Goin' to Town (*Cleo Borden*)
1936 Klondike Annie (*Rose Carlton*)
      Go West, Young Man (*Mavis Arden*)
1937 Every Day's a Holiday (*Peaches O'Day*)
1943 The Heat's On (*Fay Lawrence*)

West Side Story (1961). Music by Leonard Bernstein; lyrics by Stephen Sondheim; screenplay by Ernest Lehman from Broadway musical by Bernstein, Sondheim, and Arthur Laurents based on story by Jerome Robbins suggested by Shakespeare's *Romeo and Juliet.*

A Mirisch film released by United Artists; produced by Robert Wise; directed by Wise & Jerome Robbins; associate producer, Saul Chaplin; choreography, Robbins; production design, Boris Leven; costumes, Irene Sharaff; music director, John Green; orchestrations, Chaplin, Irwin Kostal, Sid Ramin; cameraman, Daniel Fapp; editor, Thomas Stanford; Technicolor; Panavision.

Cast: Natalie Wood (vocals by Marni Nixon) (*Maria*); Richard Beymer (vocals by Jim Bryant) (*Tony*); Russ Tamblyn (*Riff*); Rita Moreno (vocals by Betty Wand) (*Anita*); George Chakiris (*Bernardo*); Simon Oakland (*Lt. Schrank*); William Bramley (*Officer Krupke*); Ned Glass (*Doc*); John Astin (*Glad Hand*); Gus Trikonis (*Indio*); Jamie Rogers (*Loco*); Tony Mordente (*Action*); Eliot Feld (*Baby John*); David Winters (*A-Rab*); Tucker Smith (*Ice*).

Songs: "Jet Song" - Tamblyn, Jets/ "Something's Coming" - Beymer (Bryant)/ "Dance at the Gym" - Jets, Sharks, girls/ "Maria" - Beymer (Bryant)/ "America" - Moreno, Chakiris, Sharks, girls/ "Tonight" - Beymer (Bryant), Wood (Nixon)/ "Gee, Officer Krupke!" - Tamblyn, Jets/ "I Feel Pretty" - Wood (Nixon)/ "One Hand, One Heart" - Beymer (Bryant), Wood (Nixon)/ "Quintet" - Moreno, Beymer (Bryant), Wood (Nixon), Tamblyn, Chakiris, Jets, Sharks/ "The Rumble" - dance by Jets, Sharks/ "Cool" - Smith, Jets/ "A Boy Like That" - Moreno (Wand)/ "I Have a Love" - Wood (Nixon)/ "Somewhere" - Beymer (Bryant), Wood (Nixon).

In resetting *Romeo and Juliet* in the modern slums of Manhattan, the star-crossed lovers became native-born Tony and Puerto Rican Maria, with their balcony a fire escape; the Montagues and Capulets became Jets and Sharks, rival ethnic street gangs; and Friar Lawrence became a neighborhood druggist. Updated parallels are found in the rumble, the street fight between the gangs, in which Tony kills Bernardo, Maria's brother and leader of the Sharks, after Bernardo has killed Riff, Tony's best friend and leader of the Jets. At the end of *West Side Story*, however, there is no double suicide; Tony is killed by the boy Maria was to have married and Maria lives on in her grief.

The musical, which was hailed as a Broadway milestone when it first opened in 1957 with Carol Lawrence and Larry Kert, was filmed with a new cast of principals except for George Chakiris, who had played Riff, not Bernardo, in the London company. (Though the gang members and their girls were supposedly in their teens, the cleancut, well-groomed leading players ranged in age from 22 to 30.) Because of the importance of dance to the production, Jerome Robbins, credited as co-director with Robert Wise, restaged his original dances in cinematic terms using both real and studio locations. In a manner foreshadowing his *Sound of Music* opening, Wise began the film with a helicopter view of Manhattan, shot straight down, which then gets closer and closer until it zeros in on the finger-snapping, menacing Jets who then take off and dance down the streets. (These scenes were shot on location on West 64th Street, now occupied by Lincoln Center.)

While the complete original score was retained in the film, the order of some numbers was changed. "Gee, Officer Krupke" was introduced earlier to maintain the stark mood of the final scenes, and "Cool" was sung after, not before, the rumble. Also, "America" received extended choreography as well as a different lyric which emphasized Puerto Rican problems in the US rather than in San Juan.

Other film musicals based on stage musicals derived from Shakespearean plays: *The Boys from Syracuse* (1940) from *The Comedy of Errors* (1593), and *Kiss Me, Kate* (1953) from *The Taming of the Shrew* (1594).

"What Are You Doing the Rest of Your Life?" Music by Michel Legrand; lyric by Alan & Marilyn Bergman. Amorous proposal sung by Michael Dees on soundtrack of nonmusical film *The Happy Ending* (UA 1969).

"What Goes On Here in My Heart?" Music by Ralph Rainger; lyric by Leo Robin. All that bumpin' and thumpin' and jumpin', that's what. Introduced by Betty Grable and Jack Whiting in *Give Me a Sailor* (Par. 1938).

"What Have You Got That Gets Me?" Music by Ralph Rainger; lyric by Leo Robin. Question regarding the appeal of an unromantic soul, posed in *Artists and Models Abroad* (Par. 1938) by the Yacht Club Boys, Joyce Compton, Joan Bennett, and Jack Benny.

"What Makes the Sunset?" Music by Jule Styne; lyric by Sammy Cahn. Romantic series of eleven questions (two repeated) concerning the wonders of nature, asked by Frank Sinatra in *Anchors Aweigh* (MGM 1945).

"What Wouldn't I Do for That Man?" Music by Jay Gorney; lyric by E. Y. Harburg. "My Man"-type ballad of slavish devotion sung by Helen Morgan in *Applause* (Par. 1929) as she sits on the floor of her room going through photographs of her lover (Fuller Mellish, Jr.), old letters, and theatre programs. Song also sung by Miss Morgan the same year in Paramount's *Glorifying the American Girl*.

"Whatever Will Be, Will Be." *See* **"Que Sera, Sera"**

"What's Good About Goodbye?" Music by Harold Arlen; lyric by Leo Robin. After a night with Marta Torren, Tony Martin (as Pepe LeMoko) stands on his balcony—in *Casbah* (Univ. 1948)—and pleads with his departing inamorata not to leave.

"What's New, Pussycat?" Music by Burt Bacharach; lyric by Hal David. Lilting serenade in admiration of pussycat's nose, eyes, and lips, sung on soundtrack of film of same name (UA 1965) by Tom Jones.

Wheeler and Woolsey, actors. (Albert Jerome) Bert Wheeler, b. Paterson, NJ, April 17, 1895; d. New York, Jan. 18, 1968. Robert Woolsey, b. Oakland, Cal., Aug. 14, 1889; d. Malibu Beach, Oct. 31, 1938. After Broadway producer Florenz Ziegfeld brought Wheeler and Woolsey together in *Rio Rita,* which they then filmed, the comedians continued as a team in a series of RKO movies. Wheeler, who introduced "I Love You So Much" and "Dolores," played the stubby, sad-faced, squeaky-voiced innocent, and Woolsey, who looked like a scrawny owl, was the fast-talking, bespectacled con man. Wheeler returned to the stage in 1942.

1929	Rio Rita (*Chick Bean; Ed Lovett*)
1930	Cuckoos (*Sparrow; Prof. Bird*)
	Dixiana (*Peewee; Ginger*)
1932	Girl Crazy (*Jimmy Deagan; Slick Foster*)
1934	Cockeyed Cavaliers (*Bert; Bob*)
	Hips Hips Hooray (*Andy Williams; Bob Dudley*)
1935	Nitwits (*Johnny; Newton*)
1941	Las Vegas Nights (Wheeler only) (*Stu Grant*)

"When Did You Leave Heaven?" Music by Richard A. Whiting; lyric by Walter Bullock. Tony Martin's serenade to an angel in *Sing, Baby, Sing* (Fox 1936).

"When I Grow Too Old To Dream" Music by Sigmund Romberg; lyric by Oscar Hammerstein II. Waltzing, rueful ballad of parting sung by Evelyn Laye in *The Night Is Young* (MGM 1935). Also by José Ferrer and Helen Traubel in *Deep in My Heart* (MGM 1954). Hammerstein once admitted that he took eight weeks to write the eight lines in the song's refrain (six actually, since one line is repeated twice). The problem was that he wasn't exactly sure what he meant by the title phrase, since the older one gets the more likely it is that one *would* dream. "I concluded," the excessively analytical lyricist wrote, "that I must be giving the word 'dream' a special meaning, that I was thinking of it in the sense

of a lover dreaming only about the present and the future. In saying 'When I grow too old to dream,' I was really saying, 'When I grow too old to love you and to dream about loving you, I'll have you to remember, I will be remembering our love in the past.''

"When I Look in Your Eyes" Music & lyric by Leslie Bricusse. "I see the wisdom of the world in your eyes" sang Rex Harrison as he bid a melancholy farewell to Sophie the seal in *Doctor Dolittle* (Fox 1967).

"When I'm with You" Music by Harry Revel; lyric by Mack Gordon. Introduced by Tony Martin as a radio singer in *Poor Little Rich Girl* (Fox 1936), then sung by Shirley Temple (with different words) to her father, Michael Whalen. Later reprised in film by Alice Faye on the radio.

"When Love Goes Wrong" Music by Hoagy Carmichael; lyric by Harold Adamson. In *Gentlemen Prefer Blondes* (Fox 1953) gold-digging Lorelei Lee (Marilyn Monroe) and Dorothy Shaw (Jane Russell) are in Paris, down on their romantic and financial luck. Sitting at a sidewalk café they sing the mournful ballad of the chain reaction caused by their unhappy condition, and soon they've attracted a crowd including an obliging accordionist and two befezzed urchins. Now playing to the audience, the girls turn the number into a sizzling, high-stepping routine that ends with their strutting gaily into a waiting taxi as Russell stage whispers to Monroe: "No bows, honey. Eight bars and off."

"When Winter Comes" Music & lyric by Irving Berlin. Advising his beloved, "I've gotta have you to cuddle up to," the singer, like the groundhog, looks forward to being an indoor sport during the brumal season. Introduced by Rudy Vallee in *Second Fiddle* (Fox 1939).

"When You Wish Upon a Star" Music by Leigh Harline; lyric by Ned Washington. Cliff Edwards (as Jiminy Cricket) sang the plaintive ballad over the credits of *Pinocchio* (Disney 1940), which led into the cartoon tale of the puppet who came to life.

"When You're Dancing the Waltz" Music by Richard Rodgers; lyric by Lorenz Hart. Lilting invitation from Charles Collins to Steffi Duna in *Dancing Pirate* (RKO

1936), accompanied by hundreds of whirling, twirling couples.

"When You're in Love" Music by Gene dePaul; lyric by Johnny Mercer. Expansive ballad sung in *Seven Brides for Seven Brothers* (MGM 1954) by Jane Powell in her bedroom to husband Howard Keel outside her window. Song later reprised by Keel.

"When You've Got a Little Springtime in Your Heart" Music & lyric by Harry M. Woods. Prescription for everlasting youth sung by Jessie Matthews in *Evergreen* (Gaumont-Brit. 1934) to convince a director that she can impersonate her own mother on the stage. The song then becomes the theme for a production number in a London revue called *Springtime in Your Heart*. After Miss Matthews sings the piece again in a floral setting, she dashes over to a huge hourglass, turns it upside down, and transports us back to 1924 for a spirited Charleston performed by the chorus. A second turn of the glass to 1914 finds us in a surreal munitions factory in which a huge bomb-like object rhythmically descends over young girls on an assembly line and transforms them into military robots. The final turn—to 1904—features Miss Matthews and Sonnie Hale leading the dancers in a polka to the tune of "Little Brown Jug."

"Where Am I?" Music by Harry Warren; lyric by Al Dubin. Romantic disorientation ("Am I in Heaven, or am I really with you?"), expressed by James Melton in *Stars Over Broadway* (Warner 1935).

"Where Are You?" Music by Jimmy McHugh; lyric by Harold Adamson. A spurned woman's mournful lament, sung by Gertrude Niesen in *Top of the Town* (Univ. 1937).

"Where Are You Now That I Need You?" *See* **"Now That I Need You"**

"Where Is the Song of Songs for Me?" Music & lyric by Irving Berlin. Love theme in *Lady of the Pavements* (UA 1929), sung by Lupe Velez first in an elegant Paris ballroom, later at the Smoking Dog Café. In 1962 Berlin used the same waltz melody for "Is He the Only Man in the World?," in the Broadway musical *Mr. President*.

"Where Is Your Heart?" Music by Georges Auric; lyric by William Engvick. Also known as "The Song from Moulin Rouge," the waltzing piece reflects the concern of one unsure of her lover's love. It was sung in the 1953 UA film by Muriel Smith dubbed for Zsa Zsa Gabor playing Jane Avril. Originally, with a French lyric by Jacques Larue, the song was called *"Le Long de la Seine."*

"Where Love Has Gone" Music by James Van Heusen; lyric by Sammy Cahn. Ballad of romantic rejection introduced on soundtrack of film of the same name (Par. 1964) by Jack Jones.

"Whispers in the Dark" Music by Frederick Hollander; lyric by Leo Robin. Nocturnal romantic scene limned by Connie Boswell, with the André Kostelanetz orchestra in *Artists and Models* (Par. 1937). Song was originally intended for Marlene Dietrich in *Desire* the previous year, but was cut from the film.

"Whistle While You Work" Music by Frank Churchill; lyric by Larry Morey. Snow White (Adriana Caselotti) and the friendly animals and birds sing as they clean up the dwarfs' house in the cartoon film *Snow White and the Seven Dwarfs* (Disney 1937).

"Whistling Away the Dark" Music by Henry Mancini; lyric by Johnny Mercer. Before the credits come on the screen in *Darling Lili* (Par. 1969), a baby spotlight on a darkened screen picks out Julie Andrews' tiny face in the distance. As the camera slowly moves in for the closeup, we discover that she is on a London music-hall stage singing this compelling song of hope to a World War I audience. The number is repeated in much the same way at the end of the film.

"White Christmas" Music & lyric by Irving Berlin. The most popular nonreligious Christmas song of all time was introduced by Bing Crosby in a Connecticut farmhouse in *Holiday Inn* (Par. 1942). In the scene, in which Bing is teaching the piece to Marjorie Reynolds, the crooner simulates the lyric's "sleighbells in the snow" by tapping his pipe stem on the ornamental bells covering a Christmas tree. Miss Reynolds (with Martha Mears' voice) then sings a reprise with Crosby. Number was also sung by Crosby in *Blue Skies* (Par. 1946) and *White Christmas* (Par. 1954). The song's verse, understandably omitted from the movie renditions, reveals that the singer is in Beverly Hills, where the sun is shining, the grass is green, the palm trees and the orange trees are swaying, but he's still homesick for an old-fashioned, snow-filled Christmas back east.

White, Onna, choreographer; b. Nova Scotia. Broadway and London choreographer who re-created her original stage dances for *The Music Man, 1776,* and *Mame,* and who won special notice for her work in *Oliver!*

1958	Hansel and Gretel (tv)
1962	The Music Man
1963	Bye Bye Birdie
1968	Oliver!
1972	1776
1974	Mame
1977	Pete's Dragon

Whiteman, Paul, bandleader, actor; b. Denver, March 28, 1891; d. Doylestown, Pa., Dec. 29, 1967. Celebrated, durable conductor, the self-styled but misnamed "King of Jazz," who rose to fame in the 20s by giving dance music respectability. On screen, the portly, mustached Whiteman was seen only as himself and only with his band and vocalists (including Bing Crosby in his first film appearance).

1930	King of Jazz
1935	Thanks a Million
1940	Strike Up the Band
1944	Lady, Let's Dance
	Atlantic City
1945	Rhapsody in Blue
1947	The Fabulous Dorseys

Whiting, Richard A., composer; b. Peoria, Ill., Nov. 12, 1891; d. Beverly Hills, Feb. 10, 1938. Whiting began as composer of musical accompaniment for silent films; with advent of talkies he wrote such songs as "Louise," "Beyond the Blue Horizon," "My Future Just Passed," "My Ideal," "One Hour With You," "On the Good Ship Lollipop," "Too Marvelous For Words," "Hooray for Hollywood," and "I'm Like a Fish Out of Water." His collaborators included Leo Robin, Sam Coslow, George Marion, Jr., W. Franke Harling, Newell Chase, B. G. DeSylva, Sidney Clare, and Johnny Mercer. On Broadway, he worked with Nacio Herb Brown and DeSylva on *Take a Chance,* which was filmed. Maurice Chevalier, Nancy Carroll, Charles "Buddy" Rogers, Jeanette MacDonald, Janet Gaynor,

Shirley Temple, Bing Crosby, Wini Shaw, Ruby Keeler, Dick Powell, Rosemary Lane, and Frances Langford were all identified with Whiting songs. The composer was the father of singer Margaret Whiting.

1929	Innocents of Paris (Robin)
	The Dance of Life (Coslow, Robin)
	Sweetie (Marion)
1930	Safety in Numbers (Marion)
	Let's Go Native (Marion)
	Monte Carlo (Harling-Robin)
	Playboy of Paris (Chase-Robin)
1932	One Hour with You (Robin)
1933	Adorable (Marion)
	My Weakness (Robin, DeSylva)
	Take a Chance (Brown-DeSylva)
1934	Transatlantic Merry-Go-Round (Clare)
1935	Big Broadcast of 1936 (Robin)
	Coronado (Coslow)
1937	Ready, Willing and Able (Mercer)
	Varsity Show (Mercer)
	Hollywood Hotel (Mercer)
1938	Cowboy from Brooklyn (Mercer)

Whitney, Eleanore, actress, dancer; b. 1917. Tiny, dark-haired tapper who appeared in Paramount films (four with Johnny Downs) and retired at 21.

1935	Millions in the Air (*Bubbles*)
1936	Three Cheers for Love (*Skippy Dormant*)
	Big Broadcast of 1937 (specialty)
	College Holiday (*Eleanor Wayne*)
1937	Turn Off the Moon (*Caroline Wilson*)
	Thrill of a Lifetime (*Betty Jane*)
	Blonde Trouble (*Edna Baker*)

"Who Are You?" Music by Richard Rodgers; lyric by Lorenz Hart. Ardent query to the girl who has changed his life, asked by Allan Jones in *The Boys from Syracuse* (Univ. 1940). The ballad was written specially for the movie verson of the 1938 Broadway musical.

"Who Knows?" Music & lyric by Cole Porter. In a cavernous, dazzlingly white nightclub in *Rosalie* (MGM 1937), a faraway vocalist (Lois Clements with Camille Sorey's voice) sang of hoped-for marital fulfillment while descending what looked like a path cut through a snow-capped mountain. Song was then briefly reprised by Nelson Eddy dancing with Eleanor Powell.

Whoopee! (1930). Music by Walter Donaldson; lyrics by Gus Kahn; screenplay by William Conselman from

Broadway musical by Donaldson, Kahn, and William Anthony McGuire based on play *The Nervous Wreck* by Owen Davis adapted from novel *The Wreck* by E. J. Rath.

A United Artists film produced by Samuel Goldwyn & Florenz Ziegfeld; directed by Thornton Freeland; choreography, Busby Berkeley; art director, Richard Day; costumes, John Harkrider; music director, Alfred Newman; cameramen, Lee Garmes, Roy Rennahan, Gregg Toland; editor, Stuart Heisler; Technicolor.

Cast: Eddie Cantor (*Henry Williams*); Eleanor Hunt (*Sally Morgan*); Paul Gregory (*Wanenis*); Ethel Shutta (*Mary Custer*); Jack Rutherford (*Sheriff Bob Wells*); Spencer Charters (*Jerome Underwood*); Chief Caupolican (*Chief Black Eagle*); Albert Hackett (*Chester Underwood*); Marilyn Morgan (Marian Marsh) (*Harriet Underwood*); Betty Grable, Virginia Bruce (chorus); George Olsen orchestra (soundtrack only).

Songs: "Cowboys" - Grable, ranch guests/ "I'll Still Belong to You" (Nacio Herb Brown-Edward Eliscu) - Gregory/ "Makin' Whoopee" - Cantor/ "Today's the Day" - wedding guests/ "A Girl Friend of a Boy Friend of Mine" - Cantor/ "My Baby Just Cares for Me" - Cantor/ "Stetson" - Shutta, cowboys; dance by cowgirls/ "Song of the Setting Sun" - Caupolican, squaws, braves.

Ziegfeld's stage production of *Whoopee*, starring Eddie Cantor, was running about a year on Broadway when the impresario sold the screen rights to Samuel Goldwyn soon after the 1929 Wall Street crash. The agreement called for the show to close and Ziegfeld to receive credit as co-producer of the movie (actually, he functioned more as an adviser). Except for Eleanor Hunt, who had been in the chorus, the first eight featured actors in the film repeated their Broadway roles. (Albert Hackett, later to become a leading screenwriter with his wife Frances Goodrich, had also had the same part in the play on which *Whoopee* was based.) The picture, considered the best use of two-color Technicolor at the time, was Goldwyn's first musical and the first feature-length film for both Cantor and choreographer Busby Berkeley. Apart from some exterior location scenes in Arizona and Berkeley's kaleidoscopic patterns, most of the production was a static sound-stage re-creation of the Broadway show, though only three of the original 16 Donaldson-Kahn songs were retained. (Among the casualties: the classic "Love Me or Leave Me," possibly because Ruth Etting, who had introduced it, was not in the film.) In the story, hypochondriac Henry Williams,

in California for his health, unwittingly helps Sally Morgan run away from her groom-to-be, Sheriff Bob, and into the tepee of Wanenis, the Indian brave she loves.

In 1944 Goldwyn's *Up in Arms,* in which Danny Kaye made his film debut, was supposedly based on the same source as *Whoopee,* but the only similarity was its pill-taking hero.

"Why Do I Dream Those Dreams?" Music by Harry Warren; lyric by Al Dubin. Songwriter-bandleader Dick Powell sang his heart out to Dolores Del Rio in *Wonder Bar* (Warner 1934).

"Why Dream?" Music by Ralph Rainger & Richard A. Whiting; lyric by Leo Robin. Advice to stop dreaming and start romancing, introduced by Henry Wadsworth (with Kenny Baker's voice) and reprised by Harold Nicholas in *Big Broadcast of 1936* (Par. 1935).

"Why Fight the Feeling?" Music & lyric by Frank Loesser. "It's too late to run, The beguine has begun," sang romantically succumbing Betty Hutton in *Let's Dance* (Par. 1950). Music was then reprised for a dream dance by Miss Hutton and Fred Astaire.

Wilcox, Herbert (Sydney), director, producer; b. Cork, Ireland, April 19, 1892; d. London, May 15, 1977. Major British film executive who began producing in 1919, and whose most memorable musical was *The Beggar's Opera,* with Laurence Olivier. Wilcox also produced and directed all the films, both musical and nonmusical, starring his wife, Anna Neagle, including three in Hollywood. Bib: *Twenty-Five Thousand Sunsets* by Wilcox (1967).

One asterisk indicates that Mr. Wilcox was director as well as producer; two asterisks that the film starred Anna Neagle:

1930	The Loves of Robert Burns
1932	Goodnight, Vienna **
	The Love Contract
	Say It with Music
1933	Yes, Mr. Brown *
	The Little Damozel **
	Bitter Sweet **
	That's a Good Girl
1934	The Queen's Affair **
1935	Brewster's Millions
	Come Out of the Pantry
1936	Lime Light **
	This'll Make You Whistle *

1937 London Melody**
1940 Irene (US)**
1941 No, No, Nanette (US)**
      Sunny (US)**
      Spring in Park Lane**
1947 The Courtneys of Curzon Street**
1953 The Beggar's Opera
1954 Lilacs in the Spring**
1956 King's Rhapsody**
1959 The Lady Is a Square**
      The Heart of a Man (dir. only)

Wilder, (Samuel) Billy, director, producer, screenwriter; b. Vienna, June 22, 1906. Wilder came to US in 1934 as screenwriter, became director eight years later, and was responsible for such major works as *Double Indemnity, The Lost Weekend,* and *The Apartment.* His satirical gifts were noted in his comedies with songs, especially *A Foreign Affair* and *Some Like It Hot.* Bib: *Billy Wilder* by Axel Madsen (1969).

Unless otherwise noted, Mr. Wilder was director-screenwriter of following:
1934 Music in the Air (script only)
1948 The Emperor Waltz
      A Foreign Affair
      A Song Is Born (script only)
1959 Some Like It Hot (also prod.)
1964 Kiss Me, Stupid (also prod.)

Williams, Esther (Jane), actress, swimmer; b. Inglewood, Cal., Aug. 8, 1921. Hollywood's only natant musical star, she appeared in a number of colorful, spectacular, and decidedly splashy films that kept her constantly submerged and eternally smiling. A swimming champion at 15, Miss Williams was in Billy Rose's Aquacade when MGM signed her as a sports rival to Fox's skating Sonja Henie. Van Johnson was her leading man in four movies, Howard Keel and Ricardo Montalban (with whom she introduced "Baby, It's Cold Outside") in two each. She also acted in films with Red Skelton, Peter Lawford, Gene Kelly, and Fernando Lamas (her third husband).

1944 Bathing Beauty (*Caroline Brooks*)
1945 Thrill of a Romance (*Cynthia Glenn*)
1946 Ziegfeld Follies (specialty)
      Easy To Wed (*Connie Allenbury*)
1947 Fiesta (*Maria Morales*)
      This Time for Keeps (*Nora*)
1948 On an Island with You (*Rosalind Reynolds*)
1949 Take Me Out to the Ball Game (*K. C. Higgins*)
      Neptune's Daughter (*Eve Barrett*)

1950 Duchess of Idaho (*Christine Duncan*)
      Pagan Love Song (*Mimi Bennett*)
1951 Texas Carnival (*Debbie Telford*)
1952 Skirts Ahoy (*Whitney Young*)
      Million Dollar Mermaid (*Annette Kellerman*)
1953 Dangerous When Wet (*Katie*)
      Easy To Love (*Julie Hallerton*)
1955 Jupiter's Darling (*Amytis*)
1960 The Big Show (*Hillary Allen*)

Williams, Paul, composer, lyricist, singer, actor; b. Bennington, Neb., Sept. 19, 1940. A self-described jar of peanut butter, Williams has been a film actor as well as writer of such songs as "Evergreen" (with Barbra Streisand) and "The Rainbow Connection" (Kenny Ascher). He has also appeared in nightclubs, concerts, and television.

1974 Phantom of the Paradise (also *Swan*)
1976 Bugsy Malone (also singer)
      A Star Is Born (Asher; Streisand; Holmes)
1979 The Muppet Movie (Ascher)

Willson, Meredith (né Robert Meredith Reiniger), composer, lyricist; b. Mason City, Ia., May 18, 1902. Former radio conductor and Hollywood arranger who wrote scores for three Broadway musicals, two of which were filmed. Robert Preston, Shirley Jones, Debbie Reynolds, and Harve Presnell sang his songs in the movies. (Died Santa Monica, June 15, 1984.)

1962 The Music Man
1964 The Unsinkable Molly Brown

Wilson, Dooley, actor, singer; b. Tyler, Texas, April 3, 1894; d. Los Angeles, May 30, 1953. Black performer most closely identified with teary rendition of "As Time Goes By" in nonmusical *Casablanca.*

1942 Cairo (*Hector*)
1943 Stormy Weather (*Gabe*)
      Higher and Higher (*Oscar*)
1944 Seven Days Ashore (*Jason*)

"Windmills of Your Mind" Music by Michel Legrand; lyric by Alan & Marilyn Bergman. Willowy theme sung on soundtrack of nonmusical film, *The Thomas Crown Affair* (UA 1968), by Noel Harrison, introduced during a split-screen sequence involving a glider in flight with playboy-bankrobber Steve McQueen inside. "The song had to express feeling but not plot," co-lyricist Alan Bergman once explained. "You want to know why this guy is uncomfortable in his skin. We had to underline his anxiety, which is played against the glider images

. . . We thought of circles, the glider circling the sky, the circular quality of anxiety." From that came similes of a spiral, a wheel within a wheel, a snowball, a carnival balloon, a carousel, and "an apple whirling silently in space."

Wing, (Martha Virginia) Toby, actress, singer, dancer; b. Richmond, Va., July 14, 1915. Platinum-haired, pencil-eyebrowed, round-faced Toby Wing was Hollywood's epitomical chorine and coed. In musicals she is best remembered as the girl to whom Dick Powell sang "Young and Healthy" in *42nd Street*.

1932   The Kid from Spain (chorus)
1933   42nd Street (*"Young and Healthy" girl*)
       College Humor (bit)
       Too Much Harmony (bit)
1934   Murder at the Vanities (*Nancy*)
       Kiss and Make-Up (*Consuelo Claghorne*)
1936   With Love and Kisses
1937   Sing While You're Able (*Joan*)

Winninger, (Karl) Charles, actor; b. Athens, Wisc., May 26, 1884; d. Palm Springs, Jan. 19, 1969. Blustery, silver-haired character comedian who specialized in playing tycoons, vaudevillians, and deadbeats. After lengthy Broadway career, Winninger went to Hollywood, where he repeated his stage role as Magnolia's father in *Show Boat*. His screen children included Irene Dunne, Deanna Durbin, Mickey Rooney, Judy Garland, George Murphy, Gloria DeHaven, Dinah Shore, Jeanne Crain, Dick Haymes, and Dan Dailey.

1931   Children of Dreams (*Dr. Joe Thompson*)
       Flying High (*Dr. Brown*)
1936   Show Boat (*Capt. Andy Hawks*)
1937   Three Smart Girls (*Judson Craig*)
       You Can't Have Everything (*Sam Gordon*)
       You're a Sweetheart (*Chuoka Charlie*)
       Every Day's a Holiday (*Van Reigble Van Pelter Van Doon III*)
1938   Hard To Get (*Ben Richards*)
1939   Babes in Arms (*Joe Moran*)
       Three Smart Girls Grow Up (*Judson Craig*)
       Destry Rides Again (*Wash Dimsdale*)
1940   If I Had My Way (*Joe Johnson*)
       Little Nellie Kelly (*Michael Noonan*)
1941   Pot o' Gold (*C. J. Haskell*)
       Ziegfeld Girl (*Pop Gallagher*)
1943   Coney Island (*Finnegan*)
       Hers To Hold (*Judson Craig*)
1944   Broadway Rhythm (*Sam Demming*)
       Belle of the Yukon (*Pop Candless*)

1945   State Fair (*Abel Frake*)
1947   Living in a Big Way (*D. Rutherford Morgan*)
       Something in the Wind (*Uncle Chester*)
1948   Give My Regards to Broadway (*Albert Norwick*)

Wise, Robert, director, producer; b. Winchester, Ind., Sept. 10, 1914. Former film editor (*The Story of Vernon and Irene Castle*) who became director in 1944. His most successful musicals were *West Side Story* and *The Sound of Music*.

1948   Mystery in Mexico
1957   This Could Be the Night
1961   West Side Story (also prod.)
1965   The Sound of Music (also prod.)
1968   Star!

"Wish I May, Wish I Might" Music & lyric by Hugh Martin & Ralph Blane. Propulsive number heralding the arrival of prom dates at Winsocki Military Academy in *Best Foot Forward* (MGM 1943). Sung and danced to by June Allyson, Kenny Bowers, Gloria DeHaven, Jack Jordan, Sara Haden, Donald MacBride, cadets, and guests.

"Wishing" Music & lyric by B. G. DeSylva. Optimistic credo expressed by three little girls in *Love Affair* (RKO 1939).

"With a Smile and a Song" Music by Frank Churchill; lyric by Larry Morey. Chipper prescription for happiness sung in *Snow White and the Seven Dwarfs* (Disney 1937) by Snow White (Adriana Caselotti) and the animals and birds of the forest.

"With Every Breath I Take" Music by Ralph Rainger; lyric by Leo Robin. Constant amorous desire expressed by Bing Crosby singing at the Cocoanut Grove in *Here Is My Heart* (Par. 1934).

"With My Eyes Wide Open I'm Dreaming" Music by Harry Revel; lyric by Mack Gordon. Romantic disbelief registered by Dorothy Dell and Jack Oakie in *Shoot the Works* (Par. 1934). Also sung by Dean Martin in *The Stooge* (Par. 1952).

"With Plenty of Money and You" Music by Harry Warren; lyric by Al Dubin. In which Dick Powell in *Gold Diggers of 1937* (Warner 1936) looked forward to a sunny life spending money on the girl he loves. The breezy expression of romantic materialism was also sung by Doris Day in *My Dream Is Yours* (Warner 1949), and Virginia Mayo and the Blackburn Twins in *She's Working Her Way Through College* (Warner 1952). A previous gold-digger's anthem was Warren and Dubin's "We're in the Money" in *Gold Diggers of 1933*.

"With You" Music & lyric by Irving Berlin. In *Puttin' on the Ritz* (UA 1930), when songwriter-singer Harry Richman meets songwriter Joan Bennett, he gets an idea for combining their most recent musical efforts. "You play your verse and my chorus," he advises. "By a strange coincidence the words fit beautifully. You play it and I'll sing it and you tell me what you think of it." They do just as he suggests, and after singing of how much he can accomplish with his beloved by his side, Harry asks Joan if she likes it. "Like it? Oh, it's wonderful!," she exclaims. "Wonderful?," responds Harry, "Why, it's marvelous!" The song was again performed at the end of the film when Joan, on stage, is too nervous to sing, and Harry, true trouper that he is, belts it right out from the audience. (This scene may have been suggested by the real-life situation in which Al Jolson sang "Liza" from the audience to wife Ruby Keeler on stage during performances of *Show Girl*.)

"With You on My Mind" Music by Lew Pollack; lyric by Lew Brown. Lament of one still carrying the torch introduced by Ethel Merman in *Straight, Place and Show* (Fox 1938). The song's patter section, about trying to chase the blues in Harlem, was cut from the film's final print.

Withers, Jane, actress, singer; b. Atlanta, April 12, 1926. Bratty Jane Withers first won notice as Shirley Temple's kiddie tormenter in *Bright Eyes;* later was given more sympathetic but brassier roles.

1934 Bright Eyes (*Joy Smythe*)
1935 This Is the Life (*Geraldine*)
      Paddy O'Day (*Paddy O'Day*)
1936 Can This Be Dixie? (*Peg Gurgle*)
1937 The Holy Terror (*Corky Wallace*)
1938 Rascals (*Gypsy*)
1940 Shooting High (*Jane Pritchard*)
1942 Johnny Doughboy (*Ann Winters/ Penelope Ryan*)
1944 My Best Gal (*Kitty O'Hara*)

"Without a Word of Warning" Music by Harry Revel; lyric by Mack Gordon. Sudden romance revealed by Bing Crosby in *Two for Tonight* (Par. 1935).

Wizard of Oz, The (1939). Music by Harold Arlen; lyrics by E. Y. Harburg; screenplay by Noel Langley, Florence Ryerson, and Edgar Allan Woolf, adapted by Langley from book *The Wonderful Wizard of Oz* by L. Frank Baum.

An MGM film produced by Mervyn LeRoy; associate producer, Arthur Freed; directed by Victor Fleming, King Vidor (uncredited); choreography, Bobby Connolly; art directors, Cedric Gibbons, William Horning; costumes, Adrian; special effects, Arnold Gillespie; music director & adapter, Herbert Stothart; associate, George Stoll; orchestrations, Roger Edens, George Bassman, Murray Cutter, Paul Marquandt; vocal arrangements, Ken Darby; cameramen, Harold Rosson, Allen Darby; editor, Blanche Sewell; Technicolor.

Cast: Judy Garland (*Dorothy Gale*); Frank Morgan (*Prof. Marvel/ The Wizard*); Ray Bolger (*Hunk/ Scarecrow*); Bert Lahr (*Zeke/ Cowardly Lion*); Jack Haley (*Hickory/ Tin Woodman*); Billie Burke (vocal by Lorraine Bridges) (*Glinda*); Margaret Hamilton (*Elmira Gulch/ Wicked Witch*); Charley Grapewin (*Uncle Henry*); Clara Blandick (*Auntie Em*); Munchkins.

Songs: "Over the Rainbow" - Garland/ "Ding-Dong! The Witch Is Dead" - Munchkins/ "Munchkinland" - Munchkins, incl. voices of Ken Darby (mayor), Rad Robinson (coroner), Bud Linn (district attorney), Linn, Robinson & John Dodson (Lollipop Guild), 3 Debutantes (Lullabye League), St. Joseph Choir, also Burke (Bridges)/ "We're Off To See the Wizard" - Garland, Bolger, Haley, Lahr/ "Follow the Yellow Brick Road" - Munchkins, Garland/ "If I Only Had a Brain" - Bolger/ "If I Only Had a Heart" - Haley/ "If I Only Had the Nerve" - Lahr/ "Optimistic Voices" (music, Herbert Stothart) - voices of Rhythmettes/ "Gates of Emerald City" - residents/ "The Merry Old Land of Oz" - residents/ "If I Were King of the Forest" -Lahr. Unused: "The Jitterbug."

Had the original plans been carried out, *The Wizard of Oz* would have been brought to the screen with Dorothy played by Shirley Temple, the Wizard by W. C. Fields or Ed Wynn, the Tin Woodman by Buddy Ebsen, the Wicked Witch by Gale Sondergaard, Auntie Em by May Robson, and the Good Witch by Helen Gilbert. And, if some MGM hierarchs had had their way, "Over the Rainbow" would not have been in it. Fortunately, the elaborate production, which required 29 sound stages and 65 separate sets, turned out to be the most successfully realized live-action children's fantasy ever created in Hollywood, with a flawless cast, a well-integrated score, and an inventive use of special effects (including a cyclone made out of a woman's stocking and an army of flying monkeys suspended by thousands of piano wires).

In this screen treatment, Dorothy Gale, unhappy on her drab, sepia-tinted Kansas farm, is knocked out during a tornado and dreams that she is over the rainbow in the colorful land of Oz. There she meets the adorable Munchkins (played by a gang of disreputable midgets) and goes off on the Yellow Brick Road for an adventurous hejira to see the Wizard in the Emerald City. Despite the machinations of the Wicked Witch, Dorothy and her newfound friends, the Scarecrow, the Tin Woodman, and the Cowardly Lion, complete their journey only to discover that the Wizard is something of a humbug. He does, however, convince the little girl's friends that they already possess the desired brains, heart, and courage, and Dorothy wakes up from her dream, happy to be home.

The film's genesis took place in 1900 with the publication of L. Frank Baum's hugely popular children's book *The Wonderful Wizard of Oz* (which would be followed by numerous volumes in the series). In 1903 Baum adapted his story into a successful Broadway musical (music by Paul Tietjens and A. Baldwin Sloane) which starred Dave Montgomery (Tin Woodman) and Fred Stone (Scarecrow), with Anna Laughlin as Dorothy. There were two silent-screen treatments: a one-reel version in 1915 and a lengthier adaptation in 1925, with Larry Semon as the Scarecrow, Oliver Hardy as the Tin Woodman, and Dorothy Dwan (Mrs. Semon) as Dorothy.

Samuel Goldwyn acquired the screen rights in 1933 but did nothing with the property. Lyricist Arthur Freed, then anxious to become a producer, persuaded MGM studio boss Louis B. Mayer to buy the rights from Goldwyn. But Mayer, unwilling to entrust so major a project to one so inexperienced, assigned the production to Mervyn LeRoy, who had recently joined Metro, with Freed as his associate. LeRoy had difficulties with a procession of directors (Richard Thorpe, George Cukor, Lewis Milestone); when he realized Mayer would not let him direct it himself, he settled on Victor Fleming. (When Fleming was pulled off *The Wizard of Oz* to take over *Gone With the Wind,* King Vidor substituted for three weeks, during which time he supervised the shooting of the "Over the Rainbow" sequence.) The film made a star of 16-year-old Judy Garland (who had always been Freed's choice for Dorothy) and was responsible for Bert

Lahr's most memorable screen performance. As for Shirley Temple, she got to star in another no-place-like-home fantasy, *The Blue Bird,* in 1940, which Fox had hoped would rival *The Wizard of Oz.*

On television *The Wizard of Oz* has been the most frequently repeated movie shown on both CBS and NBC networks. In 1962 Filmation Associates made a cartoon feature, *Journey Back to Oz,* using the voices of Judy Garland's daughter, Liza Minnelli (Dorothy), Mickey Rooney (who replaced Peter Lawford as the Scarecrow), Danny Thomas (Tin Woodman), Milton Berle (Cowardly Lion), Ethel Merman (Wicked Witch), Risë Stevens (Good Witch), and Margaret Hamilton (Auntie Em). James Van Heusen and Sammy Cahn wrote the score for the movie, which was not released until 1974. A second Broadway incarnation of the fairy tale, all black and "modernized," was *The Wiz,* which opened in 1975 and enjoyed a highly profitable run. The songs were written by Charlie Smalls, and the cast included Stephanie Mills (Dorothy), Hinton Battle (Scarecrow), Tiger Haynes (Tinman), Ted Ross (Lion), and André De Shields (Wiz). Universal's 1978 film version, directed by Sidney Lumet, offered a teary-eyed, long-in-the-tooth Dorothy, played by Diana Ross and an urbanized Oz, filmed largely on location in New York with the World Trade Center serving as the Emerald City. Michael Jackson (Scarecrow), Nipsey Russell (Tinman), Ted Ross (Lion), Lena Horne (Good Witch), and Richard Pryor (Wiz) took part in the journey.

Bib: *Down the Yellow Brick Road* by Doug McClelland (1976); *The Making of "The Wizard of Oz"* by Aljean Harmetz (1977).

"Woman in Love, A" Music & lyric by Frank Loesser. Languid, romantic piece first sung in *Guys and Dolls* (Goldwyn 1955) in Spanish by uncredited male singer in a Havana restaurant, followed by vocal by Renée Renor, and reprised by Marlon Brando and Jean Simmons.

"Wonder Why" Music by Nicholas Brodszky; lyric by Sammy Cahn. Romantic revelation expressed by Jane Powell and Vic Damone in *Rich, Young and Pretty* (MGM 1951).

"Wonderful Copenhagen" Music & lyric by Frank Loesser. Rollicking tribute to the "salty old queen of the sea," sung by uncredited singer in a fishing boat in *Hans Christian Andersen* (Goldwyn 1953). Also reprised by Danny Kaye and Joey Walsh as they view the city's harbor for the first time.

"Wonderful, Wonderful Day" Music by Gene dePaul; lyric by Johnny Mercer. In *Seven Brides for Seven Brothers* (MGM 1954), newlyweds Jane Powell and Howard Keel ride in a horse-drawn buggy on their way to Keel's home in the Oregon mountains. As they stop to water the horse near a field of flowers, Miss Powell sings blissfully of the wonderful, wonderful day.

Wonderful World of the Brothers Grimm, The. See Hans Christian Andersen.

Wood, Deedee. *See* **Breaux, Marc.**

Wood, Natalie (née Natasha Gurdin), actress; b. San Francisco, July 20, 1938. Former child actress (*Miracle on 34th Street*) whose singing was supplied by Marni Nixon in *West Side Story* and *Gypsy*. Also sang "You're Gonna Hear from Me" (with Jackie Ward's voice) in *Inside Daisy Clover*. (Died Nov. 29, 1981.)

1952 Just for You (*Barbara Blake*)
1961 West Side Story (*Maria*)
1962 Gypsy (*Louise*)

Wood, (Samuel Grosvenor) Sam, director; b. Philadelphia, July 10, 1883; d. Los Angeles, Sept. 22, 1949. Hollywood pioneer who began with Cecil DeMille in 1915 and whose dramas include *Goodbye, Mr. Chips, Kitty Foyle,* and *For Whom the Bell Tolls.* Directed two Marx Brothers musicals while at MGM.

1929 It's a Great Life
      So This Is College
1930 They Learned About Women
1935 A Night at the Opera
1937 A Day at the Races

Woods, Harry M(acGregor), composer, lyricist; b. No. Chelmsford, Mass., Nov. 4, 1896; d. Phoenix, Ariz., Jan. 13, 1970. Associated with Jessie Matthews as creator of two of her hits, "Over My Shoulder" and "When You've Got a Little Springtime in Your Heart," both in *Evergreen.* Also wrote Rudy Vallee's "A Little Kiss Each Morning" in *The Vagabond Lover.*

1934 Evergreen (Eng.)
1936 It's Love Again (Eng.)

Woolsey, Robert. *See* **Wheeler and Woolsey.**

"Words Are in My Heart, The" Music by Harry Warren; lyric by Al Dubin. Waltzing ballad of a timid lover, first sung by Dick Powell to Gloria Stuart in a motorboat in *Gold Diggers of 1935* (Warner). Later it was used for a Busby Berkeley production number staged at a resort hotel with Powell, in a 19th-century costume, again singing it to Miss Stuart. Suddenly, they are shrunken into tiny porcelain figures in a floral arrangement, as 56 girls in white evening gowns come into view seated at 56 white baby grand pianos. The girls and their pianos (actually lightweight shells carried about on the backs of stagehands) are deployed in a variety of formations including one in which the pianos are fitted together to form a dance floor. Other musical instruments featured in Berkeley routines were violins ("Shadow Waltz" in *Gold Diggers of 1933*) and harps ("Spin a Little Web of Dreams" in *Fashions of 1934*).

"Would You?" Music by Nacio Herb Brown; lyric by Arthur Freed. Romantic invitation first played in *San Francisco* (MGM 1936) as Jeanette MacDonald waltzed in the arms of Clark Gable, then sung by Miss MacDonald at a rehearsal for a cabaret floorshow. The ballad, which replaced "The One I Love," originally slotted for the rehearsal scene, was later sung by Betty Royce (for Debbie Reynolds) in *Singin' in the Rain* (MGM 1952).

Wright and Forrest, lyricists, composers. Robert (Craig) Wright, b. Daytona Beach, Fla., Sept. 25, 1914. George ("Chet") Forrest (né George Forrest Chichester, Jr.), b. Brooklyn, July 31, 1915. Though the partners also wrote music together, their work in Hollywood was primarily as co-lyricists of previously written stage songs by Rudolf Friml, Victor Herbert, George Posford, and Richard Rodgers, as well as of songs written for the screen by Herbert Stothart and Edward Ward. In the theatre they also adapted classical compositions of Edvard Grieg, for *Song of Norway,* and of Alexander Borodin for *Kismet,* both of which were filmed. Most of their movie work was at MGM, where their songs were sung by Joan Crawford ("Always and Always"), Allan Jones ("The Donkey Serenade"), Jeanette MacDonald, Nelson Eddy ("At the Balalaika"), Ilona Massey, Howard Keel, and Ann Blyth.

1937 The Firefly (Friml)
1938 Sweethearts (Herbert)
1939 Balalaika (Stothart; Posford)
1940 Music in My Heart (alone)
      Dance Girl Dance (alone)
1941 Blondie Goes Latin (alone)

1942 Fiesta (Ward)
      I Married an Angel (Rodgers; Stothart)
1955 Kismet (Borodin)
1970 Song of Norway (Grieg)

Wrubel, Allie, composer; b. Middletown, Conn., Jan. 15, 1905; d. Twenty-Nine Palms, Cal., Dec. 13, 1973. Former saxophonist with Paul Whiteman's orchestra who wrote movie songs with lyricists Mort Dixon (''Flirtation Walk,'' ''The Lady in Red''), Herb Magidson, Ray Gilbert (''Zip-a-Dee-Doo-Dah''), and— Maxwell Anderson. Wrubel's songs were introduced on the screen by Dick Powell, Wini Shaw, Dolores Del Rio, and James Cagney.

1934 Flirtation Walk (Dixon)
      Happiness Ahead (Dixon)
1935 Broadway Hostess (Dixon)
      I Live for Love (Dixon)
1937 Life of the Party (Magidson)
1938 Radio City Revels (Magidson)
1945 Sing Your Way Home (Magidson)
1959 Never Steal Anything Small (Anderson)

Wyman, Jane (née Sarah Jane Fulks), actress, singer; b. St. Joseph, Mo., Jan. 4, 1914. Versatile leading lady, later developed into dramatic actress (*Johnny Belinda*), whose best remembered performances in musicals were with Bing Crosby (introducing ''In the Cool Cool Cool of the Evening'' and ''Zing a Little Zong''). Miss Wyman's second husband was Ronald Reagan, her third was composer Fred Karger.

1935 King of Burlesque (chorus)
1936 Cain and Mabel (chorus)
      Gold Diggers of 1937 (chorus)
      Stage Struck (chorus)
1937 The King and the Chorus Girl (*Babette*)
      Ready, Willing and Able (*Dot*)
      Mr. Dodd Takes the Air (*Marjorie Day*)
      The Singing Marine (*Joan*)
1942 My Favorite Spy (*Connie*)
      Footlight Serenade (*Flo LaVerne*)
1944 Hollywood Canteen (guest bit)
1945 Night and Day (*Grace Harris*)
1949 It's a Great Feeling (guest bit)
1951 Here Comes the Groom (*Emmadel Jones*)
      Starlift (guest bit)
1952 Just for You (*Carolina Hill*)
1953 Let's Do It Again (*Connie Stuart*)

Wymore, Patrice, actress, dancer; b. Miltonville, Kansas, Dec. 17, 1926. Tall, leggy actress-dancer usually cast in bitchy roles in Warner musicals.

1950 Tea for Two (*Beatrice Darcy*)
1951 Starlift (guest bit)
      I'll See You in My Dreams (*Gloria Knight*)
1952 She's Working Her Way Through College (*Ivy Williams*)
1953 She's Back on Broadway (*Karen Keene*)
1956 King's Rhapsody (Eng.)

Wynn, Ed (né Isaiah Edwin Leopold), actor; b. Philadelphia, Nov. 9, 1886; d. Beverly Hills, June 19, 1966. Giggling, lisping, and fluttering his hands, Ed Wynn was one of vaudeville's and Broadway's greatest clowns. His screen debut was a repeat of his stage role in *Manhattan Mary* (retitled *Follow the Leader*); later he turned to dramatic roles. Wynn, who was the father of actor Keenan Wynn, had his own radio and television series.

1930 Follow the Leader (*Cricket*)
1943 Stage Door Canteen (guest bit)
1951 Alice in Wonderland (*Mad Hatter* voice only)
1960 Cinderfella (*Fairy Godfather*)
1961 Babes in Toyland (*Toymaker*)
1965 Mary Poppins (*Uncle Albert*)

Wynn, (Francis Xavier Aloysius) Keenan, actor; b. New York, July 27, 1916. Wynn, the son of comedian Ed Wynn, was frequently cast as the brash, quick-talking talent or press agent in MGM musicals between 1942 and 1955. (Died Brentwood, Cal., Oct. 14, 1986.)

1942 For Me and My Gal (*Eddie Melton*)
1946 Ziegfeld Follies (specialty)
      Easy To Wed (*Warren Hagarty*)
      No Leave No Love (*Slinky*)
      The Thrill of Brazil (*Steve Farraugh*)
1949 Neptune's Daughter (*Joe Beckett*)
      That Midnight Kiss (*Artie Glenson*)
1950 Annie Get Your Gun (*Charlie Davenport*)
      Three Little Words (*Charlie Kope*)
1951 Royal Wedding (*Irving Klinger/ Edgar Klinger*)
      Texas Carnival (*Dan Sabinas*)
1952 The Belle of New York (*Max Ferris*)
1953 Kiss Me, Kate (*Lippy*)
1955 The Glass Slipper (*Kovin*)
1964 Bikini Beach (*Harvey H. Honeywagon*)
1968 Finian's Rainbow (*Judge Rawkins*)
1975 Nashville (*Green*)
1982 The Last Unicorn (voice of, *Capt. Culley*)

Y

"Yam, The" Music & lyric by Irving Berlin. Staccato, lighthearted new dance step described by Ginger Rogers and demonstrated by her and Fred Astaire at a country-club dance in *Carefree* (RKO 1938). Following the performance, the partners lead the dancing club members out of the dining room to the reception hall to the patio and back to the dining room. The song's recurrent musical theme, "Any Yam today?," was later used by Berlin in his wartime effort, "Any Bonds Today?"

Yankee Doodle Dandy (1942). Music & lyrics by George M. Cohan; screenplay by Robert Bruckner, Edmund Joseph, Julius Epstein (uncredited), and Philip Epstein (uncredited) from story by Bruckner based on life of Cohan.

A Warner Bros. film produced by Jack L. Warner & Hal B. Wallis; associate producer, William Cagney; directed by Michael Curtiz; choreography, LeRoy Prinz, Seymour Felix, John Boyle; art director, Carl Jules Weyl; costumes, Milo Anderson; music director, Leo F. Forbstein; orchestrations, Ray Heindorf; cameraman, James Wong Howe; editor, George Amy.

Cast: James Cagney (*George M. Cohan*); Joan Leslie (*Mary Cohan*); Walter Huston (*Jerry Cohan*); Richard Whorf (*Sam H. Harris*); Jeanne Cagney (*Josie Cohan*); Frances Langford (specialty); George Tobias (*Dietz*); Irene Manning (*Fay Templeton*); Rosemary DeCamp (*Nellie Cohan*); S. Z. Sakall (*Schwab*); George Barbier (*Abe Erlanger*); Walter Catlett (*theatre manager*); Minor Watson (*B. F. Albee*); Eddie Foy Jr. (*Eddie Foy*); Capt. Jack Young (*Franklin D. Roosevelt*); Odette Myrtil (*Mme. Bartholdi*); Leon Belasco (*magician*); Charles Smith, Joyce Reynolds (*teenagers*).

Songs: "The Dancing Master" - Huston/ "I Was Born in Virginia" - Cagney, Cagney, DeCamp. Huston/ "The Warmest Baby in the Bunch" - Leslie/ "Har-

rigan" - Cagney, Leslie/ "The Yankee Doodle Boy" - Cagney/ "All Aboard for Old Broadway" (Jack Scholl - M. K. Jerome) - Cagney, chorus/ "Give My Regards to Broadway" - Cagney/ "Oh, You Wonderful Girl" - Cagney, Cagney, DeCamp, Huston/ "I'll Be True to You" - Cagney, Cagney, DeCamp, Huston/ "Belle of the Barbers' Ball" - Cagney, Cagney, DeCamp, Huston/ "Mary's a Grand Old Name" - Cagney, Leslie; reprised by Manning/ "Forty-Five Minutes from Broadway" - Cagney/ "So Long, Mary" - Manning, chorus/ "You're a Grand Old Flag" - Cagney, chorus/ "Come Along with Me Away" - Cagney, chorus/ "Over There" Cagney, Langford/ "Off the Record" (Richard Rodgers - Lorenz Hart) - Cagney.

Dominated by James Cagney's compelling performance as the cocky, multi-talented song-and-dance man George M. Cohan, *Yankee Doodle Dandy* was among the most entertaining show-business sagas ever created for the screen. Cohan had long resisted having his story told because he was touchy about his private life, but he gave his blessing to the script—for which he was paid $100,000—because it emphasized his songs and his career as a performer rather than accurate biographical detail. (Though he was married twice, to stage star Ethel Levey and to dancer Agnes Nolan, the movie showed him wedded to only one wife, and her name was Mary.) Also, as an unabashed flagwaver, Cohan liked the idea of the picture being made as a wartime morale-booster, a factor that also appealed to Cagney. What did not appeal to Cagney, though, was the Cohan-approved screenplay, which he found too somber; only when Julius and Philip Epstein were brought in for uncredited rewrites did he agree to appear in the film.

Told through flashbacks as Cohan supposedly relates his life story to an uncommonly patient President Roosevelt, the saga begins on July 4, 1878, Cohan's birthday, covers his vaudeville days with his father, mother, and sister (a part played by Cagney's own sister), his breakthrough on Broadway, and his string of successes. After a period of crotchety retirement, the actor returns in triumph as the President of the United States in *I'd Rather Be Right* (which found Cagney imitating Cohan imitating Roosevelt) and receives a Congressional Medal of Honor for his patriotic songs, "You're a Grand Old Flag" and "Over There." The movie's most treasured sequence was the extended re-creation of the Broadway opening of *Little Johnny Jones* in 1904, with Cagney strutting, hopping, tapping, sprinting, and scaling proscenium walls.

Yankee Doodle Dandy was released in May, 1942, five months before Cohan died of cancer. Cagney, who had hoofed in only two previous film musicals, *Footlight Parade* and *Something To Sing About,* again did his George M. Cohan routine in *The Seven Little Foys* (Par. 1955), starring Bob Hope as Eddie Foy.

Yellen, Jack, lyricist; b. Poland, July 6, 1892. "Happy Days Are Here Again" (music by Milton Ager) and "Sing, Baby, Sing" (music by Lew Pollack) were Yellen's best-known film songs. Most of the lyricist's numbers were created for Fox musicals; among his collaborators were Ray Henderson, Irving Caesar, Herb Magidson, Joseph Meyer, Dan Dougherty, Sam Pokrass, and Sammy Fain. Among those who sang Yellen lyrics were Sophie Tucker (for whom he wrote special material for many years), John Boles, Alice Faye, Rudy Vallee, and Don Ameche.

1929	Honky Tonk (Ager)
1930	Chasing Rainbows (Ager)
	King of Jazz (Ager)
	They Learned About Women (Ager)
1934	George White's Scandals (Henderson-Caesar)
1935	George White's Scandals (Meyer-Magidson)
	Under Pressure (Dougherty)
1938	Happy Landing (Pokrass)
1945	George White's Scandals (Fain)

"You" Music by Walter Donaldson; lyric by Harold Adamson. Song of total adoration (which manages to rhyme "satisfy" with "that is why"), sung by the brides-and-grooms chorus in *The Great Ziegfeld* (MGM 1936) during a show on the New Amsterdam Roof.

"You and Your Kiss" Music by Jerome Kern; lyric by Dorothy Fields. Both musically extolled by Allan Jones as he serenaded Nancy Kelly on board a ship in *One Night in the Tropics* (Univ. 1940).

"You Are My Lucky Star" Music by Nacio Herb Brown; lyric by Arthur Freed. Celestial serenade introduced by Frances Langford during a radio program in *Broadway Melody of 1936* (MGM 1935); later reprised by Eleanor Powell in a deserted theatre as she imagines herself the dancing star of a Broadway show. Song was also sung by Jean Harlow and waiters in *Riff-Raff* (MGM 1935); Betty Jaynes in *Babes in Arms* (MGM 1939); in *Born To Sing* (MGM 1942); Phil Regan in *Three Little Words* (MGM 1950); Gene Kelly and Debbie Reynolds in *Singin' in the Rain* (MGM 1952); Twiggy in *The Boy Friend* (MGM 1971); and Liza Minnelli in *New York, New York* (UA 1977).

"You Are Too Beautiful" Music by Richard Rodgers; lyric by Lorenz Hart. Though he finds Madge Evans too beautiful for one man alone, Al Jolson pledges faithful devotion in *Hallelujah, I'm a Bum* (UA 1933). Number was sung while the two were dancing in her room to the music heard from a nearby ballroom.

"You Belong to My Heart" Music by Agustin Lara; lyric by Ray Gilbert. Ardent serenade sung by Dora Luz to Donald Duck in a combined live-action and animated-cartoon sequence in *The Three Caballeros* (Disney 1944). Also sung by Ezio Pinza in *Mr. Imperium* (MGM 1951). This was originally a Mexican song, music and lyric by Sr. Lara, called "Solamente una Vez."

"You Brought a New Kind of Love to Me" Music & lyric by Sammy Fain, Irving Kahal, and Pierre Norman. Song of romantic devotion sung by Maurice Chevalier to Claudette Colbert first while gliding in a gondola on a Venetian canal, then on an ocean liner, in *The Big Pond* (Par. 1930). Later in the film, with an altered lyric, Chevalier sang it as a singing commercial, "I brought a new kind of gum to you." First eight bars of song also sung by Chevalier imitators Zeppo, Groucho, and Chico Marx and mouthed by Harpo to a Chevalier recording in *Monkey Business* (Par. 1931); subsequently sung by Frank Sinatra over credits of *New Kind of Love* (Par. 1963), and Liza Minnelli in *New York, New York* (UA 1977).

"You Can Do No Wrong" Music & lyric by Cole Porter. Paean to the perfect man sung in *The Pirate* (MGM

1948) by Judy Garland to Gene Kelly after knocking him down during a fit of temper.

"You Can't Have Everything" Music by Harry Revel; lyric by Mack Gordon. Or how to achieve happiness by lowering one's expectations. Alice Faye delivered this spirited, didactic message in film of the same name (Fox 1937), accompanied by violinist Rubinoff.

"You Can't Run Away from Love Tonight" Music by Harry Warren; lyric by Al Dubin. In *The Singing Marine* (Warner 1937), Dick Powell, as a bashful Marine, obligingly sings the ballad during a moonlight weenie roast to help his buddies get their girls in the proper romantic mood.

"You Couldn't Be Cuter" Music by Jerome Kern; lyric by Dorothy Fields. Supposedly a song from a new Broadway musical, the number was sung in *Joy of Living* (RKO 1938) by Irene Dunne, the star of the show. In the scene Miss Dunne uses it to lull her twin nieces to sleep; by the time she nears the end, after singing it a second time, the actress has dozed off and the children finish the song for her. In this lively compilation of romantic praise, the music builds in emotional intensity at the end through the rapid succession of "nicer," "sweeter," "better," "smoother," and "cuter."

"You Do" Music by Josef Myrow; lyric by Mack Gordon. Performed three times in *Mother Wore Tights* (Fox 1947): 1) as a jazzy song-and-dance number by vaudevillian Dan Dailey; 2) as a slower tempoed solo by Betty Grable, also in vaudeville; 3) as an expression of affection that Mona Freeman sings to parents Grable and Dailey at a school graduation.

"You Do the Darndest Things, Baby" Music by Lew Pollack; lyric by Sidney Mitchell. Serenade by ukulele-plunking Jack Haley to unpredictable Arline Judge in *Pigskin Parade* (Fox 1936). The song may have influenced two subsequent pieces with similar titles, the Harry Warren-Mack Gordon "You Say the Sweetest Things, Baby" in *Tin Pan Alley* (Fox 1940) and the Jimmy McHugh-Harold Adamson "You Say the Nicest Things, Baby" in the Broadway musical, *As the Girls Go* (1948).

"You Don't Have To Know the Language" Music by James Van Heusen; lyric by Johnny Burke. Lively explanation why language proficiency is unnecessary when it comes to romance. Sung in *Road to Rio* (Par. 1947) by Bing Crosby, assisted by the Andrews Sisters, entertaining guests on an ocean liner.

"You Don't Know What Love Is" Music by Gene dePaul; lyric by Don Raye. Torchy lament introduced by Carol Bruce in *Keep 'Em Flying* (Univ. 1941).

"You Hit the Spot" Music by Harry Revel; lyric by Mack Gordon. Buoyant song of mutual appreciation sung by Frances Langford and Jack Oakie in *Collegiate* (Par. 1936).

"You Keep Coming Back Like a Song" Music & lyric by Irving Berlin. About a love that won't go away. Introduced by Bing Crosby in *Blue Skies* (Par. 1946) while performing at The Song Book, an open-air nightclub in New York's Central Park. Ballad also served as romantic theme for Crosby and Joan Caulfield.

"You Let Me Down" Music by Harry Warren; lyric by Al Dubin. Torchy ballad of disillusionment introduced by Jane Froman in *Stars Over Broadway* (Warner 1935).

"You Light Up My Life" Music & lyric by Joe Brooks. Gratitude for romantic illumination glowingly expressed by Didi Conn (with Kasey Ciszk's dubbed voice) in film of same name (Col. 1977).

"You Make Me Feel So Young" Music by Josef Myrow; lyric by Mack Gordon. In *Three Little Girls in Blue* (Fox 1946), love-smitten Charles Smith tells equally love-smitten Vera-Ellen, "When you smile, I'm a millionaire . . . I'm as happy as a kid with a brand new bike." To which Vera-Ellen replies, "You affect me that way too. When you're near me, you . . . you . . . you . . ." And they both sing about how love has made them feel like kids again—even though the actual singing was dubbed by Del Porter and Carol Stewart. Song was also sung by Dennis Day in *I'll Get By* (Fox 1950).

"You Must Have Been a Beautiful Baby" Music by Harry Warren; lyric by Johnny Mercer. In *Hard To Get* (Warner 1938), Dick Powell took this roundabout way of praising Olivia DeHavilland's looks while the two were gliding in a rowboat on New York's Central Park lake. Song was also sung by Doris Day in *My Dream Is Yours* (Warner 1949).

"You Never Looked So Beautiful Before" Music by Walter Donaldson; lyric by Harold Adamson. Admiringly sung by top-hatted male chorus extolling the beauty of Virginia Bruce in a midnight revue staged on the roof of the New Amsterdam Theatre. The movie was *The Great Ziegfeld* (MGM 1936). Song was also sung by Judy Garland in *Ziegfeld Girl* (MGM 1941).

"You Say the Sweetest Things, Baby" Music by Harry Warren; lyric by Mack Gordon. Alice Faye, accompanied by John Payne and Jack Oakie, introduced this uptempo ballad in *Tin Pan Alley* (Fox 1940), in which it became the first hit of the trio's music-publishing company. Later, it was sung as a romantic duet by Miss Faye and Payne on board a Staten Island ferry. The song may have been influenced by "You Do the Darndest Things, Baby," which Lew Pollack and Sidney Mitchell wrote for *Pigskin Parade* (Fox 1936); it surely seems to have influenced "You Say the Nicest Things, Baby," which Jimmy McHugh and Harold Adamson wrote for the Broadway musical, *As the Girls Go* (1948).

"You Stepped Out of a Dream" Music by Nacio Herb Brown; lyric by Gus Kahn. Production number in *Ziegfeld Girl* (MGM 1941) enabling Tony Martin to serenade a trio of visions—Hedy Lamarr, Judy Garland, and Lana Turner. As quoted in *The Busby Berkeley Book* by Tommy Thomas and Jim Terry, director Berkeley recalled, "Adrian outdid himself with his costumes for this number, as did Cedric Gibbons with his set. There were immense 60-foot-high spiral staircases in gold and silver, adorned with massive cut-glass chandeliers and fantastic trimmings. Each girl emerged from a misty cloud effect, dripping with silver sequins."

"You Took the Words Right Out of My Heart" Music by Ralph Rainger; lyric by Leo Robin. Romantic shipboard duet for Dorothy Lamour and Leif Erickson (though he didn't sing much) in *Big Broadcast of 1938* (Par.).

"You Turned the Tables on Me" Music by Louis Alter; lyric by Sidney Mitchell. In which a once calculating young lady contritely confesses that she has fallen for her former beau now that he's given her the air. Introduced by Alice Faye in *Sing, Baby, Sing* (Fox 1936).

"You Were Meant for Me" Music by Nacio Herb Brown; lyric by Arthur Freed. In *The Broadway Melody* (MGM 1929), smitten songwriter Charles King sang his latest and very personal creation—all about predestined love—to Anita Page. Then, to make sure she got the message, he confessed, "Queenie, I wrote it for you. It's you. Don't ya know what I mean?" Song was also sung by Conrad Nagel (with King's dubbed voice as a gag) to Miss Page in *The Hollywood Revue of 1929* (MGM); Bull Montana and Winnie Lightner in *The Show of Shows* (Warner 1929); schoolgirls in *Forty Little Mothers* (MGM 1940); Frank Morgan in *Hullabaloo* (MGM 1940); Dan Dailey to Jeanne Crain in *You Were Meant for Me* (Fox 1948); and Gene Kelly to Debbie Reynolds in *Singin' in the Rain* (MGM 1952).

You Were Never Lovelier (1942). Music by Jerome Kern; lyrics by Johnny Mercer; screenplay by Michael Fessier, Ernest Pagano, and Delmar Daves from story by Carlos Oliveri & Sixto Pondal Rios.

A Columbia film produced by Louis F. Edelman; directed by William A. Seiter; choreography, Fred Astaire, Val Raset; art director, Lionel Banks; costumes, Irene; music director, Leigh Harline; orchestrations, Harline, Conrad Salinger, Lyle Murphy; cameraman, Ted Tetzlaff; editor, William Lyon.

Cast: Fred Astaire (*Robert Davis*); Rita Hayworth (vocals by Nan Wynn) (*Maria Acuña*); Adolphe Menjou (*Edouardo Acuña*); Xavier Cugat (*Xavier Cugat*); Leslie Brooks (*Cecy Acuña*); Adele Mara (*Lita Acuña*); Isabel Elsom (*Maria Castro*); Gus Schilling (*Fernando*); Barbara Brown (*Delfina Acuña*); Larry Parks (*Tony*); Lina Romay (*band singer*), Fidel Castro (extra).

Songs: "Chiu, Chiu" (Niconar Molinare) - Romay, chorus, Cugat orch./ "Dearly Beloved" - Astaire, Cugat orch.; reprised by Hayworth (Wynn)/ "Audition Dance" - Astaire, Cugat orch./ "I'm Old Fashioned" - Hayworth (Wynn); dance by Astaire, Hayworth/ "Shorty George" - Astaire, Cugat orch.; dance by Astaire, Hayworth/ "Wedding in the Spring" - Romay, Cugat orch./ "You Were Never Lovelier" - Astaire; dance by Astaire, Hayworth/ "These Orchids" - delivery boys. Unused: "On the Beam."

The second movie Fred Astaire and Rita Hayworth made together at Columbia, *You Were Never Lovelier* followed their first, *You'll Never Get Rich,* by about a year. Though linked by their "You-Never" titles and the fact that Fred played a character named Robert in both, the films were totally dissimilar in plot, atmosphere, and score. The former, with Cole Porter songs, was about a Broadway dancer-director who falls for a girl in his show, gets drafted into the army, and is reunited with the girl when she shows up to appear in a GI camp show. The latter film had a more romantic theme and score (the only one Jerome Kern and Johnny Mercer ever wrote together) as it told of a dancer at loose ends in Buenos Aires who falls for the daughter of the owner of the hotel where he hopes to perform. Though based on an Argentine movie, the locale was initially switched to Rio de Janeiro (to be called *Carnival in Rio*) but complaints by the Brazilian government moved the story back to the Argentine capitol. Still, despite the movie's attempt to do its wartime bit for the Good Neighbor Policy, just about the only Latin American touches in it were provided by Xavier Cugat's accent and orchestra. Included among choreographic pleasures were Astaire's playfully brash audition for Adolphe Menjou and the ecstatic manner in which he wafted Miss Hayworth all over her elegant garden.

"You Were Never Lovelier" Music by Jerome Kern; lyric by Johnny Mercer. Dazzled by Rita Hayworth's beauty, Fred Astaire expressed both admiration and love in the title song from the Columbia film (1942), then emphasized his feelings by dancing adoringly with the lady.

"You Will Remember Vienna" Music by Sigmund Romberg; lyric by Oscar Hammerstein II. Teary, fond recollections of "Nights that were happy/ And hearts that were free" in the Vienna of their youth, sung by Walter Pidgeon, Alexander Grey, and Bert Roach in *Viennese Nights* (Warner 1930). Also sung by Helen Traubel in *Deep in My Heart* (MGM 1954).

"You Wonderful You" Music by Harry Warren; lyric by Jack Brooks & Saul Chaplin. The means through which director Gene Kelly, in *Summer Stock* (MGM 1950), explains to farmer Judy Garland how songs reveal feelings in musical comedy—which, of course, also becomes the means through which they both reveal their feelings for each other. Melody later used for Kelly's solo dance on a deserted barn-theatre stage, with the director's anxieties emphasized by the sound of his taps

on the creaking boards and on a spread newspaper. In a performance of the show being tried out, the song turns up as a vaudeville-type routine performed by Gene (in beanie and striped blazer) and Judy (in pinafore). The original lyric to the ballad had been written by Mack Gordon but it was replaced by one by Brooks and Chaplin.

"You'd Be Hard To Replace" Music by Harry Warren; lyric by Ira Gershwin. After a spat, the battling couple in *The Barkleys of Broadway* (MGM 1950) are reconciled when husband Fred Astaire tells wife Ginger Rogers how indispensable she is.

"You'd Be So Nice To Come Home To" Music & lyric by Cole Porter. Reason for romantic attachment—whether "under stars chilled by the Winter" or "under an August moon burning above"—sung in *Something To Shout About* (Col. 1943) by Janet Blair and Don Ameche.

"(If You Can't Sing It) You'll Have To Swing It" Music & lyric by Sam Coslow. Also known as "Mr. Paganini," this confession of an excessively boisterous hepcat at Carnegie Hall was written especially for Martha Raye who sang it in her screen test, in her first film, *Rhythm on the Range* (Par. 1936), and in *Four Jills in a Jeep* (Fox 1944).

You'll Never Get Rich. See You Were Never Lovelier.

"You'll Never Know" Music by Harry Warren; lyric by Mack Gordon. In a San Francisco beerhall in *Hello, Frisco, Hello* (Fox 1943), a stage backdrop at left represents San Francisco and one at right represents New York. John Payne and Jack Oakie, at the right, place a long-distance telephone call to Alice Faye and June Havoc at the left, and Miss Faye responds by singing to Payne that he'll never know how much she misses him. At the end of the film, the scene is repeated though reversed, with Miss Faye in "New York" singing to Payne in "San Francisco." Composer Warren once said that he'd written the song not only for its applicability to the period and situation, but also as an expression of the loneliness people felt during World War II. Song was also sung by Miss Faye in *Four Jills in a Jeep* (Fox 1944) and by Ginger Rogers in *Dreamboat* (Fox 1952).

Youmans, Vincent (Millie), composer; b. New York, Sept. 27, 1898; d. Denver, April 5, 1946. Of the 12 Broadway musicals for which Youmans supplied the music, four were adapted to the screen though often in altered form with additional songs: *No, No, Nanette* (three times, the first with two Youmans songs, the third retitled *Tea for Two*); *Hit the Deck* (twice); *Rainbow* (retitled *Song of the West*); and *Take a Chance* (two Youmans songs). For the screen, Youmans supplied such songs as "Keeping Myself for You," "Carioca," "Flying Down to Rio," and "Orchids in the Moonlight" (last three in *Flying Down to Rio*). The composer's lyric-writing partners included Irving Caesar, Otto Harbach, Leo Robin, Clifford Grey, Sidney Clare, J. Russell Robinson, George Waggner, Oscar Hammerstein II, B. G. DeSylva, Edward Eliscu, and Gus Kahn. His songs were sung in movies by Jack Oakie, Bernice Claire, Alexander Grey, Gloria Swanson, John Boles, Lillian Roth, Ginger Rogers, Fred Astaire, Anna Neagle, Doris Day, Gordon MacRae, Tony Martin, Jane Powell, and Ann Miller.

1930	Hit the Deck (Robin, Grey; Clare)
	No, No, Nanette (Caesar)
	Song of the West (Hammerstein)
	What a Widow! (Robinson, Waggner)
1933	Take a Chance (DeSylva)
	Flying Down to Rio (Eliscu, Kahn)
1940	No, No, Nanette (Caesar; Harbach)
1950	Tea for Two (Caesar)
1955	Hit the Deck (Robin, Grey)

"Young and Healthy" Music by Harry Warren; lyric by Al Dubin. Song of youthful ardor (in which "hate yuh" rhymes with "nature") performed by Dick Powell as part of revue in *42nd Street* (Warner 1933). The Busby Berkeley number featured chorus girls in bridal costumes appearing in a variety of kaleidoscopic effects, and ended with the camera moving through a tunnel of female legs right up to a grinning closeup of Powell and Toby Wing.

Young, Robert (George), actor; b. Chicago, Feb. 22, 1907. Durable leading man whose boyish charm at first made him something of an alternate to Robert Montgomery. In his mostly nonsinging roles in musicals, Young acted opposite Alice Faye, Jessie Matthews, Eleanor Powell, Ann Sothern, Jeanette MacDonald, and Betty Grable. Starred in television series after film career.

1932	The Kid from Spain (*Ricardo*)
1934	Hollywood Party (guest bit)

1936	Stowaway (*Tommy Randall*)
	It's Love Again (Eng.) (*Peter Carlton*)
1938	Josette (*Pierre Brossard*)
1939	Honolulu (*Brooks Mason*)
1941	Lady, Be Good (*Eddie Crane*)
1942	Cairo (*Homer Smith*)
1943	Sweet Rosie O'Grady (*Sam Magee*)

Young, Victor, composer; b. Chicago, Aug. 8, 1900; d. Palm Springs, Cal., Nov. 10, 1956. Young was a concert violinist turned pop songwriter, music director, and arranger, who scored over 300 films (mostly at Paramount). His film songs included "Golden Earrings" (lyric by Jay Livingston and Ray Evans) and "My Foolish Heart" (Ned Washington).

"Your Dream" Music by Jerome Kern; lyric by Otto Harbach & Oscar Hammerstein II. Ardent ballad whose charms were somewhat lost because of the way it was staged in *One Night in the Tropics* (Univ. 1940): on a tropical hotel veranda Nancy Kelly (or whoever) sings it to a bullfighter to get Allan Jones jealous, then Allan sings it to Peggy Moran to get Nancy jealous. The song had originally been introduced by Hope Manning and Ronald Graham in the 1938 stage musical *Gentlemen Unafraid* produced at the St. Louis Municipal Opera.

"You're a Lucky Fellow, Mr. Smith" Music by J. Francis (Sonny) Burke & Don Raye; lyric by Hughie Prince. Breezy flagwaver sung by the Andrews Sisters to departing draftees in Grand Central Station, New York, in *Buck Privates* (Univ. 1941).

"You're a Sweet Little Headache" Music by Ralph Rainger; lyric by Leo Robin. Song of affection sung to Franciska Gaal by Bing Crosby in *Paris Honeymoon* (Par. 1939).

"You're a Sweetheart" Music by Jimmy McHugh; lyric by Harold Adamson. In *You're a Sweetheart* (Univ. 1937), Alice Faye and George Murphy discovered, to their mutual surprise, that they were meant for each other.

"You're All the World to Me" Music by Burton Lane; lyric by Alan Jay Lerner. A "post-card" song in which one's beloved is likened to such breathtaking tourist sights as Paris in the spring, New York on a silvery day, the Swiss Alps, Loch Lomond, Capri in the moonlight, the view of the ocean from Cape Cod, Lake Como, Sun

Valley, and a Persian palace. Fred Astaire expressed the jaunty globe-hopping sentiment in *Royal Wedding* (MGM 1951) while gazing adoringly at a photograph of Sarah Churchill in a London hotel room, and then, defying gravity, dancing all over the room's walls and ceiling (the effect was achieved by having the camera affixed to the floor of the room, which then revolved as Astaire danced in an upright position). Composer Lane had originally written the melody in 1934 when, with a lyric by Harold Adamson, it was called "I Want To Be a Minstrel Man." Harold Nicholas sang it and danced to it with his brother, Fayard, in *Kid Millions* (Goldwyn).

"You're Always in My Arms" Music by Harry Tierney; lyric by Joe McCarthy. Waltzing ballad sung in *Rio Rita* (RKO 1929) by John Boles to Bebe Daniels, then reprised by Miss Daniels.

"You're Easy To Dance With" Music & lyric by Irving Berlin. Upbeat number of complementary couple, sung by Fred Astaire to dancing partner Virginia Dale in a New York nightclub in *Holiday Inn* (Par. 1942).

"You're Getting To Be a Habit with Me" Music by Harry Warren; lyric by Al Dubin. Amatory admonition sung in *42nd Street* (Warner 1933) by Bebe Daniels, with male quartet, during rehearsal of a Broadway-bound musical. Routine ends, rather incongruously, with Miss Daniels breaking the habit by dancing off with an actor dressed like Mahatma Gandhi. Number also was sung by Doris Day and danced by Miss Day and Gene Nelson in *Lullaby of Broadway* (Warner 1951).

"You're Gonna Hear from Me" Music by André Previn; lyric by Dory Langdon. In *Inside Daisy Clover* (Warner 1965), Hollywood producer Christopher Plummer revealed the unique singing talent of his latest discovery, Natalie Wood (as Daisy), by showing her on film to invited guests in his home. Ironically, Miss Wood's singing was dubbed by Jackie Ward.

"You're Laughing At Me" Music & lyric by Irving Berlin. Feeling that his ardor was not being taken seriously, Dick Powell sang the ballad to Madeleine Carroll while both, formally clad, were seated on a bench in Central Park. The movie was *On the Avenue* (Fox 1937).

"You're Nearer" Music by Richard Rodgers; lyric by Lorenz Hart. Adroitly rhymed sentiments ("ivy to the wall is," "winter to the fall is") addressed to an absent love. Song was specially written for the film version of *Too Many Girls* (RKO 1940), in which it was first sung by Lucille Ball (with Trudy Erwin's voice), later reprised by Frances Langford, harmonizing with Ann Miller, Libby Bennett, and Miss Erwin's voice again.

"You're Sensational" Music & lyric by Cole Porter. Socialite Grace Kelly may be considered aloof but, sang Frank Sinatra in *High Society* (MGM 1956), he's sure that he is the "proper squire" to fire her heart. The scene took place at the bar of a stately Newport estate.

"You're Slightly Terrific" Music by Lew Pollack; lyric by Sidney Mitchell. Using terms of praise associated with the silver screen ("terrific," "gigantic," "stupendous," "glamorous," "super-colossal"), Anthony (now Tony) Martin serenaded coed Dixie Dunbar at a football rally in *Pigskin Parade* (Fox 1936). Number was then used for Miss Dunbar's tap routine.

"You're the Cure for What Ails Me" Music by Harold Arlen; lyric by E. Y. Harburg. Tribute to child actress Sybil Jason's healing quality ("You're my pink of condish,/ You're my Arrowhead Springs and my Battle Creek, Mich"), sung by Al Jolson in *The Singing Kid* (Warner 1936). Also performed in the movie as a duet by Edward Everett Horton and Allen Jenkins.

"You're the One That I Want" Music & lyric by John Farrar. Propulsive song of mutual acquisitiveness introduced near end of *Grease* (Par. 1978) by Olivia Newton-John and John Travolta.

"Yours and Mine" Music by Nacio Herb Brown; lyric by Arthur Freed. On board a train in *Broadway Melody of 1938* (MGM 1937), Eleanor Powell accidentally enters songwriter Robert Taylor's compartment (which is equipped, of course, with a piano). They lose no time in becoming friends, and she even inadvertently supplies the missing words that complete the verse to the song he's writing. When Taylor urges Eleanor to sing it, Eleanor at first demurs. "After all," says she, "it's your song." "No it isn't," says he, "it's yours and mine." And so, with the composer playing, she sings about all the things they both have that make them a happy couple—shining stars, rainbows, songs of spring, summer's sunshine, the moon above, the right to fall in love, and the hope of finding their dream.

"You've Got Me This Way" Music by Jimmy Mc-Hugh; lyric by Johnny Mercer. Jaunty love song ("What are you gonna do about it/ Now that I'm in a stew about it?"), sung by Harry Babbitt, with Kay Kyser's orchestra, entertaining at a formal party in a huge mansion in *You'll Find Out* (RKO 1940).

"You've Got Something There" Music by Richard A. Whiting; lyric by Johnny Mercer. Duet of mutual attraction sung by Dick Powell and Rosemary Lane on the campus of Winfield College in *Varsity Show* (Warner 1937).

"You've Got That Look" Music by Frederick Hollander; lyric by Frank Loesser. The song's verse makes it clear that it's feather-boaed Marlene Dietrich, singing at the Last Chance Saloon in *Destry Rides Again* (Univ. 1939), who has the look that makes the men weak, not the other way around.

Z

Zanuck, Darryl F(rancis), producer, screenwriter; b. Wahoo, Neb., Sept. 5, 1902; d. Palm Springs, Dec. 23, 1979. Legendary Hollywood mogul who began as writer at Warner's, then became producer (*The Jazz Singer, 42nd Street*) and studio production chief, 1929–33. He left to form 20th Century Pictures with Joseph Schenck, which they merged with Fox Films two years later, with Zanuck as vice president in charge of production. He became an independent producer in 1956 but returned to Fox in 1962 remaining for nine years as president and later chairman of the board. Among actors in musicals with whom Zanuck was closely associated: Al Jolson, Maurice Chevalier, Dick Powell, Alice Faye, Shirley Temple, Sonja Henie, Tyrone Power, Don Ameche, Betty Grable, and Carmen Miranda. Bib: *Don't Say Yes Until I Finish Talking* by Mel Gussow (1971).

Mr. Zanuck personally produced or supervised the following; asterisk indicates he was also script writer:

1927	The Jazz Singer
1928	My Man*
1929	On with the Show
	Say It with Songs*
1930	The Life of the Party*
1933	42nd Street
	Broadway Through a Keyhole
1934	Moulin Rouge
1935	Folies Bergère
	Metropolitan
	Thanks a Million*
1936	King of Burlesque
	Captain January
	Sing, Baby, Sing
	Pigskin Parade
1937	One in a Million
	On the Avenue
	Wake Up and Live
1938	In Old Chicago
	Happy Landing
	Josette
	Little Miss Broadway
	Alexander's Ragtime Band
	Hold That Coed
	Straight, Place and Show
	Just Around the Corner
	Thanks for Everything
1939	Second Fiddle
	Swanee River
	The Little Princess
1940	The Blue Bird
	Lillian Russell
	Down Argentine Way

Ziegfeld Follies (1946).

An MGM film produced by Arthur Freed; directed by Vincente Minnelli (also Norman Taurog, George Sidney, Robert Lewis, Lemuel Ayers, Roy Del Ruth); choreography, Robert Alton (also Fred Astaire, Gene Kelly, Eugene Loring, Charles Walters); art directors, Cedric Gibbons, Merrill Pye, Jack Martin Smith; costumes, Helen Rose, Irene Sharaff; music director, Lennie Hayton; orchestrations, Conrad Salinger, Wally Heglin; music adaptation, Roger Edens; vocal arrangements, Kay Thompson; cameramen, George Folsey, Charles Rosher; editor, Albert Akst; Technicolor.

Cast: Fred Astaire; Lucille Ball; Lucille Bremer; Fanny Brice; Judy Garland; Kathryn Grayson; Lena Horne; Gene Kelly; James Melton; Victor Moore; Red Skelton; Esther Williams; William Powell; Edward Arnold; Marion Bell; Louis Bunin's Puppets; Cyd Charisse; Hume Cronyn; William Frawley; Robert Lewis; Virginia O'Brien; Keenan Wynn; Grady Sutton; Rex Evans; Charles Coleman; Joseph Crehan; Harriet Lee; Rod Alexander; Eugene Loring.

Songs & Sketches: "Ziegfeld Days" (medley) - Powell; Puppets/ "Here's to the Girls" (Roger Edens-Ralph Freed) - Astaire, male chorus; Ball, Charisse, chorus/ "Bring on the Wonderful Men" (Edens-Earl Brent) - O'Brien/ "A Water Ballet" - Williams/ "Number, Please" (sketch by Pete Barry) - Wynn, Sutton/ "Libiamo ne' lieti calici" (Verdi-Piave, *La Traviata*) -Bell, Melton, chorus/ "Pay the Two Dollars" (sketch by George White, William K. Wells) - Moore, Arnold, Crehan/ "This Heart of Mine" (Harry Warren-Arthur Freed) - Astaire, Bremer, dancers/ "The Sweepstakes Ticket" (sketch by David Freedman) - Brice, Cronyn, Frawley/ "Love" (Hugh Martin, Ralph Blane) - Horne/ "When Television Comes" (monologue by Red Skelton) - Skelton/ "Limehouse Blues" (Philip Braham-Douglas Furber) - Lee; dance by Astaire, Bremer, with Lewis, Alexander, Loring, Charisse, chorus/ "The Interview" (Roger Edens-Kay Thompson) - Garland, Evans, reporters/ "The Babbitt and the Bromide" (George Gershwin-Ira Gershwin) - Astaire, Kelly/ "There's Beauty Everywhere" (Warren-Freed) - Grayson. Unused: "If Swing Goes, I Go Too" - Astaire/ "Start Off Each Day with a Song" - Jimmy Durante/ "Baby Snooks" - Brice/ "A Bit of the West" - Melton/ "Liza" - Horne, Avon Long/ "We Will Meet Again in Honolulu" - Melton/ "Death and Taxes" - Durante, Arnold/ "Pass That Peace Pipe" - Kelly, Astaire.

The form of stage entertainment known as the revue— with its unrelated songs, dances, comedy sketches, monologues, and specialty acts—thrived on Broadway during the first half of the century. It was not, however, often attempted on the screen, though in the early days of sound there were such examples as MGM's *Hollywood Revue of 1929,* Warner's *The Show of Shows,* Paramount's *Paramount on Parade,* and Universal's *King of Jazz* (the first three displayed the talents of studio contractees, the fourth spotlighted Paul Whiteman's orchestra, with vocalist Bing Crosby and others). From then on, even films featuring well-known screen personalities appearing in specialty routines—or those based on or "inspired" by Broadway revues—felt it necessary to provide at least some semblance of story line.

Ziegfeld Follies, named for the series of legendary stage revues presented by Florenz Ziegfeld between 1907 and 1931, was the only latter-day movie created according to the basic revue format. Introduced from his heavenly abode by Ziegfeld himself (William Powell, who had played the title role in *The Great Ziegfeld*), the film offered a succession of musical and comic numbers about half of which had been previously introduced on the stage (though, oddly, none in a Ziegfeld-sponsored show). Fred Astaire, who appeared in more sequences than anyone else, was given choice assignments dancing to the elegant "This Heart of Mine" (with Lucille Bremer), the melodramatic "Limehouse Blues" (again with Miss Bremer), and the witty "Babbitt and the Bromide" (with Gene Kelly). Nonmusical highlights were "Number, Please," with Keenan Wynn as a frustrated telephone caller; "Pay the Two Dollars," another study in frustration, featuring Victor Moore and Edward Arnold; and Red Skelton's vaudeville monologue about Guzzler's Gin ("a smooooth drink"). Originally titled *Ziegfeld Follies of 1944,* the picture ran almost three hours when it was previewed late that year. Seven numbers were deleted, an elaborate "bubble" finale—with Astaire, Bremer, James Melton, and Cyd Charisse—was reshot with Kathryn Grayson, and three scenes were added. After further delays the *Follies* was released early in 1946.

Though they did not adhere to the traditional revue form, other plotless musicals have occasionally come out of Hollywood. In 1940, Walt Disney gave us a cartoon symphony concert in *Fantasia,* then followed it up with two pop-music concerts, *Make Mine Music* (1946) and *Melody Time* (1948). Director-choreographer Gene Kelly put together an ambitious feature-length program of three ballets, called *Invitation to the Dance,* which MGM released in 1956. Among the dancers in the Arthur Freed production were Igor Youskevitch, Tamara Toumanova, Tommy Rall, Belita, and Carol Haney. And MGM's two *That's Entertainment* anthologies, in 1974 and 1976, were assembled from clips of previously released films. The former, with an all-star array of narrators, was written and directed by Jack Haley, Jr., and produced by Haley and Daniel Melnick; the latter, with Fred Astaire and Gene Kelly as narrators, was written by Leonard Gershe, directed by Kelly, and produced by Saul Chaplin and Melnick.

Ziegfeld Girl. *See* **Great Ziegfeld, The.**

"Zing a Little Zong" Music by Harry Warren; lyric by Leo Robin. Zingy Dutch-accented number for lovers who imagine they're beside the Zuyder Zee. Supposedly a song from a just-opened Broadway musical, it was introduced by Bing Crosby and Jane Wyman at an opening-night party in *Just for You* (Par. 1952).

"Zip-a-Dee-Doo-Dah" Music by Allie Wrubel; lyric by Ray Gilbert. Joyous number for Uncle Remus (James Baskett) in *Song of the South* (Disney 1946), accompanied by superimposed animated cartoon birds.

Zorina, Vera (née Eva Brigitta Hartwig), actress, dancer; b. Berlin, Jan. 2, 1917 (Norwegian parents). Former dancer in ballet companies who became favorite of the musical stage in London (*On Your Toes*) and New York (*Louisiana Purchase*). Best remembered on film for her dance to "That Old Black Magic" in *Star Spangled Rhythm,* the slim, leggy Miss Zorina was the third wife of choreographer George Balanchine and was later married to composer-author-record executive Goddard Lieberson.

1938   The Goldwyn Follies (*Olga Samara*)
1939   On Your Toes (*Vera Barnova*)
1941   Louisiana Purchase (*Marina Von Minden*)
1942   Star-Spangled Rhythm (specialty)
1944   Follow the Boys (*Gloria Vance*)

MOTION PICTURE ACADEMY
NOMINATIONS AND AWARDS

There are no awards specifically for musicals. Musical films, actors and actresses in them, and directors of them, have all been nominated in categories that included nonmusicals. Following are those that were nominated; asterisks indicate winners.

Film

1929 The Broadway Melody *
      The Hollywood Revue
1930 The Love Parade
1932 One Hour with You
      The Smiling Lieutenant
1933 42nd Street
      She Done Him Wrong
1934 Flirtation Walk
      The Gay Divorcee
      One Night of Love
1935 Broadway Melody of 1936
      Naughty Marietta
      Top Hat
1936 San Francisco
      The Great Ziegfeld *
      Three Smart Girls
1937 In Old Chicago
      One Hundred Men and a Girl
1938 Alexander's Ragtime Band
1939 The Wizard of Oz
1942 Yankee Doodle Dandy
1944 Going My Way *
1945 Anchors Aweigh
      Bells of St. Mary's
1948 The Red Shoes
1951 An American in Paris *
1952 The Greatest Show on Earth *
1954 Seven Brides for Seven Brothers
      The Country Girl
1956 The King and I
1958 Gigi *

1961 West Side Story *
1962 The Music Man
1964 Mary Poppins
      My Fair Lady *
1965 The Sound of Music *
1967 Doctor Dolittle
1968 Funny Girl
      Oliver! *
1969 Hello, Dolly!
1971 Fiddler on the Roof
1972 Cabaret
1975 Nashville
1979 All That Jazz
1980 Coal Miner's Daughter
1984 Amadeus

Actress

1929 Bessie Love, *The Broadway Melody*
1931 Marlene Dietrich, *Morocco*
1934 Grace Moore, *One Night of Love*
1936 Luise Rainer, *The Great Ziegfeld* *
1945 Ingrid Bergman, *Bells of St. Mary's*
1952 Susan Hayward, *With a Song in My Heart*
1953 Leslie Caron, *Lili*
1954 Dorothy Dandridge, *Carmen Jones*
      Judy Garland, *A Star Is Born*
      Grace Kelly, *The Country Girl* *
1955 Susan Hayward, *I'll Cry Tomorrow*
      Eleanor Parker, *Interrupted Melody*
1956 Deborah Kerr, *The King and I*
1964 Julie Andrews, *Mary Poppins* *
      Debbie Reynolds, *The Unsinkable Molly Brown*

1965	Julie Andrews, *The Sound of Music*
1968	Barbra Streisand, *Funny Girl* *
1972	Liza Minnelli, *Cabaret* *
	Diana Ross, *Lady Sings the Blues*
1975	Ann-Margret, *Tommy*
1980	Sissy Spacek, *Coal Miner's Daughter* *
1985	Jessica Lange, *Sweet Dreams*

Actor

1930 Maurice Chevalier, *The Big Pond*
Maurice Chevalier, *The Love Parade*
Lawrence Tibbett, *The Rogue Song*
1936 Spencer Tracy, *San Francisco*
1939 Mickey Rooney, *Babes in Arms*
1942 James Cagney, *Yankee Doodle Dandy* *
1944 Bing Crosby, *Going My Way* *
Barry Fitzgerald, *Going My Way*
1945 Bing Crosby, *Bells of St. Mary's*
Gene Kelly, *Anchors Aweigh*
Cornel Wilde, *A Song To Remember*
1946 Larry Parks, *The Jolson Story*
1948 Dan Dailey, *When My Baby Smiles at Me*
1954 Bing Crosby, *The Country Girl*
James Mason, *A Star Is Born*
1955 James Cagney, *Love Me or Leave Me*
1956 Yul Brynner, *The King and I* *
1959 Jack Lemmon, *Some Like It Hot*
1960 Laurence Olivier, *The Entertainer*
1964 Rex Harrison, *My Fair Lady* *
1968 Ron Moody, *Oliver!*
1969 Peter O'Toole, *Goodbye, Mr. Chips*
1971 Topol, *Fiddler on the Roof*
1977 John Travolta, *Saturday Night Fever*
1979 Roy Scheider, *All That Jazz*
1984 F. Murray Abraham, *Amadeus* *

Director

1929 Harry Beaumont, *The Broadway Melody*
1930 Ernst Lubitsch, *The Love Parade*
King Vidor, *Hallelujah*
1931 Josef von Sternberg, *Morocco*
1934 Victor Schertzinger, *One Night of Love*
1936 Robert Z. Leonard, *The Great Ziegfeld*
W. S. Van Dyke, *San Francisco*
1942 Michael Curtiz, *Yankee Doodle Dandy*
1944 Leo McCarey, *Going My Way* *
1945 Leo McCarey, *Bells of St. Mary's*

1951 Vincente Minnelli, *An American in Paris*
1953 Charles Walters, *Lili*
1954 George Seaton, *The Country Girl*
1956 Walter Lang, *The King and I*
1958 Vincente Minnelli, *Gigi* *
1959 Billy Wilder, *Some Like It Hot*
1961 Robert Wise & Jerome Robbins, *West Side Story* *
1964 George Cukor, *My Fair Lady* *
Robert Stevenson, *Mary Poppins*
1965 Robert Wise, *The Sound of Music* *
1968 Carol Reed, *Oliver!* *
1971 Norman Jewison, *Fiddler on the Roof*
1972 Bob Fosse, *Cabaret* *
1975 Robert Altman, *Nashville*
1979 Bob Fosse, *All That Jazz*
1984 Carl Foreman, *Amadeus* *

Song

The one annual Academy Award (inaugurated in 1934) that most directly falls within the scope of this volume is the one with the least justification today. Apart from the impossibility of selecting a ''best'' song, this particular award, initially prestigious because of the embarrassment of riches, has simply become an embarrassment. Not the least of the reasons is the accepted practice of nominating songs that have nothing to do with the actual film but are sung over the opening or closing credits just to meet minimum eligibility requirements. And consider the following titles: ''Cocktails for Two,'' ''I Only Have Eyes for You,'' ''June in January,'' ''Love Thy Neighbor,'' ''Broadway Rhythm,'' ''I Won't Dance,'' ''I'm in the Mood for Love,'' ''Top Hat, White Tie and Tails,'' ''When I Grow Too Old To Dream,'' ''Easy To Love,'' ''I'm Putting All My Eggs in One Basket,'' ''Let's Face the Music and Dance,'' ''A Foggy Day,'' ''I've Got My Love To Keep Me Warm,'' ''Nice Work If You Can Get It,'' ''Small Fry,'' ''Two Sleepy People,'' ''At Last,'' ''I'll Remember April,'' ''Serenade in Blue,'' ''You Were Never Lovelier,'' ''A Lovely Way To Spend an Evening,'' ''One for My Baby,'' ''The Boy Next Door,'' ''Have Yourself a Merry Little Christmas,'' ''Spring Will Be a Little Late This Year,'' ''Give Me the Simple Life,'' ''It's a Grand Night for Singing,'' ''You Make Me Feel So Young,'' ''It's a Most Unusual Day,'' ''Hi-Lili, Hi-Lo,'' ''That's Entertainment,'' ''I Remember It Well,'' and ''Mrs. Robinson.'' Not one of these movie songs was ever nominated.

1934   The Carioca (Youmans-Kahn, Eliscu), *Flying Down to Rio*

The Continental (Conrad-Magidson), *The Gay Divorcee* *

Love in Bloom (Rainger-Robin), *She Loves Me Not*

1935   Cheek to Cheek (Berlin), *Top Hat*

Lovely To Look At (Kern, Fields), *Roberta*

Lullaby of Broadway (Warren-Dubin), *Gold Diggers of 1935* *

1936   Did I Remember? (Donaldson-Adamson), *Suzy*

I've Got You Under My Skin (Porter), *Born To Dance*

A Melody from the Sky (Alter-Mitchell), *Trail of the Lonesome Pine*

Pennies from Heaven (Johnston-Burke), *Pennies from Heaven*

The Way You Look Tonight (Kern-Fields), *Swing Time* *

When Did You Leave Heaven? (Whiting-Bullock), *Sing, Baby, Sing*

1937   Remember Me (Warren-Dubin), *Mr. Dodd Takes the Air*

Sweet Leilani (Owens), *Waikiki Wedding* *

That Old Feeling (Fain-Brown), *Vogues of 1938*

They Can't Take That Away from Me (Gershwin-Gershwin), *Shall We Dance*

Whispers in the Dark (Hollander-Robin), *Artists and Models*

1938   Always and Always (Ward-Forrest, Wright), *Mannequin*

Change Partners (Berlin), *Carefree*

The Cowboy and the Lady (Newman-Quenzer), *The Cowboy and the Lady*

Dust (Marvin), *Under Western Stars*

Jeepers Creepers (Warren-Mercer), *Going Places*

Merrily We Live (Charig-Quenzer), *Merrily We Live*

Mist Over the Moon (Oakland-Hammerstein), *The Lady Objects*

My Own (McHugh-Adamson), *That Certain Age*

Now It Can Be Told (Berlin), *Alexander's Ragtime Band*

Thanks for the Memory (Rainger-Robin), *Big Broadcast of 1938* *

1939   Faithful Forever (Rainger-Robin), *Gulliver's Travels*

I Poured My Heart Into a Song (Berlin), *Second Fiddle*

Over the Rainbow (Arlen-Harburg), *The Wizard of Oz* *

Wishing (DeSylva), *Love Affair*

1940   Down Argentina Way (Warren-Gordon), *Down Argentine Way*

I'd Know You Anywhere (McHugh-Mercer), *You'll Find Out*

It's a Blue World (Wright, Forrest), *Music in My Heart*

Love of My Life (Shaw-Mercer), *Second Chorus*

Only Forever (Monaco-Burke), *Rhythm on the River*

Our Love Affair (Edens-Freed), *Strike Up the Band*

Waltzing in the Clouds (Stolz-Kahn), *Spring Parade*

When You Wish Upon a Star (Harline-Washington), *Pinocchio* *

Who Am I? (Styne-Bullock), *Hit Parade of 1941*

1941   Baby Mine (Churchill-Washington), *Dumbo*

Be Honest with Me (Autry, Rose), *Ridin' on a Rainbow*

Blues in the Night (Arlen-Mercer), *Blues in the Night*

Boogie Woogie Bugle Boy (Prince-Raye), *Buck Privates*

Chattanooga Choo-Choo (Warren-Gordon), *Sun Valley Serenade*

Dolores (Alter-Loesser), *Las Vegas Nights*

The Last Time I Saw Paris (Kern-Hammerstein), *Lady, Be Good* *

Out of the Silence (Norlind), *All-American Coed*

Since I Kissed My Baby Goodbye (Porter), *You'll Never Get Rich*

1942   Always in My Heart (Lecuona-Gannon), *Always in My Heart*

Dearly Beloved (Kern-Mercer), *You Were Never Lovelier*

How About You? (Lane-Freed), *Babes on Broadway*

I've Got a Gal in Kalamazoo (Warren-Gordon), *Orchestra Wives*

I've Heard That Song Before (Styne-Cahn), *Youth on Parade*

Love Is a Song (Churchill-Morey), *Bambi*

Pennies for Peppino (Ward-Wright, Forrest), *Flying with Music*

Pig Foot Pete (dePaul-Raye), *Hellzapoppin*

When There's a Breeze on Lake Louise (Revel-Greene), *Mayor of 44th Street*

White Christmas (Berlin), *Holiday Inn* *

1943   Change of Heart (Styne-Adamson), *Hit Parade of 1943*

Happiness Is a Thing Called Joe (Arlen-Harburg), *Cabin in the Sky*

My Shining Hour (Arlen-Mercer), *The Sky's the Limit*

Saludos Amigos (Wolcott-Washington), *Saludos Amigos*

Say a Prayer for the Boys Over There (McHugh-Adamson), *Hers To Hold*

That Old Black Magic (Arlen-Mercer), *Star Spangled Rhythm*

They're Either Too Young or Too Old (Schwartz-Loesser), *Thank Your Lucky Stars*

We Mustn't Say Goodbye (Monaco-Dubin), *Stage Door Canteen*

You'd Be So Nice To Come Home To (Porter), *Something To Shout About*

You'll Never Know (Warren-Gordon), *Hello, Frisco, Hello* *

1944   I Couldn't Sleep a Wink Last Night (McHugh-Adamson), *Higher and Higher*

I'll Walk Alone (Styne-Cahn), *Follow the Boys*

I'm Making Believe (Monaco-Gordon), *Sweet and Low Down*

Long Ago and Far Away (Kern-Gershwin), *Cover Girl*

Now I Know (Arlen-Koehler), *Up in Arms*

Remember Me to Carolina (Revel-Webster), *Minstrel Man*

Rio de Janeiro (Barroso-Washington), *Brazil*

Silver Shadows and Golden Dreams (Pollack-Newman), *Lady, Let's Dance*

Sweet Dreams, Sweetheart (Jerome-Koehler), *Hollywood Canteen*

Swinging on a Star (Van Heusen-Burke), *Going My Way* *

Too Much in Love (Kent-Gannon), *Song of the Open Road*

The Trolley Song (Martin, Blane), *Meet Me in St. Louis*

1945   Ac-Cent-Tchu-Ate the Positive (Arlen-Mercer), *Here Come the Waves*

Anywhere (Styne-Cahn), *Tonight and Every Night*

Aren't You Glad You're You? (Van Heusen-Burke), *Bells of St. Mary's*

Cat and Canary (Livingston, Evans), *Why Girls Leave Home*

Endlessly (Kent-Gannon), *Earl Carroll Vanities*

I Fall in Love Too Easily (Styne-Cahn), *Anchors Aweigh*

I'll Buy That Dream (Wrubel-Magidson), *Sing Your Way Home*

It Might as Well Be Spring (Rodgers-Hammerstein), *State Fair* *

Linda (Ronell), *G. I. Joe*

Love Letters (Young-Heyman), *Love Letters*

More and More (Kern-Harburg), *Can't Help Singing*

Sleighride in July (Van Heusen-Burke), *Belle of the Yukon*

So in Love (Rose-Robin), *Wonder Man*

Some Sunday Morning (Heindorf, Jerome-Koehler), *San Antonio*

1946   All Through the Day (Kern-Hammerstein), *Centennial Summer*

I Can't Begin To Tell You (Monaco-Gordon), *The Dolly Sisters*

Ole Buttermilk Sky (Carmichael-Brooks), *Canyon Passage*

On the Atchison, Topeka, and the Santa Fe (Warren-Mercer), *The Harvey Girls* *

You Keep Coming Back Like a Song (Berlin), *Blue Skies*

1947   A Gal in Calico (Schwartz-Robin), *The Time, the Place and the Girl*

I Wish I Didn't Love You So (Loesser), *The Perils of Pauline*

Pass That Peace Pipe (Edens, Blane, Martin), *Good News*

You Do (Myrow-Gordon), *Mother Wore Tights*

Zip-a-Dee-Doo-Dah (Wrubel-Gilbert), *Song of the South* *

1948   Buttons and Bows (Livingston, Evans), *The Paleface* *

For Every Man There's a Woman (Arlen-Robin), *Casbah*

It's Magic (Styne-Cahn), *Romance on the High Seas*

This Is the Moment (Hollander-Robin), *That Lady in Ermine*

Woody Woodpecker (Idriss, Tibbles), *Wet Blanket Policy*

1949   Baby, It's Cold Outside (Loesser), *Neptune's Daughter* *

It's a Great Feeling (Styne-Cahn), *It's a Great Feeling*

Lavender Blue (Daniel-Morey), *So Dear to My Heart*

My Foolish Heart (Young-Washington), *My Foolish Heart*

Through a Long and Sleepless Night (Newman-Gordon), *Come to the Stable*

1950 Be My Love (Brodszky-Cahn), *Be My Love*

Bibbidi-Bobbidi-Boo (Hoffman, Livingston-David), *Cinderella*

Mona Lisa (Livingston, Evans), *Capt. Carey, USA* *

Mule Train (Glickman, Heath, Lange), *Singing Guns*

Wilhelmina (Myrow-Gordon), *Wabash Avenue*

1951 In the Cool Cool Cool of the Evening (Carmichael-Mercer), *Here Comes the Groom* *

A Kiss To Build a Dream On (Ruby-Kalmar, Hammerstein), *The Strip*

Never (Newman-Daniel), *Golden Girl*

Too Late Now (Lane-Lerner), *Royal Wedding*

Wonder Why (Brodszky-Cahn), *Rich, Young and Pretty*

1952 Am I in Love? (Brooks), *Son of Paleface*

Because You're Mine (Brodszky-Cahn), *Because You're Mine*

High Noon (Tiomkin-Washington), *High Noon* *

Thumbelina (Loesser), *Hans Christian Andersen*

Zing a Little Zong (Warren-Robin), *Just for You*

1953 Blue Pacific Blues (Lee-Washington), *Miss Sadie Thompson*

The Moon Is Blue (Gilbert-Fine), *The Moon Is Blue*

My Flaming Heart (Brodszky-Robin), *Small Town Girl*

Secret Love (Fain-Webster), *Calamity Jane* *

That's Amore (Warren-Brooks), *The Caddy*

1954 Count Your Blessings Instead of Sheep (Berlin), *White Christmas*

The High and the Mighty (Tiomkin-Washington), *The High and the Mighty*

Hold My Hand (Lawrence, Myers), *Susan Slept Here*

The Man That Got Away (Arlen-Gershwin), *A Star Is Born*

Three Coins in the Fountain (Styne-Cahn), *Three Coins in the Fountain* *

1955 I'll Never Stop Loving You (Brodszky-Cahn), *Love Me or Leave Me*

Love Is a Many-Splendored Thing (Fain-Webster, *Love Is a Many-Splendored Thing* *

Something's Gotta Give (Mercer), *Daddy Long Legs*

The Tender Trap (Van Heusen-Cahn), *The Tender Trap*

Unchained Melody (North-Zaret), *Unchained*

1956 Friendly Persuasion (Tiomkin-Webster), *Friendly Persuasion*

Julie (Stevens-Adair), *Julie*

Que Sera, Sera (Livingston, Evans), *The Man Who Knew Too Much* *

True Love (Porter), *High Society*

Written in the Wind (Young-Cahn), *Written in the Wind*

1957 An Affair To Remember (Warren-Adamson, McCarey), *An Affair To Remember*

All the Way (Van Heusen-Cahn), *The Joker Is Wild* *

April Love (Fain-Webster), *April Love*

Tammy (Livingston, Evans), *Tammy and the Bachelor*

Wild Is the Wind (Tiomkin-Washington), *Wild Is the Wind*

1958 Almost in Your Arms (Livingston, Evans), *Houseboat*

A Certain Smile (Fain-Webster), *A Certain Smile*

Gigi (Loewe-Lerner), *Gigi* *

To Love and Be Loved (Van Heusen-Cahn), *Some Came Running*

A Very Precious Love (Fain-Webster), *Marjorie Morningstar*

1959 The Best of Everything (Newman-Cahn), *The Best of Everything*

The Five Pennies (Fine), *The Five Pennies*

The Hanging Tree (Livingston-David), *The Hanging Tree*

High Hopes (Van Heusen-Cahn), *A Hole in the Head* *

Strange Are the Ways of Love (Tiomkin-Washington), *The Young Land*

1960 The Facts of Life (Mercer), *The Facts of Life*

The Faraway Part of Town (Previn-Langdon), *Pepe*

The Green Leaves of Summer (Tiomkin-Webster), *The Alamo*

Never on Sunday (Hadjidakis), *Never on Sunday* *

The Second Time Around (Van Heusen-Cahn), *High Time*

1961 Bachelor in Paradise (Mancini-David), *Bachelor in Paradise*

The Falcon and the Dove (Rozsa-Webster), *El Cid*

Moon River (Mancini-Mercer), *Breakfast at Tiffany's* *

Pocketful of Miracles (Van Heusen-Cahn), *Pocketful of Miracles*

Town Without Pity (Tiomkin-Washington), *Town Without Pity*

1962 Days of Wine and Roses (Mancini-Mercer), *Days of Wine and Roses* *

Follow Me (Kaper-Webster), *Mutiny on the Bounty*

Second Chance (Previn-Langdon), *Two for the Seesaw*

Tender Is the Night (Fain-Webster), *Tender Is the Night*

Walk on the Wild Side (Bernstein-David), *Walk on the Wild Side*

1963 Call Me Irresponsible (Van Heusen-Cahn), *Papa's Delicate Condition* *

Charade (Mancini-Mercer), *Charade*

It's a Mad Mad Mad Mad World (Gold-David), *It's a Mad Mad Mad Mad World*

More (Ortolani, Oliviero-Newell), *Mondo Cane*

So Little Time (Tiomkin-Webster), *55 Days at Peking*

1964 Chim Chim Cheree (Sherman, Sherman), *Mary Poppins* *

Dear Heart (Mancini-Livingston, Evans), *Dear Heart*

Hush . . . Hush, Sweet Charlotte (DeVol-David), *Hush . . . Hush, Sweet Charlotte*

My Kind of Town (Van Heusen-Cahn), *Robin and the Seven Hoods*

Where Love Has Gone (Van Heusen-Cahn), *Where Love Has Gone*

1965 The Ballad of Cat Ballou (Livingston-David), *Cat Ballou*

I Will Wait for You (Legrand-Demy), *The Umbrellas of Cherbourg*

The Shadow of Your Smile (Mandel-Webster), *The Sandpiper* *

The Sweetheart Tree (Mancini-Mercer), *The Great Race*

What's New Pussycat? (Bacharach-David), *What's New Pussycat?*

1966 Alfie (Bacharach-David), *Alfie*

Born Free (Barry-Black), *Born Free* *

Georgy Girl (Springfield-Dale), *Georgy Girl*

My Wishing Doll (Bernstein-David), *Hawaii*

A Time for Love (Mandel-Webster), *An American Dream*

1967 The Bare Necessities (Gilkyson), *The Jungle Book*

The Eyes of Love (Jones-Russell), *Banning*

The Look of Love (Bacharach-David), *Casino Royale*

Talk to the Animals (Bricusse), *Doctor Dolittle* *

Thoroughly Modern Millie (Van Heusen-Cahn), *Thoroughly Modern Millie*

1968 Chitty Chitty Bang Bang (Sherman, Sherman), *Chitty Chitty Bang Bang*

For Love of Ivy (Jones-Russell), *For Love of Ivy*

Funny Girl (Styne-Merrill), *Funny Girl*

Star (Van Heusen-Cahn), *Star*

The Windmills of Your Mind (Legrand-Bergman, Bergman), *The Thomas Crown Affair* *

1969 Come Saturday Morning (Karlin-Langdon), *The Sterile Cuckoo*

Jean (McKeun), *The Prime of Miss Jean Brodie*

Raindrops Keep Fallin' on My Head (Bacharach-David), *Butch Cassidy and the Sundance Kid* *

True Grit (Bernstein-Black), *True Grit*

What Are You Doing the Rest of Your Life? (Legrand-Bergman, Bergman), *The Happy Ending*

1970 For All We Know (Karlin-Wilson, James), *Lovers and Other Strangers* *

Pieces of Dreams (Legrand-Berman, Bergman), *Pieces of Dreams*

Thank You Very Much (Bricusse), *Scrooge*

Till Love Touches Your Life (Ortolani-Hamilton), *Madron*

Whistling Away the Dark (Mancini-Mercer), *Darling Lili*

1971 The Age of Not Believing (Sherman, Sherman), *Bedknobs and Broomsticks*

All His Children (Mancini-Bergman, Bergman), *Sometimes a Great Notion*

Bless the Beasts and Children (Devorzon, Botkin), *Bless the Beasts and Children*

Life Is What You Make It (Hamlisch-Mercer), *Kotch*

Theme from Shaft (Hayes), *Shaft* *

1972 Ben (Scharf-Black), *Ben*

Come Follow, Follow Me (Karlin-Karlin), *The Little Ark*

Marmalade, Molasses and Honey (Jarre-Bergman, Bergman), *The Life and Time of Judge Roy Bean*

The Morning After (Kasha-Hirschhorn), *The Poseidon Adventure* *

Strange Are the Ways of Love (Fain-Webster), *The Stepmother*

1973 All That Love Went to Waste (Barrie-Cahn), *A Touch of Class*

Live and Let Die (McCartney-McCartney), *Live and Let Die*

Love (Bruns-Huddleston), *Robin Hood*

The Way We Were (Hamlisch-Bergman, Bergman), *The Way We Were* *

You're So Nice To Be Around (Williams-Williams), *Cinderella Liberty*

1974 Blazing Saddles (Morris-Brooks), *Blazing Saddles*

I Feel Love (Box-Box), *Benji*

Little Prince (Loewe-Lerner), *The Little Prince*

We May Never Love Like This Again (Kasha-Hirschhorn), *The Towering Inferno* *

Wherever Love Takes Me (Bernstein-Black), *Gold*

1975 Do You Know Where You're Going To? (Masser-Goffin), *Mahogany*

How Lucky Can You Get? (Kander-Ebb), *Funny Lady*

I'm Easy (Carradine), *Nashville* *

Now That We're in Love (Barrie-Cahn), *Whiffs*

Richard's Window (Fox-Gimbel), *The Other Side of the Mountain*

1976 Ava Satani (Goldsmith), *The Omen*

Come to Me (Mancini-Black), *The Pink Panther Strikes Again*

Evergreen (Streisand-Williams), *A Star Is Born* *

Gonna Fly Now (Conti-Connors, Robbins), *Rocky*

A Word That Never Was (Fain-Webster), *Half a House*

1977 Candle on the Water (Kasha-Hirschhorn), *Pete's Dragon*

He Danced with Me/ She Danced with Me (Sherman, Sherman), *The Slipper and the Rose*

Nobody Does It Better (Hamlisch-Sager), *The Spy Who Loved Me*

Someone's Waiting for You (Fain-Connors, Robbins), *The Rescuers*

You Light Up My Life (Brooks), *You Light Up My Life* *

1978 Hopelessly Devoted to You (Farrar), *Grease*

Last Dance (Jabara), *Thank God It's Friday* *

Last Time I Felt Like This (Jabara), *Same Time Next Year*

Ready To Take a Chance Again (Fox-Gimbel), *Foul Play*

When You're Loved (Sherman, Sherman), *The Magic of Lassie*

1979 I'll Never Say Goodbye (Shire-Bergman, Bergman), *The Promise*

It Goes Like It Goes (Shire-Gimbel), *Norma Rae* *

It's Easy To Say (Mancini-Wells), *10*

The Rainbow Connection (Williams, Ascher), *The Muppet Movie*

Through the Eyes of Love (Hamlisch-Sager), *Ice Castles*

1980 Fame (Gore-Pitchford), *Fame* *

9 to 5 (Parton), *9 to 5*

On the Road Again (Nelson), *Honeysuckle Rose*

Out Here on My Own (Gore-Gore), *Fame*

People Alone (Schifrin-Jennings), *The Competition*

Winners Only

1981 Arthur's Theme (The Best That You Can Do) (Bacharach-Sager-Cross-Allen), *Arthur*

1982 Up Where We Belong (Nitzsche, St. Marie-Jennings), *An Officer and a Gentleman*

1983 Flashdance . . . What a Feeling (Moroder-Forsey, Cara), *Flashdance*

1984 I Just Called to Say I Love You (Wonder), *The Woman in Red*

1985 Say You, Say Me (Richie), *White Nights*

1986 Take My Breath Away (Moroder-Whitlock), *Top Gun*

BIOGRAPHIES

With regard to names in parentheses, in column 1 they indicate fictitious name used in the films, in column 2 they indicate whose voice or playing was dubbed.

Classical Composers, Musicians, Singers, Impresarios

Ludwig van Beethoven	Fritz Kortner	The Life of Beethoven (Ger. 1929)
	Harry Baur	Un Grand Amour de Beethoven (Fr. 1936)
	Ewald Balser	Eroica (Aus. 1949)
	Karl Boehm	The Magnificent Rebel (US 1962)
Vincenzio Bellini	Phillips Holmes	The Divine Spark (It. 1935)
Hector Berlioz	Jean-Louis Barrault	Symphonie fantastique (Fr. 1940)
Johannes Brahms	Robert Walker	Song of Love (US 1947)
Enrico Caruso	Mario Lanza	The Great Caruso (US 1951)
Frédéric Chopin	Cornel Wilde (José Iturbi)	A Song to Remember (US 1944)
	Czeslaw Wollejko	The Young Chopin (Pol. 1952)
Gaetano Donizetti	Amadeo Nazzari	Life of Donizetti (It. 1952)
William S. Gilbert	Robert Morley	Story of Gilbert & Sullivan (Eng. 1953)
Edvard Grieg	Toralv Maurstad	Song of Norway (US 1970)
George Frederick Handel	Wilfrid Lawson	The Great Mr. Handel (Eng. 1942)
Sol Hurok	David Wayne	Tonight We Sing (US 1953)
Eileen Joyce	Eileen Joyce	Wherever She Goes (Austral. 1953)
Marjorie Lawrence	Eleanor Parker (Eileen Farrell)	Interrupted Melody (US 1955)
Jenny Lind	Grace Moore	A Lady's Morals (US 1930)
Franz Liszt	Dirk Bogarde (Jorge Bolet)	Song Without End (US 1960)
	Roger Daltry	Lisztomania (Eng. 1975)
Gustave Mahler	Robert Powell	Mahler (Eng. 1976)
Nellie Melba	Patrice Munsel	Melba (US 1953)
Grace Moore	Kathryn Grayson	So This Is Love (US 1953)
Wolfgang Amadeus Mozart	Stephen Haggard	Whom the Gods Love (Eng. 1936)
	Hannes Steltzer	Die Kleine Nachtmusik (Ger. 1939)
	Gino Cervi	Melodie Eternel (It. 1940)
	Oskar Werner	Mozart (Aus. 1955)
	Pavlos Beklaris (at 7) Diago Crovetti (at 12) Santiago Ziesmer (at 20)	Mozart—A Childhood Chronicle (Ger. 1976)
	Tom Hulce	Amadeus (1984)
Jacques Offenbach	Pierre Fresnay	La Valse de Paris (Fr. 1950)
Niccolò Paganini	Stewart Granger (Yehudi Menuhin)	The Magic Bow (Eng. 1946)

Nikolai Rimsky-Korsakov	Jean-Pierre Aumont	Song of Scheherezade (US 1947)
Gioacchino Rossini	Nino Besozzi	Rossini (It. 1947)
Franz Schubert	Hans Jaray	Unfinished Symphony (Ger. 1934)
	Richard Tauber	Blossom Time (Eng. 1934)
	Nils Asther	Love Time (US 1934)
	Alan Curtis	New Wine (US 1942)
	Claude Laydu	Sinfonia d'Amore (It. 1955)
	Karl Boehm	Das Dreimäderlhaus (Ger. 1958)
	Tino Rossi	La Belle Meuniere (Fr. 1947)
Clara Schumann	Katharine Hepburn	Song of Love (US 1947)
	(Artur Rubinstein)	
Robert Schumann	Paul Henreid	Song of Love (US 1947)
Johann Strauss, Jr.	Imre Raday	The Waltz King (Ger. 1929)
	Gustav Froelich	Ein Walzer vom Strauss (Aus. 1932)
	Hans Stuewe	Der walzer Koenig (Ger. 1932)
	Esmond Knight	Waltzes from Vienna (Eng. 1933)
	Anton Walbrook	Walzerkrieg (Ger. 1934)
	Fernand Gravet	The Great Waltz (US 1938)
	Bernhard Wicki	Eternal Waltz (Ger. 1959)
	Kerwin Matthews	The Waltz King (US 1963)
	Horst Buchholtz	The Great Waltz (US 1972)
Arthur S. Sullivan	Maurice Evans	Story of Gilbert & Sullivan (Eng. 1953)
Peter Ilich Tchaikovsky	Frank Sundstrom	Song of My Heart (US 1948)
	Innokenti Smoktunovsky	Tchaikovsky (USSR 1969)
	Richard Chamberlain	The Music Lovers (Eng. 1970)
Giuseppe Verdi	Fosco Giachetti	The Life of Verdi (It. 1940)
	Pierre Cressoy	The Life and Music of Verdi (It. 1957)
Richard Wagner	Alan Badel	Magic Fire (Eng. 1956)
	Richard Burton	Wagner (Eng. 1982)

Popular Composers, Lyricists, Singers, Dancers, Musicians, Producers

All U.S. unless otherwise noted.

Ernest Ball	Dick Haymes	Irish Eyes Are Smiling (1944)
Nora Bayes	Ann Sheridan	Shine on Harvest Moon (1944)
Bix Beiderbecke	Kirk Douglas	Young Man with a Horn (1950)
(Rick Martin)	(Harry James)	
Fanny Brice	Alice Faye	Rose of Washington Square (1939)
(Rose Sargent)		
Fanny Brice	Barbra Streisand	Funny Girl (1968)
	Barbra Streisand	Funny Lady (1975)
Lew Brown	Ernest Borgnine	Best Things in Life Are Free (1956)
Eddie Cantor	Keefe Brasselle	The Eddie Cantor Story (1953)
	(Eddie Cantor)	
Irene Castle	Ginger Rogers	Story of Vernon & Irene Castle (1939)
Vernon Castle	Fred Astaire	Story of Vernon & Irene Castle (1939)
Patsy Cline	Jessica Lange	Sweet Dreams (1985)
	(Patsy Cline)	

BIOGRAPHIES

George M. Cohan	James Cagney	Yankee Doodle Dandy (1942)
Lotta Crabtree	Mitzi Gaynor	Golden Girl (1951)
B. G. DeSylva	Gordon MacRae	Best Things in Life Are Free (1956)
Jenny Dolly	Betty Grable	The Dolly Sisters (1945)
Rosie Dolly	June Haver	The Dolly Sisters (1945)
Jimmy Dorsey	Jimmy Dorsey	The Fabulous Dorseys (1947)
Tommy Dorsey	Tommy Dorsey	The Fabulous Dorseys (1947)
Paul Dresser	Victor Mature	My Gal Sal (1942)
Eddy Duchin	Tyrone Power	The Eddy Duchin Story (1956)
	(Carmen Cavallero)	
George Edwardes	Richard Greene	Gaiety George (Eng. 1948)
(George Howard)		
Gus Edwards	Bing Crosby	The Star Maker (1939)
(Larry Earl)		
Dan Emmett	Bing Crosby	Dixie (1943)
Ruth Etting	Doris Day	Love Me or Leave Me (1955)
Benny Fields	Ralph Meeker	Somebody Loves Me (1952)
	(Benny Fields)	
Fred Fisher	S. Z. Sakall	Oh, You Beautiful Doll (1949)
Bob Fosse	Roy Scheider	All That Jazz (1979)
(Joe Gideon)		
Stephen Foster	Douglass Montgomery	Harmony Lane (1935)
	Don Ameche	Swanee River (1939)
	Bill Shirley	I Dream of Jeanie (1952)
Eddie Foy	Bob Hope	The Seven Little Foys (1955)
Jane Froman	Susan Hayward	With a Song in My Heart (1952)
	(Jane Froman)	
George Gershwin	Robert Alda	Rhapsody in Blue (1945)
	(Ray Turner)	
Benny Goodman	Steve Allen	The Benny Goodman Story (1955)
	(Benny Goodman)	
Texas Guinan	Betty Hutton	Incendiary Blonde (1945)
Woody Guthrie	David Carradine	Bound for Glory (1976)
W. C. Handy	Nat ''King'' Cole	St. Louis Blues (1958)
Lorenz Hart	Mickey Rooney	Words and Music (1948)
Anna Held	Luise Rainer	The Great Ziegfeld (1936)
Ray Henderson	Dan Dailey	Best Things in Life Are Free (1956)
Victor Herbert	Walter Connolly	The Great Victor Herbert (1939)
Billie Holiday	Diana Ross	Lady Sings the Blues (1972)
Buddy Holly	Gary Busey	The Buddy Holly Story (1978)
Libby Holman	Jean Harlow	Reckless (1935)
(Mona Leslie)	(Virginia Verrill)	
Joe Howard	Mark Stevens	I Wonder Who's Kissing Her Now (1947)
	(Buddy Clark)	
Al Jolson	Larry Parks	The Jolson Story (1946)
	(Al Jolson)	
	Larry Parks	Jolson Sings Again (1949)
	(Al Jolson)	
Janis Joplin (Rose)	Bette Midler	The Rose (1979)

Scott Joplin	Billy Dee Williams	Scott Joplin (1977)
Grace LeBoy Kahn	Doris Day	I'll See You in My Dreams (1951)
Gus Kahn	Danny Thomas	I'll See You in My Dreams (1951)
Bert Kalmar	Fred Astaire	Three Little Words (1950)
Jerome Kern	Robert Walker	Till the Clouds Roll By (1946)
Gene Krupa	Sal Mineo	The Gene Krupa Story (1959)
	(Gene Krupa)	
Gertrude Lawrence	Julie Andrews	Star! (1968)
Gypsy Rose Lee	Natalie Wood	Gypsy (1962)
	(Marni Nixon)	
Joe E. Lewis	Frank Sinatra	The Joker Is Wild (1957)
Loretta Lynn	Sissy Spacek	Coal Miner's Daughter (1980)
Bob Marcucci	Ray Sharkey	The Idolmaker (1980)
(Vincent Vacarri)		
Glenn Miller	James Stewart	The Glenn Miller Story (1954)
	(Joe Yukl)	
Marilyn Miller	June Haver	Look for the Silver Lining (1949)
Helen Morgan	Ann Blyth	The Helen Morgan Story (1957)
	(Gogi Grant)	
Red Nichols	Danny Kaye	The Five Pennies (1959)
	(Red Nichols)	
Jack Norworth	Dennis Morgan	Shine on Harvest Moon (1944)
Annie Oakley	Betty Hutton	Annie Get Your Gun (1950)
Chauncey Olcott	Dennis Morgan	My Wild Irish Rose (1947)
Cole Porter	Cary Grant	Night and Day (1946)
George Raft	Ray Danton	The George Raft Story (1961)
Richard Rodgers	Tom Drake	Words and Music (1948)
Sigmund Romberg	José Ferrer	Deep in My Heart (1954)
Lillian Roth	Susan Hayward	I'll Cry Tomorrow (1955)
Harry Ruby	Red Skelton	Three Little Words (1950)
Lillian Russell	Alice Faye	Lillian Russell (1940)
Blossom Seeley	Betty Hutton	Somebody Loves Me (1952)
John Philip Sousa	Clifton Webb	Stars and Stripes Forever (1952)
Tommy Steele	Tommy Steele	The Tommy Steele Story (Eng. 1957)
Leslie Stuart	Robert Morley	You Will Remember (Eng. 1940)
Kay Swift	Irene Dunne	Never a Dull Moment (1950)
(Kay Kingsley)		
Eva Tanguay	Mitzi Gaynor	The I Don't Care Girl (1952)
Vesta Tilley	Pat Kirkwood	After the Ball (Eng. 1957)
Ritchie Valens	Lou Diamond Phillips	La Bamba (1987)
	(David Hidalgo)	
Maria von Trapp	Ruth Leuwerik	Die Trapp Familie (Ger. 1957)
	Ruth Leuwerik	Die Trapp Familie in Amerika (Ger. 1959)
	Julie Andrews	The Sound of Music (1965)
Jimmy Walker	Bob Hope	Beau James (1957)
Pearl White	Betty Hutton	Perils of Pauline (1947)
Hank Williams	George Hamilton	Your Cheatin' Heart (1965)
	(Hank Williams Jr.)	
Florenz Ziegfeld	William Powell	The Great Ziegfeld (1936)

TITLE CHANGES

U. S. Film Musicals	Retitled in England
Aaron Slick from Punkin Crick	Marshmallow Moon
Artists and Models Abroad	Stranded in Paris
Buck Privates	Rookies
College Swing	Swing Teacher Swing
Curtain Call at Cactus Creek	Take the Stage
Damn Yankees	What Lola Wants
Dancing Coed	Every Other Inch a Lady
Doll Face	Come Back to Me
Double Dynamite	It's Only Money
Earl Carroll Sketch Book	Hats Off to Rhythm
Folies Bergère	Man from the Folies Bergère
The Gang's All Here	The Girls He Left Behind
Get Hep to Love	She's My Lovely
Glamour Boy	Hearts in Springtime
Go Into Your Dance	Casino de Paree
Gold Diggers in Paris	The Gay Imposters
Hallelujah I'm a Bum	Hallelujah I'm a Tramp
Harem Scarem	Harem Holiday
The Heat's On	Tropicana
The Helen Morgan Story	Both Ends of the Candle
Here Comes Elmer	Hitchhike to Happiness
High, Wide and Handsome	Black Gold
How To Stuff a Wild Bikini	How To Fill a Wild Bikini
Icecapades Revue	Rhythm Hits the Ice
I Dood It	By Hook or By Crook
Las Vegas Nights	The Gay City
Little Miss Marker	Girl in Pawn
Manhattan Merry-Go-Round	Manhattan Music Box
Meet Me in Las Vegas	Viva Las Vegas
Million Dollar Mermaid	The One-Piece Bathing Suit
Mr. Imperium	You Belong to My Heart
The Night They Raided Minsky's	The Night They Invented Striptease
Northwest Outpost	End of the Rainbow
Off Limits	Millitary Policemen
The Petty Girl	Girl of the Year
The Powers Girl	Hello, Beautiful

TITLE CHANGES

U. S. Film Musicals

Purple Heart Diary
Riding High
Romance on the High Seas
Rookies on Parade
Royal Wedding
Sing a Jingle
Sing, Dance, Plenty Hot
Sing Me a Love Song
So This Is Love
South Sea Sinner
Spinout
Star!
Straight, Place and Show
Summer Stock
Take Me Out to the Ball Game
They Shall Have Music
Thin Ice
This Is My Affair
Three Daring Daughters
Two Girls on Broadway
Two Guys from Milwaukee
Two Guys from Texas
The West Point Story
When You're in Love
Young Man with a Horn

Retitled in England

No Time for Tears
Melody Inn
It's Magic
Jamboree
Wedding Bells
Lucky Days
Melody Girl
Come Up Smiling
The Grace Moore Story
East of Java
California Holiday
Those Were the Happy Times
They're Off!
If You Feel Like Singing
Everybody's Cheering
Melody of Youth
Lovely to Look At
His Affair
The Birds and the Bees
Choose Your Partner
Royal Flush
The Texas Knights
Fine and Dandy
For You Alone
Young Man of Music

British Film Musicals

Aunt Sally
Blossom Time
Catch Us If You Can
City of Song
The Courtneys of Curzon Street
Forget-Me-Not
Gaiety George
Going Gay
Goodnight Vienna
Head Over Heels
I Give My Heart
Jack of All Trades
Land Without Music
Lilacs in the Spring
Limelight
London Melody
London Town
One Exciting Night
The Only Girl

Retitled in U.S.

Along Came Sally
April Romance
Having a Wild Weekend
Farewell to Love
The Courtney Affair
Forever Yours
Showtime
Kiss Me Goodnight
The Magic Night
Head Over Heels in Love
Loves of Mme. DuBarry
The Two of Us
Forbidden Music
Let's Make Up
Backstage
Girls in the Street
My Heart Goes Crazy
You Can't Do Without Love
Heart Song

TITLE CHANGES

British Film Musicals	Retitled in U.S.
Pagliacci	A Clown Must Laugh
The Queen's Affair	Runaway Queen
Soldiers of the King	The Woman in Command
Spring Song	Springtime
Stardust	He Loved an Actress
The Story of Gilbert and Sullivan	The Great Gilbert and Sullivan
Sunset in Vienna	Suicide Legion
Sunshine Susie	The Office Girl
Tell Me Tonight	Be Mine Tonight
There Goes Susie	Scandals of Paris
The Tommy Steele Story	Rock Around the World
Waltzes from Vienna	Strauss's Great Waltz
Whom the Gods Love	Mozart

GENERAL BIBLIOGRAPHY

Amberg, George (ed.): *The New York Times Film Reviews 1913–1970* (Quadrangle, NY, 1971). One-volume selection.

Appelbaum, Stanley: *The Hollywood Musical Picture Quiz Book* (Dover, NY, 1974).

Bawden, Liz-Anne: *Oxford Companion to Film* (Oxford Univ. Press, NY, 1976).

Blum, Daniel, & John Willis: *Screen World* (Greenberg, NY, 1949–54; Chilton, Phila., 1955–63; Crown, NY, 1964–). Annual pictorial movie year books.

Burton, Jack: *The Blue Book of Hollywood Musicals* (Century House, Watkins Glen, NY, 1953).

Chierichetti, David: *Hollywood Costume Designs* (Crown, NY, 1976).

Craig, Warren: *The Great Songwriters of Hollywood* (Barnes, San Diego, 1980).

Crowther, Bosley: *The Lion's Share* (Dutton, NY, 1957). The MGM story.

———: *Hollywood Rajah* (Holt, NY, 1960). "The Life and Times of Louis B. Mayer."

Dimmitt, Richard: *An Actor Guide to the Talkies* (Scarecrow, NJ, 1967).

Eames, John: *The MGM Story* (Crown, NY, 1976).

Edmunds, I. G. & Reiko Mimura: *Paramount Pictures and the People who Made Them* (Barnes, San Diego, 1980).

Ephron, Henry: *We Thought We Could Do Anything* (Norton, NY, 1977).

Evans, Mark: *Soundtrack* (DaCapo, NY, 1979). "The Music of the Movies."

Ewen, David: *American Popular Songs* (Random, NY, 1966).

Fitzgerald, Michael: *Universal Pictures* (Arlington, NY, 1977).

Fordin, Hugh: *The World of Entertainment!* (Doubleday, NY, 1975). "The Freed Unit at MGM."

Fuld, James J.: *The Book of World-Famous Music* (Crown, NY, 1966).

Gifford, Denis (ed.): *The British Film Catalogue 1895–1970* (David & Charles, London, 1973).

Green, Stanley (ed.): *ASCAP Biographical Dictionary* (ASCAP, NY, 1966).

———: *Encyclopaedia of the Musical Theatre* (Dodd Mead, NY, 1976).

Griffith, Richard & Arthur Mayer: *The Movies* (Simon & Schuster, NY, 1957).

Halliwell, Leslie: *The Filmgoer's Companion* (Hill & Wang, NY, 1977).

———: *Mountain of Dreams* (Stonehill, London, 1975). The Paramount story.

Higham, Charles: *Warner Brothers* (Scribner's, NY, 1975).

——— & Joel Greenberg: *The Celluloid Muse* (Angus & Robertson, London, 1969). "Hollywood Directors Speak."

Hirschhorn, Clive: *The Warner Brothers Story* (Crown, NY, 1979).

———: *The Hollywood Musical* (Crown, NY, 1981)

Katz, Ephraim: *The Film Encyclopedia* (Crowell, NY, 1979).

Kinkle, Roger D.: *The Complete Encyclopedia of Popular Music and Jazz 1900–1950* (Arlington, NY, 1974). 4 volumes.

Knight, Arthur: *The Liveliest Art* (Macmillan, NY, 1957). "A Panoramic History of the Movies."

Kobal, John: *Gotta Sing Gotta Dance* (Hamlyn, London, 1970). "A Pictorial History of Film Musicals."

Kreuger, Miles (ed.): *The Movie Musical from Vitaphone to "42nd Street"* (Dover, NY, 1975). As reported in Photoplay magazine.

Lamparski, Richard: *Whatever Became of . . .?* (Crown, NY, 1967, 1968, 1970, 1973, 1975; Bantam, NY, 1976, 1977). 7 volumes.

Limbacher, James L.: *Film Music* (Scarecrow, Metuchen, NJ, 1980).

Maltin, Leonard (ed.): *TV Movies* (New American Lib., NY, 1980).

————: *Movie Comedy Teams* (Signet, NY, 1970).

Mayer, Arthur. See Griffith, Richard.

McVay, Douglas: *The Musical Film* (Zwemmer, London, 1967).

Meyer, William R.: *Warner Brothers Directors* (Arlington, NY, 1978).

Michael, Paul (ed.): *The American Movies Reference Book* (Prentice-Hall, Englewood Cliffs, NJ, 1969).

Mimura, Reiko. See Edmunds, I. G.

Parish, James Robert: *The Fox Girls* (Arlington, NY, 1971).

———— & Ronald Bowers: *The MGM Stock Company* (Arlington, NY, 1973).

Ragan, David: *Who's Who in Hollywood* (Arlington, NY, 1976).

Rust, Brian: *Complete Entertainment Discography* (Arlington, NY, 1974).

Scheuer, Steven (ed.): *Movies on TV* (Bantam, NY, 1980).

Sennett, Ted: *Warner Brothers Presents* (Arlington, NY, 1974). "From 'The Jazz Singer' to 'White Heat.'

————: *Hollywood Musicals* (Abrams, NY, 1981)

Shale, Richard (ed.): *Academy Awards* (Ungar, NY, 1978).

Shapiro, Nat (ed.): *Popular Music* (Adrian, NY, 1964, 1965, 1967, 1968, 1969, 1973). 6-volume "Annotated Index of American Popular Songs," 1920–69.

Solomon, Aubrey. See Thomas, Tony.

Spaeth, Sigmund: *A History of Popular Music in America* (Random, NY, 1948).

Springer, John: *All Talking! All Singing! All Dancing!* (Citadel, Secaucus, NJ, 1966). "A Pictorial History of the Movie Musical."

Stambler, Irwin: *Encyclopedia of Popular Music* (St. Martin's, NY, 1965).

Stallings, Penny: *Flesh and Fantasy* (St. Martin's, NY, 1978).

Steinberg, Cobbett (ed.): *Reel Facts* (Vintage, NY, 1978). "The Movie Book of Records."

Taylor, John Russell, & Arthur Jackson: *The Hollywood Musical* (McGraw-Hill, NY, 1971).

Thomas, Bob: *King Cohn* (Putnam, NY, 1967). Biography of Harry Cohn.

Thomas, Lawrence B.: *The MGM Years* (Columbia House, NY, 1972). "The Golden Age of Movie Musicals."

Thomson, David: *A Biographical Dictionary of Film* (Morrow, NY, 1979).

Valance, Tom: *The American Musical* (Zwemmer, London, 1970).

Warner, Jack L.: *My First Hundred Years in Hollywood* (1965).

Wilder, Alec: *American Popular Song* (Oxford Univ. Press, NY, 1972). "The Great Innovators, 1900–1950."

Wilk, Max: *They're Playing Our Song* (Atheneum, NY, 1973). Interviews with 22 songwriters.

Willis, John. See Blum, Daniel.

The New York Times Film Reviews (Quadrangle, NY). Complete, multiple-volume set.

DISCOGRAPHY
(Authorized recordings only)

Aaron Slick from Punkin Crick (Livingston, Evans; 1952). RCA 10''.

Affair To Remember, An (Warren-Adamson, McCarey; 1957). Columbia.

Alice in Wonderland (Fain-Hilliard, etc.; 1951). Disneyland.

Alice's Restaurant (Guthrie-Sherman; 1969). UA.

All That Jazz (misc.; 1979). Casablanca.

American in Paris, An (Gershwin-Gershwin; 1951). MGM.

Annie (Strouse-Charnin; 1982), Columbia.

Annie Get Your Gun (Berlin; 1950). MGM.

Anything Goes (Porter, etc.; 1936). MCA.

Anything Goes (Porter; Van Heusen-Cahn; 1956). MCA.

April Love (Fain-Webster; 1957). Dot.

Aristocats, The (Sherman, Sherman; 1970). Disneyland.

At Long Last Love (Porter; 1975). RCA (2 LPs).

Athena (Martin-Blane; 1954). Mercury 10''.

Babes in Toyland (Herbert-Leven, Bruns; 1961). Buena Vista.

Bambi (Churchill-Morey; 1942). Disneyland.

Band Wagon, The (Schwartz-Dietz; 1953). MGM.

Barkleys of Broadway, The (Warren-Gershwin; 1949). MGM.

Beau James (misc.; 1957). Imperial.

Because You're Mine (misc.; 1952). RCA.

Bedknobs and Broomsticks (Sherman, Sherman; 1971). Buena Vista.

Belle of New York, The (Warren-Mercer; 1952). Stet.

Bells Are Ringing (Styne-Comden, Green; 1960). Stet.

Bells of St. Mary's, The (misc.; 1945). MCA.

Benny Goodman Story, The (misc.; 1955). MCA.

Big Broadcast, The (Rainger-Robin; 1932). Columbia.

Birth of the Blues (misc.; 1941). MCA.

Blue Angel, The (Hollander; 1930). Regal-EMI.

Blue Hawaii (misc.; 1961). RCA.

Blue Skies (Berlin; 1946). MCA.

Blues Brothers, The (misc.; 1980). Atlantic.

Bound for Glory (Guthrie; 1976). UA.

Boy Friend, The (Wilson; 1972). MGM.

Brigadoon (Loewe-Lerner; 1954). MGM.

Buddy Holly Story, The (misc.; 1978). A-I.

Bugsy Malone (Williams; 1976). RSO.

Bundle of Joy (Myrow-Gordon; 1956). RCA.

By the Light of the Silvery Moon (misc.; 1953). Columbia.

Bye Bye Birdie (Strouse-Adams; 1963). RCA.

Cabaret (Kander-Ebb; 1972). ABC.

Calamity Jane (Fain-Webster; 1953). Columbia.

Call Me Madam (Berlin; 1952). MCA.

Camelot (Loewe-Lerner; 1967). Warner.

Can-Can (Porter; 1960). Capitol.

Can't Help Singing (Kern-Harburg; 1944). Eng. Decca.

Can't Stop the Music (misc.; 1980). Casablanca.

Captain January (Pollack-Yellen; 1936). Fox.

Carefree (Berlin; 1938). Columbia.

Carmen Jones (Bizet-Hammerstein; 1954). RCA.

Carousel (Rodgers-Hammerstein; 1956). MCA.

Charlotte's Web (Sherman, Sherman; 1972). Paramount.

Chitty Chitty Bang Bang (Sherman, Sherman; 1968). UA.

Chorus Line, A (Hamlisch-Kleban; 1985). Casablanca.

Cinderella (Livingston, Hoffman-David; 1949.) Disneyland.

Cinderfella (Warren-Brooks; 1960). Dot.

Coal Miner's Daughter (misc.; 1980). MCA.

College Humor (Johnston-Coslow; 1933). Columbia.

College Rhythm (Revel-Gordon; 1934). MCA.

Connecticut Yankee in King Arthur's Court, A (Van Heusen-Burke; 1949). MCA.

Country Girl, The (Arlen-Gershwin; 1954). MCA.

Court Jester, The (Fine-Cahn; 1955). MCA 10''.

Damn Yankees (Adler, Ross; 1958). RCA.

Damsel in Distress, A (Gershwin-Gershwin; 1937). Columbia.

Darling Lili (Mancini-Mercer; 1969). RCA.

Deep in My Heart (Romberg-misc.; 1954). MGM.

Dimples (McHugh-Koehler; 1936). Fox.

Dixie (Van Heusen-Burke; 1943). MCA.

Doctor Dolittle (Bricusse; 1967). Fox.

Double or Nothing (misc.; 1937). MCA.

Double Trouble (misc.; 1967). RCA.

Dr. Rhythm (Monaco-Burke; 1938). MCA.

Dumbo (Churchill-Washington; 1941). Disneyland.

East Side of Heaven (Monaco-Burke; 1939). MCA.

Easter Parade (Berlin; 1948). MGM.

Eddie Cantor Story, The (misc.; 1953). Capitol.

Eddy Duchin Story, The (misc.; 1956). MCA.

Emperor Waltz, The (misc.-Burke; 1948). MCA.

Everything I Have Is Yours (misc.; 1952). MGM.

Face in the Crowd, A (Glazer-Schulberg; 1957). Capitol.

Fame (misc.; 1980). RSO.

Fiddler on the Roof (Bock-Harnick; 1971). UA (2 LPs).

Finian's Rainbow (Lane-Harburg; 1968). Warner.

Five Pennies, The (misc.; 1959). Dot.

Flower Drum Song (Rodgers-Hammerstein; 1961). MCA.

Follow the Fleet (Berlin; 1936). Columbia.

Frankie and Johnny (misc.; 1966). RCA.

French Line, The (Myrow-Blane, Wells; 1954). Mercury 10''.

Fun in Acapulco (misc.; 1963). RCA.

Funny Face (Gershwin-Gershwin; 1957). Stet.

Funny Girl (Styne-Merrill; 1968). Columbia.

Funny Lady (Kander-Ebb, etc.; 1975). Arista.

Funny Thing Happened on the Way to the Forum, A (Sondheim; 1966). UA.

Gay Purr-ee (Arlen-Harburg; 1963). Warner.

Gene Krupa Story, The (misc.; 1959). Verve.

Gentlemen Prefer Blondes (Styne-Robin; Carmichael-Adamson; 1953). Stet.

Gigi (Loewe-Lerner; 1958). MGM. Also in French (Columbia), Spanish (MGM).

Girl Crazy (Gershwin-Gershwin; 1943). Stet.

Girl Most Likely, The (Martin, Blane; 1958). Capitol.

Glenn Miller Story, The (misc.; 1954). MCA.

Godspell (Schwartz; 1973). Bell.

Goin' Coconuts (Osmond Brothers; 1978). Polydor.

Going Hollywood (Brown-Freed; 1933). Columbia.

Going My Way (Van Heusen-Burke; 1944). MCA.

Good News (Henderson-DeSylva, Brown; 1947). MGM.

Goodbye, Mr. Chips (Bricusse; 1969). MGM.

Grease (Casey-Jacobs; 1978). RSO (2 LPs).

Gypsy (Styne-Sondheim; 1962). Warner.

Hair (MacDermot-Rado, Ragni; 1979). RCA (2 LPs).

Half a Sixpence (Heneker; 1968). RCA.

Hans Christian Andersen (Loesser; 1952). MCA.

Happiest Millionaire, The (Sherman, Sherman; 1967). Buena Vista.

Hard Day's Night, A (Lennon, McCartney; 1964). UA.

Harem Scarum (misc.; 1965). RCA.

Having a Wild Weekend (misc.; 1965). Epic.

Helen Morgan Story, The (misc.; 1957). RCA.

Hello, Dolly! (Herman; 1969). Fox.

Help! (Lennon, McCartney; 1965). UA.

Here Come the Waves (Arlen-Mercer; 1944). MCA.

Here Comes the Groom (Livingston, Evans; 1951). MCA.

Here Is My Heart (Rainger-Robin; 1934). MCA.

High Society (Porter; 1956). Capitol.

Hit the Deck (Youmans-Grey, Robin; 1955). MGM.

Holiday Inn (Berlin; 1943). MCA.

Honeysuckle Rose (Nelson; 1980). CBS (2 LPs).

How To Succeed in Business Without Really Trying (Loesser; 1967). UA.

Huckleberry Finn (Sherman, Sherman; 1974). UA.

I Could Go On Singing (misc.; 1963). Capitol.

I Love Melvin (Myrow-Gordon; 1953). MGM.

Idolmaker, The (Barry; 1980). A & M.

If I Had My Way (Monaco-Burke; 1940). MCA.

I'll See You in My Dreams (misc. -Kahn; 1951). Columbia.

I'll Take Sweden (Haskell-Dunham; 1965). UA.

I'm No Angel (Brooks-Ellison; 1933). Columbia.

In Search of the Castaways (Sherman, Sherman; 1962). Disneyland.

In the Good Old Summertime (misc.; 1949). MGM.

Interrupted Melody (misc.; 1955). MGM.

It's Always Fair Weather (Previn-Comden, Green; 1955). MGM.

Jacques Brel Is Alive and Well and Living in Paris (Brel; 1974). Atlantic (2 LPs).

Jazz Singer, The (Diamond; 1980). Capitol.

Jessica (misc.; 1962). UA.

Jesus Christ Superstar (Webber-Rice; 1973). MCA. (2 LPs).

Jolson Sings Again (misc.; 1949). MCA.

Jolson Story, The (misc.; 1946). MCA.

Jumbo (Rodgers-Hart; 1962). Columbia.

Jungle Book, The (Sherman, Sherman; 1967). Buena Vista.

Just for You (Warren-Robin; 1952). Columbia.

King and I, The (Rodgers-Hammerstein; 1957). Capitol.

King of Jazz (Ager-Yellen, etc.; 1930). Columbia.

Kismet (Borodin-Wright, Forrest; 1955). MGM.

Kiss Me, Kate (Porter; 1953). MGM.

Kissin' Cousins (misc.; 1964). RCA.

Lady and the Tramp, The (Lee-Burke; 1955). MCA 10″.

Lady Sings the Blues (misc.; 1972). Motown (2 LPs).

Les Girls (Porter; 1957). MGM.

Let's Make Love (Van Heusen-Cahn, etc.; 1960). Columbia.

Li'l Abner (dePaul-Mercer; 1959). Columbia.

Lili (Kaper-Deutsch; 1953). MGM 10″.

Little Boy Lost (Van Heusen-Burke; 1953). MCA.

Little Miss Broadway (Spina-Bullock; 1938). Fox.

Little Night Music, A (Sondheim; 1978). Columbia.

Little Prince, The (Loewe-Lerner; 1974). ABC.

Lively Set, The (misc.; 1964). MCA.

Looking for Love (misc.; 1964). MGM.

Lost Horizon (Bacharach-David; 1973). Bell.

Love Me or Leave Me (misc.; 1955). Columbia.

Lovely To Look At (Kern-Harbach, Fields; 1952). MGM.

Lullaby of Broadway (misc.; 1951). Columbia.

Mame (Herman; 1974). Warner.

Man of La Mancha (Leigh-Darion; 1972). UA.

Mardi Gras (Fain-Webster; 1958). Bell.

Mary Poppins (Sherman, Sherman; 1964). Buena Vista. Also in French (Buena Vista).

Melba (misc.; 1953). RCA 10".

Merry Andrew (Chaplin-Mercer; 1958). Capitol.

Merry Widow, The (Lehar-Webster; 1952). MGM 10".

Miss Sadie Thompson (Lee-Washington; 1953). Mercury 10".

Mississippi (Rodgers-Hart; 1935). MCA.

Mr. Imperium (misc.; 1951). RCA 10".

Mr. Music (VanHeusen-Burke; 1950). MCA.

Mrs. Brown, You've Got a Lovely Daughter (misc; 1968). MGM.

Muppet Movie, The (Williams-Ascher; 1979). Atlantic.

Muscle Beach Party (misc.; 1964). Buena Vista.

Music Lovers, The (Tchaikovsky; 1971). UA.

Music Man, The (Willson; 1962). Warner.

My Fair Lady (Loewe-Lerner; 1964). Columbia. Also in French (CBS), German (CBS), Portuguese (CBS).

Nancy Goes to Rio (misc.; 1950); MGM.

Nashville (misc.; 1975). ABC.

Night They Raided Minsky's, The (Strouse-Adams; 1969). UA.

New York, New York (misc.; 1977). UA (2 LPs).

Northwest Outpost (Friml-Heyman; 1947). Columbia 10".

Oh, Rosalinda! (Strauss-Arundell; 1955). Nixa.

Oh, What a Lovely War (misc.; 1969). Paramount.

Oklahoma! (Rodgers-Hammerstein; 1955). Capitol.

Oliver! (Bart; 1968). Colgems.

On a Clear Day You Can See Forever (Lane-Lerner; 1970). Columbia.

On Moonlight Bay (misc.; 1951). Columbia 10".

One and Only Genuine Original Family Band, The (Sherman, Sherman). Buena Vista.

One-Trick Pony (Simon; 1980). Warner.

Orchestra Wives (Warren-Gordon; 1942). 20th-Fox.

Out of This World (Arlen-Mercer; 1945). MCA.

Pagan Love Song (Warren-Freed; 1950). MGM.

Paint Your Wagon (Loewe, Previn-Lerner; 1969). Paramount.

Pajama Game, The (Adler, Ross; 1957). Columbia.

Pal Joey (Rodgers-Hart; 1957). Capitol.

Paradise - Hawaiian Style (misc.; 1966). RCA.

Paris Honeymoon (Rainger-Robin; 1939). MCA.

Pennies from Heaven (Johnston-Burke; 1936). MCA.

Pennies from Heaven (misc.; 1981). Warner.

Pepe (misc. 1960). Colpix.

Pete Kelly's Blues (misc.; 1955). MCA.

Peter Pan (Fain-Cahn, etc.; 1953). Disneyland.

Pete's Dragon (Kasha-Hirschhorn; 1977). Capitol.

Pinocchio (Harline-Washington; 1940). Disneyland.

Pleasure Seekers, The (Van Heusen-Cahn; 1964). RCA.

Poor Little Rich Girl (Revel-Gordon; 1936). Fox.

Popeye (Nilsson; 1980). Boardwalk.

Porgy and Bess (Gershwin-Heyward, Gershwin; 1959). Columbia.

Pufnstuf (Fox-Gimbel; 1970). Capitol.

Rebecca of Sunnybrook Farm (misc.; 1938). Fox.

Red Garters (Livingston, Evans; 1954). Columbia 10″.

Rhythm on the Range (misc.; 1936). MCA.

Rhythm on the River (Monaco-Burke; 1940). MCA.

Rich, Young and Pretty (Brodszky-Cahn; 1951). MGM.

Riding High (VanHeusen-Burke; 1950). MCA.

Road to Bali (Van Heusen-Burke; 1953). MCA.

Road to Hong Kong (Van Heusen-Cahn; 1962). Liberty.

Road to Morocco (VanHeusen-Burke; 1942). MCA.

Road to Rio (Van Heusen-Burke; 1948). MCA.

Road to Singapore (Monaco-Schertzinger-Burke; 1940). MCA.

Road to Utopia (VanHeusen-Burke; 1946). MCA.

Road to Zanzibar (VanHeusen-Burke; 1941). MCA.

Robin and the Seven Hoods (Van Heusen-Cahn; 1964). Reprise.

Rock, Pretty Baby (misc.; 1957). MCA.

Rose, The (misc.; 1979). Atlantic.

Roustabout (misc.; 1964). RCA.

Royal Wedding (Lane-Lerner; 1951). MGM.

Saludos Amigos (misc.; 1943). Disneyland.

Saturday Night Fever (BeeGees; 1977). RSO (2 LPs).

Say One for Me (VanHeusen-Cahn; 1959). Columbia.

Scrooge (Bricusse; 1970). Columbia.

Serenade (misc.; 1956). RCA 10″.

Seven Brides for Seven Brothers (dePaul-Mercer; 1954). MGM.

Seven Little Foys, The (misc.; 1950). RCA.

1776 (Edwards; 1972). Capitol.

Sgt. Pepper's Lonely Hearts Club Band (Lennon, McCartney; 1978). RSO (2 LPs).

Shall We Dance (Gershwin-Gershwin; 1937). Columbia.

She Loves Me Not (Revel-Gordon, etc.; 1934). Columbia.

Shipyard Sally (misc.; 1939). Eng. Decca.

Show Boat (Kern-Hammerstein; 1951). MGM.

Silk Stockings (Porter; 1957). MGM.

Sincerely Yours (misc.; 1955). Columbia.

Sing, Boy, Sing (misc.; 1958). Capitol.

Sing You Sinners (Monaco-Burke; 1948). MCA.

Singin' in the Rain (Brown-Freed; 1952). MGM.

Singing Nun, The (misc.; 1966). MGM.

Sleeping Beauty (misc.; 1959). Disneyland.

Slipper and the Rose, The (Sherman, Sherman; 1976). MCA.

Snow White and the Seven Dwarfs (Churchill-Morey; 1937). Disneyland.

So This Is Paris (Moody-Sherrell; 1954). MCA 10″.

Some Like It Hot (misc.; 1959). UA.

Somebody Loves Me (Livingston, Evans, etc.; 1952). MCA.

Song of Norway (Grieg-Wright, Forrest; 1970). ABC.

Song of the South (misc.; 1946). Disneyland.

Sound of Music, The (Rodgers-Hammerstein; 1965). RCA. Also in French (RCA), German (RCA), Italian (RCA), Spanish (RCA).

South Pacific (Rodgers-Hammerstein; 1958). RCA.

Speedway (misc.; 1968). RCA.

St. Louis Blues (Handy; 1958). Capitol.

Star! (misc.; 1968). Fox.

Star Is Born, A (Arlen-Gershwin; 1954), Columbia.

Star Is Born, A (Williams, etc.; 1976). Columbia.

Star Maker, The (Monaco-Burke; 1939). MCA.

State Fair (Rodgers-Hammerstein; 1945). MCA.

State Fair (Rodgers-Hammerstein; 1962). Dot.

Stop the World—I Want To Get Off (Bricusse-Newley; 1966). Warner.

Summer Magic (Sherman, Sherman; 1963). Buena Vista.

Summer Stock (Warren-Gordon; 1950). MGM.

Sun Valley Serenade (Warren-Gordon; 1941). 20th-Fox.

Sweet Charity (Coleman-Fields; 1969). MCA.

Swing Time (Kern-Fields; 1937). Columbia.

Swinger, The (misc.; 1966). RCA.

Sword in the Stone, The (Sherman, Sherman; 1963). Disneyland.

Tea for Two (misc.; 1950). Columbia.

Thank God It's Friday (misc.; 1978). Casablanca.

That Midnight Kiss (misc.; 1959). RCA.

That's Entertainment (misc.; 1974). MGM (2 LPs).

That's Entertainment Part 2 (misc.; 1976). MCA.

There's No Business Like Show Business (Berlin; 1954). MCA.

This'll Make You Whistle (Hoffman, Goodhart-Sigler; 1936). Eng. Decca.

Thoroughly Modern Millie (misc.; 1967). MCA.

Three for the Show (misc.; 1955). Mercury 10".

Three Little Words (Ruby-Kalmar; 1950). MGM.

Three Sailors and a Girl (Fain-Cahn; 1953). Capitol 10".

Three Penny Opera, (Weill-Brecht, Blitzstein; 1964). London (German); RCA (English).

Till the Clouds Roll By (Kern-misc.; 1946). MGM.

Times Square (misc.; 1980). RSO (2 LPs).

Toast of New Orleans, The (Brodszky-Cahn; 1950). RCA.

Tom Sawyer (Sherman, Sherman; 1973). UA.

Tom Thumb (Spielman-Torre, etc.; 1958). MGM.

Tommy (Townshend; 1975). Polydor (2 LPs).

Tonight We Sing (misc.; 1952). RCA 10".

Too Much Harmony (Johnston-Coslow; 1933). MCA.

Top Hat (Berlin; 1935). Columbia.

Top o' the Morning (Van Heusen-Burke; 1949). MCA.

Two for Tonight (Revel-Gordon; 1935). MCA.

Two Weeks with Love (misc.; 1950). MGM.

Umbrellas of Cherbourg, The (Legrand; 1964). Philips.

Unsinkable Molly Brown, The (Willson; 1964). MGM.

Urban Cowboy (misc.; 1980). Asylum (2 LPs).

Vagabond King, The (Friml-Hooker, Burke; 1956). RCA.

Victor/Victoria (Mancini-Bricusse; 1982). Polygram.

Waikiki Wedding (Rainger-Robin; 1937). MCA.

Welcome, Stranger (VanHeusen-Burke; 1947). MCA.

We're Not Dressing (Revel-Gordon; 1934). MCA.

West Side Story (Bernstein-Sondheim; 1961). Columbia.

When the Boys Meet the Girls (Gershwin-Gershwin, etc.; 1965). MGM.

White Christmas (Berlin; 1954). MCA.

Willy Wonka and the Chocolate Factory (Bricusse-Newley; 1971). Paramount.

With a Song in My Heart (misc.; 1952). Capitol.

Wiz, The (Smalls; 1978). MCA (2 LPs).

Wizard of Oz, The (Arlen-Harburg; 1939). MCA; MGM.

Wonderful World of the Brothers Grimm, The (Merrill; 1962). MGM.

Words and Music (Rodgers-Hart; 1948). MGM.

You Can't Run Away from It (dePaul-Mercer; 1956). MCA.

You Were Never Lovelier (Kern-Mercer; 1942). Vocalion.

Young at Heart (misc.; 1954). Columbia.

Young Girls of Rochefort, The (Legrand; 1967). Philips (2 LPs).

Young Man with a Horn (misc.; 1950). Columbia.

Young People (Warren-Gordon; 1940). Fox.

Your Cheatin' Heart (Williams, etc.; 1964). MGM.

Xanadu (misc.; 1980). MCA.

Television Musicals

Adventures of Marco Polo (Rimsky Korsakov, Warnick-Eager; 1956). Columbia.

Aladdin (Porter; 1958). Columbia.

Alice Through the Looking Glass (Charlap-Simmons; 1966). RCA.

Androcles and the Lion (Rodgers; 1967). RCA.

Cinderella (Rodgers-Hammerstein; 1957). Columbia.

Cinderella (Rodgers-Hammerstein; 1965). Columbia.

Dangerous Christmas of Red Riding Hood (Styne-Merrill; 1965). ABC.

Gift of the Magi, The (Adler; 1958). UA.

Hans Brinker (Martin; 1958). Dot.

Hansel and Gretel (Wilder-Engvick; 1958). MGM.

High Tor (Schwartz-Anderson; 1956). MCA.

Jack and the Beanstalk (Livingston-Deutsch; 1956). Unique.

Little Women (Adler; 1958). Kapp.

Olympus 7-0000 (Adler; 1966). Command.

Pied Piper of Hamlin, The (Grieg-Taylor; 1957). RCA.

Pinocchio (Wilder-Engvick; 1957). Columbia.

Rudolph the Red-Nosed Reindeer (Marks; 1965). MCA.

Ruggles of Red Gap (Styne-Robin; 1957). Stet.

Satins and Spurs (Livingston, Evans; 1954). Capitol 10".

Stingiest Man in Town, The (Torre-Spielman; 1956). Columbia.

Tom Sawyer (Luther; 1956). MCA.